ECCLESIOLOGY IN CONTEXT

Ecclesiology in Context

Johannes A. van der Ven

William B. Eerdmans Publishing Company
Grand Rapids, Michigan / Cambridge, U.K.

Originally published as *Ecclesiologie in context*

255 Jefferson Ave. S.E., Grand Rapids, Michigan 49503 /
P.O. Box 163, Cambridge CB3 9PU U.K.

Printed in the United States of America

01 00 99 98 97 96 7 6 5 4 3 2 1

Library of Congress Cataloging-in-Publication Data

Ven, J. A. van der, 1940-
Ecclesiology in context / Johannes A. van der Ven.
p. cm.
Includes bibliographical references.
ISBN 0-8028-0785-2 (pbk. : alk. paper)
1. Church. 2. Catholic Church — Doctrines.
3. Catholic Church — Membership. I. Title.
BX1746.V46 1996
262 — dc20 95-52116
CIP

Contents

II. CODES OF THE CHURCH

CORE FUNCTIONS AND CODES OF THE CHURCH

III. IDENTITY

IV. INTEGRATION

V. POLICY

Introduction

The history of practical theology is characterized by three different approaches to its object. In the first approach, which started in 1774 with the institution of the professorial chair of pastoral theology at the University of Vienna, pastoral action was considered to be the object of practical theology.

In the second approach, which arose in the middle of the 19th century, the horizon was broadened, and pastoral action was placed within the context of the church. In 1841 Graf developed an ecclesiological conception of practical theology in his *Kritische Darstellung des gegenwärtigen Zustandes der praktischen Theologie.* In 1847 Nitzsch published his *Praktische Theologie,* in which he described the object of this discipline as the "kirchliche Ausübung des Christentums." Not long afterward, the first approach again became more dominant. The action of the pastor returned to the center of attention, and practical-theological ecclesiology disappeared into the background. It was to take about a century before there was again a turn in the direction of the second approach. The subtitle of *Handbuch der Pastoraltheologie,* which appeared under the auspices of Arnold, Rahner, Schurr, Weber, and others in 1964, can be defined as being programmatic. It read: *Praktische Theologie der Kirche in ihrer Gegenwart.* The object that now functioned in practical theology was the self-development of the church. In Protestant circles, too, practical theology has ever since been founded and worked out in ecclesiology, such as in the Berlin *Handbuch der Praktischen Theologie* by Ammer and others from 1975, and the Gütersloh *Handbuch der Praktischen Theologie* by Bloth and others from 1981. Not long after its appearance the *Handbuch der Pastoraltheologie* was criticized because it had left behind the clerocentrism of the first approach, only to fall prey to ecclesiocentrism.

A third approach was heralded in 1974 with the appearance of *Praktische Theologie heute,* with which the 200th anniversary of university practical theology was commemorated. In this approach the horizon stretched further still. The church was placed in the context of society in order to contribute to the liberation of humanity and society through its evangelical praxis. Since then the object of practical theology has been the praxis of the church in the context of modern society.

This book identifies with the third approach to practical theology. We want to make a contribution to the development of ecclesiology in the context of modern society from a practical-theological perspective. The aim of this study can be further clarified by proceeding from three terms: ecclesiology, context, and practical-theological perspective.

Ecclesiology is understood to be a theological theory of the church. It distinguishes itself from a sociological theory of the church by its formal object and not by its material. The material object of both exists in the church, where it can be found in a historical and empirical sense. The formal object of ecclesiology, however, is expressed in the description and explanation of the church according to the aspect of its future from the perspective of the gospel. The vision and the mission of the church, as well as its tasks and goals, lie within this perspective. Ecclesiology is concerned both about the future of the church and about the church of the future.

In this book ecclesiology is developed by proceeding from the context of modern society; that is, society insofar as it is determined by the societal process of modernization. This process still mostly takes place in Western countries, or in the northern hemisphere. From there, however, it also influences the countries of the southern hemisphere. In this study attention is primarily focused upon the development of a theological theory of the church within the context of Western society. This means two things. On the one hand, the point of departure for this ecclesiology lies in the awareness of the relativity of the West. Proceeding from this insight into the polycentric character of present global society, it has a duty to leave any semblance of universal validity and obligation behind. It has a clear realization of its contextual limitations; however, at the same time, it is precisely in this that it sees its own specific challenge. On the other hand, this ecclesiology includes knowledge of the originality, creativity, and persuasiveness of the ecclesiologies that are being developed in the countries of the southern hemisphere, in particular the ecclesiology of liberation. It allows itself to be inspired by it, yet without believing itself dismissed from its own task: to contribute to an ecclesiology in and proceeding from the Western context.

This contextual ecclesiology is being developed in a practical-theological perspective. In this the emphasis is placed on the praxis of the church. The praxis of the church is not identical to its practice. The praxis can be described as the practice in which a transformatory orientation is active. This orientation can be distinguished by two aspects, a cultural and a structural aspect.

The cultural aspect can be defined by the term *transformatory consciousness.* It has to do with the historical insight that the church has continually undergone and is still undergoing changes. The reason is that it is continually making new contacts with elements from the societal environment around it. In the first few centuries the church took over elements from wandering charismatic-pneumatic groups found everywhere, from the pattern of association of the *collegium,* from the *oikos* household with the *paterfamilias* at its head, from the fraternal structure of the organization of civil servants, and from the hierarchical-pyramidal administrative order in the Roman empire. In later centuries it brought about contacts with elements from feudal society. Later still, the Catholic Church combined these elements with those of the state structure of the absolute monarchy. Finally, in the last few centuries, it brought about a gigantic organization, the characteristics of which were borrowed from modern state bureaucracy.

The structural aspect has to do with the transformatory mechanism that is present within the church. It points to the sociological angle from which the church can be considered as a self-regulating social context, as an organization that learns. The church is forever changing, not only because it adapts to its ever-changing environment in a passive sense but also because it is precisely this that has oriented the church toward its own tasks and goals and brought them closer. The transformatory mechanism is founded in the dialectical relationship between the church that was being changed and the church that was changing itself in this respect.

Ecclesiology that is aimed at the praxis of the church attaches great importance to both of these aspects: the transformatory consciousness and the transformatory mechanism. They are the point of departure for a transformatory ecclesiology. This is aimed at the possible and necessary change of the church within the context of modern society, with an eye to accomplishing tasks and goals that lie in its vision and mission. It distinguishes itself from an ecclesiology aimed at conservation instead of transformation, in which the consistency of the church in shape and structure comes first.

The praxis of the church can be distinguished by the level at which it is given shape. The *micro level* has to do with the church insofar as it is developed in the local, regional environment. The *meso level* refers to the church insofar as it realizes itself in the national and continental environment. The *macro level* points to the church insofar as it takes shape in the intercontinental and global society. We are not talking about a division into three levels here, but a distinction between levels. The church at the micro level cannot exist without that of the meso level, and the latter cannot do so without that of the macro level. The reverse also applies. The church at the macro level cannot realize itself independently from that of the meso level, and the latter cannot do so independently from that of the micro level. The ecclesiology in this book is primarily focused on the praxis of the church at the micro level. However, this is done without taking leave of the relations with the church at the meso and macro levels.

An ecclesiology that is aimed at the praxis of the church and not at the nature and essence of the church has to make sure of the rule-governed structure of the church from which this praxis takes shape. Otherwise one runs the risk of passing over the actual church and its praxis. The rule-governed structure of the church can be divided into several different types: episcopal, presbyterian, and congregationalist. These can be found in the traditions of the various Christian churches according to their separate elements and combinations. These churches are the Catholic, Orthodox, Lutheran, Calvinist, Anglican, Free, and Independent churches. Since it is impossible to deal with the praxis of the church in one study proceeding from all these types and church traditions, one has to make a choice. In this book a choice was made for the ecclesiology of the Catholic Church. In this we are involved not only with the negotiation of the legal system in force in this church *(ius conditum),* but also with the unlocking of ways to develop it *(ius condendum).* This latter perspective is implied in the transformatory orientation in the ecclesiology in this book. In short, what we are interested in is the praxis of the Catholic Church at a micro level. This choice stems from the practical circumstance that we are most familiar with the Catholic Church, and have collected the most knowledge about it. We do not wish to attach any surplus value to it. At the same time, however, it can be regarded as an exemplary choice. It brings numerous facets to light that may also be relevant for other denominations.

The praxis of the Catholic Church is clarified in this book by means of sociological and theological terms, with an eye to the development of an ecclesiology from a practical-theological perspective. In this, three principles are used.

The first principle has an epistemological nature. We mean the following by this. Proceeding from sociology, the church is approached from the angle of a group, network, community, association, people, movement, organization, and enterprise. This does not mean to say that the church *is* a group, network, organization, or enterprise, but that it can be *considered* as a group, organization, or enterprise. The notions in question throw a light on the church by which some facets are more sharply defined while others are more obscured. They fulfill a paradigmatic function. The same applies for the theological notions. The church is approached as *communio fidelium,* as the "church," as the Jesus movement, as the body of Christ, as the building of the Spirit, and as the church of the poor.

The second principle is that of complementarity. This means that the sociological notions mutually supplement and correct each other. It also applies to the theological notions with regard to each other. In this book we therefore do not make a one-sided choice for the church as an association, or for the church as a movement. Neither is a theologically one-sided choice made for the church as a community of believers, for the church as "church," or for the church as the church of the poor. An effort was made to bring forward the complementary character of the sociological notions and the theological notions among themselves.

The third principle is that of noncompetition. This does not have to do with the relation between the sociological and the theological notions among themselves, but with the relation between the sociological and the theological notions regarding each other. It implies that the social aspects of the church to which the sociological notions refer, and the religious aspects to which the theological notions refer, are not placed in positions of competition with regard to each other. The social aspects are not deducted from the religious aspects and vice versa. What people do in the social context of the church and what God does in the church, may not and cannot be subtracted from each other. They are not each other's negation, nor each other's counterpart. God does not cancel out the activities of people in the church, but inspires, intensifies, and orients them. God gives to the people to form the church themselves, to do the church themselves. The principle of noncompetition is founded on the insight into the immanent transcendence of God and not the absolute transcendence.

The structure of this study is as follows. First, the local church is placed within the context of the continental and intercontinental church of the macro level in Western society. This context is determined by the fundamental process of modernization. From that the general function and the core functions of the church are determined. The general function is religious communication. The core functions are identity, integration, policy, and management. They can be distinguished from the sectors of the church. The sectors are pastoral care, catechetics, liturgy, proclamation, and diacony (Part I). Next, the religious images of the church are clarified. They refer to the religious individuality of the church. They signify and re-present the salvation of God in the church. In this interpretation lies a semiotic approach, from which the religious images are conceived of as codes. The religious supercode is the church as sacrament. The function of the religious codes can be distinguished by three aspects: the codes contain religious information (cognitive aspect); they express religious experiences, emotions, and attitudes (emotive aspect); and they contain an inspiration and orientation for action in a transformatory sense (conative aspect). Through this threefold function, the religious codes give shape to the religious origin and destiny of the church (Part II).

Second, the core functions of the church (identity, integration, policy, and management) are discussed in four separate parts. The focus is particularly on the local church. Each time, the core functions are involved with one of the four dimensions of modernization. At the same time, they are involved with one of the religious codes, from which the core function in question is clarified, supplemented, and oriented. First of all, the core function of identity is dealt with, within the context of secularization proceeding from the codes *church* and *Jesus movement* (Part III). Next, the core function of integration is dealt with, within the context of individualization proceeding from the code *body of Christ* (Part IV). After that, the core function of policy is dealt with, within the context of utilization proceeding from the code *building of the Spirit* (Part V). Finally, the core function of management is dealt with, within the context of calculation proceeding from the code *church of the poor* (Part VI).

Functions and Codes of the Church

As indicated in the Introduction, the first two chapters introduce a fundamental notion: the functions and the codes of the church. The point of departure for both chapters is that the functions and codes together form the base on which an ecclesiology is built from a practical-theological perspective.

The relation between the functions and the codes is of a dialectical nature. On the one hand, insofar as one derives the functions from the position of the church in Western society today, one comes across the question, What is the religious property characteristic of the church? What distinguishes it from other societal institutions? This question cannot be answered without the religious codes, with which the church indicates what it understands itself to be. On the other hand, the clarification of the religious property characteristic of the church proceeding from the codes needs to be involved with the position of the church in present society and the functions that the church exercises in it. If one were to omit this, one would end with merely normative or aesthetic reflections. An ecclesiology from a practical-theological perspective is not served by this. It demands that the functions and the codes are mutually involved in it.

In the first two chapters, the land is made ready for building. In this the conditions are traced by which the functions and codes can adequately be discussed also with respect to their mutual connection.

In chapter 1 the general function of the church is dealt with proceeding from the societal context in which the church finds itself and the position it holds in this. This general function is religious communication. The conditions under which this general function is realized are determined by the four core functions of the church. These are identity, integration, policy, and management.

Chapter 2 begins with the assessment that both social and religious aspects are to be distinguished in these functions. The question is how these can be connected to each other. Proceeding from semiotics, an answer can be tested. This answer states that the social phenomena in the church may be interpreted as religious signs. Social phenomena refer to God's salvation as religious signs. They signify and represent the salvation that comes from God.

The question with which chapter 2 ends is: In what sense can the social aspects that are implied in the functions actually gain the character of religious signs in the praxis of the realization of the church? What does this mean for the identity, integration, policy, and management of the church? The answer to this question will be tested in the next chapters.

PART I

FUNCTIONS OF THE CHURCH

Those who consider the church in Western society have to reflect on Western society as the context of the church and on the position it holds in it. Only in this framework can one fruitfully discuss the functions of the church. If one fails to do this, there is a danger of speculation alienated from reality and of wishful thinking. However, if one were to actually concern oneself with Western society, there is a different danger. The risk that one may, in one's approach to the church, adapt oneself to Western society to such an extent that the characteristic property of the church is lost, is not imaginary. That is why critical distance is imperative. In the description of the functions of the church, this tension will always be evident.

The structure of this chapter is as follows. First, we will give a sketch of the developments in Western society that determine the context of the church. In this the process of modernization is central (chapter 1). Next, we will take a look at the position of the church in this society. We will pay attention to the church as a denomination and the church as an association. We will go into the church as a community of believers in particular (chapter 2). After that, we will determine the general function of the church in Western society. This deals with religious communication (chapter 3). Finally, we will deal with the four core functions of the church, which are aimed at the realization of the general function. These are identity, integration, policy, and management (chapter 4).

Chapter 1

The Context of the Church

The word *modern* has two meanings. It can refer to a certain time or a certain theme. In the first case, it is synonymous with "present-day" or "contemporary." In the second case, it is connected with the term *modernization.* The latter is the meaning intended here.

In this chapter we will deal with (1) what modernization entails; (2) how modernization is to be valued; and (3) what consequences modernization has for the church.

(1) Modernization

The meaning of the term *modernization* is the subject of intense discussion. Some believe that the term depends on economic modernization, like industrialization, automation, and computerization. Others, however, are of the opinion that modernization must primarily be sought in political modernization, like democratization and the social welfare state. Others point out social phenomena in particular, like the collapse of the barrier between the state and the citizen, social erosion, alienation, and isolation. Still others think that modernization is a product of the enormous expansion of science and technology.

In this chapter we will aim at the inclusive character of modernization. Our description is of a deliberately general nature. Here we understand modernization to mean the societal development that is characterized by striving to solve problems by proceeding from the perspective of rationality. We therefore approach modernization from the perspective of rationalization. It permeates the whole of societal life. We will discuss two aspects: the dimensions of modernization and the factors involved in modernization.

Dimensions of modernization

In *economic modernization,* land no longer forms the only solution for economic problems as in agricultural society, but capital does. Capital goods are employed with an aim to raising profit. With the help of technology and industrialization, a differentiated division of labor of specialized jobs is applied. The raising of production, which is a consequence of this, demands a raising of consumption. Both demand increasing control of the national and international markets for capital, raw materials, goods, and labor. By doing so, the economy becomes more large scale. It is not restricted to the industrial sector, but it also captures the agrarian sector, from which it had once emancipated itself. The agrarian sector is thus being industrialized as farms, too, are becoming multimillion-dollar businesses (Schoorl 1983). Characteristic of economic modernization are: division of economy and family, rational accountancy, investment with an eye to success on the markets mentioned, efficient use of what is formally free manpower, and methodical use of scientific and technological knowledge (Weber 1980).

In *political modernization* the control of societal problems is foremost. A large-scale economy demands a large-scale control structure. It is impossible to imagine this without the formation of national states and supranational associations that make sure that trade between individuals and groups runs as smoothly as possible. One cannot escape a highly differentiated bureaucratic apparatus, which encompasses everybody and everything. The rules, competencies, and procedures are becoming more and more formal and abstract because they have to be applied universally at a high aggregation level to the most diverse national, regional, and local circumstances. The control of the citizen therefore continues to increase (Elias 1982b).

Social modernization is determined by urbanization in particular. Migration from the country to the city is still happening all over the world. The concentration of economy and politics in the cities influences not only geographical mobility but social and professional mobility as well. Social relations are maintained primarily for their functional value. All this has consequences for the family, which is brought back to one of its so-called core functions. The social links in which the family used to be embedded are losing their meaning. This collapse of the social barrier leads to social fragmentation and individualization, which in turn also reduces social control (Heunks 1987).

Finally, *cultural modernization* is characterized by the huge expansion of information and education structures, which have an ever-increasing influence from science and the scientific attitude on daily life as a consequence. This has led to scientism, which comes down to belief in science and in scientific progress (Ravetz 1980).

Cultural modernization is also expressed in the growing autonomy of the various cultural institutions with regard to each other. Art, science, morality, law, upbringing and education, philosophy, worldview, and religion more and more have a life of their own. While they formed a whole in the pre-modern era, they now are falling further and further apart. This in turn leads to the pluralization of these forms of culture themselves.

The *process of rationalization* can be observed in the forms of culture too. The rationalization of science is the clearest sign of this. A science of science is developing (Rip & Groenewegen 1980). Education, too, is being more and more defined by rationalization. School is becoming a school of science (Wilhelm 1969). In it the emphasis is increasingly being placed on adequate information storage and rational information processing by the pupil (Gagné 1977). Art is also defined by rationalization, as can be seen in the history of music, and in the theory of harmony and morphology in particular (Popper 1978). Rationalization also applies to morality. The history of morality can be described in terms of the increase of the rational moral judgment on one's own grounds. The climax of this is held to be the self-reflexive moral judgment, which makes the moral judgment itself the object of rational criticism as well (Schluchter 1979). Finally, even religion cannot escape the process of rationalization. The history of thought about God, Christ, and the Holy Spirit and about creation, liberation, and completion is becoming more and more abstract. This also applies to thought about the church and liturgy (Weber 1920; 1969; 1980; Bellah 1973; Döbert 1973; Habermas 1982). Additionally, morality and religion are more freely disposed toward each other. Other cultural institutions, too, are more and more independently disposed to each other as a consequence of the autonomous processes of rationalization.

The question is, What holds Western society together from a cultural point of view, when cohesive values and norms and a cohesive religion are lacking? What cultural cement holds society together? Literature give three answers to this question. According to the first answer, universal values and norms are still to be found in our society, only they are formulated in a very abstract sense. For example, for Dutch society they are the importance of nature, inner-directedness, and fellow feeling (Felling et al. 1983). Some, who disagree with this, are of the opinion that from a moral point of view concrete basic rules still exist, albeit formulated negatively. These are: do not commit murder, do not steal, and do not lie (Manenschijn 1984).

Others say — the second answer — that one should not look at the values of culture, but to the normative principles present in the political order that regulate the social welfare state. At the root of this lie principles like freedom, justice, and solidarity. These hold the present society together and protect it from disintegration (Gabriel 1988).

The third answer states that there are no values or principles to hold society together — neither cultural nor political ones. The only thing that binds society is a procedural norm, namely communication. This is everywhere and always prescribed. It is the basic principle of the modern democratic welfare state. No one can or may be excluded from it. In this communication, debate takes place on the relevance of principles like freedom, justice, and solidarity and on the limits of their application. What is plausible is only the procedural norm that communication needs to take place. Nothing has been said about the concrete contents of the values and norms with this (Habermas 1982).

Factors in modernization

In economic, political, social, and cultural modernization, a number of factors are at work that are of importance in understanding the complexity of the term modernization. Modernization is anything but a monolithic phenomenon.

The first factor is that of *interdependence.* What this means is that the four dimensions of modernization are mutually dependent on each other. Contrary to what some Marxists believe, there is no simple causal line to be drawn from the economic substructure to the political, social, or cultural superstructure. In one case, economic modernization plays the role of the independent variable that influences cultural modernization as the dependent variable. In another case, the roles are reversed. The latter applies, for instance, to the balance between the economic system and the educational system. The latter is not merely a reflection of the former. The economy not only influences education, but education also influences the economy both directly and indirectly (Van Kemenade 1981; Van der Ven 1982a). However, within this web of interdependent relations, according to the opinion of some societal theorists, the causal influence of the economy on the rest of society is greater than the reverse. One talks of an economic colonization of society: the political, social, and cultural life become more and more colonies of the economy (Habermas 1982).

The second factor is *nonsynchronism.* It means that the various dimensions of modernization are characterized by a difference in rate. This not only applies to economic, political, social, and cultural modernization, but also to the various sectors within these forms of modernization. Thus, for example, the moral sector of cultural modernization in the Netherlands is characterized by various moral attitudes: from extremely conservative to extremely permissive. These can be interpreted in terms of a difference in the rate of modernization. In this way an extremely conservative moral position can go together with a highly rational economic mentality (Halman et al. 1987).

The third factor is *(non)linearity.* With this the question arises whether modernization takes place linearly or takes on other forms of development. The S-curve, for instance, belongs to the latter, which is characterized by a gradual flattening at the top. This indicates that a saturation point is reached at a certain time. Thereupon a fall may follow, which may be followed by a rise after a certain low-point has been reached (Layendecker 1984). The opposite picture is also possible: instead of an S-curve there is an exponential growth curve. One talks of linear growth when the absolute increase per unit of time is constant; exponential growth when the relative increase per unit of time is constant (Kickert 1986).

The fourth factor is *(ir)reversibility.* Does modernization always have to go ahead and is it therefore irreversible? Or can it be stopped or reversed by human intervention? Certain groups undertake all sorts of efforts to this end. The confessional educational system in Europe sprang from this, according to some researchers (Righart 1986). Or can modernization at least be regulated, so that it stagnates? According to some researchers, the Reformed Churches in the Netherlands consciously or unconsciously follow a kind of stagnation policy, especially with regard to morality and religion, while the Netherlands Reformed Church does less so, and the Catholics less yet (Peters & Schreuder 1987).

The fifth factor is labeled *the bearers of modernization.* If they have a lot of societal influence, then this encourages modernization and it quickly spreads to other societal groups. If they have only a small amount of influence, then it inhibits modernization. From a European context, a number of countries in northwestern Europe count as bearers of moral modernization (Germany, The Netherlands, and Denmark). For Ireland and the countries of southern Europe, this is clearly not the case (Dorenbos et al. 1987). In a national context, the bearers of modernization are to be found in the cities. In a categorial context, they are the highly educated and the young.

The sixth and final factor relates to *societal conflict with regard to modernization.* The societal bearers of modernization raise up other societal groups, which resist modernization. A clear example of this is the battle between the entrepreneurs of big industries and the reactionary petty bourgeoisie between 1810 and 1870 in Germany. The first group was characterized by a partial kind of modernization: economically there was modernization, but politically there was not. The second group was characterized by a complete and almost agrarian fear of the modernization that was advocated by industry and the world of banking. The partial modernization of the entrepreneurs and the antimodernism of the petty bourgeoisie may be considered the breeding ground for the failure of the Weimar Republic and the rise of the national socialism of Hitler (Peeters 1984).

(2) Critical reflection on modernization

Modernization can thus be described as societal development characterized by striving to solve problems from the perspective of rationality. In this description two terms are central, which we will now explore further: development and rationality.

Development

The term *development* takes an important place in the thought on modernization. It implies that a change takes place in society that occurs in a certain amount of time, that is irreversible, and in which one or more qualitatively new stages arise (Van Haaften et al. 1986, 29). There are at least two stages: premodern and modern. Or three of them: premodern, modern and postmodern. In the postmodern stage, the modernity is depicted as self-reflexive and self-critical (Kaufmann 1989). However, a normative problem is embedded in this division. The determining of stages always occurs in the last stage, which is judged to be the highest (Van Haaften et al. 1986, 72). If one proceeds from the dichotomy of premodern and modern, then the modern stage functions as the highest. In the trichotomy the highest is the postmodern or critical-modern stage. The question is whether this normative judgment is correct. Is modern higher and therefore better than premodern? Is postmodern better than the stages premodern and modern that go before?

A positive answer to these questions presupposes that the person answering them is in the highest stage or at least believes he is in this stage. The reason is that only from this point can the other stages be judged to be lower. It is not possible to pronounce judgment on lower positions free from one's own (putatively) high position.

With this, we have arrived at a problem that belongs to the core of modernization. Is he who determines what the highest stage of modernization is, by which the lower stages are measured, the well-educated citizen of the northern and western hemisphere? In other words: is modernization a Western bourgeois ideology? This question can be answered along the lines of two aspects: the intra- and intersocietal aspects.

The intrasocietal aspect relates to the structure of Western society. The question is, What advantage do the higher social classes have with modernization and to what degree does this enlarge the distance from the lower classes? Is modernization a process that develops by itself or is it developed, stimulated, propagated, and managed by certain groups? Does it have a kind of internal developmental logic, or is it promoted by the external developmental dynamics on which the most powerful groups wield the greatest influence? What disadvantages does this have for the lower classes in terms of their economic position, their political engagement, their social situation, and their cultural participation? Therefore, the question is whether and to what extent modernization leads to an attack on intrasocietal freedom and justice.

The second aspect points to the relationship between the societies of the northern and southern hemispheres. The question is, In what sense is modernization equal to westernization, with European and American colonization (Dorenbos et al. 1987)? It has been remarked that modernization in various societies took place in different times, without there having been talk of westernization. One could refer to Japan, Taiwan, and South Korea (Schoorl 1983; Halmen et al. 1987). Moreover, transhistorical and transcultural research has shown that modernization, taken to be rationalization, took place previous to and outside of any bourgeoisie (Weber 1920; Schluchter 1979). Yet this does not set aside the question to what extent the countries of the northern hemisphere did and still do profit from the export of modernization to the countries of the southern hemisphere. In this research the question should be asked to what extent the higher classes in these southern societies in turn profit from this export and the gap widens between the higher and the lower classes. Special attention should be paid to the question whether and in what respect certain groups are sooner the object rather than the subject of modernization, sooner the victim thereof rather than the beneficiary. Here the point is the question whether modernization leads to the attack on intersocietal freedom and justice.

Rationality

We have conceived modernization to be rationalization. What conception of rationality lies beneath this? In order to be able to answer this question, we have to take a further look at the term *rationality*.

This term can be separated into three dimensions (Weber 1980). The first is *cognitive-instrumental rationality.* It has two aspects. Insofar as the cognitive aspect dominates, it has to do with true statements regarding the state of things. For example: "x has an influence on y." Insofar as the instrumental aspect dominates, the rationality relates to statements regarding the effectiveness and efficiency of means to bring changes to the state of things. For example: "by intervening with method z, the influence of x on y decreases."

The second dimension is *normative or practical rationality.* It relates to statements regarding the correctness, in this case the righteousness of action. For example: "method z is morally permissible." More concretely: "suicide is permissible because man has the right to control his own life." Now this moral judgment may be contradicted by an opposite statement: "suicide is not permissible because life is sacred and should be respected." In these two statements rationality is at work, insofar as they contain arguments for the viewpoint in question. Since not only the points of view but also the arguments are diametrically opposed, rationality has to be further employed to regard the righteousness of the arguments critically. This is the work of normative rationality.

The third dimension is *expressive rationality.* It has to do with the authenticity of statements that express an experience, emotion, feeling, or attitude. Expressive rationality tests these statements for their emotional-biographical and interactional consistency. An example of this is: "I am deeply aware of justice as a value, but in this case I proceed purely from self-interest." The conversation partner who is confronted by this statement will want to know from the speaker how these two elements can be combined: justice as a value and pure self-interest. The partner will want to know whether he or she can still place any trust in the other's just disposition.

The rationalization that is the engine of modernization seems primarily or almost exclusively tuned to the first dimension: cognitive-instrumental rationality. This is dominant. Both other dimensions, normative and expressive rationality, hardly play a role (Habermas 1982).

Through the neglect of normative and expressive rationality, interest in intra- and intersocietal freedom and justice is pushed into the margin. Here the terms of development and rationality meet. Proceeding from reflection on the term *development,* we posed critical questions about the attack on intra- and intersocietal freedom and justice. Proceeding from the dominance of cognitive-instrumental rationality, we determined that these questions do not have sufficient chance for systematic reflection and thorough critical examination in the structure of today's society.

Dimensions of modernization

The above analysis can be exemplified for economic, political, social, and cultural modernization. In this we should consider that the pressure under which intra- and intersocietal freedom and justice function influences other facets of the personal and societal life of humanity.

Within economic modernization the excessive emphasis on the capital factor leads to neglect of the labor factor. The quality of labor is a problem. People who supply labor suffer because of this. The neglect of the labor factor applies even more to those who have been pushed out of the labor process. The unemployed share the lot of all those who are marked as nonproductive: the disabled, the young, and the aged. It leads to societal separation and segregation. Through this, a dichotomy has arisen: a class of employed and a subclass of unemployed, the owners of information and those without information respectively. From European community research it appears that more than 10% of Dutch households have to live on an income below the legal minimum. It also appears that the objective standard of this legal minimum runs equal to the SPL (Subjective Poverty Line). People below the minimum believe themselves to be poor.

These kinds of developments lead, at a global level, to structural poverty in the non-Western countries on a gigantic scale. It is estimated that one million people died of hunger in Ethiopia from 1984 to 1986. In 1992 it was reported that every day 5,000 children died of hunger in Somalia. The so-called dependency theory means that the underdevelopment of non-Western countries is a consequence of the overdevelopment of the Western countries. Critical notes can be added to this theory both in a scientific and a strategic sense. From a scientific point of view, there are internal national factors besides the external ones that play an important role. From a strategic point of view, the internal factors are susceptible to influence (Arroyo 1980). However, this in no degree lessens the validity of the dependency theory.

Within political modernization there is an enormous amount of bureaucracy in the state apparatus and institutions. The citizen feels that more and more he or she is becoming the plaything of an opaque network of institutions, competencies, and procedures. There is a real danger that democracy is being hollowed out by the increasing influence of the "fourth power," that of the civil servants and the technocrats. This would mean that the iron law of the oligarchy of Michels would come true. It states that a small, hermetically closed circle of official functionaries will take command and run things (Lammers 1984, 57ff.). Democracy would be the ideological legitimization of this technocracy. The well-educated Western citizen is a better match for these kinds of processes than the representatives of the lower classes who are in danger of getting the worst of it. Research in the Rotterdam district, the Oude Westen, has shown, for instance, how large the gap is between public institutions and the inhabitants of this district, and particularly the unemployed among them (Schippers et al. 1990).

The functionalization of the social relations in the economy and the bureaucratizing in politics lead to the symptoms of social modernization: individualization and privatization. The social barrier is subject to erosion. Community contacts are receding both in quantity and quality, not only between the allochthonous and the autochthonous but also within these groups themselves, as the research on the Oude Westen has shown (Schippers et al. 1990). Because of this, social cohesion and solidarity are disappearing. This applies to those at the bottom of the societal ladder in particular. Those who don't have work are without social networks, which are determined by the work situation. This can lead to serious forms of social and psychological alienation.

Within cultural modernization all this can lead to collective and individual loss of meaning. This loss of meaning is an important source of the psychopathology of everyday life. It rears its head in the collective or individual formation of symptoms such as hysteria on the one hand and compulsion neurosis on the other (Habermas 1982). The question of meaning occurs at the limits of life and death where individual lives come together and then separate again. Meaning is a social category (Berger & Luckmann 1967).

(3) Consequences of modernization for the church

The consequences of modernization for the church are far-reaching and very radical. They can be described using two terms: institutional differentiation and cultural generalization.

Institutional differentiation

Modern society is being characterized more and more by the independence of the economic, political, social, and cultural dimensions from each other. This also applies to the societal institutions within these dimensions, which become independent organizations that strive after their own goals, work according to their own laws, mechanisms, and procedures, and are aimed at their own effectiveness and efficiency. In short, society is branching off into more and more autonomous institutions.

This institutional differentiation is of great importance to the church. In the agrarian, preurban, premodern period, the church was the center of society and carried it. In modern society this is no longer the case. The church can no longer maintain its position as an overall institution. The other institutions have become autonomous and have emancipated themselves from the church. It has become an institution among other institutions. In this way it has been thrown back upon its religious core function, in which it distinguishes itself from other institutions. Its specific sector is religion — in this case, the Christian religion. In this it has taken on the characteristics that determine the other sectors in society. They exist within increasing institutionalization and bureaucratization. In the case of the Christian religion this comes down to increasing ecclesiasticalization (Kaufmann 1979; 1989; 1992).

The relation that the societal institutions maintain with the church in this constellation is characterized by detachedness and noncommittedness. Indeed, this applies to the institutions with regard to each other too. For the church this can be clarified by means of some examples stemming from the economy, politics, social life, and culture.

Within the economy, we can point to the gap between trade and industry and the church. Already at the beginning of this century, Weber wondered how the morality of the market could be brought into agreement with the morality of brotherhood of the church (Weber 1920). The so-called social teaching of the church, which originated in the encyclical *Rerum Novarum* (1891), made efforts to bridge this gap. It was characterized by a deductive approach, which contained much ideology, the aim of which was to restore the societal power of the church. It failed (Chenu 1979), but it made way for an inductive method. In this the church does not work patronizingly or commandingly, but rather it works searchingly and exploratively. It tries to win a place as an interlocutor among other interlocutors (Jeurissen 1989; Coleman & Baum 1991; Houtepen 1992a).

Within politics, the state and the church are no longer a unity. Throne and altar are strictly separate entities. The state treats the church as an association as it treats other associations. It takes note of the church's actions. The more these actions convince the state with the arguments used, the more elements thereof are taken up in state policy. The state does not, however, have the obligation to react to these actions. It is not bound to support the teaching of the church, nor to refute it. The state cannot enter into the religious arguments that the church advances for its points of view, in the words of the former Dutch minister of justice, De Ruiter (1985).

A clear example is the advice of the ministerial commission Government, Religion, and Worldview (Overheid 1988). The discussion revolves around the constitutional principle of the separation of church and state. This principle makes government subsidy of the church and pastoral care impossible. There is, however, an exception for institutions in which people are forced to stay by law. If these people wish to make use of the spiritual guidance of the church, the state is obliged to create finances for this. This is the case in army and penitentiary institutions (Van Gerwen 1989). For the rest, the church is aligned to politics in much the same way that all other institutions are aligned to politics. In the event that there are problems that touch upon the responsibility of the church, it can turn to politics and hope to be heard, just as any other institution would. The church is only one of the actors on society's stage, just as the government is one (cf. Bekke & Kuypers 1990).

Within social life, one finds that the cohesive function of the church has lost its force. This may be illustrated by the recent ups and downs in the field of confessional organizations. In 1960 there were still 161 national Catholic organizations, which covered the whole field of charity and welfare work, health care, education, culture and recreation, youth work, trade unions, and politics. In 1970 about 35, and in 1980 nearly 100 of these 161 organizations disappeared. Since then the process of deconfessionalization has come to a stop (cf. Duffhues et al. 1985). However, there is a fundamental problem underlying the institutions, which still shows a confessional character (education, health care, and media). It concerns the gap between the structural confessional character of the institutions and the cultural deconfessionalization of the workers in and users of these institutions. This is sometimes called the problem of paper confessional organizations (Van Kemenade 1981). The degree to which one succeeds in formulating a cohesive vision and mission for these organizations is an indication of the societal relevance of the church; the degree to which one fails is an indication of the lack of relevance. Note that it is *an* indication, not *the* indication.

Within culture we can also observe that the ties between the other cultural institutions and the church have grown looser. This may be clarified by considering the relationship between church and morality. Already in the bourgeoisie society of 17th- and 18th-century France, there was an anticlerical, laicized, secularistic morality. It then appeared that morality without the church was possible (Groethuysen 1930). Among the members of the church itself, one finds a gap between church and morality as well. Even traditional members of the church take on permissive attitudes regarding the official moral teaching proclaimed by the church (De Moor 1987). The church has lost its traditional moral power; it can no longer count on obedience and agreement as a matter of course. The time of consensus on the basis of force and power is finished. It has made way for consensus based on open communication and meaningful, argumentative conviction.

From the above it has become clear in what sense the societal position of the church has changed. It is no longer a central managing organ with an unassailable authority. It no longer finds itself in a sphere of solemnity and sublimity, which sets it above the parties and above society. It is the object of discussion, criticism, and protest, as every institution is the object of reflection, change, and conflict. The church is a partner among other partners in society — a partner with a special vision and mission. It is only a player among other players; however, proceeding from the special vision and mission, it has to play society's game (cf. Bekke & Kuypers 1990).

Cultural generalization

The institutional differentiation is coupled with a process of cultural generalization. The relationships people maintain with each other within institutions are becoming more institution, sector, and aspect bound and therefore more specialist. However, in the relationships people enter into with each other between these institutions, they have to abandon this specialist character, otherwise they cannot communicate and understand each other. That is why they abstract from their specialism and generalize at a more abstract level. Thus the institutional differentiation necessarily calls up the process of generalization (Zijderveld 1983).

In the area of values and norms, this generalization can be recognised by the general importance attached to attitudes like fellow-feeling, inner-directedness, intrinsic values, and care for nature. These abstract values and norms are the things that keep people together (Felling et al. 1983). As soon as they become more specific and concrete, people become divided. The cause is rooted in institutional differentiation. Everybody is convinced of general values like meaningful labor and care for nature. However, in the social-economic discussion, the factor of capital (the entrepreneurs) is set against that of labor (the employees) and in the debate on the environment capital and labor together stand opposite the factor of nature (the health and consumer organizations).

This places the church in a dilemma. On the one hand, if the church restricts itself to general values such as fellow feeling, inner-directedness, intrinsic values, and nature, it leaves aside the problems of modernization that occur in societal institutions. Then it ignores the processes of injustice, poverty, alienation, and loss of meaning that take place in these institutions. It would neglect its evangelical task as such. On the other hand, if the church does undertake these problems, it is entering areas where it has no authority, and it has to take sides in the conflicts of interests between and within these institutions. It would then do violence to its external universal task and to its internal unity.

How can the church get out of this dilemma? The North American episcopal conferences (United States and Canada) have been seeking a way out of this thorny problem during the past years. A good example is the letter of the bishops of the United States regarding war and peace, and in particular nuclear armament (The Challenge of Peace 1983). The process of becoming aware of the letter took three years and attracted attention by its public character. The three years were necessary because the bishops consulted a large number of experts — not only theologians and ethicists but also military people and politicians. During the same period the bishops published some draft texts to get the discussion going and to be able to process the reactions to them. This procedure was connected to the double purpose of this letter. They not only wanted to help the members of the Catholic Church in forming an opinion or judgment regarding nuclear armament. They also wanted to make a contribution to the public debate about it, outside the church. The stand taken by the bishops in the letter is characterized by the following formal structure: it makes a distinction between ethical principles on the one hand, and on the other hand, prudential judgments, in which these principles are applied to concrete situations. The bishops take the ethical principles to be absolute. These principles can be considered in argumentative communication, but basically they are beyond discussion. An example is the principle of noncombatants: citizens who do not wish to participate in battle should be safeguarded against (mass) destruction. Things are different for prudential judgments. Prudential judgments are value judgments following the tradition of Aristotle and Thomas Aquinas. They contain more than one element. One explores the problematic situation at hand. One studies its history, the context, and the developments that are to be expected in the future. In addition, the intended direct and indirect consequences and unintended side-effects are examined for all possible interventions by one's own side, the other side(s), as well as the opposite side. It is clear that no absolute certainty can be given regarding these concrete situational aspects. That is why the term is prudential judgments. People of goodwill — also within the church itself — may differ in their opinions.

An example of this is making a no-first-use statement. The moral judgment on this — whether one should or should not agree with such a statement — is of a prudential nature. People may differ in their opinions. Now the prudential judgments, which the American bishops make in their letter, are not conscientiously obligatory, even though they do call upon Catholics to take serious note of this (Van der Bruggen 1986, 207-10).

The letter greatly influenced the letter of the German bishops (Gerechtigkeit schafft Frieden 1983) and their Dutch colleagues (Vrede en Gerechtigheid 1983). The letter of the latter was preceded by a request for advice on the part of Pax Christi The Netherlands (Van der Ven 1981). The Dutch bishops did extensive consultation on this advice with experts and institutes, and held a broad round of discussions in the parishes as well. Only then did they formulate their own point of view (Van der Ven 1983b). All that is of importance in the procedure that was used to find a way out of the dilemma mentioned. This way out is through holding extensive in-depth consultations with experts and cross-sectionally with all sorts of groups. It is made up of a combination of professionalism and democracy.

Chapter 2

The Position of the Church

In the last chapter we discussed the societal context of the church. In this context the process of modernization was central and its consequences for the church were described by the terms *institutional differentiation* and *cultural generalization*.

In this chapter we will examine the position of the church itself in modern society. This position can be described using the terms *denomination* and *association.* We do not wish to suggest either that the church is a denomination or that it is an association. We use the terms *denomination* and *association* only as a perspective. We wonder what light is shed on the church if we approach it from the perspective of the denomination and the association.

Theological questions are involved in this issue. Theological evaluation of the church as a denomination leads to various ecclesiological models. At the same time, theological evaluation of the church as an association leads to critical reflection proceeding from the church as a community of believers.

In this chapter we will deal with two questions: (1) In what sense may the church be regarded as a denomination and to which ecclesiological models does this lead? And, (2) In what sense may the church be seen as an association, and what is the critical meaning of the church as a community of believers in this respect?

(1) Church as denomination

The church can be described using various terms (Yinger 1970). Some of these are: Church (= universal, established, institutionalized church), denomination, sect, and cult (Weber 1980; Troeltsch 1912). Here we restrict ourselves to these four because they give us sufficient information for our goal: the elucidation of the position of the church in Western society today. The theological evaluation of these terms leads to a number of ecclesiological models.

Church, denomination, sect, and cult

In principle the *Church* encompasses all members of society. It fulfills their personal needs, so that it contributes to personal and social integration. It maintains a consistent whole of dogmatic convictions and moral values and norms. It claims to be universal. It places emphasis on obligatory participation in religious rituals. It interprets religious leadership in terms of sacred priesthood. It demands absolute obedience to church authority.

The *denomination* can be seen as the Church's opposite. It does not contain all members of society, only a part of them. It does not meet all personal needs, but just a few of them. It does not function as the basis for personal and social integration, but as a societal institution among other societal institutions. All this means a process of transition from a uniform *depositum fidei* to a pluriform interpretation of religious understandings and moral values. This means a transformation process from universality, absoluteness, and exclusivity to inclusivity, unicity, dialogue, and communication. Coupled with this is a certain relativization of the religious ritual as well as a greater emphasis on personal commitment and engagement. On the basis of this, greater demands may be placed on the contribution of the members, who freely join and participate. Religious leadership is seen in terms of professional expertise, professional availability, and service. Finally, the autocratic structures are replaced by democratic ones (cf. Schreuder 1967).

The *sect* can also be described by contrasting it to the Church. While the Church is characterized by cultural and structural universalism, the sect restricts itself to its own circle of chosen or elected members. It throws up relatively high barriers against the reception of new members. This is done by subjecting their religion and behavior to close scrutiny. The sect is marked by an ethical radicalism that forbids easy adaptation to the ruling values and norms of the surrounding state and society. While the religious consciousness in the Church is based on the consecration of the priests, the sect has its foundation in the religious talent and aptitude of its members. In contrast to the Church the sect is characterized by a minimum of bureaucracy. In the sect, the emphasis may be placed on conversion, repentance, expectations for the future, or esoteric knowledge. Four types of sects can be distinguished based on these accents: conversionists, introversionists, adventists, and gnostics (O'Dea 1968).

The *cult* — meaning religious devotion — is a manifestation of religion in which individual spirituality plays a central part. For this purpose a loose connection is sought with others, without too much emphasis on cohesion, communication, and organization. The most important thing is the "personal path" that an individual must look for, discover, test, and follow without interference from outside concerning content, without teachings or confession, and without organizational guidance. One comes across the cult in all sorts of yoga and meditation contexts and in circles in which people are in search of themselves in the Self. From there the cult penetrates some areas of the church, even though its significance is usually only marginal. Already at the beginning of this century, some believed that the cult would be the most important religious manifestation of the religious intellectual (Troeltsch 1912). As a consequence of their specific intellectual needs and because of their intellectual-searching attitude, they could find no solace in the church (Drehsen 1988). Others point to gatherings of people from different layers of the population who share their religious experiences, such as ecstasy and healing (Thung 1976, 61).

The four terms (Church, denomination, sect, and cult) may be used in different ways to typify the church in both a historical and a systematic sense. We will take a brief look at them.

In a historical sense, the four terms are used in various combinations to describe different developments. Researchers like Pope believed that there was a straight line along which one could trace a linear development from Church to denomination, from denomination to sect, and from sect to cult (Hill 1987).

Other authors, however, are of the opinion that the historical reality is far more complex. They depict it by means of a triangle. The three points are the Church, the denomination, and the sect. The historical developments can be described in various ways by means of this triangle. Throughout history one not only comes across developments running from the Church to the denomination, like the Catholic Church in The Netherlands (Simons & Winkeler 1987). But one also detects developments from the Church to the sect, especially when the European churches emigrated to America and were established there (Niebuhr 1963; Thung 1976, 59). However, developments are also to be found from the sect to the denomination, as in the case of the Seventh-day Adventists (Dobbelaere 1988). These take place when the second generation regard the inheritance from the first generation as a means to achieve socially respectable positions (Thung 1976, 60).

In a systematic sense the four terms can be used to describe the church in terms of its present characteristics, for the church may show more tendencies of the Church, the denomination, the sect, or the cult.

Thus the church can be seen as a religious community that tries to enliven or revitalize its inheritance from the Church (=universal institutionalized church). This can be expressed by an emphasis on one or more of the following: an early occurrence of initiation rites; religious socialization, in which the accent is placed on the integrity and inviolability of the *depositum fidei;* the meaning given to feasts throughout the church year; the sacred character of the liturgy; the dominance of the sacred ministry; and the sacrosanct character of the church hierarchy.

The church can also be viewed in terms of its denominational characteristics. In this the freedom principle of the members comes first, and within this the demands that may be asked of the voluntary contribution of the members. This is expressed by the criteria for access to the sacraments; the active participation in the liturgy; and the quality and content of their belief. More attention is paid to all sorts of groups within the church than to the church as an overall institution. Already at the beginning of this century, it was remarked that the Church should move in the direction of the development of an overall association of groups (*Dachverband*) (Troeltsch 1912). Within this association, the personal motives, desires, and needs of the various groups could better be shown to full advantage (Kaufmann 1979). In addition, the emphasis is placed on dialogue and communication with other religious communities within and outside of Christianity. Pluriformity and dialogue come first.

The sect, too, makes itself known not only outside but also within the mainline churches. The word *sect* is sometimes a cause of misunderstanding. In theology it has negative shades because of connotations with heresy and secession. In sociology this is not the case. There it has a descriptive meaning. It points to the religious formation of a group, small in size, with radical religious and moral principles and great engagement. Certain traits that are characteristic of the sect in sociology are nowadays to be found in what theology calls the "basic community." To avoid misunderstanding, we will use the latter term here.

Traces of the basic community can be found on both the left and right sides of the church. In both cases there is talk of a certain sharpening of the conditions for access to and participation in the sacraments. In the Church, there are no or hardly any separate criteria regarding the sacraments. Everyone who is a member of the church — on the strength of infant baptism — may receive the sacraments. In the denomination, criteria certainly have a role to play, both formally and informally. The least thing that a particular person must do is be prepared to reflect about and communicate his or her attitude toward the sacraments. In the basic community, real standards of content, which lie embedded within demanding religious and moral principles, apply, and great commitment is demanded. Another characteristic that connects basic communities to the right and left is their sharp cultural and societal criticism, from which they determine their position in society. There is strong opposition to the values and norms of present society because it does violence to the singularity of the gospel and with that to the church. In this one can go two ways, as was indicated by Weber at the beginning of this century (Weber 1980; Habermas 1982). The first way is to turn away from society. This is the case — covertly or overtly — in more or less pietistic circles (Schwarz & Schwarz 1987) or charismatic groups. The second way is a critical turning toward and intervention in society with the purpose of transforming it (Steinkamp 1988).

Finally, we have the cult. The mainline churches sometimes have spiritual centers in which individuals explore their own religious path through mystagogical meditation, guidance, and training. The emphasis is placed not on orthodoxy or orthopraxis, but on the individual experience of the depth of one's self or of the cosmos, whether or not in reference to religious-cognitive frameworks. Some complain that the leaders of the mainline churches are mystagogically incompetent. Others wonder sceptically whether the Dutch really (want to) meditate (Schreuder 1984).

What conclusion can we draw? It cannot be denied that the mainline churches of today to a varying degree contain traits of the Church, the denomination, the basic community, and the cult. However, those who look at the church from the perspective of the denomination come to the conclusion that the characteristics of this type are most similar to those of the church. This is also becoming more and more the case in Germany, where the church has a very special public status. There is a "zunehmende Labilisierung des bestehenden Volkskirchentums" (Kaufmann 1989, 145). We are not talking about a normative argument but about a descriptive one that needs further regionally specific research.

Ecclesiological models

Supposing that our conclusion is correct, then the question arises how the church is to be theologically valued. Is it theologically acceptable and desirable that the church displays mainly denominational traits? Or should we be striving for another ecclesiological goal? With this question we move from the descriptive to the normative level.

The position of the church (Church, denomination, basic community, and cult) cannot be regarded separately from the context in which it is situated. This context is determined by economic, political, social, and cultural modernization (chapter 1). That is why the theological valuation of the position of the church is connected to that of modernization.

Here we will describe five ecclesiological models: the amodern Church, the modern and the critical-modern denomination, and the amodern and the critical-modern basic community. We are talking about five ecclesiological models, not about the opinions of five groups of ecclesiologists. The latter nearly always show combinations of aspects from the five models. The references to theological authors therefore only have an illustrative meaning for certain elements of the models, and not for the authors. The models have the character of ideal types in the Weberian sense (1980).

The first ecclesiological model can be characterized by the term *amodern Church.* There people resist modernization (chapter 1 sub 1).

At most they tolerate an "eingeschränkte Modernisierung" (Kaufmann 1992). They are aimed at the vitalization and revitalization of the Church of earlier times. They reject the central terms *development* and *rationalization* (chapter 1 sub 2). They depart from a fundamental antithesis between development/evolution and grace and between rationality and faith. Neither do they accept institutional differentiation (chapter 1 sub 3). The Church still stands in the center of society or should be restored to this position. It is the bearer of the absolute and universal truth of the *depositum fidei,* which cannot be questioned. It cannot be thought about in freedom, nor can it be discussed in dialogue with dissentients. The Church is supratemporal and supraspatial by nature. It has a sacred and ritual character. Its base lies in the divine origin of the ministry *(ius divinum),* which claims obedience to the authority of the Church. In this lies the foundation for the distinction between the two classes — clergy and laypeople. This corresponds to the distinction between the *ecclesia docens* and the *ecclesia discens* (Auer & Ratzinger 1983).

The second ecclesiological model can be described by the term *modern denomination.* In this people start from the actual fact of modernization and accept it. Development/evolution and grace are not in opposition; rationalization and faith can be harmonized. Its members accept institutional differentiation, seeing the church as an institution among other institutions with its own religious function. It has to recognize the autonomy of the other institutions and their competencies. It has to pay close attention to the limits of its own authority. The economy is left to the economic organizations; politics is left to the state apparatus; social life is left to societal associations; and culture is left to cultural institutions. Insofar as it gets involved with the problems of these institutions, it is restricted to general statements at the level of general values and norms. It adapts to the cultural generalization (chapter 1 sub 3). It departs from the hypothesis that the church is not an institution for societal and cultural criticism. Its message is: everything is politics, but politics is not everything (Kuitert 1985). At the same time it places the emphasis on the freedom of the individual members of the church. They have to make their own decisions about being (or remaining) a member of the church and to what degree they agree with its teachings. It is not wrong to make an appeal to their engagement and commitment; however, only on the condition that their freedom is guaranteed. The emphasis is on openness in communication between the individual and church tradition, communication with oneself, with fellow believers, and with dissentients. In this communication the argumentative power, together with the expressive authenticity of the opinions that are exchanged, should be central.

The third ecclesiological model can be indicated by the term *critical-modern denomination.* Emphasis on religious freedom and the personal engagement of the members of the church is typical of this model too. Here, too, the force of consensus is rejected. However, this may not degenerate into — the model places the emphasis on this — non-engagement. The church may not become a non-engaged service church or a non-engaged supplier of opportunity. The point is to guard the space between the total identification of the Church and the non-identification of the service church. Both are felt to be undesirable. The church may make an appeal to make a real choice, without, however, forcing it, and without making it a total choice.

The church is not a totalitarian institution (Goffmann 1975). At least it should not be. Otherwise it would go against institutional differentiation, which makes the totalitarian choice for one institution impossible. It would force people to make one particular totalitarian choice, while they have an infinite number of diverse roles to play in institutions that are autonomous over against each other (Kaufmann 1992). That is why partial identification is central in the critical-modern denomination (Haarsma 1983; Willems 1985), or minimal identification (Pohier 1978; 1985). A different kind of identification within the context of institutional differentiation is neither possible nor desirable.

Besides this, there is another, more fundamental difference from the model of the modern denomination. In the model of the critical-modern denomination, people are sharply aware of the negative consequences of modernization: the injustice in economic modernization, the force of the systems in political modernization, the alienation in social modernization, and the loss of meaning in cultural modernization. The church cannot and must not passively look on. To do so would mean being unfaithful to its mission. Therefore, it should look for possibilities to contribute to liberation from the needs and sufferings of modern society. It is only capable of doing this if it critically resists the process of cultural generalization. It must make concrete statements and execute concrete programs and projects. In this task, it must combine professional consultation and democratization (Van der Ven 1988b). The action of the conferences of bishops in North America is an inspiring example (chapter 1 sub 3).

The fourth ecclesiological model can be described with the term *amodern basic community.* Just as is the case in the amodern Church, people here reject modern society. Modernization implies a fundamental intrusion upon the divine origin of the church, its tradition, teaching, ministry, and liturgy. Entering into and belonging to the church have nothing to do with one's personal choice and decision. They are founded in the prevenient grace of God. This is represented in the ordained ministry. One is therefore under the obligation of obedience to the ministry. It represents Christ with its own body. A different conclusion is drawn from the difference between the church and modernity, however, than in the first model. The goal here is not the revitalization of the Church within the whole of society, but isolation from society. The church has no other option than to take itself to be a small flock, the holy few. It has to protect itself from the influences of modern society. It is better to remove the rotten apples from the basket and keep the others intact than to let the rot fester and infect the whole basket.

The fifth ecclesiological model can be labeled by the term *critical-modern basic community.* This term refers to the social formation of a religious group that is small in size, with very demanding religious and moral principles and high personal and communal devotion. The difference, however, from the amodern basic community is that they do not turn away from modern society, but go into it actively and critically with an aim to change it and reshape it with the perspective of the kingdom of God.

What is striking in this model is the emphasis that is placed on transcendence, not of the church, but of the gospel that the church has to proclaim. This transcendence is not explained by means of spatial metaphors that indicate high (God) and low (humans and earth), but with metaphors that refer to time. In this the future of God, who intrudes upon the trends of the past and present in the world of man, is central. This does not imply a total destruction of the developments in modern society, but it does imply a fundamental interruption. The coming of Christ is not to be regarded in terms of the future *(futurum),* as if the kingdom of God is an extrapolation of present trends. The coming of Christ can be taken as the advent of Christ *(adventus domini)*. This does not mean continuity with the present, but a combination of continuity and discontinuity. That is why the apocalyptic moment in eschatology may not be neglected. In that moment God judges what humans have achieved (Metz 1977).

Three different strategies can be distinguished within the model of the critical-modern basic community, always based on the existing parish. Some authors believe that critical-modern basic communities should be developed within the parish (Schneider 1982; Wess 1983; 1989); others that this development should take place separately from the parish (Steinkamp 1985; 1988); and still others make a plea for the gradual transformation of the parish to a basic community (Moltmann 1975).

(2) The church as an association

A choice for one of the ecclesiological models implies a statement about the societal position of the church. The model of the amodern Church means that the church must (again) be the center of society. The other four models imply that the church and society no longer cover each other and accept this fact. The church is not coextensive with society and does not need to be. It is part of society; it is a subsection. This means that it is not adequate to talk about church and society (proceeding from the model of the amodern Church), as is often the case now. Proceeding from the latter four models, it is better to talk of a "church in society" (Kaufmann 1992).

If the church has to be considered as a church in society, the obvious question is what kind of identity the church forms within society. In order to answer this question, we have to find out what societal formations society contains and what type the church belongs to. Concretely this means that we will research whether the church belongs to the kind of societal formation that is indicated by the term *association.* The question is therefore whether the church can be considered to be an association. Not whether it *is* an association, but what sort of perspective arises if you approach it as an association. We will also find out how this approach can be valued ecclesiologically. This will be done by seeing the church as a community of believers.

FIGURE 2.1 Societal formations in society

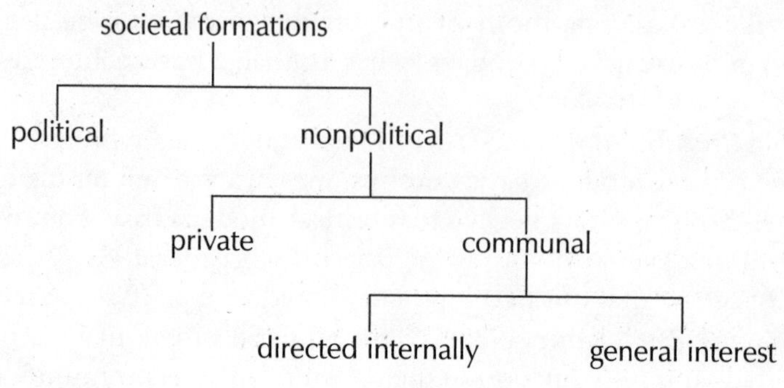

Association

In order to properly introduce the questions formulated above, it is necessary to classify the societal formations that exist (Gamwell 1984). Then the question is from which societal formation the church is to be considered.

As becomes clear from figure 2.1, two types of formations can be distinguished in every society: political and nonpolitical. The political formations can be situated at a national, provincial, or municipal level. The nonpolitical formations fall into two groups. There are formations that try to realize private or communal goals. Enterprises and companies (the private sector) belong to formations with private aims. They are directed toward growth in profit and capital. The other formations strive for the realization of communal goals (the social midfield). These can again be divided into two kinds. There are formations that are aimed at the common interest of the formations themselves and therefore are internally directed, and there are formations that are aimed at the general good *(bonum commune)*.

The latter division is of great importance for associations. Associations belong to communal formations. They can be divided into two types: associations with goals internally aimed at the community and associations aimed at the general good. Insofar as the church can be considered an association, it falls under both the first and the second category. Being aimed at the general interest is part of its identity. It belongs to the church's vision (chapter 11) and mission (chapter 12).

We will now describe some characteristics of associations and apply them to the church. In this description it is important that we make use of the sociological term for association and not of the juridical term. We are not interested in the characteristics of a civil or canonical (Catholic or ecclesiastical) association (Huysmans 1986). What matters is the description of a certain kind of social group formation, a certain kind of social formation, that can be indicated by the sociological term *association* (Scott 1957; Harrison 1960; Sills 1968; Jolles 1972; 1978).

The idea of considering the church as an association is not new (Sills 1968, 364). However, it does have a distinct history. In German-speaking countries it has been known as the *Kollegialtheorie* since the 17th and 18th centuries. In this the church is considered to be a collegium or a *societas libera et aequalis:* one may participate freely and on an equal footing. There are two versions of this theory. In the Catholic version only the bishops belong to the collegium. In the Protestant version all members belong to it. This theory was rejected by the teaching authority of the Catholic Church. This was caused by the Gallicanism, Febronianism, and Josephinism in this theory (Granfield 1982; Houtepen 1973, 90ff.; Walf 1984a, 145).

In the history of the Protestant churches the notion of the church as an association is easily identified with congregationalism. This congregationalism is itself connected with independentism. In this the right and responsibility of each local church to make its own decisions without being called to account by higher bodies is emphasized (Willis 1967; Jenkins 1974).

This history does not stop us *sine ira et studio* from checking whether and in what sense the church can be considered an association. We apply ourselves to an analytic approach. We describe the characteristics of an association and try to apply them to the church. We abandon the Catholic battle about Gallicanism, Febronism, and Josephinism and the Protestant discussion about independentism.

What is an association? An association is "a formalized autonomous social formation of cooperation between a number of people with a common, specific, and explicit aim, who joined of their own free will" (Jolles 1978, 776). Let us take a closer look at this description.

The first characteristic is that the association is a *formalized* social formation. Formalized means that the actions, reactions, interactions, and transactions between members and groups in an association are bound by rules. One cannot simply do what one wants. There is regulation.

This also applies to the church — within the Catholic Church even to quite a degree. The codex contains the written deposit of this regulation. Many ecclesiastical documents can be considered the religious legitimation of this regulation.

The second characteristic is the *autonomous character* of the association. The term *autonomous* is based on the concept of human rights. People have the right of association without being held accountable to third parties. This freedom is rooted in the constitutions of most democracies as well.

Does this apply to the church too? From the Declaration on Religious Freedom in Vatican II, one may deduce a positive answer. The argumentation goes as follows. Freedom belongs to the essence of man. This freedom has to be respected and propagated. That is why the freedom to shape religious life, which is at the center of humanity, has to be respected also with regard to its social-religious aspects. In this there is not only a philosophical matter at issue according to the Declaration, but also, and more particularly, a theological one. It is twofold. The religious freedom of humanity is founded on the side of God in the revelation in which the dignity of humankind is central. On the side of humanity, it is founded in the act of faith in God's revelation. Because this act is a human act, it is free *(actus humanus,* not *actus hominis).* The existence of religious communities has its base in this freedom. This basis also applies to the Catholic Church *(Dignitatis Humanae).*

The third characteristic lies within the word *cooperation.* One may interpret it in such a way that the cooperation distinguishes itself from social formations in which people live together. In other words, an association does not belong to the so-called primary groups in which people share each other's lives intimately, but belongs to what can be called task groups. This does not mean, however, that personal relations, feelings, or attitudes do not exist or cannot be developed in associations.

There are several kinds of task groups and therefore several kinds of (branches of) associations. Here the words *objective, subjective,* and *intersubjective* are of importance. Some task groups or associations place the emphasis on the realization of objective tasks (offering services). Others are characterized by the execution of subjective tasks (personal awareness and self-actualization). Still others engage in intersubjective tasks (encounter, discussion, contact). One can also express the difference in terms of communication. In the first, the communication is a means to achieve goals that are external to communication. In the second, the emphasis is placed on the intrapersonal communication. In the third, it is on interpersonal communication (Krefeld 1979).

This trichotomy can easily be recognized in ecclesiastical life. For example, a parish council and a pastoral care group form an objective task group; a meditation group is a subjective task group; and a pastoral encounter group is a intersubjective task group. This trichotomy can be purifying too. It prevents tendencies to regard the church as a community of people living together, a family, or relatives (Wess 1983; 1989). The church can be seen as a cooperation with three kinds of tasks.

The fourth characteristic lies in the entry of one's own *free will.* In this the freedom of choice of the individual is central. The membership is not based on birth or origin. It is not obligatory, but neither does it take place automatically. This is also expressed in terms of ascription versus achievement. Ascription relates to belonging to a group or community on the basis of biological relations (family) and/or territorial relations (village, town, country). The most characteristic of these are blood relationship and ethnicity. Achievement is determined by conducting a certain activity and/or bringing about a material or spiritual achievement.

What is implied in the characteristics of the church as a denomination or basic community, respectively, is that the church is a social formation where people join of their own free will. In a normative sense, it can be valued positively. It is founded on the philosophical and theological insight in the freedom of religion, which was just discussed. That people perform an achievement in the sense of (partial) identification and engagement is couched within the nature of the church of today. Moreover, it breaks through the narrow borders of blood relationship and ethnicity.

Joining of one's own free will does not imply that everybody — having joined — lends shape to his/her membership in the same way. Within associations one can distinguish: (1) a board, (2) professionals who are employed by the association, (3) volunteers, and (4) members. These members may be divided into various kinds: (a) virtuous members, (b) core members, (c) modal members, (d) marginal members, (e) dormant members, and (f) dead members. From this perspective people outside the association may be considered to be (g) ex-members, (h) ex-members of the first generation, (i) ex-members of the second generation, and (j) nonmembers.

This division also applies to the church. A church has (1) a church board, (2) professional pastors employed by the church, (3) volunteers who form pastoral care groups together with the pastors, and (4) church members. The latter can be split up into: (a) the great charismatic examples, from whom power and inspiration (still) stem (patron of the church, the blessed, saints), (b) core members who not only regularly take part in the liturgy but also participate in other church activities during the week, (c) modal members whose involvement is restricted to regular liturgical participation (at least once a month), (d) marginal members who only go to church a few times a year (e.g., Christmas and Easter) and participate in the rites of passage (baptism, marriage, and funerals), (e) dormant members who do not come to church, but do keep up with church news and/or make an annual financial contribution, (f) dead members whose names only occur in computer printouts, (g) ex-members who have turned their backs on the church, (h) ex-members whose parents left the church, (i) ex-members whose grandparents left, and finally (j) nonmembers (Moberg 1962, 406-11; Felling et al. 1987a, 276-77).

The last characteristic involves the *aims of the association.* Depending on the description, these aims are common, specific, and explicit. It is of importance not to take these adjectives too monolithically. They are characterized by all sorts of variations.

The common goal of an association means that the members of the association have agreed to strive after the same goal or set of goals. Present members and those who have newly joined conform to this. It keeps them together and legitimizes their togetherness both *ad intra* and *ad extra.* Naturally, this does not mean that an association is free of tensions, especially concerning the communality of the goals. This is particularly the case when the goals are complex. There are always groups that want to emphasize one aspect of the goal and other groups that wish to emphasize others. Besides this, there may be a shift in goals that stems from the play of action and reaction. These are not only caused by the (power) struggle between groups, but also because of the pressure from outside on the association (increase in members, financial means, etc.). Furthermore, the common goal does not exclude the pursuance of individual goals.

The goal or set of goals is specific. This does not mean that it is a one-issue goal. It does mean that it is not so general as to include everything and everybody. It may be complex by nature and contain more than one facet. It may be a short-term aim, or a long-term aim, or even a transcendent aim that surpasses any notion of term. It may be of a societal or cultural nature or contain a combination of both.

As we mentioned above, an association may contain an internal goal aimed at the association itself, or a goal that is aimed at the general good *(bonum commune),* the general welfare (figure 2.1). A distinction is also made between expressive and instrumental aims. In the expressive aims, the activities are an aim in themselves, for instance maintaining and promoting certain aspects of culture, music, or visual arts. One does not undertake these activities with another purpose in mind besides the value that they have in themselves. In the case of instrumental aims, certain activities are only carried out to achieve goals that lie outside them. This is the case, for instance, in associations that stand for the protection of certain interests. These need not be internally aimed interests (employer's association, union). It may also be the protection of interests for the benefit of collectives or even for the whole of society (woman's movement, environmental movement). Some associations are characterized by both expressive and instrumental aims (Gordon & Babchuk 1959).

The aim is made explicit. In its minimal meaning, "making explicit" concerns an oral agreement, while its maximal meaning encompasses having recorded the aim in a notarial document. There are all sorts of variations in between, like the description of the aim in working papers, accounts, reports, propositions for policy, work programs, etc. The fact that the aim is made explicit does not mean that it has been determined once and for all. It may be a continuous point of discussion because of the interpretation as well as the shift in the aim.

All this applies to the church too. Its goals are also communal, specific, and explicit. This does not alter the fact that these adjectives are marked by a large degree of variation, as is the case for other associations.

The communality of the aim or set of aims is expressed in the description of the essence and the task of the church in the Bible and in the scriptures of the church tradition. The official documents, like those of Vatican II, are of great importance in this. However, it is precisely these documents that are a source of discussion because of the ambivalence in them, and in *Lumen Gentium* in particular. The texts are the result of all kinds of compromises on the views of the church by conservative and progressive bishops and theologians. As a consequence, they are Janus-faced, being both hierarchical and communio-ecclesiological (Pottmeyer 1983; Conzemius 1986). The final report of the synod of bishops of 1986 also reflects this compromise (Tillard 1986).

The aims of the church are also specific, for they do not cover the whole of societal life. They are not economic, political, social, or cultural by nature. They are of a religious character. This does not mean that they are not related to the aims of the economic, political, social, and cultural life. However, they are not such that they coincide with them. The aims of the church may only be called total and encompassing insofar as they approach the whole of the societal and personal life of people from a religious perspective. This perspective itself is all-encompassing as a perspective of transcendence.

That the goals of the church have been made explicit is sufficiently illustrated by the above. Even an excess of explicitness is to be found. This has partly to do with the fact that the church has been a bureaucratic organization for centuries now. Thus the reaction of those who make a plea for a charismatic ecclesiology, which is characterized by holy anarchy and pneumatic chaos, can be explained. In this view, the blowing and sighing of the Holy Spirit must predominate, not the letter of the law (Hasenhüttl 1973; 1974).

Only an association?

Can we conclude from the above that the church is only an association? The answer is no, for two reasons. The first reason is of an epistemological nature, and the second is social-scientific.

First of all, we do not say and do not intend to say that the church is an association, but that it can be viewed *as* an association. The term *association* is not used to describe the essence of the church, but as an identifier, angle, point of view, or paradigm. It indicates the way in which we look at the church. Here we are dealing with the epistemological principle that we discussed earlier (Introduction).

Secondly, insofar as the church can be approached as an association, this in no way means that it cannot also be regarded from the perspective of other social formations at the same time. For the church can also be taken to be a people's formation, a social movement, a community, an organization, and an enterprise. In the next chapters we will take a closer look at this. We will approach the church from various perspectives: as a people's context (chapter 11), as a social movement (chapter 12), as a community (chapter 14), as an organization (chapter 20), and as an enterprise (chapter 22). However, these characteristics do not lessen our view of the church as an association. What they do is complement it. Here we are dealing with the principle of complementarity, which was also discussed earlier (Introduction).

Principle of noncompetition

A weighty argument that can be used against approaching the church as an association has a theological nature. It says that regarding the church as an association detracts from the church's religious identity, that in the end the church does not belong to the people but to God. It does not come from people but from God.

At the base of this objection lies a kind of theological dualism. The dualism stems from the following thought. Considering the church as a certain type of social formation, for example as an association, may be just, but it does not hit upon what the church really is. What God does with people in the church cannot be determined from a sociological angle. For that, theological reflection is necessary. By this idea, the meaning and range of the sociological approach are limited and curtailed. Sociology is subordinate to theology (chapter 5).

What lies at the base of this theological dualism is a kind of competitive thinking. The associative activity of people among themselves is subtracted from the unifying activity of God. Conversely, the unifying activity of God makes the associative activity of people less of a necessity and less important. More generally, what humans do is subtracted from what God does. Conversely, what God does is deducted from what humans do (Dingemans 1987, 104-5, 193).

Opposite this we can put the principle of noncompetition, which was referred to before (Introduction). In a general sense it states that God and humans do not compete. Their activities are not deducted from each other. What God does need not be subtracted from what humans do. Nor does the reverse — what humans do need not be subtracted from what God does (Schoonenberg 1969; 1986). God does not replace the activity of humans. He does not eliminate it but makes optimal use of it instead (Schoonenberg II, 1956, 149-66). In other words: what God does, humans do, what God does more, humans do more too (Schoonenberg I, 1955, 93).

If we apply this to the term *association,* we get the following: God brings people together by the fact that people come together themselves. God inspires them to togetherness by the fact that they inspire themselves to togetherness. God motivates them to a community through the fact that they motivate themselves to a community. God works in and through the cooperation of people. He acts in and through their social actions. However, God does this without being absorbed by it, or without being exhausted by it. In other words: God gives people the power of association; he gives them the power to be a community; he gives them the power to make an effort for each other; he gives them the power to express their mutual engagement. To put it differently, the association of people in the church is a sign of God's creative and liberating presence in the church.

Community of believers

We have certainly touched upon some of the most important properties of the social formation of the church by describing it as an association. However, this does not give us a description of the theological meaning of this approach. We want to bring this to the fore by critically connecting the church as an association with an approach to the church that has a rich theological tradition implied in it: the church as a community of believers. We are not, however, satisfied with a one-sided relationship. The church as an association cannot be critically valued only proceeding from the church as a community of believers, and the church as a community of believers is not allowed to be critically valued proceeding from the church as an association. Both terms can be related to each other in a critical sense. By this mutual reflection both may be supplemented and enriched.

Before we pass on to this, we first have to dwell upon the term *community of believers.* It is the translation of Latin names used to indicate the church of old: *communio fidelium, congregatio fidelium, societas fidelium, societas credentium, societas sanctorum, collectio fidelium, collegium fidelium, coetus omnium sanctorum.* The meaning of these words is that believers together form the church, founded as it is in their belief in the salvation of God, Christ, and the Spirit.

These words play an important part in the history of the church. One finds them in the texts of many fathers in patristics (Küng 1962, 20-21). Cyril of Jerusalem already stated that the meaning of the church lies in the fact that "it calls to all people and joins them" (*PG* 33.1044). Clement of Alexandria calls the church "the meeting of the chosen" (*PG* 9.437). Origen defines it as "coetus populi christiani" (*PG* 13.677) and "credentium plebs" (*PG* 12.365). Augustine sees the church as "congregatio societasque hominum . . . in qua fraterna caritas operatur" (*PL* 40.193). He sees it as "universa societas sanctorum atque fidelium" (*PL* 33.362), as "christianae fidei communio nostra" (*PL* 33.297).

In the Middle Ages the term used most to indicate the church was *congregatio fidelium.* It lays the emphasis on the social-religious character of the church. The church is the meeting of believers. Congar remarks: "ce vocable est, au XIIIe siècle, un terme purement ecclésiologique" (Congar 1970, 215). Thomas often talks of the church as a *congregatio fidelium* (*De Ver.* 29.4.8; *Comp. theol.* 1.147). "What one has to know about this," says Thomas, "is that the church is the same as association *(congregatio).* That is why the holy church is the same as the association of believers, and every Christian is as a member of the same church" (*Expos. in Symb.,* art. 9). Terms like *congregatio (coetus, collectio, universitas, societas, collegium) fidelium* have been used frequently across the centuries, but they play an important in Thomas's work (Congar 1970, 233). It is worth mentioning that the social-religious nature of the church of that day did not lessen its sacramental character, nor vice versa. There was a synthesis between the two.

This starts to change in William of Ockham. He lays the emphasis on the social-religious character of the church and not at all or less so on its sacramental nature. The religious identity does not disappear from view with this, however. He roots the church as a community of believers in the belief in God. Proceeding from this belief, the church may be critical of the pope, insofar as he is guilty of heresy. A term such as *congregatio fidelium* gains a hierarchical-critical point with this (Congar 1970, 290-95).

Against this background the term became a battle cry during the time of the Reformation and Conter-Reformation, and gained a polemic meaning. With this and similar terms, the Reformers intended to place the emphasis on the social-religious nature of the church in order to relativize or deny its hierarchical, official, and sacramental character. The Catholic theologians (precisely for this reason) avoided these terms more and more. Instead they placed the emphasis on the hierarchical structure of the church, its official nature, and the sacraments. In this way the ecclesiology was being increasingly transformed into a hierarchiology (Congar 1964, 46-84). With regard to the church as an association, their preference went more and more toward the church as a perfect society *(societas perfecta)*.

The terms *congregatio fidelium* and *communio fidelium* were not entirely forgotten, however. Thus, one reads of the church as a community of believers in the Catechism of Trent. The same applies to Vatican I (Küng 1962, 22).

The documents of Vatican II pay considerable attention to the communal belief of the members of the church in God, who joins them all together in this belief. However, one cannot say that a term such as *communio fidelium* fulfills a clear and important part. If it is used, it is usually to indicate the relationship of the bishops among themselves or the relationship of the bishops with the pope (Rikhof 1983; 1992). It is as if they (especially) form the *communio fidelium!* However, proceeding from the church's own tradition, the term should be taken in a religious-communalistic sense. It is in this direction that the term should further be developed in the future.

Church as association and as community of believers

Against this background we can now relate the terms to each other. Proceeding from the church as a community of believers, what can we learn from a critical standpoint about the church as an association? And what can we learn about the church as a community of believers proceeding from the church as an association? In what way do the terms supplement and enrich each other?

Let us begin with critical reflection on the church as an association proceeding from the church as a community of believers. In this reflection three aspects can be brought to the fore. They indicate in what way the church as a community contains an essential supplement to the church as an association.

The first aspect is of a direct religious nature. What is made explicit in the church as a community of believers but not in the church as an association is that the church as a social formation is rooted in the belief in God. This does nothing to alter the associative character of the church, as we have seen. This would mean lapsing into competitive thinking. However, the explicit reference to God as the origin and aim of the church is lacking in the term *association,* as is the reference to God as the source and destination of the church. It is in this that the religious identity of the church lies. That is why *community of believers* contains an essential, indispensable, explicit supplement with regard to the church as an association. Without this supplement, the church runs the risk of being reduced to a sociocultural association.

The second aspect has to do with the internal social structure of the church. One could say that the church as an association is a far more differentiated term than is "community of believers." It is characterized by a number of membership differentiations: members of the board, professional members, volunteer members, core members, modal members, marginal members, and dormant members. The term *community of believers* is of a more global nature; it contains none of these refinements. This globality may be regarded as a conceptual objection. It ignores the differentiated reality of church practice. Nevertheless, there is an ecclesiological advantage to this globality. The risk of exclusively making use of the term *association* may be that all sorts of damaging dichotomies arise, which may fix church life in addition. Take, for example, volunteer members set against the rest, or core members set against the rest. There is a danger, for instance, that modal members, marginal members, and dormant members are written off. In other words, the church as a community of believers keeps us aware of the fact that modal members, marginal members, and dormant members also belong to the church. The church is more than the active core of an association. The church as a community of believers protects it from association blindness: the blindness of the heart of the association.

The third aspect has to do with the internal relations in the church. We approached the church as an association proceeding from the aims of its duties. The church has objective, subjective, and intersubjective duties to perform, as was already mentioned. However important this may be, it has to be supplemented proceeding from the church as a community of believers. For it is the interpersonal involvement that forms the basis of the church. Taken from this point of view, one can say that the church is a community of brothers and sisters that is rooted in the common factor of being God's children, as Origen, for example, made clear (Ledegang 1992, 164-74). Because of this, there is cordiality and solidarity in the church. And it is for this reason that the church can be called a community of friends. Both images complement each other: the community of brothers and sisters and the community of friends. On the one hand, the church is made up of people who have not chosen each other but have found each other in one social formation. This is what "brothers and sisters" refers to. On the other hand, one joins the church and becomes part of it on the basis of a free personal decision. This does not apply to brothers and sisters, but it does apply to "friends" (Moltmann 1975, 341-44). The church is a community of companions in religion, of fellow travelers (Ruggieri 1981). This touches upon the church as the body of Christ. In this the organic solidarity of the members of the church is central (chapter 14).

Next, we have the reverse: the critical reflection on the church as a community of believers proceeding from the church as an association. In this we will scrutinize two aspects. With this we will show in what way the church as an association is a correction and enrichment with respect to the church as a community of believers.

The first aspect regards freedom in the church. From the reflection on the church as an association we may learn that the meeting of people in the church is a free and autonomous process of free and autonomous people. They join of their own choice, and they may leave of their own choice too. They determine their closeness to or distance from the church according to their own views: as core, modal, marginal, or dormant members. In accordance with their own views they change their engagement with the church in a period of time: in one period they are dormant members, in another they may be core members, and in yet another they may be modal members. The fundamental orientation of freedom and autonomy should also permeate the church as a community of believers. The church should be a place — or even the place — of freedom and autonomy. For the loss of freedom means the loss of belief (Gal. 2). At the same time it means the loss of the church as a church. The church is in essence and by its task a free community of free believers. One may say: "As a gift of God the freedom of Christians is neither available, nor manipulable, nor abolishable, if Christianity itself is not to be abolished" (Pesch 1971, 38). This insight is at right angles to group pressure and social-religious manipulation, which easily occur in closed church contexts. The church as a community of believers profits from interhuman relations between believers, which are characterized by the freedom and autonomy of the church as an association. One's own choice and one's own decision are foremost in this.

The second aspect refers to the focus of the church. The church as a community of believers runs the risk of locking itself in and shutting the world outside out. From the reflection on the church as an association, this kind of danger can be avoided by placing the emphasis on two sorts of associations, which we distinguished earlier. The one is aimed at the internal community, while the other is aimed at the *bonum commune.* The church combines both orientations. This also applies to the church as a community of believers. Proceeding from the church as an association, the church as a community of believers can break through to the external orientation of the general good. That is, it can focus on the economic suppression, political domination, social alienation and cultural loss of meaning outside of it. This continually turns the church inside out (Hoekendijk 1967).

Chapter 3

The General Function of the Church

In the preceding chapter we saw that the modernization of Western society has broken through the centrality and self-evident character of religion (chapter 1). This puts the church in a new position. It no longer covers the whole of society. Its characteristics are closest to those of a denomination (chapter 2). Since it no longer has at its command social mechanisms that support and legitimize its plausibility, the church has to shape them itself. It has to build itself up. The only way to do so is by continually bringing its religious vision and mission into communication — in short, bringing about religious communication. That is the subject of this chapter.

In discussing the term *religious communication* we will (1) pay attention to an action-theoretical approach to religious communication, and (2) place this action-theoretical approach in an interaction-theoretical frame of reference. In the former we will focus upon the actors in the religious communication, and in the latter upon the interaction between them.

(1) Religious communication from an action-theoretical perspective

From an action-theoretical perspective, religious communication can be described as follows: *the contact in which the sender sends a message to the receiver with religious meanings that are attributed to the surrounding reality on the basis of religious codes.* This description may be called action-theoretical because it lays the emphasis on the actions that the actors involved carry out as sender and receiver. In this the point is the activity of sending a particular message and receiving what was intended. What is necessary is the encoding and decoding of the message. Furthermore, one has to establish and maintain contact between sender and receiver. Finally, the point of the message is to give meanings to the surrounding reality — in this case religious meanings.

From the linguistic analysis of Jakobson (1985) we derive the insight that there are six constituent factors in this description: the surrounding reality to which the message refers; the sender; the receiver; the contact between sender and receiver; the codes; the message itself.

The surrounding reality

The message refers to the surrounding reality. It makes certain statements about it. Certain meanings are attributed to it. The surrounding reality therefore becomes a "signified" reality. Religious communication is no different. In religious communication religious meanings are attributed to the surrounding reality so that it is signified as a religious reality. In this lies the cognitive function of religious communication (generally called by Jakobson the "referential" function of communication).

For some this may not be altogether obvious. Does reality become religious through the religious meanings that we attribute to it? Does religious reality not exist beforehand, before we lend it religious meaning? If we approach this question logically, then the answer is that we do not know. Outside the religious meanings that we attribute to reality, we know nothing about religious reality. Without these religious meanings we have no access to it.

This raises the following problem: What criteria do we have available if we want to know whether messages about religious reality are true? It is true that they refer to religious reality, but — if we think logically — there is no way of checking them. We cannot trace whether they adequately represent that reality separate from the messages themselves. We cannot determine whether they represent reality the right way. The so-called representation criterion seems to have had its day.

Do other criteria exist? For belief in religious messages has to be possible without logical absurdity (Hartshorne 1948). This question has led certain authors to set up other criteria (cf. Brümmer 1981; Van Brakel & Van den Brink 1988; Van der Ven 1990c).

Thus, for example, the criterion of coherence was brought forward. Coherence implies measuring the correctness of a message against other messages. The message has to be in agreement with them, or there can be no inconsistency. In this way Grossouw defended *Revistiese* "religious creativity." Gerard Reve (a modern Dutch author) in his poetry connected his intimate relation with God and his relation with a donkey. This shocked quite a number of people: "God is not a donkey." Grossouw defended Reve by using the coherence criterion. In order to justify the image of God as a donkey, he referred to Isaiah, who defines God and the kingdom of God by means of fairy-tale animals, like the wolf, the sheep, and the panther. He pointed to the mysticism used in defining the intimate tie between humans and God, which has always been full of eroticism (Grossouw 1967). However, is this criterion sufficient in the final analysis? Even an infinite collection of messages, however great their number, can miss out on the truth!

Others live by the criterion of consensus, which implies that the eventual agreement that is reached in a community of people determines what message is true and what is not. In science this community is formed by a forum of scientists (De Groot 1968). In public life it is formed by all those who participate in the public debate *(Diskurs der öffentlichkeit)* (Habermas 1982). In religion it is formed by the language community, which makes its own religious language agreements (Dalferth 1981). However, the question is whether this can solve the question of truth. A community can get it wrong too, as history teaches us!

Still others adhere to the pragmatic criterion. They say that the image that "works" is the correct one. That is to say, the one that contributes to the improvement of the conditions of human life is the right one — in an individual as well as a societal sense. In the individual sense, the most important question is whether and in what way the religious message contributes to dealing with the suffering, death, and guilt that people have to contend with. In other words, does it contribute to contingency processing (Van der Ven 1991d)? In a societal sense, the question is whether the religious message contributes to changes in society through which the liberation of the poor can be realized (Metz 1977). If one can say that a message fulfills no practical function, then it should be banished to the kingdom of idle speculation (James 1975). But what does "practical" mean? Can a message be indirectly practical besides being directly practical? Can it be practical in the long run as well as in the short run? Besides being intentionally practical, can it be unintentionally practical?

This discussion is anything but satisfying. Since it appears that fundamental questions can be asked about all of the criteria, have we nothing to go on? Does it all finally point to the radical question: Do we know anything really and what do we really know?

There are two classic answers to this question. The first is: we know what we know, but no more than that. We know our messages and we know the images and concepts that occur within them, but we can go no further. We know the names *(nomina)* that we give to reality, but it all ends there. This is the point of view of absolute nominalism.

The second answer is: we know reality itself by the messages we create and the images and concepts that occur in them. We are capable of covering and fathoming the whole of reality with our knowledge. Reality is known to us *totus et totaliter.* This is the line of absolute realism.

Between these extremes we find the so-called moderate conceptual realism (Peters 1957). It states that we only know reality in its aspects and from perspectives. "In its aspects" means we only know aspects of reality, not the whole of reality. "From perspectives" means we only know these aspects through the perspective we took. However, being in a straight line with these perspectives, we may find the aspects of reality to which our messages refer. Due to their aspectual and perspectival character, these messages need supplementation and correction. They are subject to constant change. Knowledge is relative.

This also applies, therefore, to the messages in religious communication. They contain aspectual and perspectival information about religious reality, and demand continuous supplementation and alteration. The epistemological value of the religious messages is thus relative (De Petter 1964; Schillebeeckx 1964; Van der Ven 1990c, 150-51, 156).

The sender

The sender sends the message about reality to the receiver. He or she does this purposefully. Herein lies the distinction between communication and information, between religious communication and religious information. Communication is not only information, but intended information. It is made up of deliberate transfer of information. Looking at a monk doing his yoga exercises in full concentration provides us with information about his religious attitude and movement, but one cannot talk of religious communication. His yoga exercises are not intended for us. They do not constitute a religious demonstration. If, afterward, the monk were to explain to us what he was doing and why, then we could talk of religious communication. There is an assumption of intentionality in communication that also applies to religious communication.

We may wonder what the sender is aiming at. Does he only intend to send the receiver a message with religious meanings about reality? Does this intention restrict itself to what we called the cognitive function? Or does the sender mean to express certain attitudes, experiences, emotions, and feelings? If the latter is the case, we can talk of an emotive function. It is possible that the sender wants to make a certain assertion through much personal dedication and effort, which is contrary to what he or someone else or a whole group of people have asserted before. Then the intention is to convince. It is also possible that — in making a certain statement — the sender wants to express his own commitment and engagement. Perhaps he or she wishes to express belief, hope, and love; or perhaps instead, doubt, scepticism, irony, or even cynicism.

It is of importance to note that the terms *sender* and *receiver* refer to roles. These roles are fulfilled by people, but the people are continually changing roles among themselves. In one round of communication, person A is the sender and person B is the receiver; while in the following round, B is a sender and A is a receiver. This exchange of roles is characteristic of communication, including religious communication. It turns it into a circular instead of a linear happening. It implies two-way instead of one-way communication. It assumes reciprocity.

In principle religious communication not only stands separate from the people, but also from the functions they hold. This also applies to religious communication in the church. It is irrelevant — from a communication-theoretical point of view — whether the role of sender and receiver is taken in turns by ordained or non-ordained ministers, professionals or non-professionals, core members or marginal members, ex-members or non-members. This does nothing to alter the intentionality and reciprocity of the religious communication (Van der Ven 1990c, 59-60).

The receiver

The receiver receives the message, at least to the extent of the intention of the sender. The receiver may restrict himself to a counter-message of reception or give a reaction regarding the content. He has three choices: accept the message (partially or entirely), reject the message (partially or entirely), or remain neutral and declare it outside his domain.

What does the receiver react to, and what is the content of his reaction? Insofar as the sender only had a cognitive function in mind with the message, the receiver may accept, reject, or be neutral in a cognitive sense regarding it. However, the sender may also have had emotive intentions, wishing to express emotions and attitudes. Here, too, the receiver has three ways to react to this expression: accept it, turn away from it, or place himself beside it. Finally, there is a third possibility. The sender may have wanted to set the receiver going, to urge him to do something, to send him in a certain direction. We call this the *conative* function. There are all sorts of aids available to the sender for this purpose: adhortatives (invitations, summons), imperatives (instructions, commands), commissives (promises, threats), satisfactives (words of thanks, efforts of reconciliation, apologies), declaratives (greetings, congratulations, appointments, judgments). Here again, the receiver has three options: to accept the conative statement, to reject it, or to declare it outside his domain (Habermas 1982; De Jong 1990).

Contact

The message sent by the sender to the receiver takes place in contact between the two. This contact can be direct or indirect through physical mediation (telephone). In both cases one can talk of a psychic connection between sender and receiver that allows them to communicate and remain in communication.

This contact may only serve as a channel within which the communication takes place. In that case, it does not receive any special attention. It is also possible that the contact itself is the focus of the communication, or at least part of it. In that case, the aim of the message is to bring about the contact, to continue it, to intensify it, to check it, to restore it, or to break it off. In bringing it about, making contact is essential ("Can I have a minute of your time?"). Continuation is expressed in the wish to prolong contact ("It is important that we have a chat"). The wish to intensify contact is often a part of communication too ("We should really discuss things more often with each other"). Checking is aimed at ascertaining whether there still is any contact ("Do you get my point?"). Restoring contact has to do with renewal of contact, for example after a period of absence or a falling out ("Let bygones be bygones"). The breaking off of contact takes place within the contact too ("I really have to go now").

Being set for contact is called the *phatic function.* A nice example of taking turns phatically, recorded by Dorothy Parker, was cited by Jakobson: "'Well!' the young man said. 'Well!' she said. 'Well, here we are,' he said. 'Here we are,' she said. 'Aren't we?' 'I should say we were,' he said. 'Eeyop! Here we are.' 'Well!' she said. 'Well!' he said, 'well'" (Jakobson 1985, 152-53).

The phatic function can take on different shapes. The most usual ones are interpersonal ritual formulas. These may be positive ("Thank you") or negative ("I would like to apologize"). They are often characterized by an exchange: the action of the one demands a reaction of the other and is aimed at that ("Thank you" — "You're welcome"). Their aim is to allow the other to make contact ("do come in") or to keep the other at a distance ("you can contact my secretary"). Clear examples of this are welcome and farewell rituals (Goffmann 1977). In religious communication one comes across these ritual formulas frequently, especially in the liturgy. In a greeting: "May God be with you." In closing: "Go in peace." They also apply to other church and pastoral sectors: pastoral care, catechetics, proclamation, and diacony.

Besides this, the phatic function may take the shape of a long speech. In some situations the homily is an example of it. In such a case the preacher aims primarily at "wanting to come across" instead of at what he has to say in a cognitive sense, or what he wants to achieve in an emotive or conative sense with his homily. The important thing is to establish and maintain contact. The phatic function predominates over the cognitive, emotive, or conative function. The danger of this is that the statement comes true: the medium is the message.

Religious codes

In the message, a religious meaning is attributed to the surrounding reality. This religious giving of meaning takes place via religious signs on the basis of religious codes. The message has to be encoded by the sender and decoded by the receiver.

Anticipating our reflections on religious signification in the following chapters, we will pay attention to two terms that are central to this in a global sense: religious signs and religious codes (chapters 6 and 7).

Let us begin with an example. The message in religious communication may be as follows: the sender wishes to make known to the receiver that he experiences nature to be a gift of God. Or that the love between people refers to God's love. Or that the gesture made by the priest in the liturgy is protection given by God. To put it more abstractly: in religious communication, elements from the surrounding reality — a situation, happening, activity, process, structure — are presented as bearers of a religious sign. Through religious signification, these elements refer to the presence of God's salvation. They signify this salvation. They re-present it.

Religious communication is, therefore, a kind of intentional message of the sender to the receiver, in which religious meanings are contributed to the surrounding reality. Religious communication is not direct communication between God and humans. God does not speak to us directly. God speaks to us through the surrounding reality by means of signs, or rather the surrounding reality speaks as a sign from God. Thus, God is not dealt with directly. There is no direct *"Anrede Gottes"* (Nipow 1969, 55-73). The surrounding reality witnesses as a sign of God, who is present and speaks to us in this sign. To put it differently, the proximity of God to humanity is mediated immediateness (Schillebeeckx 1973).

The working of religious signs depends on religious codes. These are religious rules and conventions, which lie couched within religious culture and originate from religious tradition. Through knowledge of and participation in religious tradition, in which the religious codes are available, we are capable of seeing certain elements from the surrounding reality as religious signs. This can be clarified by means of the examples we just gave. Nature can be seen as a gift from God on the basis of the code of God's creation; the love between people, as the love of God on the basis of the code of God's covenant; the liturgical gesture, as protection by God on the basis of the code of God's blessing. The religious codes are the mechanism through which we make connections between the elements from the surrounding reality and the religiously signified reality.

Religious communication depends on the working of these codes. It assumes that the sender and receiver have the same religious codes at their disposal. Only then is the sender able to encode that which he wishes to communicate in the right way, so that the receiver is able to decode the message correctly. If a mutual participation in the religious tradition in which the religious codes are stored is lacking, religious communication cannot be brought about or it is scrambled. Then it is necessary to search for common ground.

If such a gap takes place in the communication itself, one may talk of the *metalingual function* of communication, as Jakobson describes it. This takes effect if the sender and receiver check whether they understand each other and find out in what way understanding can still be reached or improved.

It is clear that the problems of religious communication today lie in this function in particular. Naturally, we cannot ignore the problems of the cognitive, emotive, and conative functions. These have especially to do with the sender and receiver mixing them up and getting the three functions confused. In addition, we must not think too lightly of the phatic function. However, the metalingual function turns the scale. Due to the pluralism of worldviews in Western society today, the plausible meaning of the religious tradition of the Christian religion has been lost. In the church itself, one sees an increasing religious pluralism. This makes religious communication, which exists on the basis of a common religious tradition and the religious codes rooted within it, a fundamental problem. That is why too much attention can never be paid to the metalingual function: the function of religious coding.

This function not only surfaces in questions such as "What do you mean by creation, covenant, blessing?"; but it is also expressed in metalingual explanations about the meaning of statements like "This is revealed," "This is the word of God," "This is the teaching of the church." These questions are not about the religious reality to which the religious signs refer. They are about the religious codes. Instead of communicating in language, people communicate about language. People do not talk about God, but about talking about God. People discuss a religious grammar. This often occurs in pastoral care, catechetics, liturgy, proclamation, and diacony. In theology it happens even more. The modern emphasis on the term *revelation* in theology is an example of this (Eicher 1977).

The message itself

Communication can also be aimed at the shape of the message. In this the important point is the use, order, and sequence of the words and sentences that are used. Then communication becomes self-reflexive. Jakobson sees this as the *poetic function.* He gives a good example: "A girl used to talk about 'horrible Harry.' 'Why horrible Harry?' 'Because I hate him.' 'But why not dreadful, terrible, frightful, disgusting?' 'I don't know why, but horrible fits him better'" (Jakobson 1985, 154).

The poetic function should not be confused with poetry. The poetic function predominates in poetry, but it cannot be reduced to it. It occurs in other language activities as well, even to a large extent. The reverse is also true, for poetry cannot be restricted to the poetic function.

In religious communication we see that the poetic function predominates, for instance, in parables. It is characteristic that the parable itself — and not the reality to which it refers — draws our main attention. This also applies to the psalms. They exist for the sake of themselves.

Functions of religious communication

We have discussed six functions of religious communication. They were coupled to six constituent factors: the surrounding reality to which the message refers; the sender; the receiver; the contact; the code; and the message itself. The six functions — cognitive, emotive, conative, phatic, metalingual, and poetic — answer to these factors in the sense that if the factor in question is dominant, the function in question is dominant too. There is no religious communication in which only one of the functions occurs. We always see one particular dominant function with several subdominant ones.

(2) Religious communication from an interaction-theoretical perspective

Until now we have restricted ourselves to the action-theoretical approach of religious communication. Briefly, this entails the attribution of religious meanings to the surrounding reality in the contact between the participants in the communication. We will carry the essence of this idea on to the interaction-theoretical approach that follows.

The interaction-theoretical approach surpasses the action of both separate actors, the sender and the receiver. This happens by posing the question of what jointly moves them and what they jointly have in mind. What goals and perspectives do they have in common?

From an interaction-theoretical angle, religious communication can be described as follows: *the exchange of religious meanings, aimed at the development of an understanding and agreement within and between the participants and with religious tradition, in the perspective of religious reception, response, and reaction.*

This description contains elements that need to be looked at in more detail: the aims of the religious communication (exchange, understanding, agreement); the types (in connection with groups of participants); the orientations (intra- and interpersonally and traditionally aimed); the transcendent perspective (religious reception, response, reaction).

Aims

The term *aim* means that it is what is sought after. Whether the aim is actually achieved is another matter. Three aims with regard to religious meanings are mentioned in the description above: exchange, understanding, and agreement. These aims maintain a taxonomic relationship. This means that achieving the first goal is a condition in achieving the second; and it, in its turn, is a condition for achieving the third. They are prerequisites for each other. That is why it is no use striving for the goal of understanding if the goal of exchange has not yet been achieved. Neither is it useful to strive for agreement if the goal of understanding has not yet been reached. It is important to keep in mind the order of these goals. They should not be reversed, nor should they be set side by side, but they should be pursued one after the other (Van der Ven 1990c, 58-59).

By *exchange* we mean that the participants communicate their opinions (cognitive), feelings and attitudes (emotive), and values and norms (conative) to each other. They do this from their own perspectives. One shares one's opinions, feelings, and values with another who listens. The latter then reacts with his or her own opinions, feelings, and values, while the former listens.

In *understanding* things are taken one step further. People enter into each other's perspectives; they put themselves in each other's positions. We are dealing with the metaphor of the musical chair. The one understands the opinions, feelings, and values of the other from his angle, position, vicissitudes, background, and presuppositions, and vice versa. The understanding is based on a mutual exchange of perspectives. This brings about mutual comprehension and leads to an understanding of each other.

The aim of *agreement* takes us a step further still. People share each other's opinions, feelings, and values proceeding from the sharing of each other's perspectives. By doing so a consensus is reached. This is, of course, only partially and temporarily possible: partially, because one does not or cannot agree with someone in all aspects, and temporarily, because new data and new developments may lead to changes in opinions, feelings, values, and even perspectives. Insofar as a partial and temporary consensus is reached, one has to settle for a consensus about the dissensus (agreement about disagreement). This lies within the previous goal (understanding); however, the striving for consensus remains intact.

Types

The participants in religious communication can be divided into two groups: internal and external. The internal participants are those who feel involved and connected to the religious tradition and perhaps to the church that is the institutional expression of this religious tradition.

The external participants are those who do not regard themselves in this fashion. Subjective-autobiographical criteria are used to determine this; the distinction internal/external is not imposed on the participants from the outside. It is not based on church membership, endorsement of (parts of) the teaching of the church, or involvement with the leadership of the church. One's own experience and one's own valuation determine whether one regards oneself as an internal or external participant to religious communication. What is decisive is the degree to which one makes use of both the observer's perspective and the participant's perspective. Someone who only makes use of the observer's perspective will primarily regard himself as an external participant. Someone who also takes the participant's perspective and is able to flexibly exchange both perspectives will primarily regard himself as an internal participant.

Proceeding from this distinction, three types of religious communication may be described. In the first type, there are mainly external participants. This is characteristic of all kinds of church and pastoral activities in the areas of evangelization and proclamation. In the second type, there are both external and internal participants. This is often typical of rites of passage such as birth, marriage, and death, in which people are present who consider themselves to be nonreligious and people who consider themselves to be religious. In the third type, there are mostly internal participants in religious communication. This is characteristic of the greater part of weekend liturgy, for instance, or of group pastoral care, or catechetics. One can define the three types as follows: external, external/internal and internal.

It should be clear that the three types have an entirely different relationship with the three aims we distinguished. In the external type, striving for exchange will often be the most important aim; in the external/internal type, striving for understanding is foremost; and in the internal type, it is striving for agreement.

Orientations

Three orientations are distinguishable in religious communication. They are not mutually exclusive, athough one or the other orientation is dominant. This gives the religious communication in question a style, color, and intentionality of its own.

The first is intrapersonal orientation. The participants in the religious communication use it — consciously or unconsciously — to gain a clearer insight of themselves: who they are and what their purpose in life is. To this purpose they often go back in time, to their parents, the family situation, their childhood, youth, adolescence, the process of choosing a partner, etc. In this they reconstruct their own history in a religious sense. The relationship they maintain with the other participants in the religious communication is dominated by self-interaction (Wallace & Wolf 1991, 243). This self-interaction can be described in terms of the goals we distinguished earlier: exchange, understanding, and agreement. In their self-interaction, the participants try to reach exchange, understanding, and agreement between the "I" and the "me." Insofar as the latter is achieved — though only in a partial and temporary sense — one can speak of the foundation of a religious intrapersonal identity.

The second is interpersonal orientation. In this the participants in religious commnication converse with each other for the sake of the conversation itself. The relation to the intrapersonal orientation has a dialectical nature. On the one hand, the intrapersonal orientation is a necessary condition for the success of the interpersonal orientation. If one does not have access to one's own opinions, feelings, and values, one cannot communicate them to others. On the other hand, the interpersonal orientation is a necessary condition for the accomplishment of intrapersonal orientation. In and through the mutual clarification that arises in the interpersonal orientation, people come to self-clarification (Van Knippenberg 1987).

The third is tradition-aimed orientation. The exchange, understanding, and agreement with regard to religious meanings do not take place separately from the religious tradition, for these meanings come about in meaning-giving processes via religious signs on the basis of religious codes. These codes are stored within religious tradition. That is why religious communication is always aimed at communication in relation to the religious tradition.

This communication is characterized by the hermeneutical relationship between past and present, tradition and situation. The point is not to find a direct correlation between a text from tradition and the situation in which modern people find themselves, as if the meaning of this text would exist today in this direct correlation. The problem is more complex. The text cannot be seen apart from the societal and religious context of its own day. Likewise, the situation of people today cannot be seen separately from the societal and religious context today. The meaning of a text from the past for today thus demands a more complex procedure. If one wishes to find it out, one has to correlate the balance between the text of the past and its context with the balance between the situation of today and the present context. The point is not to find a text correlation, but a text/context correlation (Schillebeeckx 1983; 1989; Boff 1983). Religious communication is situated in the bipolarity of the text and the context of the tradition and the text and context of the situation. At various times it is more toward one or the other pole.

Transcendent perspectives

In the description of religious communication, three transcendent perspectives are mentioned: reception, response, and reaction. These three terms refer to the activity that is unleashed within people by the self-announcement of God. They refer to the human side of the communication of God's self to humanity. By the term *reception* we mean the notion that persons are addressed by God. This reception leads to a response in which a person turns to God. This also leads, however, to a reaction in which the person turns to other people and bears evidence to the meaning of religion in his or her life (Dalferth 1981).

Religious communication has two dimensions: a horizontal and a vertical dimension. The first is religious communication as a process of giving religious meaning between people. The second is communication between God and humans. How do the horizontal and vertical dimensions relate to each other? We wish to answer this question in the same way we did previously (chapter 2 sub 2), by pointing out the principle of noncompetition. If applied to religious communication, this means that communication between people does not lessen communication with God, nor does communication with God lessen communication between people. God gives people the task of communicating with each other. In this God communicates himself.

This can be clarified by means of two terms, both of which we used earlier: religious signs and religious codes. On the basis of the working of certain religious codes, the communication between people can become the bearer of religious signs. These signs refer to the presence of God's salvation for humanity. More specifically, the signs refer to God's pity, forgiveness, solidarity, love, and intimacy. They signify salvation, and in doing so, they re-present it.

This can be illustrated for the three transcendent perspectives. Reception — as we mentioned — is the awareness of being spoken to by God. This realization may take place in religious communication between people. In that case religious experience is what they gain in this communication. This can happen in a personal conversation, a sermon, a song, or a witness. They can be experienced as signs of the salutary presence of God.

The response — as we determined — is turning to God. It takes the shape of prayer. This can take place during the religious communication in which one participates. If the religious communication touches us to the depth of our being, this depth can be seen as a sign of the depth of God himself. Prayer can be taken as intrapersonal conversation with oneself, in which the mystery of one's own self is intuitively felt to be a sign of the mystery of God, in which being submerged in oneself is felt to be a sign of submergence in God, in which intimacy with oneself can be seen as a sign of intimacy with God. In this way the statement can be explained that God is not only present to humanity but is also present within humanity, that God is closer to me than my innermost being: *Deus interior intimo meo* (Augustine).

The reaction — as we have seen — is turning to other people to give expression to the meaning of belief in God. It can be given shape in proclamation and diacony. A striking sermon of God's word-with-a-small-w can become a sign of God's Word-with-a-capital-W. Inspired diacony can lead to the experience that God himself is present among our most humble brothers and sisters (Matt. 25:31-46).

In the example above, communication-theoretical and soteriological ecclesiology come together. Religious communication acuminates in diacony. Their mutual relation is of a dialectical nature. On the one hand, religious communication is a necessary condition for diacony. Without communication of the religious images, stories, and texts that encompass and undergird diacony, one cannot see its difference from secular social services. Diacony loses its identity. On the other hand, diacony is a necessary condition for religious communication. Without diacony, religious communication becomes an aesthetic divertissement. Without orthopraxis, orthodoxy becomes empty speculation (Van der Ven 1990c, 49-51).

Finally, we have the following question: Why do we speak of *transcendent* perspectives? The reason is that we cannot plan, prepare, predict, or accomplish their achievement. Religious reception, response, and reaction can only be desired; they can only be hoped for and received.

Chapter 4

The Four Core Functions of the Church

We first described the societal context of the church. For this purpose we used the term *modernization* (chapter 1). The institutional differentiation couched within modernization determines the societal position of the church, which, as we have seen, no longer covers the whole of society but primarily displays the characteristics of a denomination (chapter 2). The loss of societal plausibility makes continuous religious communication a necessity, both internally and externally. This can also be conceived as the general function of the church (chapter 3).

In this chapter we will deal with the core functions of the church. They are the conditions for the realization of the general function. We shall successively deal with (1) what the core functions are, (2) how they can be determined, and (3) what is their content.

(1) Core functions

The term *function* generally concerns the interaction between phenomena in the whole of a social context. It is not just a matter of the working of one phenomenon on another or vice versa. It is not just a one-on-one relationship. A phenomenon may have more than one function, while one particular function may involve more than one phenomenon. One can make various distinctions here. They involve frequency and duration, direction, range, and intention. We will take a more detailed look at these distinctions in order to clarify the term *core functions* (Van Doorn & Lammers 1959, 113-18; Merton 1968).

The first distinction refers to the *frequency and duration* of the working. Some functions do not occur very often, while others do (frequency). Some work for a short time, while others continue for a long period (duration). Functions with a high frequency and long duration are called *primary functions,* functions with a low frequency and short duration are understood to be *secondary functions.* A primary function is, for instance, safeguarding the evangelical mission of the church. A secondary function is the guidance of a visitor group for new inhabitants in a parish.

The second distinction is concerned with the *direction* of the working. One phenomenon may promote another, but it can also hinder it. In this it is of great importance how the other phenomenon is valued: as something good *(bonum)* or bad *(malum).* If there is talk of the promotion of a *bonum* and the hindrance of a *malum,* we call this a positive function. If a *bonum* is hindered and a *malum* is stimulated, we are dealing with a negative function. A positive function is, for example, referring to the biblical sources in a sermon. Negative functions are opposing this homiletic finding of sources and basing the sermon on the doctrinal *depositum fidei.* The distinction between positive and negative functions is of a normative nature, as is clear from the examples. One assumes a positively valued *bonum* (biblical reference in a sermon) and a negatively valued *malum* (promotion of the doctrinal *depositum fidei* in a sermon).

The *range* is a third distinctive criterion. If a phenomenon influences only one other phenomenon, one can talk of a narrow range. If it influences more than one phenomenon, it has a broad range. Within the functions with a broad range, we can distinguish between simple and complex functions. In simple functions we see a direct influence of the phenomenon on several others. In complex functions it is a combination of direct and indirect influences of a phenomenon on several others. The working of a short catechetical project, for example, on the religious cognitions of the participants is a simple function. A complex function is, for instance, the working of a long-term catechetical project guiding young parents. This not only influences their religious cognitions, but also the religious affections and attitudes of their children.

Finally, the difference between *intentional and nonintentional* functions is of importance. Intentional functions are related to the desired working of one phenomenon on another. They are sought after purposefully and resolutely. Nonintentional functions, on the other hand, are not subject to deliberation or planning. An example of an intentional function is the intended positive contribution of pastoral counseling to the religious-psychological health of the counselee. A nonintentional function is the depressing influence of a sermon.

What then are the core functions? This question can now be answered by means of the distinctions we just made. First of all, core functions have an optimal frequency and duration, which means that they are primary. Next, they are aimed at what is regarded to be good *(bonum),* and not what is taken to be bad *(malum),* which means they have a positive nature. Moreover, they have a broad range with numerous direct and indirect workings, which implies that they are complex. Finally, they contain an explicit goal, which means that they are intentional functions. Now, it is this combination of characteristics (primary, positive, complex, and intentional) that leads to the assessment that core functions are the necessary condition for the realization of the general function of the social formation they are part of. The general function cannot be carried out without them.

This means the following if applied to the church. We described the general function of the church as religious communication (chapter 3). *The core functions are the primary, positive, complex, and intentional functions that are a necessary condition for religious communication as the general function of the church.*

(2) The determination of the core functions

Before we can identify the core functions of the church, we have to answer the question how they can be determined. Various lists of core functions are available in the literature, but the disadvantage is that they are (or at least seem to be) chosen randomly. They are insufficiently or not at all justified. Usually they are borrowed from what we have called the "pastoral sectors" (Introduction). This means that the core functions of the church are actually identified with the pastoral sectors of the church. As will become clear further on, we prefer to make a clear distinction between the church's core functions and its pastoral sectors (sub 3).

A theory or theoretical model is necessary for the determination and justification of the core functions. Such a model will be discussed below. We borrow it from the work done by the sociologist Parsons. It is known as *functionalism.* Because the model has not been left uncontradicted, we will also have to discuss the criticisms to it, once we have described it. The processing of this criticism leads us to a revision of functionalism in the direction of what may be called "critical functionalism."

The choice of a model

Those who have no knowledge of the sociological discussion of the past decade will be unfamiliar with the name Parsons. Those who have followed this discussion will be unable to suppress a certain curiosity. For a long time Parsons was a leading figure in empirical-theoretical sociology. During the fifties and sixties, and especially after the revolutionary year 1968, the bottom fell out. Since then he has been severely criticized. However, from 1980 on we see that "the anti-Parsonian period is over" (Wallace & Wolf 1991, 70). This means that in the development of sociological theories, Parsons is back. The difference is that he is no longer either followed without criticism, nor completely rejected; he is dealt with through differential criticism. In short, there is a tripartition: the rise, fall, and critically reflected return of Parsons's model (Parsons 1953; 1959a; 1965; Thurlings 1980; Turner 1991; Wallace & Wolf 1991).

Parsons became known for his theoretical view of society and the social institutions. An important question in developing such a view is whether one proceeds from the individual actors in social institutions or from the institutions themselves. The importance of this question is evident for the church: Does one proceed from the individual actors in the church or from the church institution?

At the beginning of his career, Parsons developed a theory of action. In his *The Structure of Social Action* he focused upon the individual actor: the aims of the actor; the values and norms in which the aims of the actor are embedded; the methods that the actor uses to achieve the aims; and the situational restrictions the actor meets with.

After this he came to the realization that the individual actors are not alone, and he wondered how he could fit this information in his theory. To that purpose he developed two insights. The first is that the action of individuals occurs in interaction with others. This interaction is not only the result of actions by individuals, but it also influences these actions themselves. People undertake certain actions because of the expected interaction and the positive consequences that lie within them, or people omit certain actions because of the negative consequences expected. The second insight is that action and interaction take place in social institutions. They can promote or hinder them, and they can also neutralize them.

Next, Parsons was struck by the fact that the action of individual actors not only takes place in interaction and in institutions, but is itself subject to institutionalization. What does this institutionalization entail? It has to do with the fact that the actions and interactions of people are characterized by certain regularities. People act under certain conditions and according to certain patterns. They undertake a fixed number of activities, in a fixed order, within a fixed period. Where do these patterns come from? They stem from the social positions of the actors and the roles that they fulfill in social institutions. These roles are guided by certain norms, which in their turn are embedded in the culture that encompasses the social institutions and influences them.

Parsons made these discoveries when he was doing research in collaboration with Bales on small groups. While he was occupied with the social processes in these groups and the problems of leadership in them, he came across the phenomenon of institutionalization of the actions and interactions in these groups. Thus, he was able to trace certain regularities and patterns in the action of the participants in these groups.

He also discovered something else. He saw that small groups always have to contend with certain problems and that they tried to solve these problems in definite ways. What problems were they confronted with? Parsons reduced them to four groups. The first group: What are our convictions, values, and norms? The second group: What holds us together socially, and what distance or proximity do we maintain with regard to each other? The third group: What are our aims, programs, and projects? Finally, the fourth group: How do we find the necessary means such as money and personnel?

Parsons named the first group of problems *latency.* He gave it this name because he observed that the convictions, values, and norms led a dormant kind of existence. They remained latent beneath the surface — that is, until a conflict or crisis arose. Then these convictions, values, and norms awoke and started to play an important role. At this point they started to cause trouble, particularly when there was discord about them.

The name Parsons gave to the second group of questions is *integration.* The point is the binding force, the cohesion of the group. Is this shaped by mutual social relations? By what are these relations themselves determined then? How do people deal with conflicts? How are they solved? What is the leaders' place in this? Are they formal or informal leaders?

The name by which Parsons indicated the third group is *goal attainment.* This implies what people strive after, what people want to achieve. These questions come to the surface when people start to consider the actions they wish to undertake and deliberate on the programs and projects that they wish to execute.

The name of the fourth group of problems is *adaptation.* Parsons chose this name for the following reasons. He observed that the personal and material means necessary for the continued existence of the groups that he was researching together with Bales had to come from the environment in which the groups were situated. As they went in search of new members and tried to gather the necessary finances, they had to adapt to their environments to a certain degree, according to Parsons's observations.

The disadvantage of the term *adaptation* is that it may suggest passivity, as if one can only passively conform to the environment in order to draw the greatest number of means from it. This impression is incorrect. Adaptation contains both a passive and an active aspect. Besides passive acceptance of the environment, this term implies active mastery of it (Parsons 1965, 40).

One may say that latency stands for the cultural life of the groups; integration stands for the social life; goal attainment, for the political life; and adaptation, for the economic life. They form the four core functions of life in the group. Without them, a group loses its meaning and foundation (latency) and its togetherness (integration); it fails in its goal (goal attainment), and has no means of existence (adaptation).

With this the "liga" model came into being: latency, integration,

FIGURE 4.1 The structural-functional model

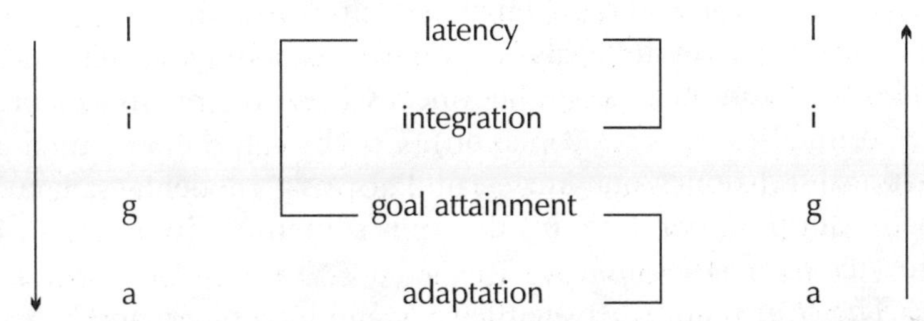

goal attainment, adaptation. It can also be reversed: "agil." "Agil" means adaptation, goal attainment, integration, and latency. However, this is not just a linguistic joke. On the contrary, those who use the liga model proceed from the notion of top-down guidance. Latency guides integration, which guides goal attainment, which in its turn guides adaptation. Those who use the agil model proceed from bottom-up conditioning. Adaptation conditions goal attainment, which conditions integration, which in turn conditions latency. In other words, the point of the liga model is the guidance from cultural life to social life, and from social life to political life, and from political life to economic life. In the agil model it is conditioning by economic life of political life, by political life of social life, and by social life of cultural life.

The terms *guidance* in the liga model and *conditioning* in the agil model are, therefore, of importance. *Guidance* means direction, regulation, channeling. They take place from the top in the liga model. *Conditioning* means that if the conditions of the lower levels are not fulfilled, then the higher levels are not brought about. They take place at the bottom in the agil model. This has been indicated by arrows in both directions in figure 4.1.

Parsons made two connections. The first is between latency and integration, the second is between goal attainment and adaptation, which is also indicated in figure 4.1. Latency and integration are of a structural nature. They are aimed at the group *ad intra.* They hold the group together. This happens by entertaining collective opinions, values, and norms (latency) and by maintaining the social relations people have (integration). Goal attainment and adaptation are of a functional nature. Their aim is *ad extra.* They maintain the relations with the outside world, the environment. They mediate between the group and its environment (mediation). The group wants to achieve certain goals in this environment (goal attainment). At the same time it borrows the means from the environment for its continued existence (adaptation). Combining the structural and functional relations, one may call Parsons's model a structural-functional one. Therefore, his theory is sometimes indicated by the term *structural functionalism*.

The connections between latency and integration and between goal attainment and adaptation may also be approached from a different point of view; that is to say, from the term *rationality,* which can be split up into three dimensions, as we have seen: cognitive-instrumental, normative, and expressive rationality (chapter 1 sub 2). Now latency and integration are characterized by the working of normative and expressive rationality. People allow themselves to be guided by convictions, values, and norms and by emotions and attitudes. They function on the basis of their sense of value and of their feelings. Goal attainment and adaptation are guided by the cognitive-instrumental rationality. In this, the determining of the state of affairs is central (cognitive) as well as the effective and efficient use of means with an eye to achieving goals (instrumental). People reckon and calculate in this; they take things into account (Parsons 1965, 35).

A third connection can be made. It concerns latency and goal attainment, which can also be found in figure 4-1. This relation is of a dialectical nature. On the one hand, there is a guiding influence from the convictions, values, and norms in latency on the programs and projects in goal attainment. On the other hand, the latter are the conditions under which the convictions, values, and norms can be realized.

Parsons believed that this model applies not only to small groups, but also to larger social formations and institutions in society. If one applies this to formations and institutions, it follows that four core functions can be distinguished. Let us give some examples from economic, political, social, and cultural life. We start off with an international business. This is an economic organization. Within it one can distinguish between internal economic structures and processes (adaptation); short-, medium-, and long-term plans (goal attainment); the social processes between and in departments and the conflicts that play a role in them (integration); and finally, the business culture that determines the climate of the business (latency). Now an example from political life: the political party. This is characterized by attention to and care for personal and financial means (adaptation); political programs (goal attainment); the social machinery for preserving the unity of the party (integration); and a structure of values and beliefs that determine party policy in the long run (latency). An example from social life is the family. An important role is played by: the housekeeping book in connection with the necessary means for existence (adaptation); the aims the family wishes to achieve, such as companionship, intimacy, recreation, and education (goal attainment); communication and conversation among members (integration); convictions and values (latency). Finally, an example from cultural life: the school. The ups and downs of a school are determined by the financial administration (adaptation); the curriculum (goal attainment); the interaction between and within school departments (integration); the philosophical identity (latency).

Parsons took one final step: he declared the model to be applicable to society as a whole. In his view, society itself can be split up into four dimensions: the economic (adaptation), political (goal attainment); social (integration), and cultural dimension (latency). The question is what happens when you apply the model to both societal institutions and the whole of society and then relate these two applications to each other. The result can be seen in figure 4-2.

The first column in this figure relates to society as a whole: adaptation, goal attainment, integration, latency. The second column relates to social institutions. We have just given examples such as the enterprise, the political party, the family, and the school. On the one hand, they belong to a certain dimension of society, as we have seen. On the other hand, each of these institutions can be split up into four dimensions: adaptation, goal attainment, integration and latency.

Proceeding from this we can introduce the term *context.* Using figure 4.2 we can distinguish several contexts. Here, we will only mention the institution as a context and society as a context. In the institution as a context the most important thing is the contextual relations between separate institutional dimensions (latency, integration, goal attainment, adaptation) and the institution as a whole. In the society as a context the most important thing is the contextual

FIGURE 4.2 Application of the structural-functional model

society	institution
latency	latency integration goal attainment adaptation
integration	latency integration goal attainment adaptation
goal attainment	latency integration goal attainment adaptation

relations between institutional dimensions (latency, integration, goal attainment, adaptation) and the dimensions of society (latency, integration, goal attainment, adaptation).

Criticism of the model

Parsons's theory was heavily criticized from very different sides. From symbolic interactionism in particular, in which the interaction between individuals is researched as well as the symbols that they use, there was sharp criticism of his work. Further Parsons was attacked by critical sociology, in which the study of change, power, and conflict in society is central. The criticism can be summed up in three points. Parsons's theory paid too little attention to the action and interaction of the individual actors (according to symbolic interactionism); social change (according to critical sociology); and the processes of power and conflict in society (again according to critical sociology).

Critical functionalism

We will describe the criticism step by step and also evaluate it point by point, in order to reach a critically differentiated consideration (Parsons 1965; Turner 1991; Wallace & Wolf 1991). At each step we will add a remark that relates to the consequences for the development of ecclesiology. This critical differentiated approach is rooted in the conviction that Parsons's theory needs revision in the direction of what can be indicated as being critical functionalism; that is, if his theory is to be useful for the further development of ecclesiology.

The first point of criticism stems from symbolic interactionism, as we mentioned (Mead, Blumer, Goffmann). They state that Parsons pays too little attention to the action and interaction of individuals. He is interested in macro- and not in micro-processes. He studies systems in collectives, not communications in dyads, triads, tetrads, or pentads.

This criticism has to be met in a critical differentiated manner. Parsons does pay attention to the action and interaction of individual people, as has become clear from the above; however, he gained more of a view of the institutionalization of this action. He continually asks to what degree this action is determined by factors that go before human freedom. It makes no sense to set structural functionalism and symbolic interactionism opposite each other polemically. Structural functionalism studies human action from the viewpoint of institutionalization. Symbolic interactionism studies this proceeding from the unicity of a person. These paradigms do not exclude each other, but rather they are complementary. What is important is that one realizes which of the two paradigms one is using and which biases are to be found in either of them. One can try to trace these biases and eliminate them or reduce them by involving the viewpoints from the other paradigm.

That is why we add the following remark for the development of ecclesiology. We strive to pay explicit attention to the aspects that are involved with micro-processes that take place between actors, and to their unicity and freedom. The basis for this lies in the action and interaction theoretical approach of religious communication as a general function of the church, which we developed earlier. In this approach, the action of the sender and receiver are central, as well as the activity involved in the message they carry out, the processes of the religious giving of meaning and coding they execute, and the contact they maintain. Central to this communication is an orientation toward mutual exchange, understanding, and the forming of consensus (chapter 3).

The second point of criticism regarding Parsons is that he has no eye for the processes of social change. This criticism comes from critical sociology (Habermas, Dahrendorf). In Parsons's view society is a structure of elements, thus goes the criticism, which are attuned to each other in such a way that the whole is kept in balance. There is unity and harmony. If the unity is broken by discord and the harmony is undone by conflict, all sorts of processes start up to restore the equilibrium. These take place in the attuning of adaptation, goal attainment, integration, and latency to each other. This attuning occurs through conditioned processes in the agil model and guiding processes in the liga model. After this everything bonds together harmoniously.

This criticism also demands a critical differentiated reaction. On the one hand, Parsons aimed at unity and peace in society and in social institutions. However, they were not a matter of course for him, but something that conjured up wonder and surprise. What holds a social institution together? Why does it not fall apart into countless units? Why is it that it continues to exist? Why is there order (cosmos)? Why is there no disorder (chaos)? These questions are not simple. They are puzzling questions — unless one has an answer ready from whatever religion.

On the other hand, it is of importance to check whether the order and harmony have to be taken in a static or dynamic sense. It is wrong to think that the equilibrium that arises after having been broken by discord and conflict would be identical to the equilibrium that existed before. The restored equilibrium is not the same equilibrium in a restored shape; it is only the balance that has returned. It has undergone — at least this is what we have to assume — an adaptive change. The equilibrium is a moving equilibrium (Parsons 1952, 36).

Furthermore, this movement can certainly be described by Parsons's model, albeit in a formal sense. One has to fix as it were two moments in history: the beginning and the end of a period in which a certain change took place. At both times the institution in question can be described by means of the agil and the liga model. The changes that took place between the two moments can be studied proceeding from the external and internal influences that the institution underwent in that period. The external influences come from the context or environment. The internal influences come from the conditioning and guiding processes within adaptation, goal attainment, integration, and latency. By relating these influences to each other, one gains insight into the structures and processes of the change.

An important objection that remains is that such a description is of a formal nature, as we mentioned. Opposite a formal theory of social change we have a theory concerning content. In such a theory one would have to indicate why certain cultural changes lead to certain social changes, why they lead to certain political changes, and why they, in their turn, lead to certain economic changes. The same goes for the reverse, why certain economic changes are the cause of certain political changes, why they are the cause of certain social changes, and why they, in their turn, are the cause of certain cultural changes. However, such a theory has not been developed yet, and is not easy to develop. We will mention only two examples. We do not dispose of a theory at present that explains the cultural revolution of, for instance, the Dutch and German Catholic church in the sixties and seventies. Neither do we dispose of a theory that, until now, gives a cohesive insight into the collapse of the former Soviet Union in the eighties and nineties. This does not mean, however, that there is no impulse to be found for the formation of such a theory (Kaufmann 1989; 1992).

Nevertheless, we would like to add the following remark regarding the development of ecclesiology. However much we lack a theory concerning content, we have to be thoroughly aware of the phenomena of social change and ecclesiastical change respectively. Indeed, the point of departure has already been discussed in the Introduction, where we mentioned that we had chosen a transformatory ecclesiology. Its program takes the change in society into account — and in connection with this, that of church formation.

Finally, there is a third point of criticism. This, too, stems from critical sociology. The question arises how Parsons deals with the phenomena power and conflict, both in society and in social institutions. In Parsons's model, power is a so-called functional requirement within goal attainment. If an institution is to adequately tune its programs to the goals it wishes to achieve, then there need to be people who have the power to guide the process. In other words, power is functional; it is a requirement. With this, Parsons closes his eyes to all sorts of other phenomena — according to the criticism — that are connected to power and positions of power. Power may be functional, but it also has to do with interests. With this it hinders the freedom and equality of people who are subject to the power. It oppresses, alienates, forces, and exploits. Power summons conflicts.

By seeing power as a functional requirement, Parsons closes his eyes to mutual rivalry between all sorts of groups in the social institutions in question. Sometimes they stand opposite each other as factions; at other times they form varying coalitions. That is why people want to exchange Parsons's system model for the parties' model. Through this, one gains an eye for the various interests that different groups pursue in opposition to and/or together with each other. Through this, attention is paid to the processes in which the groups try to capture power from each other, to retain it, or to extend it (Silverman 1970). For example, one can consider the hospital from the point of view of the parties' model. One gets a conflicting network of rival parties that are each striving after their own interests: governors, directors, heads of staff, departmental heads, doctors, nurses, psycho-social workers, pastors, helpers, volunteers, patients, and members of the family (Lammers 1984).

The criticism that Parsons pays too little attention to power and conflict is hard to refute. But it would be going too far to accuse him of having a blind spot. In his reflections on power, he pays attention to the democratic obtaining and control of power; the play between bearers of power and interest groups; the forming of compromises; and the ideologization of power in terms of general interest as a means to conceal the desire for naked power in power bearers and interest groups (Parsons 1965, 52-53, 67-68). However, these points of view need further study.

We shall, therefore, add a critical remark for the development of ecclesiology. Insofar as we use Parsons's model, we may not pass over the aspect of power. We will also have to pay sufficient attention to matters such as conflicts and leadership. In conflicts we deal with conflicts of value, interest, and power and their interaction (chapter 15). Several complicated matters are involved in leadership, among which are the ratio between power and authority; the legitimization of authority; the structuring of authority and power relations in bureaucratic organizations; and the founding of these relations in human and social theoretical reflection. It is precisely in an ecclesiology that has an exemplary involvement with the Catholic Church, that these matters have to be raised. The more so as this church is entangled in unceasing discussion about monocracy and democracy (chapter 16).

(3) The content of the core functions

We will now apply the liga or agil model of Parsons on the church, albeit with the critical remarks that we made in mind. This brings us to four core functions of the church. First we will describe them, and then we will relate them to the sectors in the church.

Core functions

We will have to make a choice: Will we make use of the agil or the liga model? We cannot discuss both models at the same time. However, such a choice is only one of sequence; it has no principal meaning. Here we will choose for the liga model. In this we have to be aware of the fact that the guidance from above in the liga model needs continuous complementation from the conditioning working from below in the agil model.

Whichever way you look at it, this means that the church has four core functions: latency, integration, goal attainment, and adaptation. However, for a clear understanding, it may be useful to translate these terms into an ecclesiological sense without detracting from their content.

Latency can be translated by *identity.* The reason is that the convictions, values, and norms that exist in the church can no longer be considered dormant. As a consequence of modernization they have lost their societal plausibility (chapter 1). They are unceasingly the topic of conversation in the church as a denomination and as an association (chapter 2). They are continually problematized in religious communication taking place between people within and outside the church (chapter 3). The church is no longer in a sleep of latency.

Integration could be translated by a term that has a long and highly intense ecclesiological history behind it, namely, the unity of the church. Yet we have abandoned this term because the term *unity* can be explained in different ways, depending on the traditionalistic or transformatory ecclesiology one chooses. Furthermore, the term *unity* may oblige us to give prominence to other *notae ecclesiae:* sanctity, catholicity, and apostolicity. Through this we would wind up in the middle of discussing these notae. In this not only their number forms a problem. There are authors who have discerned two, three, four, five, six, seven, eight, eleven, fifteen, or even a hundred notae (Küng 1967, 307; Houtepen 1983a). Then, too, the place of these notae in ecclesiology is a question in itself. This has to do with the apologetic use thereof in the traditional *demonstratio catholica.* By means of the four notae, "proof" was given that the Catholic Church was the only true church (Pottmeyer 1986). "The time," states Berkhof, "that the teachings of the notae ecclesiae were a field in which real decisions were taken, seems to have passed away forever" (Berkhof 1985, 402). That is why we drop the term *unity* and stick to the term *integration*.

Goal attainment we translate by the term *policy.* Policy better indicates what goal attainment means if we apply this term to the church. Achieving aims is part of policy. Furthermore, achieving aims has to be done in accordance with policy, to be converted into programs and projects, and to be evaluated.

Adaptation can be translated by the term *management.* It encompasses both financial and personnel management. It is about the resources that have to be drawn from the environs to keep the church going and to protect it from collapse. For this purpose a dialectical relationship with the environment is entered into, as we have seen earlier. This relationship is one of both passive acceptance and active intervention (mastery).

In short, the four core functions of the church are identity, integration, policy, and management. Identity has to do with the convictions, vision, and mission of the church. Integration refers to the cohesion, uniformity, and pluriformity of the church. Policy points to the development of church policy, programs, and projects. Finally, management refers to the financial and personnel conditions and means of the church. This division into four elements is at least globally similar to the division made by Carrol et al. (1988) and for an important part contains similarities to that of Hendriks (1990).

FIGURE 4.3 Core functions of the church

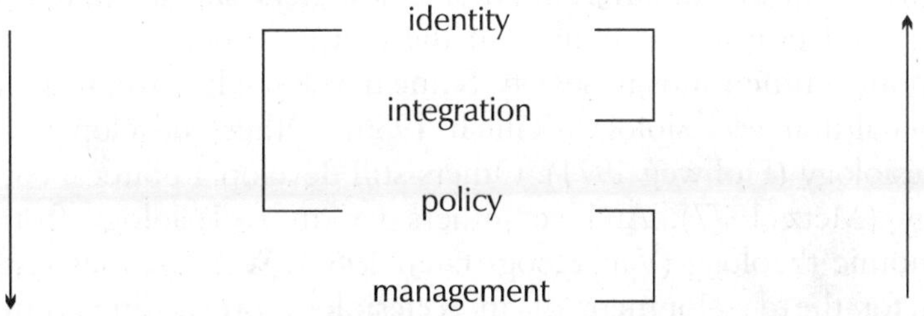

identity

integration

policy

management

Looking at figure 4.3, we can say that in the liga model a guiding force operates from identity to integration, from integration to policy, and from policy to management. The guiding force contains an if/then relationship. If the identity is adequately realized, then this stimulates integration, which stimulates policy, which in turn stimulates management. However, there is also a reverse movement. In the agil model there is a conditioning force that operates from management to policy, from policy to integration, and from integration to identity. The conditioning force contains an if not/then relation. If management is not adequately realized, then this hinders policy, which hinders integration, which in its turn hinders identity.

Likewise in connection with figure 4.3 we notice that there are a number of links to be made between the core functions: a structural link between identity and integration; a functional link between policy and management; and, finally, a dialectical link between identity and policy.

Proceeding from figure 4.2 we may ask the question: Within which dimension of society is the church to be placed? The answer has to be within that of latency in society. Thus, it is within the dimension of cultural life (Parsons 1965; Schreuder 1969; 1980). From research it is becoming ever more apparent that there is stronger two-way traffic between the church and culture than between the church and other dimensions of society (Schreuder & Van Snippenburg 1990).

This does not mean that the church does not maintain relations with the other dimensions. Apart from cultural life (latency), it is also connected with social life (integration), political life (goal attainment), and economic life (adaptation). From this point of view the differences in ecclesiological literature can be understood. These have to do with the different emphases writers on the church place on the relation of the church to the cultural, social, political, and economic dimensions in society. Some develop what may be typified as a cultural ecclesiology (Tillich 1966). Others develop a social ecclesiology (Hollweg 1971). Others still develop a political ecclesiology (Metz 1977). And yet others try an ecclesiology from an economic theology (Van Hoogstraten 1986). We, however, make a plea for the development of an ecclesiology proceeding from the cultural life of society and to relate it to other dimensions without making any one of them remote.

Further, there are several contexts to be distinguished proceeding from figure 4.2. Here, we will only make mention of the church as a context and society as a context. In the church as a context, we are dealing with the contextual relations between the separate core functions (identity, integration, policy, and management) and the church as a whole. In society as a context, the point is the relations between the core functions of the church (identity, integration, policy, and management) and the dimensions of society (latency, integration, goal attainment, and adaptation).

The latter is an important point of departure for our further reflections in the next parts. There we will deal with the four core functions one by one (Parts III, IV, V, and VI). However, each time we shall discuss the contextual relation between the particular core function of the church and the dimension of society in question. This will be done to the extent that this dimension is determined and characterized by the process of modernization. Thus, we shall link the identity of the church to aspects of cultural life in society, in this case secularization (Part III, chapter 9). The integration of the church with social life in society, here individualization (Part IV, chapter 13). The policy of the church with political life in society, that is, utilization (Part V, chapter 17). Finally, the management of the church with economic life in society — in other words, calculation (Part VI, chapter 21).

The idea that is uppermost is that these contextual relations imply limits and possibilities for the church at the same time — both dangers and opportunities, threats and challenges. In this way secularization is a limit and a possibility for identity. Individualization is a danger and an opportunity for integration. Utilization is a threat and a challenge for policy. Finally, calculation is a possible loss and a possible gain for management.

Sectors

What is the relationship between the core functions and the sectors? The core functions, as we mentioned before, form the primary, positive, complex, intended functions that are necessary for the realization of the general function of the church, that is, religious communication. It is constitutive to the church. The core functions are, as indicated, intended; they contain aims for the church. These are pursued and realized by carrying out tasks. These tasks form a structure of activities in certain sectors. The sectors are the areas or fields in which the activities are executed (Kickert 1986, 100).

The relation between core functions and sectors is, therefore, not direct. It contains three intermediary links: goals (implied in the core functions), tasks (aimed at the realization of the goals) and activities (aimed at the execution of the tasks). These activities take place in the sectors.

What sectors can be distinguished in the church? We have already mentioned the following: pastoral care, catechetics, liturgy, proclamation, and diacony. Jumping ahead of the description of these sectors in Part V, we can already give short definitions of them here. Pastoral care means rendering help and guidance in easing the flow of religious communication. Catechetics relates to the accompaniment of learning processes with an eye to religious communication. Liturgy is made up of executing the ritual of religious communication. Proclamation refers to the presentation of the gospel with an eye to religious communication in public. Finally, diacony implies contributing to the liberation of people from material and spiritual distress within the broader context of religious communication. It is worth noting that we have described each of these sectors in terms of religious communication (chapter 18).

It will come as a surprise to some that we have mentioned these five sectors in particular: pastoral care, catechetics, liturgy, proclamation, and diacony. There are other lists. Some have four sectors (Haarsma 1970a; Bloth et al. 1981). Others have three (Rössler 1986; Zulehner 1989-1990; Hiltner 1958; Zerfass 1974). Also, one notices that there are not only differences between but also within these groups

FIGURE 4.4 Core functions and sectors of church development

	pastoral	catechetics	liturgy	proclamation	diacony
identity					
integration	com-	muni-	ty	build-	ing
policy					
management					

of three or four. We will stick to our group of five because the sectors mentioned (pastoral care, catechetics, liturgy, proclamation, and diacony) cannot be reduced to each other.

Core functions and sectors

There is another particularity that clings to our list. It offers no separate place for church development and community formation. The reason is that we relate the core functions and sectors to each other in such a way that church development and community formation come to the fore in an organic fashion without needing a separate space in the list of sectors.

The relation between the core functions and sectors is depicted by means of a matrix. As figure 4.4 indicates, the vertical axis is made up of the four core functions, while the horizontal axis has the five sectors.

As can be seen in the title of figure 4.4, we take church development to be all-encompassing. It encompasses all core functions and sectors together. It is given shape in this whole.

With this we take up a new stance in a discussion that has been going on for a number of years now and has not yet led to any satisfactory solution. This discussion has to do with the question of the relation of church development to pastoral care, catechetics, liturgy, proclamation, and diacony. In the literature three different points of view are distinguished. According to some, church development is superordinate, and thus the sectors have to be placed beneath it. The activities in these sectors are guided from church development. According to others, church development is coordinative and has to be placed at the same level as the other sectors. Here there is no guidance from church development. According to yet others, church development is subordinative and its place is beneath the other sectors. In the latter view, church development is not seen as guiding but as creating conditions. It provides conditions for the execution of tasks in the sectors. A guiding influence leads from the sectors to church development.

In figure 4.4 we take up a stance that may break through the impasse that characterizes the discussion we just described. The reason is that we involve a more abstract point of view. Proceeding from this viewpoint, church development encompasses all core functions and sectors in one whole. Proceeding from this figure, it is unimaginable that church development could stand apart from matters like identity, integration, policy, and management. However, it is equally unimaginable that church development could be realized independently of pastoral care, catechetics, liturgy, proclamation, and diacony.

At the same time, figure 4.4 leaves special room for community formation. Community formation has to do with the development and guidance of social networks within the church. It can be considered to be a part of the core function of integration. In the matrix, it permeates the five sectors mentioned as proceeding from integration: pastoral care, catechetics, liturgy, proclamation, and diacony. Community formation is not realized separately but within the activities in these sectors.

Another advantage that comes to the fore is in the insight within figure 4.4, that all activities in all sectors (pastoral care, catechetics, liturgy, proclamation, and diacony) are entirely determined by the core functions (identity, integration, policy, and management); and, on the other hand, that these core functions are only realized in these sectors. This insight perceives the core functions and sectors as one whole. It provides the church and pastoral action with a unity of vision.

PART II

CODES OF THE CHURCH

In the preceding part we discussed the societal context of the church and determined its position as a denomination. Within this context we dealt with the functions of the church, distinguishing one general and four core functions. The general function is religious communication. The core functions are identity, integration, policy, and management.

In Part II we will pay attention to the fact that these functions contain social and religious aspects (chapter 5). In order to determine the relation between these aspects, we will consult semiotics. We will ask ourselves the question under which conditions the social aspects can take on the character of religious signs (chapter 6). Insofar as social phenomena can be interpreted as religious signs, it is necessary to pay attention to the ground on which religious signs function: religious codes. In this we will be particularly interested in going into the question of whether the church as a sacrament can be considered as a supercode (chapter 7). Since religious codes are used for various purposes, we will take a look at each one separately (chapter 8).

Chapter 5

Social and Religious Aspects

Two aspects can be distinguished in the functions of the church: social and religious. The social aspects refer to the social relations, processes, and structures that are necessary to realize the functions of the church. The religious aspects refer to the religious identity that is shaped in these functions. This identity bears on the relationship to God. The problem is, How is one to determine the relation between the social and religious aspects?

In this chapter we pose the following questions: whether (1) only the social aspects are relevant, or (2) only the religious aspects are, or (3) the social and religious aspects together are relevant. If the latter is the case, it is of importance to know whether (4) the social aspects are subordinate to the religious aspects, or (5) we can speak of coordination.

(1) Social aspects

It is possible to describe the functions of the church from the viewpoint of the social aspects only. The general function — religious communication — can be handled from the angle of communication between people, disregarding the religious dimension. The core functions (identity, integration, policy, and management) can be approached from a Parsonian angle, without paying attention to their religious identity. In the history of the church and ecclesiology this has often occurred and still occurs. We will give two examples here: the church as a society and the church as a bureaucracy.

Church as society

For a long time the church was seen (and sometimes still is seen) as its own society, equally as independent as the state and independent with regard to the state. That is why it was defined as a perfect society *(societas perfecta). Perfect* means "autonomous" here. It is equally perfect as the state, and equally independent as the state. However, at the same time it was seen to be more perfect than the state; for in contrast to the state, it was deemed to have a divine origin and a divine purpose. This made the leaders of the church even more unassailable with regard to the state (Granfield 1982; Lakeland 1990; Raedts 1990).

The most marked examples are to be found during the period of the Counter-Reformation in the 16th and 17th centuries. The following statement made by Bellarminus can be held to be exemplary. According to Bellarminus, the church is as visible and as tangible as the senate of the Roman people or the kingdom of France or the republic of Venice. Here the church is exclusively approached from a social angle. This also becomes clear from the definition of the church. According to Bellarminus, the church is the meeting of people who are united through the confession of the same Christian faith and the celebration of the same sacraments, under the administration of legal pastors and especially of the Vicar of Christ on earth, the bishop of Rome (Bellarminus 1721, 102).

The residue of this opinion can still be found today. One may find it, for example, in the Constitutions of Vatican II on the Church (*Lumen Gentium* 8) and on the Church in Today's World (*Gaudium et Spes* 40). In both documents the church is called *societas constituta et ordinata.* The church, according to the Constitution on the Church in Today's World, was established by Christ and built up as a society and equipped with suitable means with an eye to the visible and social unity of the church. Thus, it — being at the same time the external visible group and the spiritual community — keeps pace with the whole of humanity (*Gaudium et Spes* 40). The documents of the Special Synod of the Dutch bishops held in Rome in 1980 also contain numerous indications that this opinion still has its effects (Bijzondere Synode 1980). The church is seen as a society, and the Dutch church is seen as a subsidiary that is in trouble and therefore requires course correction (De Grijs 1985).

What comes to the fore in this example is which social aspects can be distinguished in the functions of the church, if one regards it as a society. In this way, for instance, the social visibility of the church is set forth. This is of importance to describe the church in its identity with regard to its social environment. In addition, the cohesion of the people in the church and the basis on which it rests — the same Christian faith, and the same sacraments — are emphasized. This is of importance for the integration function. Besides this, the focus is on the structural relations between the various sections of the church. These regulate the traffic between the ordinary people in the church, the administration of legal pastors, and the supreme leadership of the pope. This is relevant for the policy function. Finally, the external relation of the church to the state is regulated. The church is a properly functioning and clearly structured organization like the state. It is equally autonomous as the state, and that is why it does not tolerate any interference. Here again, the identity of the church in relation to its social environment appears before the footlights, but now within the aspect of social power and prestige.

Church as bureaucracy

In the footsteps of the sociologist Weber, theologians are starting to regard the church as a bureaucracy. This does not mean that the church bureaucracy is only a modern phenomenon but only that the study thereof is a recent development. It has been pointed out that in the late Roman Empire, the church had already become bureaucratized. This is to be regarded as a happy circumstance, because the church is said to have survived the fall of the Roman Empire through this. Since then the bureaucratization of the church has increased more and more (Laan 1967). This applies to the church of the 19th and 20th centuries in particular (Kaufmann 1979; Gabriel & Kaufmann 1980).

Striking similarities are to be observed between the church and (other) bureaucratic organizations. We can point out the greater amount of attention paid to the functions fulfilled by people than to the people themselves; the distribution of competencies, rights, and obligations across several functions; the hierarchical distribution of these competencies, rights, and obligations across functions; the rules for the execution of these functions; and the impersonal, official character of the execution thereof. If one also looks at the divisions in the church and (other) bureaucratic organizations, one can point out remarkable parallels. There are divisions for enlistment and recruitment of personnel; education, formation, and training; personnel matters; building matters; financial matters; juridical matters; purchase; production; sales; communication; market research; public relations; and advertising.

In all these matters the policy and management function of the church is under discussion. They are approached only from the social aspects in the church as a bureaucracy. One cannot find a trace of the religious aspects.

One might wonder whether the bureaucratic church is opposed to the real nature of the church. The identity of the church depends on the openness to God, the Father, the Son, and the Spirit. In being children of God, members of the church find values like freedom, equality, and brother- and sisterliness. These are brought to nothing by the rigidity and power structures in the bureaucracy. Some see only an unbridgeable gap between church and bureaucracy (Weber 1920). Others believe that the church should use its bureaucratic apparatus in a positive sense to realize freedom, equality, brotherliness and sisterliness, step by step. The pneumatological understanding (the church as a creation of the Spirit of God) can function as a source of inspiration to realize this gradual transformation (Spiegel 1969).

Social aspects only?

These are two examples of the social aspect of the functions of the church. However, something remarkable should be mentioned. We came across some religious reflections. The church was called not only a perfect society but a more than perfect society. For it was deemed to have a divine origin and purpose. In *Gaudium et Spes* of Vatican II, the church was called both a visible society and a spiritual community. In the church as a bureaucracy, we came across some religious considerations too. We found a gap between the church as a bureaucracy and the church as the creation of the Spirit. The way to bridge this was through the church becoming more a creation of the Spirit, step by step. From this it appears that the social aspects are not the only ones. Upon further consideration, one automatically, as it were, comes across the religious aspects of the church.

(2) Religious aspects

We will now turn to another extreme. The functions of the church can be described exclusively or mainly in terms of their religious aspects. The general function — religious communication — can be considered in its vertical dimension only: the communication between God and humanity. This also applies to the core functions. Quite a number of examples can be taken from the history of the church and ecclesiology, from which it appears that the church was exclusively or mainly viewed from the angle of its religious identity. As an example we will consider the invisible church.

Invisible church

The origin of the characterization of the church as invisible can be found in a statement made by Augustine. Many people are to be found within the church, according to Augustine, while they seem to remain outside it; and many are to be found outside the church, while they seem to be within it (*De Baptismo* V.38). With this the distinction between the visible and the invisible church was made. The visible church is the institutional church, to which one belongs on the basis of externally observable membership. The invisible church is the community of believers who have been called together by God to become a church. Not all of those who are members of the institutional church belong to the church as a spiritual community of believers. Especially in reformatory tradition this distinction played and still plays an important role.

Around the turn of the century, the reformatory theologist Sohm made this distinction into a separation. According to Sohm, the church is the covenant people of God summoned in faith. One cannot read who belongs to the people of God from the social reality of the church. Belonging to the church is only the work of the Spirit, as the church itself is only the creation of the Spirit. The real authority in the church stems, therefore, from the Spirit. The church is essentially a pneumatocracy, according to Sohm, and not an autocracy, aristocracy, or bureaucracy (Heinz 1974).

The distinction between the visible and the invisible church plays an important part in our time, as can be seen, for instance, in the work of the theologian Barth. The visible church is observable to everyone, the believing and the unbelieving alike. The essence of the church that exists in the assembly of the living community of the living Lord, however, is only accessible with the eyes of faith. The assembly of the community based on the mercy of God, the power of Jesus Christ, and the mission of the Spirit is a mystery. It is hidden, just as God's own essence is hidden. It may be approached only in faith (Barth IV/1, 1955, 726ff.). The influence of Luther can be felt in this expression. He spoke preferably of the *Deus absconditus* and in parallel of the *ecclesia abscondita* (Congar 1970).

Religious aspects only?

Here the identity of the church in opposition to the social context is given so much emphasis that the relationship with its context disappears from view. It seems as if there is no relationship at all; that is, the true essence of the church is hidden from whatever kind of social determining of position exists. Nevertheless, Barth places a certain value on the visible church. He does not wish to lapse into what he calls "ecclesiological docetism." Docetism belongs to Christology. It has to do with the neglect of the humanity and corporality of Christ. Ecclesiological docetism does not affix any value to the social shape of the church. Barth is opposed to this. The church as the living community of the living Lord is realizing itself in the here and now, according to him, in the externally observable shape of the institutional church.

One assumes that the distinction between the visible and the invisible church has its origin in the religious-political situation that has arisen since the fourth century in particular. It was then that Christianity became the state religion. Besides those who were Christians because of their convictions, many people became members of the church for economic reasons, under political pressure, or as a social-cultural convention. That is why it is postulated that not everyone who belongs to the visible church belongs to the real church, the invisible church, the spiritual community of believers. Now that the time of the state church is over, the distinction has lost its value. The church displays the characteristics of a denomination. It is a voluntary church. There is absolutely no talk of economic, political, or cultural force in becoming a member of the church. Now that the visible church is liberated from social pressure, it is no longer necessary to set it against the invisible church (Berkhof 1985, 391-92).

(3) Social and religious aspects

We can draw no other conclusion from the above than that the functions of the church have to be approached using both the social and the religious aspects (cf. Jossutis 1976). Just how important this is can be indicated by means of an example: the church as *communio*.

Church as communio

Usually, the religious aspects are the center of attention in the church as *communio*. The church is regarded as the community of the faithful *(communio fidelium)*, in which everyone participates proceeding from his or her own faith in freedom and equality. This freedom and equality are based on the charismata that everyone within the church has received, and still does. These are the gifts of God to perform activities in the fields of proclamation, liturgy, and diacony. As believers, ministers are a part of this community. They have been appointed to serve the community. Official service can be seen as one of the charismatic gifts of grace (Haarsma 1991, 178-90). The church as a community of the faithful is nourished by the charismata. By these means the community lives in touch with God, with the Father, the Son, and the Spirit (Rikhof 1981, 229ff.).

Nothing can be subtracted from the religious depth of this view. However, special social aspects are involved in the church as *communio* — aspects such as the openness, equality, and reciprocity of the relations in the community and their extensiveness, closeness, and depth. Aspects such as leadership, authority, and power are equally at issue if one regards the church as *communio*. Neither can one escape having to deal with matters like conflict perception, conflict treatment, or conflict solving.

The necessity to consider the social aspects of the church as *communio* becomes greater if one involves the administrative layers present in the church. The local church does not exist on its own. It maintains relations with higher echelons. And it is precisely in these vertical relationships that all sorts of distinctions arise concerning competence, leadership, authority, and power.

All these matters would be hidden from the eye if one were to view the church as *communio* in its religious aspects only. If one were nevertheless to come across them, it could result in astonishment, surprise, or even aversion (Rikhof 1983; 1990; 1992). The church as *communio* is anything but free from struggles of power and conflict; in fact, it is highly charged with power and conflict. That is why one has to involve the social aspects as well as the religious ones in a treatment of the church as *communio*.

(4) Subordination

Now that we have seen that the functions of the church, involving both their social and religious aspects, have to be dealt with, we have to determine the relations among these aspects. One of the ways to connect the aspects to each other is in terms of subordination. Within ecclesiology this means that the social aspects are subordinate to the religious ones. Usually there is no explicit mention of such subordination; however, it is implicitly couched in the language game used in this context. It can be defined by words like "certainly" and "really." The social aspects are "certainly" of importance, but the religious aspects are "really" the most important.

The varieties of this language game are abundant. For example: the social aspects bear only upon the empirical church, while the religious aspects bear upon God's appeal to the church (Rahner 1964, 99); the social aspects refer to the church as a problem, while the religious aspects refer to it as a mystery (Auer & Ratzinger 1983, 29-31); the social aspects are expressed in sharply defined, bare concepts, while the religious aspects are expressed in rich, imaginative metaphors (Zirker 1984, 17-35); the social aspects are fragmentary, while the religious aspects represent the surplus value of the church (Henau 1989a, 18); the social aspects bear upon the church-with-a-little-c, while religious aspects bear upon the Church-with-a-capital-C (Haarsma 1981, 7); the social aspects refer to the truth of consensus, and the religious ones to the truth of Christ (Dingemans 1987, 105).

Noncompetition

A kind of theological dualism underlies the subordination of the social aspects to the religious ones. This implies that according to its religious nature the church eventually develops apart from its social-historical situation. The social-empirical aspects are "certainly" of importance, but they "really" do not have any influence on the religious identity of the church.

This theological dualism can be seen as a kind of reaction to the sociological reductionism that reduces the church to its social-empirical appearance only. The church is no different as a group from other groups, no different as a community from other communities, no different as an organization from other organizations. Nothing specific is left to the church. In reaction to this, we often end up with the other extreme: theological reductionism. By this we mean the refusal to recognize or make use of the parallels between the church and other social formations for fear of injury to the religious identity of the church. Through this the church is reduced to only its religious aspects (Gustafson 1961, 99ff.; Komonchak 1976). The church then becomes a group that essentially distinguishes itself from other groups, a community that essentially differs from other communities, an organization that has an essentially different character from other organizations. The church is not really a group, a community, or an organization. It is something in its own right, an entity *sui generis,* not comparable to anything. This theological reductionism places the church's character of grace above its social-historical and social-empirical self-realization (Schillebeeckx 1982).

Competitive thinking underlies this sociological and theological reductionism. What is said about the social aspects of the church is deduced from religious aspects. What is said about the religious aspects is deduced from the social aspects.

Let it suffice to refer to the principle of noncompetition (Introduction). In a general sense, this principle states that God and humanity do not compete. The activities of the two cannot be deduced from each other. This principle implies that what God does, humanity does too; what God does more, humanity does more too (chapter 2 sub 2). Applying this to ecclesiology, it means that God calls people together in the church by the fact that they call each other together. He inspires the church by the fact that the people in the church inspire each other. He purifies the church by the fact that the people in the church purify each other. God gives the people the ability to call each other together, to inspire, and to purify the church themselves.

(5) Coordination

Subordination does not supply us with an adequate connection between the social and the religious aspects that are linked to the functions of the church. Is this the case for coordination then? Coordination is often defined as double-sided. The functions of the church may be understood from two equivalent angles. Proceeding from the sociological angle, the social aspects come to light; while from a theological angle, the religious aspects do so. The point here is not one of inferiority or superiority, but of equivalency. Coordination may be split up into two models: the nonsequential and the sequential model.

Nonsequential

In the nonsequential model the sociological and the theological approaches alternate continuously. A good example of this is the research done by Derksen into parish development. In this research one finds all sorts of approaches, which continuously move through and about each other, depending on the aspects that are being dealt with: juridical, historical, sociological, theological, or empirical. The result is a rich variety and continually alternating views on the general function of the church: religious communication (Derksen 1989).

The disadvantage of the nonsequential model, however, is that it lacks a clear structure. The various disciplines are continuously mixed up. One may speak of the model as indiscriminate multidisciplinarity. The objection to this is that it does not become clear whether a connection is made between the various approaches and what it is (Heckhausen 1972).

Sequential

The sequential model does not have this disadvantage. It is characterized by a two-phase structure: first we study the social aspects of the functions of the church, after which we look at the religious ones. Much practical theological research follows this two-phase model (Van der Ven 1990c; 1991c; 1992a). A good example is the research done among the inhabitants of an old quarter of the city of Rotterdam, called the Oude Westen (Old West). The research was done by a practical theological research group in Kampen (the

Netherlands). In the first phase, the needs and interests of the inhabitants were charted in a social-empirical sense. For this purpose sixty focused interviews were held. In the second phase, reflection on the results of the interviews proceeded from a theological point of view. For this purpose the interview material was read theologically using three motifs: the kingdom of God, Jesus Christ, and the Spirit. A practical goal was kept in mind with all of this: the development of pastoral care in the context of the urban mission of the church (Schippers et al. 1990).

Bridging concepts

One of the most difficult questions within the two-phase model concerns the transition from the first to the second phase. How does one go about this transition without doing violence to the socio-scientific analysis in the first phase and the theological analysis in the second? This question can be put more concretely by checking what concepts are used to connect the first and the second phases. We give two examples of such bridging concepts below: coherence and meaning, and history and history of salvation.

Coherence and meaning

In the investigations of the Kampen research group, the bridging concepts *coherence* and *meaning* were used. These concepts were to be found in the border between the first and second phase. On the one hand, the empirical interview material was ordered by means of these terms in the first phase. On the other hand, they functioned as the point of departure for the theological reflection on the interview material in the second phase.

How should we consider the bridging concept of coherence and meaning? This question can be answered by proceeding from the image of humanity and society that is hidden beneath it and from the definition of religious that lies within it. In psychology, both terms are characteristic of an image of humanity that radiates balance. In sociology, they are typical of an image of society that is marked by consensus. In the theory of religion, they stand for religious acceptance and consolation. The question is whether and how these psychological, sociological, and religious theoretical choices can be justified. Can we not just as well take the bridging concepts from a critical psychology, sociology, and religious theory, in which change and liberation are central? Is this not the obvious choice if we want local pastoral care to be developed in the direction of the urban mission of the church? Or if one wants to transform church and society in the direction of the message of the kingdom of God?

History and history of salvation

In the *Handbuch der Pastoraltheologie* two other bridging concepts were used: *history* and *history of salvation.* The term *history* orders the social-empirical aspects of the study in the first phase, while the term *history of salvation* is the point of departure for theological reflection in the second phase. Whereas the Kampen research group drew its terms from the social sciences and philosophy, the *Handbuch* derived them from fundamental theology (Arnold et al. 1964).

There are problems attached to this choice as well. These have to do with the three aspects that are inherent in the terms *history* and *history of salvation.* In the first place, one can place the emphasis on doom or salvation in history. Next, one can place the accent on humanity's share or God's share in the history of salvation. Finally, one can focus attention on the continuity or divine discontinuity between history and the history of salvation (Schillebeeckx 1977a, 686-701). The *Handbuch* shows no awareness of this problem — so we find — and simply ignores it.

Bridging

We close this chapter with a conclusion and a question. The conclusion is as follows: *ecclesiology should be developed proceeding from the coordination of the social and the religious aspects of the functions of the church.* The above discussion leaves us no other choice. This leaves us with a question, however: With the help of which concepts can the study of social aspects and religious aspects be bridged? The terms *coherence* and *meaning* as well as *history* and *history of salvation* turned out to raise too many questions. Other proposals have been made of late. A plea has been made for concepts like human subject, liberation, justice, and community through liberation (Nipkow 1975; Mette & Steinkamp 1983). However, these proposals are also characterized by a certain arbitrariness. The question is whether we should or should not choose a more abstract approach. Do bridging concepts really hit the mark? Should we not look for a formal bridging theory? Is such a formal bridging theory available?

Chapter 6

Religious Signs

In the last chapter we found that the social and religious aspects of the functions of the church demand a coordinative rather than a subordinative approach. The question that we have not yet answered is how the study of the social aspects and the religious aspects can be connected. Since the bridging concepts we discussed in the last chapter were inadequate, we will raise the question to a higher level of abstraction — from the level of concepts to that of formal theories. We will examine two formal bridging theories: hermeneutics and semiotics. Hermeneutics offers a perspective from which the study of both social and religious aspects can be made clear. Proceeding from semiotics as the doctrine of signs, we can indicate how to make the connection. The social phenomena can be conceived as religious signs. As religious signs they refer to the reality of God's salvation. In this they signify this salvation and represent it.

In this chapter we will (1) decide whether a connection can be made from the perspective of hermeneutics between the study of social aspects and the study of religious aspects, (2) determine how the connection can be made from semiotics as the doctrine of signs, and (3) discover what connection exists between the sign and signified reality.

(1) A hermeneutical perspective

A fundamental problem in bridging the social and the religious aspects of the functions of the church lies in the diverse nature of the disciplines involved — sociology and theology. How can sociology and theology be related to each other, or be connected to each other? Hermeneutics may contribute to the solution of this problem in the view of many practical theologians (Tracy 1981; Browning 1983; 1987a; 1991; Van der Ven 1990c; Fowler 1987; 1990; Joncheray 1992; Ménard 1992). In this we have to make a distinction, however, between traditional and new hermeneutics.

Traditional hermeneutics

It is often asserted that while sociology aims at descriptive prediction, presents hard facts, and arrives at objective judgments, theology aims at valuing speculation, presents soft facts, and arrives at subjective judgments. One cannot imagine a greater contrast: description versus valuation, prediction versus speculation, hard versus soft, objective versus subjective. Regarded in this way, an ecclesiology that endeavors to connect the social and religious aspects of the functions of the church is an impossible if not hopeless task.

Is this contrast correct? From a dichotomizing philosophy of science, which sets the empirical sciences against the alpha-sciences, it is. The empirical sciences explain reality, according to this view, while the alpha-sciences try to understand it. The explanation of reality in the empirical sciences assumes an attitude of dissoluteness and distance. The researcher registers, measures, and tests in a neutral fashion. He or she does not yield to personal feelings and beliefs; they are irrelevant. By contrast, the understanding of reality that is characteristic of the alpha-sciences stems from the personal participation of the researcher in the object of study. He or she is personally involved with it and feels one with it. One can talk of a subjective unity. Description takes place from the perspective of the observer, while understanding takes place from the perspective of the participant. A sharper difference is hard to conceive.

This dichotomization is not only characteristic of the position taken by the positivists on the side of the empirical sciences. It is not in the least typical of the position taken by traditional hermeneuticists on the side of the alpha-sciences (Schleiermacher, Dilthey, Heidegger, and Gadamer). Traditional hermeneutics originates from the Romantic period of the 19th century (Ricoeur 1987, 36). It proceeds from the irreconcilable contrasts between: repeatable and nonrepeatable phenomena; systematically explainable and unique occurrences; nomothetic and idiographic knowledge; quantitative and qualitative methods; know-how and art (Ricoeur 1987; Pannenberg 1973, 157-69; De Groot 1968, 360ff.; Simonton 1990).

New hermeneutics

Proceeding from a complementary scientific view, however, these contrasts do not add up. Explaining and understanding are not each other's negative. They supplement each other. The one implies the other. This can be further worked out from new hermeneutics.

New hermeneutics proceeds from the insight that every scientific research is subject to the tension between two poles: the subject and the object of study. On the one hand, the object cannot be approached separately from the involvement of the subject with the object. On the other hand, the subject has to be optimally aware of this involvement. The subject has to be as open as possible to the object by temporarily postponing this involvement, as it were, and putting it between brackets. This never works completely, but the endeavor is of essential importance.

In this tension between the subject and the object of research lies the complementarity of the observer and the participant perspective. No empirical social scientist presents hard facts that are separate from the personal position and the surrounding culture by which he or she is influenced. No empirical social scientist has an Archimedean point above him, from which he can survey and check the social reality in an absolutely objective sense. Where else could such a point be but in his own head? One's personal involvement with the object of study cannot be undone. It cannot be cut out from the research, no matter what shape the involvement may take, be it weak or strong, negative or positive.

We are not dealing with a general phrase here, but a phenomenon that can be concretely pointed out in its fundamental aspects in the research process. First of all, the personal involvement of the researcher comes up in the choice of the subject for research and in the selection of the aspects that can be distinguished therein. Then, it influences the legitimization of the choice of the subject and the aspects in it. Furthermore, it plays a role in the dynamics and the motivation from which the researcher tackles the research. Next, it works on in the ideas developed and generated with regard to the object of study. Moreover, it is expressed in the lapidary, often slogan-like formulations used in the research, which point to a (necessarily) uncritical moment in the research. Finally, it manifests itself in a kind of attitude of orthodoxy and intolerance regarding different research of other researchers. Here, there is no talk of an inferior kind of research that would look bad in contrast to a superior kind of research. The aspects mentioned determine the research *tout court* (Ricoeur 1987, 225-28).

This personal involvement influences the formulation of the problem, the setup of the research design, the analysis, the interpretation, and the evaluation of the data. The methodical technical collection and methodical technical processing of the data fall outside this. These can be considered as merely instrumental and objective (Weber 1968).

Using all of this, the sharp contrast between the observer's and the participant's perspective, the hard and soft method, and the objective and subjective approach are relativized. They are regarded as being complementary to each other.

This complementarity is itself based on mutual implication. This means that in explaining reality objectively, one automatically comes across aspects that should be considered for subjective understanding; and in understanding something subjectively, one automatically comes across aspects that should be considered for objective explanation. This implicative relation rests on the fact that the two poles attract each other: the object and the subject of study. Understanding has as its point of departure the fact that the object cannot be approached separately from the involvement of the subject. Explaining has its point of departure in the fact that the subject has to be as aware as possible of this involvement, and has to put this involvement between brackets. The point is the polar tension between subject and object. It is the polar tension between understanding and explaining. They cannot and may not be done separately from each other (Ricoeur 1987, 131-64).

With this understanding we go beyond the sharp contrast between sociology and theology. It is surpassed within a hermeneutical perspective that connects the two. Sociology and theology become complementary to each other. This complementarity is based on mutual implication. This is precisely the case in the study of phenomena like religion and the church. This means that in socio-scientific research on the church, one automatically comes across aspects that demand further theological study. And conversely, in theological analysis of the church, one automatically comes across aspects that require further socio-scientific clarification.

(2) A semiotic connection

Hermeneutics does offer an adequate angle for the proposition that the study of social aspects and the study of religious aspects of the church can be connected to each other. But it does not solve the problem of how they are to be connected.

To adequately approach this problem we will take a closer look at what Ricoeur called the semiological challenge (Ricoeur 1987, 35). He believed that a number of insights that had developed within hermeneutics could be deepened and further developed in a semiotic frame of reference. The term *semiotics* is derived from *semeion,* the Greek word for "sign." Semiotics means the doctrine of signs. It is the science that is involved with the study of signs, signification, and the giving of meaning. We believe that the social and religious aspects can be connected to each other by regarding the social aspects as religious signs from the perspective of semiotics. In order to clarify this, we will need to discuss the terms *sign* and *religious sign*.

Sign

There are various opinions on what a sign is. These can be reduced to two main traditions that can be distinguished within semiotics: the Peircian tradition, which refers to the American Charles Sanders Peirce (1839-1914); and the Saussurian tradition, which refers to the Swiss Ferdinand de Saussure (1857-1913). The most important differences — insofar as they are of interest to us — are related to two questions. The first is: Is attention paid to non-linguistic signs besides linguistic ones? Linguistic signs lie within words, sentences, and texts such as stories, parables, prayers, and letters. Nonlinguistic signs are, for example, natural phenomena, bodily attitudes and movements, objects, and forms of art. The second question is: Does the sign character, linguistic or non-linguistic, lie in the signs themselves, more or less independent of humans? Or does the sign character come about in interaction with humans as signifier? In other words: Is the human share as *homo semioticus* within the communicative context in which he finds himself sufficiently taken into account? In the Peircian tradition both questions are positively answered — more so than in the Saussurian tradition (Grabner-Haider 1975; De Pater 1978a; 1978b; Lukken 1991). In the Peircian tradition attention is paid to both linguistic and non-linguistic signs. Further, the emphasis is placed on the interaction between signs and signifier and on the communicative context within which signification takes place. That is why we take the Peircian tradition as our point of departure (Peirce 1985; Morris 1985; Van Zoest 1978). This has already proved to be fruitful in the area of exegesis (Van Wolde 1984; 1989; 1990a; 1990b), practical theology (Bastian 1972), and liturgy (Geerts 1990). Within the Peircian tradition the semiotics of Umberto Eco in particular will be our guide (Eco 1979a; 1979b; 1990).

What is a *sign?* Peirce gave the following classic definition: "something which stands to somebody for something in some respect or capacity" (Peirce 1985, 5). There are four aspects to be discerned in this: the sign (the first "something"), the denotatum (the second "something"), the interpreter (present in "somebody"), and the code (in some respect or capacity).

There is a "something" that functions as a sign. This "something" can be all sorts of things. All possible things, processes, structures, and actions can be signs. One can classify them into certain categories. Spatial things can be a sign (buildings, rooms), tactile actions (embrace, caress), linguistic statements (words, sentences, texts), paralinguistic expressions (use of voice), bodily attitudes and movements (facial expression, standing, sitting, walking), types of fashion (clothing, hairstyle), interactional relations (interaction rituals, types of communication, organizational processes), cultural styles (manners, norms, values), aesthetic expressions (musical morphology, theory of harmony, counterpoint). Everything can be a sign.

The sign is "something" that stands for "something," according to Peirce. This second "something," that which the sign stands for, is the *denotatum.* The sign refers to it; it represents it. In contrast to the sign, the denotatum is absent; it is not observable. It is present only insofar as the sign represents it. The denotatum is the signified reality.

What functions as denotatum cannot be determined without information from the linguistic and nonlinguistic context within which the sign finds itself. It can be concrete or abstract, material or spiritual, imaginable or unimaginable. It can exist or not exist. It can be fictional or real. It can belong to the past, present, or future. It can be acceptable or abject.

Another element has to be added to this. "Something" (sign) stands for "something" (denotatum) "to somebody." This somebody is the *interpreter,* the one who interprets something as a sign of something else. The result of this interpretation is the interpretant (not to be confused with the interpreter!). Peirce called the *interpretant* an equivalent sign that is located in the mind of the observer of the sign, the spirit of the interpreting person. The preacher who is preaching a sermon on the book of Job and is manifesting a certain facial expression in this, is observed by a hearer who is thinking to himself, "he looks so vulnerable." This thought, "he looks so vulnerable," is the interpretant. It is the mental concept in the complex pattern of thought of the interpreter. The interpretant is located in the mind of the interpreter.

We have to add a fourth element as well: "something" stands for "something" for "somebody" "in some respect or capacity." Where does this "in some respect or capacity" come from? In most cases it stems from the codes that underlie the signs. A code is a whole set of rules, agreements, and institutionalized habits on the grounds of which we interpret something to be a sign of something else. It lies couched within the cultural tradition of which the interpreter is a part. In other words, a code contains the structure of cultural mechanisms on the ground of which we see something as a referent to something else. Without knowledge of the code, we lack that which enables us to recognize the sign as a sign. "On the ground of which": this is characteristic of a code. That is why Peirce uses the word *ground.* For that matter, codes are often the grounds of a sign, but not always.

Religious sign

Proceeding from the above, it is natural to conceive of the relation between the social and religious aspects of the church in a semiotic sense. From the definition of Peirce this can be understood as follows: the social phenomena in the church (sign) refer to God's salvation (denotatum), at least to those who see it as a sign (interpretant), on the ground of conventions that lie within the religious tradition (codes). Let us take a look at the four elements separately (sign, denotatum, interpretant, codes).

The social phenomena in the church function as religious signs. This is the main statement that we want to focus on here. The religious aspect is not added to it. It does not come on top of the social phenomena. It is precisely these themselves that are interpreted as referring to God's salvation. To this purpose all categories mentioned can be considered in principle: spatial, tactile, linguistic, paralinguistic, bodily, fashion, interactional, cultural, and aesthetic phenomena. Everything can become a religious sign: the greeting ritual, the word of the preacher, the prayer over gifts, the story of the last supper, the circle around the altar, the bread, the wine, the ritual dress, the liturgical music, the candles, the incense, the mission, and the blessing.

The denotatum to which the social phenomena refer as religious signs is God's salvation. This can be indicated in various ways. In the New Testament fifteen different images are used: safety, protection, return, reconciliation, peace, restoration, forgiveness, sanctification, support, community, love, freedom, newness, fullness, and liberation (Schillebeeckx 1977a, 436-468). This means that social phenomena as religious signs can refer to this fifteenfold richness of God's salvation.

The interpretant is the indispensable link in the whole. The fact that the social phenomena are interpreted as religious signs can be reduced to the interpretant, which is present in the mind of the interpreter. The religious signification takes place in the mental apparatus of the interpreter. Religious signification is a mental process. This not only applies to the religious interpretation of liturgical dress and incense, but also to belief in the presence of the Word of God in the words of the Bible and in the words of the minister. It equally applies to belief in the presence of Jesus under the signs of bread and wine. With this we do not wish to hold a mentalistic view, as if there were nothing else than this mental process (Stillings et al. 1987). We only wish to say that this belief does not occur outside or above this mental process (cf. Duroux 1955; 1963; Chenu 1964).

The last element is the religious code. It plays a fundamental role, for where it is lacking, religious signification of social phenomena is impossible. The religious code is the basis (ground) thereof. The religious tradition is the cultural cradle for the religious code. Insofar as the interpreter is part of this religious tradition, he has the basis for religious signifying at his disposal. If this is not the case, then religious signification will not happen.

(3) The connection between sign and signified reality

Within the Peircian tradition three kinds of signs are distinguished: iconical, indexical, and symbolic signs. This distinction has to do with the various ways in which they relate to the signified reality (denotatum) and is of direct importance for the connection between the social and religious aspects of the church, particularly insofar as the social aspects are viewed as religious signs.

Iconical signs

Iconical signs are characterized by the fact that they are similar to the reality to which they refer. The point is the similarity between these signs and the reality that they represent in a depicting manner. Iconical signs are portraying signs. That is why they have a certain suggestive power. A sign in a store on which there is a circle with an opening on it, from which an arrow extends, has more suggestive power than a sign saying "exit." If this sign is accompanied by the figure of a walking man, then the suggestive power is further enhanced. The iconical signs are determined by figurative qualities that are similar to reality.

There are numerous religious iconical signs. In the Bible one continuously comes across them in images, similes, metaphors, and parables such as the shepherd and the sheep, the charitable father and the lost son. Religious rituals are chock-full of them too. The eucharistic prayer is represented as a mimesis of the last supper of the Lord. The greeting of peace is the image of the peace God makes. The blessing represents the blessing of God. The anointing represents the anointing by God. The community of people depicts the community of God with the people.

Indexical signs

Indexical signs are characterized by the proximity of the sign to the signified reality. There are points of contact or tangent planes between them, or at least there have been. Indexical means that the signified reality has exercised a certain influence on the coming about of the sign. The wreath of smoke rising above the houses points to the existence of a fireplace somewhere in the area. The fresh tracks of a hare in the forest tell us that the animal has just taken to its heels. The typical skin condition that characterizes Lyme disease indicates that some time ago a tick caused a bacterial infection.

Indexical religious signs also exist. A good example is the deed Pope John XXIII performed at the opening of the Second Vatican Council when he replaced the papal tiara by the episcopal miter. Thus, the replacement of the ritual dress in some churches by the *tenue de ville* is an indexical sign of the desired adaptation of the liturgy to modern life. The retention of Gregorian chant can be regarded as a indexical sign of the attachment to an aesthetically refined liturgical tradition.

Symbolic signs

Symbolic signs are signs that come about on the ground of agreement, conventions, or generally applicable rules that either are or are not made explicit. Their relation to the signified reality is indirect and detached. They are more or less abstract by nature. This is different for the iconical and indexical signs. The iconical signs contain a similarity to the signified reality and are therefore located closer to it. The indexical signs have been in contact with the signified reality, which has left visible traces. They have been influenced by it. The symbolic signs are characterized by a certain arbitrariness. They refer to the signified reality according to agreement, but not on the basis of intrinsic connections. They are based on consensus.

There are a great many religious symbolic signs. In meditative, reflective, and discursive texts, which play a large part in religion, they often have a strong presence. One need not think only of words like "one person and two natures," "transubstantiation" or "real presence." Words like creation, redemption, grace, and history of salvation also belong to this category. Their religious referential power is derived from the fact that the religious community has determined that they have a religious referential meaning on the ground of the religious tradition. They are religious signs-by-agreement. In this way creeds and council texts come about.

Iconical, indexical, and symbolic signs

The first two, iconical and indexical, are the most direct, proximate, and concrete. And of these two, the iconical signs are the most flexible, plastic, inventive, and rejuvenating. Something may unexpectedly become an iconical sign because one suddenly sees a similarity to reality in it that one had not seen at first. Iconical signs may be new, original, unexpected, and fresh. They may generate new meanings, and they may make new interpretations possible. This is less so, if not at all the case, for the indexical and symbolic signs. The symbolic signs are the most indirect, remote, and abstract.

Now it is not so that signs are either iconical, or indexical, or symbolic. They usually contain all three aspects in them, but only one aspect dominates: the iconical, the indexical, or the symbolic. This often depends on the angle from which one regards the sign.

More often one can talk of a composite sign. The green sign on which a man is depicted with an arrow including the words "pass here," contains a combination of several signs. The green is a non-linguistic symbolic sign. It is based on the agreement that green signs mean one is allowed to drive/walk on. The man is an iconical sign. The similarity with the reality is clearly expressed in it. The arrow is an indexical sign. Its direction is directly influenced by the direction in which one is expected to go in reality. Finally, the words "pass here" are a linguistic sign, of which the meaning has come about on the ground of agreement.

These insights are of importance for religious signs, which can often be regarded as composite signs. They contain combinations of iconical and symbolic aspects in particular. In the community of people in the church lies an iconical aspect, insofar as it depicts a similarity to the community of God with the people. However, there is also a symbolic aspect in it, insofar as the meaning of this sign is set down in the Bible, in tradition, and in the confessions. Fixed expressions like "community of believers" and "the body of Christ" refer to this. They can be viewed as a kind of religious consensus, if not a kind of religious codification.

It is precisely the combination of iconical and symbolic aspects that makes religious signs undergo continuous stress. The iconical character of these signs affords them a certain freshness, originality, and newness. It is the source of continuous invention. The symbolic character holds them to agreements already made, to fixed rules and conventions that are in force. The religious signs are located in the midst of the tension between invention and convention. In new iconical signs the invention dominates. According to the degree to which they have become a steady habit, the symbolic convention dominates. In other words, with new iconical signs the analogous relation between sign and signified reality dominates. The similarity or analogy plays the most important role in this. In the traditional symbolic signs, the logical relation between sign and signified reality dominates. The logic in this rests on formal agreements and rules (cf. Van Wolde 1989, 25-26; 51-52).

Chapter 7

Religious Codes

We came to the conclusion that the social and religious aspects of the functions of the church deserve to have a coordinative rather than a subordinative treatment (chapter 5). After that we found a way to connect both aspects to each other. We viewed the social phenomena as religious signs that refer to the signified reality of God's salvation (chapter 6). In this chapter we will take a further look at the basis of this religious signification: the religious codes.

The following questions will be discussed: (1) What are religious codes? (2) What functions do they exercise? (3) Under which conditions? And finally, (4) In which contexts do they exercise these functions?

(1) Religious codes and supercodes

In the last chapter we described codes as the basis (ground) on which the process of signification takes place. In this a distinction can be made between codes and supercodes.

Codes

Codes can be viewed as rules, agreements, and institutionalized habits that form the mechanism on the ground of which things, situations, happenings, and actions are seen as signs. Without a code there is no connection between sign and signified reality (denotatum), nor between sign and interpretant. Without a code there is no sign, no signified reality, no interpretant.

This also applies to religious codes. They form the mechanism on the ground of which social phenomena and happenings are viewed as signs that refer to the salvation of God. These codes are part of the conventions of the religious culture that lies within the religious tradition. Knowledge of and participation in this tradition are necessary to set the mechanism going. Without this knowledge and participation, social phenomena cannot be experienced, recognized, and interpreted as signs of God's salvation. The religious codes are located in the consciousness of the people, at least insofar as the religious tradition is reflected in it. If they disappear from there, then the possibility of experiencing and understanding religious signs is also lost.

Supercodes

Codes work within supercodes. These are wholes of codes that give cohesion to the codes and organize their mutual relations. Within these wholes one can point out hierarchical structures. Let us take a look at an example and build the hierarchical structure from the bottom up.

We will start with the codes related to facial expressions. These are involved when we believe we see gladness, sadness, anger, or disappointment on someone's face. Being able to read someone's face is a question of interpretation. These interpretations are organized by an equally large number of codes — the codes for gladness, sadness, anger, and disappointment. These codes organize the interpretation of the facial expressions in terms of feelings. Together they can be called the supercode of facial expressions.

The supercode of the facial expressions is itself a part of the kinesiological codes. Besides the codes of the facial expressions, the codes related to posture and physical movement also belong to them. In posture the point is the sign character for the position of the head, for example, or the neck, the shoulders, the upper body, etc. One can tell psychic attitudes from this such as willingness, aggression, and stubbornness. In physical movement the point is the character of the sign of walking, bending, jumping, etc. We interpret them in terms of psychic attitudes such as hurry, condescension, joy. Together the codes for facial expressions, postures, and physical movements are the kinesiological supercode.

The kinesiological supercode itself is part of the nonverbal interaction codes. Besides the kinesiological codes, these include also the proxemic and gestural codes. The proxemic codes regulate the bodily and spatial proximity and distance. These function as signs of intimacy or alienation. The gestural codes are involved with body language. These entail gestures typical of "a real civil servant," "a real sergeant-major," "a real professor." Together with the proxemic and gestural codes, the kinesiological codes form the supercode of nonverbal interaction.

The supercode of nonverbal interaction together with the supercode of verbal interaction — which represents a field of its own — makes up the supercode of interaction.

Finally, at this high level of abstraction other supercodes can be distinguished besides the supercode of interaction. For instance, the architectural, economic, political, social, cultural, and aesthetic supercodes belong to this level. The religious supercode is also part of this.

Ecclesiological supercode

Within the religious supercode we can distinguish theological, christological, pneumatological, and ecclesiological supercodes. How can we characterize the ecclesiological supercode? In the Introduction we gave the codes that seem important to us within the framework of a transformatory ecclesiology. These are: people of God, body of Christ, building of the Spirit, Jesus movement, church of the poor, and community of believers. Which of these is suitable as a supercode?

An ecclesiological supercode has to be general enough to contain all these codes. One can find several suggestions in ecclesiological literature.

The first option can be found in the *symbolum apostolicum.* Following the church we find the term the *communio sanctorum.* Sanctorum has to do with *sancti:* the believers who are connected to each other through the community. Sanctorum also has to do with *sancta:* believers who participate in holy things, that which is sacred (Barth IV/1, 1955, 728). One can therefore view the *communio sanctorum* as the basic formula of the church, as the ecclesiological supercode (Moltmann 1975, 314-44).

A second option is the church as *communio fidelium.* Fidelium refers to *fides:* the belief in God — Father, Son, and Spirit. A more encompassing ecclesiological supercode than this trinitarian basic formula is well nigh unimaginable (Rikhof 1981a, 229ff.).

A third option is the *church as sacrament.* That the church is sacrament means that it is "a sign and instrument, that is, of the communion with God and of unity among all men," as the Vatican states (*Lumen Gentium* 1).

A number of arguments can be brought forward for the opinion that the church as sacrament is the preeminent ecclesiological supercode. The first argument is that the church shares in the original sacrament itself: Jesus the Christ is the original sacrament of God. The church, according to the Fathers of the church, is a derivative original sacrament: the sacrament of the moon (*mysterium lunae*) that receives its light from Jesus Christ, who himself is the sun. The face of God can be seen in his face (Boff 1987a, 35).

The second argument goes further still. It refers to the trinitary depth that lies within the church as sacrament. Christ is not in himself the original sacrament of God; Christ is the original sacrament of God in and through the Spirit. The sending of the Spirit is the eschatological original sacrament of the future of the kingdom of God that has already begun and is aimed at its fulfillment. The church that participates in the original sacrament of the sending of the Spirit is therefore itself also aimed at this fulfillment (Moltmann 1975, 224-31).

The third argument is that the church as sacrament encompasses five other approaches or codes that we mentioned earlier: the *communio fidelium,* the people of God, the body of Christ, the messianic Jesus movement, and the church of the poor. Especially liberation theology pays attention to the latter. In solidarity with the poor, the church brings about its sacramental function: it is precisely in this that it is the sign and instrument of the salvation of God. Conversely, where the church allows the suppression of the poor to exist or even legitimizes it, it is an anti-sacrament. The church's task is political sanctity. This task implies waging a battle against poverty proceeding from the solidarity of God with the people. In this political sanctity, the church executes its sacramental function (Boff 1987a, 41-46; Klein Goldewijk 1991, 281-82).

The interesting thing about the church as sacrament is that this expression in its entirety can be interpreted in a semiotic sense. "Sacrament" here means that the church refers to the salvation of God *(significative salvation historical)*. At the same time sacrament points to the vehicle of salvation that the church encloses: it is this vehicle *(instrumental salvation historical)*. This is what Vatican II says in *Lumen Gentium* about the church as sacrament (Koffeman 1986). These two aspects join with the semiotic approach of the church. *Sacrament* means "sign" just as the Thomistic principle says: *"sacramentum est in genere signi"* (Schillebeeckx 1964, 301). The sign function of the church means that the church refers to God's salvation *(significative salvation historical)*. This sign function also implies that the church signifies and represents God's salvation, that is, it makes it present *(instrumental salvation historical)*. In short, the church as sign is a reference and vehicle. As a sign, the church is a sacrament.

(2) Functions of religious codes

Codes can fulfill three functions: a cognitive, an emotive, and a conative function. Eco denotes these as the informative, expressive, and instructive functions (Eco 1979a, 54-57, 203, 241-43). We have a preference for the terms cognitive, emotive, and conative because terminologically they link with the first three functions of religious communication (chapter 3 sub 1).

Cognitive

Codes contain knowledge about the signified reality (denotatum), to which the signs refer. They offer an angle from which reality can be approached, they put it in a certain light, and they divulge a certain aspect of it. They give information.

Now religious codes provide religious information. They state that the church is the people of God, the body of Christ, and the building of the Spirit. This is not knowledge that the church can champion. It cannot derive rights from it. If it did, it would disown the peculiar character of religious information. That the church is the people of God, the body of Christ, and the building of the Spirit does not mean that it can take the credit for this. It is the case because of the gift of grace by God. This means that it *may* be the people of God, the body of Christ, and the building of the Spirit (Kuitert 1992, 196).

The religious knowledge that contains the codes can be distinguished according to three aspects. This distinction lies within the threefold structure of each religion (Schillebeeckx 1977b). The structure of the Christian religion in particular is found in creation, liberation, and completion.

From the aspect of creation, the religious codes bring the church into contact with God, who grounds it in Christ and the Spirit. God is at the origin of the church — not in a historical but in a qualitative sense. God preserves and protects it, cares for it, and has it much at heart. God creates and re-creates it continuously, not chronologically or evolutionistically, but kairologically — in other words, from moment to moment. The church is at stake every moment for God. He calls it to life again and again, and challenges it likewise. At the same time God spares it and forgives it.

This gives the church anything but reason for pretensions and claims. It stimulates the awareness of receptiveness, openness, and dependence with regard to God. It intensifies the notion of gratuity. It stimulates an attitude of meekness. It contains a source of consolation and a perspective of mercy in situations of chaos and hopelessness. This applies to the authorities in particular. The story of creation contains an appeal to the leaders to be careful not to overestimate their power or to misuse it. What also applies to church leaders is this: "they are like everybody else taken from the earth, their stars and destiny long determined, their judgement on good and evil always premature, for it is reserved unto God, the deadly violence (. . .) a brand on their blazon, that stamps their existence to Gnadenfrist" (Houtepen 1992b, 57).

Proceeding from the aspect of liberation, the religious codes confront the church with its own deficiency, want, guilt, and sin, in which it is caught and from which it has to be freed. They stimulate the notion that the church is playing below its own measure and needs continuous correction, purification, and reformation. What we are dealing with here is a mixture of incapacity and culpable inadequacy, finiteness and responsibility, contingency and guilt.

Even though the church is called the mother of all believers and the bride of Christ, occasionally this mother and bride is also a whore (Barth IV/1, 1955, 772). Origen was still in a position to say that whores are outside the church and that the heretics and the godless are always busy "setting up a whorehouse, a brothel at every turn" and that Christ protects the church from prostitution and "has placed the necklace of obedience around its neck" (Ledegang 1992, 124). In our time, however, we see more clearly to what extent the church itself has been unfaithful to its own calling and task and how it soils and defiles them. That is why the external and internal criticism vented on the church is often so sharp. The silent "criticism by number" of those who are disappointed in the church and have simply turned their backs on it also belongs to this.

This criticism is aimed at several points, as Congar has indicated. One of those is the confusion of aims and means. Because of this confusion, the accumulation of financial and institutional means begin to control the church, and evangelical aims are placed in a tight corner. In addition, this criticism is aimed at the traditionalism in the church: being stuck to outdated historical forms that have been passed down. People accuse the church of a narrow and restricted historical perspective and historical slowness (Congar 1968).

Criticism can be formulated in a more fundamental sense, as Barth did. Barth sees a twofold religious corruption in the church. The first is the *"Fremdhorigkeit."* Through this the church has begun to serve other strange gods, such as those of a certain institution or a certain philosophy. The church is then degraded to a mondial church, state church, *Volkskirche,* or culture-bound church. In this way the church is secularized: it desanctifies itself. The second is self-glorification. Through this the church makes itself an idol, a golden calf. The church aims its energy at itself in that case, instead of at the gospel. In this way the church becomes sacralized: it consecrates itself (Barth IV/1, 1955, 747-65).

There is no security against this corruption, no guarantee, no insurance, unless the church continuously reforms itself and places itself under the criticism of the gospel. By nature the church is *ecclesia semper purificanda,* according to Vatican II (*Lumen Gentium* 8). By nature it is *ecclesia semper reformanda.*

This reformation can only take place if it finds its source in the belief that God liberates the church in Word and Spirit to its true essence. The church cannot pull itself up out of the swamp. It must turn in prayer to God, who has wanted its origin and destiny, and who guides and preserves it. The church may allow itself to be judged, consoled, and encouraged by God (Schillebeeckx 1968).

From the aspect of completion, the religious codes inspire the church to hope for the future promised by God. Not through extrapolation, as if the future were to be entirely deduced from the trends in the past or present. Nor through prediction, as if the future were to be predicted from a network of connected factors. The future that has been promised the church and to which it is aimed is not the *futurum,* but the *adventus.* The *futurum* develops linearly from the present; the *adventus* is what is coming to us. This is determined by the unpredictable, incalculable, unexpected. It is characterized by the gratuity of God.

The future that is promised the church does not mean that its present structure and order will be maintained nor that its size and shape will remain the same. The future is larger than the past and the present of the church. Or more precisely, Christ is larger than the church. Finally, God is greater than Christ. That is why the future of the church is seen from the perspective of the convergence of all these communities, groups, and individuals who are aimed at God in their belief. This breaks through and surpasses the limits of the church. This insight stems from the fact that the church and the kingdom of God are not the same. The church is oriented toward the kingdom of God and will be completed by it on the basis of creation and liberation (Schillebeeckx 1989).

Emotive

Codes also give expression to feelings, emotions, and attitudes. They stimulate the feelings and experiences and shape them. This also applies to the religious codes. Religious codes give expression to religious experiences, feelings, and emotions. The feelings we are dealing with here may be aimed at ourselves or at others. They belong to the deeper layers of human existence. They have a certain high-mindedness in them. They are feelings of earnest. They are involved with *la vie serieuse* (Durkheim 1925). They also contain a combination of emotional activity and passivity. They have something about them of active receptiveness and active tolerance, and of passive courage and passive decisiveness. Furthermore, they contain a positive and a negative pole. The negative pole tells us that something is wrong. It confronts us with suffering and evil. It raises feelings of sadness and sorrow and of tragedy and guilt within us. The positive pole tells us there is redemption, that suffering and evil will be abolished, will be surpassed. It calls on feelings of release, relief, joy, and gratitude within us. The emotional conflict between the negative and the positive is not resolved; the gap is not bridged. What does come about is a feeling of reconciliation and a feeling of hope (James 1902, 331).

The cognitive and emotive function of religious codes are each other's correlates. The cognitive aspects are characterized by complexity: creation, liberation, and completion. The emotional aspects are also characterized by complexity: depth, earnest, high-mindedness; activity and passivity; the negative and the positive. Conflicts lie within this complexity: the cognitive conflict of creation and liberation, the emotional conflict of the negative and the positive. These conflicts are raised by the religious codes in the sense that they are "raised to a higher, religious plain." The cognitive conflict of creation and liberation is raised in the perspective of completion, while the emotional conflict of negativity and positivity is abolished in the perspective of hope.

Conative

Codes also contain an incentive, appeal, and instruction. They indicate how one should deal with the reality to which they refer — whether one should act in a preventive or intervening sense, or whether an action should be left. A certain kind of regulation is stored within codes, like inspiration and orientation, or a kind of direction, like imperative or corrective.

This applies to religious codes as well. These not only contain religious information and are not restricted to the expression of religious emotions. They also have a stimulating, motivating, appealing, and correctional working. They show us the way, push us on, and urge us to reversal.

Here again religious codes lead to modesty and unpretentiousness. The cognitive function implies that the statement "the church is the people of God" has to be understood as "the church may be the people of God." The conative function means that this statement has to be understood as "the church still has to become the people of God." Similarly, "the church may be the body of Christ," and "it still has to become the body of Christ." Finally, "the church may be building of the Spirit," and "it still has to become the building of the Spirit" (Kuitert 1992, 195).

What way do the religious codes point out to us? What orientation do they offer? For the answer to these questions, we restrict ourselves to the religious codes, which are relevant for the development of a transformatory ecclesiology. In this we find our point of departure, as has been observed in the Introduction. Within this restriction three aspects can be distinguished in the regulatory orientation. The first aspect is involved with the direction in which the church has to develop internally *(aspect ad intra).* The second aspect points to the road the church must take with regard to the outside world *(aspect ad extra).* The third aspect refers to the way in which the church has to use time (temporal aspect).

The *aspect ad intra* contains the call for an evangelical way of treating each other within the church. This evangelical task involves the following elements: humanity, equality, freedom, and cohesion.

The first element contains the appeal for respect for the humanity of the members of the church, and admonishes us not to walk all over them or pass them by. It is precisely their personal humanity that deserves regard. This lies within the religious code that states that the people in the church are a chosen race, a royal priesthood, a holy nation, God's own people (1 Pet. 2:9-10).

The second element follows from this: the call for the promotion of equality among the people in the church. This equality is founded in the church as a community of believers. It has its base in the community of brothers and sisters of our common brother Christ, in the communality of the children of God, as Origen put it (Ledegang 1992, 164-74). There is no longer male and female, no longer slave or free, no longer Jew or Greek. All are one in the Messiah Jesus (Gal. 3:26-28). This evangelical charter is at right angles to the divisions in the church between the superior and inferior, such as the ordained and the non-ordained, clerics and laymen, men and women. Because it goes back to a pre-Pauline tradition, it deserves the recognition of evangelical originality (Schillebeeckx 1985, 45).

The third element lies in this: the task of promoting the freedom of people within the church and attuning church order to it. This has to be handled and structured in such a way that people are not patronized or subjugated. They have to feel that they can stand on their own two feet and walk upright with their heads held high. This is implied in the biblical verse: "You were called to freedom" (Gal. 5:13). A code such as *building of the Spirit* calls upon the church to break through stagnation and rigidity, and work on freedom, dynamism, and creativity (chapter 20).

The fourth element involves the cohesion of people in the church. This has to be based on relations of a socio-religious and not (only) an institutional nature. The socio-religious cohesion has to be purposefully developed and promoted. It gives people the feeling that they really are part of a community and not just a cog in a bureaucratic machine. This lies within the code of the body of Christ. In that the organic unity has priority over the institutional framework.

The *aspect ad extra* contains the appeal for an evangelical approach to people outside the church. This evangelical call involves the following elements: the external focus of the church, its open borders, and solidarity.

The first element involves the focus of the church. The church should be primarily aimed at what is happening outside of it and not at what is happening within it. It should not be locked up within itself, but should throw open its windows and doors. With this a choice is made for mission goals over survival goals, for the purpose of giving over the purpose of gaining (Schillebeeckx 1968a, 160). This choice lies within a code like *people of God.* People of God is in principle coextensive with "the peoples." This choice also lies within the church's aim at the kingdom of God (Commissaris 1977).

The second element involves the border traffic between church and society. One can open and close one's borders. In the case of open borders, streams of people are going in and coming out and with them their opinions, attitudes, networks, and connections. If the borders are closed, one cannot talk of border traffic. The barriers have been let down, passports are scrutinized, and imports and exports are strictly regulated. Special codes answer to this, as we can learn from the science of organization (Katz & Kahn 1978, 64-66, 434-35). Proceeding from the code *societa perfecta,* the border traffic between church and society is watched very closely. From the code *people of God,* however, this border traffic is viewed as essential for the realization of the task of the church (chapter 11).

The third element, which naturally presents itself in open border traffic, is the position of the church regarding the problem of the organization of society. Formally the church has a choice between a neutral and a solidary position. From a neutral attitude, it will try to take up an intermediary position between opposing interest groups. From a solidary position it will take its option for the poor seriously. The latter lies within codes such as *church as Jesus movement* and *church of the poor.* Proceeding from the gospel, the church has no other choice (chapter 12 and 24).

Finally, proceeding from the *temporal aspect,* the question arises how the church should use time: past, present, and future. In this it has a choice between a static or a dynamic view of time. In the Introduction a reference was made to a traditionalistic view of the church, which is expressed in historic restrictedness, narrowness, and slowness. Opposite this is a transformatory ecclesiology that accepts the continuous change of the church as a historic fact and takes it as its point of departure for further development. A code like *building of the Spirit* links with this and stimulates the church in this direction (chapter 20).

Cognitive, Emotive, Conative

Codes never fulfill these three functions at the same time or to the same degree. At times the cognitive function dominates, later the emotive one does, and on other occasions the conative function does. This applies to religious codes too. If the cognitive function has the upper hand, religious knowledge and thought are set in motion. If the emotive function dominates, religious poignancy predominates. If the conative function is dominant, we are stimulated and urged to religious action.

(3) Conditions of religious codes

The question now is under which conditions the religious codes exercise the functions we just mentioned. We distinguish three such conditions. We will call them by the names we have borrowed from the theory of development: *phylogenetic, ontogenetic,* and *actual-genetic* conditions (Koops 1981). The phylogenetic conditions involve the development of the religious codes in the cultural and religious history of humankind; the ontogenetic conditions involve their development in the history of individual people; and the actual-genetic conditions involve their development in the here and now.

Phylogenetic conditions

Phylogenetic conditions relate to the changes that codes go through during history. At a certain moment certain codes arise. Initially, they take up a peripheral place. After a while they may disappear, maintain their peripheral place, or take up a more central position. Later they may lose this central position and become marginal or disappear. It is also possible that they return after a time and start a new life. And then they may go on to lose meaning. In short, codes are determined culture-historically.

A striking example of this is nightclothes. In the dim past one either slept with all one's clothes on or one took them all off. This variety could also be found in the monastic orders. The Cistercians slept in their habits and kept their belts tight. They held this to be a sign of ascesis. The rule of Cluny allowed monks to sleep naked. In neither of the above cases were there any special nightclothes. Some centuries later, the nightshirt became fashionable in the upper class of society. It can be seen as a sign of restriction and discipline. Afterward this habit trickled down to the lower classes. Later still pyjamas appeared on the scene, which were to replace the unsightly nightshirts by a more attractive design. So one could say that the disciplining was esthetically veiled. Today, however, nightclothes fulfill other functions. They do not necessarily point to restriction or shame, but can also fulfill a biological-hygienical function. Moreover, in a certain context, nightclothes can function as alluring and seductive. Sleeping naked has also come back into fashion. One may view this as a sign of individual open-mindedness or a sign of relational accessibility and intimacy (cf. Elias 1982b, 221-28).

Phylogenetic conditions are also of importance for religious codes. Historical ecclesiological research has shown that religious codes related to the church rose in a certain period and disappeared in another. In the New Testament 96 codes refer to the church (Minear 1960). Among them are codes such as *fighters against Satan* and *slaves of God*. In the first century after Christ, these codes relied on cultural and religious plausibility. The belief in demons and devils was spread far and wide. The code *fighters against Satan* could rely on this. At the same time society was characterized by the dichotomy between slaves and the free. The code *slaves of God* was founded on this societal structure. In our time the belief in demons and devils has disappeared. Slavery, too, is a thing of the past. With this the plausibility of these codes has expired.

The problem is to find which religious codes can rely on a certain cultural-historical plausibility nowadays. What should we do with codes like perfect society, divine institute, mystical body? Do they not belong to a period that has already passed? Does a code like *community of believers (communio fidelium, congregatio fidelium)* not better fit the cultural social context in which the church finds itself at present (chapter 2 sub 2)? Kuitert invented a new code: "giver of opportunity." The church gives us the opportunity to pass on and appropriate the Christian tradition of faith. This code refers to the giving up of claims and power by the church (Kuitert 1992, 204).

Ontogenetic conditions

While phylogenetic conditions are involved with the development of religious codes in the cultural and religious history of humanity, ontogenetic codes refer to their development in the history of the individual. What is present phylogenetically in culture can in principle gradually be absorbed, learned, and understood by the individual — at least if the development of psychological stages is taken into account. However, what is absent phylogenetically in culture cannot be developed ontogenetically by the individual.

This insight is of importance for the religious codes. If, for instance, the codes *church as a mystery* and *perfect society* no longer live in the general religious cultural consciousness, they cannot be developed in the consciousness of individuals either. At least not to the extent that they can be actualized in certain situations and fulfilll a cognitive, emotive, and conative function. No evangelization, proclamation, or catechetics program can do a thing about this.

Insofar as religious codes are present in the religious cultural consciousness, they can also be transferred to individuals. This has to be done in such a way that they can really be learned and appropriated. In this the ontogenetic development stages have to be taken into account. Religious codes of a high level of abstraction cannot be understood or actualized by children who have not yet reached the formal-operational development stage (±12 years old) (Piaget & Inhelder 1978).

Actual-genetic conditions

Actual-genetic conditions are related to development of the religious codes in the here and now. The point is the time- and place-restricted micro-processes that take place in the interaction between individuals and their immediate environment. While "actual" relates to the working of religious codes *in actu,* "genetic" refers to the development conditions for this actualization. The question that arises here is under which conditions in the here and now are the religious codes going to turn on or take on a glow, as it were. Two actual-genetic conditions can be distinguished: recognition and stimulation (Eco 1979a, 221-24, 241-43).

The recognition takes place if the one "something" is spontaneously seen as a sign of the other "something" (the denotatum). Thus, if you are Dutch, you will spontaneously see the link between the orange football shirts of eleven football players on television and "our boys." The compound code of "orange shirt/House of Orange/Dutch nation" turns on immediately here. The words spontaneously and immediately indicate that the actualization of the code works without a hitch. However, this does not mean that this actualization is not based on learning processes. The spontaneity is acquired spontaneity; the immediateness is learned immediateness. As soon as a Dutchman sees an orange shirt on the screen, a learned semiotic automatism starts to operate.

One can talk of stimulation if one is entering into a situation where one expects certain codes to be actualized. One does not need to be entirely aware of this beforehand. Often we are dealing with expectations that take place in the border between unconsciousness and consciousness. However, in questioning afterward, these expectations are at least reconstructable and communicable.

Let us give an example. Someone has been moved in reading the psychoanalytical interpretation of the Mona Lisa of Leonardo da Vinci by Freud (1985, 143-233). He decides to travel to the Louvre in Paris with the expectation that he will be moved by the piece of art itself. Standing in front of the picture, he sees the same things Freud saw in the painting. He is touched by the same emotion as when he was reading: the tragedy of the loneliness and the limitedness of love. What is happening here? The reader has been "programmed" in such a way that the semiotic relation between the brush strokes and the emotion he has learned to attach to the Mona Lisa by reading Freud's essay has really been actualized. The depth psychological codes that Freud used turn on spontaneously. However, the flashing on of the codes does not happen by accident. What was behind it was a desired self-stimulation.

Recognition and stimulation often occur in the field of religion, and precisely in mutual interaction. The gesture of blessing, the kiss of peace, religious music, the biblical sermon: one takes part in them and undergoes them to be stimulated by them. This also explains the disappointment and frustration felt when the gesture of blessing is experienced as a routine, the kiss of peace as an automatism, the music as cheap, and the sermon as rubbish: the recognition and stimulation sought for are not achieved. The actualization of the religious codes has failed.

(4) Contexts of religious codes

Religious codes do not have eternal value. They come and go with the periods that characterize the history of a culture. Within the same period, however, their place and meaning can strongly differ. The culture in which the codes are embedded is not a unity. It is made up of different subcultures. These subcultures are the various contexts within which the different codes function. From there they get their meaning. This can be elucidated by means of the following distinctions: inclusive and exclusive codes, central and marginal codes, and attracting and repelling codes.

Inclusive and exclusive codes

There are codes that are used in certain contexts and not in others. They are exclusive. In this way a code like *perfect society* is used in a traditionalistic context, but not in a transformatory one. This also applies to the code *church factory (fabrica ecclesiae)*. This code refers to the church foundation, the aim of which was to look after acquisition, maintenance, management, and alienation of so-called temporary goods (Huysmans 1986, 173-74). It indicates the church's financial machinery in which everything runs smoothly and efficiently. All the wheels and cogs are set for a balanced budget, sufficient returns, and sound investment (cf. Morgan 1986). The code *church factory* was quite alive in, for example, the Flanders of the poet Guido Gezelle in the second half of the 19th century (Van der Plas 1991). Even though it is no longer mentioned in the Codex of 1983, it still determines the thought and doings of people in traditional Catholic areas (Walf 1984a, 171). The reverse is the case for a code like *the giver of opportunity.* Within a traditionalistic view of the church it is not used, but in a transformatory one it is.

There are also inclusive codes. They are used in both contexts, albeit they have different meanings. To find these out, one has to take a further look at the nonlinguistic and linguistic contexts within which they function. Examples of this are: *communio,* body of Christ, and creation of the Spirit. These can function in both a traditionalistic and transformatory context (Rikhof 1983; Koffeman 1986; Moltmann 1975). In a traditionalistic context "communio" refers primarily to the *communio episcoporum,* "the body of Christ" refers to an official corporalistic structure of the church, and "creation of the Spirit" refers to a strongly hierarchically controlled, charismatic church. In a transformatory context "communio" primarily indicates the *communio fidelium,* "body of Christ" indicates the equality and mutual dependency of the members of the church, and "creation of the Spirit" indicates the flexibility and creativity from which church structures are relativized again and again. Inclusive codes have a complex content. They can easily cover and gloss over differences. Because of this they call up misunderstandings and become the object of church discussion and dispute.

Central and marginal codes

It is often the case that the place of the inclusive codes in the various subcultural contexts is different. In one context certain codes take up a central spot and others are more marginal, in another context the latter have a central significance and the first are in the margin.

In the context of a traditionalistic view of the church, a code like *the church as a mystery* fits in with the endeavor to continue and legitimize the status quo of the church. One withdraws it from critical reflection, discussion, protest, and reformation by calling it a "mystery." A code like *people of God,* on the other hand, has a merely marginal function. A characteristic example is the final text of the Synod of bishops of 1985. This text mentions the code *people of God* only once, and merely in an enumerative sense (Willems 1986). Something similar applies to the policy program of the diocese of 's-Hertogenbosch in the Netherlands. This program says that the code *people of God* should be placed within the framework of the *church as a mystery* (Bouwen rond de hoeksteen 1989, 9). Thus it is relativized. In the *church as a mystery* the hierarchy plays a determining role (Witte 1991).

In the context of a transformatory view of the church, it is precisely the code *people of God* that takes up a central position. The Constitution on the Church of Vatican II devoted its entire second chapter to this (*Lumen Gentium* 9-17). In this document the church is placed within the whole of the history of salvation. The general priesthood of believers is emphasized. The *consensus fidelium* and the charismatic gifts of the whole people of God are thrown into relief. The catholicity of the whole people of God is brought up for discussion separately. After that, all sorts of groups with which the church as the people of God has to do are discussed: Catholic and non-Catholic Christians as well as non-Christians. The entire exposition is rounded off with the mission of the church as the people of God. This same constitution, however, has not left the code *church as a mystery* unmentioned. Nor does it take up a marginal position. On the contrary, the entire first chapter is devoted to this. However, the angle from which the church as a mystery is approached has nothing to do with a restrictive hierarchical perspective. The church is placed within the framework of that which makes up the real mystery: God's salvation in the gospel of Jesus (Smulders 1966).

Attracting and repelling codes

Certain codes attract each other and others repel each other. This, too, depends on the contexts within which they are used. In the context of a traditionalistic view of the church, codes like *perfect society, divine institution,* and *church as a mystery* often occur together and strengthen and influence each other. In the context of transformatory ecclesiology, codes like *community of believers, people of God, Jesus movement, building of the Spirit,* and *church of the poor* attract each other and determine each other mutually. Examples of codes that repel each other are *perfect society* and *church factory* on the one hand, and *giver of opportunity* on the other.

Chapter 8

Aims of Using Religious Codes

We started this part with a discussion of the relationship between the social and the religious aspects of the church (chapter 5), determining this relationship in terms of semiotics. We took the social phenomena in the church to be religious signs (chapter 6). In this religious signification, religious codes play a central role (chapter 7).

We will now examine the fact that although in principle religious codes go unnoticed, they are purposely made explicit in certain situations when one no longer lives, thinks, feels, and acts proceeding from these codes without being aware of them. It is then that they precisely become objects of conversation, discussion, and reflection. This is the case when they have become a problem. This happens when clashes occur — clashes between various religious cultures or subcultures in which the codes lie; clashes with new codes in religious cultures or subcultures; clashes with codes from nonreligious cultures or subcultures. In all these kinds of cases, religious codes are problematized. They become objects of deliberation, negotiation, study, research, and policy. One starts to use them consciously. In this process, different aims can be sought after.

In this chapter we will discuss questions about whether the aims of religious codes involve (1) religious self-attribution, (2) religious socialization, (3) evangelization, (4) religious legitimization, or (5) religious ideologization.

(1) Religious self-attribution

Religious self-attribution by means of religious codes takes place if one's own religious identity is made explicit for whatever reasons. This can be elucidated by proceeding from the following terms: attribution, self-attribution, and individual and collective religious self-attribution.

Attribution

Not only individuals but also groups and communities go through processes of attribution. These take place when remarkable happenings arise. One may wonder where these incidents come from (cause) and what their purpose is (*causa finalis* or aim). One can situate the cause and the *causa finalis* within the reach of oneself, one's own group, one's community, or outside of these. If one places the cause with oneself or one's own collective, then it can be called *internal attribution.* If the cause is placed outside this, it can be called *external attribution.* For instance, if a romance fails, external attribution usually takes place because one sooner lays the blame on the other than on oneself. If a football team wins, however, the strength and dexterity of one's own club is usually commended. The latter is an example of collective internal attribution (Luhmann 1978).

Self-attribution

Attributions only relate to incidents that occur on the outside, even though one may have had a hand in it, as appears from internal attribution. Self-attributions have to do with one's own individual or collective identity. One asks oneself the question where this identity comes from and what its meaning and purpose are. Here, too, there are two possibilities: internal and external attribution. The origin of one's identity can, for instance, be placed with the parent(s) (external attribution) or with one's own unicity (internal attribution). The striving of the Dutch people for freedom can be explained by the commercial interests that they had to defend in the competitive world market as a seafaring nation (external attribution). This same endeavor can be explained by the basic motives of the Dutch nation itself, which was born in the battle for liberation against Spanish domination (internal attribution).

These self-attributions are not bound to the momentary here and now. They are not instant attributions. They lie in codes, scripts, and grammatical rules that are themselves couched in the cultural traditions and contexts in question. In self-attributions, elements from these codes, scripts, and grammatical rules are taken up, made explicit, and combined (cf. Lindsay & Norman 1977; Izard et al. 1984; Frijda 1986).

Individual religious self-attribution

In individual religious self-attribution, religious meaning is attached to one's personal identity. Examples of this are child of God, image of God, one with a calling, loved one, follower, witness. In these religious images, personal identity is placed within the area of tension between God's part (external attribution) and the human part (internal attribution). The first images are characterized more by external attribution, and the latter more by internal attribution. With "child of God" the emphasis is more on God as the *causa finalis* of religious identity; with "follower" and "witness" it is more on the activity of the believer. There are also dyadic and triadic religious self-attributions. An example of a dyadic religious self-attribution is marriage as a covenant (Pieper 1988). An example of a triadic religious self-attribution is the following verse from the New Testament: "where two or three are gathered in my name, I am there among them" (Matt. 18:20).

Collective religious self-attribution

In collective religious self-attribution, groups and communities lend religious meaning to their identity. They place this identity in the area of tension between the activity of God and that of the collective itself. A remarkable example is "chosen people." Through the influence of the Old Testament, this self-attribution is actively present as a code or script in the religious tradition of Western culture. Three different nations applied this to themselves in three different contexts: the Dutch people in the battle for liberation against Spain (Schama 1988), the American people in the program of the New Frontier in the President's State of the Union Address (Bellah & Hammond 1980), and white South Africa in the system of apartheid (Pieterse, Scheepers, and Van der Ven 1991). Opposite the ideological function of this code, we find its emancipatory use by basic communities in the framework of liberation theology (Gutiérrez 1974; Boff 1987a).

Also within the church one frequently comes across collective religious self-attributions. The most striking examples are community of believers, people of God, Jesus movement, body of Christ, building of the Spirit, and church of the poor. These can also be viewed as codes or scripts that enable the church to question its own identity and find an answer.

The need for collective religious self-attributions in the church comes to the fore when special circumstances occur. From the research on attributions in general and self-attributions in particular, these can be distinguished — in a hypothetical sense — according to the following characteristics. The happenings in question have not only an objective relevance but also an emotional one; they are not superficial but deeply radical by nature; they can have both a positive and a negative meaning; they take place on the social and communal plane; they are hard to control and to keep under control; they touch upon one's feeling of self-esteem (Spilka et al. 1985).

It is not hard to concretely imagine certain happenings that rouse the need for collective religious self-attribution in the church. They can be negative happenings like conflicts and polarizations, or positive occurrences like intense cultivation of community and successful communication. They may also be processes that take place between the church and other social institutions. With this there may be negative occurrences such as financial, political, social, or cultural tensions, or positive happenings like mutual adjustment and cooperation.

Through such self-attributions, the church is capable of relocating its identity inwardly and outwardly, preserving its unity, determining its mission, plotting its course, developing its policy, and executing its programs and projects. If it lacks such self-attributions in times of tension and crisis, we have to fear for the church's vitality, energy, power of attraction, integration, continuity, and even its survival.

(2) Religious socialization

The generation that produced the collective religious self-attributions has a duty to pass these on to the next generation. This happens in religious socialization. This process encompasses upbringing (primary socialization) and education (secondary socialization). The generation of "goers" introduces the generation of "comers" to the convictions, values, and norms of the church and accompanies them in the internalization thereof. These convictions, values, and norms can take on all sorts of shapes, like myths, stories, images, notions, ideas, testimonies, doctrines, and theories. In this process all sorts of things happen. The adults answer the questions of the young, present and inform, give motives and reasons, resolve problems, refute objections, discuss criticism, and react to objections and protests (cf. Berger & Luckmann 1967).

Where do these questions, problems, objections, and criticisms come from? The answer is as simple as it is far-reaching: they stem from the fact that we are dealing with two different generations here. We do not wish to go off on the old hobbyhorse of the generation gap. The point is the difference in generation that is given in the term *generation* itself. A generation is a collection of people who go through the same happenings during the same phase of life and interpret this proceeding from the same succession of cultural periods. The difference between the generations can be seen as their being confronted with the same happenings in *different* phases of life proceeding from a *different* succession of cultural periods. The occurrences with which the generations are confronted are identical, but the phases of life and the succession of cultural periods from which they experience and interpret these events are different. Whether one is young or old makes quite a difference in the experiencing of what is occurring in the society of today. Whether one has a short-term perspective or a long-term perspective in which a number of cultural periods during which one has lived come together, is of decisive importance (Mannheim 1928). Thus the generation that was born at the beginning of this century experiences unemployment in the nineties as the herald of a possible repetition of the economic crisis in the thirties; the generation born in the forties experiences it as the crisis of the social welfare state; the generation born in the seventies experiences it merely as a lack of opportunity on the labor market. The same generation from the beginning of the century sees church politics in the nineties as a liberalization of church policy in the long run; the generation from the forties sees it as being unfaithful to Vatican II (1962-1965) and the Dutch Pastoral Council (1968-1970); the generation from the seventies merely interprets it as church conservatism.

This difference in generations that characterizes religious socialization, too, implies that there is no simple transfer of convictions and values. The answering of questions, the giving of motives and reasons, the solving of problems, the refuting of objections, and the discussing of criticism: all intrinsically belong to religious socialization. This means that all sorts of religious codes that have a certain degree of plausibility for the adult generation need to be made explicit and to be discussed. On the basis of this they are compared to each other, analyzed, evaluated, criticized, and possibly rejected.

This also applies to the religious codes that are used for the religious self-attribution of the church, like community of believers, people of God, Jesus movement, building of the Spirit, etc. Here critical questions may be brought up for discussion, such as: Is the church the people of God, the body of Christ, and the church of the poor, or should it become this, or may it become this? These kinds of questions dampen the pretensions of the church and restrict its claims to power.

(3) Evangelization

The church is not only involved with itself, nor solely with its own survival. It is also aimed at society and at the people in society outside it. In this we also find the church's essence and goal: the proclamation of the gospel. This proclamation is both linguistic and nonlinguistic by nature. It takes on the shape of an explicit proclamation of the Word and diaconal presence. The primitive form in which this proclamation is realized is dialogue — dialogue with society and with people and groups in society, but also dialogue with other religions and philosophies of life (Dialogue and Proclamation 1991).

Precisely in this dialogue numerous opportunities present themselves in which the church has to account for the faith it preaches and the hope that gives it life. In this it cannot simply fall back on the self-evidence of religious codes. On the contrary, the codes need to be made explicit, elucidated, and differentiated. They require further substantiation, argumentation, analysis, and evaluation, as well as a critical sorting and selection.

This outward orientation returns to the church itself too. The questions, problems, objections, points of discussion, and criticism do not leave the essence of the church untouched. They demand permanently critical self-reflection on the part of the church: critical self-reflection on its speech and action and its doings. That is why the *missio externa* implies a *missio interna* at the same time (Heidenreich 1988). The basis of this is the church as *ecclesia semper purificanda* (*Lumen Gentium* 8).

This applies all the more strongly insofar as evangelization is aimed not only at the linguistic aspects, which lie in orthodoxy, but also at the nonlinguistic aspects, which are couched in orthopraxis. The continuous reformation that the church needs is precisely involved with the way and degree in which it contributes to liberation to freedom, equality, and solidarity within the perspective of the kingdom of God. Ever the question has to be asked whether the *anuncio* of the good news goes hand in hand with the *denuncio* of structural sin, which is implicit in the inhuman relations in society. The question must also arise whether it really contributes to *transformacion,* which is individual and social conversion and structural change (Mette 1990).

Against this background both the *missio externa* and the *missio interna* lead to a problematization of the religious codes that the church uses for itself. They continually criticize the identity of the church (religious self-attribution) as well as the transfer to the next generation (religious socialization). Therefore it is not a linear relationship that connects religious self-attribution, religious socialization, and evangelization, as if the results of religious self-attribution and religious socialization have to be determined before evangelization can begin. Rather, one can speak of a cyclic or spiral-shaped process. Evangelization itself leads to further reflection on religious self-attribution and religious socialization because of the dialectics between the *missio externa* and the *missio interna.* Through this, religious self-attribution and religious socialization are placed under permanent criticism (Van der Ven 1984a; 1984b).

(4) Religious legitimization

After religious self-attribution, religious socialization, and evangelization, we land at a meta-level with religious legitimization. The questions, problems, objections, and points of criticism that were brought up for discussion will now be systematized. The treatment and answering thereof will also be systematized. For this purpose they are placed at a higher level of abstraction and stripped of their concrete, personal, and local characteristics. They go beyond the face-to-face relations and transcend the circumference of the local community. They are caught in abstract terms and theories, in formal arguments and systematic evaluations.

Religious self-attribution, religious socialization, and evangelization are the tasks of the church community and of all the members who belong to it. Religious legitimization is the work of specialists: the theologians. They examine the suppositions from which the questions, problems, and points of discussion were brought forward and examine the answers given of old by the church, taken from tradition. They work out unexpected similarities and differences; choose new angles and perspectives; and develop, analyze, and evaluate the logic, dialectics (art of reasoning), and rhetoric (art of convincing) of the church. They build in self-reflexive feedback mechanisms (if one says this . . . , then one has to say this too).

A striking example is the catholicity of all sorts of social institutions. Especially since the sixties this has come under enormous pressure, both structurally and culturally. The structural expansion of the system not only appeared to have reached its limits, but in many institutions a process of phasing out had also started: a great number of institutions have put aside the title Catholic. Besides this there was a hollowing out of culture because all the convictions, values, and norms that had held the entire structure together started to show all sorts of tears and cracks. It began to lose its cultural plausibility (Duffhues et al. 1985; cf. Billiet 1988). Since the seventies, however, one can find traces of a process of legitimization in the sense described above. If we apply this to the Catholic University of Nijmegen, we see that in the beginning of the seventies the report on catholicity by the Schillebeeckx commission appeared. In the middle of the eighties, the board of governors of the university published a statement on its Catholic foundation and identity. In 1992 a new statement appeared from this board; this dealt with the support and profile of Catholic identity.

Similar processes can also be found in the church. One can see ecclesiology — including the one in question — as an attempt at religious legitimization of the church using the means of theology. In this we systematically examine the questions and problems with which the church is confronted in the context of the society and culture of today, and attempt to draw a path for the future of the church, as well as a path for the church of the future.

Discussions and conflicts are not excluded from this either within the church or within theology or ecclesiology. On the contrary, a dichotomy is perceivable in ecclesiology, as has been remarked in the Introduction. The one is traditionalistic in its setup, while the other is transformatory. Both have the intention to contribute to the systematic treatment of the social and cultural problems of the church, and through this sketch a perspective for the church; however, they proceed from differing points of departure and perspectives.

The problematization of the religious codes to which the church helps itself increases because of this. Through ecclesiological discussion it becomes clear that some codes are used exclusively in one view of the church, and other codes are used exclusively in others. This means that some codes are central to one view of the church and others are peripheral in the other view of the church, and vice versa. The fact that some codes attract and others repel each other is all the more reason to subject these codes and their functions to further research.

(5) Religious ideologization

That we are only now discussing religious ideologization does not mean that sequentially or chronologically it holds last place. Elements of religious ideologization are sometimes already present in religious self-attribution, religious socialization, and evangelization. More often they pop up in the religious legitimization. The lines between religious legitimization and ideologization are not always easy to draw. Often they flow into each other.

Yet in an analytical sense, it is important to separate the two as clearly as possible. That is why we will now discuss religious ideologization separately. In order to do this satisfactorily, it is necessary first to discuss the terms *ideology* and *ideologization* (the process of forming an ideology), before applying them in a religious sense to the church. Both terms have three meanings (Merton 1968, 510-62).

Ideology and ideologization

In its broadest sense, the term *ideology* has to do with a structure of opinions and values regarding certain situations, occurrences, processes, and structures in social life. Thus, one can talk of an ideology of an institute, organization, or company or of an ideology that underlies a certain policy. In such cases ideology does not imply anything more than view, usually a long-term view. Sometimes it is also a view in which a certain image of humanity or society lies (Kagenaar 1975). Often ideology is associated with a system of normative choices that cannot entirely be fathomed rationally (Kickert 1986, 48).

Ideology has a more restricted meaning when it is brought into connection with a certain social group in society. It then refers to a whole network of opinions and values that are characteristic for the position this group holds in society, and that differ from those of another group. Thus farmers, workers, tradesmen, and owners could each have their own ideology. In this view, opinions and values are determined by noncognitive, social factors (Weber 1980; Berger & Luckmann 1967).

An even more restricted meaning lies within the term when it is especially applied to the opinions and values of dominant groups in society. The idea is that these groups want to maintain the dominant position they hold by certifying that their opinions and values are generally valid. For this purpose they try to make them prevalent and acceptable to all groups. In this way they not only strive to preserve their dominant position but to strengthen and extend it (Mannheim 1960). In this sense Marx gave a classic description of ideology in *Die deutsche Ideologie:* "in every era the ruling ideas are the ideas of the ruling classes" (Marx 1971, 373).

This raises the question of what term should be used to denote the opinions and values of groups striving to emancipate themselves from the dominant group. For this purpose we can use the term *utopia.* Ideology and utopia then function as contrastive terms (Mannheim 1960). Ideology is connected to the ruling classes, and utopia is connected to the striving for emancipation of the under class(es). Ideology looks backward, as it were, while utopia looks forward. Ideology defends the existing reality, while utopia problematizes it and attacks it (Ricoeur 1987).

Religious ideology and ideologization

Can we also speak of religious ideology and religious ideologization, and does it occur in the church? If one checks the three meanings of ideology, one gets the following answer.

Ideology as a view of the church, in which lie certain opinions and values regarding humanity and society, has been in existence as long as the church has existed. Ecclesiology can be seen as the attempt at systematic elucidation of and critical reflection upon that view.

Ideology bound to certain groups within the church has also existed as long as the church has. We find this phenomenon already in the Christian communities in the New Testament — leaders against members, Jews in Jerusalem against Jews in Palestine, Jews in Palestine against Hellenistic Jews, Jews against non-Jews, charismatics against non-charismatics (Heinz 1974) — as well as in the church in the course of its history (Weber 1980).

The question of whether ideology, bound to the dominant group or groups within the church, occurs can be answered by distinguishing between the two types of power with which the church has to do. The first is the power in the relationship of the church to society or to the state. The second is the power within the church itself.

Power in the relations between church and state

The ideologization that stems from the position of power of the church in its relation to society or to the state belongs in the Western world *grosso modo* to the past. This does not mean that it is no longer present in the thinking of the church; in fact, it is still active in a more concealed shape.

In the Middle Ages certain periods can be pointed out that are very clearly characterized by a hierocratic ideology. According to this ideology the leadership of the state falls to those who are ordained, and at their head is the leader of the church, the pope. The leaders of the state are believed to have received their power from the church, for instance the emperor, who was ordained for that purpose. They are also presumed to carry out their duties in agreement with the church (Congar 1970, 176ff.). Opposite the hierocratic ideology, however, a reverse tendency is also observable: the caesaropapist ideology. This implies the complete subordination of the priestly, or papal power to the worldly, or imperial power (Weber 1980).

According to some authors, the Concordat of Worms in 1122 brought an end to both the hierocratic and the caesaropapist tendencies in principle. The conclusion of the Investiture Controversy in this Concordat led to a structural balance between the church and the state (Kaufmann 1989; 1992), albeit a shaky one. During the course of history it continually saw various shifts in power, especially during the Reformation and the Enlightenment. In response to the Enlightenment, the church (once more) returned to the conviction that though it may not be above the state, it certainly was not under it. Where the state is characterized as a *societas perfecta,* the church is a *societas perfecta* too. Perfect does not mean whole in the sense of sacred, but of autonomous. The church is as independent as the state, as we have seen earlier (chapter 5 sub 1). At the same time, however, it was believed to be more than perfect, because it has — as the theologians of Vatican I taught — a spiritual origin and spiritual goal (Granfield 1982).

Even though Vatican II did not use the term *societas perfecta,* the church as *societas constituta et ordinata* is prominently present (*Lumen Gentium* 8; *Gaudium et Spes* 40). The pastoral constitution says that church and state are two independent and autonomous entities (*Gaudium et Spes* 76). Over against that we also have the ecclesiological renewal that Vatican II brought, which is made up of an emphasis on the church as the people of God. Against this background the ambiguities of the texts of Vatican II are pointed out (Walf 1984a; 143-51). Some believe that this ambiguity is not just a minor flaw. Nor is it the result of a compromise poorly worked out. It is supposed to have to do with the nature of the church itself. A deeper ambiguity is supposed to lie within this, because the church is a city or society in a class of its own: *civitas Dei* (Milbank 1990, 389-92). One can see how radically the question of power determines the church in this. Some see the remainders of an obsolete power ideology in *societas.* Others believe that the church cannot and may not be defined as anything other than its own autonomous *civitas.*

Power in the church

With regard to power in the church, we also find both proponents and opponents. The one side accuses the other of obsession with power, while the latter believes that it is precisely this that will preserve the essence of the church from its undoing. The question of power within the church can be approached from two angles sociologically: a monocratic and a democratic angle (Weber 1980). In monocracy the leadership is made up of one man, while in democracy the authority of the leadership falls to the members of the community. A great number of intermediate forms are possible between these two. Thus, the monocratic form is softened by fraternal colleges and advisory bodies. These do not, however, effect the fundamental distinction between monocracy and democracy (chapter 16 sub 3).

Proceeding from a monocratic angle, one makes use of notions that support sacred power *(potestas sacra)* in the church. These notions are drawn from the doctrine of God, Christology, and the working of the Spirit in the history of the church. Concerning the doctrine of God, the emphasis is placed on the divine institution of the church grounded in *lex divina.* Ministry in the church is based on this *lex divina* (Listl 1983). As far as Christology is concerned, reference is made to the foundation of the church by Christ. Just as Christ is the head of the church as its founder, the ordained minister represents the leadership of Christ to the church (Auer & Ratzinger 1983, 144). Concerning the working of the Spirit in the history of the church, the doctrine of *successio apostolica* is in focus. This connects the present office of the bishop to that of the apostles in the apostolic age (Javierre 1968).

From a democratic angle, a pneumatological and charismatic approach are often chosen. In the pneumatological approach, the dynamism and freedom of the Spirit, which is given to the church and which lives on in it, are central. In the charismatic approach, the point is that this Spirit is a spiritual gift of grace to each believer (Haarsma 1991). Against this background the liberty and equality charter of the letter to the Galatians forms the central focus (Schillebeeckx 1985). Here ministry is viewed as a function besides other functions in the church. Its service character is emphasized, just as all other charismata have this character of service for the development of the church (Willems 1985; 1986). Instead of the minister's place as "opposite" believers in the church, its unifying function is pushed forward. This unity derives from keeping together both the separate church communities and the church communities among themselves (Wess 1989).

The renewal of the church cannot be brought about by theological ideology criticism alone, of course. It is not enough to critically regard the foundation of ministry in the doctrine of God, Christology, and the history of the church, or to replace them by pneumatology and the doctrine of the charismata. Nor is it sufficient to endeavor a kind of synthesis and to found the christological and pneumatological approaches to ministry and church in the theology of the Trinity (Philipon 1966). However, one would go too far in doing away with the contribution made by theology by seeing it as wishful thinking. It is not right to do away with the renewal of theological thinking about the church as a "reversal of reality" (Wess 1989, 670). For reflection on power in the church is not without meaning. It problematizes the various opinions, deprives them of their obviousness, and brings them into communication with each other.

Ideologization can be recognized by the following elements. The first is lack of contact with reality, a lack of empathy with the practice. The second is that the terms that are used are reified; that is, they are not seen as referring to processes that take place in people's heads, but appear to be independent entities that have a life of their own. The third element is that the meaning of the reality of practice and that of the terms is reversed. The terms are felt to be more important. The practice is twisted and adapted to the terms. The fourth element has to do with the closed-mindedness from which reality is entered into. This is characterized by: dichotomization in thought that is forced on reality as a *claire obscure;* a lack of critical reflection and critical self-reflection; intolerance with regard to different opinions; logical inconsistency that comes from the confusion of normative and descriptive statements, unmentioned presuppositions, circular arguments, invalid deductions, and illegitimate conclusions; and irrationality, which can be recognized by fideism and fundamentalism (Ricoeur 1987).

Summary of Parts I and II

In Parts I and II we have dealt with the functions and the codes of the church in a general sense. Part I has to do with the functions, while Part II discusses the codes of the church. These give us the building blocks for the development of a contextual ecclesiology in a practical theological perspective.

In part I the functions of the church are placed within the society of today and within the position that the church holds in this society. The societal context is that of modernization, institutional differentiation, and cultural generalization (chapter 1). The position of the church is especially that of the denomination and association. Due to the drastic negative consequences of modernization, the church has to take on not an anti-modern, nor an a-modern, but a critical-modern stance with regard to society. The image of the church as a community of believers calls upon us to do so *(communio fidelium, congregatio fidelium)*. In this the transcendence of God is central as the foundation of the faith of the church, as is the focus on freedom, liberation, and solidarity (chapter 2). Because of its social position and its critical-modern attitude, the general function of the church can only be seen in terms of religious communication, both *ad intra* and *ad extra* (chapter 3). This general function can only be realized if the core functions that the church has to fulfill are actually executed. These core functions are: identity, integration, policy, and management (chapter 4).

In Part II attention is focused on the fact that two aspects — social and religious — can be distinguished in the functions of the church. The question is how these relate to each other. They can only be regarded in a coordinative sense over against each other and not in a subordinative sense (chapter 5). The question then arises in what way they can be connected to each other in a coordinative sense. The solution, taken from semiotics, is that the social phenomena in the church are viewed as religious signs that refer to the salvation of God for humankind. These signs signify this salvation and represent it (chapter 6). In this religious signification, the religious codes take up an important place. Examples of religious codes are community of believers, people of God, Jesus movement, body of Christ, building of the Spirit, and church of the poor. "Church as sacrament" can be regarded as the ecclesiological supercode. These codes form the mechanism on the ground of which social phenomena can be interpreted as religious signs. It is of importance to keep the functions of the religious codes — the cognitive, emotive, and conative functions — in mind. These functions are realized under different conditions and in different contexts (chapter 7). The different aims of using the codes can also be distinguished: religious self-attribution, religious socialization, evangelization, religious legitimization, and religious ideologization (chapter 8).

Parts I and II can be viewed as a clearing of the land on which the following chapters can build. They also supply the materials with which the next chapters can be built.

The question with which parts I and II close and which will be dealt with concretely in the next chapters is: In what sense can the social aspects that can be distinguished in the functions of the church become, in the concrete practice of the everyday church, the bearers of religious signs that signify and represent the salvation of God?

Core Functions and Codes of the Church

Part I has made it clear that the church is focused on four core functions: identity, integration, policy, and management. They are the themes of the following four parts. They can be dealt with from the top down (liga model) and from the bottom up (agil model). The two approaches are complementary to each other. That is why we must not lose sight of the conditioning function according to the agil model (chapter 4) in the treatment according to the liga model, which we opted for.

Part II ended with the question in what sense the social aspects that are implied in the core functions of the church may assume the character of religious signs that refer to the salvation of God.

This question will be asked regarding the four core functions in the following parts. A religious code will be discussed with each core function — two will be discussed with core function identity — on the basis of which the church as a social phenomenon can become a religious sign. For *identity* these religious codes are the church as the people of God (chapter 11) and the Jesus movement (chapter 12); for *integration* it is the body of Christ (chapter 14); for *policy* it is the building of the Spirit (chapter 20); for *management* it is the church of the poor (chapter 24). This does not mean that there is a one-to-one relationship between the core function and the code. The full richness of the codes does not merge into each core function, and their meaning is not exhausted by it. We are only dealing with accents we have introduced.

In this the dialectical relationship between the core function and the code has to be kept in sight. On the one hand, because the code in question is dealt with proceeding from the core function, it is placed in a special light and a special facet is brought forward. On the other hand, an influence extends from the code to the core function insofar as it is clarified regarding its deeper meaning proceeding from the code and is supplemented, criticized, and corrected from there. This will be indicated by means of the religious code through reference to its cognitive, emotive, and conative meaning (cf. chapter 7).

Every core function will be placed in its own societal context, and more particularly according to the aspect that has special relevance for the core function in question. In this way attention will be paid to both the threats and the challenges that lie within the societal context. Thus, we will deal with the context of secularization in our discussion of identity (chapter 9); with the context of individualization in integration (chapter 13); with the context of utilization in policy (chapter 17); and with the context of calculation in management (chapter 21).

Part III deals with the core function of identity. As we mentioned, it is placed in the context of secularization. Then the religious convictions of the church will be discussed. These are the hard core of the identity of the church. The pluriformity within this identity will then be oriented to the personal understanding of the church, its vision (the church as the people of God). This is dialectically related to its mission (Jesus movement). In its vision and mission the question of the religious individuality of the church, by which it distinguishes itself from other social contexts and societal institutions, is raised.

Part IV discusses the core function of integration. This is situated in the context of individualization, which itself is a consequence of the urbanized and industrialized society. We will check to see to what degree these societal processes allow or even demand group and network formation at the same time. The question is in what sense the church can link up with and stimulate the group and network formation that supply the basis for the formation of a community in the church (body of Christ). We will dwell at length on the religious treatment of conflict, which is necessary within the formation of a community and regarding religious leadership and ministry.

Part V discusses the core function of policy. It is localized in the context of utilization. It has to do with the increase in pleading for one's own needs and own interests. The church has to undertake this insofar as these needs and interests can be placed in the perspective of a declaration of solidarity, which lies in the vision and mission of the church. In order to deal with this adequately, the church needs effective policy development. The policy organization within which the policy development has to be carried out has to surpass the present borders of the juridically set church structure. It has to develop in the direction of an innovative organization (building of the Spirit).

Part VI calls our attention to the core function of management. This is embedded in the context of calculation, in which the pros and cons of all sorts of choices are continually weighed against each other and a calculated decision is made. The church has to handle this critically and creatively through care for quality in its service. The development of personnel in the local church has to be looked into in connection with this. This also applies to financial management. The vision and mission of the church have to function as a guide in this (church of the poor).

PART III

IDENTITY

The very nature of the church is expressed in its basis and identity. Without this basis and identity it would float in a vacuum and would dissolve into the societal environment surrounding it. The relationship between these two terms needs further explanation.

The *basis* has to do with the relationship of the church to the Christian tradition. Within this is the choice for one of the specific Christian traditions, the most prominent being the Catholic, Eastern, Lutheran, Calvinistic, and Anglican traditions. The local church may wish to found itself on an ecumenical basis, proceeding either from a specific tradition or between two or more traditions.

The basis is determined with the foundation of the local church. The possible change of the basis can be seen as the most decisive matter in which the local church can involve itself. It touches upon its very foundation. One speaks of this as a church schism or secession. These do not take place without highly intense, traumatic processes that can tear individuals, groups, institutions, and collectives to pieces.

Merely discussing the basis, without a problematization leading to church schism and secession, has a positive sense insofar as it contributes to reflection. Such reflection is necessary because a choice made once — however far it is removed historically — can never serve as an undisputed, settled, completed matter. Even if the choice goes back many, many generations, it has lost its (absolute) self-evidence due to the processes of modernization and secularization. The ecumenical movement also exercises its influence, criticizing the separateness of the Christian traditions and denominations.

We do not mean here that the basis has to be viewed as a constantly open question that has to be answered either this way or that. The issue here is the necessity for continuous reflection on the basis.

While the basis of the church can be found in the writings of the specific Christian tradition, the *identity* has to be formulated again and again. The identity is not set, but changes together with the historical and societal context in which the church finds itself. We do not wish to assert that it is only a changeable variable. However, it cannot be found outside the changing context; it cannot be determined separately from this context.

That is why we start this part with a discussion of a dimension of the societal context that deeply affects the identity of the church: secularization (chapter 9). Next, we focus on identity itself. This has its basis in the religious convictions that the church cherishes. In this it gives an answer to the question: What do we believe? Religious convictions determine the view of the church regarding personal and societal reality, and direct and guide practical interaction as well (chapter 10). On the foundation of these convictions, the church develops a perspective of what it is itself. In this it endeavors to answer the question: Who are we? What is important here is the church's vision of itself. This can be given expression in the church as the people of God (chapter 11). On the basis of this, the church community constructs a notion of its task. This is aimed at the question: What are we striving after? This raises the point of the mission of the church that finds its expression in the church as Jesus movement (chapter 12).

This division (context, convictions, vision, and mission) should not be conceived in a linear sense. It is not the case that the next step in the chain is deduced from the results of the previous step. We do not deny that the vision of the church, for example, has an influence on its mission. But it is not true that the vision first has to be clarified entirely before mission can be developed from it. The clarification of mission also influences the awareness of the vision. In other words, the relationship between the four aspects has to be taken in a cyclical, or, better yet, in a spiral sense.

Chapter 9

The Context of Secularization

In order to determine the identity of the church, we shall first dwell upon the societal context in which it finds itself, in this case that of secularization. This context also influences the identity of the church. It does not determine it. But because the church is in interaction with its context, an influence does extend from this context to the church's identity.

In this chapter we will ask ourselves: (1) what the term *secularization* means, and (2) how the church deals with it.

(1) Secularization

There are authors who refuse to use the term *secularization.* The reason is that its meaning is unclear because so many things are described by it (Kaufmann 1989, 121). Indeed, if you check the history of the term, you come across a tangle of meanings. Still, this does not have to lead to a distancing from the term, at least on the condition that one clearly states what one understands the term to mean. We use the term here in a macro-sociological sense. This means that we consider secularization from the angle of the development that society as a whole is undergoing, namely, that of modernization, and therefore not from the viewpoint of the church. In the latter case, matters like the liquidation of church goods, the separation of church and state, the decrease in church participation, and the drop in the number of church members would have to be discussed. Here we will ignore all of this (cf. Lauwers 1974).

Proceeding from a macro-sociological point of view, then, one can distinguish a cultural and a structural dimension. The cultural dimension has to do with the consequences of rationalization of the worldview. The structural dimension is connected to the consequences of institutional differentiation, which we spoke of earlier (chapter 1 sub 3).

Cultural dimension of secularization

The cultural dimension is given an impressive description by authors in the tradition of Weber (1978; 1980). They have noted that the natural, societal, and personal reality is being more and more demystified *(entzaubert)*. Religious-scientifically this means more and more desacralization. To put it semiotically, it means less and less interpretation as a religious sign. Theologically it means there are fewer and fewer traces of God. Natural reality appears to be under the ever-increasing control of the laws of nature in a natural-scientific sense. Societal reality is being exposed more and more according to sociological patterns and regularities. Personal reality can be described and predicted more and more according to psychic factors and mechanisms. Natural, societal, and personal reality are being increasingly desubjectivized, objectivized, and de-deified (Dux 1973; 1982; Laeyendecker 1992; Van der Ven 1992b). The total worldview is being increasingly rationalized (Habermas 1982).

This rationalization also penetrates religion. In this way the meaning of life proceeding from the belief in God can take on two shapes, from a theoretical point of view. The first shape has to do with the meaning of life proceeding from the belief in God as personal, the second from the belief in God as impersonal (higher power, supreme being). The difference is that the meaning of life proceeding from the belief in a personal God is characterized by subjectivization and that which proceeds from belief in God as impersonal is characterized by desubjectivization and objectivization. Research was done into these two forms in 1979 among the Dutch population. Table 9.1 contains data relating only to those people who were members of one of the churches in the Netherlands (in 1979: 58% of the population). The scale runs from 1 (strongly disagree) to 5 (strongly agree).

From this table one can see an identical pattern for the members of the Dutch churches. On average they attach a greater value to the

TABLE 9.1
Meaning of life

	Cath.	NRC	RCN	Other
Meaning of life proceeding from belief in a personal God	2.95	3.24	3.76	4.33
God as impersonal	3.79	3.92	4.04	4.65

Cath. = Catholic
NRC = The Netherlands Reformed Church
RCN = The Reformed Churches in the Netherlands
Other = other Reformed Churches

Source: Peters & Schreuder 1987, 213

meaning of life proceeding from the belief in God as impersonal than from the belief in a personal God. It does not make any difference whether they are members of the Catholic church (Cath.: 3.79 and 2.95), the Netherlands Reformed Church (NRC: 3.92 and 3.34), the Reformed Churches in the Netherlands (RCN: 4.04 and 3.76), or the other Calvinist churches (Other R.: 4.65 and 4.33).

What is striking is that Catholics systematically score lower than members of the Protestant churches. Both types of religious signification of life — proceeding from the personal and the impersonal God — show a rising line: members of the Catholic Church, the Netherlands Reformed Church, the Reformed Churches in the Netherlands, and other Reformed Churches.

Structural dimension of secularization

The structural dimension is connected to institutional differentiation. What this means is that more and more areas in society have become autonomous institutions. This applies to economic, political, social, and cultural life. These autonomous institutions bring along their own partial frames of signification: economic, political, social, and cultural. Most of these systems of signification are separate from any philosophy or religion whatsoever; however, some are embedded in a philosophical tradition, while others are embedded in a religious one. This means that signification, philosophy, and religion no longer coincide (Kaufmann 1989, 146-71; Hijmans & Hilhorst 1990).

There is signification with and without philosophy. Signification without philosophy exists in deriving life-fulfilling meanings from values like economism ("my career comes first"), familialism ("my family is the most important thing I have"), and hedonism ("I am led by what I like"). In these examples there is a complete lack of more complex, further-reaching, or deeper-going convictions. Such signification without philosophy occurs frequently (Döbert 1984; 1986).

Signification with philosophy is characterized by a complex of convictions regarding the individual and societal life and cosmos, from which one proceeds to give meaning to one's existence. Thus there is also philosophy with and without religion. Within nonreligious philosophy one can be open to the surprising and wonderful aspects of human nature (birth) or nature as a whole (landscape); however, one does not link this to transcendence. One does have a notion of mystery-with-a-small-m without wanting or wishing to speak of Mystery-with-a-capital-M. Nonreligious philosophy is characterized by the perspective of immanence. Religious philosophy originates from a perspective of transcendence. Within religious philosophy individual and societal life, nature, and the cosmos are brought into connection with God.

From the research we just discussed, it appears that the Dutch population attaches a greater value to nonreligious than to religious philosophy on average. The average score for nonreligious philosophy is 2.98, and for Christian religious philosophy it is 2.21 (Felling et al. 1986, 59).

That the church is having a hard time with the trend that appears from these data is demonstrated by the control it is tempted to exert from time to time. An example is the theologoumenon of anonymous faith in God or anonymous Christianity, which states that those who are open to that which is unexpected, or surprising, in life or in nature, already believe in God unawares, or in the God and Father of Jesus (Rahner 1976; 1978). The objection to this approach is that the Mystery of God is an extension of the mystery of life and nature to the believer but not to the unbeliever. The realization of the mystery in human existence is not awareness of the mystery of God for the unbeliever. Here the danger of religious colonization lies in waiting (Willems 1967, 111-12; Knitter 1988; 1990).

TABLE 9.2

Belief in God as personal and church membership: %

very religious church members	18
religious church members	23
religious nonmembers	7
nonreligious church members	14
nonreligious nonmembers	22
very nonreligious nonmembers	16
Total	100

Source: Schreuder & Van Snippenberg 1990, 26

Two processes come out of institutional differentiation in this way: the pluralization of signification, philosophy, and religion and the marginalization of the Christian religion within all of this.

These processes go together with yet another process, which seems to be contrary to them: the increasing institutionalization of the Christian religion. We are dealing here, however, with a paradox that can be readily understood proceeding from the phenomenon of institutional differentiation. As all areas of society are increasingly being institutionalized, so, too, is Christian religion; it is being institutionalized further and further. This is happening at the same time as pluralization and marginalization, which can be explained by the same process of institutional differentiation. In other words, the church is being churchified (Kaufmann 1979; 1989).

Proceeding from the institutionalization of religion, one can assume that belief in God occurs more among people within the church than outside of it. Is this actually the case? From research among the Dutch population carried out in 1985, some remarkable statistics come to light.

From table 9.2 it appears that (18% + 23% =) 41% of the Dutch population believe in God as a person and are members of a Christian church. Further, it appears that (22% + 16% =) 38% do not believe in God and are not members of a church. If one adds these percentages together, we find that (41% + 38% =) 79% of the population belong either to the category of religious church members or to that of nonreligious nonchurch members. In other words, only 21% are left, to which the dividing line religious/church member and nonreligious/nonchurch member does not apply. What is this 21% composed of? No less than 14% belong to a church, but feel nonreligious. They are sometimes called ecclesial atheists (Zulehner 1988). Only 7% feel religious without actually belonging to a church.

This 7% is in glaring contrast to the eloquence with which theology declares that there is belief outside the church (Rahner 1976; 1978). In an empirical sense this is a considerable disappointment. Even if the percentage is higher for other countries, one has to guard against generalizations concerning nonecclesial belief that are too broad (Bibby 1987). In a theological sense, the church may then be of relative value (Hoekendijk 1967; Willems 1967; 1985). In actual fact it appears that where the church drops out, belief disappears within a shorter or longer time. In the classic words of the French sociologist of the thirties, Gabriel le Bras: "It is not so that the people no longer go to the church because they do not believe; they no longer believe because they do not go to the church" (Schreuder 1980b, 147). For the youth, too, there is a very strong connection between belief and church membership (Andree 1983, 237).

(2) Church and secularization

How does the church handle secularization? Three strategies can be traced: deductive, inductive, and reductive (Berger 1979). These can be considered as a reaction to the cultural dimension of secularization: the rationalization that is expressed in the disenchantment of the world and the desacralization of the worldview. The deductive strategy reacts to this with antirationalization, while the inductive and reductive strategy accept the rationalization. The inductive strategy wants to retain the perspective of transcendence in this, albeit in a transformatory manner. The reductive strategy eliminates the perspective of transcendence. Criticism on this trichotomy has been aired on various sides (Gaede 1981; Claassen 1985; Van Gerwen 1990). Yet for heuristic reasons, it can render us service. We will discuss the trichotomy here and then take a look at some combinations.

Strategies

In the *deductive strategy* the church is founded on a complex of convictions that are deemed to have an unchangeably eternal value. These automatically give their meaning for individual and societal life if they are applied to concrete situations. They lie embedded within holy texts that have to be interpreted proceeding from the holy traditions that have been kept and passed on from generation to generation. The latter are guarded by holy ministers, who make infallible decisions if an "undivine" discussion arises with regard to the interpretation. These texts, traditions, and ministers together possess a holy authority that cannot be questioned (Weber 1980).

In the *inductive strategy,* the church works in a different way. It takes religious experience as its point of departure. In this it works via two procedures and then tries to involve the two procedures with each other. In the first procedure, it checks to see what religious experiences underlie the texts of the religious tradition and what relations it has with the context of that time. In the second procedure, it checks to see what religious experiences lie in the stories of the people of today and how they relate to the context of modern culture and society. After this the two procedures are combined with each other. In the text/context correlation that then arises, the tradition criticizes the situation of today, which in its turn criticizes the tradition itself. Through this a religious-transformatory process is set in motion (Schillebeeckx 1989).

The *reductive strategy* brings about the relationship between tradition and situation in such a way that the perspective of transcendence falls away. By doing so, the religious tradition is reduced to micro or macro ethics, depending on whether one places the emphasis on the individual or on society. All that is left is a metaphor from the religious tradition, which expresses the conditions for individual or societal existence — a metaphor that inspires one to individual self-development or societal liberation, without the relation to God being symbolized in prayer or in the liturgy (Döbert 1973; 1984).

Which strategy is used the most? In 1989 this question was put before a random sample of 255 pastors from the three largest churches in the Netherlands (Van der Ven & Biemans 1992a). In 1980-1981 it had already been put before a random sample of 235 teachers at Catholic primary schools in the diocese of Rotterdam (covering most

TABLE 9.3

Deductive, inductive, reductive strategy in %

	pastors	teachers at primary schools
deductive	78	41
inductive	88	97
reductive	40	62

Source: Van der Ven & Biemans 1992a; Claassen 1985, 98-99

of the province of Zuid-Holland in the Netherlands) with an eye to their catechetical duties (Claassen 1985).

A striking difference comes to the fore in table 9.3. The pastors on the whole are closer to tradition than the teachers. They place more emphasis on the deductive strategy (78% versus 41%), less on the inductive strategy (88% versus 97%), and still less on the reductive strategy (40% versus 62%). An explanation for this is not hard to find. The pastors are theologians whose education is characterized by a scientific study of the texts from tradition. Moreover, they bear full-time responsibility for the progress of Christian tradition in the church of today and are obliged to continually be accountable to "superior" higher organs.

Something else catches our eye in this table. The inductive strategy turns out to be dominant in both groups. 88% of the pastors and 97% of the teachers at the Catholic primary schools choose the approach in which tradition and situation are related to each other. The second choice is different. The pastors have a preference for the deductive strategy (78%), while the teachers prefer the reductive strategy (62%). The third choice is the mirror image of the previous: the reductive strategy scores 40% with the pastors, and the deductive strategy scores 41% with the teachers.

Combinations of strategies

The extremely high percentage of teachers who chose the inductive strategy (97%) gives us occasion to delve deeper. Suppose we base ourselves on the 97%, what combinations are left to teachers to make

TABLE 9.4

The inductive strategy in combination with the deductive and the reductive strategy in %

		deductive strategy	
		–	+
reductive strategy	–	(1) 16	(3) 22
	+	(2) 43	(4) 19

Source: Claassen 1985, 99

within the choice they made for the inductive strategy? In table 9.4 four groups have been distinguished within the inductive choice: group (1) rejects the deductive and reductive strategy entirely, choosing only the inductive strategy; group (2) rejects the deductive strategy, opting for a combination of the inductive and reductive strategy; group (3) rejects the reductive strategy and combines the inductive with the deductive strategy; finally group (4) does not reject any strategy and combines all three. In table 9.4 the percentages are given of four groups of 235 teachers of the Catholic primary schools mentioned in the diocese of Rotterdam in the Netherlands.

From this table we can see that group (1), which chooses a "purely inductive strategy," is only 16% of the total. It is the smallest group. Group (2), however, which advocates a combination of the inductive and the reductive strategy, comprises 43% of the respondents. It is by far the largest group. Group (3), which opts for a combination of the inductive and the deductive strategy has only 22%. Finally, group (4), which prefers a combination of all three strategies, contains 19%.

From this table it becomes clear that the "purely inductive strategy" (group 1) is a good theological design, but it does not occur very often, being the choice of only 16% (at least among these teachers). It loses to the "reductive-inductive strategy" (group 2). This is the dominant choice (43%). The strategies of the other two groups can be regarded as reactions to this dominance. They emphasize a supplement to the inductive approach proceeding from the deductive approach: group (3) merely proceeding from the deductive approach (22%) and group (4) proceeding from the deductive and reductive approach together (19%).

The dominance of the reductive-inductive strategy of group is not without its problems. Insofar as it inclines toward trading the transcendence perspective for a micro- and macro-ethical frame of reference, it may lead to an excavation of the religious identity of the Christian tradition and of the church.

Chapter 10

Convictions

In the last chapter we set the problem of the identity of the church in the societal context of secularization. What emerged was that secularization exercises an influence on identity or at least it is able to do so. We ran across the pluralism of three strategies: the deductive, the inductive, and the reductive. Among these the reductive-inductive strategy holds a dominant position. In this context there is an active trend toward trading the transcendence perspective for a micro- or macro-ethical frame of reference. This can lead to the undermining of religious convictions and with that the religious identity of the church — all the more reason to make it the center of attention.

In this chapter we will look at the following questions: (1) In what sense do convictions make up the core of the religious identity of the church? (2) What are these convictions? And (3) From which sources do they stem?

(1) Convictions as the core of religious identity

In order to make clear that convictions form the core of the religious identity, we need a theory of religion. For this purpose we shall choose a theory of religion that is not restricted to one aspect of religion, such as the cognitive, emotive, conative, communal, or ritual. It has to be sufficiently inclusive to cover the whole of the field of religious identity. The theory of religion of the cultural anthropologist Geertz meets these requirements.

According to Geertz, religion can be described as follows: a system of symbols that establishes powerful, pervasive, and long-lasting moods and motivations in human beings, through the formulation of convictions concerning a general order of existence, as well as clothing these convictions with such an aura of factuality that the moods and motivations seem uniquely realistic (Geertz 1969).

One can focus on a number of elements from this description. First of all, convictions are active in religion that formulate a general order of human existence. These convictions function as order *(nomos)* as opposed to the increasing threat of disorder *(chaos)*. This disorder is of a varied nature: cognitive, emotional, and normative. One can speak of cognitive chaos if one is inundated by contradictory data, messages, opinions, and interpretations about reality. This easily leads to emotional chaos, because of which one is incapable of structuring the confusion of experiences and emotions. An example would be when one is confronted by suffering and death. This can in turn lead to normative chaos in which one may not be able to distinguish good from evil, or understand why good is good and evil is evil and why one should do good and not evil. Now it is religion that brings order to chaos. The religious convictions structure the cognitive, emotional, and normative housekeeping.

Next, these convictions activate certain symbols. These symbols describe how reality works (descriptive). They also indicate whether or not and how we have to act (normative). They provide a model for reality.

Furthermore, these convictions cause certain moods that correspond to the content of the symbols, insofar as these contain a model of reality. These moods have a complex structure because they have to do with the depth of existence (cf. James 1902). They are composed of positive and negative emotions, such as sad joy and glad sorrow. That is why we can always talk of earnestness and high-mindedness (cf. Durkheim 1925).

These convictions and moods lead to motivations, which imply an orientation toward the actual realization of the model for reality by action. Through this, religion becomes "applied religion" of everyday life.

Another fact in this description of religion strikes us. It has to do with the definition that convictions are clothed with an aura of factuality. Because of this, the description states, the moods and motivations seem to become uniquely realistic. What Geertz means here can only be gleaned from the whole of his theory of religion, in which the ritual aspect of religion holds a central position. The earnestness of the ritual play allows the convictions that are expressed in the ritual to make a pertinent impression. In this they refer the participants to the true reality. They are not involved with ordinary reality with its daily routines and worries. The convictions that are raised to consciousness by the penetrative power of the ritual are precisely what break through the structure of daily life that is taken for granted. What is thoughtlessly taken for granted to be true, good, and beautiful in daily life is broken through in the ritual. The rituals make such a powerful presence of the convictions concerning the true reality that the moods and motivations that stem from them confirm the impression of actual realism.

The elements that are active in religion are, therefore, convictions, symbols, moods, and motivations. They are actualized in the context of the communal ritual. It is of importance to note that they are only conceived of as elements of religion. In other words, only the four elements together represent what religion is, not one separate element and not without the context of the communal ritual.

At the same time we can derive the insight from this description that within the whole of religion and its communal-ritual context, convictions fulfill a central role. They activate the symbols. They evoke the moods, and together with the frames of mind they lead to motivations to act. This theoretical insight is also confirmed in an empirical sense (Felling et al. 1987b, 38-41).

(2) The content of religious convictions

Now that we are going to deal with the convictions that underlie the religious identity, we are confronted by the question whether all convictions are equally important. Can distinctions be made? Or, better yet, an order of rank?

Such an order of rank can either be material or formal by nature. If it is of a material nature, we run the risk of having it as the subject of discussion and conflict right from the very beginning. What is higher or lower? Are, for instance, convictions concerning creation of a higher theological rank than those concerning liberation? Some authors believe that answering these questions on the theology of creation should precede those of other theological treatises (Houtepen 1992b). By contrast, others believe that it is precisely liberation theology that should be given priority (Klein Goldewijk 1992).

In order to escape such a discussion, one can choose a formal order of rank. An example of this is to be found in the theory of culture and religion by Parsons. He believes that the convictions within the philosophical or religious identity of a culture can be distinguished by four formal levels having to do with ultimate reality, the ultimate order, the spheres of life, and activities (Parsons 1965, 964-71). We believe that this distinction is applicable to the convictions within the religious identity of the church.

Ultimate reality

At this level the convictions are involved with the question of what ultimate reality the particular worldview or religion represents, or to which ultimate reality it refers.

This is an important question for ecclesiology because it gives it an opportunity to point out that the ultimate reality to which the church refers cannot, in any case, be the church itself. The question forces the church to transcend itself. With this the focus is shifted from the church *ad intra* to the church *ad extra.* Attention is focused outward and upward.

The ultimate reality to which the church refers and which it represents is special and complex by nature. It is not *dingfest* or *handgrifflich* present. It is interwoven in stories, parables, and proverbs of wisdom. It does not exist outside of these texts. The church does not contain or encompass it; the church is only aimed at it, waiting, expecting, and hoping. The ultimate reality that is its origin and base is not the way other realities are, for it is a beckoning and receding perspective: the kingdom of God. This perspective is characterized by the bipolarity of the involvement of God and humanity with each other. There is no divine reality separate from a human one. There is only a composite perspective of God's salvation for all people, in particular the "least of these" (Matt. 25:40). The church refers to this perspective as a sacrament. The church is the sacrament of this salvation. It signifies this salvation, it re-presents it (chapter 7 sub 1).

In the perspective of the kingdom of God, two main lines are couched. One is that of creation. It dates back to the belief of the Canaanites that God is the king of creation and of the fertility of the earth. The second main line is that of the history of salvation. It dates back to the stories of the exodus from Egypt, the passage through the desert, and the entry into the promised land. These two main lines are continually connected to each other in many, many texts. Each time they point to the belief in God who created the world and who is actively present in this world with an eye to the salvation of his people. There is no polarization between creation and liberation. Rather, one should talk of a polarity between the two main lines that belong together (Perrin 1963; 1976).

Jesus also belongs to this perspective. He proclaimed the message of the kingdom of God in word and deed, and heralded it by his person. He made it visible in speeches, parables, and blessings and made it tangible in table communion and miracles. In this he, too, combined and involved the two main lines with each other. In his proclamation, he constantly referred to the presence of the creator God who allows the sun to rise above both good and evil, and grants both groups the fertility and coolness of the rain (Schüssler Fiorenza 1983). At the same time he linked with the eschatological future outlook of Deutero-Isaiah, post-exilic prophecy, and the apocalyptics (Schillebeeckx 1974; Merklein 1983; Van der Ven 1990c, 80-95).

Now it would be a misconception to believe that the reference to the ultimate reality within the identity of the church is a uniform, monolithic matter. God and the kingdom of God proclaimed and depicted by Jesus are the object of divergent images, stories, and interpretations. They are interwoven in divergent texts. They do not exist outside of these texts; at least they are not accessible outside these texts. Also and precisely in the church of today, one can talk of a pluralism of visions and interpretations. We will illustrate this by means of the convictions with regard to God, to God and suffering, and to Jesus.

Research into images of God among 638 students of the University of Nijmegen in the Netherlands in 1990 brought a rough trichotomy to light. The students were found to have theistic, panentheistic, and pantheistic images of God at their disposal. The theistic and the pantheistic image are each other's opposite. The theistic image emphasizes the distance and inequality between God and the world; in contrast, the pantheistic image emphasizes the unity and equality

TABLE 10.1
Images of God

	population (N = 638)	subpopulation (N = 328)
theism	2.11	2.67
indiv. panentheism	2.35	3.12
soc. panentheism	2.32	2.91
cosmol. panentheism	2.22	2.80
ontol. panentheism	2.78	3.23
pantheism	2.60	2.88

Source: Van der Ven 1992b

between God and the world. The panentheistic images of God are somewhere in between. They stress the proximity of God to man and the world, without God merging into this proximity (Hartshorne 1948; Hartshorne & Reese 1953; Tillich 1966; Tracy 1988). These panentheistic images could be separated into individual, social, cosmological, and ontological images. Within the panentheistical images the proximity of God is emphasized: in the individual image to the individual person, in the social image to society, in the cosmological image to nature, and in the ontological image to existence *tout court* (Van der Ven 1992b). In table 10.1 the average scores of the entire research population and of a subpopulation of students who consider themselves to be religious are shown. The scale runs from 1 (strongly disagree) to 5 (strongly agree).

From this table it appears that the highest priority of both populations is given to ontological panentheism (2.78 and 3.23) and the lowest to theism (2.11 and 2.67). It is also interesting to find out that the second priority is pantheism (2.60) for the entire population and individual panentheism (3.12) for the religious subpopulation. Here, therefore, the ways separate! In addition, the score of the religious subpopulation for individual panentheism (3.12) comes very close to that of ontological panentheism (3.23). It appears that there is no significant difference between the two. Herein lies empirical support for the image of God set forth by Tillich (I, 227-28), who believed that God should be regarded as the basis for personal existence (in-

TABLE 10.2
God and suffering

	score	sd
Apathetic God	2.10	.73
Retaliative God	1.66	.67
Pedagogical God	3.04	.68
Solidary God	3.40	.59

Source: Van der Ven 1990c, 222

dividual panentheism) and at the same time for existence *tout court* (ontological panentheism). To put it differently: God is the grounds for one's personal existence, because he is the grounds for existence *tout court.* The table, however, points out that there is no reason to suppose that this is, or should be, the only image of God!

Research was also done on images of God in relation to the suffering people undergo. From this it appears that again there is real religious variety. Four different images appear to play a fundamental role. The first refers to a God who is unmoved with regard to the innocent suffering of people. It does not touch him; it means nothing to him. This is the image of the *apathetic God.* The second refers to the suffering one feels one has deserved as punishment for the evil that one is guilty of and that one has done to someone else or to oneself. This the image of the *retaliative God.* The third implies that one believes that God has not wanted the suffering, but has fitted it to his plan for humankind and has given it a fitting destination. This is the image of the *pedagogical God.* The fourth image has to do with the experience that God truly suffers along with the sufferer. This is the image of the *solidary God.* Table 10.2 contains data from research into these images among a population of 158 core church members, held in the region between Nijmegen and Tilburg in the Netherlands in 1988. It presents the average scores on a five-point scale together with their standard deviation (sd).

What strikes us in this table is the extremely low score for the image of the retaliative God (1.66). It indicates a very strong rejection. Following this is the image of an apathetic God (2.10). This score also implies a rejection. The image of the pedagogical God holds some

TABLE 10.3
Belief in Christ

	score	sd.
ascension	4.09	.73
descension	3.38	.70
liberation	3.55	.79

Source: Van der Ven 1992a, 120

doubt (3.04). The image of the solidary God, however, is granted approval (3.40). It is interesting to note that it is precisely this image that has the smallest standard deviation (.59). The respondents disagree the least about the religious meaning of this image. There is less agreement with regard to the other images (.67, .68, and .73).

Finally, an example from christological research. In 1990, 218 members of Catholic parishes in Ottawa (Canada) answered a series of questions regarding images of Jesus. The factor analysis of these answers resulted in three images. The first is the image of *ascension.* The image of ascension says that Jesus has shown us how to love God and our fellow humans in the way he lived and that in this, God's love for man is shaped. The second is that of *descension.* In the image of descension the sending of Jesus as the Son of God by God is central, as well as his lordship over all that the earth contains and his judgment about what happens on earth (Schoonenberg 1991). The third image has to do with *liberation.* The core of this image is formed by the solidarity of Jesus with the suppressed in their battle for justice and freedom. In table 10.3 one finds the average scores with regard to the three images.

It becomes clear from this table that the image of ascension gets a relatively strong agreement score (4.09). This also applies to the image of liberation. It also gets agreement, albeit to a lesser extent than with ascension (3.55). Things are different for the image of descenion, which lies more within the area of doubt, although it is clearly on the positive side of it (3.38). From the standard deviation, it appears that the degree of consensus about the three images does not greatly differ (.73, .79, and .70).

What conclusions may we draw from these illustrations regarding the images of God, of God and suffering, and of Jesus? First, the convictions that underlie the religious identity of the church are not one massive datum or monolithic block, but instead there is a variety of images. Secondly, the scores point out that these images vary as to the degree of agreement or rejection. Some images, like the ontological image of God, the image of the compassionate God, and the christological image of ascension, are valued positively. However, others, like the theistic image of God and the image of the retaliative God, are valued negatively. Thirdly, the standard deviation gives us the degree of mutual consensus and dissensus within this agreement or rejection. In short, one can talk of an obvious pluralism of convictions at the level of ultimate reality. How we can deal with this pluralism will be discussed in the following chapters.

Ultimate order

At this second level, we deal with convictions that give an answer to the question about the ultimate order that a particular philosophy or religion represents. To which ultimate order does it refer? With which ultimate order is it engaged? This can be the existing order. However, if the existing order is viewed as disorder *(chaos),* then the ultimate order can also be be a future order to be accomplished (*cosmos* in an eschatological sense). Some upper-class churches in the United States interpret the existing order as *cosmos* and view the church as the vehicle to maintain and strengthen this order. Lower-class churches, however, take the existing order to be *chaos* and view the church as a vehicle for the establishment of an eschatological *cosmos:* a new city, a new society, a new world (or, to put it more religiously, the new Jerusalem, the kingdom of God). In this vision the church is a sign and instrument of liberation. In short, religious convictions about *cosmos* and *chaos* are class bound; at least they can be class oriented to a greater or lesser degree (Weber 1980). This is not a necessity, however, since religious representatives of the higher classes can also be oriented toward the establishment of a new *cosmos* of freedom and justice for the lower classes.

Again, we shall illustrate this by means of some research results. These have to do with the degree to which belief in God — the ultimate reality — and being a member of the church influence the

TABLE 10.4

Belief in God, churchliness, and conservatism in %

	Non-conservatives	Economic conserv.	Cultural conserv.	Outspoken conserv.
VNN	58	28	7	6
NN	48	21	21	11
NC	36	24	25	15
RN	31	11	31	26
RC	27	15	35	23
VRC	11	7	44	38
Total	35	18	28	20

Source: Felling et al. 1986, 103

way in which people take a position with regard to the existing order. The question is whether believers and members of the church have or do not have a conservative position regarding the existing society.

In table 10.4 one finds the six categories mentioned that we came across earlier (table 9.2): very nonreligious nonchurch members (VNN), nonreligious nonchurch members (NN), nonreligious church members (NC), religious nonchurch members (RN), religious church members (RC), very religious church members (VRC). They have been divided among four groups: the nonconservatives, the economic conservatives, the cultural conservatives, and the outspoken conservatives. The latter hold both economic and cultural conservative convictions, while the nonconservatives hold neither economic nor cultural conservative convictions. Economic conservatism is measured by means of items that measure the opposition to levelling of incomes, government intervention, and influential trade union politics. Cultural conservatism is measured by means of items that measure opposition to civil liberties, interference with life, and changes in the role of women. The data in table 10.4 originate from research done among the Dutch population in 1979.

If one regards the two outer columns, it appears that the nonconservatives (35% in total) can be found especially among the nonreligious and nonchurch members, and that the outspoken conservatives (20% in total) can be found among the religious church members in particular. However, this convenient picture becomes distorted when one looks at the two middle columns. It then appears that the economic conservatives (18% in total) are clearly underrepresented among the religious church members. The cultural conservatives (28% in total) are, however, clearly overrepresented among the religious church members. In other words, from an economic point of view, religious church members are anything but conservative, while from a cultural point of view they clearly are conservative.

Here again we notice that we cannot speak of a uniform, monolithic image. At the level of the ultimate order there is also a variety of convictions. Again we refer the reader to the following chapters concerning the question of how we are to deal with this pluralism.

Spheres of life

The convictions at the level of the ultimate order influence the convictions concerning the spheres of life. One can imagine spheres of life such as family life, professional life, recreational life, and public life in the political sector of society. Convictions regarding these spheres of life partially determine the religious identity of the church. Which convictions do people in the church hold regarding these spheres of life?

We will illustrate the importance of this question by means of some moral convictions that have to do with the spheres of life mentioned: convictions concerning family life (familialism), professional life (economism), recreational life (hedonism), and public life (criticism of society). Familialism is characterized by a primary aim at family life and the raising of children. Economism places the professional career at its center, or rising on the social ladder. In hedonism striving after enjoyment, pleasure, and lust is central. In criticism of society, finally, the change of society from the perspective of social justice is the focal point.

The first column in table 10.5 has to do with research carried out in 1989 among 537 members of the most important movement of renewal in the Dutch Catholic Church, the so-called Acht Mei-Beweging (The 8th of May Movement). It contains the scores of these members regarding the moral convictions just mentioned (Van der Ven 1991b). These scores are set off against the average scores of the

TABLE 10.5
Moral convictions

	The 8th of May Movement	Dutch pop.	Cath. pop
familialism	3.2	3.7	521
economism	2.8	3.5	512
hedonism	3.2	3.5	494
criticism of society	3.9	3.1	492

Source: Van der Ven 1991b, 340; Felling et al. 1983, 94; Peters & Schreuder 1987, 208

total Dutch population in the second column (Felling et al. 1983). To this was added a third column, which displays the average factor scores of the Catholics in the Netherlands (Peters & Schreuder 1987). The latter have to be read with a maximum deviation of ±100 from 500, which is considered to be the standardized average factor score of the total Dutch population. An example may clarify this. In the second column we find the score for the Dutch population on the familialism scale (3.7). In the third column this was set at 500. On the basis of this, one can see that the average Dutch Catholic (521) agrees a lot more strongly with familialism than the average Dutch citizen (500). Another example: the score of the Dutch population on the hedonism scale (3.5) in the second column was set at 500 in the third column, so that one can see that the average Dutch Catholic (494) is less aimed at hedonism than the average Dutchman (500).

From this table it appears that the members of the 8th of May Movement feel criticism of society to be the most important thing (3.9) and economism to be the least important (2.8). However, criticism of society is given the lowest value by the Dutch population (3.1), while familialism is at the top (3.7).

We can compare the priorities the Dutch Catholics give to these moral convictions. Their lowest priority is criticism of society: their score for criticism of society (492) is lower than that of the Dutch population (500), which already was the lowest with regard to the other moral convictions (3.1). The highest priority of the Dutch Catholics is given to familialism; their score for familialism (521) is higher than that of the Dutch population (500), which itself was already the highest with regard to the other moral convictions (3.7).

The image that comes to the fore from this is, therefore, that the Dutch Catholics are more familialistic and less societally critical than the Dutch population. The 8th of May Movement deviates from this to a considerable degree. It is less familialistic and more societally critical than the Dutch population. One may conclude that the Dutch Catholics and the 8th of May Movement are each others' mirror image with regard to the Dutch population. The average Dutch Catholic stands to the "right" of the average Dutchman, while the average member of the 8th of May Movement stands to his "left."

Again we can talk of obvious variety. The moral convictions at the level of spheres of life do not display a uniform picture. They differ with regard to the four spheres of life we distinguished (family, profession, recreation, and public life). They also display a different picture among the various groups in the church.

Activities

The term *activities* serves to indicate the level of performance of activities and achieving of results, to which the convictions in question attribute a certain meaning. This is the lowest level of the philosophical or religious identity of a culture. One can imagine such activities as caring for house mates, raising children, maintaining relations with parents, siblings, and friends, carrying out professional duties, executing societal duties, rendering services to the distressed, and carrying out tasks in the church. The religious meaning of this kind of activity is often summarized under the keyword *vocation* in the religious tradition. Thus the educational and professional activities, for example, are seen by Luther as vocation.

One can ask oneself whether and to what degree these activities still have a religious meaning. Do we not find that secularization as a consequence of the rationalization of the worldview has penetrated so far that this religious notion of vocation has been lost? It appears from research that leaders in the sectors of economy, politics, and management do not spontaneously bring their professional responsibilities into connection with God or the transcendent. They understand it to be immanent (Kaufmann 1989, 148-51).

As a test case, we will take an activity that did not occur in the list above, and would hardly seem to be an activity, but is so nevertheless: meditating. One could say that if there is one activity to which any one religious meaning has yet to be attached, it is meditating. If there is one activity to which a "calling" is felt, then it has to be opening oneself meditationally to the mystery or Mystery of life.

Now proceeding from the tradition of Weber, we find that meditating is determined by two contrasts: that between activity and passivity, and that between turning away from and turning toward the world. Weber does not see meditating as active intervention in the world, but as passively relating oneself to the world. This passivity can take on two shapes. The first is that in which one delivers oneself to the existing order in the meditation (turning toward the world). The second is that in which one turns inward upon oneself and away from the existing disorder (turning away from the world). This approach does not do justice to the breadth and richness of meditation and mysticism. There is also a critical-political form of mysticism (Steggink & Waaijman 1985, 31). However, it does bring forward important variants of meditation and mysticism (Weber 1980; Habermas 1982, 293).

We shall consult research done in 1979 among the Dutch population. In this research the question was asked whether one practiced certain types of meditation. About 10% gave a positive answer, while the rest were negative. This answer can be connected with the religiosity and church membership of the respondents and with the two contrasts we just mentioned: activity versus passivity and turning away versus turning toward the world.

From this research it appears that meditating occurs slightly more often among believers and church members than among nonbelievers and nonchurch members. Further, it appears that to a certain extent meditating goes together with praying and reading the Bible. Finally, it appears that those who meditate feel that they are more religious and award religion a more important place in their lives than those who do not (Schreuder 1984, 137).

How do those who meditate position themselves with regard to the society around them? Are they characterized by an attitude of activity or passivity, of turning away or turning toward the world? One can endeavor to find an answer to this question by checking, for example, whether or not they participate in demonstrations or action groups. Proceeding from the tradition of Weber, it is obvious to

FIGURE 10.1 Loglinear analysis effect model: meditating

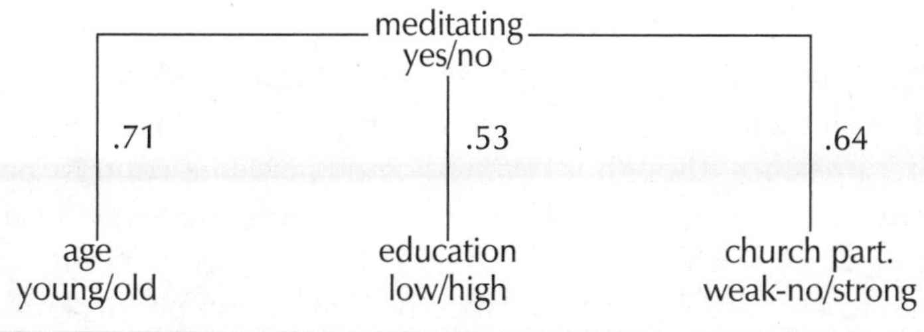

suppose that they would take up a neutral or negative position with regard to demonstrations or action groups. However, from the research mentioned, we do not find a negative or neutral connection, but only a moderately positive connection between meditating and participating in demonstrations and action groups. 18% of those who meditate join in such political activities as compared to 5% of those who do not meditate (for the Dutch population). From the test of significance, we find that this division is not based on chance (Schreuder 1984, 140). In this research one can thus find a certain degree of empirical support for a critical-political spirituality.

Furthermore, one may wonder what moves those who meditate to do so, and which factors incite them. In figure 10.1 three factors that have the most influence on meditating, according to research, have been placed together: age, education, and church participation.

The following things strike us in this figure. The factor of education (.53) remains the furthest below the equal proportion of probability of 1.00, which it has with the other two factors. What this means is that education determines the proportion of probability the most and therefore influences meditating the most. Having undergone higher training therefore incites people the most to practice meditation. After this we have church participation (.64), and finally age (.71). What does this mean? People with higher educations feel the most need to distance themselves from time to time, come to themselves, ponder upon things in peace, and be open to the out-of-the-ordinary. They feel the most need to interrupt the treadmill of daily life from time to time, to break away from it. Through their education, they have been given the chance to put things more at a distance, to be more reflective (Schreuder 1984).

What has this to do with the religious identity of the church and the people in the church? As we said, meditating shows a significant connection to religiosity and church membership. It does occur everywhere: within and outside of religion, within and outside of the church. But within religion and within the church it has a significantly greater presence, though it is not a lot greater. The contrast between activity and passivity and the contrast between turning toward and turning away from the world seem to be passé. Meditating appears, at least to a certain degree, to go together with active political militancy. However, the most important thing is that people meditate especially for some peace and to distance themselves; they want to be able to reflect. With this goal the religious meaning of meditating has more or less faded into the background. The notion of meditation as a vocation has become second rate.

Now we can survey the whole of the convictions at the four levels (ultimate reality, ultimate order, spheres of life, and activities). From this we can draw two conclusions. The first refers to the pluralization of the religious convictions at all levels. The second relates to the influence of secularization as a consequence of rationalization, which affects the religious meaning of convictions. We will take these conclusions into account in the following chapters.

(3) The sources of religious convictions

Where do religious convictions come from? From which sources do they stem? This question may be surprising since the religious convictions that are present in the church and determine its identity belong precisely to the life of the church. The religious convictions in the church stem from the church itself, one is inclined to say. However, with this answer the church threatens to become reified. The church is not an independent phenomenon: it does not exist without the people within the church. Neither do religious convictions exist independently of the people in the church. The people are the ones who have certain religious convictions, they are the ones who discuss them among each other, and they are the ones who pass them on from generation to generation. That is why the relevant question is how people arrive at these religious convictions, where they derive them.

Now there is no unequivocal answer to this question. Various sources act upon each other at different moments in the course of people's lives. They can be divided into two groups: early religious socialization and present religious practice.

Religious socialization

From research it has become sufficiently well known that early religious socialization exerts a great influence on the religious convictions. The most important factors are the personal religiosity and church participation of the father and mother. We are dealing here with the religious attitudes, religious practices, and church practices of the parents, which act as an example for the child and which also determine his or her religious convictions. This is true not in the sense that the parents consciously posit an example that the child has to follow but in the sense that the unconscious character of the religious processes that take place in the family are picked up by the child as an example (Welten 1991; 1992). There are indications that the example of the mother is stronger than that of the father (Andree 1983, 245).

There is, of course, conscious influencing in religious education, in which the child is explicitly involved with churchgoing, praying, reading the Bible, religious conversations, and Sunday observance. Much influence comes from praying with children, churchgoing, and religious conversations; the greatest from praying with children, especially praying before going to bed (Andree 1983, 253).

In religious education, one can speak of a variation in religious guidance. One can leave the child to him- or herself, but one can also stimulate the child to varying degrees. It is yet to be decided what degree of guidance leads to what degree of religiosity. It probably lies somewhere between *führen* and *wachsen lassen* (Litt 1940).

Besides the primary religious socialization in the family, there is the secondary religious socialization at school. This takes place in the special school in particular. Within such a school religious education is also given. Usually, the school only strengthens what has been brought about in the family. What a family lacks in religiosity cannot be compensated for by the school (Greeley & Rossi 1966; Feldman & Newcomb 1969).

TABLE 10.6
Religious socialization and practice (eta)

	pantheism	individual panentheism	ontological panentheism
religious socialization			
religiosity father	.23	.39	.24
religiosity mother	.26	.45	.29
church part. father	.25	.35	.18
church part. mother	.22	.35	.21
religious upbringing	.18	.29	—
religious guidance	—	.20	—
confessional schooling	—	.18	—
religious education	—	—	—
religious practice			
religious experience	.26	.41	.41
religious activities	.31	.45	.37
praying	.45	.75	.44
church participation	.25	.63	.27

Source: Van der Ven 1992b

Religious practice

Present religious practice, too, is of influence on religious convictions. It is not that it initiates them, but that it promotes, strengthens, and intensifies them. Religious practice involves being open to and receiving religious experiences, doing religious activities (such as reading the Bible, meditating, reading religious books), praying, and participating in church.

Table 10.6 contains data concerning the influence of early religious socialization and present religious practice on religious convictions. The data originated from research among students of the University of Nijmegen in the Netherlands, which we dealt with before (table 10.1). Now we have limited the religious convictions to the three most prominent ones: pantheism, individual panentheism, and ontological panentheism. *Pantheism* has to do with the belief in God as coincidental with the whole of human and natural life. *Individual panentheism* refers to belief in God, who is present in and around one and is personally involved with each specific human being. *Ontological panentheism* points to belief in God, who is the source and basis for human existence *tout court,* without, however, merging into it. The factors in religious socialization are: the religiosity of the father and mother, the church participation of the father and mother, religious upbringing, religious guidance, confessional schooling, and religious education. The factors in present religious practice are being open to religious experience, doing religious activities, praying, and church participation. The connection between religious convictions on the one hand, and religious socialization and practice on the other, is indicated by the measure of association (eta), which runs from .00 to 1.00.

Within religious socialization, the religiosity of the parents is the most important factor, as appears from this table. That of the mother (.26, .45, and .29) is indeed a little greater than that of the father (.23, .39, and .24). This difference applies less to their church membership, which for that matter is of slighter importance. Religious upbringing is again of less relevance than the church membership of the parents. It is entirely lacking with ontological panentheism. Religious guidance only influences individual panentheism. The same applies to confessional schooling. Religious education has no influence whatsoever.

Within religious practice, praying is the most important factor (.45, .75, .44). The second most important factor for pantheism is the whole of religious activities (.31). For individual panentheism it is church participation (.63), and for ontological panentheism it is religious experience (.41).

Sources of religious experience

We will take a special look at this last factor. For, if it is true that the religious experience functions as a source of religious convictions, then naturally the question arises about the source of this religious experience itself. Where do people receive religious experiences? Here we give the results of research into the religious experiences of people who are closely connected to the weal and woe of the church: pastors, pastoral managers, and volunteers.

In table 10.7 we find the results of a factor analysis of the answers to 25 items of a total of 432 pastors, managers, and volunteers in the

TABLE 10.7

Sources of religious experience

	score	sd.
liturgy	3.8	.63
personal emotion	3.2	.83
global problems	2.9	.93

Source: Van Gerwen 1990, 128

Netherlands in 1986. It appears that three factors come into play: personal emotion, liturgy, and global problems. The most important items involved in personal emotion are love for your companion, friendship, physical love, listening to music, and art. The most important items involved in liturgy are celebration of the Eucharist, funerals, messages from the pope, and the baptism of a child. The third factor is made up of global problems. Belonging to this group in particular are the nuclear threat, exhaustion of natural resources, and poverty in the Third World.

From this table it appears that liturgy is the greatest source of religious experience (3.8), and that the unanimity about this is also the greatest (sd. .63). Personal emotion follows. Only in a moderate sense does it form a source of religious experience (3.2), with a lesser degree of consensus (sd. .83). As far as global problems are concerned, the respondents doubt whether they are a source of religious experience (2.9). There is a great lack of agreement (sd. .93).

We cannot be surprised that liturgy comes to the fore as the greatest source of religious experience, at least not if we use Geertz's theory of religion (1969). In his description of religion, which we dealt with at the beginning of this chapter, we speak of convictions that are clothed with an aura of factuality. According to Geertz, this takes place in religious ritual.

Chapter 11

Vision

Until now we have paid attention to secularization in this part because it is the societal context within which the identity of the church has to be brought to development (chapter 9). Next, we discussed the religious convictions that form the core of the identity of the church. We came across two problems in this: first, the pluralization of religious convictions, and second, the influence of secularization on it (chapter 10).

In this chapter we face the challenge of properly approaching these problems proceeding from the vision of the church. In this vision the church indicates what it conceives itself to be, how it deals with itself, and, of course, how it deals with all those various groups — including their various convictions — that the church contains within it.

Earlier on we mentioned that in a social sense the church can be considered from several perspectives: association, people's union, movement, community, organization, and enterprise (chapter 2 sub 2). We believe that of these social formations *people's union* is the most eligible to clarify the identity and the vision the church has of itself. The term *people* refers to a manifold and many-colored social formation that gives all sorts of groups space and holds them together at the same time, as we will make clear further along. This binding force can be found in the social-cultural identity in particular, to which the term *people* refers. People and identity thus imply each other (Thurlings 1977, 197).

Beginning from the church as a people, we will further try to clarify the religious identity of the church in the perspective of the church as the people of God. This is certainly one of the most important codes. According to some authors, it is the most important (Küng 1967, 139).

The question is whether there is a perspective in the church as a people and as the people of God from which we can adequately deal with the pluralization and secularization of religious convictions. Are infinite pluralization and secularization possible, or should a certain orientation be given to it? We shall try to clarify where the religious identity of the church can be found proceeding from three functions of the code *people of God*.

In this chapter we thus will ask ourselves (1) in what sense the church can be considered a people, and (2) what the code *people of God* means in this.

(1) People

In order to be able to check in what sense the word *people* is applicable to the church, we will first have to discover its meaning. We will do this by describing a number of its characteristics. After that, the application can be tested.

What is "people"?

The word *people* calls up all sorts of associations — often negative ones — because it has so often been ideologically abused during the course of history — especially in the 19th and 20th centuries — and still is. This is why many authors either avoid the term or use it only in an ideology-critical sense. They make use of it as a kind of catchword to show that each time it is used, it is meant to legitimize certain interests of a certain group, nation, or state. Those who allow this to act upon them may have difficulty dealing with the fact that this word is used to indicate the vision the church has of itself.

This brings us to an analytical approach to the term *people.* This means that we will dissect it into a number of characteristics, to the extent that it becomes clear under which conditions the term is used in an ideological sense, and under which conditions it can be applied in an ideology-critical sense. To our minds there is no better analysis of the term *people* than that of Weber. We will present the most prominent aspects that he distinguished and add a number of other facts (Weber 1980, 234-42).

One thing is very clear to Weber — it is too important not to mention this beforehand — all attempts to find evidence for the ethnical solidarity of a people in a common descent are built on quicksand. One would then pass over the countless sexual relations that have existed between the peoples within living memory and the mixed marriages that have sprung from them with all the consequences this has had for their descendants. In order to hide this fact from view, all sorts of myths are made up about the genesis of a people; and many a yarn is spun about ethnic identity and the importance of ethnic purity, their aim being to promote the ethnic interests of their own group (Eisinga & Scheepers 1989). A people cannot be determined by common heredity. The genealogical argument refers to the dark caverns of myth-creating ideology.

What a people is should be described not in historical, but in social categories. The proper terms are *mutual attraction* and *repulsion.* Members of a social formation who regard themselves as a people feel attracted to each other. They isolate themselves from other social formations that in their turn regard themselves as separate peoples. The mutual attraction and repulsion call each other up and strengthen each other. The mutual attraction can be defined as the internal dimension, while the mutual repulsion is the external dimension. In other words, the word *people* has to be conceived of in an intra- and interethnic sense.

Now the question is by means of which categories the internal and external dimension can be described. Let us first mention the two categories that are often put forward but that are unsound: language and religion.

Language is often called the heart of a people. However obvious this may seem, this fact harbors a number of problems. The terms *language* and *people* do not cover the same reality. A common language can be spread across several peoples; furthermore, within one people several language communities may exist. All this becomes more complex through the sliding scale between language and dialect. For there are communities who consider themselves a people on the basis of their dialect, while — for an outsider — they belong to a larger, dialect-transcending language community. That is why we will further disregard language.

The second category that is unsound is religion. Religion is often defined as the core of the common connection of the people. However, here again some problems present themselves tht are analogous to those of language. The terms *religion* and *people* do not cover each other at all. In one people several religions may occur and one religion can be practiced by several peoples. Here, too, the picture is complicated by the various partially or completely seceded organizations and groups within religion. The phenomenon of the state church is an example of this. This aspect also has to be left aside.

What, then, does make up the identity of a people if the genealogical, linguistic, and religious categories are no good? By means of which categories can the internal and external dimensions be adequately described?

The social category of the mutual connections is certainly of importance. The members of a people feel connected to each other in contrast to members of other peoples. A "we" consciousness prevails opposite a "them" consciousness. There is a kind of homely feeling, especially if one finds a fellow countryman in foreign parts. Over against the outside world they feel they belong to one family, being brothers and sisters. Every member of a people equally shares in this, no matter which class they come from, whether they are rich or poor, or whether they do managerial or menial work. It permeates all social layers and all generations. Proceeding from this internally and externally oriented notion of community, in which everybody shares equally, the ideological leap toward an idea of blood relations and common origin was made. However understandable this may be, it remains an ideology.

What is even more important is the cultural category of everyday life. In this peoples distinguish themselves from each other. We can mention simple, but influential opinions and behaviors in this context with regard to manner of living, housekeeping, clothing, daily routine, bodily care, head dress (hair style, beard), body odor, communication between companions, interaction between parents and children, relations among children, division of roles in the family, use of holidays, use of days off, nursing of the ill, undertaking; these cultural factors are the things that give people the feeling that they belong to one people and not to another.

Ritual factors can also be counted as belonging to the cultural category of everyday life. Rituals of greeting and departure belong to this, as well as paying visits and receiving visitors, morals and customs. However, the larger congregations, meetings, feasts, ceremonies, and celebrations are also part of this. They give expression to convictions, opinions, and values that are commonly felt.

The social, cultural, and ritual aspects are the core of the identity of a people. They determine this identity both within and without. However, there are circumstances in which they are applied in an ideological sense that — at least in a strict sense — lies outside this identity: politics, police, and military matters.

Thus it can happen that the social, cultural, and ritual aspects are used for political ends. This is the case, for instance, if an attempt is made purposely to turn various groups of people into one people. This nation building is itself part of the formation or strengthening of the national state. It is felt to be necessary both for internal cohesion and for international relations. For this purpose special projects and programs are sometimes organized, education and media are manipulated, and national ceremonies are given an extra shine (Schoorl 1983, 152-54). This is not without its dangers. Chauvinism may take a leading role. Sometimes a populist leader, who is regarded as a father to all the people, will come forward. The people itself can be reduced to a silent majority that is thought to express itself in the words of the charismatic leader.

There are circumstances in which the formation of political plans results in the formation of a police power. This entails placing the monopoly of violence that is characteristic of a national state in the hands of the executive power unchecked. All this is done for the sake of the protection of the people, according to the doctrine of national security. It demands that national dissidents among the people be eliminated. As a consequence the authorities of the legislature and judicial power may be injured.

The formation of a police power can also go hand in hand with the formation of a military power, in order to strengthen the belief of the people in themselves as well as to take a stand against other peoples, nations, or states. We will not have seen the last time that a people was called upon as a people to enter the arena and go to war.

As one considers this description, one may have some difficulty thinking about the meaning of the church as a people and as the people of God. Nevertheless, we will have to take the path trodden, as one may rightly wonder whether the following suggestive statement made by Weber also applies to the church: "And behind all 'ethnic' contrasts we find somewhere quite naturally the idea of the 'chosen people'" (Weber 1980, 239).

Church as a people?

Now that we are considering in what sense the church can be viewed as a people and that implications lie within this, we will leave out the genealogical and linguistic aspects. The genealogical argumentation is built on ideological quicksand, as we have seen, and the linguistic approach to the term *people* is not adequate.

The problem is difficult enough as it is. On the one hand, it appears that the church as a social-religious formation does not fall together with one people. We already pointed out that within a people several religious traditions and denominations may occur. And, in addition, the church transcends the borders between peoples at the same time, because of which it is able to take correctional action against nationalism and ethnocentricity. In other words, church and people do not cover the same reality. On the other hand, it is true that in certain countries, regions, or areas, the church can really display, sometimes to a great extent, the characteristics of a certain people, or section of the people. This not only applies in a historical sense. One thinks of Catholic Brabant and Limburg in the Netherlands and Catholic Bavaria in Germany. The situation of the church in Poland can be called exemplary. The local church can also be marked to a great extent by a section of the people or by a population group from which it is composed. Parishes often differ from each other in that they are marked by different sections of the people or population groups. This applies all the more if a certain ethnic minority determines the identity of the local church.

We have called the social, cultural, and ritual aspects the core of the identity of the people. By analogy this applies to the local church. What distinguishes this from other churches in the same or other denominations as well as from groups outside of any ecclesial context, can often be brought back to a "we" feeling, an awareness of belonging together. Social-cultural aspects play an important role in this. These are expressed in opinions and behaviors regarding things that are viewed as self-evident, such as lifestyles, styles of interaction, types of action, customs, and usages. The ritual aspects also influence the identity of the church: the forms and structures of liturgy, the way of preaching, and the way a feast is celebrated. Together the social, cultural, and ritual aspects can be called the "spirituality" of the church. It gives the church its own look and determines its distinctive features.

Often this spirituality has a long history that the church cherishes and that it deals with carefully as a precious inheritance. The people in the church construct and reconstruct this history continuously. According to their notions it goes back to certain persons (a patron, leaders, pastors, or members), certain actions (foundation, building of the church, or church development), or certain happenings (time of economic crisis, war, or renewal). Therefore it is of importance to pay proper attention to the history of the spirituality of the church (Hopewell 1987; Carroll et al. 1988, 21-47).

The other aspects that we have mentioned deserve some critical discussion. It is not that the local church is guilty of political, police, or military behavior; however, one cannot turn a blind eye to certain phenomena that take place in the church both at a micro- and macro-level, as well as in its relation to the national state. At the least, certain interpretations of certain phenomena could or should be food for thought.

Let us start with a phenomenon that belongs to the political aspect: populism. It has been said that since the fifties some bishops and clergy have become populists, who try to make large groups of people dance to their ecclesial and pastoral pipes (Boff 1987a, 54). However, there are claims that this phenomenon can be observed today too, at all levels of the church, even at the highest (Gabriel 1988b).

One can also come across certain characteristics of chauvinism in the relation of the church to the national state, because of which nation building and church building can almost become identical. Because of this the church may directly or indirectly promote ethnocentrism. The latter can be illustrated by means of research done on the relationship between belief, church participation, and ethnocentrism. It is a relationship that already has a long international research tradition behind it, particularly in the United States. Recently, this relationship was researched in South Africa (Pieterse et al. 1991) and the Netherlands (Eisinga & Scheepers 1989).

Figure 11.1 gives further information about the situation in the Netherlands. The question is whether religion has a significant influ-

FIGURE 11.1 Christian belief and ethnocentrism

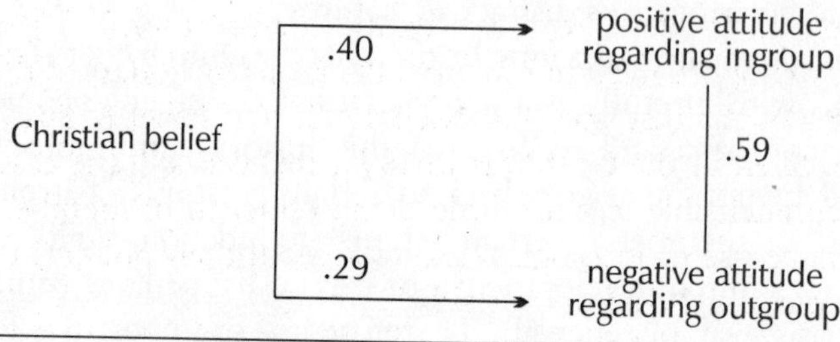

ence on both the internal and the external dimension of ethnocentrism. The internal dimension has to do with positive attitudes toward one's own ingroup, while the external dimension has to do with negative attitudes toward outgroups (other peoples or population groups).

The regression coefficients in this table indicate to what degree belief influences positive attitudes toward the ingroup and negative attitudes toward the outgroup. This influence is strong (.40) in one instance and moderate (.29) in another. Moreover, the correlation between the two dimensions appears to be very strong (.59).

Research was also done to see to what extent church membership contributes to ethnocentrism. In this research, membership was split up into core, modal, and marginal members. An important difference came up in the research. The modal members had high scores, while the core and marginal members had relatively low scores. The modal members, therefore, have a stronger positive attitude toward their own ingroup and a stronger negative attitude toward the outgroup than the core and the marginal members. Consequently, we can talk of a curvilinear relation between church membership and ethnocentrism (Eisinga et al. 1990).

A phenomenon connected to this that probably belongs to its background is that of closed versus open religious attitudes. The closed religious attitude is characterized by dogmatism, while the open religious attitude is characterized by tolerance for the convictions and opinions of dissentients. From a research in Dukenburg (Nijmegen, the Netherlands) what came forward was that a more closed religious attitude was found in modal members and that core and marginal members had a more open religious attitude. Here, too, we come across a curvilinear relation, but now it is between church membership and an open/closed religious attitude (Peters 1977, 79).

In a direct sense there are no military aspects to the church, in contrast with the past. There are, however, in an indirect sense. Take, for example, the support given to military operations by leaders of the church in terms of the just war (Jeurissen 1993; Van Iersel & Spanjersberg 1993). Even in the Gulf War in 1991, this was still the case. It is equally reprehensible if it has little or no criticism of members of state who make use of ideological expressions in their political or even war rhetoric, like "God on our side."

(2) Church as people of God

In the above discussion the point has already been made implicitly that pluralization and secularization of religious convictions in the church do not develop infinitely. They have to be oriented toward a certain vision of the church and be supplemented and possibly corrected from there. This orientation can occur proceeding from the religious code *people of God*.

However, the meaning of this code itself cannot be determined separately from the historical context in which it originated and the history attached to it. That would be a sign of false semiotic romanticism. *People of God* contains no automatic guarantee that the church will follow the right track of its own accord if it allows itself to be led by this code. That is why it is necessary to sketch the outlines of the history of the code. After doing that, we shall determine its cognitive, emotive, and conative functions (chapter 7 sub 2).

History of "people of God"

The designation "people of God" is indissolubly tied to the origin and the history of the people of Israel. Much is still unclear; however, we can give a simple sketch that suffices in the framework of our explanation.

When the monarchical government in Egypt stretched across all of Palestine in the 14th century before Christ, one could find a kind of dichotomy in the country. The citizens led a prosperous existence in the cities, while the peasants led a slave's existence in the country and in the mountains. During the course of the 13th and the 12th centuries, however, Egypt gradually began to lose control; the cities collapsed and the peasants went through a technological revolution. Because of this, more and more peasants' revolts against the monarchy and the cities broke out. For this purpose all sorts of groups — families, clans, and tribes — joined together to get out from underneath the rule of the monarchy and the cities. They had a movement "separate from Egypt" in them, a striving to get "out of Egypt." This motif applied all the more to those groups which had originally come down to the north of Egypt from Canaan. The movement "out of Egypt" had even stronger roots in them. When the Philistines managed to drive the Egyptian army out of the southwest of Palestine during a migration of the peoples along the coast that was occurring at the same time, this indirectly helped the peasants' movement. It felt supported by their resistance. However, the Philistines were not satisfied with what they had achieved. They wanted to have all of Palestine under their control, both the cities and the peasants' land. This moved the peasants to close ranks more firmly than ever. The families, clans, and tribes forged a covenant. With this agreement they hoped to ward off possible attacks from the Philistines and other powerful neighboring peoples and repay them with the same warlike methods and means. The motive for this alliance was political in nature; the cement was religious. Thus came into existence the religious-political power, the people of Israel, that tried to establish and maintain itself in opposition to its powerful neighbors (Negenman 1986, 42-46).

On the basis of these religious-political data, a religious self-attribution and legitimization gradually developed (chapter 8). In this the choice that the people of Israel had made for YHWH religion was connected to the realization that YHWH on his part had chosen the people of Israel. The relationship between the people of Israel and YHWH was experienced and depicted as mutual. The covenant between the tribes was at the same time experienced as a covenant between YHWH and Israel (Josh. 24:21-24). The stately proclamations were as follows: "I will take you as my people, and I will be your God" (Exod. 6:7). From a historical perspective, it was the people of Israel that developed first and then the people of God; theologically, from God's perspective, the people of God is primary, according to Boff (1987a, 58-59).

In the definition of Israel as the people of God, we gradually begin to see two different lines. The first is imperialistic. As Israel sees only itself and no other people as the people of God, it imagines itself to be superior. The expansion that takes place under David and Solomon is viewed as the extension of the power of God over other peoples. They take the view that the power of God, who joins in the fight on Israel's side, will rule over all peoples.

The second line is universal. In this Israel becomes aware of the fact that God is the God of all peoples and that Israel is only one people among these peoples. This realization implies a certain relativization. However, within this Israel becomes aware of its vocation toward the peoples: a vocation of universalism (Pixley 1984).

What shape does this vocation take on? One can trace three orientations. The first is centripetal by nature. It involves the idea that the peoples will advance toward Jerusalem on a pilgrimage or should do so (Isa. 2:2-4; Ps. 87; Jer. 3:17). The second is decentral by nature. It is expressed in texts that say that the peoples can participate in the revelation of God's being king in their own towns and cities (Isa. 45:18-25). The third is centrifugal. Even though it is not always very perceptible, one can find it in the texts concerning the mission of the suffering servant for the peoples (Isa. 42:1-9), the mission of Jonah, and a number of psalms (e.g., Ps. 117). In this the universal subservience of Israel to the peoples is expressed (Vogels 1986).

"People of God" in the New Testament

What meaning does "people of God" have in the New Testament? Although the term does not occur in the Gospels, it played an important role implicitly in the action of Jesus. His proclamation was determined by the message of the kingdom of God. In this message he took up an old tradition that went back to the peasants' revolts, in which the rights of the poor were central. The monarchy was rejected because it was the cause of exploitation and oppression. The attempts that were later made to establish a monarchy for Israel itself were also opposed proceeding from this tradition, as appears from the stories about Gideon (Judg. 8:22-23) and Samuel (1 Sam. 8:4-18). Jesus preached the kingdom of God without earthly kingship because the poor were closest to his heart. In this kingdom, according to Jesus' message, there will be no titles or badges, no places of honor, no power and esteem. He who is most subservient to the poor shall be the great power (Mark 10:41-45). The gospel is for the poor (Luke 4:18; 7:22). This is its essential meaning (Pixley 1984).

The relationship between the first Christian communities and the old Israel is not explicitly clarified by this. The question is inescapable: What is the meaning of the title "people of God" with which the people of Israel and now these Christian communities define themselves too?

Initially, the communities understood themselves to be the true, faithful people of God and not as the new people. They believed that through their belief in Jesus, they had been taken up into a covenant with God, to the extent that the promises of the Old Testament were realized in them. Because they took the Twelve to refer to the twelve tribes, they viewed themselves as being in continuity with Israel as the people of God.

A change came over them through the missionary work done by Paul among the Gentiles. Initially, Paul did his work of proclamation among his fellow Jews. He appeared in synagogues (Acts 13:5,14; 17:1-2). He did not restrict himself to Jews in this, because he knew he was called upon to proclaim to both Jews and Gentiles (Acts 9:15). Later, however, resistance to him from the Jews grew. This gradually pushed him toward the Gentiles exclusively (Acts 22:18-21). Thus he became the apostle to the Gentiles (Acts 26:17). Paul's breaking away from the Jewish community and his mission as an apostle of the Gentiles are outlined in three stories of Paul's Damascus experience in Acts 9, 22, and 26 (Schillebeeckx 1974, 295-310).

All this had far-reaching consequences for the relations between the Christian communities and Judaism. The relationship became more and more tense. On the one hand, Paul remained faithful to God's promise to and election of the Jewish people. He did not deprive it of the title "people of God." He did make use of the traditions that were alive within Judaism at the time, namely, that being a child of Abraham in the flesh offers no guarantees of God's salvation, since only being a child of the promise counts for God (Rom. 9:8), and salvation would fall only to a small remnant of Israel, seeing the unfaithfulness, callousness, and obduracy of many (Rom. 9:27; 11:5-7). Finally, Israel had as its duty to be a light to other peoples and to lead them in the service of God, so that they, too, could receive the salvation of God. In the latter lies a call to Israel for universalism. On the other hand, however, Paul reversed the perspective of election and universalism. He did not propose that when Israel was collected around Mount Zion, the people would flock to it for the sake of their own salvation, as Jewish tradition would have it. He proclaimed that Israel would gain salvation only when the peoples had been offered salvation (Rom. 11:5-16). In this dialectical manner Paul found a way to reconcile the Jewish people and the Christian church with each other, at least in his letter to the Romans (Schillebeeckx 1977a, 552-55).

Functions of the church as people of God

Against this background it is of significance to try to recover the meaning of the church as people of God in the context of present society. We will do this by describing the functions of this religious code for today's church. In this we will distinguish a cognitive, an emotive, and a conative function (chapter 7 sub 2).

Cognitive

We would like to point out two important aspects here. The first involves the religious insight that God stands at the origin of the church as people of God. It is God who calls, collects, and perpetuates the people together; he is the one who gives the people salvation and a future. That is why the salvation that stems from God and that he has predestined for his people is not the church's prerogative but his own. The salvation of God is greater than that which the church can contain and encompass. God's salvation is all-surpassing and universal. The church is only a sacrament of this salvation. It is not the salvation itself, but it signifies and re-presents it. Moreover, God's salvation has not been completed. It is realized in and through the vicissitudes of his people in the perspective of the promise of the kingdom of God. The church does not have a patent on this either. God's salvation is its end, its destination.

An aspect of breadth has to be added to this transcendent aspect of God's salvation. This aspect of breadth lies in the relationship of the church to Israel, as was already pointed out in the comments above. The meaning of this relationship is that the church may and has only to view itself as the people of God in continuity with Israel, at least insofar as it answers to its evangelical mission. With this it has to appreciate the vocation that Israel was and is called to. Earlier this vocation was described from three orientations. Besides the centripetal there are also the decentral and centrifugal orientations. In the decentral orientation we are concerned with the realization of the people of God among the peoples themselves. In the centrifugal orientation we are concerned with the mission of the suffering servant to the peoples. This is given particular expression in the New Testament verses on the commission of the apostles by Jesus (Matt. 28:18-20), of which it is assumed that they go back to a direct commandment made by Jesus (Vogels 1986). The subservience of the church comes foremost in this. It is not as if it only has to bring something. In dialogue with the peoples it has to discover what treasures lie buried in the whole of the people of God, which is present in the peoples and of which it is only a part. What we understand as the people of God is the total of all those people, groups, and collectives who try to direct their lives and actions to God and his salvation for all, and especially "the least of these who are members of my family" (Matt. 25:40), as it is said in the gospel (Boff 1987a, 63).

Emotive

The code *people of God* meets the requirement of all sorts of peoples and population groups to express their own social-cultural and ritual identity in a Christian sense. Through this they can develop their own spirituality: their own religious aspirations, forms of expression, language and text, dynamics, and style. It is not only a question of religious wording or coloring; the social-cultural forms even penetrate the structure of the identity and the convictions themselves. They make the church into "something that is ours." To the extent that one could say, proceeding from a personal intrinsic impulse: "the church is all of us together," "the church is what we are," this is what essentially appeals to groups and collectives in the code *people of God*.

This raises the problem of the enculturation or inculturation of the church. The term *enculturation* comes from cultural anthropology and was introduced into missiology. The term *inculturation* is a Catholic invention *(catholicisme inculturé)* that has penetrated into official texts such as the apostolic adhortation *Catechesi Tradendae* (1979) from Catholic missiology. How far does the enculturation of the church go? The cultural form that is actually dominant in the church is the Western one, that is to say, the Western form of culture, mainly from before modernization. In the Catholic Church this is the Vatican form of culture in particular, which additionally shows signs of an amodern established church or even state church (chapter 2 sub 1). The term *enculturation* sooner represents a desideratum than an actual reality (Bosch 1991).

It is of vital importance to the church to sufficiently comply with this desideratum. Without the Christian religion being integrated into the cultural forms of the people, or the population group in question, it would remain essentially alien and would be alienating. There is a danger that double systems of religion will come into being. In a double system the traditional, official Christian form of culture functions next to a local, regional, or national form of culture, without links being made. This is characteristic of countless expressions of popular religion, which are shaped separately and independently from the official religion, to the detriment of both. It is also possible that people start to develop a kind of double bind with all the negative consequences this has (Schreiter 1984).

In this issue of enculturation we are dealing not only with a problem for non-Western countries. The churches in the Western countries have to contend with this too. In this the church has the task of restructuring Christian religion in form and content to the degree that "modern" people feel the church to be their church, or their people of God, in a critical-evangelical sense. This requires fundamental changes. It applies not only to the church organization and structure but also to the ritual forms of expression in liturgy, and above all to the content and interpretation of the Christian belief itself. Only then can one say "this is our church." It is precisely in this that the emotive function of the code *people of God* lies.

Conative

There are aspects in the code *people of God* that act adhortatively, regulatively, or even correctively upon the church, or should do so. In this we are referring not only to the misuse that is possibly made by the church as the people of God in the fields of politics, police, and military. It is obvious that such misuse will have to be shown up, as we have already discussed earlier. Here, however, we are dealing with things we have looked at only from a positive point of view, but which contain a number of dangers at the same time. These lie in the opportunity to conceive of the people of God in such a harmonious sense that all sorts of actual divisions between groups that exist in the church are hidden from the eye in a veil of romanticism. In the code *people of God,* for that matter, we find the inspiration and orientation to trace these dangers and to discuss them. We will mention two of them.

The first danger is that the division that actually exists between the clergy and other members of the church — in a structural sense between the clergy and the laity in the Catholic Church — is hidden from view. The totality of the church as the people of God seems to remove this division. The "church is us together" places such an emphasis on the "us" that the division between "us" and "you" in the church is nearly lost sight of. The division may and cannot exist, but of course it does nevertheless.

Here the history of the terms *people* and *people of God* can guard us from organizational blindness. Thus, at the end of the twelfth century Etienne de Tournai wrote that there is not one people but two within the church, namely the people of the clergy and the people of the laity (Congar 1964, 32). According to medieval insight, the clergy deal with liturgy and the sacraments and the laity are concerned with the matters of the world. Following Gratianus's view, the laity have the duty to subject themselves to the clergy, to obey them, to follow their orders, and to honor them (Boff 1987a, 62). After Vatican II all this may sound somewhat surprising. This council dedicated all of chapter II of the constitution about the church to the one people of God (*Lumen Gentium* 9-17). In other words, before all distinctions in the church there is first and foremost a fundamental connectedness and equality (Semmelroth 1966). This was a revolutionary act for the history of the Catholic Church (Alberigo 1984). However, even though the setting may be different, those who claim that medieval thought is a thing of the past have not been keeping up with the actuality of the church.

In other words, the code *people of God* does lay the emphasis on the whole of the church. It should not, however, cloak the divisions that actually exist. It calls upon us to trace them and to check under which conditions they can be removed. To put it differently, the church may not only be a people of God, it still has to become the people of God! The question is whether this can be accomplished in a way that is not democratic. We will not go into this question here any further, but refer the reader to the following part (chapter 16).

The second danger involves the actual division that exists between the rich and the poor classes within the church. This, too, threatens to disappear from the view of the totality of the church as the people of God. Those who talk of "the church is us together" are tempted to place so much emphasis on the "us" that "you" who live on the edge of society disappear from view.

Here it is significant to complement the description of "people" in this chapter with an analysis of "people" in which the *plebs* are central and not the *populus*. In this the mass of people stands opposite the elite. Those who are serious about this meaning of "people" can do nothing else than to understand the church as the people of God proceeding from the perspective of the church of the poor (Boff 1987a, 66-71). We will try to clarify what this means in the last part (chapter 24).

Cognitive, emotive, conative

Those who allow the three functions to act upon them cannot escape the notion that the church has fallen somewhat in arrears regarding the task God has given it. Proceeding from the cognitive function, there is a danger that the transcendence and the breadth aspects are corrupted. Proceeding from the emotive function, the lack of enculturation comes to light. From the conative function, the danger arises that the divisions between the clergy and the laity and between the rich and the poor are covered up. One has to conclude that the church as the people of God contains other implications too. The church as the people of God is also a church of pilgrims, a church underway, and a church of sinners, as we will illustrate.

That the church is making a way for pilgrimage can be gathered from the constitution about the church of Vatican II. There it is called proceeding right across the temptations and tribulations (*Lumen Gentium* 9). This description expresses the experience that the church is in the dark, that it is stumbling, and that is forever falling and getting up. The church is marked on the inside by defect, shortage, finiteness, and guilt (Congar 1965a).

The church is an *ecclesia mixta,* a mixed church of saints and sinners, as was already formulated by the Fathers (Congar 1970, 14-15). This mixed character is not to be conceived as that of a church of both saints and sinners, but as that of a church in which all the members are characterized by saintly and sinful features. All of us are sinners, as Augustine put it in reference to Romans 3:23 and 5:18 (Rahner 1966, 442). This fact also applies to the ministry. They, too, are saintly and sinful at the same time *(simul justus et peccator).* The more influential their position in the church is, the more they harm the sanctity of the church (Congar 1968, 83-84, 108-19).

One cannot escape the insight that the church itself is sinful. Some people, however, have a different opinion. Individuals are indeed both saintly and sinful at the same time, according to this view, but this refers only to sin in the church and not the sin of the church. By linking sin exclusively to persons, one can give it a place within the church and at the same time claim that the church itself is holy. This view also lies in the decree on ecumenism of Vatican II (Berkouwer 1970, 163). According to it, the church remains subject to sin in its members *(in membris suis)* in its earthly pilgrimage (*Unitatis Redintegratio* 3).

Yet this approach falls short of the actual situation in which the church finds itself. Not only the persons in the church are to blame, but also the church itself. In its entirety it is continually below par, which was drawn up in the perspective of the people of God. One cannot point out places in the church that have not been injured or corrupted, according to Haarsma (1967, 333-35). For sinners really belong to the church; they are not excluded from the formation of the church. They are in the lap of the church *(in ecclesiae sinu),* as Vatican II puts it (*Lumen Gentium* 14). This marks the quality of the church itself. In patristic times the church is sometimes depicted as an adulterous woman or as a whore. It is sometimes compared to the fallen Jerusalem, Sodom and Gomorrah, Tyre and Sidon. Only proceeding from the sinful quality of the church itself can it say of itself: holy and at the same time always called upon to purify itself *(sancta simul et semper purificanda),* according to Vatican II in the constitution about the church (*Lumen Gentium* 8). With this statement the Catholic Church has finally well nigh literally made reformatory care for the *ecclesia semper reformanda* its own (Schillebeeckx 1989, 213).

Chapter 12

Mission

We placed the identity of the church in the context of secularization (chapter 9). After that we looked at its core, which is made up of the religious convictions (chapter 10). These convictions find their orientation in the vision of the church as people of God (chapter 11).

The vision of the church cannot be viewed separately from its mission. What obviously follows the question of how the church regards itself is what moves the church, what it strives after. We have already been confronted with this question in our treatment of the church as the people of God, when it became clear that the church as the people of God had to be understood as the church of the poor.

The discovery of the mission of the church dates from this century. Before that, mission was only brought into connection with the spreading of the Christian faith in non-Christian regions. This task was exercised by the apostolic chair in the Catholic Church and by special societies in the Protestant churches. A change came about during the course of this century culminating, in 1961, in the declaration of the World Council of Churches in New Delhi, in which mission was viewed as the heart of the church. Its counterpart was the constitution about the church of Vatican II. In it mission is founded in the church as sacrament (*Lumen Gentium* 1). One no longer spoke of church and mission, but of the mission of the church (Bosch 1991, 372).

It is important to determine further the core of mission because more than a dozen interpretations are to be found in the literature (Bosch 1991, 368-510). Besides that, it is important to scrutinize the conditions under which mission can be realized. Without insight into these conditions there is the threat of wishful thinking.

We now wish to deal with both matters (core and conditions) in conjunction with each other. This will be done by involving the term *movement* in our reflection. On the one hand, this term can serve to clarify the core of the mission: the church on the move within the perspective of the kingdom of God. On the other hand, it can provide insight into the conditions under which mission can be brought about. There is also another important point. Using the term *movement* links mission with the Jesus movement that underlies the church and of which it may and must be witness. The church's duty is to preserve the memory of the Jesus movement and to continue it as *sequela Jesu*.

In this chapter we will deal with the following questions: (1) What does the term *movement* imply? (2) What is the Jesus movement made up of? (3) How was the Jesus movement given shape in the first communities? And (4) What is the meaning today when we use the term *Jesus movement* as a religious code for the church?

(1) Movement

It seems a trivial remark to begin with, but movements rise in certain periods, lead a shorter or longer existence, and then disappear again. However trivial it is, the insight into the factors that underlie the rise, continuance, and fall of movements is an entirely different matter. There are all sorts of opinions about this.

Rise of movements

One can generally distinguish four theories in the literature that explain the rise of movements. Some authors believe that they exist at right angles to each other, while others believe that they complement each other. The insights that lie in these theories are greatly relevant to (religious) movements within and outside the church as well as to the church as a movement itself.

According to the *deprivation theory,* the rise of movements can be understood proceeding from the feeling people have that something is missing in their situation. Several types of deprivation can be distinguished: physical (malnutrition), economic (unemployment), political (oppression), social (isolation), and cultural (loss of meaning). The latter can be subdivided into psychic, moral, and religious aspects since one can experience a lack of psychic strength, moral power, or religious depth (Glock 1973). Proceeding from these types of lack, people develop an equal number of movements, at least if they have the right ideas available. These ideas serve as vehicles to adequately verbalize their lack and to define the desired change. They therefore have an expressive and a utopian function. Without such ideas, movements would not come about (Schreuder 1981).

Proceeding from the perspective of the deprivation theory, one can point out a great number of movements within the church. In the churchly basic communities in Latin America, the endeavor to remove the economic, political, social, and cultural deprivation plays an obvious role (Boff 1987a). In Western society there are also quite a few movements in which the church participates directly or indirectly. We can mention the Third World movement, the Fourth World movement, the peace movement, the women's movement, and the environmental movement as examples. However, we can also point out specifically religious movements that have arisen because of some kind of religious deprivation. Thus it appears that participants in the Jesus movement feel attracted by the movement because of social, psychic, moral, and religious deprivation (Mauss & Petersen 1973). Similar conclusions were drawn in the research done on religious movements in the Netherlands. Thus, the Moral Rearmament movement initially wanted to improve the spiritual atmosphere in the Netherlands Reformed Church because the members felt it to be superficial and without content (De Loor 1986). And as far as the new religious movements in the Netherlands are concerned, the members of these movements appear to be fully alive to the notion of spiritual emptiness of the secularized culture. At the same time they display a strong urge to belong to something socially (Van der Lans 1981).

The so-called *elite theory* starts on the other side, as it were. It bases itself not on the notion that deprivation brings people together in a movement, but on the presence of an elite who have authority. This opens people's eyes, inspires them, and shows the way to a solution to all the wrongs in which people are involved. This theory does not deny the presence of deprivation, for it is this deprivation that has to be dealt with. However, the elite, not deprivation, are the drive of the movement. Without an elite, a movement does not exist (Etzioni 1968).

Indeed, the elite play a prominent role in all sorts of movements, also within the church. The emancipation and renewal movement in the Catholic Church in the Netherlands cannot be understood without the contribution of the elite. Already at the beginning of this century this manifested itself in several organizations of Catholic intellectuals, like the Thijmgenootschap, founded in 1904, and the Radboudstichting, founded in 1905. It was even more clearly expressed in the contribution of Catholic intellectuals to the renewal of the church and pastoral care in the decades that followed. It concerned areas like mental health care, marriage and family, ecumenism, and the typical identity of Catholic institutions (Simons & Winkeler 1987). The Dutch Pastoral Council from 1968 to 1970 is unimaginable without the contribution of the intellectual elite (Goddijn 1973, 149ff.).

The *resource mobilization theory* is very close to the elite theory. No more than the elite theory does it see deprivation as the dominant factor in the rise of a movement. However, it places less emphasis on the elite than on the presence of a close organizational network of groups (resources), which stimulates people to assemble together and march in the streets (mobilization). Such an organization not only contains a network of groups that are well tuned to each other and are adequately coordinated, but the tasks set before them are carried out professionally. There is a hierarchy of aims that have to be achieved successively. These are structured from low to high. In this the aim is constantly focused on the most achievable and therefore the relatively lower goals because the achievement of aims gives a feeling of success. This is necessary for the survival of the movement, for the participants in the movement — according to this theory — make cost-benefit analyses: what they invest in the movement has to lead to results. For this purpose regularly recurring (small) successes are of eminent importance.

Proceeding from the perspective of the mobilization theory, interesting light is shed on the activities of the church. This is particularly the case when new initiatives are taken, such as the building of a new church, the establishment of an association, the beginning of a new group, or creatively taking advantage of the social environment with campaigns. In all this one can recognize the outlines of a movement. The (scanty) manpower and financial means are continuously brought into action in new places again and again to meet the new requirements; therefore, it is of importance that (small) successes are regularly achieved. A large number of ordinary processes within the church can be made more clear in a surprising manner by proceeding from this idea (Duffhues 1991). The church is a church on the move (Van Bilsen 1962).

The *interaction theory* can be viewed as a mediating theory in comparison to the previous ones. On the people's side, it bases itself on deprivation. The theory assumes that people are in search of a solution. On the side of the movement, it bases itself on the existence of a kind of organization that gives opportunities for the collective awareness of deprivation and for the campaign to remove it. Because potential members come into contact (interaction) with actual members, a process of information, transformation, and conversion arises. This may lead to the joining of the movement (De Loor 1986, 240; Van der Lans 1981).

It is not a foregone conclusion which of the theories is right about the rise of movements. Rather, they are to be regarded as interesting hypotheses, which have to be tested separately using concrete cases. The view that several elements from these theories may well go together has been demonstrated by the movement of Moral Rearmament (De Loor 1986).

Continuance of movements

It is not self-evident that once movements have arisen they continue to exist for a shorter or longer period of time. One is right in being surprised about this: Why do they not disappear instead of continuing to exist? Several factors are involved, both cultural and structural.

The cultural factors have to do with the system of ideas that gives wings to the notion of being liberated from the feelings of deprivation and the inherent ideals attached. As long as these ideas remain relevant for the participants in the movement, they keep the movement going. If this no longer is the case, after a certain period of time an ideological vacuum may occur. This compels people to find new sources for their ideas and to reformulate their form and content. It can be necessary to adapt the ideas to the changed circumstances and/or to reduce the goals that they contain to lower, more achievable proportions. In addition, it may be necessary to subject the movement to a process of shifting of aims. If this succeeds, it contributes to the continuance of the movement. Imagination then rules. If this does not succeed, then it can lead to a serious crisis in the movement.

An example of the latter case may be found in the Catholic pillarization and depillarization in the Netherlands. The Catholic pillarization can be seen as the institutional composition of the movement of the Catholic population group to remove its economic, political, social, and cultural deprivation. The ideas that gave direction to this were drawn from the neo-Thomistic doctrine of human beings and society. When this doctrine was cracking at the seams in the sixties and the intellectuals were incapable of closing the ideological gap, the pillar started to totter. The depillarization had started (Duffhues et al. 1985; Simons & Winkeler 1987).

The structural factors have to do with informal and formal organization. An organization continues to exist on the condition that the informal networks it contains remain intact. In this the social relations between family members, friends, acquaintances, neighbors, and colleagues are of crucial importance. These meet the need to belong and foster a sense of community. Without such social-emotional patterns, it is hard for a movement to survive.

Besides the informal organization, there is also a formal one. It is made up of the coordination of activities, the formalization of tasks and responsibilities, and the exercising of leadership. This formal organization is characterized by a gradual systematization of the legitimization of campaigns and ideas; the development of a certain kind of esprit de corps; the recruitment of leaders, staff, and members; the spreading of information; the development of programs and projects; the contacts with other organizations and nonmembers; and the raising of funds. The development of a "social movement organization," as it is called in the literature, is essential for the continuance of a movement. Even if it did not function as the flywheel of the movement, as is suggested by the mobilization theory, it still is a necessary condition for the survival of the movement (De Loor 1986). For that matter, such a movement organization also holds a certain ambivalence within it. On the one hand, it is the guarantee of the continued existence of the movement; but on the other hand, it can contribute to the fossilization of the movement, as we shall see shortly.

Fall of movements

As we mentioned, movements not only arise and exist, but they also disappear. They do not have eternal life; they are not immortal. The question is which factors contribute to the fall. Several theories are in circulation about this too. The first three link with the deprivation, elite, and mobilization theories that explain the rise of movements. The fourth contains a perspective that is separate from the above.

The first is the *emancipation theory*. This implies that the movement ceases to exist when the deprivation is removed and the movement has achieved its aim. This applies to the labor movement, for instance, in the social-economic field, for the movement of full suffrage in the field of politics, and for the Catholic scout movement (formerly "the movement," for short) in the pedagogical field. This does not (yet) apply to other movements, such as the women's movement and the environmental movement, and the equal rights movement in the United States and South Africa.

In this way the phenomenon of pillarization and depillarization, which we just discussed, can be explained. Proceeding from the emancipation theory, yet another light is shed upon matters. Sectarianism can be viewed as the attempt of certain population groups (particularly Catholics and Reformed Protestants) to regain their lost ground societally. When this process of emancipation was completed in the sixties, the removal of traditional religious barriers began (Thurlings 1978; Righart 1986).

Proceeding from the emancipation theory, we can not only explain why movements in church circles disappear, but also why others continue to exist. Their aim has not yet been achieved. An example of this is Pax Christi. This movement continues to exist because its point of departure lies in the experience that the world is still far removed from justice and peace (deprivation). It cannot be denied, however, that besides deprivation elements, mobilization and movement organization elements play a role. It is precisely as an organization that Pax Christi mobilizes certain people in certain places with an eye to certain achievable aims.

Besides the emancipation theory, the *elite theory* can also be mentioned as an explanation, albeit in the opposite direction. As we said, it implies that a movement comes about if an elite guides it. Now we can add that the movement will only continue to exist as long as the elite wishes it and makes the means for it available. If the elite sees nothing more in it and withdraws or ceases to exist itself — by whatever cause — the movement is finished (Etzioni 1968).

Again this can be illustrated by means of the renewal movement in the Dutch Catholic church. When the intellectual elite called it a day in the sixties, this movement lost its intellectual and creative base. Partially because of this, it got into difficulties (Goddijn 1973, 149ff.; Van der Ven 1985a, 14; Simons & Winkeler 1987).

Yet another explanation for the fall of movements can be drawn from the *mobilization theory,* albeit again in the opposite direction. If the resources display a descending line and the financial and personal means drop, the movement itself enters the danger zone. If the organizational network crumbles because of these and other factors, the movement grinds to a halt.

Separate from the theories mentioned so far, there is a fourth theory that explains the fall of movements. It proceeds, however, from an entirely different perspective. It does not deal with the disappearance of the social formation that was embodied by the movement, but with this formation becoming stronger and stronger until the movement as a movement disappears. The social formation in this theory takes on such strong organizational shapes that the movement as a movement is suffocated. The movement organization overpowers the movement and crushes it to death. Now we have arrived at the *deterministic oligarchy theory* of Michels.

According to this theory, movements replace the ideals they have found to be too radical after a time by more realistic aims. At the same time members' attention shifts from the outside world, which was the initial focus of change, to the inner world and to the movement's own doings. This is coupled with the development of an organization on its own, including the processes of formalization, bureaucratization, and professionalization. Eventually, this leads to a centralization of the decision making, which results in the establishment of a small group of people who make the decisions. According to this iron law, in due course an oligarchy comes out of every movement. With this development, the movement as a movement signs its own death warrant.

One can see the oligarchy theory as an expression of the ambivalence that is inherent in every movement organization. It can supply the movement with the continuance it needs, but it can also fossilize or suffocate it (Duffhues 1991, 24). For that matter such a fossilized system can itself provoke a new movement (Lammers 1984, 115).

It is not certain that the theories that try to explain the fall of movements are mutually exclusive. It is possible to imagine a combination of several elements from these theories. Thus it is obvious that the achievement of the emancipation goal leads to a reduction of the availability of resources and of the engagement of the elite.

With this body of concepts it is possible to understand the movement that rose up around Jesus and was given shape in the first communities in the New Testament (sub 2 and 3). In addition, it is possible to clarify the meaning of the church as a Jesus movement (sub 4).

(2) Jesus movement

In the last few decades exegetes have gained more of an eye for the movement in the New Testament. Jesus' conduct, his attraction for people, the gathering of pupils, and the group formation around him: all this can be conceived of as a movement. In this we can discern the movement of wandering charismatics, the Pharisaic movement, and the Jesus movement itself. It makes sense to stop and look at this more closely.

Movement of wandering charismatics

Jesus' life and works predominantly took place in the country. Jerusalem did form the scene of his suffering and death; however, his daily preaching, parables, disputes, table companionship, laying on of hands, and healings took place in rural rather than in urban areas. He moved from one place to another, drawing people's attention, surrounding himself with followers, and raising up smaller or larger multitudes.

Jesus was a preacher who went from place to place, just as other preachers did. He belonged to what are known as wandering charismatics. What they had in common was that they gave voice to and received approval from people without possessions, without a roof above their heads, without any family ties. In short, from pariahs. In this atmosphere of wandering preachers, ethnic radicalism and eschatological expectations regarding the coming of the Son of man or Messiah could assume large proportions. Along with this, people were often opposed to the established powers in Jerusalem. Not only the caste of high priests of the temple and all other groups that lived off the temple had to suffer for it, but also the wealthy class of Sadducees, who were, moreover, seen as collaborators with the Romans (Theissen 1977; 1979).

Pharisaic movement

This movement is the context in which Jesus' life and works took place. Within this context, he was especially close to the Pharisaic movement without actually merging into it. The Pharisees were caught up in a battle with the Sadducees. The Pharisees were the party of the poor and oppressed of the country, while the Sadducees came from the groups of the powerful and rich of the cities. The Pharisees felt they were connected to the synagogues, which were spread across the country and attracted many people. The Sadducees were connected to the temple of Jerusalem, which functioned less and less as the center of Jewish spirituality. The Pharisees were represented by their scribes and rabbis, who had no power whatsoever. The Sadducees were represented by their own leaders and the high priests, who bathed in luxury. The Pharisees had an "elastic" view to a certain extent, because they had their own actualizing interpretation of the oral Torah or Mishnah next to the Torah as the basis for their doctrine and life. The Sadducees, however, restricted themselves to the Torah only. Against this background, the Pharisees understandably laid their emphasis on the combination of liturgy and social justice. They denounced the ritual devotion to duty in the temple without doing justice as false piety and hypocrisy. For the kingdom of God could not be accomplished, in their view, as long as injustice continued unimpeded.

Jesus followed in this line. He, too, took strong action against the rulers and powerful who oppressed the people. He, too, condemned the temple cult, because it did not go together with care for the "least of these who are members of my family." He was also attracted to the intimate experience of God that lay in the Pharisaic religious consciousness and in which God is personally near to his people and to each individual. Partly proceeding from this tradition, he felt intimately connected to God, his "Abba."

How is it, then, that so many disputes occur with the Pharisees in the New Testament? Where do the anti-Pharisaic statements come from? This cannot be explained by proceeding from Jesus' historic action. These are texts that have to be understood from the postwar period after the Jewish war from 66 to 72. In that time Pharisaic rabbinism fossilized, leading to all sorts of discussions within Judaism itself, in which several Jewish groups, among them Jewish Christians, took part. The statements, therefore, stem from Jewish internal criticism within which the Jewish Christians played their own role. By degrees this led to a cooling and hardening of the relationship between Pharisees and Christians (Schillebeeckx 1985, 23-32; 1989, 169-70).

Jesus movement

Even though Jesus is close to the Pharisaic movement, the Jesus movement itself does not merge into that of the Pharisees, since it displays a radicalization and transcendence. For Jesus accepted those people who had been religiously and societally marginalized and were considered outcasts. The kingdom of God could only be realized where salvation was given to all, without considering the person, even without a religious consideration of the person, according to his message. Therefore Jesus traveled around without any prejudice, doing good, granting boons to all, healing anybody, joining at the table of those who were shunned, speaking to those who had been found guilty or even sinful, and giving forgiveness to those who had been cast off religiously. The movement's deepest base was of a religious nature. It lay in the notion that God, not human beings, is the one who brings about the reconciliation of all people in his kingdom of justice and love. Jesus embodied in his person, his life, and his works the unconditional acceptance and becoming whole of all humanity through God. The parables of the lost sheep, the lost coin, the lost son, the Pharisee and the publican, and the workers of the eleventh hour bore witness to this. Jesus took away the low self-contempt of people he met. He drew up the leper. He made people laugh. He brought the people together in the brotherly and sisterly sharing of the bread and fish. In short, through his actions Jesus did pioneering work in the universal reconciliation of the kingdom of God. He was the promised Messiah (Schillebeeckx 1974).

In Jesus' actions everything revolved around God. In the language of his time, it was "the kingdom of God." In this time it was not customary to define God directly as "God." This God who allows the sun to shine on both the good and evil and who excludes no one was a dissident God for official Judaism of the time. His being dissident was based on his absolute freedom, which broke through all rules and procedures. Proceeding from this absolute freedom, he was a continual surprise as a dissident God. The Jesus movement was borne by this surprise of divine gratuity. The first messianic communities are characterized by belief in this dissident God of Jesus (Schillebeeckx 1989, 130-41).

As a wandering preacher, Jesus appeared to attract people and started to develop a movement. He struck a sensitive chord with his proclamation of the kingdom of God. He touched the souls of his fellow Jewish people. However, he did introduce some emphases of his own. He dissociated himself from the the Sadducees, whose ideas about the kingdom of God consisted of dealing with the Roman rulers and making compromises with an end to accomplishing as much political and religious autonomy as possible for Israel. He also dissociated himself from the quietism of the Essenes, who were waiting in peace and quiet for the right moment in the future to establish God's kingdom by force. He also turned his back on the revolutionary groups, to which the Zealots belonged, who were in favor of immediate revolution through violence. Jesus had the greatest affinity with the Pharisaic view, in which the kingdom of God was depicted as something that had already begun but that took place in secret, and that has to be taken onto one's shoulders and borne as a yoke. It exists in doing deeds of social justice for the service of the poor and oppressed, especially for widows, orphans, and foreigners. Without this justice, the kingdom of God will not come into its own. For that, *metanoia,* which opens people up to follow the Torah or law and *halacha* (tradition of interpretation) is necessary. But Jesus radicalizes the view of the Pharisees, as we mentioned. He proclaims the good news to the cripple, the outcast, and the poor as well. Moreover, he not only proclaims the kingdom of God, but he displays it in his own person, his actions, his healings, and his table companionship. He gives visible and tangible shape to it in his life and works. He performs the praxis of the kingdom of God. This is what raised up the people and stirred them (Sandmel 1969; Rhoads 1976).

(3) Jesus movement in the first communities

The Jesus movement developed into group formation around Jesus. Among the Jews who spoke Hebrew (Aramaic), this movement led to groups that can be called "messianic communities." Among Diaspora Jews, who spoke Greek, groups were formed that can be defined as "pneumatic communities." This does not mean that a clear distinction can be made between these messianic and pneumatic communities, for we are dealing with the same presence of Jesus in these communities: during his lifetime as the messiah Jesus and after his death living in his Spirit. The crucial question is in what sense the Jesus movement is given shape after that, in the Pauline and post-Pauline communities.

Messianic communities

The people who joined Jesus in the first wave of the Jesus movement felt themselves attracted to radical ethics and religion for their time. The ethically and religiously radical ideas that Jesus proclaimed in alignment with the Pharisaic movement adequately expressed their feelings of deprivation as well as their utopian desires. In the Jesus movement, they were drawn along by the dissident God whom Jesus preached about and embodied in his own person and actions.

Proceeding from the world of thought of the Jews was a strong suggestion to regard Jesus as the Messiah. In the Jewish tradition of the day, however, there were several messianic notions. The first involves the messianic eschatological prophet. This figure was regarded to have been the one anointed by God, on whom God's Spirit rested, and who would bring the glad message of God's lordship and with it the liberation of Zion. The second notion goes back to national-dynastic Davidic messianism. This movement was aimed at the restoration of the royal house of David. In this an eschatological undercurrent is present, because it was hoped that the messiah from the line of David would bring definite liberation to Israel. The third notion can be defined with the term "prophetic-sapiential Davidian messianism." This stems from the Wisdom Literature, in which the messiah had the characteristics of the wise man Solomon and would act with authority because of his wisdom and bring peace. The fourth notion has to do with the expectation of two messianic figures in Qumran: a priestly messiah from Aaron and a royal messiah from Israel, who would merge into one figure during the period of Roman occupation. The messiah was seen as the expected priest-king. Finally, there is the notion of the "son of man." This came from an entirely different tradition and originally had nothing to do with messianism. The messiah was seen as a historic figure with salvation-historical significance from eschatological features. The son of man, however, was conceived of as a heavenly figure. He was regarded as a heavenly judge for the godless and a figure of salvation for the holy rest of the pious. Later the figure of the son of man was combined with that of the national, Davidic messiah (Schillebeeckx 1974, 359-85).

When it became clear to the groups around Jesus that they had to regard him as the messiah, this entire world of notions was playing a part in the background. However, it had a meaning of its own. The emphasis came to rest on the notion of the messianic eschatological prophet. He was to be sent to bring the glad message to the poor, to help the unfortunate, to liberate the prisoners, and to proclaim the redemption of those in shackles (Isa. 61:1; Luke 4:18; 7:22). This prophetic messianism was dominant, even though certain elements from other messianic notions were combined with it in a transformatory sense. Thus there were some communities that connected the dynastic-Davidic messiah figure to it, without, however, taking on its narrow national meaning, which was rejected because it was in complete contradiction with Jesus' life and actions. They were interested in a universal interpretation. From the resistance of Jesus to this national-dynastic meaning, we can also understand the secret of the Messiah in the Gospel of Mark. It is the expression of Jesus' reservations about the messiah title in Davidic-dynastic terms and the redefinition made by him in an eschatological-prophetical shape. With this redefinition, elements from sapiential-Davidic messianism were also useful. Characteristics from the wise and peaceful figure of Solomon were imputed to the eschatological prophet. It is against this background that Jesus is seen as the anointed messiah, Christ: "Jesus, who is called the Messiah" (Matt. 1:16; 27:17). This religious-functional name gradually became his proper name: Jesus Christ (Schillebeeckx 1974, 386-422).

Pneumatic communities

The first wave of the Jesus movement was especially made up of Jews who spoke Hebrew (Aramaic). The second wave, however, was centered around Diaspora Jews, who spoke Greek. The Hebrew (Aramaic)-speaking Jews felt attracted to the movement of Jesus through the experience of the historic Jesus. The power of attraction for the Greek-speaking Jews in the Diaspora did not lie in the personal meeting with Jesus — for they had never had contact with him. It lay in the experience of the presence of the Spirit of Jesus. In the awareness of these followers, God had not left Jesus at his death, but turned him into a life-creating and life-giving Spirit (1 Cor. 15:45). Jesus was present in this group of followers in his Spirit. One can define these groups as pneumatic communities.

Several pneumatic groups populated the Mediterranean coast at the time; however, the Christian communities distinguished themselves from other pneumatic groups through their specific belief in the presence of Jesus in his Spirit. The intense experience of life from and in the Spirit of Jesus was central to them. These communities lived through the Spirit and according to the Spirit. The members of these communities therefore called themselves spiritual people (Gal. 6:1). The foundation of this was the baptism in the Spirit. All those baptized in these communities formed the one pneumatical people of God. They were fulfilled by the Spirit. This also applied to the community in Jerusalem, for that matter. The pupils were so full of the Spirit that they seemed drunk, according to Peter's speech in Acts 2. For them the prophecy of Joel has been fulfilled; the Spirit has been poured out over them: sons and daughters prophesy, young men see visions, and old men dream dreams (Acts 2:14-22).

The religious union that Jesus himself had founded continued to exist in these communities in an anamnetic-pneumatic sense. In the memory handed down (anamnetic) Jesus was present in his Spirit (pneumatic) for his followers. This anamnetic-pneumatic experience was the basis for fundamental freedom, equality, and solidarity in these communities. Thus it is written in the charter of freedom in the

Epistle to the Galatians: "As many of you as were baptized into Christ have clothed yourselves with Christ. There is no longer Jew or Greek, there is no longer slave or free, there is no longer male and female; for all of you are one in Christ Jesus" (Gal. 3:27-28). In this an egalitarian view of the community as brotherhood and sisterhood comes to the fore. For every kind of discrimination is removed: of Jew against Gentile, of male against female, of the free against slaves. These communities form a prophetic-pneumatic community, founded in the baptism in the Spirit.

This baptism in the Spirit could lead to the notion that the fullness of the salvation promised had already been realized. The communities were sometimes fully alive to an actualized eschatology. The aspect of future salvation in the kingdom of God disappeared completely because of this. This sometimes led to an abundance of ecstatic processes such as healings and glossolalia, which Paul was later to correct (Schillebeeckx 1985, 42-47).

Pauline and post-Pauline communities

We have seen that the messianic and pneumatic communities were characterized by the enthusiasm of the Jesus movement. But how was this for the Pauline and post-Pauline communities? Can we still talk of a messianic and pneumatic élan? Or did the Jesus movement light on calmer water? Is there really any Jesus movement left?

For Paul the Spirit formed the foundation of the life of the community. He spoke to the community of Corinth as follows: "Do you not know that you are God's temple and that God's Spirit dwells in you?" (1 Cor. 3:16). At the same time, this Spirit was seen as the Spirit of Christ (Rom. 8:9), of the Lord (2 Cor. 3:18). He added the following for the Galatians: "And because you are children, God has sent the Spirit of his Son into our hearts, crying, 'Abba! Father!' " (Gal. 4:6). The most striking expression of the Spirit as the basis of the community is found in the first epistle to the Corinthians. According to Paul there is no community without the activity of the Spirit. In this activity the community finds its living and unifying principle: "Now there are varieties of gifts, but the same Spirit; and there are varieties of service, but the same Lord; and there are varieties of activities, but it is the same God who activates all of them in everyone. To each is given the manifestation of the Spirit for the common good. To one is given through the Spirit the utterance of wisdom, and to another the utterance of knowledge according to the same Spirit, to another faith by the same Spirit, to another gifts of healing by the one Spirit, to another the working of miracles, to another prophecy, to another the discernment of spirits, to another various kinds of tongues, to another the interpretation of tongues. All these are activated by one and the same Spirit, who allots to each one individually just as the Spirit chooses" (1 Cor. 12:4-11).

Despite this strong pneumatological foundation of the community, there are traces of a certain kind of regulation to be found in the leadership Paul gives. We will make use of a term that we introduced earlier: the Jesus movement begins to display the features of a *movement organization*.

Now the relationship between the pre-Pauline and the Pauline communities (including the post-Pauline ones) has to approached subtly. Some pre-Pauline communities display hardly any or only a very low degree of organization. On the other hand, others have a relatively high degree. This immediately strikes us when we look at matters like the social relations, the structures of authority, and the processes of admittance and expulsion. Some communities are more hard lined and social-ethically radical; others are more flexible. Smaller communities give rein to their members; larger ones take regulatory measures. Communities that are under great influence from wandering Christian charismatics place the emphasis on baptism in the Spirit, while more sedentary communities place it on baptism with water as a (verifiable) sign of baptism in the Spirit (Theissen 1977, 21-26).

This variety has to be kept in mind to prevent the too-easy setting up of pre-Pauline communities opposite Pauline ones. Nevertheless, a certain trend in the direction of movement organization in the Pauline communities cannot be denied. This can be clarified as follows.

The first thing that strikes us in the Pauline literature is that the communities in the cities are made up of representatives from the broad middle class. The upper class cannot be found there, nor can the lowest one. One cannot speak of a typical rural deprivation, such as characterized the first wave of the Jesus movement (Schillebeeckx 1985, 70). In general it holds true that social and religious movements in the first century exercised an attraction to the middle class in particular (Theissen 1977, 34-46).

Further, it appears that life in the communities was characterized by a certain amount of discipline. One sees Paul slowing down the pneumatic movement of the first generations to a certain extent. He corrected the realized eschatology that was among them, proceeding from his own parousia eschatology: he shifted the emphasis from "already" to "not yet" concerning the coming of Jesus (Schillebeeckx 1974, 328-58). With this he restored the irrational ecstasy found in some pneumatic communities to surveyable proportions. He was afraid that it would lead to chaos (Schillebeeckx 1985, 44).

This applied to prophesying and speaking in tongues in particular. Here there were two matters at stake. In the first place, Paul was concerned about the image of the communities in the eyes of his Roman-Hellenistic fellow citizens. He wanted to prevent them from being scared by the irrational behavior of the Christians. In the second place, however, Paul wanted to guard the communities from falling to pieces. There was a danger that individuals and small groups who prided themselves on their talents of prophesy and glossolalia were going to make this a criterion for the real possession of the Spirit. Because of this, all kinds of disintegrating processes could arise in the communities. That is why he wanted to restrict and restrain the glossolalia (Theissen 1983, 269-340).

Not only disciplining but also structuring the organization characterized these communities. Doctrinal teaching and disciplinary instructions were issued; conflicts were dealt with and solved in an orderly fashion; leaders performed their duties of proclamation, admonition, and guidance. This did not involve a hierarchical organization structure, as the church later determined. The ministry in the Pauline and post-Pauline communities in the New Testament is not an *ordo* in the sense of the Roman rank of senators, as the church was later to use this term. There was functional leadership for the development of the community (Schillebeeckx 1985, 50-72). We will return to this later (chapter 16).

Finally, one cannot deny a certain tuning in to the societal context. Paul adapted his communities to their environments to a certain degree, albeit that the personal religious-critical point remained intact. As a consequence, there is tension between two poles in this tuning: adaptation and identity. Economic, political, and social aspects were involved. The economic aspect has to do with slavery. It belonged to the societal system of the time. At the same, however, the community lived by the Christian charter of freedom: "There is no longer slave or free" (Gal. 3:28). That is why Paul instructed the communities to tolerate the tension between freedom for slaves in the communities and slavery in the world. The political aspect refers to the relation of the Christian community to the state authority. Paul rejected any kind of revolution toward the state authority. With this, for that matter, Paul continued the tradition of the Jews from the Diaspora, which entailed civic loyalty, albeit under rejection of the cult of state authority (Schillebeeckx 1977a, 526-27). The social aspect involves the division of roles between men and women and the discrimination that lies in this for women. Paul set men above women. He cannot be cleared of religious ideologization when he founds the subordination of women in the subordination of men to Christ and the subordination of Christ to God (1 Cor. 11:3). One can ask oneself what led Paul to this ideologization. Some authors say that Paul used the subordination of women to emphasize the difference between the sexes, in order to avert the danger of homosexuality (Theissen 1983, 161-80). Whatever may be the case, Paul added a fundamental relativization to his religious ideology: "But if anyone is disposed to be contentious, we have no such custom, nor do the churches of God" (1 Cor. 11:16). What strikes us here is the word *custom.* According to Schillebeeckx, "they are therefore respectful customs. . . . The theologisations of Paul should not be taken to mean more than he meant them himself" (Schillebeeckx 1977a, 540).

In the disciplining, structuring, and tuning of the communities to the societal context, we can trace features of what we earlier defined as a movement organization. In such an organization the ambivalence that we discussed earlier in a general sense is recognizable. It holds a certain tension. On the one hand, one can ask oneself to what extent the Pauline and post-Pauline organization provides the necessary conditions for the continuity of the Jesus movement. On the other, to what extent it fixates them and strips them of the character of a movement. Here we do not remove the tension as if one could solve it. It makes more sense to clarify the task of the Jesus movement for the church of today proceeding from this tension.

(4) Church as Jesus movement

Now we want to try to expose the meaning of the term *Jesus movement* for the church of today, by conceiving of it as a religious code for the church. Hence the title: church as Jesus movement. The question is, of course, whether this title does not contain a contradiction in terms. Are not the Jesus movement and the church opposite to each other? The sharpness of this question is not blunted if we are to realize that the church is not the Jesus movement, but can be considered as the Jesus movement paradigmatically (epistemological principle; see Introduction). Does the paradigm of the Jesus movement really fit the church? As Alfred Loisy said: Jesus did proclaim the coming of the kingdom of God, but what actually came is the church (Loisy 1903, 153). We cannot escape defining the limits and possibilities of the use of the code *church as Jesus movement* after having clarified its functions.

Functions

Earlier we mentioned three functions of religious codes: the cognitive, emotive, and conative functions (chapter 7 sub 2). Now we will apply this distinction to the code *church as Jesus movement*.

Cognitive

The religious information that lies in this code has to do with the origin of the Jesus movement in Jesus himself. It is a movement around his person that issued from him. After his death, this movement did not cease to exist. Jesus is present in the church in an anamnetic-pneumatic sense. Anamnetic means that the church keeps his memory alive. Memory is an active, vital category. It not only refers passively to the past, but it also involves putting the awareness of what occurred in the past, in a way that allows it to act upon the present. Anamnetic-pneumatic means that the Spirit of Jesus is actively present in this memory. He arouses, stimulates, and strengthens this memory. In this memory the Spirit creates the church on the move.

In this memory the church is not only active with the Jesus movement of the past, but from there it is also aimed at the future. The Jesus movement is focused on the messianic period in the perspective of the liberative lordship of God. It brings the perspective of liberation for all those who are weighed down by suffering and distress. It implies the promise of reconciliation within it: of each person with him- or herself, of all people with each other, of the living among themselves and the living together with the dead, and of all humanity with the whole of nature. It orients itself toward the great metaphors of the eschatological final completion: the resurrection of the body, the new city, the kingdom of God, the new heaven and the new earth (Schillebeeckx 1989, 152).

Emotive

In these metaphors that indicate the destination of the Jesus movement lie the desire and yearning of humankind for becoming whole in and from God. They form the expression of the hope for wholeness that will only proceed from the parousia image "Maranatha" ("Come, Lord Jesus"). With this the emotive function combines two aspects.

The first aspect is of an expressive nature. The Jesus movement gives expression to the emotiveness of the individual as well as the emotiveness of people in relation to each other. It gives it a destination. This involves not only the circle of friends and acquaintances but also all those who announce themselves as fellow believers, at hand and far away, in the present and past, among the living and the dead. It focuses individual and collective emotional energy at a goal that answers the deepest aspirations of the individual and all people together: God, everything to everyone.

The second aspect is of a receptive nature. The achievement of this goal cannot be planned, predicted, or commanded. It demands an active-receptive attitude, which is nourished from prayer. In this we may repeat what Jesus taught us: "Our Father, your kingdom come."

Conative

The Jesus movement also implies a mission. This mission turns the church away from itself and makes it center its attention outside itself. It turns the church inside out.

This means that it is of importance that the church looks beyond itself and its own structure and organization, as it were, each time the suffering and distress of humanity demands it. It has to consider itself a movement organization that has only one aim: not only to move out of the way of the Jesus movement but to actively stimulate it. This requires a sharp eye for the suffocating and fossilizing factors that are present in the church organization, particularly for the effect of oligarchization described by Michels. Where the church neglects this mission, it corrupts the Jesus movement and with that itself (Congar 1968).

What has to keep the church going as Jesus movement is the restless search for ways of liberation of the "least of these who are members of my family," among whom Jesus himself is present. In addition to this, we have to answer the question: "Lord, when was it that we saw you hungry and gave you food, or thirsty and gave you something to drink? And when was it that we saw you a stranger and welcomed you, or naked and gave you clothing? And when was it that we saw you sick or in prison and visited you?" (Matt. 25:37-39).

Limits

However essential these functions may be, we have not yet clarified the conditions under which the code *church as Jesus movement* can effectively be realized. There are several limitations that cannot be underestimated as well as a number of opportunities and challenges. Both involve the mission of justice and solidarity, which lies in the Jesus movement.

The first limit lies in the relationship between the church and present society. It implies that the societal power of the church to realize justice and solidarity is restricted. This is the consequence of a dilemma. The more the church cherishes ideals that lie far from the status quo, the more its support from society will wane, so that its potential for change loses power. The more it strives after aims that promote the status quo, the more unfaithful it is to the gospel of the kingdom of God. The influence that the church is able to exert in Western society is no more than that of a larger or smaller volunteer association (chapter 2 sub 2). It only has an effect, insofar as it carries public opinion, which in its turn is influenced by other groups and organizations. Proceeding from public opinion, influence can be gained over the political organizations. The path runs through the alignment of several societal groups and organizations to public opin-

FIGURE 12.1 Path analysis of solidarity

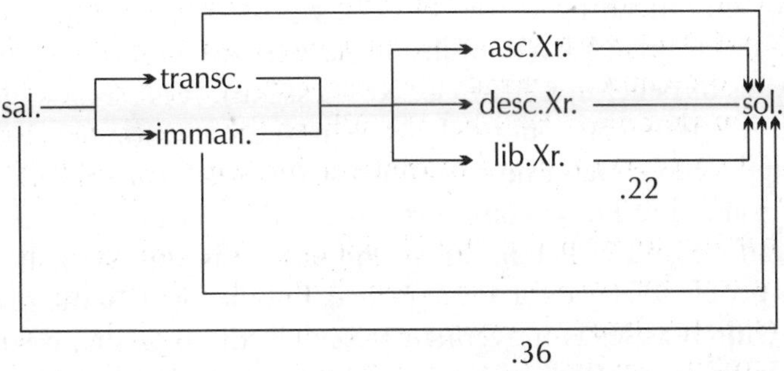

ion and through this to the policy-makers. The path runs up the sometimes steep slope of discussions, lobbying, negotiating, making compromises, reopening negotiations, and making new compromises. There is no other way (Thung 1976; Jeurissen 1993).

The second limit lies in the church itself. The question is whether there is enough support in the church for changing society in the direction of justice and solidarity in the perspective of the kingdom of God. And to what degree this support — insofar as it is present — is inspired and nourished by the Christian faith of the members.

In figure 12.1 we have connected some data from a research project carried out among members of Catholic parishes in Ottawa, Canada. Here the attitude of societal-critical solidarity is placed in the center of attention. It appeared to have moderate support from the parishioners researched in Ottawa (3.15 on a five-point scale). We checked to what extent this attitude was influenced by the belief of the parishioners in God and in Christ. For this purpose we set up a causal model. From left to right, the factors in this model are: saliency (sal.: the degree in which the belief is felt to be important to the parishioners); transcendent belief in God (transc.: belief in God who transcends human existence); immanent belief in God (imman.: belief in God, who is the foundation of existence); belief in the ascendent Christ (asc.Xr.); belief in the descendent Christ (desc.Xr.); and belief in the liberating Christ (lib.Xr.). And finally, the societal-critical attitude of solidarity itself (sol.). Next, we tested the model empirically in a path analysis. In this it appeared that the variance of the attitude of solidarity could be explained for 19% (R^2.19).

What this figure brings out is that the attitude of solidarity is explained by only two factors: salience (β .36) and agreement with the image of the liberating Christ (β .22). Both types of belief in God (transc. and imman.) have no influence whatsoever. Neither do the other types of belief in Christ (asc.Xr., desc.Xr.). It is remarkable that the two religious convictions that are most alive among the parishioners appear to contain no stimulus for the development of an attitude of solidarity. These convictions involve belief in a transcendent God (transc.) and belief in an ascendent Christ (asc.Xr.). Neither inspires people to strive for social justice. In other words: the margins for the church as Jesus movement are small; the margins within the church itself are small!

Opportunities

This does not mean, however, that the margins actually present — however small they are — should not be used for their best purpose. How this can be done will be clarified here by means of some terms from deprivation, elite, mobilization, and interaction theories, which we discussed earlier.

First of all, it is of importance to trace those types of deprivation which are really present in church and society. This is not always easy because they are often cloaked in a culture of silence, as it has been described by Freire (1972). An inspiring example is the work done by a research group from Kampen (the Netherlands) in the Oude Westen quarter of Rotterdam, to which we have referred before (chapter 5 sub 5). This quarter counted some 10,000 inhabitants in 1988, with a relatively high percentage of allochthonous people. More than 500 people participated in the local parish activities, which amounted to 5% of the total population. By doing interviews, the researchers tried to find out what the needs of the people were. They came across specific vital, social, and spiritual needs, which they have since then tried to deal with adequately in activities centered around community formation, neighborhood development, and individual case work. Without effective support from the supra-local body of representatives, such an undertaking cannot succeed. However, without the effort of the local church, such an undertaking simply cannot be brought about (Schippers 1990).

The tracing of deprivations, however, is not enough. It is a matter of finding the words, together with the people, and developing the ideas with which they can give adequate expression to their distress and suffering according to their feelings. It is also of importance that these ideas offer a perspective of liberation. The ideas are precisely what make the deprivations the engine for action. Without ideas the deprivations stay dumb and blind.

A second point now comes to the fore. The accompaniment and guidance of these kinds of processes require societal experience, organizational insight, and expertise. In other words, it is a matter of acquiring organizational professionality. With this we hit upon the insights provided by proceeding from the perspective of the elite theory. Without professional leadership, a movement does not come about. At least, it evaporates without professional leadership, particularly because of the complexity of the societal context on which it is trying to exert an influence.

The church may view itself — and this is the third point — as a mobilization organization that functions as a flywheel for the movement. Earlier we saw that movements can be approached and explained proceeding from both the perspective of deprivation and the angle of the mobilizing organization. The time has passed that these perspectives were set polemically opposite each other. Now they are rather to be seen as complementary.

Some marginal notes have to be placed with this organizational angle. An organization that makes resources available to give wings to the movement is an important matter. With this, as we mentioned before, the point is developing or making available an organizational network of groups and of financial, spatial, and personal means. This is not only useful and necessary for the initiation of the movement but also for its continuance. Without a sturdy organizational infrastructure, it will fall apart in the long run. Without a movement organization, it crumbles.

It is of importance that the ideas that are alive in the movement are translated into more concrete projects and goals of action, which are achievable and contain a ready chance for success. Examples of such aims are the enlargement of accessibility of social service organizations; exerting pressure on policy-making organizations; setting up and implementing so-called parental education, educational home visiting projects, community education, and community organization (Van der Veen 1982).

However, we have to keep in mind the inherent ambivalence of the movement organization. On the one hand, it can stimulate the permanence of the movement as a movement; on the other hand, it can suffocate and fossilize it. Because of this, the movement as a movement disappears. This brings us to the oligarchical theory of Michels. To prevent this from happening, the movement organization should not be set up in a bureaucratic sense, but according to the model of the innovative organization, which we will discuss later (chapter 20).

Finally, we can never pay enough attention to the interaction between the members of the movement among themselves and between themselves and outsiders. Earlier we saw that internally a movement exists by the grace of the informal communication structures, because of which a notion of belonging and a "we" feeling arises. However, taking care of the interaction *ad extra* is important too. It fosters goodwill, enlarges the accessibility of the movement for outsiders, and attracts those interested. An influence of enlistment exudes from it. It gets people on the move.

Church on the move

Insofar as the church brings about the development of movements, as we outlined above, and places them in the perspective of the proclamation of the kingdom of God, it is giving shape to the church as Jesus movement. Naturally, we cannot talk of the flaming and pulsating energy of the charismatic wandering preacher Jesus within it. We no longer live in the time of the Jesus movement in the communities of the first generations. The flame of the prophetic charisma burns a little lower, and the light of the pneumatic charisma has been set on a lower candlestick. After the religious virtuosos Jesus and Paul, we live in a period of the routinization of charisma *(Veralltäglichung des Charisma).* This becoming commonplace is, in general, characteristic of the generations that come after the actions of the charismatic leaders (Weber 1980, 142ff.). It also applies to the church of today (Avis 1992).

In this routinization, charisma becomes institutionalized, as it were, because rules are drawn up for living together, for the ritual, for mutual communication, division of labor, executing tasks and activities, rights and duties, recruitment, succession, and fund-raising.

Yet the history of the church has known many moments with a strong resurgence of the prophetic-pneumatic charisma. The movement that stemmed from Francis is a model for this (Schreuder 1967). His inspiration stretches from the twelfth century to the basic communities in Latin America of the present (Boff 1987a). In other words, the degree to which the church is open to the Jesus movement varies in time and place. Even when the messianic margins are small, they can and should be used effectively.

PART IV

INTEGRATION

Having discussed the core function of the identity of the church in the last part, we will now deal with integration. This is necessary because it is not at all obvious why the church should not disintegrate and fall apart into all sorts of subdivisions and elements. The question is: What holds it together?

The answer one could give is its identity. Yet this does not suffice, for we have seen how much the identity of the church is determined by a far-reaching pluralization of religious convictions. We did indicate that these convictions can be oriented to the vision and mission of the church and can be supplemented and corrected from there. But the collectiveness of convictions does not take place in individuals, or in a number of individuals who have nothing to do with each other. It has its ground in interpersonal interaction. It has its foundation in social relations, processes, and structures. From there the content of the convictions themselves is given shape. Identity and integration are intertwined: the convictions guide the integration via the mission and vision of the church, while integration has a conditioning effect on the convictions via the mission and vision of the church. Both are the prop and stay of the church. Together they are the structural core functions of the church (chapter 4 sub 2).

We start this part in the same way as we started the last part. First, we place the question of integration in the societal context of today, but now from the perspective of individualization. Here the church comes across all sorts of limits and challenges (chapter 13). Next we go into the group and network processes that take place in the church and that supply the grounds for the formation of community in the church. We will pay special attention to the church as body of Christ (chapter 14). As group, network, and community formation processes never go without conflict, we will also take a look at the conflicts that occur in the church. Here we will also pay attention to the treatment of conflict in a religious perspective (chapter 15). Finally, we will deal with the function of religious leadership in the church. With this we will also discuss the ministry (chapter 16).

Chapter 13

The Context of Individualization

The process of individualization that permeates the whole of Western society can be regarded from several perspectives: ecological, economic, sociological, juridical, and psychological. Proceeding from the ecological viewpoint, a central part is played by the relationship of humans to the natural environment and to demographic factors. Proceeding from the economic angle, what catches the eye are matters such as land and raw materials, capital and capital goods, labor and the labor market. In the sociological perspective, the focus is on the development of society according to social-structural and social-cultural aspects, as well as the consequences thereof for the relations between people and their way of life. Proceeding from a juridical point of view, the increasing bringing of matters *sub judice* and the legalization of society are set in a special light. In a psychological approach, attention is paid to the development of the cognitive, affective, and attitudinal aspects of the interhuman formation of relationships and of the individuals within this. Here, we choose the sociological perspective, without principally shutting out elements from the other perspectives. Especially the ecological and economic viewpoints cannot be separated from the sociological frame of reference. Within this perspective we will focus on the phenomenon of urbanization, since this significantly influences the process of individualization.

In this chapter we will deal with questions about (1) what urbanization implies, (2) what influence it exerts on individualization, and (3) which consequences this has for the church.

(1) Urbanization

In order to be able to understand the process of urbanization, it is necssary to distinguish between the primitive, preindustrial, industrial, and postindustrial society. The distinctive criterion of this division lies in the technological development in the relation of humanity to the natural environment (Schoorl 1983).

Primitive society

Primitive or archaic society was characterized by the invention of simple tools and the use of fire. It was made up of collectors, hunters, and fishermen. It was small in size but self-supportive. It had no division of labor other than sex and age. It was social-culturally homogenous (there were no social strata). Kinship determined one's belonging to certain groups and maintaining relations (ascription), not achievement. The context of community had a strong face-to-face character. It was borne by common moral and religious codes. The balance between the settlements and societies among themselves was symmetrical.

Preindustrial society

The transition to preindustrial society was determined by the domestication of plants and animals. Instead of the collection of plants, there was cultivation: horticulture. Instead of the hunting and catching of animals, there was care for and breeding of animals: husbandry. Humankind actively took the production of food into their own hands. This meant increasing control of the natural environment. In this preindustrial society — including both the villages and the towns — had its foundation. The preindustrial villages are here dealt with in connection with the towns because they can be regarded as being complementary to them.

This preindustrial village society was sedentary. It had the knowledge and the techniques to produce more food than was strictly necessary. This made food surplusses possible. These could be used by people who were not at work in the agrarian sector but who lived in the preindustrial towns (never more than 20% of the population for that matter). This made a division of labor between the agrarian and nonagrarian sector possible. However, the peasants did not make produce for the market with an eye to the maximization of profit: they handed over part of their products, as it were, to others. They were peasants, not farmers. The village communities were less autonomous and symmetrical with regard to each other than the primitive societies.

The preindustrial towns originated between 2000 and 1000 B.C. in Mesopotamia. They were small in size compared to industrial cities of today: fewer than 10,000 inhabitants, and sometimes even fewer than 5,000 inhabitants. They were characterized by a compilation of non-agrarian activities, which brought with it a certain division of labor and specialization in themselves. The difference in social layers (social stratification) is partially based on this. They had an upper and a lower layer, as well as pariahs, who were partly kept at a distance because people were afraid of them, and partly felt to be useful to do the dirty and/or unclean work. There was little or no social mobility: those who belonged to a certain layer stayed in it all their lives. The upper layer profited from the production surplusses of the lower layer and from that of the peasants in the countryside. It held the top economic, political, military, juridical, and religious positions. The lower layer provided people for the lower functions, like civil servant, merchant, artisan, or soldier. The upper layer lived in the center of the city, the lower layer in the districts surrounding it, and the pariahs in the corners of the city. Here, too, the social connections were based on kinship in particular (ascription) and not on achievement. Within this system the extended family was an important social datum. It often functioned as a production and consumption unit. However, there were specialists who functioned in specific functions in society, especially in trade and handicrafts. Finally, the religious institutions held an important place in these preindustrial towns.

Industrial society

The most prominent characteristic of the industrial society lies not in the production of food, but of energy. This was made possible by the revolutionary development of science and technology, which led to the growth of modern industrial cities with no fewer than 20,000 (or 100,000) inhabitants.

Urbanization is the process of the increase in the share of the total population that lives in the cities. One speaks of over-urbanization if this increase is greater than social-economic growth can cope with. Within this the so-called primate cities, which are many times bigger than the other cities, started to develop. These have a tendency to suck in investments away from the surrounding urban areas and the country. The phenomenon of passive urbanization, through which all sorts of villages are gradually drawn within the city limits, is connected to this. Thus, the urbanization of the global population between 1920 and 1960 — with cities of at least 20,000 inhabitants — rose from 14% to 25%, in Latin America from 14% to 32%, in Europe from 32% to 41%, and in North America from 38% to 57%.

Urban society is a kind of society that is based on industry, which is characterized by large, densely populated settlements of socially heterogenous groups and people. The presence of industry can be viewed as a necessary condition. The size of the settlements, the population density, and the heterogeneity of the social stratification determine the degree of urbanization.

Urbanization itself can be explained as proceeding from two main factors: the natural growth of the population, particularly in the Third World countries, and migration. The latter has to do with the movement from the country to the cities, through which the rural areas become emptier and the urban areas more crowded. The causes of migration are manifold. First of all, there are so-called push-and-pull factors. The push factors involve the phenomenon of overruralization. More people live in the country than the economic situation requires, so people are driven to the towns. The pull factors draw people to the city because of employment, social services, educational institutions, and possibilities for recreation. Besides these social-economic forces, they are also drawn to the city by social-cultural and psychic factors. The social-cultural factors involve wanting to escape the values, norms, and habits that control country life and the social control this entails. The psychic factors refer to the hope people have in their transition to the cities in which they expect that their primary material and spiritual needs will be met (De Goede 1983).

Postindustrial society

Some authors add the postindustrial society to this analysis. It is not so much based, they say, on the industrial sector and industrial technology as on the service sector. The postindustrial city is largely cloaked in mist, but there are authors who believe they can already sketch its outline. First of all, the business service sector within the service sector (accountants, lawyers, and advisers) holds a central position. It generates all sorts of jobs and brings with it a special kind of infrastructure: the availability of information technology, a high quality labor market, the proximity of other specialized services, access to high-quality international communication networks, and the proximity of airports. Next, information technology itself influences the urban economy, due to the importance of global networks, through which one can directly participate in the world economy. That is why we also speak of the informational city. The international level is increasing in significance, as is the urban level, while the national level is losing relevance. A worldwide hierarchy of cities is on the rise. Further, the number of modern households is increasing in the postindustrial city, that is to say, households made up of single workers or double income families, with or without children. These are dependent on a sufficiently dense network of services.

Another characteristic of postindustrial society is the enlargement of the assortment, because of the reduction of the user value and the increase of the symbolic value of goods. Through this the emphasis is placed on the lifestyles that are thought to radiate these goods and the meaning they are deemed to have for the sense of self-valuation and identity. The city is increasingly becoming a theater where one looks around in order to be seen. Finally, due to economic recession, the loss of industrial jobs, and the increase in the size of ethnic minorities, the postindustrial city is becoming a city of the permanent underclass. This may lead to the formation of ghettos (Kloosterman 1992).

(2) Urbanization and individualization

The increase in scale through which urbanization is determined, entails the extension and bureaucratization of the industrial and service sectors. At the same time it brings with it an increasing collectivization of government facilities. This also involves an inclination to strengthen the division of labor, which characterizes the industrial city in contrast to the preindustrial city. Every function and subfunction, task and subtask is more and more being carried out by separate people. This, in turn, leads to the fact that the relationships people have with each other are mostly based on their functional roles. All of this together determines the urban way of life. The individualization that stems from this, however, can at the same time be seen as the source and origin of group and network formation in urban society.

Urban lifestyle

Urban lifestyle is characterized first of all by the segmentation of human relations. Since everybody fulfills many roles, one only invests part of oneself in all one's relationships. If only in a physical sense, it would be impossible to involve oneself entirely in each of the relationships determined by the roles (De Goede 1983). This is sometimes defined as the narrowing of relations, which are primarily secondary instead of primary by nature (Dekker 1987, 119).

Next, one also takes up a reserved and distantiated position, because of the great number of relations and the limited amount of time and energy available. One protects oneself against too great a number of appeals. Because of this the attitude of reserve can sometimes move toward distrust. This can lead to the feeling of homelessness, that is, that one does not belong anywhere.

Further, the functionality of human relations lies in this. It is not expressiveness that determines the urban lifestyle. In this people express the feelings they have for other people, the attention, the sympathy, the care, the responsibility, and the attraction. Instead of this, we look primarily to the usefulness of the relations we have. With this, a balance of costs and benefits is made up: how much will this cost me, and what will I get in return?

This leads us to a characteristic that is defined by the term *abstract solidarity* as opposed to *traditional solidarity*. Traditional solidarity is characteristic of village society. In this the entire network of relations of the family with the parents and the grandparents, uncles and aunts, brothers and sisters, nieces and nephews is embedded in that of the neighborhood and the village. The relationships within this are based on ascription. Abstract solidarity, however, is based on functionality. Among other things this means that the people one has relations with may be at quite a geographical distance from one's own area. Due to the lack of the traditional solidarity, relationships can easily change and fluctuate too. They are based on achievement. They take place in the bureaucratic extensions of the mega-institutions that characterize the urban way of life. They are not so much characterized by the spontaneity of authentic feelings as by a kind of "keep smiling culture" (Zijderveld 1983, 116). The relations are controlled, civilized in an emotional sense; they are domesticated (Elias 1982b).

Does this mean that the urban society implies a hard lifestyle that spares no one and nothing? One finds a certain amount of romanticism in some articles. In these the homeliness of the community in the preindustrial society *(Gemeinschaft)* is set against the coldness of the industrial society *(Gesellschaft)*. *Gemeinschaft* is founded, it is said, in the solidarity of blood, place, language, will (consensus), spirit, kinship, neighborliness, and friendship. *Gesellschaft* is presumed to be based upon all-permeating contract-mindedness, focus on efficiency, calculation, mercantilism, and competition (Tönnies 1987).

But this is the consequence of a trick of the eye. Because of this the preindustrial, industrial, and postindustrial societies are too one-sidedly depicted. What we need to do is take a sharper look at things, according to some critics.

The preindustrial society did have spontaneous charity. This was, however, the expression of a certain system of society that was not inferior for its calculation to the abstract solidarity of industrial urban society. It was aimed at the contact of the wealthy class with the wandering poor or beggars. It stemmed from a balancing of pros and cons, according to what research has brought to light. The advantage of giving meals and alms lay in the fact that the hordes of pariahs were made dependent upon the propertied class. Through this they were made useful and employable for certain functions. In addition, the fear of the well-to-do for these wandering bands was dampened and restricted. The disadvantage was that this charity hurt the pocketbooks of the rich. Whether the system of charity was worth this high price depended on the calculation of costs and benefits thereof. The system had a strong and a weak side. The strong side was that any moneyed gentleman was obliged to be charitable. The church kept an eye on this (social control) and legitimized it by means of the doctrine of charity. The weak side was that one never knew whether or not one's rich neighbor would hold to this duty or would continue to do so. If this was not the case, one had to bear the whole burden of charity.

This made it tempting to try to get out from underneath this social obligation. However, if one were to decide to do this, it might tempt the neighbor to do the same, as a consequence of which the whole system would collapse. Through this one would be subjected to an even greater disadvantage. One would have to fear robberies, arson, and destruction of the manors by the wandering vagabonds in that case. On the grounds of this kind of calculation of costs and benefits, people usually decided to carry out their duty of charity. According to this theory, one can view the modern welfare state with its extensive network of collective facilities as a continuation of this system. Analogous principles underlie this state: the insurance of the collective against the needs of its members (De Swaan 1990).

Today's society is also too one-sidedly depicted by the dichotomy of *Gemeinschaft* and *Gesellschaft.* According to some authors, a transition is taking place from a materialistic to a postmaterialistic society. The materialistic society is characterized by the investment of practically all its energy into the achievement of sufficient material prosperity for all. The markets for raw materials, semimanufacture, products, labor, capital, service, and consumption are central to this. As soon as the battle for material existence is won, however, the materialistic attitude makes room for the postmaterialistic one. This is characterized by the appreciation of what follows the struggle for material life: self-development, self-realization, personal growth, and the development of the inner person (Inglehart 1990).

For that matter it would be incorrect to think that postmaterialism is the dominant lifestyle in the Western society of today. In most countries one can speak of a mixture: people combine elements from the materialistic and postmaterialistic attitude. From longitudinal research it appears that there is a slight rise in the postmaterialistic attitude and a slight drop in the materialistic one (Halman 1991, 145). However, there is still a great deal of discussion as to how durable — in the short and/or long term — the development in the direction of a postmaterialistic attitude will be. The question is whether or not it will be influenced in a negative sense by all kinds of societal fluctuations, such as economic recession and unemployment (Clarke & Dutt 1991).

The balance between cultural conformity and cultural independence is often taken as an indication of the materialistic and postmaterialistic attitude. The materialistic attitude is presumably ex-

TABLE 13.1
Conformity and independence

age	education	conformity	independence
high	low	.31	-.26
high	high	-.22	.04
low	low	.23	-.06
low	high	-.37	.31

Source: Halman et al. 1987, 264

pressed in the indiscriminate copying of traditional values and norms. The postmaterialistic attitude is supposedly connected to giving priority to personal preferences and making personal choices. In table 13.1 are given the average scores of different age and education groups on the cultural conformity and cultural independence scale, which were used in the context of European value research.

What strikes us in this table is the contrast between the combination of high age and low education on the one hand and low age and high education on the other. On the conformity scale they are opposites (.31 versus -.37), as they are on the independence scale (-.26 versus .31). Further, it appears that education is decisive with regard to conformity. Among people with a high age and a high education, a negative attitude can be traced (-.22); among people with a low age and a low education, however, there is a positive attitude (.23).

Group and network formation

Even though the process of individualization permeates the whole of societal and personal life, this does not mean that it results in an absolute monadization and atomization. The question is, How can this be?

Authors like Blau and other structuralist sociologists in the United States have tested an answer. They believe that the increasing division of labor that is characteristic of urban society is at the same time the source of group and network formation. How do they view this connection? For this purpose they introduce a missing link between the division of labor and group and network formation. This link is increasing interdependency. The reasoning is: the increasing division of labor strengthens mutual dependency between people (interdependency) due to the ever-increasing specialization. This interdependency leads to people searching out each other and making contact, which they do in groups and networks. Now the latter is of importance because the integration of society does not come about on the ground of functional contacts alone. It demands that people have physical, actual, personal contact with each other, that they meet each other as concrete people (actual social association and affiliation). Well, then, this occurs in groups and networks (Wallace & Wolf 1991).

Whether this is a sound theory still has to be seen. It can be criticized from a theoretical as well as an empirical point of view. This does not alter the fact that group formation occurs frequently in urbanized society. A whole process of formation of groups is observable, in which people participate not in a functional but in a personal sense: economic groups (class or job), political groups (local, national, and international), social groups (family, relatives, and ethnicity), social-emancipatory groups (women or elders), social-recreative groups (sports, spare time, and holidays), educational groups (aimed at the individual or society), cultural groups (film, theatre, and arts), psycho-social groups (illness, unemployment, and mourning), philosophical groups (convictions, values, norms, and religion). These processes of group formation have an even stronger presence in non-Western countries, which are also characterized by a high level of modernization. Japan is the clearest example of this, particularly concerning the family and the relatives. In a comparable sense this can be found in Latin America (basic communities) and countries like India (De Goede 1983).

There is something to be added to this. People not only take part in just a few groups, let alone one single group. They are members of many groups. Through this participation in many groups at the same time, they make connections between the groups. They make a web of relations between groups to which they belong (web of group affiliations). They form a network. Now one could say that these ties are not nearly as strong as they were in the kinship and neighborhood communities in the pre-industrial society. It cannot be denied that they are weaker; however, this weakness is also their strength, the so-called strength of weak ties. For people with strong ties in very dense networks with friends who all know each other are cut off from information from and contacts with larger collectives. People with weaker ties in less dense networks, however, do not have this disadvantage. They have access to a larger number of contacts to which larger, looser networks give more opportunity (Wallace & Wolf 1991).

(3) Church and individualization

Which reactions to the process of individualization are possible on the part of the church? Because we can view individualization as one of the consequences of modernization, the reactions to it can be defined in terms of modernization. We distinguish three types: amodern resistance, modern adaptation, and critical-modern exchange.

Amodern resistance

The first reaction is amodern resistance. This implies that one is opposed to the process of individualization, and that right across the board one wishes to see society restored in the life of the *Gemeinschaft* in the pre-industrial sense. This is depicted proceeding from a certain kind of romanticism as a *heile Welt,* a "paradise lost." This is sometimes stimulated by the symbols and structures of the church, which still strongly remind us of the rural period. It particularly applies to descriptions like pastor (shepherd) and flock and for the territorial borders of one local church over against those of another. The territorial principle can be seen as a result of the agrarian society, in which ground has a vital value (Laan 1967, 48). The beginning of parishes has to be sought in the country. Initially, the cities had no parishes: the *presbyteroi* worked under the guidance of the *episkopos* without being allocated their own area, and people went to whatever church they liked. When the Christian faith started to extend from the cities to the country, pastoral care was clearly defined into separate areas and was appointed to separate parish *presbyteroi* (Van Bilsen 1962, 87ff.; Schillebeeckx 1985). Since feudal times, the pastor of a parish was pastor and landowner at the same time. For the members of the parish he was a leading figure not only religiously but also agriculturally (Greinacher 1968, 113).

The desire to return to the golden age is as understandable as it is unreal. It is understandable because the church is dependent on group and community formation. Without this it does not exist; it is an institutional bubble. Moreover, because of its vision (people of God) and mission (Jesus movement), it cannot tolerate people falling into loneliness and alienation (chapters 11 and 12). However, the desire for a "paradise regained" is unreal. Attempts at restoration of a community that radically ignores the modern division of labor have no chance of success. The division between the living and the work area, which contains fundamental problems for the church, cannot be undone by the church. This also applies to the other divisions that characterize urban society, like that between classes (strata) and races (ethnicity). The same applies for other matters that were mentioned in the previous chapters, like the radical functionalization, bureaucratization, and segregation of society. These processes have been taking place for centuries already and are societal-structural by nature. They work entirely outside the reach and power of intervention by the church.

Modern adaptation

Does this mean that the church has to adapt to modern society without criticism? It is a second possible reaction. According to some, the church can do nothing structural in urbanized society. It can only help people to keep their heads above water in this society. It should abandon the prophetic task of cultural and societal criticism (challenge) and restrict itself to support, consolation, and encouragement (comfort). With this the tension between comfort and challenge has ended. The primary task of the church should lie in the religious guidance of the individual biography, in particular mourning and the rites of passage (Glock et al. 1967; Bellah et al. 1985).

Besides considering these opinions about the church, it is of importance to look at the actual practice of the church, at least of its pastors. For this purpose we submitted a number of questions to a sample of 255 pastors from the three larger Dutch churches (the Catholic Church, the Netherlands Reformed Church, and the Reformed Churches in the Netherlands) concerning the way they actually spend their time. In table 13.2 we see the areas of activity that we discovered in a long list of activities through factor analysis. These

TABLE 13.2

Time spent by pastors in % (N = 255)

	Cath.	Neth. Ref.	R. Neth.
liturgy	22.3	23.1	22.9
pastoral care	18.7	20.3	20.4
visiting	11.3	9.0	10.8
catechetics	8.3	12.4	12.5
diacony	3.7	1.7	2.6
development and mission	1.6	2.2	1.5
church dev. and volunt.	16.5	14.0	14.5
financial campaigns	1.5	0.7	0.5
meetings	6.6	6.0	5.9
study and reflection	9.5	10.7	8.5

Source: Van der Ven & Biemans 1992a

run from liturgy to study and reflection. The three columns contains the average time spent by the pastors from the three churches (in percentages).

From table 13.2 it appears that most time is spent on five pastoral tasks: liturgy; pastoral care; church development, including guidance of volunteers; catechetics; and making visits (house visits, occasional visits, visits to new members, etc.). Two groups of activities that are limiting conditions for the above and on which a relatively large amount of time is spent are study and reflection, and meetings. If we restrict ourselves to the top two in this table, then we see that most time is spent on liturgy and pastoral care. There are no important significant differences between the denominations on this point.

From this table one can read that the pastors — of whatever denomination — spend most time on comfort (liturgy, pastoral care, church and community development, and visits) and little time on matters of challenge (development and mission, diacony).

Now one may remark that these figures do show the actual time spent by pastors, but not the time desired. In other words, it may be that they make challenge their priority, but that outside pressure and/or pressure of time forces them to comfort. This remark cannot be set

TABLE 13.3
Priorities of pastors (N = 255)

	Cath.	Neth. Ref.	R. Neth.
liturgy	1.7	1.3	1.6
pastoral care	1.7	1.7	1.6
visiting	3.2	2.7	2.5
catechetics	2.6	2.0	2.2
volunteer guidance	2.1	2.0	2.2
diacony	2.7	2.9	2.9
development and mission	2.7	3.0	3.0
church development	3.1	3.0	3.3
financial campaigns	2.9	3.1	3.3
meetings	3.0	3.1	3.1
study and reflection	2.4	2.2	2.3

Source: Van der Ven & Biemans 1992a

aside. From research it appears that the most prominent problem with which pastors have to deal is the pressure of time, as we shall see further along (chapter 23; table 23.1).

The question now is: What is the desired time from the pastor's point of view? Table 13.3 gives us a definite answer to this. It contains the same list of areas of activity as table 13.2, albeit that church development and volunteer work have been split up. The three columns contain the average scores of prioritization of these areas by the pastors. In order to interpret the scores, one can use the following classification: from 1.00 to 1.80: very high priority; from 1.81 to 2.60: high priority; from 2.61 to 3.40: moderate priority.

From this table the same top two come to the fore: liturgy and pastoral care. They form the top priority of the pastors of whatever denomination. If one looks at the top three, they are again the same for the three denominations: liturgy, pastoral care, and volunteer guidance (albeit that for both Protestant churches the latter is equal to catechetics). Within the time they wish to spend, comfort is central too. That is where the priority of the pastors lies. Challenge (diacony; development aid, mission) is clearly felt to be less important. It has only a moderate priority.

Critical-modern exchange

Another reaction is possible: the critical-modern exchange. In this people do not try to restore the wholeness of rural community life, nor do they adapt themselves without criticism to present societal surroundings. The critical-modern exchange is more differentiated than the contrast between resistance and adaptation suggests. Two sides can be distinguished in it.

On the one hand, people criticize the factors in society that lead to gradual isolation and alienation through the process of individualization. One has to have a sharp eye for the mechanisms that are the cause of this. Proceeding from the vision (people of God) and the mission (Jesus movement) of the church, one tries in coalition with other groups to contribute to the liberation of people from this situation of need. Examples of this are diaconal groups for the relief of structural need; educational groups for conscientization; participation in local church and societal organizations; support of national and international aid organizations; churches aimed at being of service to the industrial society; and types of categorical pastoral care, particularly institutional pastoral care, such as industrial, youth, school, student, penitentiary, hospital, and military pastoral care.

On the other hand, one also tries to expand and to help to develop, as much as one can, the possibilities for community formation that the present society offers. What the church seizes upon for this are the formation processes of the groups that we just mentioned: economic, political, social, social-emancipatory, social-recreative, educational, cultural, psycho-social, and philosophical groups. The processes of network formation between these groups also offer an equal number of chances and challenges, as we have seen, for the church.

Several authors urge us to consider the local church as a small umbrella organization *(Dachverband),* which has space for the many kinds of groups that we just spoke of (Kaufmann 1979; Wess 1989). We are not dealing with a new idea here. This proposal was launched at the beginning of this century already (Troeltsch 1912; Drehsen 1988), and rightly so. In the present society it appears that only the church that works with the network formation of groups has any spirit. With this the five factors that Hendriks developed proceeding from a social-psychological and group-dynamic perspective are of eminent

TABLE 13.4

Groups in parishes in the archdiocese of Utrecht

	N = 344	%
parish administration groups	344	100.0
charity and diacony groups	332	96.5
liturgy groups	268	77.9
mission/development groups	218	63.4
visiting groups for the sick	158	45.9
catechetics groups (youth)	156	45.3
service groups for the sick	146	42.4
welcoming groups	142	41.6
laity liturgy groups	127	36.9
district contact groups	122	35.5
liturgy groups (children)	121	35.0
initiation groups	90	26.2
church and society groups	63	18.6
house visiting groups	56	16.3
catechetics groups (adults)	49	14.2
peace groups	37	10.8

Source: Derksen 1989, 84-110

importance, namely, climate; guidance; structure (relations between groups); aims/tasks; identity. These factors contain an equal number of grips for the development and optimalization of the group and network formation in the local church. The point is to have an open, free, cooperative, positive climate; a participative and service-oriented style of leadership; an informal, direct, intensive communicative structure between groups; a lucid survey of clear, concrete, common, inspiring aims and tasks; and a clear concept of identity concerning vision and mission (Hendriks 1990).

One may wonder what groups the church actually houses. In the archdiocese of Utrecht (the Netherlands) research was done on this question in 1985. The data were collected from all 344 parishes in this diocese. In table 13.4 we find a summary of them. In the first column one finds the number of particular groups in the diocese; in the second column, the percentage of parishes in which the groups occur.

From this table it appears that each parish has an administration group. This is not surprising since every parish has to have an administration group according to ecclesiastical law; however, this does not apply for all other groups. In this light the percentage of charity and diacony groups is extraordinarily high (96.5%). The liturgy groups follow with a high percentage too (77.9%). This percentage is even higher if one adds the laity liturgy groups (36.9%), liturgy groups (children) (35.0%), and initiation groups (26.2%), even if (possible) double countings are subtracted. Under this we have the mission/development groups that are represented in nearly two-thirds of the parishes (63.4%).

From the high percentages for the charity, diacony, and mission/development groups on the one hand, and the liturgy groups on the other, one can draw a hypothetical conclusion. The tasks with which the groups in the local church occupy themselves modify the skewed image that arose from the figures on the actual and desired time spent by pastors. The pastors especially emphasized liturgy and pastoral care. The groups bring the image into balance through the great attention they pay to societal tasks like charity, diacony, missionary, developmental, and peace work. Here it becomes clear that the life of the local church cannot be read by what the pastors do, but by what activities are carried out by the whole of the community.

Chapter 14

Community Formation

In the last chapter we placed the problem of integration as a core function of the church in the context of the societal process of urbanization and individualization. We indicated that the church can react to this in various ways. One of these reactions is the critical-modern exchange in which individualization is seen as a limit and a chance, as a risk and a challenge (chapter 13).

Against this background in this chapter we will trace what possibilities the church has to stimulate integration. These possibilities lie in the processes of group and network formation that take place in the urbanized society and that create conditions for the formation of a community in the church. Here a problem that we described earlier arises, the pluralization of religious convictions (chapter 10 sub 2). How can the formation of community and pluralization be related to each other? We shall try to explain that there is a perspective in the religious code *body of Christ,* in which we can find a way out of this problem.

In what follows we will pose these questions: (1) What is the relationship between group, network, and community formation? (2) How do community formation and pluralization relate to each other? And (3) What is the meaning of the church as the body of Christ?

(1) Group, network, and community formation

As our point of departure we take the developments we described in the last chapter. On the one hand, the process of urbanization and individualization presents itself. On the other hand, processes of group and network formation also need to be seen. These create conditions for community formation in the church. We will not restrict ourselves to the groups and networks of volunteers and core members, who are the bearers of the ecclesiastical and pastoral sectors and who give shape to church policy (chapter 4 sub 3). What we are interested in are all groups and networks of people who participate in church life in whatever way (as core, modal, marginal, or other members) in either an active or a passive sense.

Group formation

Some see the church as a group of followers of Jesus. In order to be able to value such a characterization of the church, it is necessary to describe further what a group is. A group contains at least two members — a dyad — and a maximum of fifty (Van Krefeld 1979). There is an optimum between this minimum and maximum. This optimum depends on the degree to which one desires frequent and direct contact (face to face) between the members themselves without intermediary people. For some this number can be five people; for others it may be between five and ten people.

Group formation depends on three aspects: the degree of interaction, the action, and the affection between people who come together in a social connection of five to ten people or more (Homans 1961; Deaux & Wrightsman 1984).

First the *degree of interaction.* This can be further determined as direct (face to face) and frequent interaction. The direct character of the interaction is the distinctive criterion between the group, on the one hand, and two other terms that refer to collectives: the social category and the masses. The term *social category* refers in no way to interaction. It refers only to a chance collection of individuals without relationship, without connection. Social categories are, for example: men, women, students, workers, middle-class people, the churchly. The term *masses* refers no more to direct interaction than social category does. Often no connection whatsoever is present; one speaks of "the amorphous masses," for example. If there is cohesion, it comes about because a certain person is addressing the masses, and his speech brings about order in an ideological and social sense.

The interaction can vary in its frequency. Some groups come together often, say one, two, or three times a week; others come together little or hardly at all, perhaps one, two, or three times a year. The level of frequency determines not only the degree of interaction but also the kind of action and the intensity of the affection. For the execution of an objective action like working out the church budget, high frequency is not necessary. For subjective and intersubjective actions in religious encounter groups like those that take place in pastoral group work, relatively high frequency is necessary.

Next we have *action.* Action has to be seen in relation to interaction. For interaction in a group is aimed at the execution of certain actions with an eye to achieving certain goals. A distinction can be made between objective, subjective, and intersubjective actions, aimed at achieving objective, subjective, and intersubjective goals, as we indicated earlier on (chapter 2 sub 2).

Finally, we have the *affections.* Due to the collective execution of actions and because of the frequent, direct interaction that arises as a result of this, affective processes always occur too. The nature and the tendencies of these processes are determined by various factors: the emotional proximity and distance of the members among themselves, which call up feelings of sympathy or antipathy; the emotional processes of transfer, through which mutual projections of love and hate take place; social control, through which processes of mutual emotional adaptation and resistance take place; the development of power, leadership, and authority; the uniformity and pluriformity of convictions, values, and norms through which people feel mutually connected or separated.

All these factors determine the emotional processes in the group in mutual connection. Where people do not form a group but only a category or mass, these kinds of processes do not take place. However, the more intensively people come together, the more the processes of mutual attraction and repulsion, bonding and loosening increase in intensity. Within this process centripetal and centrifugal forces are always at work. Group formation, therefore, always leads to positive, negative, and/or ambivalent feelings.

It is important to take note of this last point, since ecclesiological reflections sometimes lapse into a kind of group romanticism. If the church is considered to be a group of followers of Jesus, it goes through the same emotional processes that every group goes through, with all the positive, negative, and/or ambivalent feelings inherent in these processes. It does not live in a *heile Welt,* a "whole world." Just like every other group, it is subject to mechanisms of sympathy and antipathy, of emotional projections, of social control, and of power and counter-power formation.

Which kinds of groups present themselves within the area of the local church? The answer is: in principle all the kinds we mentioned earlier (chapter 13 sub 2). These are economic groups (class or occupation), political groups (local or regional), social groups (family, relatives, and ethnic), social-emancipatory groups (women or elders), social-recreative groups (sport, leisure time, and holidays), educational groups (aimed at society or persons), cultural groups (film, theatre, and art), psycho-social groups (illness, unemployment, and mourning), philosophical groups (convictions, values, norms, and religion). Naturally, churches vary in the numbers and sorts of groups that occur within their area. However, that is not the point here. What is important is that we learn how to take on the perspective of group formation. That is to say: to learn to see that the local church is not made up of separate individuals but of individuals who all belong to several groups.

Within this, the ecclesial-pastoral groups are a subset. They function within the church sectors in the composition and execution of church policy: administration, pastoral care, catechetics, liturgy, proclamation, and diacony groups, for example (table 13.4).

Network formation

The word *network* refers in English to "work in which threads, wires or the like, are arranged in the form of a net," according to the *Shorter Oxford English Dictionary.* It can also refer to a network of personal and group relations in a figurative sense. The word group *relations* is ambiguous. It can refer to relations between individuals within groups (Veen & Wilke 1986, 172) or to relations between groups (Duffhues et al. 1985). Here we use the term to indicate relations between groups; therefore, we take the local church to be a network of relations between groups. This is more than a collection of groups. The difference is that "collection" indicates only the existence of groups next to each other, while "network" refers to relations between the groups.

What are the characteristics of a network? We will mention only two here: density and strength. Networks can vary in that there are

FIGURE 14.1 Density of networks

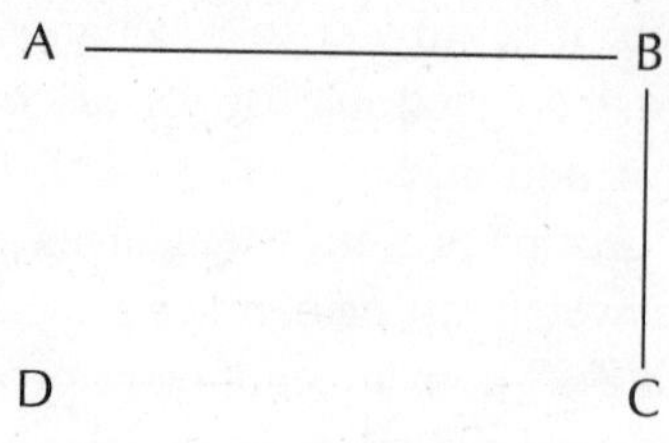

more or less dense as well as more or less strong networks (Turner 1991, 549-57).

Density implies two aspects: the number of groups and the number of relations between groups. The number of groups can be two, five, fifteen, fifty, a hundred, five hundred, or even more. Density also applies to the area that the local church covers. Those who are surprised by the number of five hundred or more should remember that we have taken on the group perspective from which the area of the church can be regarded as a network of groups. We are concerned with the total number of possible groups, of which the ecclesial-pastoral groups are only a subset.

The number of relations between groups is also of importance. One can speak of a relation between two groups if at least one person participates in both groups at the same time. Thus one group can maintain only a few relations with other groups, another can maintain many relations with several groups, and yet another many relations with many other groups. With this the degree of connectedness or isolation of the groups becomes clear.

By connecting the number of groups and the number of relations to each other, one can determine the density of networks. The example in figure 14.1 contains some illustrative data. There are four groups — A, B, C, and D — and two relations — A-B and B-C. The density can be expressed by a number that indicates the proportion between the relations that actually occur and the number of possible relations.

In this figure the factuality of the two relations (A-B, B-C) stands opposite the possibility of six relations (A-B, B-C, C-D, D-A, A-C, B-D). The density of the network in this figure is therefore (2 : 6 =) .33.

FIGURE 14.2 Strength of networks

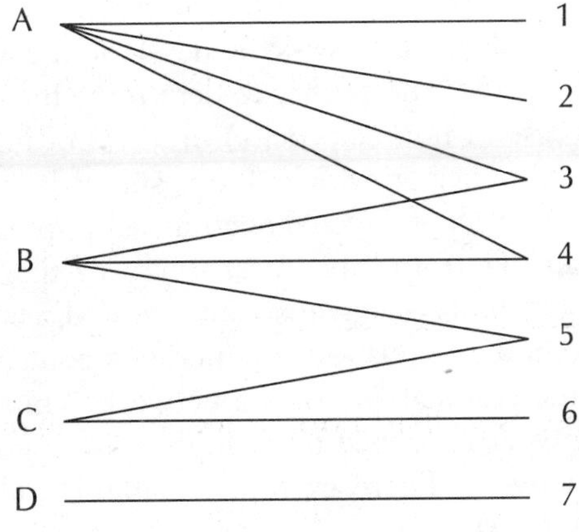

The *strength* of a network is expressed by its multiplicity. Multiplicity implies that a distinction can be made between singular and plural relations between groups. In singular relations, one can speak of one person who participates in two groups; while in plural relations, there are several people. In figure 14.2 this is clarified. On the left one finds the groups A, B, C, and D, and on the right one sees the members 1, 2, 3, 4, 5, 6, and 7. There are lines between A and 1, 2, 3, and 4; between B and 3, 4, and 5; between C and 5 and 6; and between D and 7 only.

The strength of the networks in this figure can be determined as follows. The relation between groups A and B has a multiplicity of 2 because members 3 and 4 participate in both groups. The relation between groups B and C has a multiplicity of 1 because only member 5 participates in groups B and C. Group D has no relation whatsoever because its members — exemplarily member 7 — participate in only one group.

By connecting the data with each other over several years, one can trace the development of networks in terms of density and strength. One can determine its course in terms of rises and drops (cf. Duffhues 1991, 241ff.). This can lead to gladdening or bewildering insights. We may assume that the social formations (among them the church) are more vital and attractive the more their network of groups is denser and stronger.

A large number of refinements can be added to all of this. Thus, for instance, one can pay attention to the presence of the reciprocal character (one-sidedness or two-sidedness) of the relation of one group to another. Next, one can try to determine the direction of the relation (in the case of nonreciprocity) in terms of influence: Which group exerts an influence on which? If one succeeds in answering this question, one may speak of directed relation, as opposed to undirected. Further, one can determine the accessibility of the groups among themselves. Accessibility is greater the more direct relations and smaller the more indirect relations the network contains. Finally, one can determine the vulnerability of the network. This can be formulated by tracing what influence dropping out of a group has on the ties within the network. There are four possibilities. Dropping out of a group can: (1) increase the connections; (2) leave them unchanged; (3) decrease them; or (4) break them. The group in question then is: (1) a weak group; (2) a neutral group; (3) a strong group; or (4) an articulation group, which gives expression to the connection: when it ceases to exist, the network ceases to exist (Felling & Hüttner 1981; Turner 1991, 549-57).

Community formation

Within living memory, the church has been depicted as a community. The question is what being a community entails, and how it can be stimulated. Two theories are in circulation about what a community constitutes. The first comes from Tönnies (1987), which we saw earlier on, and the second from Parsons (1959a, 250-79; 1959b, 152-79; 1965, 45-46).

As we indicated earlier, Tönnies developed a theory regarding the relationship between preindustrial and industrial society (chapter 13 sub 2). The first he characterized with "community" *(Gemeinschaft)* and the second with "society" *(Gesellschaft)*. The community is an organic unit, while the society is mechanic. In the community, people live together on the grounds of direct, personal relations and in mutual solidarity. One can speak of a "will of common being" *(Wesenwille)*. This mutual connectedness is expressed in family and relatives, village and town, through common patterns of value and religious convictions. In the society people associate with each other on the grounds of considerations of efficiency. Their interactions take place in the limited liability company, the big city, and the bourgeois and industrial society. One can speak of a "will of choosing" *(Kürwille)*. In the *Wesenwille,* affectivity and spontaneity play an important role; in the *Kürwille,* rationality, thought, and calculation do so. Thus, the structure of the community and the society also differ. In the community, custom, habit, and religion are dominant, while treaty, contract, law, and public opinion rule in the society. This dichotomy between community and society permeates all of social life. Within the economy, we find the contrast between village and town and between production and trade; within politics, between people and state and between aristocracy and democracy; within culture, between religion and science and between church and sect. In this historical interpretation of the transition from the preindustrial to the industrial society, one feels a certain nostalgia for the early community and has a certain uncomfortable feeling about the present society. Tönnies had a great influence on later thought. His dichotomy between community and society is part of the foundation of dichotomies that later were developed by other sociologists, like family and market, country and city, sacred and secular, primary and secondary groups (Goddijn 1981).

The meaning of community in Tönnies's sense *(Gemeinschaft)* is often implicitly or explicitly attributed to the church. The mutual relations are taken to be affective and noncognitive, spontaneous and not calculating, expressive and noninstrumental, concrete-solidary and nonstrategic. These relations are deemed to be based on family and kinship ties and neighborliness. They are held together by common usages and customs and not through treaties, contracts, or (church) legislation. The pattern of values is viewed as uniform and nonpluriform; the community, as integrating and nonindividualizing, as self-evident and nonreflective, as transcendent and nonimmanent.

It cannot be denied that a certain nostalgia for the past shines through in this view, leaving aside whether such a community did in fact ever exist. The risk of a romanticizing illusion or a limited perspective is not imaginary. Whatever way we look at it, this view of the church as a community no longer suits the urban society of today. It has no sense of reality. The church community in Tönnies's sense is a thing of the past.

Parsons's theory concerning community looks a lot simpler. One could well-nigh call it an empty theory. In short, it comes down to the following: All interaction between people, wherever and however it takes place, is executed in physical space, a local context, and ecological environs. This can be further worked out for three kinds of interaction: residential, professional, and jurisdictional interaction. The communication processes in the family belong to the residential interactions: these take place in the physical space in and around the home. Social relations in the neighborhood also fall under residential interactions: they take place in a geographically determined neighborhood or district. Professional interactions are connected to the practice of a job: these occur at the place of work, in the factory or office. The jurisdictional interactions relate to the legally determined unit one belongs to, such as the municipality, the province, or the state. All sorts of communication processes result from this, in which all kinds of legal interests, rights, and duties are at stake. These jurisdictional interactions are determined locally as well. They take place in buildings, in which the offices of the registration service, inland revenue, or social security service are localized. Now according to Parsons, "community" refers to this aspect of locality. It follows that a family can be called a community; likewise a neighborhood is a neighborhood community. However, a department in a company or an entire company can be called a community, proceeding from the viewpoint of the interactions that locally take place within it. Thus, one would have to speak of the "company community." Other professional organizations, too, can be considered communities, proceeding from this perspective of locality. One would have to speak of the "school community," the "university community," the "hospital community," etc. Finally, jurisdictional entities can also be called communities, proceeding from this viewpoint: the "village community," the "urban community," or the "national community." Against this background one can also speak of a "church community." However, this term means no more than that interactions take place in the physical space of the area that the church covers: a certain neighborhood, district, or city.

Church community as network of groups

The community in Tönnies's sense belongs to the past, while the community in Parsons's sense is an empty term. Can a third view be developed?

We believe we can clarify the church as community proceeding from the perspective of group and network formation, which we dealt with earlier. The church community can be described proceeding from the angle of the varying density and strength of networks of groups that find themselves in the area that the local church covers. As we mentioned before, density has to do with the relationship between the factual and the possible relations between groups. Strength has to do with the multiplicity of these relations: the number of people that bring them about.

The question is whether it is correct to apply this network perspective to the church. For certain groups in the church, this is definitely the case, especially for ecclesial-pastoral groups. The network perspective provides a further definition of the view according to which the parish is a community of working groups, as Derksen put it (1989, 55-111). With this view we are concerned with administration, pastoral care, catechetics, liturgy, proclamation, and diacony groups. In short, these are the groups in the ecclesial-pastoral sectors (chapter 4 sub 3). Proceeding from this network perspective, one can determine the density and strength of the relations between these groups. But the other elements we mentioned earlier, such as the reciprocity, influence, accessibility, and vulnerability of the working groups, are also of importance here. With this perspective, the network development of the working groups can be charted over a number of years and the increase or decrease of the ecclesial-pastoral community formation can be determined. Proceeding from such a diagnosis, community formtion can also be stimulated in a positive way.

We have to realize, however, that the network formation of the working groups only has to do with pastoral volunteers and active core members. However interesting this may be for the ecclesial-pastoral sectors, the question arises whether all other members of the church (modal, marginal, and sleeping members) fall outside this. Does the network perspective restrict itself to the ecclesial-pastoral working groups? Or can it be applied to the local church as a whole?

Liturgical community as network of groups

This question applies most stringently for liturgy. In liturgy — according to tradition — the church comes together as a community. Liturgy is "at the same time an association of brothers in one-mindedness and an organic group, bearing distinct functions" (Martimort 1961, 88-89). It is a celebration of communion *(celebratio communitatis)*, according to Vatican II (*Sacrosanctum Concilium* 21). "It is certain that among themselves the community of believers, which forms a unique body, is founded in the Eucharistic meal" (Löhrer 1964, 304). That is why we focus the question whether the network perspective is applicable to the whole of the local church in regard to liturgy. The question is as follows: Does the network perspective sufficiently cover the "community" that comes together in liturgy?

For clarity's sake, the hypothesis that is formulated here does not state that the church community is a network of groups in liturgy. The hypothesis only says that the church community can be *regarded* as a network of groups in liturgy, in accordance with the epistemological principle mentioned earlier (Introduction). The advantage of the network perspective is that from there the variation in community formation in liturgy can be charted and described. We will clarify this by means of some examples.

We begin with the individual, who finds himself in a church unknown to him and in unknown liturgy, such as may be the case in a foreign country. Let us assume that the other people in this liturgy — the local population — are connected to each other in all sorts of ways. The foreigner, however, will not gain any community experience in this liturgy, simply because he does not maintain a face-to-face relation with anybody in this church. In the terminology used: he does not form a group with anybody. This does not mean that he cannot gain different kinds of experiences from this liturgy, for example existential, esthetic, or religious experiences.

The other extreme is a church service with a large congregation of people who do not know each other, as in a church for the passerby in the international company and tourist trade. In the terminology used, we are not dealing with amorphous masses because the ritual and rhetoric appearance of the minister(s) bring order and coherence to them. The people are spoken to, the aim of their coming together is articulated, and shape is given to their desires and motives. However, community formation does not take place, simply because there are no groups with frequent and direct interactions that participate in the service. Suppose couples and families take part. Then one can speak of groups, but they are loose groups. It is precisely in a church for passersby that everybody is unknown to everybody else. One cannot speak of community formation, because there are no network relations between the groups. One does not gain community experience there, which does not mean to say that existential, esthetic, or religious experiences cannot be gained.

Now let us look at regular weekend liturgy in ordinary churches, in which some hundreds of people participate. Proceeding from the hypothesis of the network perspective, churches differ from each other to the degree in which this liturgy is characterized by community experience and community formation. These differences can be traced back to the density and strength of the relations between the groups of people who participate in the liturgy and come into contact with other members from other groups. One can speak of density and strength to the extent that the liturgical participants take part in two or more groups in settings of family, neighborhood, school, friends, colleagues, and acquaintances proceeding from economic and political organizations, social and recreation clubs, or cultural and artistic contexts. The strength and density of the network are expressed in easily observable matters, like noticing each other, looking at each other, greeting each other, getting into contact with each other, talking to each other, and making engagements with each other before and/or after the service. Naturally, the social-liturgical (and other eccesial) experiences people have have an effect on the network formation itself. Liturgical weekend celebrations in which this network density and strength hardly occur or do not occur at all, are characterized by a lack of connectedness. One misses the cohesion, the integration: "it is as disjointed as grains of sand," as experienced ministers might put it.

The rights of passage liturgy is another example. In dealing with the funeral of someone with a network of great density and strength, one gains a penetrating sense of community fellow-feeling from this liturgy. However, there can also be a low density and strength, as a consequence of the existence of only indirect relations and meager multiplicity between the groups that participate in the liturgy. The people who participate in the funeral service and who are only connected to each other through the deceased will hardly gain any community experience from such a service, or none at all. Here, liturgical theory and practice come into conflict. However beautiful the phrases about liturgical community formation may sound, people experience such a funeral as cold and unmoving.

Another example in which the theory of liturgists clashes with pastoral practice is the following. Certain authors argue for having rites of passage, such as baptism and marriage, take place in ordinary weekend celebrations. Sometimes this leads to positive reactions, sometimes to frustrations, as experience has taught us. Why is this? The cause can be clarified from the network perspective. In such a service, two networks come together: the network of the ordinary weekend liturgy and that of the rites of passage, here that of the family of the child to be baptized or of the couple being married. If the network of the rites of passage is part of the network of the ordinary weekend liturgy, an intensified sense of community can arise. If the rites of passage network maintains no relations whatsoever with that of the weekend liturgy — except perhaps a couple of simple relations — this leads to frustrations. This is expressed in statements like: "it is just as if two separate companies are sitting in the church."

One last example: the liturgy in ecclesial basic communities can contain an intense community-forming experience. This can be understood proceeding from the density and strength of the network of groups from which one participates in this liturgy. For one can speak of a high multiplicity: a large number of plural, direct relations between a large number of people in the various groups in the basic community.

We hope we have made the relevance of the network perspective clear by means of the liturgy, in which the church community most strongly manifests itself according to liturgical theory. We believe that this angle is not only compatible with the community formation in liturgy but that it also makes it easier to conceptualize, explain, and research. It is able to portray and predict the variations in community formation and to stimulate community formation itself from this.

(2) Community formation and pluralization

We already ran across the pluralization of convictions in the church in our discussion of identity (chapter 10 sub 2). Here we said that such pluralization had to be oriented toward the vision and mission of the church and could even be corrected from there (chapters 11 and 12). Now we would like to discuss the integration aspects that this entails, for pluralization is not only a problem for identity but also for integration. The question is how we can approach this proceeding from community formation. We shall deal with this question using the terms *consensus* and *confession*.

Consensus

The point of departure in our approach is that community formation in the church demands that one strive after consensus formation in case of pluralization. This means two things. The first is that the pluralization be recognized and acknowledged, not suppressed or neglected. One can speak of suppression if one ends or tries to end it through words of power. One can speak of neglect if one leaves it for what it is and disregards it. The second is that one initiates, develops, and stimulates processes that are aimed at the achievement of mutual consensus.

The supposition in this is that communication is the only desirable and passable route to carry out effectively the search for consensus. Consensus in the church can be realized only through communication. It cannot be imposed, commanded, ordered, or sanctioned. Why is this?

We can approach this question by proceeding from the various ways in which people affiliate with groups. Some kinds of group affiliation are based on coercion, others on exchange, and yet others on normative agreement (Thurlings 1977, 127-50). This distinction goes back to the trichotomy in coercive, exchange, and normative organizations, as described by Etzioni (1964; Gross & Etzioni 1985). We can apply it to the affiliation of people with groups, partially because groups cannot be viewed separately from the organizational context in which they occur. This theory holds that the affiliation to a concrete group or organization is primarily characterized by one of the three types of bond, but sometimes by (one of) the others in a secondary sense.

The first bond is based on *coercion.* This consists of the fact that one undergoes external pressure to participate in the group in question. In addition, one is forced to follow certain externally imposed rules of the group. The order that one finds in such a group exists only by the grace of subjection. Because of this, the order is in continuous danger. As soon as the opportunity arises, people resist and a revolt comes about. This is aimed at the leadership of the group or system of which the group is a part. If the revolt is quashed, a strengthening of the coercion follows, until liberalization is made possible after a cooling-down period. Different kinds of coercion can be distinguished: physical coercion (in prisons or the army) and mental coercion (in philosophical and religious sects).

The second bond is based on *exchange.* In this the emphasis is placed on the profit one experiences in accommodating oneself to the rules of the group. Profit means that one has reached the conclusion that the advantages of belonging to the group outweigh the disadvantages. A cost-benefit analysis has taken place in which one aims at the maintenance or maximalization of one's personal interests. The bond is regarded as profitable. Some speak of a secret between ego and alter that underlies this kind of group affiliation. This secret implies that ego offers someting to alter that has more value to alter than to ego, and that alter on his or her part gives something back to ego that again has more value to ego than to alter himself or herself (Thurlings 1977, 143). Proceeding from the exchange mechanism, one can also view all sorts of feelings that present themselves in group life. If one can speak of symmetrical exchange, and if scales of exchange are in balance, feelings of satisfaction, gratitude, harmony, and unanimity develop. However, the scales of exchange can also become unbalanced. Thus ego can turn to anger if alter does not give that which ego believes he has a right to. In a different situation ego can start to develop feelings of guilt if he notices that his advantage is at the expense of the rightful interests of alter. If ego, however, has unexpected advantages — more than is his share — without alter being short-changed, he feels like he is in the seventh heaven (Frijda 1986). The clearest examples of bonding on the basis of exchange can be found in the profit and nonprofit organizations. People accommodate themselves to the rules of the company or organization because they make their living there. The exchange relation also applies to personnel in the pay of the church.

The third bond is based on *normative agreement.* This exists in the personal bonding to the group on the grounds of personal engagement with the values and aims of the group. The bonding is of a moral nature. One feels called upon from the depth of one's being to participate in the group. The kind of group bonding can be especially found in organizations that are concerned with advancing education, art, culture, morals, ideology, or religion.

Sometimes the affiliation with certain groups or organizations goes through a development. Thus, the affiliation with the church has developed since the fourth century from a primary normative bonding to a primary coercive bonding (theocratic state church). In the transition from the established church to the denomination and basic community, it again develops into a primary normative bonding. Probably the affiliation with schools and universities nowadays is developing from a primary normative to a primary exchange bonding. Insofar as this is correct, an example of this can be seen in what is called the economic colonization of society, in the case of schools and universities (Habermas 1982).

Since the affiliation of the ordinary members to the church is primarily of a normative nature, the pluralization of convictions cannot be approached by proceeding from the formation of consensus on the grounds of coercion or exchange. These simply have no results. Ordinary members just cannot be compelled; one cannot sanction them in a physical, financial, or mental sense. This is different for those who are in the pay of the church.

Let us take a look at what the effect is if the church does try to settle an ongoing discussion by means of words of power. Most illustrative is the Catholic Church's ban on the anticonception pill, as it is worded in the encyclical letter *Humanae Vitae* of 1968. Demographic research has shown that many Catholics have set aside the ban. In 1969, 72% of the Catholics in the United States rejected sex before marriage. In 1985, sixteen years later, this rejection had dropped to 33%, which meant a decrease of no less than 39% (Gallup & Castelli 1989, 79). American researchers like Greeley point out that with the ban on the pill becoming known, the number of church members fell. Indeed, with its becoming known, but was it also *because* of its becoming known? A temporal connection — fact A and B take place at the same time — does not imply a causal relation; it does not mean that fact A is the cause of fact B. Not only the Catholic but also the Protestant churches displayed a drop in church membership during the same period. From this we can conclude that it was not the ban on the pill that was the cause, but the far deeper process of secularization in all of society (Van Hemert 1991). In other words, pure words of power appear to have no direct effect: people do not hold themselves to an ecclesial order if they do not personally agree; neither do they see it as a direct reason to leave the church.

In the meantime, however, the encyclical letter has hurt the plausibility of the church. The prestige of the church and church authority among Catholics and in the public eye has suffered. This pinches all the more because there were very different views in the world episcopate at the time of the publication of *Humanae Vitae.* In addition, a plea was made to discuss this matter openly and to develop an open argumentative process of communication in the church (Haarsma 1981).

The only desirable and acceptable way to achieve consensus exists in the fact that the plurality and pluralization of convictions are themselves made the objects of communication. The normative bonding to the church leaves us no other choice. The reason is that the members of the church themselves are concerned with the church on the grounds of their own convictions and affiliate themselves with it on the basis of personal agreement. There is no consensus that can be commanded physically, financially, or mentally. Consensus can only be brought about through communication (Osmer 1990; Fuchs 1990; Avis 1992).

We do not wish to deny that church leadership has its own place in this communication process. It can, may, indeed must perform with authority in this process. But what does this mean? It does not mean wanting to end or ending the process through this, as if the consensus could be based on "believing at command" (Huizing & Bassett 1976). It does mean that the content of what it has to communicate and the way in which it does this have to be convincing in themselves. An appeal to the sacred ministry that one holds and/or support from the Spirit do not annul the demand for intrinsic strength of persuasion. The support of the Spirit does not replace reason, nor does it make reasonable communication superfluous. That is why the arguments on the grounds of which church leadership formed its opinion have to be taken into account and discussed and judged for their strength of persuasion. Church leadership cannot and may not withdraw from the communication process (Komonchak 1976).

It is good to revive our memory of a number of elements from the theory of religious communication. As we saw earlier, communication can be realized only through the taxonomic aims of mutual exchange, taking each other's perspective and striving after consensus. With this we have to take the threefold orientation into account: intrapersonal, interpersonal, and tradition-oriented communication. The communication has to be open to the transcendence perspective that lies in the religious reception, response, and reaction (chapter 3 sub 2). Finally, from the treatment of the identity of the church we draw the insight that the communication has to be oriented towards the vision (people of God) and mission (Jesus movement) of the church (chapters 11 and 12).

Confession

Insofar as consensus is achieved, it can take the shape of confession, in which the local church or a group in the church expresses its collective faith. Now one should not let oneself be misled by all sorts of connotations that the term *confession* easily calls up. These suggest that a confession is transhistorical and transcultural, universal and eternal, based on total consensus, impersonal, and contains the integral faith. If one goes back in time, however, and researches how confessions came about and how they functioned, little or nothing is left of these epithets. This can be clarified as follows.

Confessions are not transhistoric or transcultural by nature. It appears that they have been very much determined by their time and culture. Rahner refers to two short formulas that have already appeared in the New Testament and that function as confessions there. The first applied to Christians among Jews: "Jesus was the Messiah" (Acts 9:22). The second applied to Christians among the Gentiles: "you turned to God from idols, to serve a living and true God" (1 Thess. 1:9). Without the Jewish and Gentile conceptual universe of the time, they cannot be understood (Rahner 1967). What is also important is the formula of confession found in Acts: "The God of our ancestors raised up Jesus" (Acts 5:30). This formula occurs in nearly the same shape in another six speeches in Acts. However, it gets a different introduction depending on whether those in attendance were Jewish or Gentile. The Jewish audience is first taken back to Abraham and the Exodus (Acts 13:16-41), while the Gentile audience is taken back to the creation of the world (Acts 17:24). The religious confessions give evidence of the necessary enculturation in a certain time in a certain place (Lang 1978).

Confessions are neither universal nor eternal. The oldest apparent confession we know that is recognized by all Christian churches is the Twelve Articles of the apostles. This apostolic confession (*Symbolum Apostolicum*) does bear the image of universality, but historical research has greatly relativized this. In reality the Twelve Articles (other confessions in the Syrian church have seven articles) were drawn up in the seventh or eighth century in Gaul. It was, in fact, a provincial confession from a western country for catechetical and liturgical use. Since the Gallic liturgy exerted a great influence on the Italian liturgy after Charlemagne's reign, the confession was also introduced in Rome. Eventually it was taken over and accepted by the whole of the western church as a confession. Now it is true that traces of the confession have been recovered in the ancient Roman confession of the third and fourth century. The latter was, however, only a member of a family of mutually different confessions, which were found in Italy, North Africa, Spain, and Gaul during that time (Heron 1978). Originally there were a greater number of confessions. These formed a binding means for the local churches to profess their common faith *(medium fidei)*. Their primary significance is doxological and not doctrinal. Later they developed from *medium fidei* to *norma fidei* (rule of faith): from an expression of faith to a norm of faith. Later still their meaning was narrowed down from *norma fidei* to principle of doctrine *(norma doctrinae)* and finally to a criterion of orthodoxy *(norma orthodoxiae)*. The *credo* ("I believe") did, in fact, develop into *docemus confiteri* ("we teach that which has to be professed"). The fixation on the *Symbolum Apostolicum* as *norma orthodoxiae* deprived and still does deprive the local churches of their own creative, expressive, and communicative power.

Confessions are not based on total consensus either. Let us take the other confession that is recognized by all Christian churches: the *Symbolum Niceno-Constantinopolitanum* from 381 (included in the Missale Romanum as *Credo*). We know that the confession of Nicea from 325 came about as a consequence of the conflict, which divided the churches at the time over the doctrine of Arius. It was based on anything but consensus, and it did not help to gain consensus among the parties that were involved in the conflict (Kannengiesser 1978). A further fifty years of discussion were held on all parts of the symbolum, which was drawn up in 381 in Constantinople, before it was declared the standard confession in 431 in Ephesus (Houtepen 1983a). Something similar applies to the confessions of the Protestant churches in the Netherlands. They have three so-called Forms of Unity, which are made up of the Belgic Confession from 1561, the Heidelberg Catechism from 1563, and the Canons of Dort from 1618.

In the latter the petition (remonstration) of the Arminians, who defended the free will of man, was set aside and Gomarus's side was chosen. The Remonstrant doctrine was in effect condemned. Here again, a confession stemmed from a conflict (Vischer 1978).

Confessions need not be impersonal. Bishops wrote their own, personal confessions when they entered into the office of bishop, for instance. Augustine wrote his *Enchiridion*, and Luther his own paraphrase of the apostolic confession. Lately, some Catholic theologians have kept their end up too (Van der Linde 1978). Among them we can mention Rahner (1967), Schoonenberg (1969, 194-95), and Schillebeeckx (1977a, 782-83). Rahner later wrote (a draft for) three confessions, in which he placed three different emphases: an existential and a social emphasis, and one aimed at the future (Rahner 1970).

Finally, confessions do not integrally contain the faith. This would be an impossible demand, which is not even fulfilled in the New Testament. Numerous confessions that occur in the New Testament have a liturgical origin. They are of a doxological, not a doctrinal nature. They often contain a special angle from which aspects of the faith are illuminated, like the kenotic hymn of Philippians 2:6-11 and the logos hymn of John 1. An interesting example of this can be found in the baptismal confession in Acts 8:37: "I believe that Jesus Christ is the Son of God." This sentence belongs to the story of the conversion of the Ethiopian minister and his baptism by Philip. However, the sentence must have been added later, as appears from the fact that it is missing in many manuscripts. The original text, therefore, had no real credo shape. The amorphous acceptance of the "gospel of Jesus" apparently sufficed (Lang 1978).

Rahner is therefore of the opinion that confessions may and must have a provisional character and that they are changeable, for they always express the faith inadequately (Rahner 1965a). One can produce two reasons for this. The first reason is that they contain only a perspectual and aspectual approach to reality: the mystery of God in Jesus (cf. chapter 3 sub 1). The second reason is that they are always expressed in a special language and conceptual universe that are bound by time and place. They are not eternal, and cannot be so (Rahner 1967).

Against this background, a confession cannot be regarded as the end point and completion of a communication process that contains everything and everyone. Rather, it is a moment of crystallization, in which the local church or a group in the church articulates belief in God's salvation in Jesus in its own way. The formulation has to be open, appealing, central, personal, and existential. It does not close off the communication process but stimulates it instead. This is strikingly rendered in the following quotation: "the deliberate acceptance of the common formula of faith does not guarantee a subjective and inter-subjective absolute certainty that the person in question really is a believer. In addition, the formula that has been achieved and commonly accepted, is never so 'clear' that it can provide its absolute meaning from within itself and that it cannot be given, nor does it indeed require any further interpretation" (Rahner 1965a, 109). In the double meaning of "never so clear" (transparent and completed) lies the necessity for permanent communication.

(3) The church as the body of Christ

Having discussed the church community as a network of groups, as well as the communication that permeates this community, we will now go in search of the meaning of the religious code *body of Christ.* What light does it shed on the community formation in the church, or on the church as a community? We shall first give an outline of the meaning of this code in the New Testament, and afterward in the *Wirkungsgeschichte* of it. Next, we will go into the functions of this code.

Body of Christ

The definition of the church as the body of Christ occurs only in the Pauline corpus in the New Testament. There is a difference between the meaning of this image in the epistle to the inhabitants of Rome and the First Epistle to the Corinthians on the one hand, and those to the inhabitants of Ephesus and Colossae on the other.

In the Epistle to the Romans and the First Epistle to the Corinthians, the church as the body of Christ deals with the mutual relations in the community. Thus, the Epistle to the Romans reads: "For as in one body we have many members, and not all the members have the same function, so we, who are many, are one body in Christ, and individually we are members one of another" (Rom. 12:4-5). In the First Epistle to the Corinthians one finds this further worked out: "For just as the body is one and has many members, and all the members of the body, though many, are one body, so it is with Christ. For in the one Spirit we were all baptized into one body — Jews or Greeks, slaves or free — and all were made to drink of one Spirit. . . . If one member suffers, all suffer together with it; if one member is honored, all rejoice together with it. Now you are the body of Christ and individually members of it" (1 Cor. 12:12-27). All emphasis here is placed on the cohesion and collaboration of everyone in the body of Christ that is the church.

The eucharistic meal is probably the point of departure for this symbolism. As the First Epistle to the Corinthians puts it: "The cup of blessing that we bless, is it not a sharing in the blood of Christ? The bread that we break, is it not a sharing in the body of Christ? Because there is one bread, we who are many are one body, for we all partake of the one bread" (1 Cor. 10:16-17). It is precisely because of this that we are part of Christ's own body. Besides that, there is a kind of analogy with baptism, according to the First Epistle to the Corinthians: "For in one Spirit we were all baptized into one body — Jews or Greeks, slaves or free — and we were all made to drink of one Spirit" (1 Cor. 12:13). In this way the church's being the body of Christ is based on its being connected through baptism and being united in the Eucharist (Küng 1967, 236-59).

Thus we are always dealing with the person of Christ, who is depicted according to his visible shape: his body. Our union with Christ is presented in a concrete fashion: we are the members of the body of Christ.

Another image comes to the fore in the two other epistles: Christ as head of the body. Thus, the Epistle to the Ephesians states: "And he has put all things under his feet and has made him the head over all things for the church, which is his body, the fullness of him who fills all in all" (Eph. 1:22-23). The same emphasis on Christ's being the head can be found further along: "But, speaking the truth in love, we must grow up in every way into him who is the head, into Christ, from whom the whole body, joined and knit together by every ligament with which it is equipped, as each part is working properly, promotes the body's growth in building itself up in love" (Eph. 4:15-16). This emphasis comes starkly to the fore at the end of the epistle: "For the husband is the head of the wife just as Christ is the head of the church" (Eph. 5:23). We also find this emphasis in the Epistle to the Colossians: "He is the head of the body, the church" (Col. 1:18). When the writer warns the members of the church, who practice an excessive asceticism, he says: "and not holding fast to the head, from whom the whole body, nourished and held together through its ligaments and sinews, grows with a growth that is from God" (Col. 2:19).

In the emphasis in the epistles to the Ephesians and Colossians on Christ's being the head, an element of superordination and subordination comes to the fore in the symbolism of the body of Christ. This hierarchical relationship between Christ and the church not only serves spiritual purposes, as in the Epistle to the Ephesians, which says that the church as a body draws strength from Christ as the head (Eph. 4:15-16). There are also parenetic and spiritual-disciplinary undertones in this. Those who indulge in excessive asceticism are put in their place by an appeal to Christ as the head (Col. 2:19).

In the epistles to the Ephesians and Colossians, the body of Christ is more clearly that of the risen body than in the Epistle to the Romans and the First Epistle to the Corinthians. It has become the pleroma of the Godhead. The risen Christ is set above the heavenly lordships and powers. From there Christ, *pleroma* of the Godhead, showers his gifts on the church. The perspective of Christ here is from above to down below. Christ is, after all, the head of the body that is the church. Christ fulfills the hegemony of the head over the body (Cerfaux 1966).

In the history following the New Testament, the emphasis was primarily placed on Christ's being the head, as this was set forth in the epistles to the Ephesians and the Colossians. In this two tendencies can be traced. The first is spiritual by nature. It places the emphasis on the spiritual aspects of Christ's being head. Christ is the source of personal faith; he nourishes and shapes it. The second is of an organicistic-institutional and therefore hierarchical-corporatistic character. The body symbolism is worked out from a certain kind of nature-related originality, in a way that the church appears as an organ, with members and a head, that works harmoniously. Within this, a specific function is assigned to each member, albeit within the greater whole of the church that is held together in harmony by the church hierarchy (Koffeman 1986).

In the past decades two elements, which we just mentioned, have been at the center of attention: Christ's being the head and the sacramental base of the body of Christ. These two elements have given rise to all sorts of discussions and disputes. In the encyclical letter *Mystici Corporis* of 1943, both elements were strongly emphasized and exclusively worked out in the direction of the Roman Catholic Church. Because of this, the church as body of Christ was identified with the Roman Catholic Church, including its juridical order (Head) and sacramental structure (baptism, Eucharist, and priesthood). Thus it was declared that there was no better, more excellent, or more divine name for the church than "the mystical body of Christ" (*Mystici Corporis* 13). In actual fact, the encyclical letter tried to harmonize the concept of the church as *societas perfecta* with that of the mystical body of Christ (Dulles 1974, 48). This document can be seen as a carryover from a trend that already had a strong presence in Vatican I, as appears from the draft of the constitution on the church worked on by Von Kleutgen. Here too, the church as the mystical body of Christ was central (Semmelroth 1966, 456).

Against this background, it is important to trace carefully what Vatican II says about the church as the body of Christ. What strikes us is that the council does not use the term *Corpus Christi Mysticum* in the Latin text, in the chapter that explicitly discusses the church as the body of Christ (*Lumen Gentium* 7). In the Dutch translation the title "The Church as the Mystical Body of Christ" was incorrectly used at the head of the chapter. The text does make use of the adverb *mystice:* "By communicating his Spirit, Christ's brothers, called together from all nations, were mystically (*mystice*) constituted as his body." In the next chapter, which deals with the visible and invisible spiritual church, the term *mysticum Christi corpus* does occur (*Lumen Gentium* 8). One can hardly see anything other than an intentional or unintentional inconsistency (compromise) in this.

The structure of the text in number 7, which is made up of eight paragraphs, is meaningful. The first three paragraphs refer to the church as the body of Christ in the spirit of the Epistle to the Romans and the First Epistle to the Corinthians. The emphasis is on mutual cohesion and connectedness. With this baptism and the Eucharist are discussed. The following three paragraphs, including the final paragraph, place Christ's being the head of the body, the church, at the center of attention, entirely in the spirit of the epistles to the Ephesians and the Colossians. Therefore, the text combines the two orientations that are present in the New Testament. However, in the seventh paragraph a new perspective is set forth. It deals with the Spirit in the church (Cerfaux 1966, 354).

It makes sense to dwell on this for a moment. What is said is: "In order that we might be unceasingly renewed in him (cf. Eph. 4:23), he has shared with us his spirit who, being one and the same in the head and in the members, gives life to, unifies and moves the whole body in such a way that his work could be compared by the holy Fathers with the functions that the principle of life, that is, the soul, fulfills in the human body." One can at least see it as a first, shy attempt to connect a christological and pneumatological foundation of the church.

Besides this, we are struck by the dynamic orientation of the text quoted. The Spirit, communicated through Christ, makes the body live and move. Earlier in the text — in the fifth paragraph — it says that "While still pilgrims on earth, tracing in trial and in oppression the paths he trod, we are associated with his sufferings" (*Lumen Gentium* 7). Here, the other image is anticipated that is central to this church consitution and that comes up for discussion further along in the constitution: the church as the people of God. What is said of the church as the body of Christ is that it moves forward on earth in trial and oppression (*Lumen Gentium* 7). What is said of the church as the people of God is: "moving forward through trial and tribulations" (*Lumen Gentium* 9).

Other than in the encyclical letter *Mystici Corporis*, the church as the body of Christ in the constitution of Vatican II is not identified with the Catholic Church. The only thing that is said is that the church as the mystical body of Christ (and here the word *mystical* does occur!) subsists *(subsistit)* in the Catholic Church: the church is not the Catholic Church, but it is present within it. This leaves room for the presence of the church as the body of Christ outside of it (*Lumen Gentium* 8).

The question is now raised: What is the relationship between the two great images that apppear in the text quoted according to Vatican II: body of Christ and people of God? There is a difference in opinion concerning this.

Some authors believe that the symbolism of the church as the people of God is the central term of Vatican II. They regard it as a criticism of the central place the church as the mystical body of Christ held in the previous decades. This also became clear from the fact that the draft text during the council, which was dominated by the church as the body of Christ, was rejected. After various other versions, it was eventually replaced by the final text, in which the church as the people of God was attributed a prominent significance. This occurred without the church as the body of Christ disappearing from the text, as we have seen. In this view, both images are ultimately seen as each other's critical correction and complement (Semmelroth 1966).

Other theologians have a different opinion. They believe that Vatican II reached a true synthesis by placing the two images in an intrinsic relation to each other. This relation implies that the people of God is seen as the genus that refers to both the people of the old covenant and the people of the new. It is applicable to the community of the Jews as well as to that of Christians. Then the image *body of Christ* is viewed as the *differentia specifica.* Within the broader terminology of people of God, it indicates the specificity of the Christian church: for this is the people of God in the shape of the body of Christ; as the body of Christ it is the people of God; the church is the people of God, that is, the body of Christ (Küng 1967, 259).

Still other authors believe that Vatican II did not reach a synthesis at all and that the constitution on the church left the two images next to each other. The council did not integrate the two terms. On the contrary, the relation between the two is unsure and unclear (Rikhof 1981, 49).

From this survey of the constitution of Vatican II and the discussion about this, it becomes clear that the images *people of God* and *body of Christ* are anything but unproblematical. The disputes that take place about them can be described in the terms we used earlier to indicate the importance of the context of religious codes: inclusive and exclusive, central and marginal, attraction and repulsion (chapter 7 sub 4). This can be clarified as follows.

The battle is about the question whether the code *body of Christ* can be interpreted in such a way that it gets an inclusive meaning instead of an exclusive one. Here we are dealing with the differences between the two orientations in the New Testament on the one hand, and the encyclical letter *Mystici Corporis* on the other. The first group of authors brings this problem up for discussion explicitly. It refers to the exclusive meaning of the code *mystical body of Christ* in the encyclical letter, but it comes to the conclusion that the codes *body of Christ* and *people of God* do not exclude each other in the council text but that they do criticize each other. The second group sees the meaning of the code *body of Christ* as inclusive. The third group hesitates because it deems the relationship of this code to other codes, particularly *people of God,* to be poorly worked out.

Furthermore, the questioned is raised whether the code *body of Christ* should be attributed a central or a marginal meaning. The authors mentioned all believe that it should be seen as a central code. The question is, however, whether it should be seen as equally central, less central, or more central than the code *people of God.* The first group regards the code *people of God* as more central. The second group sees them both as equally central. The third group is not capable of forming a rounded judgment, due to the obscurity in the council text.

The process of attraction and repulsion plays a role too. The first group sees tension between the two codes. It regards them as each other's critical complement. This can mean that the codes attract and repulse each other at the same time. The second group proceeds from a maximum of attraction. Here, too, the third group hesitates. It believes that Vatican II did not clearly define the relationship between the two.

The importance of the context of the religious codes, which has been clearly given with the above, becomes evident even more in the period after Vatican II. The second group of authors, which believed that Vatican II brought about a synthesis, have had to come to the conclusion — even if it was brought about at all — that it was short-lived. It is more probable that the third group of authors is right. Vatican II left the discussion about the relationship between the two codes undecided, which meant as a consequence that the meaning of the codes shifted with the shifting of the church contexts.

The groups in favor of change replaced the coordination of the codes *body of Christ* and *people of God* with a setting aside of the code *body of Christ* and a preference for the code *people of God.* The connotations with the code *mystical body of Christ* in *Mystici Corporis* but also the church constitution of Vatican II are probably the cause of that. The code *people of God* has gained a negative, irritating value for conservative groups (Witte 1991). Thus, the final report of the extraordinary meeting of the synod of bishops in 1985 used the wording *people of God* only once, in an enumerative sense, as we indicated earlier (chapter 7 sub 4). Instead, the church was especially designated by words like *communio* and *mystery* (Willems 1986). As far as the term *communio* is concerned, one has to realize that this can refer to the *communio fidelium,* the *communio ecclesiarum,* and the *communio episcoporum* (Pottmeyer 1986). It is precisely the later reference to the *communio hierarchica* that is often implicitly or explicitly raised and stands in sharp contrast to the *communio fidelium* (Rikhof 1983; 1990; 1992).

Functions

Now we will try to expose the meaning of the code *body of Christ* for community formation in the church. In accordance with the distinction we made earlier, we will deal with the cognitive, emotive, and conative functions for that purpose (chapter 7 sub 2). Naturally, we will have to take up a position in the discussion that we just reported on. We do this from the perspective of a transformatory ecclesiology (Introduction).

Cognitive

The image of the members of the body that Christ is gives us insight into the specific nature of the church. The church as a community finds its origin and destination in the participation of each of the members in Christ rather than in the community that it forms itself. Participation in Christ is the foundation and the aim of communality and connectedness in the church. The church as a community exists by the grace of the community that Christ founds and offers gratuitously. He leaves it to the church to form itself as a community.

This does not make the processes of group and network formation unnecessary; however, it does relativize them — not in the sense of making them less important but of relating them to, and involving them with, Christ. They find their own meaning and their own shape in their orientation on the body of Christ. Otherwise one would come into conflict with the principle of noncompetition (Introduction).

In this orientation on Christ, the church distinguishes itself from other social formations that are defined with the image of the body. Thus one can talk of the body of the state, the legislative body, and the administrative body. A meeting or commission can be defined as a body. One sometimes speaks of companies in a biological sense: the company is an organism with a certain kind of soul; it has a head; there is a company core where the heart beats; there are processes at the foot of the company; the company has cells. What separates the church from all these formations is that it is the body of Christ: it stems from him and is aimed at him.

This does not mean that the body of Christ and the church are identical. "This church (. . .)," according to Vatican II, which earlier in the same number defined it as the mystical body of Christ, "subsists in the Catholic church" (*subsistit: Lumen Gentium* 8). There is also a church outside of it. The church can take no credit for it. It does not have exclusive rights. It can make no claims to universality hold. Even proceeding from the code *body of Christ*, it is obliged to focus on other churches and the world outside of it.

Emotive

The power of expression of the church as body of Christ immediately catches the eye. The image gives expression to mutual connectedness and connectedness to Christ. In this there is a continuous exchange between currents: outward and inward, from the bottom up and from the top down. In this image, people give to and receive from each other, with an eye to their personal growth and the growth of the community of Christ. This is done in such a way that giving is receiving and receiving is giving.

This image is further worked out in the visionary praxis of the community in Acts: "They would sell their possessions and goods and distribute the proceeds to all, as any had need. Day by day, attending the temple together and breaking bread in their homes, they partook of food with glad and generous hearts, praising God and having favor with all the people" (Acts 2:45-47).

The breaking of the bread holds an important position here. The image *body of Christ* is applicable in two senses. To put it briefly, the church is the body of Christ in the breaking of the bread, in which Christ himself is present under the signs of bread and wine. In semiotic — and proper sacramental — terms this can be interpreted as follows. On the one hand, the community itself, which has come together in the Eucharist, is a sign of Christ; it signifies and re-presents him. On the other hand, it is precisely the bread and wine in this celebration that become a sign of Christ: in this they signify and re-present him; they refer to him and make him present to the community. The double meaning of "body of Christ" means that here the community as a sign and the signs of bread and wine interlock. In other words: "In the meal of the Lord the community is constituted as a body" (Küng 1967, 258).

It is striking that in the code *people of God* the categories of time come first, and that the categories of space come first in the code *body of Christ.* The people move through the times, while the body depicts the unity of the social formation in the here and now. Does this mean that the church as the body of Christ is not on the move? Vatican II referred us to the fact that the church as the body of Christ, "is still moving forward," as we already mentioned (*Lumen Gentium* 7). However, does this mean that it is also tested? That it stumbles or falls? That it falls short of Christ? The body of Christ falling short of Christ? It is hard to imagine. The image does not seem to leave any room for that. This impression is confirmed if one places an emphasis on the organic character of the body, as if the growth of the church as the body of Christ would take place in a "natural" way, without any personal effort, ripening organically simply through sufficient eucharistic food and drink.

Conative

This visionary expression needs supplementation. The clearest indication of this can be found in the First Epistle to the Corinthians. The ornate comparison of the church with the body, which Paul holds up to the Corinthians, has a clearly parenetic purport. He admonishes them to become one body. He urges them to become the body of Christ. He presses for unity, mutual help, and attuning (Küng 1967, 262-63). The meaning of this can be explained by a number of considerations.

The first one that is necessary is the recognition of the pluralism in the church. Before one can call upon *communio* — if that should occur at all — it is necessary to research the distinctiveness and separateness and make it the object of communication. This is important in order to be able to answer the following question: What do we and do we not agree upon, and if not why? Often the drawing up of the *status questionis* is hard to do and takes a lot of patience and dedication. It demands the achievement of two taxonomic aims, which we described earlier: exchange and understanding on the grounds of a change of perspective (chapter 3 sub 2). This implies breaking through individual and collective prejudices: ecclesial egocentrism and sociocentrism. It requires decentering the church (cf. Piaget 1975).

Acknowledgment of pluralism has to follow its recognition. We are not dealing with fashionable permissiveness, but with an attitude and way of acting that lie in the community formation of the New Testament itself. Pluralism can be found everywhere in it: "The church communities in Palestine which created the synoptic tradition, the municipality of Jerusalem as we know it from Acts, the missionary center Antioch, the urban mission communities of Paul in Thessalonica, Corinth, Philippi, and Rome, the urban parishes in Ephesus and Colossae, the communities of John in Asia Minor: they have no unity of organization, no uniformity of doctrines, no codex of liturgical rites, no identical 'halacha' in reading scripture, no equal pattern of social behaviour. Yet they acknowledged each other in this pluralism as 'people of God', churches of the Lord, people anointed with the Spirit" (Houtepen 1983a, 284).

Finally, we must mention striving for the further formation of consensus. The communication within and between the churches should not stop at the recognition and acknowledgment of pluralism. The striving should be aimed at the stimulation of unity and community. In this striving it is preferable not to call upon *communio* but to contribute to it through discussion and reconciliation. A negative effect can issue from appeals, which can be experienced as the declaratory politics of claiming the initiative to speak for oneself and the implicit attribution of shortcomings to the other party. It is often the case that church leaders are themselves responsible for discord. It is, therefore, also their responsibility to restore the *communio*.

Chapter 15

Treatment of Conflict

In this part we placed the core function of integration of the church within the context of the societal process of individualization (chapter 13). The group and network formation that occur within this process were taken as points of departure for the treatment of community formation in the church. With this we discussed the problem of pluralization, which had already come up for discussion in the previous part. We tried to make clear that the only way to deal with this adequately lies in steadfast communication and the formation of consensus (chapter 14).

The problem now is what has to be done if communication and formation of consensus fail and pluralization leads to conflict. This can vary depending on the kinds of conflict. It is also of importance to keep an eye out for the religious identity of the church with this conflict.

In this chapter we will discuss the following questions: (1) What are the most important characteristics of conflicts? (2) What types of conflict treatment are there? And (3) In what does the religious orientation of conflict treatment lie?

(1) Characteristics of conflicts

Instead of giving (or being able to give) a definition of what conflicts are, we will restrict ourselves here to the description of some of their characteristics that are of importance to the church. We will do this by making a number of distinctions. With this description we shall see that it is not only a question of the objective existence of conflicts. But what is decisive is that we interpret certain processes as conflicts in interhuman and societal interaction in a subjective way. This applies to church processes too. In short, conflicts are cognitive constructs regarding social processes (Rabbie 1979; Hendriks & Stoppels 1986; Van der Ven 1986; Van Iersel & Spanjerberg 1985; 1993).

To begin with, conflicts can have either a destructive or constructive nature. Destructive conflicts have a negative effect on the church. They reduce the energy and diminish the effectiveness; they injure the cohesion, coordination, and cooperation. They damage the church, if not ruin it. Constructive conflicts, however, can lead to new, fresh approaches to tasks, increase cohesion and cooperation, raise the members' sense of satisfaction, and increase the feeling of vitality. They can lead the church to an unexpected view of its vision and mission, to a new, original way of acting (cf. Daft 1989, 458-60).

The constructive or destructive nature of conflicts is mainly a matter of interpretation and valuation. It is often the case that conflicts are already placed in a negative light beforehand, and are therefore judged to be destructive from the outset. This especially applies to a community such as the local church. The term *conflict* is often valued so negatively that the person who initiates it is viewed as the violator of unity. Even if he only manifests that which has been latently simmering beneath the surface for quite some time. Because of this he is easily given the blame for the conflict and the burden of proof is one-sidedly placed upon him. In other words, conflicts that from a business point of view may be constructive are often regarded as being destructive due to the fear of conflict and the danger of disintegration.

Here we have in passing introduced the distinction between manifest and latent conflicts. Manifest conflicts are more or less close to the surface, visible to both insiders and outsiders. This is not true for latent conflicts. They simmer beneath the surface in such a way that one really has to have inside information to be able to recognize them. Sometimes one or more of the parties are aware of the presence of the latent conflict but have reasons to leave it at that. Sometimes they are not aware of it. The latter can be caused by two things. It may be that they simply do not recognize the latent conflict. It is also possible that proceeding from a normative preoccupation ("there may be no conflicts"), they cannot bear it emotionally.

That conflicts in the church are easily viewed as destructive and are therefore often — consciously or unconsciously — kept latent is connected to another distinction. Conflicts may originate from differences in interests or in values. Differences in interests occur if two parties run into each other in their striving to gain financial-economic means or power. One can divide them into financial conflicts and power conflicts. Value conflicts refer to differences that lie in carrying through one's own personal religious convictions, values, and norms against the wishes of (an)other group(s). It is often felt that financial and power conflicts do not belong within the church, although they are certainly present. People fear that value conflicts cannot be handled or resolved. This is reason enough to shun both interest and value conflicts as long as possible.

There is another reason why people in the church are so cautious and careful — not to say overcareful — about conflicts. It has to do with the fear of the change from business conflicts to aggressive-escalating conflicts. The parties in a conflict can behave like business opponents; however, often — at least that is what is feared — one sees them becoming enemies. This fear is not always just. Research shows that conflicts need not necessarily imply enmity and aggressive behavior. Many conflicts are characterized by objective differences between parties that are not each other's enemies, but each other's opponents.

With this short introduction we have introduced four pairs of terms that are useful in analyzing and dealing with conflicts in the church: constructive and destructive; manifest and latent; interest and value; businesslike and escalating. We must add to this list a fifth pair of terms: correct and incorrect. What we mean by this is correct or incorrect perception. One can say a conflict is correctly perceived if it is rooted in objective differences in interests or values. However, one might be seeing things; that is, one may believe one has a conflict when in fact there is none.

When is one seeing things? This question cannot be solved by those who believe what they perceive to be true. Only an outsider is capable of this — an outsider who has enough knowledge of the people and matters that are involved in the conflict and who does not go along with the fallacy of the party or parties in question. This sometimes gives the discussions that lead to the "dis-covery" and "dis-illusionment" of the wrongful perception a painful or even tragic character.

There are several cases in which one may speak of an incorrect perception of the conflict. The first case is simple: one sees a difference where there is none at all — let alone a conflict. People sometimes "invent" differences. This is not because of their wild imaginations, but due to all sorts of defense mechanisms that play a part in the processes that occur within and between people. These have to do with one's unconscious wish to protect oneself against inner fear and guilt. Inner fear and guilt are often rooted in a great or overly great sense of responsibility in connection with the duties one has at heart and in which one consciously or unconsciously is afraid that one falls (or will fall) short of the mark. Proceeding from this fear, one begins to see other people as a threat because one is afraid of being overruled and overpowered, or accused and charged. One sees other people as a danger, while from a business perspective there is no reason for this. This often occurs in a religious or church context (Uleyn 1969).

The second case of an incorrect perception of conflict is that one sees a conflict where there is actually an easily solvable difference. The difference that one sees is there objectively, but one does not have an eye for the opportunities that are there for the taking, as it were, to get the problem out of the way. This can be achieved simply by removing the difference or changing the circumstances. One need not intervene in the relationships between the parties because a change of condition is already enough. Thus the discord that may exist about the allocation of financial means to various working groups within the church can often be solved by drawing up an impartial, rational allocation procedure. This is better than starting all kinds of complicated rounds of discussions about the size of the amounts and the desired and achievable change thereof.

The third case occurs if one believes that a certain theme is the source of conflict while in fact it revolves around a different matter. Thus one may think that the fight about the liturgical order of service is a liturgical value conflict. What one does not see here is that it is, for example, a power struggle between the working groups in the church and/or between working groups and ministers and administrators.

One can speak of a fourth case if one thinks one sees a conflicting difference between parties, while in fact it all comes down to one party and an entirely different party or even two totally different parties. Often the difference between two parties at the level of the local church is a reflection of the difference between one of these parties and another party who is at a higher level (deanery, diocese). One believes one sees a so-called horizontal conflict instead of the vertical conflict that is really at stake. The latter has to do with conflicts between two or more hierarchical levels (Daft 1989, 445-46).

(2) Treatment of conflict

In the treatment of conflict a distinction can be made between the rules that can be followed as a guide and the internal dynamics in the treatment of conflict. The rules define the boundaries within which one has to operate in dealing with the conflict. The internal dynamics have to do with the processes that occur in this.

Rules

In the above discussion one already finds a number of ways of dealing adequately with a conflict. A number of rules can be derived from this. These can be formulated descriptively and regarded normatively at the same time, seeing them as stemming from theory and research concerning the adequate treatment of conflict. For in the term *adequate* lies a normative moment. We group the rules into three kinds: rules connected to perception, attitude, and handling of conflict.

The first group has to do with the *perception* of conflict. The following rules are found in this: seeing that there are no conflicts where there are no differences; seeing that there are no conflicts where easily solvable differences occur; seeing that conflicts appear to be aimed at a certain theme while they are actually focussed on a different problem; seeing that conflicts appear to be taking place on a horizontal level while they are vertical conflicts in actual fact.

The second group refers to the *attitude* from which one faces conflicts. In this we are dealing with an attitude that answers to the following characteristics: constructive and not destructive; business-like and nonescalating.

The third group refers to the *handling* of conflict itself: keeping

FIGURE 15.1 Types of conflict treatment

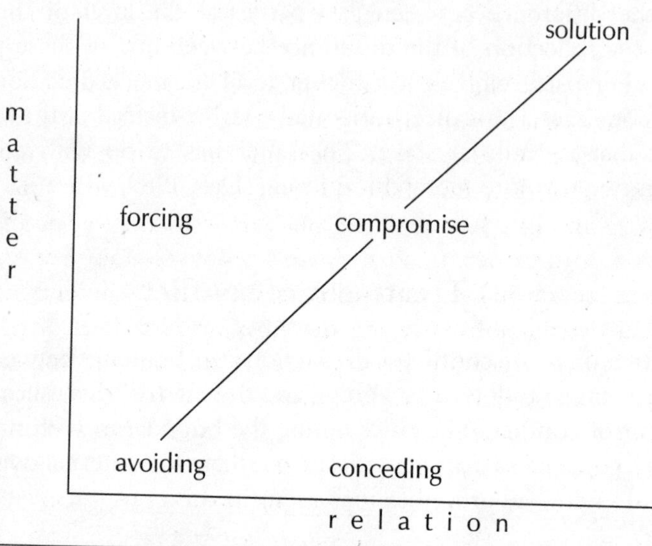

conflicts latent if they need to be kept latent (for whatever reason); making them manifest if they can and should be made manifest; handling them as interest conflicts if they present themselves as interest conflicts; and handling them as value conflicts if they manifest themselves as value conflicts.

Dynamics within two dimensions

In drawing up these rules nothing has been said about the internal dynamics that lie within the treatment of conflict. They are only a guide, giving the boundaries within which one has to operate. Further discussion is necessary concerning the playing field within these boundaries and the dynamic processes that take place.

We can do this by distinguishing two dimensions in these dynamics: the matter in question and the relationship between the parties that are involved in the conflict (Prein 1976; Blake & Mouton 1984; Rondeau 1990). Proceeding from the first dimension of the matter, one emphasizes the financial, power, or value problem in question; one tries to solve it as adequately as possible. Proceeding from the dimension of the relations involved, one tries to do as much justice as possible to the parties' staying together. Various positions can be taken up along these two dimensions, as indicated in figure 15.1.

If one keeps to the center of both dimensions in such a way that maximum justice is done to them, the treatment of the conflict results in a real solution. One can then speak of a maximum treatment of the matter and of the relationships. Often, however, a real solution is not possible and one has to satisfy oneself with an acceptable compromise for both parties. In such a case a midway solution is reached in which as much justice as possible is done to the interest of the matter and the relations between the two parties according to their own assessment. One can then speak of a transaction. Sometimes, however, one chooses to deal with the matter only. The handling of the conflict then comes down to forcing the issue. This occurs when there is strong competition and one of the parties strongly dominates. If one chooses exclusively for the relations, however, this comes down to conceding. One adapts oneself entirely to all the demands of the parties. One "runs with the hare and hunts with the hound." If one chooses for a minimum of care for both the matter and the relation, the lack of interest can be characterized as avoiding the issue. One can speak of running away, withdrawal, and apathy.

Internal dynamics

By means of these terms the internal dynamics of the treatment of conflict can now be described. It is often the case that processes of conflict in the church are consciously or unconsciously kept latent because people are afraid of party formation and disintegration. If they are consciously kept latent, there may be a case of what figure 15.1 calls "avoiding the issue." This can only continue until one of the parties involved raises the alarm and makes the theme a point on the agenda of the working group, the team, or the church board. There are two possibilities in such a case: either one tries to avoid raising it to the level of "policy" and supports this with some kind of argument (in short, legitimizing not the action, but the lack of it); or a real process of conflict starts up. Then it can go two ways. On the one side, the matter can get the upper hand. This may be a financial problem (budget), a power problem (authority), or a normative matter (aim of pastoral work). The more the matter dominates and one of the parties pushes forward its opinion, the more we can speak of forcing the issue. The relationship with the other party involved carries little or no weight at all. It revolts or drops out in its opposition. It can also happen that the relations between the parties gets the upper hand. The more this is the case, the more one can speak of hushing up, covering up, or conceding. Both parties are satisfied, confidence is restored, and the matter is disregarded.

What can also happen is that the consultation process swings one way (the matter) and then the other (the relations). This is particularly the case when we are dealing with complex problems that touch upon the vision and the mission of the church and that cannot be easily solved. One often sees processes of conflict moving to and fro between the matter and the relations. Sometimes one or both parties feel the need to resolve the conflict in the maximal possible sense. This is done in such a way that the most possible justice is done to both the matter and the relations. This can place quite a weight on the consultation process, certainly where it concerns complicated problems that contain many complex sides and ones in which outside forces also have an influence. If the ideal image of the maximal solution is proposed with enough intensity, it can put a certain amount of pressure on the consultation process. It can call up counterreactions from people who do not find the ideal image desirable and/or achievable. It can lead to anger or to apathy and even make people leave. In many cases the process will eventually result in a compromise. It is of importance to check from which side an attempt is being made to reach the compromise: from the minimum effort of avoiding the issue or the maximal ideal image of the solution, and besides this the effort for the matter or for the relations.

All the concepts in figure 15.1 do not account for the fact that the parties in question can solve the conflict by ending it. Ending here means that the parties part company because they separate or are separated from each other. If they separate themselves, one can speak of an independent decision of one of the parties or of both. If they are separated, then this is usually the result of an outside decision by order of the powers that be. The latter regularly occurs in the practice of organizations. The so-called structural separation is considered to be one of the conflict-limiting techniques (Daft 1989, 462).

(3) Treatment of conflict in religious perspective

In order to gain an insight into the religious orientation that is involved in the treatment of conflict in the church, we will now focus on the New Testament. A distinction has to be made between interecclesial conflicts, which in fact arose between Paul and the apostles, and intraecclesial conflicts, which involved life within the local church (Schillebeeckx 1985). We will take a further look at both. After that we will try to make an evaluation.

Interecclesial treatment of conflict

The most striking interecclesial conflict involved the dispute between Paul and Barnabas, on the one hand, and the leaders of the church in Jerusalem — Peter, James, and John — on the other. This conflict was about the question whether Christians in Antioch, who were Gentiles originally, should undergo circumcision like the Christians earlier, who were Jews originally, had. The consultation took place in Jerusalem and is known in history as "the council of Jerusalem." One could say that a real solution was found in the sense of figure 15.1: the matter everything revolved around was done full justice and the relations between the parties — as far as we know — was honored to the full. The solution was that circumcision was not obligatory for the Gentiles. This collective decision was sealed with "the right hand of fellowship," according to Paul (Gal. 2:9). The solution that was found here concerned not only a detailed matter of practice but a deeply fundamental value conflict involving the intrinsic structure of the relationship between the Jews, the Gentiles, and the Christians.

Paul himself saw this solution to be the final result of a consultation among equals. However, in the later reconstruction in the book of Acts, it was not presented as a decision from mutual consultation but as a solemn decree that was communicated on the authority of "the brothers, both the apostles and the elders," via a letter by appointed delegates "along with our beloved Paul and Barnabas" to "the believers of Gentile origin in Antioch" (Acts 15:22-29). Paul and Luke, the author of the Acts, appeared to have placed different emphases on the report of this council as well as on the ecclesiological legitimization of it.

That even then a council did not solve all problems became clear shortly thereafter when a second interecclesial conflict arose. The consultation in Jerusalem had not only led to a solution concerning the matter of circumcision, but also of the division of labor between Peter, James, and John on the one hand, and Paul and Barnabas on the other. Paul summarized the decision as follows: "we should go to the Gentiles, and they to the circumcised" (Gal. 2:9). But what happened when this division of labor was thwarted? For according to the Epistle to the Galatians, Peter turned up in Antioch, a community in the area of the Gentiles. There he partook of the meals with Christians who had been Gentiles. This was detestable to the Jews and Christians from Judaism. Nevertheless, Peter continued to do so. This changed when Jewish Christians from James's circle arrived in Antioch from Jerusalem. Peter then stopped this practice of openness and respect, just as did the other Jewish Christians who sat down at the same table. Even Barnabas stopped doing this. This was quite a shock to Paul. Once again the credibility of Christianity as opposed to the lifestyle of the Gentiles was at stake. Paul spoke sharply to Peter: "If you, though a Jew, live like a Gentile and not like a Jew, how can you compel the Gentiles to live like Jews?" (Gal. 2:14). From that time on Peter and Paul avoided each other, and Paul and Barnabas left each other's company too.

This conflict appears not to have been resolved or settled then — at least we do not have any data about it. If this is correct, then it appears that in one of the first Gentile-Christian communities in the New Testament, one could speak of the kind of treatment of conflict that was called structural separation in the discussion above. The bitterness in Paul can still be traced in the way in which he accused the Jewish Christians, who shared their meals with Gentile Christians in Antioch "for fear of the circumcision faction" (Gal. 2:12), of hypocrisy. Of Barnabas he said, "even Barnabas was led astray by their hypocrisy" (Gal. 2:13).

Intraecclesial treatment of conflict

Besides these interecclesial conflicts which involved relations between Paul and the other apostles, there are also numerous intraecclesial problems and difficulties in the New Testament. We need only follow Paul's report regarding the processes that were going on in the communities of Galatia and Corinth. How much this moved Paul, appeared from one of the first verses of the Second Epistle to the Corinthians: "For we do not want you to be unaware, brothers and sisters, of the affliction we experienced in Asia; for we were so utterly, unbearably crushed that we despaired of life itself. Indeed, we felt that we had received the sentence of death, so that we would rely not on ourselves but on God who raises the dead; he who rescued us from so deadly a peril" (2 Cor. 1:8-10).

What was going on there? After Paul's last visit, it seemed that preachers had appeared in Galatia who had tried to win over the Gentile-Christians to an interpretation of the gospel from the Jewish Christian communities. In this not only the circumcision but also the upholding of other Jewish laws played an important role. This missionary work had as its aim, or at least as a consequence, that Paul's authority was undermined. The tone of the Epistle to the Galatians is hard: Paul was to the point. Already in one of the first verses he tells the Galatians: "I am astonished that you are so quickly deserting the one who called you in the grace of Christ and turning to a different gospel — not that there is another gospel, but there are some who trouble you and want to pervert the gospel of Christ. . . . As we have said before, so now I repeat, If any one proclaims to you a gospel contrary to that what you received, let that one be accursed. Am I now seeking human approval, or God's approval? Or am I trying to please people? If I were still pleasing people, I would not be a servant of Christ" (Gal. 1:6-7, 9-10). A little further along he forces the issue of the difference between the Gentile-Christian interpretation (the Spirit, the faith) and the Jewish-Christian interpretation (the law, the flesh) even more: "You foolish Galatians! Who has bewitched you? . . . The only thing I want to learn from you is this: Did you receive the Spirit by doing the works of the law or by believing what you heard? Are you so foolish? Having started with the Spirit, are you now ending with the flesh?" (Gal. 3:1-3). Paul threw all his weight into the balance as well as his personal relationship with the Galatians: "Friends, I beg you, become as I am, for I also have become as you are. . . . [You] welcomed me as an angel of God, as Christ Jesus. . . . Have I now become your enemy by telling you the truth?" (Gal. 4:12, 14, 16). The epistle is sharply worded. Whether Paul was successful with it is not known.

What was going on in Corinth in comparison to Galatia? The problems in Galatia had to do with the insurgence of Jewish-Christian preachers, who were trying to win over the Gentile Christians. In Corinth the people were in danger of becoming tempted by the rhetorical performance of the handsome, charismatic Apollos and accepting a mixture of Hellenistic philosophy and mysticism. Some members of the community had gone so far as to be completely in the power of Apollos, and had turned away from Paul (1 Cor. 4:18). Here, too, Paul went all out, without being too sharp in a relational sense, as he had been in the Epistle to the Galatians. He left no room for misunderstanding: no doubt Apollos had a greater gift of eloquence or erudition (1 Cor. 2:1) and he himself was weak, nervous, and of a fearful nature (1 Cor. 2:3). Nevertheless, the wisdom that Apollos brought was only the wisdom of the (Hellenistic) world (1 Cor. 1:18-31), while the Christian wisdom, which was only foolishness in the eyes of the world, represented the true wisdom (1 Cor. 2:4–6:21).

What kind of conflict treatment did Paul apply here? By setting the gospel, as he had proclaimed it, and the doctrine of Apollos opposite each other and by showing the arguments for and against them, he tried to convince the Corinthians. He did not try to persuade them — for that was precisely what he believed Apollos was up to. No more than with the Galatians did Paul aim at a treatment of conflict that resulted in compromise (in the sense of figure 15.1). He was not one to compromise. He strived after a general and completely satisfying consensus for both parties — the maximum solution. For this purpose he communicated and argued with a passion.

The question whether Paul succeeded in his intention cannot be answered with any great certainty. However, in all probability his sharp performance did not fall on good ground. In any case, it appears that his relationship with Corinth was fundamentally disturbed. Before he wrote his Second Epistle to the Corinthians, he appears to have paid a visit to his community there. It had not been pleasant, and even a bit sad (2 Cor. 1:23; 2:1). It had ended up with a painful incident (2 Cor. 2:5; 7:12). He therefore wrote his second epistle "with many tears" (2 Cor. 2:4). Afterward it appears he sent the far milder Titus, who came from the circles of Gentile-Christians, to Corinth (2 Cor. 7:5-6, 13-14; 8:6, 16-19, 23; 12:18). After he managed to solve the problem there (2 Cor. 2:6; 7:5-16), Paul was very pleased (2 Cor. 2:1-13; 7:5-16) and could now contentedly travel to Corinth (Schillebeeckx 1985, 118).

If one compares Paul's and Titus's performances in Corinth (reconstructed from the sparing data we have), it appears that Paul indulged in a certain degree of forcing the issue in the sense of figure 15.1. Titus, however, found a kind of balance between "the matter" of the gospel and "the relationship" with the members of the community. He succeeded where Paul failed.

Evaluation

If we summarize the data from the New Testament, we see that four kinds of conflict treatment come to the fore: solution based on a general consensus (council in Jerusalem); separation of parties (Peter and Paul in Antioch); forcing the issue (Paul regarding Corinth); and compromise (Titus in Corinth). Two of the four kinds are worth further consideration: solution and compromise. Both other kinds (separation and forcing the issue) will not be considered further because they offer no further perspective. Separation can sometimes be necessary because there is no other way out, even if it leaves the parties with sorrow and bitterness. Forcing the issue not only fails to solve anything but also leads to obduracy, which requires treatment in itself, as appears from Paul's case.

The council of Jerusalem is, of course, central. The consensus that was reached there, and that was satisfying to all parties, did full justice to the matter of the gospel and may be seen as a guideline for every treatment of conflict. In order to connect this with previous chapters: one can say that the vision (people of God) and mission of the church (Jesus movement) were tuned to the integration of the church (body of Christ) and vice versa, in a harmonic way in this council decision. For the issue under discussion — circumcision — touched upon the relationship between the Jewish people as the people of God and the church as part of the people of God. It belonged to the core of the gospel that Jesus proclaimed and through which he was recognized and acknowledged as Messiah in the Jesus movement: liberation from the law to the freedom of the kingdom of God. This essential issue was brought to a happy conclusion in collectiveness and mutual connectedness, so that the church as the one body of Christ could remain intact, and Christ was not torn. In short, for truly essential matters they were one!

Yet at the same time and in all matter-of-factness, we must

remark that the council also drew up an important work schedule. This was meant to stop the formerly opposing parties from getting in each other's way once the council was over — to stop them from thwarting each other. This seems to be part of things: the exalted decision, taken in unanimity, need not stand in the way of practical agreements. On the contrary, the strategic decision demands an operational measure, in this case a territorial division. Paul said pithily: "we should go to the Gentiles and they to the circumcised" (Gal. 2:9). It is possible — we do not know for sure — that the decision to divide the territory was taken at the same time as the essential decision to lift the law of circumcision. It would not have been the last time a practical agreement had stimulated the taking of a principal decision in a climate of unanimity.

Having said all this, we do not imply that the formation of consensus in less essential matters should not be an important aim to strive for. It is important, but not as important. That is why it is also possible to be satisfied with a temporary compromise in less essential matters — a compromise that is not eternally binding and that can be broken if new data or facts present themselves, a compromise that is supple and flexible, without the striving for the solution of complete consensus disappearing from view entirely. This is probably how Titus's mission ended.

Closing a compromise demands negotiation. People often think that this is not allowed in the church. If striving for consensus as an endeavor is not undone by it, then it is hard to see why negotiation should be unbecoming in the church. Negotiating means nothing more than striving to do as much justice as possible to both the matter and the relationships, step by step. In practice it is often hard to do more.

Closing a compromise can be legitimized in a theological sense by proceeding from the eschatological perspective of the nearing of God's salvation, in which there is tension between "already" and "not yet." If one lets go of the tension, there is a possibility of landing in the "already complete" of realized eschatology. Paul took action against this possibility in Corinth, not only because of the danger of hysterical situations but especially because of the risk of party formation and schism. Realized eschatology, in which people believe to have God's salvation in their grasp, can lead to ecclesiological fanaticism. It destroys the church (chapter 12 sub 3). The other possibility is that if one lets go of the tension, one lands in the "not at all complete" of apocalyptic chiliasm. Daily life is postponed, as it were. The expectation of the end of time, which is just around the corner, makes daily life unimportant. Often aggressive tendencies are hidden behind this. This, too, can lead to disintegration (Sierksma 1978, 216-51).

Closing a compromise can be legitimized in an ethical sense proceeding from the term *prudence*. Prudence does not mean cautiousness but sensibility. According to Aristotle, it is an intellectual virtue involved with the consideration of aims that have to strived after in the practice of life and with the calculation of the means that have to be brought into action for that purpose. Prudence, in the words of Aristotle, has to do with sensible management concerning, for instance, the family and the state. Prudence comes down to the management of home economics (Aristotle, *Nicomachean Ethics* VI, V).

The virtue of prudence implies that one does three things before one resorts to a certain action in a certain situation. The first is that one becomes aware of and reflects upon the aim one wants to achieve, including the values that lie in this aim. The second is that one should carefully inform oneself about the situation in which the action in view will take place: how the situation arose during the course of history; which present-day factors determine it; in which direction it will develop in the future, independent of whatever possible action. To an important degree, this information is based upon subjective and/or objective estimates. Subjective estimates stem from personal intuition or feeling. Objective estimates are made on the basis of calculation of probability. The third is that one tries to make subjective and objective predictions of the direct, indirect, and unintended effects of the various actions one could perform in the particular situation. By weighing the pros and cons of the various actions against each other and by bringing them into relation with the aim in view, an image arises of the choice one has to make. The realization of such a process of choice, which is preceded by insight, forms the core of the virtue of prudence (Van der Ven 1985c, 93-94; Van Iersel 1982). One can put it like this: in prudent action that which is desirable (aim) and that which can be achieved (situation) are involved with each other. Prudence takes place between ideal and reality (Mette 1978; Van der Ven 1985b). Prudence is thus a strategic-tactical term (Thomas, *Summa Theologica* II-II, 48, 50).

Troeltsch pointed out at the beginning of this century what the consequences are of the neglect of the art of negotiation and of the closing of compromises. They are idealistic fanaticism on the one hand, and fatalism and cynicism on the other. He developed an ethic of compromise, which contains important insights for the church. What Schleiermacher defines as "the rules of pastoral art," were worked out by Troeltsch in his ethical-ecclesiological doctrine of compromise. In it we find elements like insight into the relativity of one's own position, tolerance and respect for that of others, and the provisional character of compromise (Drehsen 1988, 586-612).

Chapter 16

Leadership

In this part (IV), the integration of the church is central. We placed it in the context of the societal processes of urbanization and individualization (chapter 13). In this it appeared, however, that group and network formation also occur. We chose them as the point of departure for our consideration of the church as a community, in the context of which we also approached the church as the body of Christ (chapter 14). The pluralization of convictions can put the church under a certain amount of pressure and can negatively influence the formation of consensus. This is certainly the case if the pluralization leads to conflicts (chapter 15). The figure of church leadership continued to play a role in the background. In this chapter we will put this topic in the forefront.

During the course of this chapter we will try to find answers to the following questions: (1) What kind of leadership actually exists in the church of today, particularly the Catholic Church? 2) What kind of leadership can be found in the New Testament and in the early church? (3) What insights can be derived from that era for church leadership today? and (4) How can we view the ministry on that basis?

(1) Leadership in the church

Those who try to find an answer to the question what kind of leadership actually exists in the church, and particularly the Catholic

Church, need to have a theory of leadership at hand. By means of terms from such a theory, one is able to draw up a description of the kind of leadership that comes across in the church and to set it off from other kinds. Through this, one gains sharpness and precision.

For such a theory, we shall turn to authors in the tradition of Max Weber, first dwelling upon the distinction that is made between power and authority in this tradition, then distinguishing four types of authority.

Power and authority

The words *power* and *authority* entail an entire ecclesial discussion. They are words of contradiction mainly because descriptive and normative statements are used interchangeably. On the one hand, one hears that power does not belong with the church and should not be there (normative). On the other hand, one finds that in actual fact the structure of the church is controlled through power (descriptive), even holy power *(potestas sacra)*. The reverse holds for authority. On the one hand, people regret that there is no or insufficient authority in the church and make a plea for true authority as something desirable (normative). On the other, the church leadership posits that it certainly acts with authority (descriptive). In short, what is power, what is authority?

In this kind of discussion in which two terms cause confusion, it sometimes helps to introduce a third, more neutral term, in order to be able to define clearly the two other terms. Following Weber, the third term is *influence.* Weber's point of departure lies in two different phenomena that he registers in daily life. The first phenomenon is that some people exert an influence on other people. They influence their way of experiencing, feeling, thinking, being motivated, and acting. This kind of influencing, which involves the perceptions, emotions, cognitions, motivations, and behaviors of the people in question, Weber calls *power.* Power divides people into two groups: rulers and subjects, the more and the less powerful. This kind of power occurs everywhere: in the family, in education, in trade and industry, in politics, and in the church too. What then is authority? According to Weber, authority is the influencing that is acknowledged, wanted, honored, and accepted by the people in question. Authority is always respected power, legitimized power. Influencing appears in two shapes: power and legitimized power. Legitimized power is called *authority* by Weber. Power without legitimization is *naked power;* while power with respect, or with legitimization, is viewed as *authority* (Avis 1992).

One may well wonder how much naked power and how much authority can be found in the church. Naked power can be recognized by the actual influence the church leadership exerts, without this being respected. Here we are not dealing with the juridical influence that is attributed to it in the codex, but with real, effective influence. Authority can be recognized by the degree to which people respect this effective influence — not that which should be respected morally, but that which is actually respected.

Proceeding from this distinction between naked power and authority, one can draw up two general hypotheses. The first is that naked power has a disintegrating influence in the church. The second is that authority has an integrating function. The reasons are clear. Naked power is influence without respect. It does not bind people; it sooner repulses them, certainly in a normative institution like the church (chapter 14 sub 2). Authority, however, is influence with respect. People acknowledge the influencing and desire to be influenced.

Authority

The term *authority* can be separated into four different types, proceeding from the tradition of Weber. Weber himself worked out three types: charismatic, traditional, and legal-rational. Others added a fourth type, functional-rational, partially on the basis of Weber's work. These types are also relevant for the description of leadership in the church (Weber 1980; Thung 1976; Sonnberger & Van der Ven 1992).

In *charismatic authority* leadership is acknowledged on the basis of exceptional or even extranatural or supernatural gifts attributed to it. The founders of the religions and of new movements within these religions are often attached to charismatic authority. Jesus himself is an eminent example of this, but so are people like Francis and Ignatius, who stood at the beginning of religious movements of renewal in Christianity. Charismatic authority is personal authority.

Sooner or later the charisma becomes routinized to a certain extent when the charismatic founder is succeeded by people appointed by himself or by followers. The authority that is attached to the new leaders is no longer based on their personal gifts, but on the tradition that has arisen in the meantime. This *traditional authority* has its roots in the conviction that the leader should be obeyed because this "always has been the case" and because "that is just the way things are." It corresponds to the earlier directions given by the founder and to the values, norms, and conventions that have been rooted in the particular tradition. Traditional authority is authority built on the past.

Opposite this traditional authority we have *legal-rational authority.* Here the respect shown to the leader is not based on the force of tradition, but on the formal rules concerning succession that hold in the particular community. These rules are recorded in writing in regulations, canons, constitutions, and laws. If the leader in question has risen to the position he now holds because the procedures in question have been carefully followed and finished, then he really "deserves" respect and acceptance by the members of the community. Legal-rational authority is formal authority.

Functional-rational authority implies that the authority of the leader is accepted because he has expertise and expert assessment in a particular field. He is known as a professional who therefore deserves to have respect and acknowledgment. Functional-rational authority is expert authority (Wilke 1979).

Does one also find these types of authority in the church? One comes across two different opinions in literature about this. They can be defined as the views of simplicity and complexity. We will give a short description of them here.

In the view of *simplicity,* the various types of authority occur exclusively within the various church communities. Thus, charismatic authority occurs only in the charismatic churches and in the Pentecostal Movement; traditional authority occurs in traditional churches, like the Eastern Orthodox churches; legal-rational authority occurs in the Catholic Church; and functional-rational authority occurs in liberal Protestantism.

In the view of *complexity,* the various types occur in all churches, albeit that one church is especially characterized by one type and another church by another type. Thus, charismatic authority is characteristic for charismatic churches and the Pentecostal Movement, but in this elements may also be present from, for instance, traditional authority. Thus, the Eastern Orthodox churches are mainly characterized by traditional authority, but besides that there may also be elements from charismatic authority. Legal-rational authority may be characteristic of the Catholic Church, but one may also find elements from charismatic, traditional, and functional-rational authority. Functional-rational authority may determine the shape of the liberal churches in Protestantism, but features from charismatic and legal-rational authority may also be traced.

The view of complexity can be further worked out for the Catholic Church. It is indeed the case that legal-rational authority is characteristic of this church. For the emphasis on requirements for preparation to the ministry, the procedures for admission to the ministry, the criteria for ministry practice, and the division of power across the various ministerial levels are central to the Catholic Church structure. It is precisely this officialdom that makes people believe that authority and power are the same, more so than in charismatic, traditional, and functional-rational types of authority. Those who have ended up in a ministerial position following the formal-legal channels deserve acknowledgment, respect, and acceptance on the basis thereof; more or less separate from the personal way in which they give concrete shape to the ministry. It is precisely this personal interpretation, which is of less importance in the legal-rational type of authority, that tips the scale with the other types of authority. In the charismatic type, we look to the extraordinary or supernatural giftedness of a particular person; in the traditional type, we look to the personal connection to tradition; and in the functional type, we look to the professional quality a particular person commands. While the emphasis in the legal type is on business and formal-official procedures, the other three are characterized by more personal prestige (Moberg 1962; Laan 1967).

However, authority and the exercise of authority in the Catholic Church are not restricted to the legal-rational type. Charismatic, traditional, and functional-rational elements are also connected to it. Thus one speaks of the professional charisma of the church official. Support from God's Spirit has been beseeched for the ordinand, so that he can execute his ministry, inspired by the Spirit (Weber 1980). The traditional type of authority lies in the ordination of the minister by the bishop, who is deemed to be connected to the apostolic tradition and

TABLE 16.1

Types of authority in the Catholic Church (N=413)

	score	sd
charismatic	3.35	1.05
traditional	2.76	1.29
legal-rational	2.55	1.17
functional-rational	4.32	.66

to the apostles themselves through the *successio apostolica*. Hence one can say: without tradition, there is no ministry. Finally, one also comes across functional-rational elements, even of old. The professions of doctor, notary, and priest in the Middle Ages can be regarded as the first forms of professional practice (Parsons 1968). The Council of Trent can be viewed as the founder of the professional educational structure, which was felt to be necessary for the adequate exercise of office. The regulations now in force in Sapientia Christiana are an offshoot of this.

What attitudes do ordinary church members show with regard to the four types of authority in the Catholic Church? In table 16.1 one finds the data of two groups of respondents from two comparable communities in the Netherlands and Nordrhein-Westphalia in Germany, specifically Oosterhout (Noord-Brabant) and Kleve, which have been combined in this table. The data were collected by Klaus Sonnberger in the context of the research project "Participation and Church Development" within the department of empirical theology at the University of Nijmegen, the Netherlands. The respondents were given a number of questions in which the four types of authority defined by Weber were operationalized. The scales run from 1 (very strongly disagree) to 5 (very strongly agree). We must note here that the research population was primarily made up of modal and core members.

A clear prioritization comes to the fore in table 16.1. The functional-rational type of authority is felt to be highly desirable (4.32), and we are also struck by the low standard deviation (.66). Therefore, one can speak of a great degree of consensus with regard to a very strong preference for a typically modern kind of authority:

TABLE 16.2
Correlations of types of authority

	legal
charismatic	.41
traditional	.77
functional	.16

$p \leq .05$

that based on professionalism. At a distance we see the charismatic type of authority (3.35), about which people have their doubts, albeit in a positive sense, and which is surrounded by a large degree of dissensus (1.05). Following this, again at a distance, is the traditional type of authority (2.76), which people also have doubts about, but now in a negative sense, and which is surrounded by an even greater amount of dissensus (1.29). The lowest place is held by the legal-rational type of authority (2.55), which people reject, and which is again characterized by a great deal of disagreement (1.17).

Nevertheless, not all has been said. The legal-rational type of authority can enter into certain relations with one or more other types of authority. Through this, it may lose its strikingly negative valuation to a greater or lesser extent. In table 16.2 we find the coefficients of the correlations between the legal type of authority on the one hand and the charismatic, traditional, and functional types on the other. They again have to do with the research in Oosterhout and Kleve.

In table 16.2 it appears that the legal-rational type of authority has a significant connection with the three other types of authority. However, the correlation coefficient of one of the three, the functional type (.16), remains below the threshold of relevance (.20). Thus we are left with the correlations with the charismatic type (.41) and the traditional type (.77).

Some sociologists from the tradition of Weber note that the connection between the legal type of authority on the one hand, and the charismatic and traditional types on the other, has the function of masking the fact that the Catholic Church is entirely characterized by a certain kind of legal-rational type of authority, the monocratic type. The connection between this monocratic, legal-rational type of authority and the charismatic and traditional types hides the erosion that the structure of the church suffers. It disguises the lack of acknowledgment and respect from which the actual structure of power suffers. Some authors believe that the church is aware of these elements and makes use of them. That is why they speak of strategies: the strategy of charismatization and of traditionalization. Accordingly, the sociologist Gabriel posits that all this refers to "firstly, the charismatization of the person of the pope in particular, but also in a derived sense of the bishops and priests, and secondly the strategy of traditionalization in the sense of a conscious stimulation of the devotional, popular piety of the people which has been handed down and of an organization of mass religiosity" (Gabriel 1988b, 35). Here, charismatization and traditionalization are viewed as functions of the ideologization of the structure of the Catholic Church (chapter 8 sub 5).

(2) Leadership in the early church

It appears from all of this that the leadership of the Catholic Church is quite a problem. In such a situation, the obvious thing to do is to turn to the New Testament and the early church, to see how leadership in the church was developed in the first Christian communities. We shall first put a number of data on the early church together, and then try to expose their significance for the church of today.

The early church

It is not necessary here to take a detailed look at all sorts of texts and groups of texts in the New Testament. We refer the reader to exegetical publications for that purpose. Here we will restrict ourselves to the conceptualization of the results of synthetic studies in this field (cf. Schnackenburg 1961; Heinz 1974; Hahn et al. 1979; Schillebeeckx 1980; 1982; 1985; 1989; Hainz 1982; Lohfink 1986; Kertelge 1986).

In the conceptualization we have in mind, there are a number of central terms, as is indicated by figure 16.1: spontaneous and functional, informal and hierarchical, decentral and central, fraternal and vertical. These terms have been ordered in a binary fashion in figure 16.1, and in such a way that pair by pair they form each other's opposite. We are dealing with contrasting pairs: spontaneous versus functional, informal versus hierarchical, decentral versus central, and fraternal versus vertical. Moreover, these contrasting pairs have been placed in a tree structure, so that it becomes clear to which semantic or conceptual domain each term belongs, and from which it gets its meaning. A binary-structured tree diagram has the advantage, as semiotics teaches us, that the total semantic and conceptual field is covered. In addition, the terms gain greater clarity if their meanings are described proceeding from their mutual opposition. Because of this, we can oversee matters and gain insights (Eco 1979a, 73-84).

We begin by establishing that no community in the New Testament can be found in which one cannot speak of some kind of structure. By structure we mean in a general sense a lasting attuning of actions and interactions of people in a social whole, through which this whole takes shape. "Structure" involves the durability of actions and interactions in a social whole (Van Doorn & Lammers 1959, 77-81). In a certain permanent state, the members of the community perform all sorts of actions and interactions with an eye to the development of the community.

This lasting structure of actions and interactions can be divided into two types: a spontaneous and a functional structure. The *spontaneous structure* is primarily based on the experiences, feelings, and attitudes that originate in the extraordinary charismata. In the *functional structure,* certain rational considerations play a role, particularly with regard to the choice of certain means with an eye to certain goals. It sooner stems from pastoral aims and motives. It is founded on the ordinary charismata (for the distinction between ordinary and extraordinary charismata, see sub 3).

A spontaneous structure can be found in the pre-Pauline communities, and especially in Antioch. We know this indirectly from the epistles of Paul, the Acts, certain traditions in the Gospel of Mark, and other texts from the New Testament. These communities were characterized by a strong pneumatic emotiveness, prophetic inspiration, and charismatic community formation on the grounds of a realized eschatology (chapter 12 sub 3). These were the foundation for a charismatic-egalitarian ecclesiology: those who were filled by the

Spirit exercised authority in the community. This is represented in figure 16.1 by "spontaneous structure" (1).

In contrast to the pre-Pauline communities, we find a functional-pastoral structure in the later apostolic communities, and particularly in the Pauline and post-Pauline ones. Two sides can be distinguished in this structure. On the one hand, it had the external shape of an important social formation in its time, the *oikos,* the Greco-Roman family house, to which, besides the immediate family, the servants, slaves, and other people belonged. Usually this implied the larger houses of well-to-do citizens, who threw open their homes for community meetings. Thus the community came together in the *oikos* of Aquila and Prisca in Ephesus (1 Cor. 16:19). Because the space was limited due to the dimensions of the house, the members of the community had direct, face-to-face contact with each other.

On the other hand, the hierarchical structure surrounding the *paterfamilias,* which was characteristic of the *oikos,* was broken through to form a different social formation of that time: the *collegium.* A *collegium* can be regarded as a free society, an association of equals, who held meetings in the house of one of its members. It had a free and democratic order. The later apostolic, Pauline, and post-Pauline communities were characterized by the internal order of such a *collegium.* They mostly came together in the *oikos* of one of the members of the community, according to the internal structure of a *collegium.* Insofar as the community members came together in a synagogue, the *collegium* structure was applicable, since the synagogue was modeled on this structure. Within this structure people provided themselves with informal pastoral rules for the adequate performance of duties inside and outside the community and for the treatment of conflicts. Thus, Paul's performance was characterized by all sorts of doctrinal, moral, and disciplinary instructions, the purpose of which was to channel the unbridled freedom of the pure charismatic communities into the development of the community. His performance was functional-pastoral by nature (chapter 12 sub 3). It is of importance to note that the rules and instructions mentioned were not of a formal but of an informal character, and seemed to differ from community to community. So one can speak of all kinds of services that were performed in the community, like those of apostles, prophets, teachers, miracle workers, healers, helpers, administrators, speakers in tongues, and interpreters (1 Cor. 12:28-30). However, there was no set list of services, let alone a list of formal offices. In figure 16.1 this is called the "informal-functional structure" (2).

In the postapostolic communities in the New Testament, however, changes gradually started to occur. In the pastoral-functional structure, a tendency toward formalization started to show up, as appears from a few Pastoral Epistles (1 and 2 Timothy, Titus, and 1 Peter). People were not entirely unprepared for this, since in some later postapostolic communities a certain amount of systematization and uniformalization started to become visible. In this way the list of services, which encompassed nine different types of service in the First Epistle to the Corinthians, is reduced to five in the Epistle to the Ephesians, which was written around A.D. 90. These services were rendered by apostles, prophets, evangelists, pastors, and teachers (Eph. 4:11). The community still came together in the *oikos* of one of the members; however, the internal structure was not so much drawn from the democratic *collegium* as from the order of the *oikos* surrounding the *paterfamilias.* He was called the *presbyter-episkopos,* which means as much as the (no doubt circulating) chairmanship of the presbyterion, probably made up of the heads of the households. With this hierarchical structure, the emphasis was also placed on the obedience that all owed to the presbyterion and the presbyter-episkopos, taking it away from the *oikos* organization. Along with this a religiously legitimized androcentrism was introduced too: women were not members of the group of the heads of the households! The tendency toward formalization was even more strongly present in the noncanonical writings from about the same date as the Pastoral Epistles, such as the epistles of Clement and the epistles of Ignatius of Antioch. The Pastoral Epistles still had teachers and prophets next to the presbyters and the episkopos. In the noncanonical epistles (not in the *Didache*!) it appears that their authority has been entirely absorbed by the presbyters and the episkopos. However, an important element deserves special mention. The hierarchical structure was not of a central but of a decentral nature. The hierarchical *paterfamilias* was the pivot of the community, without his having to be accountable, however, to a higher, more encompassing organ. In other words, the church was a community of mutually equal local communities. In this sense the church structure of the New Testament is called congregationalistic (McKenzie 1976). In figure 16.1 this is called the "decentral-hierarchical structure" (3).

This decentral-hierarchical *paterfamilias* structure has to be limited with respect to the central form that the hierarchical administration assumed in the course of the second and third centuries. During these two centuries, an ever-increasing tendency toward centralization of government of the local churches arose. This tendency originated in the urban and provincial centers. For this purpose the structure of civil service in the cities and provinces of the Roman Empire in particular were taken over. With this we must note that this centralization had the nature of an *entente*, as it is known in management science. An entente is characterized by the meeting of governors of an equal level for the exchange of information regarding matters each of them is authorized to regulate autonomously and besides this to reach a consensus on matters that concern all of them together. The entente structure can be understood by means of a Venn diagram: only the area where the two circles dissect each other requires a collective definition of opinion; what falls outside this belongs to the authority of the individual governor. The entente structure, therefore, has a fraternal structure (Keuning & Eppink 1986, 136-39). The episkopoi came together in a fraternal sense to inform each other on matters that concerned their own area, and to consult and make decisions on business that concerned them all. This is called the "fraternal-central structure" in figure 16.1 (4).

In the meantime, all sorts of developments arose in the second and third centuries that led to the extension of all kinds of administrative intermediate levels between the episkopoi. In some areas, as in the church of Egypt (in contrast to Africa), an order of rank started to arise between bishops, metropolitans, and patriarchs. This development was enhanced during the course of the fourth century by the increasingly close ties that grew between the church and the Roman Empire. It was then that the administrative intermediate levels between the bishops and the churches they led started to take on a pyramid-like nature. This was especially the case after the Edict of Milan in 311 when Christianity became a so-called permitted religion *(religio licita),* provided with rights that were equal to those of other religions. This became even stronger from 380 on, when Christianity became the state religion. So at the end of the fourth century, there were the following patriarchates: Jerusalem, Alexandria, Antioch,

FIGURE 16.1 Tree diagram of the structure of the church

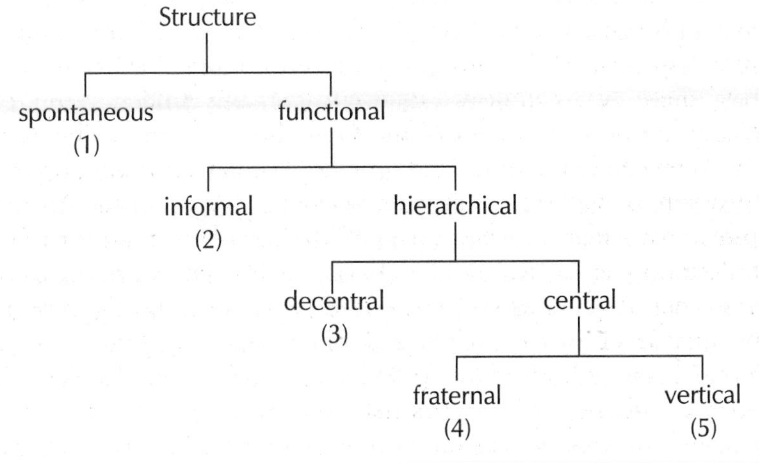

Constantinople, and Rome. The church ceased to be a community of horizontally related communities; it became a pyramid-like structure, built vertically (Alberigo 1984; Schillebeeckx 1989.) This is called "vertical-central structure" in figure 16.1 (5).

The tree diagram in figure 16.1 represents a conceptualization of the historical development of the leadership of the church, which gradually moved from type 1 to type 5. It cuts off the approach that moves in the opposite direction. If one follows the reverse route, then one proceeds from the present pyramid-hierarchical structure back to the New Testament to find as much evidence as possible for the justification of the present church order. Three steps have to be taken for this purpose. One proceeds from the "one office" in the present church, the office of bishop. This office is represented as "upwardly differentiated" in the direction of the office of pope and "downwardly" in the direction of the offices of priest and deacon. Next, one goes back to the New Testament from the office of bishop to the "office of apostle," traveling the line of the *successio apostolica.* The present bishops are deemed to be the direct successors of the apostles. Finally, the step is taken from the "office of apostle" to the "office of Christ," which holds the doctrinal, priestly, and pastoral office in itself (Auer & Ratzinger 1983).

Significance for the present

As we mentioned, the tree diagram follows the direction of historical development, and not the reverse. However, if one wishes to draw some kind of orientation for the church of today — for that is what we are interested in — then we are left with two different methods of handling the data from the early church.

The first method implies that greater importance has to be attached to the earlier developments in the early church than to the later developments. This means that greater importance is attributed to the ecclesial structures of authority at the top of the diagram (types 1 and 2) than to the lower structures (types 3, 4, and 5). Thus, Küng attributes a certain priority to the Pauline epistles, which is precisely where one finds type 1 and especially type 2. He ascribes less importance to Acts and the Pastoral Epistles, which are characterized by type 3. His argumentation is threefold. First of all, the first types have a greater historical proximity — chronologically — to the proclamation of the gospel by Jesus than the latter. Next, they also have a greater proximity — theologically — to the "matter" of the gospel than the latter. Finally, what speaks in favor of the first types is the authenticity of the authorship of Paul (Küng 1967, 209).

There are, however, fundamental problems connected to this approach. The first problem is that in this way one lands in the pitfall of a canon within the canon, whether one wants to or not. This implies that one isolates some writings in the canon of the writings of the New Testament, to attribute a special value to them. Opposite this we have the fact that the precise meaning of the concept *canon* is that the writings of the New Testament form one whole together. All sorts of texts belong to this, such as prophetic, narrative, instructive, confessional, doctrinal, and apocalyptic. Together they form the New Testament (Tracy 1981). This has greater significance than the arguments that Küng sets forth concerning his preference for the epistles of Paul.

Moreover, there is something irrational about these arguments themselves. As far as the historical argument is concerned, why should that which is chronologically most proximate be the most adequate? It can be, but need not necessarily be. Sometimes distancing (in a chronological sense too) is a better condition for the correct interpretation of happenings. The later interpretation of history sometimes brings certain facets to light that have remained covered or disguised in an earlier reflection. Further, the theological argument is not unquestionably sound. It harbors the danger of a circular argument in it: what one feels to be theologically adequate can be found in the epistles of Paul, and that is why one believes these epistles are theologically adequate! Finally, one can now see why the authenticity of the Pauline epistles forms its own argument. This argument is actually a variation of the first, which involved historicity.

There is, however, yet another objection that can be brought against Küng's approach. If one consistently reflects upon his method of work, one lands in ecclesiological biblicism. One declares one model that is found in the Bible to be directly applicable to today, without taking the differences in the societal and church context between then and now into account (Frankemölle 1981).

Let us then take up the second method to deal with the data from the New Testament and the early church. Over and against the hermeneutical method of text correlation, which lies in Küng's method of work, we have the method of text/context correlation. In the method of text correlation one proceeds from a present-day problem and tries to find a suitable (correlating) answer directly from the Bible. In the text/context correlation things are somewhat more complicated. It is aimed at the correlation between the relation of the text from the early church to the context of its time on the one hand, and the relation of the "text" of the present-day church to the present context. Therefore, we are dealing with a correlation between the past relation (text/context) and the present relation (text/context). In other words: the way the church of the past related to its context is an example of the relation the church of the present should have. This does true justice to the Bible, and more particularly to the Bible as canon, in which so many different texts and contexts occur (Boff 1983; Schillebeeckx 1989).

What do we see when we take a further look at the models of the structure of the church in the tree diagram of figure 16.1? Each time the church altered its structures and adapted itself to the societal and ecclesial context that it came across in a certain place at a certain time. Thus, for example, it took over the charismatic structure from the many charismatic and pneumatic movements that could be found along the Mediterranean at the time (type 1). With an eye to a kind of pastoral functionalization of the duties and services in the community, it took over the internal structure of the *collegium* (type 2). Later still, it took on the decentral-hierarchical structure around the *pater-familias* in the *oikos* (type 3). In the second and third centuries, it adapted itself to the hierarchical administrative system of the civil servants in the cities and the provinces of the Roman Empire (type 4). Finally, it allowed itself to become part of the pyramid structure of the empire as a permitted religion and later as the state religion during the course of the fourth century (type 5).

Two principles

Surveying all of this, one discovers that two principles function as guides to the continually new structure of the leadership in the early church: ecclesiality and contextuality. These principles have mutual connections. They can serve as an orientation for the further development of the church.

The principle of *ecclesiality* implies that the ecclesial structure is tuned to the development of the church community. This means that the ordering of the church is made subordinate to its aims and tasks. It is a function of the realization of the vision (people of God) and the mission (Jesus movement) of the church (chapters 11 and 12). Everything that stands in the way of this realization or does not optimally stimulate it in the ecclesial structure is eligible for change. The church is not there for its own purpose. It stands as sacrament of the salvation from God, focused on the reality outside of it: God and the salvation of humankind (*Lumen Gentium* 1). This sacramental structure takes precedence over all other structures of church order.

The principle of *contextuality* implies that elements from the surrounding societal formation are taken up into the structure of the church, insofar as they serve the church's development. Just as the early church took over elements from its environment (the pneumatic movements, the *collegium,* the *oikos,* the administrative organization, and the empire), the church of the present has to ask itself which elements from the societal organization of today are useful. This has to happen without any violence being done to the vision and mission of the church. The matter of the gospel has to be guaranteed and served by it. The church as the people of God has to continue on its journey. The church as Jesus movement has to be able to continue.

(3) Leadership in the church of today

The types of authority that we described earlier, proceeding from the tradition of Weber, will now be filled in from the principles that we just drew up. To refresh our memories, there were four types of authority: charismatic, traditional, legal-rational, and functional-rational. By relating the principles of ecclesiality and contextuality, which we have just described, to these types, we hope to develop some relevant insights for leadership in the church of today.

(a) Charismatic authority

Ecclesiality

The leaders of the church are not the only bearers of charisma; in principle all members are, as exegetical research into the pre-Pauline and Pauline communities has shown. The later development in the church does not imply that charisma has disappeared from view but rather that charisma as a "gift," given to all, has been reduced to the "property" of a certain group, the leaders: "The development of the ministry in the early Christian churches was not so much . . . a historic shift from charisma to institute. It was a shift from the charisma of many to a specialised charisma of but a few" (Schillebeeckx 1985, 125).

How should one regard these charismata? According to Weber, with charismata we are dealing with extraordinary, extranatural, or even supernatural gifts that mark someone as a charismatic (Weber 1980, 140-42). Küng, however, makes a distinction between ordinary and extraordinary charismata. The ordinary charismata can be divided into higher and lower charismata. The higher ones are faith, hope, and love. The highest is love (1 Cor. 13:13). The lower ones fall into three categories: proclamation, aid, and leadership. The extraordinary charismata are, for instance, glossolalia and miraculous cures. Due to their eccentricity, they have to be specially judged on their relation to Jesus and to the church. The extraordinary charismata have to be judged proceeding from the ordinary charismata. The ordinary charismata settle the matter (Küng 1967, 210ff.). As a supplement to Küng, the following has to be added: the extraordinary charismata fall under the judgment of the ordinary charismata. The ordinary charismata, however, in their turn (together with the extraordinary charismata), fall under apostolic authority, as is made plausible by the rhetorical analysis of the First Epistle to the Corinthians (Smit 1989).

Weber places the emphasis on what Küng calls the extraordinary charismata, and Küng places it on what he calls the ordinary charismata. The difference between the two can be explained proceeding from Weber. Weber introduced a term, as we mentioned before, to define what happens if the charismatic leader of a movement no longer exists: *the routinization of charisma* (chapter 12 sub 4). The extraordinary charisma of this leader is replaced by the ordinary charisma of his successor(s). Type (1) in figure 16.1 has to do with the extraordinary charisma, which is described by Weber, and type (2) has to do with the ordinary charisma, to which Küng refers and which is defined by Weber with the term *routinization of charisma.* The initial, extraordinary excitement and emotion are gradually replaced by a more realistic, well-considered inspiredness; the fever is replaced by a calmer, more balanced emotion; the spontaneity is replaced by a more adapted motivation, which is more involved with reality (Avis 1992). The emphasis comes to rest upon the higher charismata of faith, hope, and love and on the lower charismata of proclamation, aid, and leadership.

Church leaders today are called to inspired, moving, motivated, expressive religious leadership. This leadership belongs to the lower charismata. It forms one whole with the other lower charismata (proclamation and aid). Together with these charismata, it is aimed at the realization of the higher charismata: faith, hope, and love. These charismata are the gifts of mercy of everyone in the church community. The highest charisma is love (1 Cor. 3:13).

Contextuality

Proceeding from the principle of contextuality, one should pay the greatest amount of attention to the ordinary and the higher and lower charismata without there being a gap with the extraordinary charismata.

The ordinary, higher, and lower charismata form the necessary spiritual soil for the church. They are constitutive for the church.

They determine its life. The higher charismata are the most important element in this. Without faith, hope, and love, the church would simply cease to exist. Together with the lower charismata (proclamation, aid, and leadership) they are the source for the specific religious identity of the church, which distinguishes it from every other societal institution and gives shape to its vision and mission (chapters 11 and 12).

The charismata are also the source of the integration and unity of the church, for they are there for the development of the church. Together they form the one body of Christ (chapter 14). Without this charismatic-spiritual soil, church life would become hollow, and the church itself would degenerate into a barren institute. That is why it is important that the members of the church bring about the development of their own religious inspiration and motivation and, proceeding from this, participate in the execution of the duties of the church. Even though the ordinary charismata have precedence over the extraordinary, the distance between them should not be unnecessarily enlarged. Thus, the charisma of healing can be seen as the effect of prayer on the psychosomatic unity that humans form. Psychic liberation can free the healing powers in the body. The charisma of glossolalia can be regarded as the expression of intuition and feelings proceeding from the deeper emotional layers in humans, which have not been put into any rational wording as yet. In this gift of tongues, one can see similarities to the gift of tears, stemming from the same emotional layers, and being equally without a comprehensible articulation (Schoonenberg 1985).

It is the duty of the leaders of the church to stimulate and encourage the ordinary, higher, and lower charismata in particular, which are rooted in the religious inspiration and motivation of its members. For this purpose, they must have the necessary charismata, the necessary religious inspiration, and motivation themselves. The religious leaders should propagate their charismata, transmit their inspiration, and spread their motivation around them. That is what lends their appearance of authority. This is where the difference lies between power and authority, to which we referred at the beginning of this chapter. Without charismata leaders degenerate into officials (Etzioni 1964, 61ff.).

(b) Traditional authority

Ecclesiality

We are dealing here with the relation between the leaders of the church and tradition, and especially apostolic tradition. The question is, however, what this connection signifies. There are two possible views on this.

In the first view, apostolicity refers to the so-called *successio apostolica* in which the emphasis is placed on the unbroken chain that is supposed to exist between the disciples in the Gospels, through the bishops during history, down to the bishops of today. In this view the bishops are the successors of the apostles on the grounds of a divine institution, as was defined by Pius XII (Auer & Ratzinger 1983, 184).

In the second view, apostolicity is not exclusively attributed to the bishops, but to the church as a whole. Several arguments are involved. The doctrine of *successio apostolica* ignores the fact that the New Testament did not have a hierarchical-pyramidal office of bishop. Besides this exegetical argument, there is also a historic one. The history of the church does not have an unbroken *successio,* as the doctrine suggests. There have been abbots (non-bishops), who had the authority to ordain priests. The most prominent argument, however, is of a dogmatic nature. It is the church that is called apostolic, as appears from the symbolum: *credo apostolicum ecclesiam* (Küng 1967, 408). The focus here is the belief in the praxis of the imitation of Jesus by the church in agreement with the tradition of the apostolic testimony and the apostolic service (Schillebeeckx 1985, 120). It is up to the church leaders to lead the church community in this praxis of imitation and to point out a passable route for the future, proceeding from the apostolic tradition.

Contextuality

In order to clarify what this apostolicity means for the church of today, we recall the term *text/context correlation,* which refers to the hermeneutical parallel between the relation of the apostolic church to its latter-day societal context and the relation of the present church to the present context. In other words, as far as the apostolic tradition is concerned, faith demands the development of a leadership structure that relates to the present context as the apostolic leadership structure related to the latter-day context. As we have seen, the apostolic church had a considerable variety of elements of church structure, which it drew from the succeeding societal formations in which it found itself. We mentioned the pneumatic movements, the *collegium,* and the *oikos.* In the postapostolic church we can add the administrative organizations and the organizational structure of the empire. This contextual variety contains the hermeneutical key to the development of a societal-plausible structure for the church of today, as we shall see further along. With this we shall have to take care that the vision of the church (people of God) and its mission (Jesus movement), which we unearthed from the apostolic writings, are guaranteed and stimulated (chapters 11 and 12); and in addition, that the church as a community (body of Christ) can continue to grow (chapter 14).

(c) Legal-rational authority

Proceeding from the theory of Weber, the focus in legal-rational authority is on the respect that leaders deserve on the basis of the fact that they gained their office in a legal manner and exercise it in a legal fashion. Formal rules have to be applied. This gives legal security and cultivates a positive sense of justice. It calls for acknowledgment, commands respect, and makes authority acceptable. The legal-rational type of authority depends on legal procedures and rules. It depends on formalization.

Problems with legal-rational authority

One can easily establish that the Catholic Church is characterized by a considerable degree of formalization. However, it is precisely in this formalization that a number of problems lie. These can be divided into two kinds: structural and foundational. The structural problems involve the organizational balance of tension in the order of the church that is in force, while the foundational problems involve the foundation of the order itself.

Structural problems

Proceeding from a sociological viewpoint, the actual structure of the legal-rational authority in the church raises problems that have to do with the following aspects: the degree of formalization, the degree of centralization, and the degree of hierarchization.

As far as the degree of formalization is concerned, people wonder whether the balance between informal and formal leadership is not too much to the disadvantage of informal leadership and in favor of formal leadership. From this one can understand that the cohesion of the church is under threat, as is the case for other institutions, if the formal leaders do not give enough space to informal leaders (Etzioni 1964, 58-67).

The degree of centralization also raises objections. One wonders if the subsidiarity principle is sufficiently shown to good advantage in the present church order, even though it is recognized as a principle by the official church (Listl 1983). This raises the question whether the capacity present in the lower levels in the church is sufficiently recognized and its creativity utilized. People fear that the integration of the church will be damaged, as is the case with other social formations, if the potential present at the different levels is suffocated (Daft 1989, 180).

Finally, the degree of hierarchization is a problem too. By this we mean the existence of long lines in a steep organization, in which everything from the top down and from the bottom up has to pass through all kinds of intermediary levels. A plea has been made for shorter lines in a flat organization, so that the vitality and concreteness of the communication processes in the church may increase. If one neglects to do this, this can lead to the draining of the body of the church, at least parts of it, as occurs in other institutions that are too steep in their organization (Morgan 1986, 39-76).

However important they may be, the structural problems mentioned (formalization, centralization, and hierarchization) are not typically characteristic of the church. They occur in all larger and more complex institutions, in profit-making organizations (enterprises and factories), as well as in non-profit organizations (schools, universities, and associations). In all these institutions, people are struggling with questions like: to what extent do the lines of responsibility have to be fixed juridically (informal versus formal); to what degree does the administration have to be carried out proceeding from the periphery or from a single fixed point (decentral versus central); to what extent is the central board to be shaped according to the model of entente or according to that of a hierarchical pyramid (flat versus steep)?

We just mentioned that these three structural problems are not typical of the church. But this does not mean that they do not occur in the church. We came across them in the early church too. In figure 16.1 the contrast between informal and formal lies in the relation between types (2) and (3); the contrast between decentral and central, in the relation between types (3) and (4); and the contrast between flat versus steep, in the relation between types (4) and (5). This enhances the insight that it is not only useful but also theologically legitimate, and even necessary, to involve oneself carefully with these problems. They were already problems in the early church.

Problem of foundation: monocracy or democracy

However important the structural problems may be, they do not strike at the core: the foundation of legal-rational authority in the church. Proceeding from an analytical-sociological viewpoint, we are confronted with a binary choice. Formal-rational authority can be rooted in monocracy or democracy. Monocracy is characterized by the existence of a single head as leader of the community; while in democracy, the administrative power, both formal and factual, lies with the members of the community (Weber 1980).

Proceeding from the science of social administration, one can distinguish different variations within monocracy and democracy. Monocracy can, on the one hand, turn into autocracy if the leader rules arbitrarily on his own, albeit within the borders of the law, but as he sees fit. One speaks of a theocracy if the power of the leader is rooted in a transcendent power. On the other hand, monocracy can be softened by creating coordinative and subordinative structures. One speaks of a coordinative structure if leaders with equal authority meet, consult each other, and make decisions together. Monocracy then develops into a polycracy. One also speaks of the principle of fraternity that is built into the system of monocracy (episcopal fraternity). There are subordinative structures if advisory bodies are added, which are (partially) made up of the ordinary members of the organization. Their duty is to give advice, whether it is called for or not. One can speak of the synodal principle, which can be applied at three levels: diocesan, provincial, and national. This principle is more firmly applied by the radical synodalists than by the moderate synodalists (Roes 1991). It leaves the monocracy untouched, however (Van Braam 1986, 322-25).

Democracy also has different variations. It can be participatory democracy or representational democracy. In participatory democracy, the members exert direct influence (direct democracy); while with representational democracy this happens through representatives (indirect democracy). However, these variations do not affect the difference between the basic shape of the monocracy and that of the democracy (Van Braam 1986, 326-31).

Ecclesiality and contextuality: democracy

Insofar as the literature departs from the two principles we mentioned earlier (ecclesiality and contextuality), we plead for the democratization of the church. In a general sense, the plea is as follows: the development of the church in the present society (ecclesiality) is served by the church's adaptation of church structure to the dominant structure of that society, democracy (contextuality). Along with this, we distinguish between material, formal, and fundamental democracy. Material democracy refers to concrete kinds of state and state systems in modern society, for example the American, German, French, or Dutch systems. Formal democracy has to do with the procedural agreement that the direct or indirect participation of the members of the community in the administration is constitutionally and/or legally arranged. Fundamental democracy points to a form of living together *(Lebensform),* in which freedom, equality, and fraternity are central and the people bear a collective responsibility (Van Braam 1986, 326-27).

The proposal was forwarded to approach and determine the problem of democratization of the church, proceeding from fundamental democracy as a form of living together (Lehmann 1971). Further, a proposal was formulated that bore the title: the New Testament constitution for church life. The articles of this constitution deal with the freedom of Christians, the equality of Christian brothers, Christian fraternity, the order of service in the Christian communities, the degree of historicity of the church ministry, and authority in the church (Pesch 1971).

Objections to democracy

Besides pleas for the democratization of the church, one also finds objections in the literature. These are not aimed against fundamental democracy, but against the principles that underlie material and formal democracy. With these objections, manifold exegetical, historical, dogmatical, and empirical arguments are involved. Furthermore, all kinds of practical considerations play a role, as well as reasoning from common sense, and rational thought. As far as the content of the arguments is concerned, they sometimes involve the relationship between church ministry and the ministry of Christ, or the intraecclesial functions of church ministry, or the specific identity of ministry in the relations between the churches, or the task of the ministry in the relation between the church and society, or, finally, the tasks of the ministry in the traffic between church and state. We restrict ourselves here to the description of five objections to the principles that underlie material and formal democracy, and that concern the core of the matter, in our view. We will also check to see in what sense these objections are sound.

First objection

The first objection is that the church does not originate in the people, but in Jesus and through Jesus in God. The absolute initiative lies with him. The church's source is not in the sovereignty of the people, but in that of God. That is why the church cannot and may not adapt itself to the shape of government that is in force in present society: democracy. It has to resist the pressure that is being put on it from this society. Otherwise it would forsake its divine origin.

This is the classic sovereignty objection. The question is whether it has any validity. Five different levels were distinguished in representative democracy. The first is that of legislative labor in the strictest sense. The second level is determined by the constitution that underlies legislative labor and forms a context for it. The third level involves constitutional principles, which in their turn underlie the constitution.

Particularly the division of power is essential (legislative, administrative, and executive power). The fourth level is characterized by ethical principles, as they have been set down in human rights (individual and social basic rights). They belong to what we earlier defined as fundamental democracy. The fifth level — which we are involved with here — is the level of transcendence. Recent research has shown that the democratic constitutional state is rooted in legislative labor and constitution, and via this in constitutional and ethical principles. However, the question about the foundation of constitutional and ethical principles themselves goes a step further still. It has to do with the foundation of fundamental democracy itself in something that carries and supports it. In some constitutions and reflections on constitutions, it appears that the latter foundation is religiously symbolized. In this symbolization a transcendent point of reference is alluded to. In this allusion reference is made to the transcendent origin and destination of the democracy: God is portrayed both personally and apersonally in this. This has been shown, albeit in distinctly different ways, in the constitutions of the United States, France, Germany, and the Netherlands (Piret 1992). For this reason, the democracy of the state cannot simply be played off against the foundation of the monocracy of the church in God. The acknowledgment that God is at the origin of the church and is also its aim in no way implies a choice against a democratic form of government proceeding from this viewpoint. It is not the intention of those who advocate the democratization of the church to deny the divine origin of the church (Greinacher 1990; 1992).

Something has to be added to this. The insight that God is at the origin of the church can be respected or neglected in the practice of both monocracy and democracy. One cannot assert that the monocratic structure of the church in the past has been a guarantee against fundamental errors, mistakes, guilt, and sin. Neither can one say that only a democratic structure leads to purity and holiness. The church is an *ecclesia mixta,* whether or not it is monocratic or democratic. Neither structure guarantees purity or holiness. For it is God's initiative in Jesus that underlies the purity and holiness in the church; guarantees for this cannot be provided by people or human communities. They have the task to bring about as best they can only the purity and holiness that God desires in the church (chapter 11 sub 2).

Second objection

The second objection is related to the first. It again has to do with the question of sovereignty. However, now we are not focusing on the origin of the sovereignty, but on the proxy as a consequence of the sovereignty. The objection is that the church has no proxy with regard to the gospel as the Word of God. It does not own the gospel. It does not have the gospel at its disposal. This is at right angles to democratic structure, which proceeds from the doctrine of the self-determination of the people. The objection is that the church cannot and may not adapt to the democratic form of government of the present society, on pain of the loss of the divine proxy that it has only under trust and which it may not transfer.

This side of the objection of sovereignty (being the proxy and not the origin) demands further discussion too. We just introduced the necessary distinctions in levels regarding the democracy. At the level of legislative labor, an ordinary majority of votes is necessary in general. Alterations at the constitutional level are subject to a series of complicated procedures and require a qualified majority. Changes, however, at the third level, which would set at nought the constitutional principles, are simply out of the question in the context of a democracy. Correction or (partial) lifting of these principles would mean that the democracy itself is abolished. The same applies more strongly to the level of ethical principles: the individual and social basic rights of man. Changes at this level of fundamental democracy — in the sense of partial or total abolition — are an absolute violation of democracy. It would simply cease to exist because of this.

Now the self-determination of the people in representative democracy goes as far as the level of legislative labor and — via complicated checks and balances — to that of the constitution. The constitutional principles at the third level have the status of constitutional nondissolution. Finally, the ethical principles at the fourth level are off-limits; they are sacred. They have the status of constitutional immutability. Hence the symbolization of the transcendent core of fundamental democracy at the fifth level, which we just described.

Proceeding from this distinction, the objection of the right of self-determination of the people loses its force. The people in a democracy are bound to the constitutional and ethical principles of the third and fourth levels, which themselves are rooted in the level of transcendence. The people are bound to this, as the church community is bound to the gospel (Schillebeeckx 1989, 236).

Third objection

The third objection contains a combination of the first objection (concerning the origin) and the second objection (concerning proxy). Only now these objections are caught in more legal terminology. The objection implies that the offices of the pope and the bishop exist in the church by divine law *(ex iure divino),* as is determined by the Codex (i.e., canon 330). As is the case for all matters that return to divine law, such as the *depositum fidei* and the sacraments, the hierarchical administrative structure is felt to be irreversible. It cannot be undone, even if pressure is brought to bear upon it from the type of government of the present society (Listl 1983, 92-94).

It is of importance to note that the doctrinal authority of the church itself is developing in this area. Trent voiced condemnation *(anathema sit)* of all those who denied the divine foundation of the hierarchical trinity (bishop, priest, and deacon). Vatican II, however, took on a more abstract standpoint. During this council, it was not determined that the trinity of the ministry in the church was based on a divine institution, but that the ministry itself was. Not the trinity of the ministry, but the ministry itself comes from God (*Lumen Gentium* 28). Here we find that a later council relativizes an earlier one (Küng 1967, 477).

The question is where the divine foundation of the ministry goes back to historically. It is assumed that it goes back to Jesus' establishment thereof. However, proceeding from exegetical research, one cannot maintain that the office of bishop, which is considered to be the core of the ministry, can explicitly be found in the New Testament. The bishops cannot simply be regarded as the successors of the apostles: "Although it is probable that during Jesus' life on earth the Twelve were a fixed group and Simon Cephas had a leading position in it, one cannot find references to successors of the Twelve or of other apostles in the New Testament," according to Schoonenberg (1968, 296). On the contrary, the New Testament shows a most pluriform picture of government in the community, as we indicated above (figure 16.1). One finds (1) the spontaneous-charismatic model, (2) the informal-functional model, (3) the decentral-hierarchical model, as well as (4) some initial steps toward the fraternal-hierarchical model. The hierarchical-pyramidal model (5) can be viewed as the result of a late and definitely postapostolic and post–New Testament development.

Also, in a systematic sense, one should handle the doctrine of *ius divinum* in a dynamic way, rather than in a static one. Since the church continually appears to adapt its organizational structure to the surrounding society, as we find in exegetical and historical research, this doctrine has to be regarded as historic too. The communities of the New Testament simply have no knowledge of it. The doctrine had no role to play in the decisive initial history of the church simply because it did not exist. They could not foresee its coming into force in the church's later history. Through the influence of Greek thought on the philosophy of law in the west, it gradually started to develop in the juridical thought of the church (Corecco 1983, 13). It is precisely the contingent-historical definiteness that makes its value historically relative. Thus we are equally incapable of making eternal predictions about whether this doctrine will remain in force or should do so. As Rahner says: "If it is the case that there always will be religion in the future, it will always be there as a societal variable too. This variable will also depend on the profane order of the global society in its historical concreteness. As Christianity has neither a concretely obliging picture of this profane society, nor the power to prophesy over it, it cannot make any prediction as to the concreteness of its own societal-ecclesial shape for the future" (Rahner 1965b, 86-87).

Fourth objection

The fourth objection entails that the church ministry has and should have a singular position as an "opposite" *(Gegenüber)* with regard to the church community. In this it represents Christ's being the head as opposed to the church as the body of Christ. It represents him in person *(in persona).* This would be disposed of in a democratic church. The democratization would do away with this representation and with it the incarnation of Christ's being head of his body, the church.

This is another classic objection. Again, however, the question is whether this rings true. We can note that representative democracy (at least in the Netherlands) is characterized not by monism, but by dualism between the administration and the representative body. The "opposite" is not done away with; it is structurally couched in representative democracy. Within this dualism both the administration and the representative body are held to the constitutional and ethical principles (levels three and four) we just discussed. It is hard to see why such a formation cannot equally well be applied to the structure of the church.

Fifth objection

The fifth objection is that representative democracy is not applicable to the church because it implies a party system. Such a system would supposedly endanger the unity of the church. It is precisely this unity that is one of the fundamental characteristics *(notae ecclesiae)* of the essence of the true church *(ecclesia vera).* If the church is to be the true church, then it must resist the pressure of democratization that stems from society. It is the church's essence that is at stake.

What we can bring against this objection is that it has no eye for the empirical reality that actually exists in the church. The church of today (just like the church in former centuries) is entirely marked by pluralism. Vatican II acknowledged this too. Next, one cannot ignore the fact that there are parties within the church, even though they may not be institutionalized. There is no order or congregation without parties. In some of them a democratic order has been taken on to handle adequately the phenomenon of party formation (Steggink 1991). One cannot imagine a council without party formation. Council texts in general can often be interpreted as compromises between parties. The determination of such texts comes about through voting.

Even if the party system is not taken up as an objectionable side of democratization, it still is seen as a problem for the unity of the church, as appears from the above. However, this objection should not be exaggerated. The party system and unity are not diametrically opposed to each other. Just as a representative democracy is characterized by a fundamental consensus with regard to constitutional and ethical principles (levels three and four), so too one would expect a democratic church to have a fundamental consensus with regard to fundamental religious convictions (Haarsma 1981).

Here we can draw the most important insight from Vatican II

with regard to the "hierarchy of truth" (*hierarchia veritatum* in *Unitatis Redintegratio* 11). Freely translated, this states: the more the religious convictions concern the core of the faith, the more possible consensus is and the greater its need; the further they are from this core, the more one can live with the dissensus (Van der Ven 1982a; Witte 1983; 1986a; 1986b). If in the latter case a decision has to be made, then the opinion of the majority can be an essential basis to move the decision in one way or another, as was suggested by Rahner (1972b, 64). One should perhaps wonder whether the introduction of the party system is rather more a matter of practical efficiency than of dogmatic orthodoxy (Küng 1973).

Democracy and participation

From the above it appears that the relationship between the church and democracy has not been clarified to the point that sufficient consensus about it exists. This does not mean to say that the church can or may cut itself off from the significance democracy has for the development of the church in the society of today. The principles of ecclesiality and contextuality demand that the church be permanently engaged with it. However, as long as the necessary consensus is lacking, the church has to at least give shape to fundamental democracy. This is made up of a form of life, as we mentioned earlier, which is based on the freedom, equality, and fraternity of people in the church, who collectively bear responsibility for it. Fundamental democracy links with themes like the freedom of the children of God, the equality of Christians, and the solidarity of "the least of my brothers and sisters." These themes have a basis in convictions such as the gift of the Spirit to all in the charismata, the sense of faith of the faithful, and the general priesthood of the faithful (Lehmann 1971).

This fundamental democracy as a form of life implies maximum participation by ordinary members in the development of the church at a local level. Without this, the church lacks its necessary legitimization. Without this, it lacks the basis for its further development. Precisely from the vision of the church (people of God) and its mission (Jesus movement), the greatest significance should be awarded to the participation of ordinary members of the church. In what ways this can be stimulated will be clarified in the following part (chapter 20).

(d) Functional-rational authority

Functional-rational authority is characterized by the systematic and explicit use of scientifically justifiable knowledge, insights, skills, and attitudes that have been reflected on for exercising leadership. All this is expressed in the the pastoral professionalism of the church. It is rooted in academic-theological training and professional culture among the members of the pastoral-professional group, resulting in a pastoral-professional code and a pastoral-professional organization or association (Mok 1973; Van der Krogt 1981).

Ecclesiality

Emphasizing the principle of ecclesiality is not unnecessary. For a problem we often hear of that is connected to professionalism is the danger of the enlargement of the distance between the professional and the community, in this case the church community. This danger is not imaginary. It is inherent in professionalization that the body of knowledge that is used by the professional is made more scientific. Because of this, a cognitive gap can arise between the professional and the church community. Some try to bridge this gap by participating in the process of proto-professionalization: in order to develop adequate contact with the professional, professional jargon is used more and more (De Swaan 1982; 1990). Further, it is typical of professionalization that the professionals come together in their own professional associations, to raise the standards of training and to increase the quality of professional duties. A social gap with the church community can arise as a consequence. To avert the danger of both cognitive and social distancing, it is important to make pastoral professionalization come from the church community and remain aimed at it (Van Gerwen 1988a).

What this implies can be worked out in all sorts of directions, as will appear in the following two parts. In a general sense, however, we can state here that the aim of pastoral professionalization is to purposefully, effectively, and efficiently give shape to the vision of the church (people of God) and its mission (Jesus movement). Purposefully means with a certain aim and with a fixed but flexible course. Effectively implies that the aim is achieved in a sufficiently satisfying way. Efficiency means that the available means are used in a sensible manner. Without professionalism the realization of the vision and the mission of the church moves within the circle of wishful thinking (Van der Ven 1985a, 21-28).

Contextuality

Functional-rational authority forms an important, even necessary demand in today's society, which is characterized by the fundamental processes of modernization and rationalization. Therefore we cannot ignore the demand for pastoral professionalization.

Particularly in pastoral care within institutions like those of health care (clinical pastoral care), judicature (penitential pastoral care), and the armed forces (military pastoral care), we see a growing need for professionalization. This has two causes. On the one hand, the pastors themselves have a need for the enlargement of their scientific knowledge and insight, scientifically justifiable skills and attitudes. On the other hand, they are under the pressure of legitimization, due to the increasing scarcity of financial means, which compels them to clarify the relevance and use of their work in comparison to that of other professionals (e.g., doctors, psychotherapists, and social workers). Without a demonstrable contribution to the health and welfare of the people who are entrusted to their care, the latter is impossible. Even though criteria like effectiveness and efficiency only are applicable in a limited sense in pastoral care and service, it does not mean that one should not make clear what can be made clear (Van der Ven 1991e).

One can also trace the need for professionalization in what is called basic or general pastoral care. Thus, the association of pastoral workers has made a top priority of professionalization, having made room for scientific research in this area.

Yet we are not dealing here with a subject that does not have its problems. On the one hand, one can trace a professionalization movement, but on the other, one finds a kind of countermovement. People sometimes take the view of a contrast between professionalism and charisma and between professionalism and spirituality.

However, setting professionalism and spirituality opposite each other testifies to a lack of perspective. Those who think through both terms see that they are complementary. Here, complementary means that they supplement each other because they imply each other and call up each other. This can be illustrated by the ideas of the pastoral-theologian Haarsma. In 1964, the year in which the professorial chair of pastoral theology was established in Nijmegen (the Netherlands), the sociologist of religion Schreuder made a plea for the professionalization of pastoral ministry in his inaugural speech (Schreuder 1964). A year later Haarsma joined the call for professionalization. He tried to remove the objections against professionalization, which proceeded from the term *charisma*: "Not only does charisma not exclude study, design, and training in professional skills, it requires them, just as God's gift to man" (Haarsma 1965, 281). Some years later he made known that a way had to be chosen that combined both matters for the solving of the crisis in which the pastoral ministry found itself: prophetic charisma and professionalism (Haarsma 1970b; 1981). At the tenth anniversary of the professorial chair, he again made a plea for a connection between professionalism on the one hand, and charisma, prophetism, and spirituality on the other (Haarsma 1975).

(4) The ministry

The question we are going to discuss now is: What is the relationship between the insights we gained in the last chapter and the ministry? How can the four aspects of authority (charismatic, traditional, legal-rational, and functional-rational) and the ministry be involved with each other? In order to answer this question, we will explore what the term *ministry* means, how the ministry and ordained ministry relate to each other, and what ordination implies.

Ministry

The question is whether the nonordained minister fulfills a function that can be called an office. Because we are dealing with a directly ecclesial structural problem here, we refer to the description of the Codex. It states that: "An ecclesiastical office is any function constituted in a stable manner by divine or ecclesiastical law to be exercised for a spiritual purpose" (Can. 145, 1). In continuation of this, Canon 228, 1 adds the important statement that: "Qualified lay persons are capable of assuming from their sacred pastors those ecclesiastical offices and functions which they are able to exercise in accord with the prescriptions of law." From this we can conclude that not only the ordained minister but also the nonordained pastoral worker can be considered to occupy an ecclesial office in the ecclesial-juridical sense of the word. To this we can add that this interpretation was set down in a public report on the pastoral worker of a working group made up of bishops and theologians (Ernst & Van der Ven 1987, 33; Huysmans 1986).

Now it is possible to connect the insights with regard to ecclesial leadership (charismatic, traditional, legal-rational, and functional-rational) to the canonical description of the ecclesial office. Someone who holds an ecclesial office must give leadership to the church community in a way that meets the requirements of performing authoritively in a charismatic, traditional, legal-rational, and functional-rational way. That is to say, an evangelically inspired, apostolically oriented, democratically participational, and pastoral-professional performance. This applies to both the ordained and nonordained pastor.

Ministry and ordained ministry

What is the relationship between the ministry and the nonordained ministry? This question can be approached in terms of both the differences and the similarities. If one emphasizes the differences, then one has to deal with financial aspects (remuneration), administrative aspects (pastoral organization), aspects of church order (criteria of admission), and sacramental aspects (liturgy). The financial aspects imply that the present economic infrastructure of the church make the remuneration of the priest easier than that of the pastoral worker. The administrative aspects involve the difference in competence between the minister and the pastoral worker, which determines their difference in being used or not. As far as the criteria of admission are concerned, the ordination is open only to unmarried men, who wish to remain so. It appears from research carried out in 1992 that 84% of the Catholics in the Netherlands are of the opinion that priests should be allowed to marry and 66% think that women should be allowed to be ordained as priests (Uitgave 1-2-1, 12/6/92, 5-6; Schepens 1992). Finally, the execution of the sacramental liturgy by the ordained minister is held to be an act of the hierarchically ordered ecclesial institution of salvation.

One can also emphasize the similarities between the ordained and nonordained ministry. Here two fundamental matters have to be dealt with: the contents of the leadership they fulfill and the sacramental significance of this leadership.

As far as the contents of the leadership are concerned, the criteria that we just drew up do, of course, apply to both the ordained and the nonordained ministry. The requirements of an evangelically inspired, apostolically oriented, democratically participational, and pastoral-professional performance applly to both. It is not right to consider some of these aspects to be more important for the nonordained pastor (a democratically participational and pastoral-professional performance) than for his ordained brother. But it would be equally incorrect to do the opposite and find certain aspects more relevant for the ordained minister (an evangelically inspired and apostolically oriented performance) than for his nonordained colleague. There is no reason not to declare all four aspects applicable to both.

The sacramental significance of the ministry can be clarified by two aspects. The first aspect is that what one could call a "religious-semiotic effect" may stem from the performance of the ordained as well as the nonordained minister. This means that the actions of both are a sign, or at least can be a sign, of God's salvation. In such a case, they signify this salvation and re-present it. This arises in, for example, an individual pastoral counseling, a group discussion, a catechetical meeting, a diaconal meeting, or a religious speech. In this activity a sacramental happening is executed: *"sacramentum est in genere signi."* In this context their performance can be called pastoral-sacramental (chapter 7 sub 1).

From here a connection can be made with the four aspects that we distinguished in religiously authoritative performance. The more the way they work meets these four aspects, the greater the chance the so-called pastoral-sacramental happening we just mentioned will occur. The more they handle people in evangelically inspired, apostolically oriented, democratically participational, and pastoral-professional fashion, the greater the pastoral-sacramental density of their work is. We have now formulated a hypothesis that can be considered for empirical-theological testing.

The examples we gave take place in the nonliturgical sector: pastoral care, catechetics, diacony, and proclamation. Let us now turn to the liturgy. This is the second aspect. In principle, both the ordained and the nonordained minister can function as presider within the liturgy, albeit that this covers a limited area for the nonordained minister in the context of the church order in force. However, provided that he is given the proxy, the pastoral worker can in principle function as minister of baptism (Can. 861, 2 and 230, 3); qualified witness to a marriage (Can. 1112: depending on Rome's agreement); and distributor of communion (Canon 230, 3).

Here, too, a connection can be made with the aspects of the religious authoritative performance of the ordained minister and the pastoral worker. The more their functioning in the liturgy meets the demands of an evangelically inspired, apostolically oriented, democratically participational, and pastoral-professional performance, the greater is the chance of liturgical-sacramental density in their leadership. This hypothesis also is eligible for empirical-theological testing.

Ordination as sacrament

Until now we have emphasized the similarities between the ordained and the nonordained minister in particular. However, what makes them different from each other is indicated by the words *ordained* and *nonordained.* This raises the question: What does "ordained" mean?

Ordination can be viewed as the liturgical celebration of the assigning of the candidate for the ministry by the church community, including the ministers present in communion with other church communities. In this liturgical ritual, three separate rites take place: (a) the rite of the invocation of the Spirit *(epiclesis),* in which the church community asks for the further development of the candidate; (b) the rite of the hand, which can be seen as the rite of indication with the hand *(cheirotonia)* or as the rite of the laying on of the hand *(cheirotesia);* (c) the rite of acknowledgment and acceptance *(acceptatio)* by the community (Lima 1982; Luyckx 1981; Houtepen 1984; Schillebeeckx 1985, 140-42).

In what does this ritual of ordination differ from the installation ritual of the pastoral worker? It is possible to set the three rites (epiclesis, rite of the hand, and acceptatio) beside each other and to lend a different meaning and weight to them. It is then that the similarities between the ritual of ordination and the ritual of installation catch the eye. Both rituals are characterized by the invocation of the Spirit (epiclesis) and acceptance by the community (acceptatio). However, if one places the emphasis on the mutual connection among the three rites, then one sooner hits upon the differences between the rituals of ordination and installation. In the mutual involvement of the three rites, one finds that the rite of the hand takes up a central position. It colors and determines the other two. It is precisely the rite of the hand that appears to determine the specificity of the ritual of ordination and makes it differ from the installation ritual of the pastoral worker (Ernst & Van der Ven 1987, 65-66).

PART V

POLICY

In the two previous parts we discussed the core functions of identity and integration. In this part we will deal with the core function of policy. This is necessary because the vision and the mission of the church, which determine the identity of the church, have to be worked out and executed in a policy plan, policy programs, and projects. The integration of the church, for its part, requires that an adequate policy organization is shaped.

As in both the previous parts, we will begin with the societal context within which this core function can be realized. In the broader context of modernization we will deal here with the societal process of utilization. What this means in a general sense is increasing the endeavor for the satisfaction of one's own needs and the realization of one's own interests. This brings up the question of how the church handles this process in its policy and how it should do so (chapter 17). Next, policy development will come up for discussion. Here we will focus on questions that have to do with the formation and implementation of policy (chapter 18). After that, we will devote a number of reflections to the formal policy organization in which the formation of policy takes place (chapter 19). We end this part with the development of the policy organization with an eye to the enlargement of the participation in policy by members of the church, paying attention to the church as the Building of the Spirit (chapter 20).

Chapter 17

The Context of Utilization

The church has to realize its policy in the context of the societal process of utilization. By this we mean that people face the societal institutions in which they participate more and more from the viewpoint of their own needs and their own interests. People consider them more and more from the aspect of the rights and claims they can make of them and of what use they are to them.

In this chapter we will ask the following questions: (1) Where does utilization come from? (2) In what sense is the church confronted with utilization? (3) How should it react to this, proceeding from the perspective of solidarity?

(1) Factors of utilization

Where does utilization come from? One cannot give a monocausal answer to this question. We are dealing with a multiplicity of factors. These can be placed in the general process of modernization, and within this, particularly in the processes that take place in the areas of economy and politics.

Modern economy

By modern economy we mean the market economy, or the mixed economy respectively, in which the market on the one hand, and the state on the other, determine economic life. Both have a great influence on the daily routine of individuals and groups.

The influence of the market economy in the daily routine is recognizable in the utilitarian lifestyle and pattern of behavior, which is characterized by exchange. In this exchange, the central endeavor is to make the exchange as asymmetrical as possible to one's own advantage. What the ego gets from it is the only thing that counts, irrespective of the rightful interest of the alter, and in spite of the (thorny) situation in which the alter finds itself. Proceeding from this viewpoint, the intention to make the exchange as symmetrical as possible can nevertheless be seen as advantageous for oneself in the long run. If the ego expects to remain in contact with the alter for a period of time, it has to act from another attitude than one in which it could say: "I will never see him again."

The contribution of the state consists in providing a social safety net for all those who get caught in the wheels of the ruthless market. For this purpose, the social-legal structure of the welfare state was developed. The care of the socially deprived is no longer in the hands of individuals *(caritas).* The system of the social state looks after this care. This has consequences for one's daily routine, as appears from the following quotation: "A sense of responsibility for the suffering of others goes together with the conviction that these people have to be helped: but not by anyone in particular. 'Something has to be done' — not by the witness, but by something else, by 'it', by the hidden subject of all these passive sentences: the state. The state is the abstract, universal and anonymous supporter of all members in society" (De Swaan 1990, 260). This way of thinking and acting is sometimes defined as the ethics of abstract solidarity (Zijderveld 1983, 112ff.). These ethics also have consequences for the way in which the person in question himself ("the witness" in De Swaan's sense) handles the welfare state: "This social consciousness also provides a permanent and fundamental legitimization of claims to indemnification, benefits and financial support, the more so where the apparatus of the state and the means are effective and available" (De Swaan 1990, 260).

Modern politics

Modern politics also work as a driving force for utilization. To an increasing degree they are characterized by the process of democratization. If one conceives of the term *democracy* in a formal sense, the relation to utilization is not easy to understand. In a formal sense, democracy suggests only the people's power of expression and the procedures that need to be implemented in it. In a material sense, however, the terms *democracy* and *democratization* cannot be viewed separately from the tension between equality and inequality in society. Neither can one separate them from the will to gain more equality by negating the inequality, which is seen as a matter of justice. In this the focus is on the transfer of the power of expression of the more powerful to the less powerful. Without tactical and strategical operations aimed at the maximalization of one's own interests, this transfer does not come about. This implies discussion, negotiation, and struggle. In this attempt, one always finds conflicts of interests, which one tries to resolve for the benefit of the emancipation of one's own group.

By placing the process of utilization in the context of modernization and the influence of the modern economy and politics within it, we hope to have escaped the moralization of the term, as if it is reprehensible and degrading in itself. Utilization is not primarily a normative but a descriptive and explanatory term — at least that is the way it is presented here. Moreover, a moralizing approach would have little effect, since utilization — as will have appeared from this short representation — is rooted in the fundamental societal process of modernization. This does not alter the fact, of course, that one can or should pass evaluative judgment on it, at least in the context of ecclesiology. However, before we pass on to this in the continuation of this chapter, we believe it is a good idea to look first at the content of the term, where it comes from, where one finds it, how it works, and what effects it has. A premature evaluative judgment can foster moralization as well.

(2) Church and utilization

The church is confronted with the process of utilization in all kinds of ways. People are not only members of the church and not only feel connected to the church from merely ideal motives. Naturally, ideal motives certainly play a part too. But these are probably never (entirely) separated from the endeavor to satisfy one's own needs and realize one's own interests at the same time. Bonds between people are always of a complex and ambivalent nature. Unselfishness and selfishness never occur in an entirely pure shape. This also applies to the church. To put it unambiguously, people wonder: "Does the church make me any the wiser?"

Social stratification of the local church

Now the church is not confronted by one need. The sorts of needs vary according to the groups of people that are within the church. In order to trace the needs, one has to develop insights into the various groups and their different needs.That is why we engage ourselves with the social stratification of the local church.

The term *social stratification* has to do with the dividedness of society across several societal groups or strata (*stratum* means "scattered"). Social inequality functions as an important angle in this stratification: the groups in society are unequal groups. They differ in material prosperity, power, and prestige. This leads to the forming of several subpopulations and to the development of an order of rank among them. What we mean by subpopulation here is the degree to which the members display common values, norms, and behavioral tendencies. The development of an order of rank exists to the extent to which people determine the societal value of the subpopulation to which they belong in comparison to other subpopulations (Turner 1984, 56-69). Mostly people pay attention to differences in age, sex, education, profession, and income; societal power; knowledge and information; and, finally, lifestyle. Lifestyle includes, for instance, language use, style of consumption, social aspirations and interpretations, collective feelings of inferiority and superiority, collective stereotypes, and in- and out-group perceptions (Berting 1981).

In what follows we will give some examples of the size of local churches, their age structure, people's length of residency, their social-economic situation (education and profession), their social-cultural background, their religious and ecclesial orientation, church participation, and pastoral participation. By way of example, we will add some notes regarding the needs and interests of people in discussing each of these factors.

To clarify matters we will present some tables from the research project called "Parish, Social Context and Church Involvement. A

Research in Seven Parishes" (Van Hemert & Spruit 1984; Van Hemert 1991). Even though the data come from research in 1983, the systematics present in them made us decide to show and discuss the data here for illustrative purposes. The researchers tried to order Dutch Catholic parishes by means of a computer program on the basis of three characteristics: the size of the citizenry, the size of the parish, and the level of church attendance. The result was a division of 1,616 parishes across seven groups (Van Hemert 1991, 65). These groups were then divided according to the degree of urbanization. Three of the seven groups belong to the urbanized area (≥ 50,000 inhabitants), two of them to medium-sized cities (10,000 to 50,000), and the last two to rural areas. The researchers described the prototype of each of the seven groups. The three urban prototypes are (I) the District Parish, which is found in a new residential area, (II) the Industrial Parish, which lies in an older industrialized area, and (III) the Central Parish, which lies in the downtown area. The two parishes from the medium-sized cities, which they described prototypically, are called (IV) the Reconstructed Parish, which gives an impression of the process of change in the average parish in the traditionally Catholic Province of Brabant (the Netherlands), and (V) the Diaspora Parish, which lies in the traditionally Protestant and secularized Province of Groningen (the Netherlands). The two rural types of parishes are (VI) the Village Parish and (VII) the Agricultural Parish, the latter of which no longer has its own minister. Approximately 325 respondents were randomly selected from the address files of these seven parishes. The questionnaires were handed to the respondents at home and were collected there too. The average response was 46.6%, with fluctuations between 35% and 68%. The total number of respondents was 1,038 (Van Hemert 1991, 64-66).

Size

A first look at table 17.1 tells us that there are enormous differences in the size of these parishes. This especially applies to Parish I on the one hand, and Parishes V, VI, and VII on the other. Parish I contains 14,000 parishioners, while the three latter parishes contain 1,900, 2,000, and 900 parishioners respectively. However the difference between these last three parishes likewise catches the eye. The Diaspora Parish V with its 1,900 parishioners contains only 5% of the inhabitants

TABLE 17.1
Size of the seven parishes

	Urban par. I	II	III	Med. par. IV	V	Rural par. VI	VII
Inhabitants community × 1000	86	59	87	11	37	2	19 (com.) 1.6 (core)
Parishioners × 1000	14	8	4	4	1.9	2	0.9
Parishes in community	6	4	5	2	1	1	5

Source: Van Hemert & Spruit II 1984, 3

of the community (more than 37,000). The two rural parishes (VI and VII) cover a far greater part of the population of the community or heart of the village in size. The number of parishioners in Parish VI is nearly identical to that of the number of inhabitants of the community, while the population of Parish VII with its 900 members corresponds to almost 60% of the number of inhabitants of the heart of the village (more than 1,600).

Completely different needs can present themselves in relation to the size of the local church. If we restrict ourselves to social needs, for example, the members of the local church in Parish I, the District Parish, cannot simply fall back on all sorts of obvious structures from their urban environment for their need for social contacts. The situation in the two rural parishes (VI and VII) is different. There still are a lot of social contacts in neighborhoods, clubs, and associations there.

Naturally, these differences influence the making of policy in the local churches. Parish I, the District Parish, which is a very large parish with 14,000 parishioners, will probably have to take great pains with the development of a personal/social infrastructure. This entails large-scale operations. Equally, Parish V, the Diaspora Parish, will probably have to put a lot of energy into the building of social networks. The reason here is not the large size of the parish (1,900 parishioners) but its Diaspora character (5% of the inhabitants of the community are

TABLE 17.2

Age structure in %

Age	Dutch pop.	urban par. I	II	III	med. par. IV	V	rural par. VI	VII
16-24	21.5	19.3	19.4	21.6	17.3	13.7	20.2	13.2
25-34	22.2	34.5	21.8	11.2	24.0	21.1	20.2	21.7
35-44	18.7	26.1	13.7	24.1	20.2	21.7	18.7	22.8
45-54	14.5	9.2	18.6	18.1	17.3	16.0	11.3	16.4
55-64	12.9	5.0	21.0	14.7	16.4	15.4	17.2	15.9
65-75	10.3	5.9	5.7	10.3	4.8	12.0	12.3	10.1

Source: Van Hemert & Spruit II 1984, 5

parishioners). Parishes VI and VII, however, can probably make use of the very surveyable social structure of the village community or the heart of the community respectively.

From this perspective, the question of whether a parish has to engage in community formation is not a matter of free choice. The question is whether sufficient social infrastructure is present in the local church. If it is indeed present, as it is in the villages, the development of the community is less necessary than when it is absent, as in the anonymous District Parish. Here a varying number of degrees of freedom exist for the different parishes.

Age structure

Age structure is of great importance for the making of policy in the local church. There are young and aging parishes. It is precisely with an eye to the survival of the parishes that insight into the age structure and the orientation of policy on the younger age categories is of great significance. At the same time, however, the aging of Western societies demands specific adaptations by the church and pastoral policy. In table 17.2 we find the age categories of the respondents to the research in the parishes mentioned, set off against the Dutch population in the first column.

This table presents a clear picture of the distribution of parishioners across the different generations. De-ecclesiasticalization is highest among the younger generation. The category of parishioners ≤ 35 is smaller on average than the same category of the Dutch population. Two exceptions can be traced: in the category 25-34-year-olds, which make up 22.2% of the Dutch population, Parish I, the District Parish, contains 34.5% of the parishioners and Parish IV, the Reconstructed Parish, contains 24.0% of the parishioners. The reason is that the District Parish contains many students, while the same age category is overly represented in the Reconstructed Parish. With the exception of the category 65-75-year-olds, the category of ≥ 35 is on average greater than the same category of the Dutch population. Here, too, an exception has to be made for Parish I, the District Parish. The categories 45-54-year-olds (9.2%) and 55-64-year-olds (5.0%) are smaller than the identical categories of the Dutch population (14.5% and 12.9% respectively). Once more, this has to do with the lopsided distribution of the population in the student quarter. Something special is going on in the category 65-75-year-olds. In the table they form a smaller contingent in nearly all parishes than the particular category of the Dutch population (10.3%), with the exception of Parishes V (12.0%) and VI (12.3%). The reason is that during the period in which the members of this category were born, the percentage of Catholics in the whole Dutch population was lower than in more recent times. Nevertheless, from the smaller size of the category of the young on average and the larger size of the category of elders on average, one has to draw the conclusion that relatively the parishes are aging. In a more general sense, we can assert that age and participation in church activities display a strongly significant correlation: the younger people are, the less they participate; and the older they are, the more they participate. Better yet, proceeding from the age category, one can predict to quite an extent the degree of church participation (Van Hemert 1991, 109-10).

What is the significance of this finding for the conducting of ecclesial policy? Let us discuss, for example, some strategies that local churches sometimes use to deal with the various religious needs that are related to the different age categories. In pastoral practice people often depart from the idea that all people have a latent need for religion. To evoke this need, people make an effort to lay an adequate connection between the content of the Christian faith and the present context of experience. This often occurs across all sectors: pastoral

TABLE 17.3

Length of residency in %

residency	Dutch pop.	Urban par. I	II	III	Med. par. IV	V	Nonur. par. VI	VII
born	30.5	27	45	39	50	17	54	36
before '75		39	46	37	27	45	28	37
1975-79		22	6	14	18	23	12	17
1980-		13	4	10	5	15	6	10

Source: Van Hemert & Spruit II 1984, 8

care, catechetics, liturgy, proclamation, and diacony. With this people make a choice for the inductive strategy (chapter 9 sub 2). However, as we saw, the inductive strategy contains two extreme variants: the deductive-inductive and the reductive-inductive variant. It appears from research that the reductive-inductive variant is used far more often than the deductive-inductive variant (table 9.4). It may be that the choice for one of the two variants has to do with the specific age structure of the parish. Concretely, one can ask oneself the question: Does Parish I, the District Parish, perhaps choose for the reductive-inductive variant and do Parishes III and VI, the Central Parish and the Village Parish, choose the deductive-inductive variant? These are interesting questions for empirical theological research.

Length of residency

The length of residency of parishioners can be of importance to the local church and the continuity of policy. In table 17.3 one finds four categories of length of residency. The first involves people who have lived in the parish since birth, the so-called autochthonous population. The second refers to people who already lived in the parish before 1975. The third gives the category of people who moved to the parish between 1975 and 1979. Finally, the fourth concerns those came to live there after 1980. Let us remember that the data are from 1983.

What strikes us in this table is the relatively high average percentage of autochthonous people among the respondents in the parishes: 38% against 30.5% of the Dutch population (measured in

1975). There are, however, two parishes where the percentage of autochthonous people is clearly smaller: Parish I, the District Parish, which lies in a new residential area where a relatively large number of students live (27%), and Parish V, the Diaspora Parish, which lies in a city that grew strongly in the postwar period (17%). The last two lines of the table give the percentages of people who have come to live in the parish since 1975. Here, too, Parishes I and V catch the eye, with (22% + 13% =) 35% and (23% + 15% =) 38% respectively.

What is the meaning of these data? One can make use of two perspectives. Proceeding from the first perspective, one orients oneself from the people to the church; proceeding from the second, one orients oneself from the church to the people. Within each of these perspectives, one can check to see to what extent church policy takes the needs of the people into account. The first is the needs/church perspective; the second is the church/needs perspective.

Proceeding from the needs/church perspective, one can ask the question whether the length of residency has consequences for the needs of the people in relation to the church. By *needs,* we mean, among other things, information, liturgical celebrations, pastoral services, and belonging to the church community. Even though one may believe otherwise, it appears that length of residency has hardly any influence on the participation in or valuation of the parish community (Van Hemert 1991, 106ff.).

However, proceeding from the church/needs perspective, things are different. A great number of difficulties for church policy are related to length of residency. The percentage of removals amounts to over a third on average during a period of less than ten years. In a number of large cities, this percentage is far higher because approximately 20% of the population changes its address each year. This has consequences for matters like house visits by the minister and welcoming committees; extended house visits; after-care in rites of passage such as baptism, marriage, illness, death, and mourning; continuity of religious socialization, etc. The question is whether parishes are sufficiently attuned to their floating population.

Educational level

Educational level is a factor that people often take into account implicitly or explicitly in the policy of the local church. In table 17.4 a

TABLE 17.4
Educational level in %

	Dutch pop.	I	II	III	IV	V	VI	VII
prim. ed.	24.6	9.3	28.3	14.9	25.5	19.4	26.1	29.3
sec. ed.	59.1	64.4	62.5	56.1	58.8	66.1	63.3	60.3
tert. ed.	16.2	26.3	9.1	28.8	15.7	14.5	10.5	10.3

Source: Van Hemert & Spruit II 1984, 6

survey is given of the educational levels of the respondents to the research.

From this table it appears that the average educational level of the respondents from the seven parishes differs only to a small extent from that of the Dutch population. The average percentages of the respondents of the seven parishes together are: primary education 21.8%, secondary education 61.6%, and tertiary education 16.5%. Only the lowest educational level shows a clear difference: 24.6% of the Dutch population against 21.8% of the parishioners (difference: 2.8%). This can probably be explained by the fact that people with lower training are generally underrepresented in written questionnaires.

Between the parishes, however, differences of educational level are great. Parishioners with a low training level are found relatively frequently in Parishes II, IV, VI, and VII and relatively little in parishes I, III, and V. Parishioners with a medium level are found relatively frequently in parishes I, II, V, VI, and VII. The higher level can be found mostly in parishes I and III and hardly at all in parishes II, VI, and VII. The two extremes here are parishes I, the District Parish, with relatively few lower and relatively many higher-educated people, and Parish VII, the Agricultural Parish, with relatively many lower and relatively few higher educated people.

Let us also take a look at these data proceeding from the needs/church perspective. People often think that differences in educational level have an influence on the need for church participation, like participation in church celebrations. Those who are better educated are presumed to be more modernized and therefore less

TABLE 17.5
Profession in %

Profess.	tot.	urban par. I	II	III	med. par. IV	V	nonur. par. VI	VII
untra.	15	6	21	9	24	10	19	17
trained	33	37	39	22	22	49	33	24
low/med.	21	33	22	30	18	20	12	17
self-em.	13	3	1	7	16	9	18	25
higher	19	21	16	31	20	12	17	13

untra.= untrained; low/med.= lower and medium employee; self-em.= self-employed; higher= higher employee

Source: Van Hemert & Spruit li 1984, 7

churchly. However, from research it appears that this suspicion does not have strong verification. In national research, a moderately negative correlation between education and churchliness was traced (Felling et al. 1986, 84-85). In the parish research reported here, this correlation is lacking altogether (Van Hemert 1991, 111).

Now let us reverse our point of view. What comes to the fore proceeding from the church/needs perspective? One can guess that the difference in educational level is expressed in church policy. This applies, for instance, to the liturgy, the language used, and the length of the sermon; to the choice of catechetical projects; to the preparatory talks for the rites of passage; and to the training of volunteers. It is not impossible to conceive of a correlation between the educational level on the one hand, and the choice for a people's church or denominational self-opinion of the local church on the other. One can also attach a certain period of time to the possible influence of the educational level on the church's self-opinion. In research it has been demonstrated that the Catholic intellectuals in the period 1951-1955 experienced a switch from a people's church approach to a denominational approach to the church in the Netherlands. In this they were followed by the Dutch bishops in the period 1961-1965. The latter have undone an important part of this switch since the seventies (Simons & Winkeler 1987).

Profession

The distribution of the parishioners among the various professions is also of importance for the policy of the local church. In table 17.5 the distribution for the seven parishes is given. In the first column the totals of the seven parishes together are given in percentages.

In order to give the interpretation of this table some perspective, one can ask to what extent certain professional groups dominate the local churches. In other words: Are local churches class churches (Weber 1980)? Let us successively examine the workers (untrained and trained); the middle class; the self-employed (farmers and tradesmen); and the higher professional group.

We start off with the workers. Which of the seven parishes is a workers' parish? If one adds the percentages of the untrained and trained workers together, then it appears that the workers form the so-called modus in each of the seven parishes (the category with the highest percentage): (6% + 37% =) 43%, (21% + 39% =) 60%, (9% + 22% =) 31%, (24% + 22% =) 46%, (10% + 49% =) 59%, (19% + 33% =) 52%, and (17% + 24% =) 41%. Only in Parish III is the percentage in question equal to that of higher professions (31%).

One could also draw up a sharper criterion; for example, the untrained and trained workers encompass 50% or more parishioners (≥ 50%). It then appears that Parish II, the Industrial Parish, with (21% + 39% =) 60%, Parish V, the Diaspora Parish, with (10% + 49% =) 59%, and Parish VI, the Village Parish, with (19% + 33% =) 52%, can be characterized as worker parishes.

How do matters stand for the middle classes in the seven parishes? A quick glance at the table tells us that they do not form the modus in any of the seven parishes. However, Parish III, the Central Parish, is close with 30% (the higher professions are the modus with 31%). They also score a relatively high percentage (33%) in Parish I, the District Parish (the trained workers are the modus with 37%).

Proceeding from the insight that the self-employed (farmers and tradesmen) have often been considered as brakes to modernization, one can ask the question: In which of these parishes do the self-employed form the modus? The answer is that only in Parish VII, the Agricultural Parish, do they reach the highest percentage (25%). In addition, they pass the 10% level only in Parish IV, the Reconstructed Parish, and Parish VI, the Village Parish, with 16% and 18% respectively.

Finally, do the churches have people with higher professions? Are they elitist churches? The table tells us that only in Parish III, the Central Parish, do they form the modus (31%). This percentage, however, is equal to that of the workers (9% + 22% = 31%); while the smallest possible distance to the percentage of medium employees (30%) relativizes the elitist character even more. The Central Parish is therefore controlled by three groups approximately equal in size: workers (31%), employees (30%) and higher professionals (31%), to which a remainder category of self-employed may be added (7%). The researchers make mention of a strong polarization in this parish. The question is whether this is related to the three-class character of this parish. There appear to be two neighborhoods in this parish, one of the well situated and one of the workers, that are involved in a continuous battle of interests and values (Van Hemert & Spruit I 1984, 24-26). The Central Parish cannot really be called an elitist parish, but it is a parish with a relatively large group of the elite.

The global conclusion is that there are some worker parishes (II, V, and VI) as well as one parish in which farmers and tradesmen set the tone (VII). From this we cannot simply deduce that parishes II, V, VI, and VII are class churches, for the other classes keep their ends up too. Parish III is characterized by a conflicting balance between the classes in question.

The representation of the various classes in the parishes does, of course, have an influence on pastoral policy. In a direct sense this applies to the financial infrastructure of this policy. There are poor and rich parishes, parishes where a lot is possible and where very little is possible. At stake are the needs of the parishioners and the degree to which church policy is capable of meeting their wishes and desires. Also, the content of the needs is partially determined by the class to which one belongs. Those who belong to the lower classes are more strongly motivated to change the societal status quo than those who represent the higher class, who are more strongly oriented toward the development of egalitarian relations (Felling et al. 1983, 176-77).

Social-cultural background

Many things can be counted as part of the social-cultural background, for example, a preference for politics, broadcasting company, and

TABLE 17.6
Localism

	score	N
3 parishes in cities	3.71	257
2 parishes in medium-sized places	3.93	238
2 parishes in villages	4.05	357
total	3.90	852

Source: Van Hemert 1991, 79

papers; attitudes regarding moral values and norms, moral hot issues; attitudes with respect to family, upbringing, education, and one's own living environment; and ethnocentrism and racism. It is of great importance for the policy of the local church to have an insight into these factors, and to do research from there regarding which needs lie within them and how one can deal with them adequately.

We will restrict ourselves here to a single example, namely attitudes with regard to one's own living environment. This is also defined as *localism.* People vary with regard to localism. Some appreciate having good contacts with their neighbors because they feel it is necessary for a livable situation. They find what is happening in their local environment equally as interesting as what happens in the national news. They believe that they can live well only in places where there is a community. They find that people in cities live at cross purposes. Others, however, do not agree with this or have a more qualified opinion. This attitude of localism is important because it can influence the kinds of needs people have with regard to their local environment. Besides this, localism can be a supportive attitudinal pillar for the church as a local community. A parish that really wants to fulfill the function of a local community but that is made up of members who score poorly on the localism scale will see its bottom drop out. In table 17.6 the average scores of the seven parishes can be found regarding localism. The data are grouped for the three urban, two semiurban, and two nonurban parishes. The scale runs from 1 (entirely disagree) to 5 (entirely agree).

From this table it appears that the two nonurban parishes score the highest. They display a strong to very strong localism (4.05). The two semiurban parishes have a strong attitude of localism (3.93). The three urban parishes, however, have a weaker one (3.71).

From further analysis, it appears that certain groups stand out within these parishes, both in a positive and a negative sense. Housewives (with or without a job on the side) seem more interested in their own living environment. This also applies to pensioners. Other groups, like the unemployed and those unfit for work, however, have far less interest. They seem not only to be estranged from their work environment but also from their living environment. The students who live in the parishes are far less oriented toward what is taking place in the direct social sphere of life. If one looks at the professional level, one sees that untrained workers have a far stronger attitude of localism while people with higher training have a far weaker one (Van Hemert 1991, 85). Finally, localism appears to correlate poorly with church participation (see table 17.8). This is remarkable since American research demonstrated a strong correlation (Van Hemert 1991, 89-95).

These data can be of importance for the policy management of the local church. If it really wishes to fulfill a local community function, then this will be more easily achieved in the nonurban parishes than in the urban parishes. Furthermore, one will sooner find support from housewives (with or without a job on the side) and pensioners in general than from the unemployed, those unfit for work, or from students. In general, more support will be found among untrained workers than from people in higher functions. Regarding the unemployed and those unfit for work, the local church can focus its diaconal policy on the (presumable) need for contact, encounter, community, and solidarity of this group.

Religious and ecclesial orientation

Just as social-cultural background, so religious and ecclesial orientation is of importance for church policy. It can, for that matter, be viewed as an aspect of social-cultural background. Usually the religious and ecclesial orientation go together, but not always (chapter 9 sub 1).

The researchers put some questions of self-judgment before the respondents. The wording was as follows: "Do you regard yourself to be religious?" and "Do you regard yourself to be Catholic?" (Van

TABLE 17.7

Religious and Catholic in %

religious & Catholic	tot.	urban par. I	II	III	med. par. IV	V	nonur. par. VI	VII
r/c	78	62	75	71	85	83	84	91
nr/c	4	6	2	7	5	2	5	4
r/nc	8	13	13	8	3	9	5	2
nr/nc	10	20	10	14	7	6	6	4

Source: Van Hemert & Spruit II 1984, 11

Hemert & Spruit I 1984, Appendix 5, 4). In table 17.7 the answers are given to these two questions, and in a special relation to each other. For this purpose, four groups of answers were formed: (1) religious and Catholic (r/c), (2) nonreligious and Catholic (nr/c), (3) religious and non-Catholic (r/nc) and (4) nonreligious and non-Catholic (nr/nc). The first column shows the average of the seven parishes together.

What comes to the fore in this table is a strong connection between religious and Catholic (r/c) as well as between nonreligious and non-Catholic (nr/nc). Together they represent (78% +10% =) 88% of the respondents. The middle categories (nr/c and r/nc) contain the rest (4% + 8% =) 12%. The non-Catholic believers (r/nc) can be found in the urban areas in particular: Parishes I (13%), II (13%), III (8%), and the urbanized Parish V (9%). One might be led to believe that one would find the nonreligious Catholics (nr/c), in particular, in rural areas, because of the social control. However, one finds the highest percentages among two of the three urban parishes, Parishes I (6%) and III (7%). It is possible that the social need to belong plays a role in the urban parishes rather than the mechanism of social control (Van Hemert & Spruit II 1984, 11).

Finally, as can be expected, one finds the most non-Catholics in the urbanized parishes. From the total number of respondents, 18% (10% + 8%) regard themselves as non-Catholic. In Parish I this is (13% + 20% =) 33%, in Parish II this is (13% + 10% =) 23%, and in Parish III this is (8% + 14% =) 22%. In this survey we have to consider the fact that the respondents were taken from the address lists of the parishes themselves.

From this table it appears that religious and ecclesial orientation do not always go hand in hand. Sometimes people are oriented toward religion from their own need, but not toward the church. Sometimes people turn toward the church because of their own need — from wherever this need may stem — but not toward religion. In most cases, however, the needs will run parallel, being either equally positive or negative.

Here lies an important factor that has to be taken into account for church policy. This can be clarified by an example relating to the need people have for the rites of passage: the liturgies of baptism, first communion, marriage, and the funeral. The need for these rites can vary in four ways. One may be dealing with a religious/ecclesial need, a nonreligious/ecclesial need, a religious/nonecclesial need, or even a nonreligious/nonecclesial need.

Pastors deal with the situation in different ways. Here we shall look at some guidelines from a letter of the diocese of Breda (the Netherlands). They relate to three possible situations that may arise and the way in which pastors are expected to react.

(a) "During the request for the sacrament the religious motivation has been found to be *lacking* and it has appeared impossible to evoke this through catechetics. In this case it is a good idea to bring people to the insight that receiving the sacrament is not meaningful. With this a different offer of pastoral service can be made."

(b) "There is *a difference of insight* between the pastor and the person who asks for the sacrament. The pastor deems himself responsible for the administration of the sacrament according to the faith of the church. The person who asks for the sacrament feels justified to ask for the sacrament. The pastor, however, doubts whether the religious motivation is sufficient. If an agreement cannot be reached through discussion, and the validity of the sacrament is not under discussion, the pastor can best follow the conscience of the person."

(c) The third situation is characterized by a consensus between the pastor and the person who asks for the sacrament: "If the sacrament cannot be administered according to the faith of the church, the pastor of the church can be close to the people in various situations of life in *word and prayer.* If a ritual is involved in this, the distinction with the sacrament must be made clear" (Ernst 1989, 9).

Church participation

The last matter we will look into here is church participation. It is of great importance to take into account the fact that people show very divergent manners of church participation. We can distinguish five different types. (l) A certain group gives shape to its participation in church happenings by reading the parish paper. This group has no further needs. (2) A different group goes to church a couple of times a year, particularly at Christmas time. The need for a Christmas celebration marks the church membership of this group. (3) Yet another group contributes to the church financially. In so doing the group expresses its sympathy for the weal and woe of the church. People wish to contribute to its upkeep. (4) Still another group participates regularly in church services several times a month. It is made up of regular churchgoers. (5) Finally, there is an active core group, which carries out all kinds of volunteer work in an executive, pastoral, or managerial sense.

The researchers found a definite connection between the groups we just mentioned in the data they collected from the seven parishes. After further analysis it appeared that the first and second group nearly entirely coincide. That is why the two groups have been lumped together under the heading "reads parish paper" in table 17.8, which means we have four groups in toto. The connection between these four groups appeared to be cumulative. This means the following. Those who belong to group (1) only read the parish paper. Those who are part of group (2) not only read the parish paper but also give a fixed financial contribution. Group (3) is made up of people who not only read the paper and make a financial contribution but also regularly go to church several times a month. Finally, group (4) does all that groups (1) to (3) do but also actively participates in volunteer work during the week. A group (0) appears to precede the four groups. The people who belong to it are to be found in the address lists of the seven parishes but do not take part in any of the above activities. In table 17.8 one finds the distribution of the groups across the seven parishes altogether.

One can also read this table proceeding from the group division we made earlier on (chapter 2 sub 2). Group (0) contains sleeping

TABLE 17.8
Church participation

	N	%	cum. %
0 nothing	39	5	5
1 reads parish paper	197	23	28
2 makes a fixed contribution	258	30	58
3 goes to church 3 or 4 times a month	232	27	85
4 is a parish volunteer	126	15	100
Total	852	100	100

Source: Van Hemert 1991, 68

members or members on paper only (5%). Groups (1) and (2) are formed by the marginal members (23% + 30% = 53%). Group (3) is made up of the modal members (27%). Finally, group (4) contains the core members (15%).

It is of importance not only to aim church policy at those whom the pastor sees in church regularly (group 3 and 4: 27% + 15% = 42%) or at those with whom he works (group 4: 15%); for the majority is made up of marginal members (53%), and that is not even counting the members on paper only (5%).

Sometimes one comes across the view that it is not right to divide the members of the church into such groups. People might fall into a kind of concentric thought. The pastor would be the center; the inner circle would be formed by the core members; the middle circle, by the modal members; and the outside circle, by the marginal members and possibly by the members on paper only. In such a scheme of concentric circles, the essence would be more or less church participation: the core members participate the most, the marginal members and the members on paper participate the least, and the modal members are somewhere in the middle. The danger is not imaginary, according to this view, that reality is marked by a scheme, so that the complexity of the church community is hidden from view. Thus a plea is made to allow the specificity of the various groups to be shown to full advantage and not to make it dependent upon the center/periphery perspective (Schneider 1982). In addition, researchers point out that this perspective shuts the door on all the kinds of religious

TABLE 17.9

Pastoral participation in seven parishes in %

	tot.	urban par.			med. par.		rural par.	
		I	II	III	IV	V	VI	VII
volunt.	17	11	15	17	12	22	12	26

Source: Van Hemert & Spruit II 1984, 15

activities that take place outside the church and for which church policy has no eye (Feige 1990).

For that matter, the division between core, modal, and marginal members need not necessarily lead to a concentric idea of things. An illustration of this is the research into ethnocentricity and an open or closed religious attitude. From this research, it appeared that the modal members deviated from the marginal members on the one hand, and from the core members on the other. They showed themselves to be more ethnocentric and closed in their attitudes than both other groups (chapter 11 sub 1).

Pastoral participation

We would like to take a special look at one aspect from the whole of church participation: pastoral participation. By this we mean the activities of parishioners as volunteers in the broad area of pastoral work. Table 17.9 presents the percentages of the volunteers in the seven parishes. The first column contains the percentage of all active parishioners of the seven parishes together.

What strikes us about this table are the relatively high percentages of volunteers in parish V, the Diaspora Parish, with 22%, and Parish VII, the Agricultural Parish, with 26%. How can they be explained? The answer to this question cannot be given with any certainty. Nevertheless, we can formulate some suppositions.

Diaspora parishes, like Parish V, are often characterized by a great number of volunteers. The situation of this one parish of 1,900 members in the greater municipal context of 37,000 inhabitants obliges them to put their shoulders to the wheel with united force

TABLE 17.10
Number of church members x 1,000

	1975	1980	1985	1990
Catholic Church	5,460	5,617	5,533	5,560
Netherl. Ref. Ch.	3,038	2,812	2,710	2,534
Reformed churches in the Netherlands	878	867	828	784

Source: Van Hemert 1991, 3

(table 17.1), for they have scarcely any or no infrastructure at all to fall back on.

If a parish no longer has a pastor of its own, like Parish VII, it is compelled — if it wishes to survive — to go to work itself. The Agricultural Parish has come to be in such a situation. We are dealing here with a parish that is not found in the ecclesial but in the pastoral Diaspora, you might say. This can bring potential capacities and talents to the surface.

The percentage of volunteers in Parish I, the District Parish (11%), Parish IV, the Reconstructed Parish (12%), and Parish VI, the Village Parish (12%), can be called relatively low with respect to the general average (17%). Parish II, the Industrial Parish, and Parish III, the Central Parish, hold a medium position (15% and 17%). We would also like to mention here that the average participation of volunteers in the seven parishes (17%) is higher than the average participation of volunteers in a general societal context in the Netherlands, which is 14.7%. Regarding the latter, we can add that the more people are churchly, the more they participate in volunteer work in a general societal context (Van Hemert 1991, 14).

The future

Having given data from the seven parishes, which, as we mentioned, were collected in 1983, we will now end this survey by looking to the future. We will do this by presenting some figures with regard to church membership over the last twenty years. Besides this, the data with respect to church membership distributed over certain age categories are of importance.

TABLE 17.11

Index figures — church members and churchgoers (1975 = 100)

	church members			churchgoers		
	1975	1980	1985	1970	1980	1985
Catholic Church	100	103	101	100	80	59
Netherl. Prot. Ch.	100	93	89	100/100	94/93	88/86
Reformed Church	100	99	94	100/100	93/80	82/62

Source: Van Hemert 1991, 5

The first group of data relates to the number of members of the larger denominations at four points in time: 1975, 1980, 1985, and 1990. In table 17.10 we have the total number of members, with no distinctions between core members, modal members, and marginal members. The data relate to the three largest denominations in the Netherlands, and come from the statistics of these churches themselves.

From this table it appears that the number of Catholic Church members decreased somewhat during the first half of the eighties. The Netherlands Reformed Church has been having to cope with a steady decrease for far longer. The Reformed churches in the Netherlands saw a decline in membership from the middle of the seventies.

In addition, it is important to regard the data that have to do with weekend churchgoers. The three larger churches do annual counts of church attendance. The figures of table 17.10 have been transformed into index figures in table 17.11 for the church members in 1975, 1980, and 1985. The index figures for the churchgoers have been added to this. The number of church members and the number of churchgoers from 1975 have been set at 100. With the two Protestant denominations, the first figure relates to the visitors of the Sunday morning service, and the second to those of the Sunday afternoon and Sunday evening service.

From this table it appears that the Catholic Church, as we just indicated, shows a slight decline in the number of church members during the first half of the eighties (from 103 to 101). But there is a very strong decline in the number of churchgoers (from 100 in 1975 to 59 in 1985). The Netherlands Reformed Church, however, shows

TABLE 17.12
Modal members within the Dutch population in %

Age	Catholic	Netherl. Ref.	Ref. Ch. Neth
15-24	6.3	3.3	4.8
25-34	5.2	3.4	4.7
35-49	10.4	4.5	5.1
50-64	17.4	6.5	5.5
65-	18.4	8.4	6.3

Source: Knippenberg 1992, 250

a parallel decline in the number of church members (from 100 to 93 and 89) and the number of churchgoers (from 100 to 94/93 and 88/86). The Reformed churches take up an intermediate position. They display a slower decline in the number of church members (from 100 to 99 and 94) than the number of churchgoers (from 100 to 93/80 and 82/62). In their case, the Sunday afternoon and evening services are out of favor (from 100 to 80 and 62).

It is important to check what the distribution of age is among these churchgoers. In table 17.12 the percentage is presented per age category of the share of modal members in the whole of the Dutch population within the age group concerned across the three larger church denominations. The age categories are: 15-24, 25-34, 35-49, 50-64, and 65 and older. The data are from 1985/1986.

From the distribution of these percentages across the age categories, we can deduce an image of the future. Those older than 50 among the modal members in the Catholic Church cover 17.9% of the Dutch population within their age group; the 15- to 35-year-olds cover only 5.8%. This implies a very strong decline. The modal members in the Reformed churches in the Netherlands, which the third column refers to, display a more stable image. There, 5.9% (those over 50) are set off against 4.8% (15- to 35-year-olds). The modal members in the Netherlands Reformed Church hold an intermediate position: 7.5% (older than 50) against 3.4% (15- to 35-year-olds). All in all, we cannot expect that the decline of the number of modal members will stabilize in the short term.

The unusually strong decline that the Catholic Church is going

TABLE 17.13
Catholics from 0 to 6 years old in %

	1975	1980	1985	1990
Catholics	10.0	7.8	6.9	6.6
Dutch population	10.8	8.9	8.5	8.7

Source: Van Hemert 1992, 6

through can also be observed from the development of the number of Catholics who belong to the age category 0 to 6 years old. The columns in table 17.13 relate to the following points in time: 1975, 1980, 1985, and 1990. The first row contains the percentages of the share of the Catholics from 0 to 6 years old in the total number of Catholics; the second row contains the percentages of the number of Dutch from 0 to 6 years old in the whole of the Dutch population.

What this table brings out is that the number of Dutch children from 0 to 6 has dropped in a relative sense between 1975 and 1985 (from 10.8% to 8.5%), but the last five years there has been a very slight increase (from 8.5% to 8.7%). The number of Catholic children from 0 to 6, however, does not run parallel to this. The decline we see in the figures between 1975 and 1985 (from 10.0% to 6.9%) has continued during the last five years (from 6.9% to 6.6%). Moreover, it appears that the number of Catholic children of the same age lags further and further behind the total number of Dutch children. The difference was only 0.8% in 1975 and 1.1% in 1980, while it came to 1.6% in 1985 and climbed to 2.1% by 1990.

(3) Church, utilization, and solidarity

We have discussed above the process of utilization. By this we meant the increase in the attempt to satisfy one's own needs and to realize one's own interests. We paid attention to the social stratification of the local church community because this brought to light the inequality between all sorts of groups of people. This inequality, in its turn, generates or strengthens the divergent needs and interests.

The question now is how the church has to deal with this.

Should it go about blindly confirming, or does it have criteria that allow it to make priorities? In order to be able to answer this question, we will make a distinction between the various kinds of needs and will dwell upon the normative implications of this distinction.

Kinds of needs

There are various kinds of needs (economic, political, social, cultural, and religious), which in addition are of an unbalanced nature among the various population groups. The economic needs of those who live below the poverty line (more than 10% of the Dutch population) can be valued differently than the desire of the middle class for more material prosperity. The political needs of ethnic minorities can be judged differently from the needs of those with university training, who complain about a lack of influence on policy and management. The social needs of widows and orphans can be evaluated differently from those of people who are already socially integrated, who strive after even greater community experience. The cultural needs of untrained, unemployed youths weigh heavier than the wish for additional training of those who have already made it. The need of the less educated for a proper repertoire of Dutch hymns throws more into the scale than the desire of the religious intellectual elite for the beauty of Gregorian chant.

Something has to be added to this. The economic, political, social, cultural, and religious needs we distinguished can be either passive or active by nature. Passive needs have little motivational power and do not or hardly get people going. However, through actively present needs, people are stimulated to make up for the lack they feel and to undertake all sorts of activities. It is possible that needs change during time: they go from active to passive and vice versa. They can be influenced from the outside. Thus, passive needs can be evoked and stimulated in the direction of greater activity, just as active needs can fall into a state of sleep through outside influences.

Furthermore, needs can have either a subjective or an objective character. Something can be defined as a need if it is experienced as a need. However, such a subjective experience of need may not come about, while one is able to determine that there certainly is a need proceeding from an objective analysis. A process of communication can be set in motion concerning such an objective need with the people or groups in question. In this way one can prevent a need from being forced on them. People are therefore not manipulated from a false awareness in the direction of a true awareness. The point is the recognition of the need in question by the people themselves proceeding from their own perspective (Giesecke 1979; Freire 1972; Negt 1971).

Normative implications

The distinction between passive and active, subjective and objective, manifest and latent needs does make it clear that separate needs do not exist. There are only interpreted needs. The term *needs* refers to certain data in individual and societal life that we observe, define, interpret, and evaluate as needs. In other words, there are no needs outside the frame of reference from which one sees, feels, recognizes, and values them. What always plays a part in this is an image of humanity, of society, of religion, and of the church. What we see, understand, and judge to be needs depends on our convictions about which needs have to be fulfilled. Our value judgments indicate what humans cannot actually do without, what is their due, what they need. In other words, normative criteria are always involved (Van der Ven 1985c, 199-200).

In the literature, one finds a distinction that can serve for the prioritization of needs: the division between primary and secondary needs. The primary needs are food, water, health care, shelter, clothing, work, and education. The satisfaction of the material needs (food, water, health care, shelter, and clothing) is necessary for simple survival. The satisfaction of the need for work implies that all who are capable of work should have sufficient paid work. It provides the opportunity to be able to look after one's material needs. Moreover, it contributes to the development of human society, insofar as the work meets quality standards. The realization of the need for education forms a necessary condition for the sensible way in which to handle the fulfillment of the primary needs. In addition, it contributes to the cultural, moral, and spiritual cultivation of humans and prepares them for bearing responsibility in society.

Besides the primary needs that deserve the highest priority, there are secondary needs. These are made up of desires and wishes in the social-cultural field, like spare time, recreation, holidays, corporate life, and art (Tinbergen et al. 1977, 66-68).

Proceeding from the vision of the church (people of God) and its mission (Jesus movement), the distinction between primary and secondary needs forms an important guide for the prioritization of the needs (chapters 11 and 12). In the code *people of God* one finds the notion of the church of the poor. In the code *Jesus movement* one finds the orientation toward the "least of these my brothers and sisters" (Matt. 25:40). The kingdom of God starts with them. In them it has its beginning, its origin, and its destination (chapter 24).

Chapter 18

Policy Development

In the last chapter we discussed the problem of utilization. It relates to the increase in the endeavor to satisfy one's own needs and to realize one's own interests. We traced various kinds of needs by taking a closer look at the social stratification of the local church. We established that the church has to set priorities in the contribution it has to make to the satisfaction of the needs. This prioritization has to be carried out proceeding from the vision and the mission of the church (chapter 17).

In order to transfer this prioritization into practical action, the church has to convert it in terms of the making of policy. Two aspects can be distinguished in the making of policy: the formation of policy and the execution of policy. In the formation of policy the policy is prepared, developed, and established. In the execution of policy, it is given concrete shape in practice. The experiences that are gained through this execution are fed back to the formation of policy. This process from policy formation to policy execution and back again is expressed in the so-called policy cycle.

In this chapter we will pay attention to questions of (1) policy formation, (2) policy implementation, and (3) the policy cycle.

(1) Policy formation

Policy formation in an explicit sense is often the object of reflection and discussion in the local church. The core questions that are connected to this come down to the following: Can and may the local church work on policy formation? And how can it work on policy formation? The question of whether it can or may do so relates to the points of departure of the policy formation, while the question of how it can do so relates to the working out of policy formation.

Points of departure

Policy formation can be described as the endeavor of actors to achieve certain ends with certain means, with an eye to the accomplishment of change in the future. This description contains some terms that require clarification: ends and means, actors, change, and future. As will become clear, these terms refer to certain notions that lie within them. The term *ends and means* refers to the instrumental rationality in relation to the normative and expressive rationality; *actors* refers to the social support; *change* refers to the transformatory power; *future* refers to the tension between *futurum* and *adventus.* We shall discuss these notions by distinguishing a number of kinds of plans that are connected to these notions and in which policy formation becomes concrete. The advantage is that in making these distinctions, an equal number of choices for the local church arise. Because of this, the broad notion of policy formation becomes manageable (Commissaris 1977; Van Doorn & Van Vught 1978; Van Vught 1979; 1982; Van de Vall 1980; Dunn 1981; Bosman 1981; Blommestein et al. 1984; French & Bell 1984; Van Hoesel 1985; Kickert 1985; 1986; Daft 1989).

Instrumental rationality

We have just described policy formation as the endeavor for the achievement of certain ends by certain means. However simple this description may sound, it contains a barrel-load of problems. To begin, one may wonder whether the thought that underlies this definition is that once one has set oneself certain goals, one need only choose and implement the correct means to achieve the goals. However, the correct means do not exist. There are only better and poorer means, and that is why the effectiveness and efficiency of the action to achieve the goals in question may vary. Effectiveness and efficiency are never at a maximum; they are only optimal. At most they are the best possible effectiveness and efficiency. Let us define the idea of optimal attunement of means to aims as the assumption of instrumental rationality.

The question is whether this assumption is not based on myth. For those who engross themselves in policy formation, as it develops in the everyday life of the local church, see that other processes also take place. A master plan in which the entire policy of the church community could be filed under the optimal attunement of the means to the aims simply does not exist. One finds only incremental forms of policy. In other words, the policy of the church is formed through new ways to solve the problem, which are added to the existing ones every day; they grow, as it were. One need only look at the way in which people usually choose a new method of catechetics. People decide to introduce it because it meets certain objections that certain groups had to the last method, without the catechetical aim that lies behind it being problematized.

However, the assumption of instrumental rationality is put under further pressure when we see that the formation of policy in the parishes is also determined by all sorts of lobbies and coalitions. Certain groups wish to push through certain changes against the wishes of other groups. For this purpose they form ad hoc relations and make mutual compromises: "if you scratch my back, I'll scratch yours." One need only consider how experiments are carried out or broken off with respect to liturgy.

Finally, formation of church policy is also influenced by ecclesial regulations. In this the central question is not about which means one needs to achieve the aims one has in mind in the most effective and efficient way, but with which means one is allowed to achieve them. In other words, which means are permissible? People allow themselves to be guided by the rules of administration that are applicable in a particular case. Thus a pastoral worker who has been appointed for youth pastoral care is not allowed to hold his sermon in the place of a homily in the youth liturgy, but in the place of the opening address. This is simply because the ecclesial regulations order it.

All this means that instrumental rationality is curtailed by the incremental, coalition, and administration processes that take place every day (Dunn 1981; Geurts & Vennix 1989). Is it just a question of being curtailed and not of being dispelled? There are authors who do indeed believe that nothing is left of instrumental rationality in the daily practice of policy formation. They mark it down as a complete myth. This is because the practice is entirely marred by irrationality.

This irrationality has several causes, according to these authors. The problems with which people are confronted in policy formation are far too complex to be placed within the mold of instrumental rationality. Moreover, the information about all these problems is so extensive that people are simply incapable of dealing with it. Furthermore, the criteria are lacking with which the information can be adequately ordered and selected. Finally, we are short of methods and procedures to be able to judge the alternative policies on their merits and drawbacks.

The irrationality of policy formation is expressed in the reduction of complexity that the administrators apply. Reduction of complexity is a euphemism for "muddling through." Administrators are often found to base their policy on anything but rational considerations. The three things they use are: routine, habits, and rules of thumb. If one bases oneself on routine, then one falls back on ways of acting one had close at hand in the recent past — without much consideration for aims and means. If one appeals to habit, then one legitimizes oneself by referring to a vague and global approach from the distant past, in which it is not at all clear whether this applies to the situation of the here and now of the present problem. If one relies on rules of thumb, then one appeals to a number of rules that have not been reflected upon, which are deemed to belong to the collective conventions of a particular group, in this case administrators, pastors, and volunteers. If one wishes to legitimize these conventions, then one refers to the (putative) body of knowledge of academic professionals, thereby bringing authority to bear upon the matter. One cannot speak of rationality, according to this view.

Let us give some examples of rules of thumb in church policy borrowed from the American best-seller *Twelve Keys to an Effective Church.* The rules are as follows: the local church should aim itself at two or three specific goals; visits by ministers and pastoral volunteers should take place every week; the weekly services have to be set up holistically (unity of music and message), planned by a real group, and led by an inspired, emotionally involved minister; one should invest in people and not in programs; strong religious leadership is necessary in the local church; effective processes of decision making should be held; there should be two or three really good programs;

the church should be easily accessible; it should be architecturally visible and recognizable; there has to be a parking lot; the church has to be large enough; the church has to properly address the people concerning their financial contribution (Callahan 1983).

These rules of thumb meet with criticism because they are in no way rooted in theological and/or social scientific theory and research. They appear to belong to the simple strategy of the church growth movement. Besides that, all sorts of problems with which church policy-makers are so often confronted are entirely hidden from view, such as the development of programs and projects in the fields of pastoral care, catechetics, liturgy, proclamation, and diacony. Moreover, it does not become clear how the various groups of people (core, modal, marginal, and nonmembers) are to be motivated, and what this means in terms of organization and management (Dietterich 1991, 19-21).

Is instrumental rationality indeed a myth? Is it perhaps an ideology that serves as a cover for the irrationality of church administrators? Does it try to take on the aspect of the royal ermine robe of the God Reason?

Yet, there is a way out of the dilemma between rationality and irrationality. This is made up of two aspects. First, one has to recognize the irrational processes that take place de facto in the daily practice of policy-making, and take them seriously. This means that one pays attention to merely incremental solutions, coalition influences, administrative regulations, routine, habits, and rules of thumb. The second aspect is that one decides to hold these processes up to a critical light and to make them the subject of argumentative communication, proceeding from rationality as a human capacity. The first aspect, therefore, relates to the rational recognition of irrationality, while the second relates to the critical analysis of it. In this way, instrumental rationality functions as an option from which one can actually judge the effectiveness and efficiency of the making of policy (Etzioni 1988).

Normative and expressive rationality

The question is, however, whether the perspective of instrumental rationality is sufficient. It forms only one aspect of rationality, which also encompasses normative and expressive rationality (chapter 1 sub 2). If instrumental rationality functions without the other two, there is the danger that the whole of policy formation gets in the way of the functional, system, and cybernetic planning. In these three types of planning, the aims of policy formation are fixed; they cannot be negotiated. The only thing that has to happen is that the right means are used to achieve the aims in view. In functional planning, the focus is on the realization of one goal. System planning is aimed at maintaining a balance between all the aims. This can be done, for example, by attending to the mutual tuning of the input, the throughput, and the output. Cybernetic planning has a somewhat more complex structure. It works with feedback, which provides information on the results of policy, so that this can be taken into account in the next policy cycle. Its purpose is improving the achievement of the aims once they have been set. An example of functional planning is setting up an adequate procedure for group pastoral care, so that the effectiveness is raised. An example of system planning is the division of financial means across five sectors of pastoral policy, in which an allowance has been made for the sources of the means, like collections, stipends, financial contributions to the church by the people (input), the way in which they are used (throughput), and the results (output), so that a balance arises. Finally, an example of cybernetic planning is the continuation of policy formation per year, in which the judgment of the results of the previous year count as the starting point for the policy of the next.

What is wrong with these examples? Nothing as such, but there is something missing, and that is permanent reflection on the aims themselves. In these types of planning, the aims are not up for discussion. Nevertheless, it is necessary to subject them continually to critical research and to check to see whether they require supplementation, adjustment, or correction. Perhaps they may even need to be eliminated. For aims are not universal, eternal entities that are not subject to change themselves. They are formulations made by people at a certain time in a certain place with regard to that which they believe is worth striving for in that time and place. Due to shifts in the societal context, in the church itself, and in the views regarding its vision and mission, the aims have to be looked at critically again and again.

Without activating normative and expressive rationality, this kind of examination is not possible. For it does not aim at how certain goals must be achieved, but at which goals must be achieved and why. In normative rationality, the values and norms in question, and justice in particular, are at stake. Proceeding from this, the aims under discussion can be placed in an objective-critical light. In expressive rationality, the intersubjective clarification of the aims is involved. Through this, the participants place themselves in each other's positions, which allows them to understand and comprehend why certain goals have certain subjective meanings to certain people. Normative and expressive rationality surpass the aim/means relation of instrumental rationality. They demand a kind of policy formation in which there is room for normative planning and expressive-participative planning.

Social support

Who are the actual makers and bearers of church policy? Is it a single person, or a small group at the top of the local church? A council somewhere in the middle, or the community itself at the base? Which processes take place between these layers: top-down or bottom-up processes? These questions can be answered by localizing different types of planning on a continuum.

On one side of the continuum, one finds command planning. Here, we are dealing with a greatly centralized, forceful, and bureaucratic manner of policy formation. Thus a church council can issue directives with the firm conviction that these can be transferred into programs and activities without hesitation. In the middle area of the continuum, we find corporative planning. In this a number of more or less institutionalized groups, or in a more limited sense the leaders of these groups, take part in the planning. In the local church this kind of policy formation takes place if the pastoral team and the church council consult the permanent committees and working groups for the purpose of determining a policy plan. On the other side of the continuum, we find community planning. Broad categories of people from the base participate in this. An important element in this community planning is advocacy planning, in which special allowance is made for the position of groups that are at the bottom of society and therefore have no voice. In this kind of policy formation, people stick up for these groups and bring their interests to the fore (hence we speak of advocacy). However, because the interests of the groups differ among themselves, it is not always easy to reach a consensus. Moreover, people who live on the edge of society usually get the worst of it, no matter how many "advocates" step into the breach for them. Their interests are easily made subordinate to the "general" interest. Sometimes it is necessary to secure their interests via so-called conflict planning.

Transformation

We described policy formation as the endeavor of actors for the planning of change. However, one can have smaller or larger changes in mind. Changes also vary in their transformatory power. Once again the notion of a continuum can help us to order our ideas.

On the one side of the continuum, we find tuning planning, adaptive planning, and contingency planning. Tuning implies that one attunes policy to the changed needs of people. Adaptation is aimed at the control of crises from its environment that affect the church. Its main purpose is to bring the injurious consequences back to minimal proportions. With contingency planning people try to get ahead of crises and cut them off before they break out. The activities that people undertake are keeping tabs on the trends that occur, making extrapolations of these trends for the future, endeavoring to make predictions on the basis of this, determining which possible injurious consequences they may have for the church, and, finally, meeting these injurious consequences as adequately as possible. Therefore we can say that contingency planning is preventive planning. Let us look at some examples. An example of tuning planning is the introduction of new hymns in liturgy because people find the existing hymns a bit dull. An example of adaptive planning is the introduction of various liturgical celebrations for different groups, in order to reach all kinds of people who have become estranged from the church. An example of contingency planning is the development of multi-ethnic programs in the various pastoral sectors, before one can speak of ethnic problems in the particular parish.

On the other side of the continuum, we can distinguish the following: re-orienting planning, re-creating planning, and radical planning. These kinds of planning surpass the existing aims and frameworks of the church. The re-orienting planning aims at the development of a relatively new direction the church has to take. This involves re-orienting. It is made up of frame bending: people do not take a new course but reset the course, making a course correction. Re-creating planning has to do with the creating and implementing of new aims and a new course. The existing aims are not placed in a new order of priority, but they are replaced by new ones. Here we can speak of frame breaking. Radical planning goes one step beyond both of these. Here the decision is made to blow up the existing organization in a structural sense. That is why radical planning is closely related to counter planning. The revolutionary planning of the guerilla movement serves as a model in this. An example of re-orientation planning is the reprioritization of adult catechetics with respect to catechetics for children (from the second to the first place or vice versa) or of diacony with regard to catechetics. An example of re-creating planning is given by Dieterrich (1987). If a church is stuck in a fatal crisis, it can gain an entirely new lease of life, as it were, through expert guidance. Fatal crises can stem from fundamental conflicts around the succession of ministers and church administrators, the course of church policy, and interpersonal tensions that are running high in the pastoral team (Adam & Schmidt 1977). Radical planning does not occur in the ordinary churches in Western society.

Reallocative planning and innovative planning belong to the middle area of the continuum. Reallocative planning involves the redivision of personal and financial means over the various areas that the church organization covers and across the different programs that belong to it. Innovative planning goes one step further, dealing not with redivision of the means across existing programs, but with withdrawing means from these programs in order to make new programs possible. Examples of this are spending less time on catechetics and more on diacony (reallocative planning); withdrawing money from liturgy and proclamation in order to bring about the development of a new program for unemployed youths (innovative planning).

Futurum and adventus

Policy formation always has to do with bringing about change in the future. But the question is: What do we know of the future? And if we know little or nothing about it, in what sense do we think we can influence the future by taking measures now?

These are fundamental questions. They deal with the insecurity of the future, which is, of course, something with which policy formation always has to do. It makes no sense to deny this or camouflage it. The point is to find a way to handle the insecurity of the future.

Several strategies can be distinguished for handling this insecurity. They can be clarified by means of three terms from system theory: system, system borders, and environment. A *system* is a structured whole of elements that distinguishes itself from its environment as an entirety. The area where the system and the environment meet is defined as the *system borders* (Kickert 1985). Proceeding from this perspective, the church can be considered as a system and the societal context as its environment. The system borders can be found where the church and the societal context touch each other.

The first group of strategies involves insecurity regarding the environment. This can be reduced in two ways: by predictions about the environment and by influencing the environment. In predictions, a connection is made between two or more variables, so that from the presence of the one variable, the presence of the other variable can be predicted. In this we are always dealing with statements of chance: there is a greater or smaller chance that the other variable occurs when the one is found. These sorts of predictions are of great importance for the formation of church policy. They can be deduced from empirical research reports concerning religion, church, and pastoral work. The insecurity regarding the environment can also be reduced by its being influenced indirectly. One also comes across this strategy in the church. Thus, the bishops try to influence politics regarding moral matters like abortion, suicide, and euthanasia. By doing so, they try to free the church (the system) of opinions and practices that occur in society (the environment) and that can penetrate the church from there.

The second group of strategies is made up of the closing of the system borders (between the church as a system and society as an environment). This only succeeds to a certain extent. People can always turn to this strategy when it is feared that the influences from the environment — possibly despite efforts to influence it — are starting to penetrate the system. Through this strategy the system changes from an open one to a closed one. In the business community, one comes across system delimitation, when we see people turning to buffer formation of products through stocks, in order to brave the unpredictable fluctuations of the market. One also comes across a variety of border patrols within the church. During Vatican II the borders of the Catholic Church were open; in the period that followed, they gradually closed. This was expressed through increasing regulation, codification, and setting of policy.

The third group of strategies involves the system itself. If the injurious influencing from the environment cannot be prevented, the environment itself cannot be influenced and the delimitation of the system does not work or is insufficient. We are then left with only one possibility: we must learn to live with the insecurity in the system itself. It is just a fact of life that a number of phenomena take place without having been predicted, prevented through influencing, or repelled through system delimitation. In what way can the system learn to live with the insecurity? The answer is that it has to bring about the development of a capacity to make flexible adjustments.

Policy formation and flexibility need not have a strained relationship. They can be seen as each other's opposite number if one views policy formation and flexibility in an absolute manner. Policy formation would then come down to total and detailed control of the future, while flexibility would be made up of the total release of every kind of regulation. Policy formation is associated with the impenetrable black of Kafka's bureaucracy, and flexibility with the transparent blue of the ocean. These, however, are extremes. In reality, both policy formation and flexibility are viewed less absolutely. Policy formation lies somewhere between controllability and uncontrollability. It belongs to the genus of goal-oriented influencing — which belongs to human action *(actus humanus)* itself. The opportunity of goal-oriented influencing cannot be denied — it would deprive man of his freedom. At the same time, however, it is bound by conditions and limitations — human freedom is bounded freedom. Proceeding from this boundedness, people come to the insight of the importance and necessity of flexibility in policy formation.

Flexibility can be seen as a dimension of policy formation. It has to do with the degree to which one is not involved with only one activity for the realization of aims, but with a set of alternative actions; and also with a set of alternative reactions to these actions and the interactions and transactions that are implicit in it. In other words, we are dealing with a broad scale of alternatives that can be used interchangeably depending on the changing circumstances in the environment, in the border traffic, and within the system itself. There is also the possibility that yet other alternatives can be developed in connection with the existing alternatives, in order to tackle the varying challenges more efficiently and effectively. Flexibility does not mean nonplanning; it means smart planning (Kickert 1985, 187).

Justice is done to the tension between the future as *futurum* and the future as *adventus* with this flexible formation of policy. *Futurum* has to do with the future insofar as it can be extrapolated from certain trends in the past and present, from which an image of the future can be projected. *Adventus,* however, refers to the nonprojectable character of the future, to its unpredictability, incomprehensibility, originality, and newness. Humankind does not have the future as *adventus* under control, but is oriented toward it as something that has yet to occur. Hope and desire lie in this. The tension between *futurum* and *adventus* does not imply control of the future but openness for the future.

In theological literature, we can find two starting points to symbolize this openness to the future in a religious sense. The first is the theme of eschatological reservation. Everything humanity does, prepares, and plans is marked by provisionality because God, who is the absolute future, will interrupt and restructure all our achievements in an unexpected and gracious manner. The *adventus* is thus not the destruction of the *praesens,* but it does place it under the criticism of the dangerous memory of Jesus. Jesus' praxis of solidarity with the living and the dead holds as a criterion of this dangerous memory. Because of this, all our doings are placed under the reservation of the future of God's solidarity with one and all. Proceeding from God's solidarity, our actions will be subjected to the last judgment (Metz 1977; Peukert 1978).

The second theme is *kairos.* The difference between *chronos* and *kairos* is that *chronos* stands for quantitative, measurable, dividable time, and *kairos* for qualitive, immeasurable, undividable, gratuitous time. *Chronos* is the time that can be drawn as a line from the past through the present toward the future. *Kairos,* however, is always present in the here and now. It forces itself upon you; it befalls you and surprises you. It is the actual-present *praesens (hodie)* that can be defined as a point (Tillich 1966). The term *kairos* leads to dealing with time in the present in a religious way and to tracing the signs of the times in the present and to discovering traces of God, who comes to meet us in the here and now.

Against this background, flexible church policy formation can be regarded as a kind of anticipatory planning. It can be seen as the foreshadowing of the unexpected character of God's salvation in the future, the foretaste of the unexpected and unpredictable kingdom of God. Church policy formation that lacks this all-penetrating feature of flexibility only leads to eschatological oblivion *(Zukunftvergessenheit),* through which it passes over the gratuitousness of the present (Bitter & Engelert 1984).

Working out

People are confronted not only with the question of whether policy formation may be done and can be done in the church, but also with the question how they can give it shape. In exploring this latter aspect, we base our discussion on the idea that the average local church can be found somewhere in the middle of the two continuums that we just distinguished. As far as the social base of policy formation is concerned, it is located between command and community planning: somewhere in the neighborhood of corporative planning. In certain cases it also makes use of advocacy planning. As far as the tranformatory power is concerned, the range is far greater. The parishes probably cover the whole field from tuning planning up to and including re-creating planning. The types of planning that are located in this area can be used as perspectives from which church policy formation can be understood, developed, and evaluated. Thus it can be approached from the angle of tuning, adaptive, and contingency planning, from the view of reallocation and innovation planning, and from the perspective of re-orienting and re-creating planning. Each time a different light falls on policy formation proceeding from these perspectives, as it concretely develops.

In the concrete working out of policy formation, we have three means at our disposal: the policy plan, the program, and the projects. The policy plan involves the total pastoral policy in the medium range (3 to 5 years). The program can be situated within the policy plan and has to do with the total pastoral policy in the short run (1 to 2 years). The projects are located within the program and are especially aimed at a certain function, sector, goal, method, or target group in the short run (1 to 2 years).

Policy plan

The functions that a policy plan fulfills can be defined as important for policy formation and with that for the development of the church. They can be described as follows. The policy plan implies a systematic clarification and critical consideration of the aims that the church strives after. It gives structure to the aims of the pastoral policy sectors, through which these can become a surveyable and integrated whole. It contains a definition of tasks from which itemized tasks can be assigned to individuals, groups, and collectives. It creates the opportunity for interim adjustment and course correction. Finally, it provides us with an instrument for regular evaluation.

What are the contents of a policy plan? In global terms it is made up of four parts: (A) normative, (B) descriptive, (C) strategic, and (D) condition-setting. In the normative part (A), the plan indicates what the aims are of the church and pastoral work. In the descriptive part (B), it describes what the present situation looks like. In the strategic part (C), it sets out the path that has to be taken proceeding from the present situation to approach or achieve the aims respectively. In the condition-setting part (D) a definition is given of which conditions are necessary for this and how they can be realized. It is clear that the linear relationship we have sketched between the four parts has to be conceived of in a cyclical-iterative sense: the parts influence each other (cyclical) again and again (iterative).

Let us briefly define what elements these parts are made up of. Where possible we refer the reader to the relevant chapters in the book. The normative part (A) contains the following subparts: (a) vision of the church (chapter 11), (b) mission of the church (chapter 12), (c) concept of the community (chapter 14), (d) concept of leadership (chapter 16), and (e) aims of the policy sectors (chapter 18 sub 1). The descriptive part (B) exists of: (f) description of the present profile of the church and pastoral work (aims, sectors, and strategies), (g) description of the present environment of the church (societal environment, church environment), (h) description of the future environment, and (i) description of the strong and the weak sides of church and pastoral work, proceeding from the present and future environment. The strategic part (C) concerns: (j) description of the strategic gap between the normative and descriptive parts in its most prominent aspects, (k) choice of programs, program units, and projects for the bridging of the strategic gap (chapter 18 sub 2) and (l) description of the method of evaluation to be used (chapter 18 sub 3). The condition-setting part (D) relates to: (m) the organizational structure (chapter 20), (n) the personal conditions (chapter 23), and (o) the financial means (chapter 24). Just so the reader has a clear understanding of things, we wish to emphasize that this list is intended to fulfill a heuristic rather than a prescriptive function (Keuning & Eppink 1986, 319-63).

Program

The program can be located within the policy plan and contains the survey of the whole of the connected activities in the church and pastoral work in the short run. Therefore it is looked into or reviewed at least once every two years. It describes the total service package of the five sectors, including their aims: pastoral care, catechetics, liturgy, proclamation, and diacony. Pastoral work can further be divided into individual and group pastoral work. The reasons why we do not count church development and community formation as parts of these sectors were mentioned earlier (chapter 4 sub 3).

Aims of pastoral work

Individual pastoral work is aimed at the guidance of personal developmental and learning processes of individuals under the aspect of the questions of meaning, worldview, religion, and Christian faith. The emphasis can be placed on pastoral work as care or counseling (Van der Ven 1991e).

The motivation for individual pastoral conversation lies in personal and relational crises, mourning, loss of meaning, a need for an orientation in life and faith, and important life events such as birth, formation of relations and marriage, illness, and death.

In group pastoral care, the focus is on the guidance of interaction processes in groups tackling questions and themes in the fields of meaning, worldview, religion, and Christian faith. The emphasis lies either on the interpersonal or on the intrapersonal interaction. On other occasions, interaction with the Christian tradition from which the theme in question is being treated can be the focal point. This means that group pastoral work is characterized to a differing degree by the so-called encounter group, personal counseling in a group context, and the so-called thematic interaction method.

In contrast to group pastoral work that is primarily aimed at the development of affective processes, the aim of catechetics lies especially in the development of cognitive learning processes, without neglecting the affective and attitudinal aspects. The catechetics of the sacraments (baptism, communion, and marriage) holds an important position in this. In addition, catechetics can supply course and formation work, lectures, and series of lectures. The focus may be on introductions to the Bible and biblical texts, spiritual and mystical texts, or actual ethical and religious themes. A special place is taken by themes in the fields of social justice, war and peace, the third world, the environment, multi-ethnicity, and interreligious dialogue.

Liturgy and preaching hold an important position. In liturgy the creative ritual shape of the expression of the Christian faith is central. In preaching the most essential matter is the text/context correlation between the Scripture that is read in the liturgy on the one hand, and the present personal and societal experience of existence on the other.

Liturgy can be divided into weekend liturgy and the rites of passage. In the weekend liturgy, the church community comes together to give expression to its common faith in a ritual manner and to establish itself as a church community. The more this expression of faith comes about, the more a collective excitement arises, a "common passion," a "general fever" (Durkheim 1925). In the rites of passage, the church community focuses on individuals who are going through an important life event and wish to give expression to this in a ritual-religious manner, as with birth, marriage, and death (Scheer 1991). There are large groups — the marginal members — that wish to be part of the church only for the rites of passage. They go to the church only on occasion. In fact, one should not say that they wish to participate in the liturgy only "on occasion," but that they wish to participate proceeding from the kind of self-evidence that stems from the deeper meaning of the life events themselves. Proceeding from this viewpoint, we are fundamentally mistaken in speaking of marginal members (Rössler 1986, 202).

Proclamation, like diacony, is aimed at people and institutions outside the church. The point is to clarify the meaning of the gospel in cultural publicity. That is why it is of importance that the church participates in the public debate on matters of general interest and on problems in which people are involved. It can also take the initiative in starting a public debate, for instance, by throwing open lectures and organizing panel discussions. Here we can mention: the economic colonization of society; political alienation; the challenge of Europe and the whole of the Western world; social erosion; multi-culturalism; awareness of culture and values; ethical problems like abortion, euthanasia, and suicide; and the place and meaning of civil religion.

Diacony is aimed at the development of involvement and solidarity with the weakest in today's society, proceeding from the perspective of the kingdom of God. In diacony it is important to give shape to the personal involvement in actions and projects with an eye to making a contribution to social justice. These may relate to the direct environment of the church itself, or they can also be measured on a larger scale: national, European, Western, and global. The focus may be on the support of projects in underprivileged districts in larger cities, in distressed Western countries, or in Third World countries that are below the poverty line.

Projects

Within the program we find one or more projects. These are especially aimed at a certain function, sector, aim, method, or target group in the short run (1 to 2 years). Let us briefly dwell upon these elements, using examples. Concerning the functions, we can think of identity, integration, policy, and management. In integration special attention may be given to group, network, and community formation (chapter 14 sub 1) and treatment of conflict (chapter 15). The sectors have just been mentioned: pastoral work, catechetics, liturgy, proclamation, and diacony. The pastoral aims can be distinguished in their cognitive, affective, attitudinal, motivational, and social aspects. The methods can be divided into sectors and aims (chapter 18 sub 2). Finally, the target groups are in principle all the categories that were discussed earlier in the context of social stratification (chapter 17 sub 2; chapter 22 sub 2).

Projects are to be developed by combining some elements from the functions, sectors, aims, methods, and target groups with each other. Thus a project can aim at the contribution of the church to the public debate regarding euthanasia and suicide, proceeding from its own vision and mission (function), within proclamation (sector), with an eye to the development of a cognitive clarification of the meaning of the gospel (aim), using the panel discussion (method), especially for teachers from primary and secondary education (target group). Further along, we will mention an example of project development in the field of youth pastoral work (chapter 18 sub 3).

(2) Policy implementation

Now that the policy formation as such has been realized to the extent that we can speak of a policy plan, a program, and one or more projects, we can step over to the execution of policy. This contains a great many aspects that we will not be able to deal with in detail. However, we would like to pass some of them in review: the external and internal conditions, the methods and means, the points in time, and the effects.

External conditions

The external conditions relate to the circumstances in the local church that influence the policy plan, program, or project from the outside. Through these conditions they may be promoted and favored, but also hindered and impeded. Here we may consider conditions of both a structural and a cultural nature.

Structural factors are, for example, official church policy at a supralocal level that asserts its influence at the local level; the pressure of church policy administrators at a supralocal level; or the pressure of conservative or progressive groups in the local church. The factor of power is important in this. One should remember, however, that it is not necessarily the person who holds a formal position who has power, but the person who exerts effective influence on people in reality (Letterie 1979). One may hold a high position in the formal organization but may equally determine the thought and action of others in the informal organization.

Cultural factors can equally stimulate and impede the execution of program and projects. These relate to convictions and views regarding the church. They can exert a strong influence if conflicts threaten to arise about the vision and mission of the church, for instance. Taking on and bearing conflicts is just not done in the church. The reason is that conflicts are too often and too easily seen as a threat to the unity of the church and, along with this, as a threat to its identity. They are insufficiently seen as a sign of the pluriformity in the church and of the life and vitality of the church (Boff 1985). The reformation of the church, which is its permanent duty according to Vatican II, does not take place without conflict. In fact, the reformation of the church depends on conflicts and their balanced treatment. Being without conflict is often a sign of the low frequency and meager intensity of interactions between members in the church (Rosenthal 1980). The neglect of conflict and its repression can be viewed as a sign of inactivity in the church, or at least as slight involvement with the church (chapter 15).

Internal conditions

The internal conditions relate to the number of means that are available for the execution of policy. The personal and financial means as well as the time available are the focal points here. Naturally, the three are connected. They determine the feasibility of the program and the projects to an important extent. The personal means relate to the availability of both pastoral professionals and pastoral volunteers. Without sufficient means, one cannot even begin. The wonderful prospects that lie in the codes *people of God, Jesus movement,* and *body of Christ* remain intangible if they are not concretely involved with the internal conditions.

Methods and means

Methods and means vary depending on the ecclesial and pastoral aims in the policy sectors to which they relate. By methods, we mean the procedures and techniques that are used to achieve the aims that have been set. The means mostly have to do with the video, audio, and written material on the basis of which the route to the aim is followed. We will give some examples.

Van Knippenberg developed a procedure for religious communicative self-research for pastoral work. It has to do with group pastoral work based on the following specific aims: paying attention to, reflecting, and communicating on the religious theme in question. The methodical elements are exploring, analyzing, and processing the religious theme (Van Knippenberg 1987, 90-113). Since this procedure could also be used in the context of individual pastoral work, Van Knippenberg and Kemper wrote a handbook for its application in such work. Smeets further worked out this handbook and enriched it, making frequent use of written material. He calls this procedure "guided self-pastoral work" (Smeets 1990).

Quite a number of curricula were developed for catechetics, on the basis of which catechetical teaching/learning processes were given shape in a church or school context. Various kinds of curricula can be distinguished depending on the different aims and different types of curriculum organization.

As far as the aims are concerned, we can distinguish three kinds: knowledge of content and insight aims, as in the curriculums of mourning and religion (Vossen 1985), prayer (Siemerink 1987), and suffering (De Jong 1990); procedural aims, which are directed not at knowledge of content and insight, but at the learning of religious and/or moral strategies, as in the curricula on the environment and creation (Hermans 1986), and war and peace (Van Iersel & Spanjersberg 1993); and developmental aims, in which neither contents nor procedures are central, but the stimulation of the developmental stages of the participants, as in the curricula regarding moral development (Roumen, Hermans & Van der Ven 1991).

As far as the different types of curriculum organization are concerned, we can also distinguish three kinds. The first can be defined as the *experience curriculum.* In this type, the needs of the participants are central as well as the interest they have for certain themes, as in a curriculum on labor and unemployment (Van Schrojenstein Lantman 1990). The second kind is the *scientific structure curriculum.* The base of this is made up of the structure of the discipline that underlies a certain theme, as in a curriculum about religious experience (Van Gerwen 1985). The third is the *elaboration curriculum,* in which one alternately zooms in and out on thematic parts. By zooming in, all sorts of details are clarified; and by zooming out, they are continuously placed within a larger context, as in a curriculum on religious metaphors (Hermans 1990).

In liturgy, we also find that all sorts of methods and means are used. Thus, the liturgy can be celebrated according to the official ritual, but it can also deviate from this. In the latter case it can be more oriented toward experience, toward society, or toward the Bible. In liturgy focused on experience, the personal experiences and feelings of the participants, their personal life history, their world, are central. Liturgy aimed at society focuses on the religious thematization of societal problems and dilemmas like war and peace, underdevelopment, labor and unemployment, the environment, racism, and emancipation (Laeyendecker & Thung 1978; Osendarp & Ferron 1985; Siemerink 1992). In liturgy aimed at the Bible, the larger parts of a biblical book, an entire book, or even a number of books from the Bible serve as a guide (Scheer 1985a; 1985b).

Besides this, we can distinguish various homiletical methods: the sermon as kerygma, didache, martyrion, argument, and homily. With the sermon as argument, we can speak of a linear communication; and with the homily, of interactional communication (Dingemans 1991). Further, a sermon can be aimed at the Bible or at situations, or try to form a correlational bridge between the Bible and the situation (Pieterse 1987).

In the field of proclamation, a large number of methods can be distinguished at various levels. Here we will restrict ourselves to the public arena in which the Christian religion can contribute, along with other religions and philosophies, to the clarification of societal problems at a local, national, or global level. The methods used are discussion programs with citizens, governors, and professionals; panel discussions; information programs; initiation programs; identification programs; and, finally, liturgical programs (Van Leeuwen 1985; Ter Steeg 1985).

In the area of diacony we also come across all sorts of methods. We can mention the following: diacony as the efficient management of diaconal funds; diacony as professional care and counseling; diacony as diaconal management; diacony as solidarity (Steinkamp 1985; 1988); diacony as an *alliance habitus* or style of action (Van den Hooge & Van Gerwen 1991; Jäger 1986).

This description of the methods in the sector of diacony must necessarily remain general because of its nature. It needs to be further worked out and concretized. An example in the field of diacony concerning war and peace may clarify this. Let us assume that the mission of peace of the local church is not only the concern of the parish peace group, but that this group endeavors to interest others in this subject. It hopes to be able to influence the liturgy group in this sense and the larger whole of the church community via the liturgical service for peace. What steps does such a group have to take if it wishes to succeed in its intention? In order to answer this question, we can draw up a tree diagram for decisions. This contains six components: formulation of the concrete task; broadening of the base; negotiation with ministers and administrators; negotiation with the liturgy group; working out the setting of the task; and evaluating the setting of the task. In this tree diagram of decision with its six components, we find eleven questions to be answered and sixteen activities to be carried out. Here we are dealing with diagnostic questions (like, Did we achieve what we set out to achieve in a particular component?) Besides this, agogic questions (like, How can we develop the negotiation process within the particular component as adequately as possible?) are central. Questions of decision making (like, Which activities should be given priority and in what sense, considering the present situation of the one that is arising?) play an important part too. Furthermore, the tree diagram of decision contains six possibilities for a dead end, in which the peace group runs aground and its endeavor has to be seen as a mission impossible (Van Iersel & Spanjersberg 1993).

Even though we did not view community formation as a sector but as a function of the church, we would nevertheless like to explore some distinct methods here (chapter 4 sub 3). Within these methods one can introduce a dichotomy: community development and community education. In *community development* the important thing is to develop participation in church activities. An aid in this is community organization. This is characterized by the development of, for example, a network of councils (for pastoral work, catechetics, liturgy, and diacony). In *community education* the development of formation processes is central, with an eye to the raising of participation. Here, the point is the teaching/learning processes through which people develop the skills, abilities, and attitudes that are necessary for participation (Van der Veen 1982; Dijkstra 1989). An instrument that is used by some local churches is the extended house visit. By doing this, people try to strengthen the church as a community at the neighborhood level. At the same time it has a signaling function: one quickly and directly traces whether there are any necessities or requirements, problems or conflicts, that demand care and treatment (Baart, Bakkers & De Loor 1985).

Points in time

By points in time we mean determining the duration of the program and the projects, as well as setting forth a sequence for the various activities involved. This is very important because it promotes control and communication. If the program is divided into convenient time units, this makes them discussible. Boundless wholes of pastoral activities that no one can make head or tail of can only lead to endless discussions. The phases in time intended here prevent this from happening.

The phases in time can be described by means of a matrix, in which the horizontal axis relates to the duration in weeks or months, and the vertical axis relates to the list of activities. Filling in the cells in the matrix demands the making of time estimates. For this purpose we have three types to consider: a pessimistic (tp), an optimistic (to), and a real time estimate, based on real expectations (te). This provides us with three different types of time data. One can combine them to make a composed time estimate that is sufficiently balanced (tb). For this purpose one uses the time data in a simple statistical formula (Van Doorn & Van Vught 1978, 202):

$$\text{tb} = \frac{\text{tp} + \text{to} + 4\text{te}}{6}$$

This can be clarified by means of an example. Suppose that the peace group we just discussed wants to push the liturgical group to interest the whole community in the theme of peace via a liturgical service of peace. The balanced composed time estimate *(tb)* can be calculated accordingly in the following way. The time estimate *tp* comes down to 10 months, *to* comes down to 2 months, and *te* comes down to 3 months. The application of the formula results in: *tb* = (10 + 2 + 12)/6 = 4 months (16 weeks).

Effects

In the *traditional approach* to determining and evaluating effects, we find three central questions: Were the necessary means sufficiently made available and were they used purposefully (resource approach)? Did the internal organization run smoothly enough (internal process approach)? Were the aims set actually achieved (goal approach)? Of the three questions, the latter seems to be the most important. It is

TABLE 18.1
Liturgical celebrations

	1985	1986	1987	1988	1989
weekend lit.*	769	674	740	682	714
baptism	76	90	73	86	71
receiving com.	118	125	121	114	91
confirmation	67	67	51	46	38
marriage	12	12	15	15	6
funeral	59	77	62	71	75

* = number of participants per counted weekend

Source: In *Gezamenlijke Verantwoordelijkheid 1990*, 8

the most logical one too: goals can be considered as effects being strived for, and people want to know whether they are being achieved. This does not mean, however, that the first two questions can be neglected. For assuming that the aims were achieved, but that the resources were used too lavishly, one still has reason to reflect. Or suppose that the goals were reached, but that the internal organization had to deal with all sorts of conflicts (internal process). Then it is necessary to scrutinize the whole. The aim can never be to achieve the goals whatever the cost (Daft 1989, 98-104).

In the *modern approach* the term *effect* is extended and worked out in four aspects: output, range, judgment, and results. Perhaps these terms seem a bit too businesslike. However, it is important to reserve any opposition to them for the moment, because in practice one is confronted by them whether one likes to be or not (Ezerman & Mastenbroek 1991, 151ff.). Let us take a look at the terms one by one.

What we mean by *output* here is the number of services provided in hours or shifts. Thus one can ask how many sessions for individual pastoral care were held in a certain period. Hospital administrators are interested in the number of contacts made by hospital ministers with patients during a period of three months. The same question can be put to parish ministers. Besides this, we can determine how many meetings were held within the context of group pastoral work and catechetics. In liturgy the number of weekend services can be determined. As far as the data for the rites of passage are concerned, these can be traced from the files on baptism, marriage, and funerals. According to the Codex these records have to be present in the local church and have to be carefully kept by the minister (Can. 535; Toepassingsbesluiten 1988 Codex; Regeling 1989). Table 18.1 contains the data of the various liturgical celebrations of the Nijmegen parish of John and James in the Netherlands.

From this table it appears that the weekend liturgy has been stablizing at approximately 700 participants during the last few years, while there were still 1,157 in 1977. The Nijmegen district Dukenburg (the Netherlands) where the parish of John and James Church can be found has 26,000 inhabitants of which 67% are registered as Catholics. This means that only 4% of these Catholics go to church during the weekend, while the national average in 1990 was somewhere between 13.0% and 14.0% (Van Hemert 1991, 4; 1992, 24). On the other hand, more than 600 parishioners are active as volunteers (in *Gezamenlijke Verantwoordelijkeheid 1990*, 7-8).

The term *range* relates to the categories of people and the numbers of people who participate in the meetings or make use of the services. As far as the categories of people are concerned, all kinds of divisions, which we distinguished earlier in the context of social stratification (chapter 17 sub 2), may be relevant. Examples of these are: age, sex, societal class, political preference, social-cultural orientation, and church membership (marginal, modal, and core membership). Within this and over and above this, the number of users or participants can be determined.

The word *judgment* refers to the valuation of the quality of the meeting or the service by the users or participants. While this valuation is often only incidentally expressed — in connection with a "good" or "bad" meeting or celebration — it can still be tackled systematically. This is sometimes defined by the term *constituency approach.* In this case, "constituency" refers to all those who are involved with the local church (Daft 1989, 104-6).

Now the value of a meeting or celebration can be explained by means of several aspects. An example: one may impute a greater or lesser amount of importance to it; have participated in it with interest; have enjoyed it; have felt the level of cognitive complexity to be too high or too low (Van Gerwen 1985, 201ff.). Another example: one may have found the meeting to have had a more or less personal significance; have gone to a great or small amount of trouble for it;

have found it stimulating for further reflection (Siemerink 1987, 273-76). Besides this, one can ask what the participants thought of the conversation methods in the separate meetings and how they experienced the meetings as a whole (Van Knippenberg 1987, 135, 188-90).

Finally, we have the *results.* This is a term that has to used with care, for the eventual results of pastoral work cannot be measured. This is true for two reasons. First, the personal attitude of people to the Christian faith eventually transcends every kind of description or conceptualization; therefore, it is withdrawn from any kind of measurement or test. Here, the core of human freedom is at stake, which cannot by its very nature be pinned down, Secondly, the personal attitude toward the Christian faith is a gift of mercy from God proceeding from a theological point of view. Here the core of the transcendent gratuity of God is at stake. This cannot be harnessed in theories and notions, or by measurements and figures. It does not allow itself to be measured (Van der Ven 1982a, 642-45).

What can be measured is the degree to which the conditions that are required for a religious attitude can be reached. These are not sufficient conditions, but necessary conditions. The necessary conditions are cognitive, affective, attitudinal, motivational, and social conditions. Everything here revolves around the conditional results. Let us take a look at the following example. In 1988 a theodicy program in pastoral work, catechetics, liturgy, and diacony was simultaneously carried out in parishes in the region between Nijmegen and Tilburg (the Netherlands). The participants displayed 20% progress in the cognitive area. The average score for the affective change was 4% (Van der Ven 1990a). The number of participants in whom a process of attitudinal change could be traced at the end of the program was 44% (Van der Ven & Ven der Tuin 1990, 233). Naturally, one cannot gain a measurement of the results expressed in figures for every celebration and meeting. But we do not need it. A systematic collection of qualitative data, collected by means of concise forms that people are asked to fill in, can serve us well.

Now by combining output, range, judgment, and results of meetings, one gets an image of the vitality of the church and the pastoral work. In this matter it is important to keep a close eye on the fact that we are dealing with a comparative image.Comparison always takes place implicitly or explicitly proceeding from past experiences with the church and experiences with sister churches. Desired experiences play a role too. With the latter, convictions about what the church should be (vision and mission of the church) are the main focus.

(3) The policy cycle

The policy cycle provides for feedback proceeding from the execution of policy (sub 2) to policy formation (sub 1). It belongs to what we earlier called "cybernetic planning." In this instrumental rationality plays an important part. This does, however, have to be supplemented, as we argued earlier, proceeding from normative and expressive rationality. First we shall describe which components make up the policy cycle and which two kinds of elements it contains. Along with this, a selection is made from the literature that we believe is relevant for church policy (Dunn 1981; Etzioni 1988; Geurts & Vennix 1989). After that we shall illustrate all of this by means of an example: the project of youth pastoral care.

Components and elements

The policy cycle consists of seven components: (a) the problem that has to solved; (b) the alternatives for the solution that are at hand; (c) the optimal alternative on which the policy is based; (d) the implementation of this optimal alternative in the concrete practice of policy execution; (e) the monitoring of the execution; (f) the report of the execution; and finally (g) the evaluation of the execution proceeding from the question whether the problem in (a) was actually solved. All these components together form the policy cycle.

By means of the components in figure 18.1 we can discern two kinds of elements within the policy cycle. The first kind relates to methods for the preparation of policy decisions; the second kind relates to the policy decisions themselves. It makes sense to distinguish these two, since preparation and decision making assume two different roles in principle. This distinction in roles heightens the critical insight in the various tasks and responsibilities. It contributes to the content of rationality, which we earlier chose as an option for the making of policy.

The distinction in elements can mean that one assigns them to

FIGURE 18.1 Policy cycle

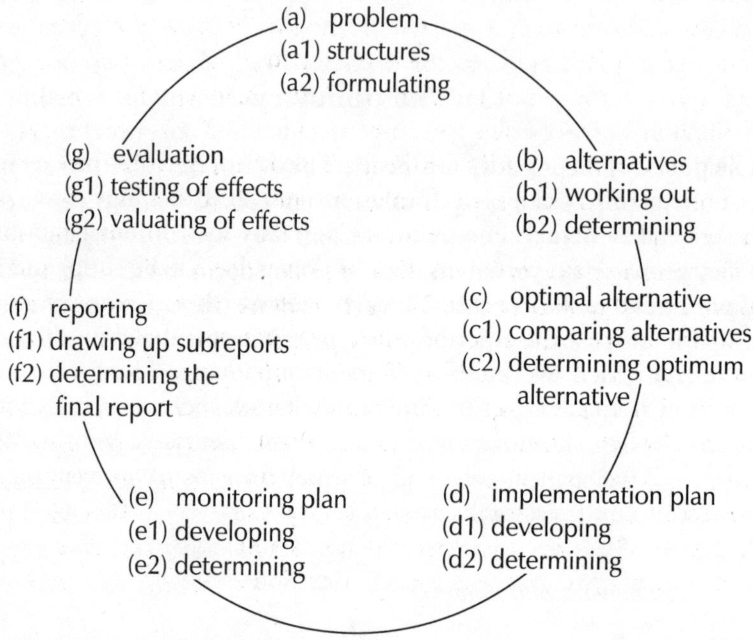

two distinct groups: those who prepare policy and those who decide policy. This is not necessary, however. The same people can — and often have to — fulfill several roles: one moment they are preparing policy, while in the next they are deciding it. It is not the distinction in persons that is essential, but the distinction in roles.

The methods that are employed for the preparation of policy decisions are: (a1) structuring of problems; (b1) working out of alternatives; (c1) comparing of alternatives; (d1) developing an implementation plan for the execution of policy; (e1) developing a plan for monitoring through which the execution of policy can be watched; (f1) drawing up subreports on execution; and (g1) testing the effects.

The policy decision relates to: (a2) formulating the problem; (b2) determining the alternatives; (c2) choosing the optimal alternative; (d2) determining the implementation plan; (e2) determining the monitoring plan; (f2) determining the final report; and (g2) valuating the effects (figure 18.1).

Besides the roles of preparer and decider of policy there is, of course, the role of policy executor. For after the monitoring plan has been determined, execution takes place. Reports are made on the execution. From the perspective of the policy cycle, the execution of policy takes place between the determination of the monitoring plan (sub e) and the reporting (sub f). One may wonder whether the distinction in three roles (preparer, decider, and executor) makes the policy cycle unnecessarily top-heavy. This is not the case. It is essential that the three roles be kept strictly separate. However, this can happen in such a way that people are aware that they are fulfilling the role of policy preparer one moment, that of policy decider the next, and that of policy executor later still. This can be done, though it may be more desirable to have the roles of policy preparer and decider fulfilled by one person, and the role of policy executor by another.

The whole has to be viewed in a cyclical-iterative sense. Cyclical means that the seventh component (g) can pass into the first component (a) and start a new cycle of policy formation. Iterative implies that the cycle can be gone through several times. This depends on the degree to which the problem persists as a problem and it is felt that its importance warrants renewed attention from the perspective of policy.

Example: project of youth pastoral care

An example will clarify the above. Let us assume that the local church experiences the intergenerational gap between "coming" and "departing" as a problem. The ministers and administrators are somewhat concerned that the generation of 16- to 24-year-olds make up only 15% of the total number of Catholics. Because the same generation forms 21.5% of the entire Dutch population, we can talk of its underrepresentation by 6.5% (Van Hemert 1991, 163). Let us further assume that the ministers and administrators do not panic at this prospect. They are aware that this is not just a matter for Catholics. They know the church participation figures of the youth in general, which run through all churches. They are also aware of the fact that of all the religious churchly people in the Netherlands 31% belong to the 18- to 34-year-olds, and of all the nonreligious, nonchurchly people 53% belong to this age category (Felling et al. 1981, 71). Moreover, they realize that we are not dealing with a purely Dutch problem here, since the more religious and churchly oriented United States displays a similar, albeit less serious picture: there, too, one finds a proportional reduction in the number of youths in the churches (Gallup & Castelli 1989, 26-27).

Against this background they decide to check how to react to this from the perspective of policy (phase a). In order to make this research work, the problems are structured by distinguishing a number of aspects, such as defectiveness of religious education in the family and religious formation at school; the inaccessibility of the liturgy for this generation; the influence of scientism on the attitude to life, especially among youths in higher education; and finally, the taboo of religion with the youth broadcasting companies (phase a1). On the basis of this, people reach a formulation of the problem: How can the threshold of the local church be lowered for the young (phase a2)?

After that, research is done on the alternatives that can stimulate a lower threshold in the church for the young (phase b). For this purpose a number of alternatives are collected. In the field of liturgy: the foundation of a youth choir that functions flexibly, and the development of a creative youth liturgy. In the field of catechetics: the development of attractive youth projects. In the area of group pastoral care: the provision of youth projects with attention to personal biography; direction of family projects for the young and their parents. In the field of diacony: guidance of youth groups for questions in the areas of relationships and work. In the area of management and administration: the engagement of a youth pastor. These alternatives are carefully reviewed. Some, like the direction of family projects for the young and their parents, are crossed off the list because they feel that this would sooner enhance the problem than decrease it (phase b1). The rest are systematically set down on a list and ordered (phase b2).

We then arrive at the moment when the optimal alternative has to be chosen (phase c). For that purpose the pros and cons of the remaining alternatives have to be discussed. With this the similarities and differences have to be determined as systematically as possible. In addition, they are compared to the degree of desirability and achievability (phase c1). This weighing process finally results in an unequivocal choice. Here, the choice falls on engaging a youth pastor for the duration of three years, whose duty will be to provide a well-defined and approachable pastoral service for youths (phase c2).

Then an implementation plan has to be developed (phase d). For this, all possible variants are regarded to flesh out the project in a concrete sense (phase d1). This eventually leads to the determination of the implementation plan, in which the following matters are taken up: the external conditions (approval from the diocese); the internal conditions (financial base); the methods and means (further determination of aims, contacting of target groups, phasing of the project by content, and providing textual material); and, finally, the determining of a time schedule (phasing in time). They determine in the plan itself that a flexible manner of working will be adhered to (phase d2).

So as not to lose control of the project, they decide how the monitoring of the project has to occur (phase e). For this purpose, all sorts of possibilities are looked at, like the use of randomly selected audiotapes of conversations between the youth pastor and youths; interviews with youths; a short, exploratory questionnaire among youths during the project; some monthly discussion evenings with youth with regard to the project; monthly work reports by the youth pastor (phase e1). Finally, a combination of two methods of work is chosen on the basis of considerations of achievability: the questionnaire and the monthly report (phase e2).

Then the actual execution of the project begins. Reports are made on its execution (phase f). These are prepared by means of subreports, which are considered as process reports (phase f1). On the basis of this a (brief) summarizing final report is formulated and determined toward the end of the project (phase f2).

Finally, they turn to the evaluation (phase g). Here use is made of the constituency approach, which means in this case that especially the satisfaction of the participating youths is asked about, but also of the youth pastor, the other pastors, and the group of pastoral volunteers (phase g1). On these grounds they are capable of judging and valuing the effects and able to link them to the problem that was initially set (phase g2).

They then decide to start a new project that links up with the last one. The problem that the new project has to solve has to be further determined due to the experiences that were gained from the previous project. That is why they decide to subject the new project to further reflection, before continuing the cycle of the new project (phase a).

Chapter 19

The Formal Policy Organization

At the beginning of this part of the book we paid attention to the societal process of individualization. This is characterized by striving for the satisfaction of one's own needs and realization of one's own interests (chapter 17). Insofar as this endeavor deserves support, proceeding from the vision and mission of the church, it has to be given sufficient room in the church's policy implementation (chapter 18).

Policy implementation, however, contains a great number of organizational implications. It demands that all sorts of tasks be clearly described (functionalization), in the context of the policy plan. It requires tasks to be adequately tuned to each other (coordination). Finally, they have to be aimed at the goals of the policy (finalization). These three matters (functionalization, coordination, and finalization) assume the presence of a properly functioning policy organization (Lammers 1984).

Now a policy organization does not just pop out of a hat, nor is it possible to create it from nothing as it were — at least not within the church. It is embedded in the structures of the church and bears the tradition of centuries with it. That is why it is necessary to check what are the most prominent outlines of the existing policy organization. We are not seeking continuation of the staus quo; however, we want to take a critical look at how it is structured and how it works. Only after we have gained some insight into this does it make sense to turn to the theme of the development of the policy organization, which will be dealt with in the following chapter.

In the present chapter we will try to answer the following questions: (1) What are the most important characteristics of the policy organization of the Catholic Church in force at a local level? and (2) How can they be understood proceeding from an organizational analysis.

(1) Description of the formal policy organization

Here we will give a description of the most important elements of parish law in the Catholic Church according to the Codex Iuris Canonici from 1983. We shall successively deal with the following: the pastor and his fellow workers, the finance council, the pastoral council, and the pastoral group of clergy and laity.

The pastor and his fellow workers

According to the Codex, the center of the policy organization of the local church is formed by the pastor. He performs the tasks of teaching, sanctifying, and governing in the parish, together with other priests or deacons and laymen (Can. 519). He has to be a priest (Can. 521 §1). The responsibility for policy formation and policy implementation lies in his hands, formally speaking. He gives guidance to the parish and is held accountable to the bishop concerning this matter (Can. 519).

No matter what special circumstances hold in a parish, this principle is not deviated from. For example, if the pastoral care in a parish is provided for by several priests, then one of them has to be appointed as moderator. He is held accountable to the bishop (Can. 517 §1). There may be only one pastor or moderator in the same parish (Can. 526 §2).

If a dearth of priests makes the participation of others, such as deacons or a group of laymen, necessary, then it again holds that a priest has to be appointed who is provided with the powers and faculties of a pastor. He supervises pastoral care (Can. 517 §2). The Codex states that if there is a dearth of priests or other circumstances, the same pastor can be entrusted with the care of several neighboring parishes (Can. 526 §1).

A pastor can therefore work together with other priests and deacons as well as with laymen. We will come back to the latter later on. Does the theologically educated and professionally trained pastoral worker enter into this cooperation too? Generally speaking, the position of the pastoral worker is brought into connection with the room provided for in the Codex concerning the permanent or temporary engagement of professionally trained, nonordained persons to some special service of the church (Can. 231 §1 and §2). In the Dutch regulations, the pastoral worker is described as follows: "a man or woman, who is recognized by the bishop, because he or she meets the conditions, set by the bishop, and as such is appointed in the parish on the basis of a contract of employ and in virtue of the pastoral mission by the bishop" (Algemeen Reglement 1988, art. 10). This appointment can be interpreted as an office, as we saw earlier (chapter 16 sub 4). Some, however, believe that such an interpretation only leads to a canonical-juridical play on words, which is sooner obfuscating than elucidating (Eijsink 1988). It is certain, however, that in this ministry we are not dealing with the ordained ministry. That is why the pastoral worker is not authorized to perform activities that go back to the ordained ministry.

What are his or her duties? According to the Dutch rules, one has to distinguish two groups of tasks in principle: nonsacramental liturgical and sacramental liturgical tasks. In principle the pastoral worker is authorized to perform all tasks that do not directly concern the sacramental liturgy. These tasks encompass the following areas: individual and group pastoral care, catechetics, community and church development, proclamation, diacony, and the nonsacramental liturgy. As far as the sacramental liturgy is concerned, a distinction can be made between preparation for and presiding over the celebration of the sacraments. The pastoral worker is authorized to prepare people for the sacraments that are relevant to the parish (baptism, confirmation, penance, eucharist, marriage, and anointing of the sick). Besides this, he or she is authorized to perform a few sacramental liturgical tasks under certain conditions. Thus, he or she can be empowered by the bishop to preside over the liturgy of a baptism. He or she may have the authority to function as an official ecclesial witness at a marriage if the bishop is granted permission by the Holy See through the conference of bishops. Further, the pastoral worker has full powers for preaching; however, not for doing the homily (Letter from the bishops of Groningen et al. 1990; Meijers 1991; Van der Helm 1992; *In Christus' naam* 1992).

In the diocese of Haarlem (the Netherlands) the function of pastoral assistant has arisen (Letter from the bishop of Haarlem 1990).

In Germany a kind of hierarchization among professionally trained laypeople has developed. The pastoral assistant is on top, followed by the parish assistant, and finally the parish helper. In the diocese of Haarlem (the Netherlands), we can speak only of a pastoral assistant (Walf 1984b, 134-35; Eijsink 1988).

In five of the seven Dutch dioceses an attempt is being made to arrange pastoral teams that are made up of one or more priests, deacons, and pastoral workers. However, so as not to detract from the central position of the pastor, which we mentioned earlier, the bishops make explicit mention of the fact that the pastoral team in the parish or parishes is led by the pastor (Letter from the bishops of Groningen et al. 1990).

What comes to the fore in all of this is that the pastor is not alone. As we stated earlier, he may work together with other priests or deacons and with pastoral workers in a pastoral team. Besides this, however, he and his team are assisted by some other colleges.

Finance council

In accordance with the Codex, a finance council *(consilium a rebus oeconomicis)* has to be present in every parish. It is formed by laypeople who aid the pastor in the administration of parish goods (Can. 537). According to Dutch regulations, this council "manages the parish's financial means and takes care of the purposeful use thereof for the benefit of the parish" (Algemeen Reglement 1988, art. 24, par. 1). Besides this, it has the duty to "advise the pastor, other priest(s), deacon(s) and pastoral worker(s) on pastoral policy" (art. 24, par. 2). According to Dutch regulations, there are at least four other members in this council besides the pastor, who is the chairman, who are appointed by the bishop. One of these members is appointed vice-chairman by the bishop on his nomination by the finance council — having heard the pastoral council. The vice-chairman can replace the pastor in his capacity as chairman if the pastor deems this necessary or desirable (arts. 25 and 26).

Pastoral council

There is another college that can support the pastor and his pastoral team. It is called the pastoral council *(consilium pastorale)* by the Codex. In contrast to the finance council, which has to be present in every parish, it is up to the bishop whether a pastoral council has to be established in every parish. This is done after the bishop has listened to the presbyterial council and if he judges it to be opportune (Can. 536 §1). It possesses a consultative vote only, and it is governed by norms developed by the bishop. According to Dutch regulations, the pastoral council is established on the request of the finance council (Algemeen Reglement 1988). Its duties are advising the pastor and his team on pastoral policy; nominating candidates for the finance council; and advising the finance council on economic policy (art. 40). The pastor is the chairman of the pastoral council. He can be replaced by the vice-chairman (art. 47). The meeting has at least ten members, who are appointed by the bishop (art. 43). By diocesan law, the council has the following members: the pastor, other priest(s), deacon(s), and pastoral worker(s) (art. 44, par. 2; art. 47, par. 3). To avoid the danger of nonengagement because of its purely advisory character, the Dutch regulations state that the finance council may depart from the advice or proposition of the pastoral council only if it has held prior consultations with said pastoral council (art. 40, par. 3). The finance council is not dependent on the approval of the pastoral council; all that is obligatory is consultation (Huysmans 1986, 170). We should note here that such consultation is urged concerning the nomination of candidates for the finance council and advice on economic policy, but not concerning pastoral policy.

Pastoral group of clergy and laity

Besides the finance council and the pastoral council, there is yet another college that aids the pastor and his team (beyond the Codex): the pastoral group of clergy and laity. In analogy to the examples in Belgium and Ghana, the pastoral group of clergy and laity arose during the eighties and is developing rapidly at the moment (Hoeben & Nooren 1984). For this reason its formal status has not yet risen above the regulations of some specific Dutch dioceses. The provisional statute for the pastoral group of clergy and laity in the diocese of Breda (the Netherlands) is as follows: "the pastoral group of clergy and laity is a group consisting of Catholic volunteers and those who do pastoral work on the basis of a diocesan mission, who look after the pastoral care in a parish, under the guidance of a priest, who is provided with the powers and faculties of a pastor" (Voorlopig Statuut 1992, art.

1.1). It looks after the pastoral care by coordinating the pastoral activities that take place in the parish and by participating in their guidance and execution. Its aim is to contribute to the continuity of the mission of the local church (art. 2.1). Its duties are the development of pastoral policy and the stimulation of its implementation; the support of people and working groups that are active in the various sectors; and the division and execution of pastoral tasks with due observance of the distinct offices, powers, and faculties (art. 2.3). This regulation seems to go further than giving guidance to the execution of policy because it also adds policy formation to the tasks of the pastoral group of clergy and laity (Huysmans & Scholten 1986). However, one should consider what the juridical foundation is for the pastoral group of clergy and laity and what its juridical limitations are. The pastoral group of clergy and laity works under the guidance of the pastor, according to the provisional statute. In reference to the Codex, the statute states that it gives expression to participation in the mission of the church (Can. 204 §1) and to the stimulation of parochial communion in the church (Can. 529 §2), and lends its cooperation in the practice of pastoral care (Can. 519). The canonical meaning of the terms *participation* and *cooperation* is that the faculties and tasks of the pastoral group of clergy and laity do not detract from the guidance of the pastor and his powers and faculties.

(2) Analysis of the formal policy organization

As we just saw, the policy organization in the local church contains four colleges: the pastoral team of the pastor and his fellow priest(s), deacon(s), and pastoral worker(s); the finance council; the pastoral council; and, finally, the pastoral group of clergy and laity. Let us first make an organizational analysis of the whole of this structure and then of the separate positions of the colleges.

Proceeding from the organization typology of Mintzberg, the church and the local church within it can be viewed from several perspectives. On a global and national scale, two types are applicable as Mintzberg described them: the missionary organization and the bureaucratic organization. At a local level, however, the church can be regarded as an entrepreneurial organization. These perspectives apply not only to the Catholic Church, for that matter; they apply by analogy to a great number of Protestant churches as well (Fichter 1961; 1988; Rudge 1968). Let us take a closer look at the three perspectives (missionary, bureaucratic, and enterprising organization) (Mintzberg 1979; 1989).

Missionary organization

The church as a missionary organization is made up of a social context that is characterized by the endeavor to propagate, both inwardly and outwardly, the convictions, values, and norms that bind the members together. The members identify with these convictions and ideas. In connection with this, they identify themselves with the organization itself. They feel inspired and motivated by it. They find that their organization is unique and that it distinguishes itself from all other organizations, even similar ones. The missionary organization has a formalized program to promote the presentation of and identification with the convictions and values it propagates. This program is made up of the propagating of the message outwardly and the socialization and internalization of the message for members inwardly. The missionary organization sees the message as binding and absolute. Deviations are not tolerated. The only thing that is allowed is the interpretation of the message.

The missionary organization captures the spirit of its members by means of their common values (Mintzberg 1991, 232). It has the features of what has been called elsewhere the "total institution": it penetrates and determines all aspects of the entire personal and societal life of the members (Goffman 1975). It also contains the characteristics of the "greedy institution," which is never satisfied and desires and demands more and more from its members. This can imply that the professionalism that is present in the organization loses to the tenacity with which the convictions and norms are held on to. As typical representatives of the missionary organizations, Mintzberg sees not only religious contexts like the convent, or socio-ideological contexts like the kibbutz. One also comes across them in the business community, like McDonald's, which appears to be selling an entire ideology with its Big Mac (speed, purity, friendliness, and quality), which stimulates the personnel to go all out.

This latter example makes it clear that the missionary organization can enter into relations with other types of organizations, like the bureaucratic and the enterprising organization. Pure missionary organizations do not occur in reality, just as bureaucratic and enterprising organizations do not occur in a pure form. The different types of organizations overlap each other. The missionary organization is rather to be viewed as a perspective from which certain features of a certain organization — like the church — strike us. In other words, the church is not a missionary organization, but it can be viewed as a missionary organization (Mintzberg 1991).

Bureaucratic organization

Within the whole of the church as a missionary organization, a structure has developed that displays the features of a bureaucracy to a large extent. Mintzberg makes a distinction between three kinds of bureaucracies: machine, divisionalized, and professional bureaucracies. The differences these types exhibit are certainly applicable to all sorts of aspects of the church, but we will concentrate on the bureaucracy in general here. We would like to note that the typification of the church as a bureaucracy certainly does not apply to the Catholic Church alone (Moberg 1962; Gabriel & Kaufmann 1980; McSweeney 1980), but also, for instance, to the Protestant churches (Spiegel 1969; Fichter 1988), like those in South Africa (Pieterse 1983).

The bureaucracy is characterized by a steep organization, which contains an entire hierarchy of administrative layers and intermediary layers. Each of them possesses its own juridically determined powers and faculties. People interact with each other according to set procedures and communicate according to formalized rules and standardized patterns. The lines of command run from top to bottom, and the lines of responsibility from bottom to top. Everything passes all the intermediary stations. What controls a bureaucracy is the endeavor to control: everything has to be kept under control as much as possible. Insecurity has to be avoided as much as possible. The leaders at the top are therefore continuously occupied in refining control in their organization. By doing this they try to hold the whole apparatus together. One of the consequences is that the people in the organization are treated more as if they are means (Mintzberg 1979; 1991; Weber 1980; Lammers 1984; Chanlet 1990).

The structure of the Catholic Church contains many aspects of a bureaucracy. Its hierarchical structure seems like that of the well-oiled machine of a multinational corporation: with an administrative center on its own territory in Rome and a worldwide network of branches across continents, countries, states, provinces, and dioceses; with a network of diocesan branches across vicarates, regions, districts, and parishes; all is determined and described in a universal, continental, national, and diocesan codification and set of rules, which concern matters like powers and faculties, appointments, and task descriptions (Van Gerwen 1990). Here is a single example that gives us some impression of what this entails: the figures for 1990 show that the number of Catholics approached a billion. 9.5% live in Africa, 7.2% in North America, 11.6% in Central America, 2.3% in the Antilles, 28.6% in South America, 9.3% in Asia (of which 0.4% live in the Middle East), 30.7% in Europe, and 0.8% in Oceania. 17.7% of the world population was Catholic (Annuarium 1992). A year earlier, the total number of dioceses across the entire world amounted to 2,545. The average number of pastoral units (mainly parishes) per diocese was 157, which contained an average of 2,270 parishioners. The total number of parishes on a global scale was 399,210 (Annuarium 1991).

Both from a historical and sociological perspective, it has been remarked that the enormous apparatus that the Catholic Church has built mainly stems from the period 1850 to 1950. In this period the church developed into a bulwark so as to offer resistance to the heathen spirit of the Enlightenment, the French revolution of 1789, and the revolution of 1848. It wished to protect Catholics from the religious views of deism, pantheism, atheism, and immanentism, and from the political systems of liberalism and socialism. Against this background, the declaration of the infallibility of the pope by Vatican I can be understood. The church felt faced with an emergency situation and felt the need for strong, central authority (Houtepen 1973). It placed the emphasis on neoscholastics in order to have unambiguous doctrinal formulas at hand to make a stand against the hostile spirit of the times (Welte 1965). It drew up concordats, founded nunciatures, enlarged its influence in the area of the appointment of bishops, and tightened the reins on the bishops (Aubert 1974; McSweeney 1980; Gabriel & Kaufmann 1980; Raedts 1990; Van Harskamp 1986). The bureaucracy of the church was as perfect as the state bureaucracy. It marked Catholicism as the specific historical and contextually determined shape in which the Catholic Church reacted to the Enlightenment defensively and offensively at the same time (Kaufmann 1989; 1992; Van der Ven 1993).

Entrepreneurial organization

The pastor in his parish is the end point of this hierarchical structure. This means that all that falls "below" him, includes nothing substantial. Above him there is a broad and extensively spun-out bureaucratic network of juridical relations; below him the structure ends, and we cannot speak of real regulation. The conclusion that the structure comes to an end below him means that all matters concerning policy formation and policy implementation that announce themselves are centered around his position and attached to his position.

The pastor

In the organizational analysis proceeding from the theory of Mintzberg, the pastor can be viewed as someone who fulfills the role of the entrepreneur in an entrepreneurial organization. Even though this image in no way meets the self-image of the individual pastor, the perspective of the entrepreneurial organization can shed light on matters that otherwise would have been left untouched. We do not wish to portray this as an ideal image. On the contrary, the focus is only on a description of some features — next to others — that are attached to the office of the pastor in an objective sense. The development of an ideal image will be discussed later (chapter 20).

The entrepreneurial organization contains a simple structure. Here *simple* means "plain," "not intricate," "surveyable," "functioning from one clear center." This implies that the power to make all important decisions lies in the hands of one man. There is no shared, let alone scattered responsibility. It is not an obvious choice to make a distinction between policy formation and policy implementation within such a structure, nor between strategic decisions — within policy formation — in the long run (policy plan) and tactical decisions in the short run (program and projects). It is not at all obvious that the emphasis should be placed on education, formation, and training within such an organization.

The parish can be regarded — however one-sided it may be — from the perspective of a one-man business rendering services. Proceeding from this angle, one can view the pastor as someone who offers services to those who wish to make use of them: liturgical and other pastoral services. From this viewpoint he can be conceived of as the embodiment of a church in terms of care and service. The parish is, at least juridically, the work area of the pastor, who cares for his parishioners; it is his field of office (Huysmans 1986, 185-84, 208). This was the approach to the parish that resounded in the Codex of 1917 proceeding from the medieval parish tradition (Van Bilsen 1962), and that remained intact in the Codex of 1983. Although the latter also makes mention of the fact that the parish is a community of believers besides an institution of pastoral care (Can. 515 §1), this does not detract from the structure of the one-head parish organization.

Now it is sometimes asserted that the lack of bureaucratic regulation in the area "below" the pastor has the advantage of flexibility. The parish itself could then decide on the spot what organizational structure it wishes to develop under the circumstances in a certain time and place (Huels 1986). However, other authors believe that serious objections are attached to this. Due to the central position of the pastor, the parish can be likened to a one-man business. Because of this, there is a danger that all kinds of strategic decisions in the long run get mixed up with the tactical decision in the short run, and that policy formation becomes entangled in policy implementation. It is also said that being tied to one person sets severe restrictions on the parish that can lead to the talents and capacities of people being seriously curtailed. It is also a very risky structure since everything depends on the decisions, as well as the health, moods, and whims, of one person (Mintzberg 1979, 305-13). It can undermine the legal security as well as the continuity of the parochial organization (Huysmans 1986, 201-9).

The cause lies in the juridical gap in the area of parish organization (Van Gerwen 1990, 176). Rahner had the following to say in the final part of his four-volume *Handbuch der Pastoraltheologie:* "Democracy in the church first of all very simply means that the laity also have to actively and responsibly participate in the life and decisions of the church. More precisely it means that such active participation in church life has to be institutionalized by human ecclesial law, because people only take on real responsibility and actively participate where they are supported by a law and are not continually dependent on the whims of those in power" (Rahner IV, 1969, 754).

Priests and deacons

How do things stand with the fellow priests of the pastor and with the deacons? The relationship with the fellow priests is of an ambivalent nature, at least in a juridical sense. On the one hand, there is the principle of priestly fraternity that lies in the particular canon of the Codex. Pastoral work from a team perspective can be regarded as the expression of this principle. This can be seen in the stipulation that pastoral care in one or more parishes can *in solidum* be entrusted to several priests (Can. 517 §1). On the other hand, the canon speaks of a moderator who gives guidance to the college of priests and who can be held accountable by the bishop. We have to note here that the priests do not take turns at leadership, nor is it democratically chosen. This places the other priests in a hierarchical position with regard to the moderator (Can. 517 §1).

How is the position of the deacon to be interpreted? Quite rightly there have been remarks that the Codex is characterized by a lack of attention for the deacon. Vatican II established the so-called permanent deaconry, or rather it re-established it (*Lumen Gentium* 29). The council decided that permanent deacons could not marry, but could be married before they were ordained. Their duties lie in the area of liturgy, proclamation — including the homily — and pastoral work in the broadest sense. These tasks are of a supportive nature (Möller 1990; Nissen 1991). However, the Codex restricts itself to a number of stipulations concerning the formation, ordination, and tasks of the deacon. We learn nothing of his position. An exception has to be made for the stipulation we mentioned earlier: in case of a dearth of priests, the care for the parish can be entrusted to him — or to some other person or community of persons (Can. 517 §2). However, a pastor has to be set above him by appointment. Also, the addition "to him or some other person or to a community of persons" relativizes the position of the deacon to a considerable degree (Huels 1986).

The pastoral worker

According to the stipulation of the Codex, the pastoral worker is temporarily or permanently appointed for a special service in the church, for which purpose he or she has acquired "the appropriate formation" (Can. 231). However, no matter how important the function or office of the pastoral worker is, he or she cannot be viewed as anything else than a layperson according to the Codex. He or she belongs to the "lay members of the Christian faithful" who are an "assistant" to the pastor in the practice of pastoral care (Can. 519).

Here the subordination of the pastoral worker to the pastor is clearly expressed. In most Dutch dioceses an attempt is being made at forming pastoral teams in which the pastoral worker has a seat next to the pastor, the other priests, or the deacons. However, the guidance of the team is left to the pastor. This is even more clearly expressed in the regulation of the diocese of Den Bosch (the Netherlands), which localizes the pastoral worker in the pastoral group of clergy and laity (Letter from the bishop of Den Bosch 1990, 24).

A latent conflict lies within this practice that is not of a personal but of a structural nature. It can be viewed in various ways. One could say that the principles of two organizational structures clash here: those of the bureaucratic and those of the professional organization (Mok 1973; Van der Krogt 1981). One could also say that two different organizational cultures clash. What is characteristic of the one is the metaphor of the machinery apparatus; while for the other, it is the metaphor of the brains (Morgan 1986). It could also be said that two types of authority collide here (Weber 1980): the legal-rational and functional-rational types (chapter 16 sub 1).

The fact that the latent conflict is of a structural nature means that it does not depend on the difficult character of the pastoral worker to become manifest; but it is due to his or her reconciliatory character that it remains latent. Neither is the authoritarian character of the pastor to blame, if the conflict rise to the surface; it is due to his reconciliatory character that it remains submerged. In other words, the conflict is of a suprapersonal nature; it has to do with the structure of the organization.

Yet one can trace a gap in the Codex through which perhaps juridical regulations can be provided for in the (distant) future, which will resolve this (latent) conflict. For this purpose a detour will have to be taken: the detour — *mirabile dictu* — through the ecclesial judge. In the Codex, a stipulation has been made stating that the laity — men and women — may function in the office of ecclesial judge (Can. 1421 §2). The stipulation concerning the ecclesial judge, who participates in the power of jurisdiction of the church and can nevertheless be one of the laity, relativizes the strict connection between the power of jurisdiction and that of ordination. The question is whether the function of the pastoral worker would profit more from the further disjointing of the connection between the power of jurisdiction and that of ordination. The pastoral worker could then perform a guiding role in the church without being ordained. However, there are many historical and systematical-theological pitfalls here (Walf 1984a, 139-40; Eijsink 1988).

Finance council

The position of the finance council can be clarified by means of the four models that are distinguished in the theory of the non-profit organizations. These models will be presented in order of decreasing authority and involvement. The first is that of the *executive board,* which exerts direct influence on the execution of policy and also contributes to it in an active sense. The second is the *policy-forming board,* which waives all activities in the area of policy execution and restricts itself to policy preparation and making decisions about policy. The third is the *supervisional board,* which involves itself with neither policy execution nor policy formation. It only sees to it that the policy formation — by third parties — actually takes place and tests it, albeit only in a marginal sense. For the rest it fulfils an advisory function. Finally, the fourth is the *condition-making board.* It occupies itself purely with the financial and organizational conditions within which the policy formation and policy execution — carried out by third parties — take place (Keuning & Eppink 1986, 247-49).

It is clear that the Codex makes a choice for the fourth model. The finance council aids the pastor in the administration of parish goods. The Dutch regulations make a choice for a combination of the third and fourth model. The finance council gives advice concerning the pastoral policy (third model), and further it has the task to create conditions in a financial sense (fourth model). What is clear is that the responsibility for pastoral policy formation and policy execution lies elsewhere: with the pastor.

Pastoral council

The position of the pastoral council is only of an advisory nature, as we mentioned before. What does this mean from the viewpoint of fundamental democracy and participation, which we dealt with earlier (chapter 16 sub 3)? Proceeding from the socio-scientific viewpoint, we can discern various levels of participation. Looked at in order of increasing participation these are: (1) being informed on matters of policy; (2) having a say in matters, which means that one can think about matters and give advice on them; (3) being able to consult with the makers of policy, which implies that one can talk to them about matters of policy; (4) active participation, which implies the opportunity to make decisions too; and finally (5) being able to co-manage the particular means and institutions (Van Braam 1986, 326). The power of the pastoral council generally does not exceed level (2), which encompasses having a say in matters and giving advice. It possesses the authority to consult, which refers to level (3), if the finance council wishes to deviate from the economic advice or nomination that the finance council received from the parish council. One cannot, however, speak of further authorities in the areas of consultation (level 3), active participation (level 4), and co-management (level 5).

Pastoral group of clergy and laity

The regulations in the diocese of Breda (the Netherlands) regarding the pastoral group of clergy and laity can be viewed as the formal deposit of the presence of volunteers in the parish who carry out pastoral activities. The motives for the set of rules are formulated in terms of co-responsibility. This co-responsibility can be regarded as the shape in which the laity can give expression to their being a subject of the church. Moreover, they contribute to the continuity of the local church through this (Ernst 1992, 184).

At the same time, we have to note that the cooperation of volunteers calls up problems with relation to the professional pastoral workers. These problems involve the allocation of tasks, the bearing of responsibility, being held accountable, and the division of powers and faculties (Ernst 1992, 186). Now the tense relationship between professionals and volunteers is a problem that generally occurs in volunteer organizations. It is not typical only of the church (Aves 1973). The juridical structure within which it occurs in the church is, however, specific to the church. For whatever way one looks at it, the pastoral group of clergy and laity works "under the guidance of a priest, who is provided with the powers and faculties of a pastor" (Provisional statute 1992). The question is whether this structure meets the conditions within which the local church factually functions at present. This is the point of departure for the following chapter.

Chapter 20

Policy Organization Development

In this part we placed the increasing endeavor for the satisfaction of one's personal needs and the realization of one's own interests in the context of the societal process of utilization (chapter 17). Insofar as this endeavor can be judged as positive proceeding from the vision and mission of the church, it has to be negotiated in the church's policy development (chapter 18). This policy development takes place within the formal policy organization of the church (chapter 19).

The question is whether this formal policy organization sufficiently meets the conditions in which the self-realization of the local church actually takes place nowadays. This is the question with which we closed the last chapter. These conditions have to do with the environment of the church, the large number of volunteers that it utilizes, and the style of leadership that this demands. All this requires the development of the policy organization in the direction of a so-called innovative organization. It can also involve the religious code *building of the Spirit,* in which we have a special guideline for policy organization development.

In this chapter we will look at the following questions: (1) In what sense does the local church have to develop in the direction of an innovative organization? and (2) What inspiration and orientation lie in the church as the building of the Spirit?

(1) The church as an innovative organization

We wish to defend the proposition that the local church would benefit from the formation of an innovative organization. First, we shall dwell upon the term itself, and then list the arguments in its favor. Finally, we shall discuss some indications for the development of this organizational form.

Innovative organization

Innovative organization is characterized by an organic structure in which people relate to each other and attune their tasks to each other in a natural fashion. Their aim is to execute their activities together and lend each other support if problems occur. They utilize each other's strong points and supplement each other's weak sides. They find that anticipating each other's problems and tuning to each other's capacities are of great importance. There is little formalization, centralization, or hierarchization. It is a flexible organization that is divided into functional units that continually arrange varying project teams.

The metaphor that applies to this organization is not the palace — as with the bureaucracy — but the tent: "A tent can be picked up and moved at will" (Mintzberg 1979, 433). The innovative organization can therefore be called an "adhocracy." The adhocracy is not some kind of disposable organization (Hendriks 1990, 99-100). The term *adhocracy* is borrowed from the futurological reflections in the book *Future Shock* by Alvin Toffler, who believed he had observed a turn-about in all kinds of larger and smaller organizations in the United States, from bureaucracy to adhocracy (Mintzberg 1979, 432; Keuning & Eppink 1986, 263). Toffler worked out this turn-about further by means of the architectural term *modulization.* In modulization the architect designs a kind of skeleton of a house and gives the actual inhabitants the choice of the places of the doors, the walls, and with that the division of the rooms and halls. So the frame is permanent, but the separate modules or blocks can be placed, ordered, or arranged by every inhabitant according to his or her own wishes. In application to the organization, this means that there is a permanent organizational skeleton present within which all sorts of ad hoc projects (adhocracy) can be founded, exchanged, or terminated (Toffler 1971). While the term *adhocracy* emphasizes more flexibility, the term *innovative organization* places greater emphasis on the renewal and transformation that should issue from this kind of dynamic organization. One can use the terms interchangeably according to Mintzberg (1991, 202). This organization consists of a network of flexible organizational elements, which people continually regroup to take on new challenges from the environment (Fortuyn 1992).

Arguments

Now that the word *environment* has been used, we will first dwell upon arguments that can be brought to bear on the development of an innovative organization, proceeding from the environment of the local church. Then we shall shift our attention from the environment to the organization itself, which in fact lies in the functioning of the church itself: the volunteer church. This, too, demands an innovative organization and applies to the style of leadership that is implied in the volunteer church.

Environment

In some theories in organizational science, the environment is held to be an important or even deciding factor. The environment determines, to an important extent, the organizational form that lies in the enterprise or institution, as well as the direction in which it develops, or has to develop respectively. This approach is characteristic of the so-called contingency theories. In the theory of organization, contingency relates to the changing circumstances in the environment that bring along with them insecurity for the organization. There are four factors that exert an influence on the organization from the environment: stability, complexity, diversity, and hostility. These lead to four hypotheses. We shall apply them to the church one by one (Mintzberg 1979, 267-87).

Hypothesis 1: The more unstable but dynamic the environment is, the more the organization requires flexibility and informal, unartificial, natural, organic relations between people and groups. This applies most strongly to the church; for the time of societal peace and stability, in which the church could thrive as a matter of course, is far behind us. The time of the state and established church has passed.

The church is confronted by the societal process of modernization, which is shaking, pulling, and pushing the church on all sides (chapter 2 sub 1).

Hypothesis 2: The more complex the environment is, the more the organization benefits from decentralization. This hypothesis strongly applies to the church too. For not just one or two factors are influencing the church from the outside, but many, almost inextricable factors exert an influence on the church over and above themselves or out from underneath themselves. The influence is direct and indirect, latent and manifest, positive and negative. Examples of this are secularization, religious and philosophical pluralism, the proliferation of the church in denomination and basic community, dechurching, depillarization, individualization, utilization, and finally calculation (chapters 1, 2, 9, 13, 17, and 21).

Hypothesis 3: The more diverse the needs in the environment are, the more the organization is benefited by differentiation. By handling its structure flexibly, it raises its effectiveness and efficiency. This, too, applies to the church. Earlier we described how much the church's environment is characterized by differentiated economic, political, social, cultural, and religious needs. Furthermore, we described how different these needs were for the various groups that make up its environment. We were dealing with groups that vary in age, length of residency, educational level, profession, localism, ecclesial and religious orientation, church participation, and pastoral participation (chapter 17 sub 2).

Hypothesis 4: The more hostile the environment is, the more the organization leans toward centralization; the less hostility there is, or if there is none at all, the more it leans toward decentralization. As far as the church is concerned, one cannot speak of a hostile environment, certainly not in comparison with periods of laicism, anticlericalism, and antipapism in the past. One should rather speak of three different attitudes: benevolence in those involved with the church, acceptance of the importance of the church for others than oneself, and indifferentism (Geffré & Jossua 1983; Kaufmann 1989).

From all of this, we can draw the conclusion that the development of the policy organization of the church would benefit from a free, organic, flexible, loosely formalized, and decentralized structure. This is typical of the network of ad hoc organizational forms of the innovative organization that we just described.

Volunteer church

We turn from the environment to the organization itself and wonder what kind of structure lies in the actual functioning of the local church. With this we will pay attention to the free choice on the basis of which people decide to be a member of the church. Next, we will look into the fact that the engagement of the volunteers is the mainstay of the local church to a large extent. Both mark the local church as a volunteer church: the free choice of the members of the church and the active commitment of volunteers. Both lead to the conclusion that the development of an innovative organization is an absolute must.

We need not dwell upon the free choice for membership for long. Earlier we asked the question from which kind of bond people participate in church life. The answer we gave proceeding from the theory of Etzioni was: not from a bond based on coercion or profit, but based on one's own personal decision. Proceeding from this viewpoint, the church is not a coercive or exchanging organization, but a normative organization. It exists by the grace of approval and agreement (chapter 14 sub 2). To this we would like to add a remark about the structure of a normative organization. From research it appears that normative organizations are more flexible and less hierarchical than coercive and exchanging organizations. They have fewer administrative layers. They are less steep, more flexible, and more dynamic (Hall et al. 1967, 126; Mintzberg 1979, 136).

Let us now turn to the active commitment of volunteers. Earlier we mentioned the colleges that are active within the structure of the church: the pastor and his team, the pastoral group of clergy and laity, the finance council, and the pastoral council (chapter 19). Everybody knows, however, that many other people are active in informal councils, committees, and groups. Their activities take place within the sectors of pastoral care, catechetics, liturgy, proclamation, and diacony (chapter 4 sub 3).

Before we draw conclusions from this, it is a good idea to find out how many volunteers are active in the particular sectors. Table 20.1 provides information on: (a) diacony and pastoral care; (b) catechetics; (c) liturgy (concerning content); (d) liturgy (execution); (e) church building and other buildings; (f) information and contact, and (g) management and finances. The data were collected in the Netherlands in 1987.

TABLE 20.1
Volunteers per parish

Sectors	(a)	(b)	(c)	(d)	(e)	(f)	(g)	Total
Volunteers	23	9	23	97	23	29	33	190

Source: Witteman-Devillee et al. 1989, 35

What this table brings out is that the average number of volunteers per parish in the Netherlands in 1987 was 190. The liturgy is the most important field, involving more than half the volunteers, (23 + 97 =) 120 people. If we restrict ourselves to the pastoral policy sectors in the strictest sense (diacony and pastoral care, catechetics and liturgy, without the execution of liturgy), then we find that (23 + 9 + 23 =) 55 pastoral volunteers are active on average per parish. If one adds the volunteers who take care of the execution of liturgy, then the total number is higher: (55 + 97 =) 152 people per parish.

It is important to see that the voluntary character of the Dutch Catholic parish is greatly increasing. Let us restrict ourselves to policy sectors (a), (b), and (c) for the moment. We see that there is a significant growth during the course of the past twenty years. In 1971 some researchers reported that in total 209 nonordained workers were active in the pastoral field in all the parishes together throughout the Netherlands, of whom 35 were laypeople (nondeacon and nonreligious). It was noted that the phenomenon had started in 1969 and had greatly expanded by 1970 (Tettero 1972). By 1987 the numbers had increased substantially, to 55 per parish, as we mentioned before. If we take sectors (a) to (g) together, we can establish that in relation to the total number of parishioners, the total number of volunteers grew by 44% on average between 1977 and 1987 (Witteman-Devillee et al. 1989, 29-30).

One can express the importance of the efforts of volunteers in another way too. Estimates of the time invested by volunteers vary between 17,000 and 33,000 hours of work per parish in the Netherlands per annum. These can be set against the number of hours of work per pastor per annum. If one sets the actual working week of a pastor at 50 hours and bases oneself on 46 weeks per year, then the total number of hours a pastor works per annum is 2,300. This means that the volunteers do the work of 7 to 14 pastors per parish (Scholten 1988).

From our earlier organizational analysis, it appeared that the formal context introduced by the official ecclesial regulations displays a vacuum. The parish with the pastor as its pivotal center is the keystone of the national and global bureaucracy. Parish law itself, however, does not go any further than the juridical description of the powers and faculties of the pastor and the colleges around him. It is as if the pastor is covered "from above" by a bureaucratic canopy, while there is a yawning gap "below" him. It is as if there is a dense juridical lattice from above, of which he himself is the last piece, and the parish below disappears in a juridical vacuum. In short, the ecclesial regulations do not cover the efforts of the many volunteers who carry the church and ensure its continuity. It passes over them.

The conclusion we can draw from this is that the local church requires an organizational structure that adequately deals with the efforts of volunteers and flexibly channels them to a loosely formalized whole. It has to handle the talents and capacities of the volunteers in a dynamic fashion so that they feel remunerated and are stimulated to continue with their work. This is the only way that the church can take creative advantage of the new challenges that keep popping up in its environment.

We would like to add something to this. From research it appears that contexts of volunteers vary depending on to what extent they display the features of a social movement. The fewer features of a movement they have, the more centralized and formalized they look. The more they are characterized by the features of a movement, the less central and formal is the image (Sills 1968, 368). We talked about the church as a movement earlier on, and in connection with this about the mission of the church as a Jesus movement (chapter 12 sub 4). The more the church as a volunteer church emphasizes its mission as a Jesus movement, the more flexible, dynamic, and innovative it becomes. At least the more flexible, dynamic, and innovative it has to become to do justice to the Jesus movement.

Style of leadership

The hypothesis that the local church benefits from the development of an innovative organization can also be argued from the style of leadership that the church of today needs. According to Kurt Lewin, styles of leadership can be divided into autocratic and democratic styles. This distinction is important because both autocratic and democratic styles occur in the church (Hollweg 1971). This is putting it mildly because the leadership in religious institutions appears to have an almost intrinsic tendency toward an autocratic style. Church leaders speak of "higher" things; that is why they seem to act "from above." If these leaders legitimize the rightness of their sayings from the Bible, the church tradition, or the ministry, the autocracy easily transforms itself into a theocracy, according to Weber (1980).

Now one might call this an exaggerated representation of matters, especially because a purely autocratic or purely democratic style does not occur. That is why it makes sense to take a look at some intermediary types. For this purpose we shall consult the division into four styles of leadership developed by Likert (1967; Taylor & Bowers 1972).

The first style is called the *exploitative-authoritarian style.* Here the leader imposes his will on the members of the group(s) with whom he works. This style of leadership leads to poor communication, the avoidance of controversies, a lack of responsibility, apathy, and party formation.

The second style is defined as *enlightened-authoritarian.* It, too, is characterized by the dominance of the leader, but once in a while he asks for advice from the members of the group on an individual basis. This leads to competition among group members, which leads to differences in (moral) rewards and (moral) sanctions that the leader provides to the individual members. It can also lead to the fact that (displeasing) information is kept from the leader and from other members because there is a fear of sanctions. This means that mutual trust is kept to a minimum and a climate is created in which the taking of risks is avoided.

The third style is described as the *consultative style.* In this style the leader stimulates the asking and giving of advice in the group, both in the relationship of the members to himself and among the members themselves. This style leads to an opening of the communication channels and to the reduction of withholding information. It provides the members of the group with the opportunity to exert influence on the decisions that the leader makes. It gives people the feeling that the members can bring some weight to bear on matters. In the meantime, the leader remains the only one to make the decisions.

The fourth style is called the *participative style.* It can be divided into four characteristics: support, goal emphasis, work facilitation, and interaction facilitation. *Support* means that the leader is friendly and easy to approach. He pays attention to what the members of the group have to say. He is prepared to listen to their problems. *Goal emphasis* implies that the leader encourages group members to do their best and maintains high standards in the execution of his work. He himself sets a good example by working hard. *Work facilitation* means that the leader encourages the group members to take action without waiting for detailed indications or approval on his part. He helps in the organization of labor and in the making of plans of action and working schemes. He demonstrates how work can be improved. He suggests new ideas for solving problems that people come across in their work. Finally, *interaction facilitation* entails that the leader encourages the group members to work as a team. He stimulates them to exchange views and ideas with each other. He organizes meetings in which the group members can really come to grips with all sorts of matters (Taylor & Bowers 1972).

Likert defends the hypothesis that the participative style is the most effective and efficient one. This type of leading is, in actual fact, guidance. It leads to better results because the leader may make decisions in an authoritarian manner (exploitational or enlightened); he may involve group members through consultation in his decisions; but he nevertheless depends on their willingness and cooperation in executing them (Lammers 1984, 93).

This reason applies particularly to the local church. The pastoral professional — ordained or nonordained — can accomplish nothing without the willingness, acceptance, and cooperation of the volunteers who support the church. Even if he wanted to do so, he could not. That is why people are rightly trying to develop the local church in the direction of a participative style (Dietterich 1987; Hendriks 1990).

The Catholic Church at the local level has to be organized in such a way that the participative style of leadership can truly be developed. The innovative organization is the most suitable for this purpose. It promotes a natural kind of interaction, cooperation, and coordination. It exists in a flexible network of organizational forms that can be continuously placed in different configurations. That is why it is flexible and dynamic. From there the members can take on every new challenge that comes from the environment with courage and creativity. The structure has to be developed in such a way that it does not clash with the bureaucratic organization above it, or disappear into the vacuum of the entrepreneurial organization below it.

Development of the innovative organization

We will now give two indications for the further development of the church in this direction. The first relates to the handling of the network of groups in the innovative organization in a manner that allows for optimal cooperation. The second relates to the placing of these groups in a matrix organization.

Cooperation between groups

Given the fact that the work of the local church is done by a large number of groups, it is worth looking into how they work together. Groups can be divided into cooperative and competitive groups. Cooperative groups want to work together; competitive groups want to do battle, particularly where power is concerned. Both groups occur in the church. In order to make both groups work together, it is necessary to know what is characteristic of cooperative and competitive groups (Boekestijn 1979).

The first characteristic is that cooperative groups do not or hardly make use of the scheme of the in-group and out-group. They identify themselves poorly or not at all with their own group (us), nor do they find the other group (them) threatening or dangerous. The reverse holds for competitive groups. They have a highly developed notion of the in-group and out-group. Thus it appears that groups that are trying to make a new place for themselves in church life behave competitively. This is understandable: they have to gain attention, space, and means from other groups, or else they will not develop. The task of the pastoral team, of course, is to take account of this adequately.

Next, the cooperative groups have a low profile insofar as it concerns the tracing of their own tasks and their own territory. The competitive groups, however, place a greater emphasis on their own competence. They brook no infringement of their territory by other groups. In some churches we find that the pastoral team makes pastoral decisions, the finance council makes financial decisions, and the pastoral council makes decisions regarding policy execution; each works separately from the other. In other churches, however, there is more general discussion between the groups; and people try to reach decisions collectively. In yet other churches, there is a system of different layers for decision making: it starts with the group with the least responsibility and ends with the group with the most.

Further, the cooperative groups display no or hardly any aggression toward the other group, nor do they feel frustrated by the other group. This is different for the competitive groups. These groups are characterized by feelings and expressions of aggression to the other group, just as they also feel frustrated by the other group. This can often be observed in the pastoral field. All sorts of groups like catechetical and liturgical groups, which are dependent on other groups concerning policy and finance, feel frustrated when they do not "get their way." The aggression that comes out is expressed in the meetings with the other group, in discussions afterward in their own group, and in possible correspondence in which numerous labels, distortions, and projections can be made or used. It does not take a leap of the imagination to see that the more powerful group can and will be used as a scapegoat by the less powerful one. Least of all is the church a community of saints; it is instead an *ecclesia mixta* (chapter 11 sub 2).

Finally, the aspect of power plays an important role, as has already become clear from the examples. Power is not a well-loved subject within ecclesiology. It is assumed that it does not exist in the local church, or at least that it should not exist. However, if one puts one's ear to the ground to hear what is really going on in pastoral practice, one cannot escape the aspect of power. For some groups simply have more power than others.

How can one deal with the power in groups? In order to be able to answer this question, it is necessary to know how power in groups works. Otherwise there is the danger that one falls into moral appeals. An important factor in the relations between groups has to do with the question of whether there is a larger or smaller difference in power between them. Let us assume there are two different situations, one with little difference in power and one with a lot.

We can speak of a situation with little difference in power if there is little or no social-psychological distance between, for example, the pastoral team, the pastoral group of clergy and laity, the finance council, or the pastoral council, on the one hand, and the committees and working groups on the other. In such a situation, with little difference in power, people tend to lean toward reducing the difference further still. This happens on both sides.

This is not so in the case of a large difference in power. This occurs when, for instance, the liturgy council feels it is being put in its place by the pastor, who is being holier than the pope in his interpretation of the Missale Romanum. This is purely from a management rationality perspective (chapter 18 sub 1). Or take the case in which the finance council lets the diacony council know at every meeting that they have financial control. In a situation where there is a large difference in power, the powerful group has the tendency to want to increase the distance from the other group. The less powerful group endeavors to bridge the power gap, with the consequence that the social-psychological gap widens even more (Wilke 1979).

How should one deal with the latter? We can mention several ways. The most obvious, of course, is to reduce the distance through one's own behavior and one's own contributions in discussions. One can do this by continually inviting the less powerful groups to clarify their opinions and presuppositions and by supporting them in their clarification. Further, individuals who function as key figures in the group(s) can be talked to concerning their influence in this matter. Finally, one can also turn to metacommunication. Through this, one makes the communication itself the subject of communication. For that matter, we can note that not everybody is happy with meta-communication. One can accept it as an opportunity to improve communication, but one can also reject it and disqualify it (Watzlawick et al. 1967). The refusal of meta-communication forms an absolute boundary in the communication: it cannot be moved, let alone be surpassed (cf. Van der Ven 1990c, 61-69).

Matrix organization

One can raise the cooperation between the members of groups and between groups by placing them in a matrix organization. A matrix organization is based on principles like taking effective and efficient advantage of new developments in the environment; flexibility; a changing composition of the groups; ad hoc provisions; short lines in the relations between groups; functional cooperation. It can be viewed as a combination of so-called line organization and project organization.

In line organization a distinction is made in a vertical sense between upper management, middle management, and executive workers. The relations between these groups can be set out on a line running from high to low. Via middle management, upper management gives instructions to executive workers. Middle management is executive with respect to upper management and managerial with regard to executive workers. Besides this, line organization makes a distinction in a horizontal sense between staff positions (staff organization) and services. Staff positions are characterized by professionality. They do not find themselves on a vertical line; they are horizontally oriented with respect to the vertical line, being the professional support, guidance, and advice to upper management and middle management respectively. The same holds for the services. They are not on a vertical line either. Just like the staff positions, they are horizontally oriented to the vertical line, fulfilling all kinds of services (administrative, financial, documentation, and domestic departments). Line organization forms the basic pattern for every organization (Keuning & Eppink 1986, 81-82). This also applies to parochial organization, as appears in figure 20.1. In this the principal part of the organigram of the Parish of John and James in Nijmegen (the Netherlands) has been given. The organigram is divided into sectors: catechetics, liturgy, diacony, pastoral care, and organization. We have supplemented it with a single element (services) in connection with the sector organization, which we will explain later.

From this figure, it appears that the parish council has the leadership. It goes beyond the finance council, as described in the Codex. It bears the final responsibility in all kinds of matters, especially pastoral and financial ones. Middle management is formed by the sector-bound councils: catechetics, liturgy, diacony, pastoral care, and organization. It is remarkable that a sector council for proclamation is lacking. The sector councils are responsible for the coordination of the working groups. The working groups do the executive work, performing the activities that are necessary to give concrete shape to the policy. Besides this, they have a signaling and advisory function for the sector council in question, according to the explanation added to the organigram. Over 600 parishioners are active in this whole. This comes down to more than 3% of the total number of registered

FIGURE 20.1 Organigram line organization

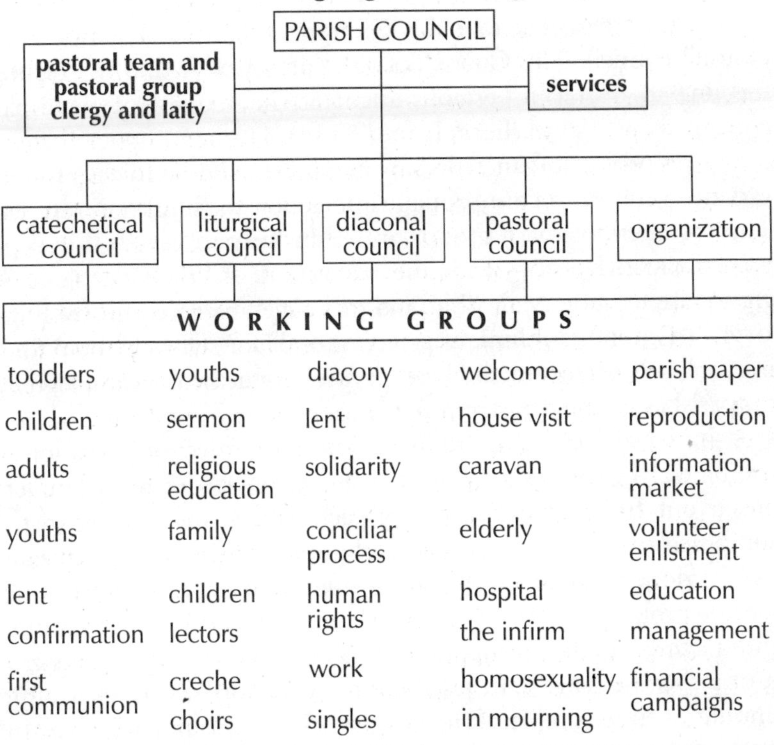

Catholics of this parish, which number 17,420 in all (in *Gezamenlijke Verantwoordelijkheid 1990,* 7-8).

The pastoral team and the pastoral care group of clergy and laity fulfill a staff function. They are not set on the vertical line but on the horizontal line, which is aimed at the line relation between upper management (parish council) and middle management (sector councils). They support, guide, and coordinate the sector councils.

The services are lacking in this organigram, at least formally. They are materially present under the head of the organization. Proceeding from organizational science, the sector of organization (parish paper, reproduction, information market, volunteers, management, and financial campaigns) does not fulfill a line function, since it is made up of a number of services. That is why it would be better to reposition the sector of organization in the organigram from the vertical line it is on now to the position of services on the horizontal line, which we added to the organigram.

It is remarkable that the Church of John and James has no pastoral council. The Codex does not prescribe it, and the bishop is the one to decide its establishment at the request of the finance council, as we saw earlier (chapter 19 sub 1).

In a project organization in its purest shape, project groups of varying composition are brought into action to fulfill different tasks. The members of these groups are exclusively involved — in a pure project organization — with the realization of "their" project. The groups are temporary, flexible, and maneuverable (Keuning & Eppink 1986, 141). One can think of project groups for self-help, help for the unemployed, environmental campaigns, multicultural campaigns, aid for parishes adopted in Latin America, etc.

In the matrix organization the line and project organizations are combined. That is to say, the line organization remains completely intact, but from time to time project groups are formed that are composed of members from several groups of the line organization. This is done with an eye to performing specific tasks and resolving specific problems. This happens without the members being entirely withdrawn from the line organization. Their work in the project group is of a specific nature. It has a limited duration and takes a limited amount of time. The latter means that only a certain part of the time it spends on the organization as a whole is allocated to the project group (Keuning & Eppink 1986, 140-42). In figure 20.2 the line organization is combined with an imaginary project organization to form an imaginary matrix organization.

In this figure the sector-bound councils of the line organization are displayed on the horizontal axis and the project groups are on the vertical axis. Here "organization" is replaced by "proclamation." The project groups are composed of one or more members of the sector councils or groups that fall under the sector councils. Each cross (x) indicates that one or more of the members from the deliberation groups has a seat in the project group. The project groups themselves are established if a specific task has to be carried out, for which the input from the sector councils is useful or necessary. They are liquidated when the task is accomplished. One can view the matrix organization as a concrete kind of innovative organization that is necessary to give shape to the base of the church.

FIGURE 20.2 Organigram matrix organization

	catech.	liturgy	diacony	past.	procl.
self-help	x	x	x	x	x
unemployed youths	x	x	x	x	x
environm. camp.	x	x	x	x	x
multicult. camp.	x	x	x	x	x
adopted parish	x	x	x	x	x

(2) The church as building of the Spirit

As in the previous parts, we will again try to determine the relevance of one of the religious codes that refers to the religious identity of the church and represents it. In the case of the church's core function of policy, the code is: building of the Spirit. We shall first try to expose the meaning of this code and then discuss its functions.

The Spirit

The code *building of the Spirit* stems from the messianic and pneumatic communities among the first generations of Jewish and Gentile Christians that were under the spell of the Jesus movement (chapter 12 sub 3). These communities remembered what Jesus had done (*anamnesis*) either because they had met him themselves or because they had heard eyewitnesses talk about him. This anamnesis roused a spiritual excitement in them, which they themselves interpreted as the gift of the Spirit of Jesus (*pneuma*). The communities can therefore be called anamnetic-pneumatic communities (Schillebeeckx 1985, 42-47; 1989, 176-77). They lived in and from the Spirit. They formed a community on the basis of baptism in the Spirit — their baptism in the name of Jesus, who was in their midst as Messiah. They experienced their spiritual life as a new life. This newness is expressed in the first letter to the Corinthians: "Thus it is written: 'The first man, Adam, became a living being'; the last Adam became a life-giving spirit" (1 Cor. 15:45).

We just stated that a certain spiritual excitement took possession of these communities, which they saw as the gift of Jesus' Spirit. In semiotic terms, this means that they saw their own spiritual strength as a sign of Jesus' strength; their own spiritual inspiration as a reference to Jesus' inspiration. Their own strength and inspiration signified and represented Jesus' powerful and inspiring closeness to them (chapter 6).

Through this there was no exchange between the human spirit and Jesus' Spirit nor with God's Spirit. Proceeding from the anamnetic-pneumatic signification, Jesus' Spirit penetrated the human spirit, laid claim to it, and shaped it, without its dissolving into the human spirit, however. The first letter to the Corinthians is clear about this: "But, as it is written, 'What no eye has seen, nor ear heard, nor the human heart conceived, what God has prepared for those who love him' — these things God has revealed to us through the Spirit; for the Spirit searches everything, even the depths of God. For what human being knows what is truly human except the human that is within? So also no one comprehends what is truly God's except the Spirit of God. Now we have received not the spirit of the world, but the Spirit that is from God, so that we may understand the gifts bestowed on us by God. And we speak of these things in words not taught by human wisdom but taught by the Spirit, interpreting spiritual things to those who are spiritual" (1 Cor. 2:9-13).

The Spirit was seen as a gift of Jesus as Messiah by these communities: a messianic gift. In this gift there was fulfillment of what had been proclaimed by the messianic prophets in the Old Testament according to this viewpoint: "For I will pour water on the thirsty land, and streams on the dry ground; I will pour my Spirit upon your descendants, and my blessing on your offspring. They shall spring up like a green tamarisk, like willows by flowing streams" (Isa. 44:3-5). The distribution of the Spirit was understood as the sign that the eschatological happening was soon to occur or that it had already started in actual fact. Thus the Old Testament prophecy states: "Then afterward, I will pour out my spirit on all flesh; your sons and your daughters shall prophesy, your old men shall dream dreams, and your young men shall see visions. Even on the male and female slaves in those days, I will pour out my spirit" (Joel 2:28-29). These verses can be found in the sermon that Peter preached, according to the Acts, directly from the experience of the Spirit at Pentecost. With this quotation he indicated that what Joel had proclaimed had become reality in the Pentecost experience. In this experience they felt filled by the Spirit and taken unto him, so that they started to talk in strange languages. This surprised the people who had flocked to them because everyone heard them speak in their own language. But according to Peter, "Indeed, they are not drunk, as you suppose, for it is only nine o'clock in the morning. No, this is what was spoken through the prophet Joel" (Acts 2:15-16). Here Peter interpreted the linguistic excitement of the apostles proceeding from the frame of reference of Old Testament prophetism and saw it as a sign of the presence of God's Spirit in them, as a sign of the eschatological happening in actuality.

With the experience of the presence of the Spirit, one should not think in subjectivistic or animistic terms. The Spirit was not primarily experienced as a kind of personified being that assails humans like a demon, or takes possession of them and drives them to all sorts of activities in speech or action. The Spirit was sooner seen as an impersonal force *(dynamis)* that is present in humans, and that pulls and pushes them. This *dynamis* was tangible in wisdom, hope, courage, endurance, joy, and charismata. The latter is of importance: the charismata were felt to be the strength of the Spirit *(dynamis pneumatos)* (Rom. 15:13). In the charismata the strength of the Spirit is given expression (Bultmann 1965, 158-159).

Charismata

The gifts of the Spirit, however, displayed an image with several meanings. On the one hand, there were the ordinary gifts, which stemmed from the strength of the Spirit. All those who had been baptized had them at their disposal. The charismatic way of life from the Spirit was simply part of the Christian existence, as the Acts states: "Repent, and be baptized every one of you in the name of Jesus Christ so that your sins may be forgiven; and you will receive the gift of the Holy Spirit" (Acts 2:38). Paul did not even see the gift of the Holy Spirit as a consequence of conversion and faith; he reduced the faith itself to the strength of the Spirit: "For all who are led by the Spirit of God are children of God. For you did not receive a spirit of slavery to fall back into fear, but you have received a spirit of adoption. When we cry, 'Abba! Father!' it is that very Spirit bearing witness with our spirit that we are children of God" (Rom. 8:14-16). In short, the faithful live "in the Spirit."

On the other hand, however, there were people who seemed to be special bearers of the Spirit *(pneumatikoi)*. Those who practiced glossolalia and prophecy belonged to this group. Earlier we saw that

Paul did not work against them directly, but he did try to reduce their influence because they called up dangers inwardly and outwardly. Inwardly, they caused discord and religious competition. Outwardly, the church was losing face in the Gentile environment. This channelization and restriction can be conceived of as the routinization of the charismata (chapter 12 sub 3).

This routinization did not detract from the fact that the gifts of spiritual strength among the various members of the communities were present to differing degrees. In Acts there is reference to the choice of "seven men of good standing, full of the Spirit and of wisdom" (Acts 6:3). It continues as follows: "They chose Stephen, a man full of faith and of the Holy Spirit, together with Philip, and Prochorus, and Nicanor, and Timon, and Parmenas, and Nicolaus, a proselyte of Antioch" (Acts 6:5). Here Stephen is mentioned separately as a man full of the Spirit, apart from the others. Further along this is repeated: "he was a good man, full of the Holy Spirit and of faith" (Acts 11:24).

Furthermore, various spiritual gifts were active in the communities. Paul makes mention of them at the beginning of chapter 12 of the first letter to the Corinthians: wisdom, knowledge, faith, gifts of healing, the working of miracles, prophecy, discernment of spirits, glossolalia, and interpretation of glossolalia (1 Cor. 12:8-10). At the end of the chapter, Paul returns to these charismata, but he adds some services as well: "Now you are the body of Christ and individually members of it. And God has appointed in the church first apostles, second prophets, third teachers, then deeds of power, then gifts of healing, forms of assistance, forms of leadership, various kinds of tongues" (1 Cor. 12:27-28). He appears to have placed them in an order of rank, and a multiple one at that. The services of apostles, prophets, and teachers are more important than the charismata of deeds of power, gifts of healing, forms of assistance, forms of leadership, and glossolalia. The most important of these services is that of the apostles; and of the charismata, glossolalia is the least important (Smit 1989). The low rank that glossolalia holds becomes even clearer in the sequel of the letter. What Paul had emphasized earlier comes to the fore even more strongly: the charismata had to be aimed at mutual love, the community, and the development of the community. In the following chapter, he places love in the top rank, even above faith and hope (1 Cor. 13:1-13). In chapter 14, he gives a detailed account of why prophecy outranks glossolalia (vv. 1-25). Finally, he gives a set of rules for prophecy and glossolalia during the meetings of the community: no more than two or three people per meeting for prophecy and glossolalia separately; everybody has to wait his or her turn; the prophecies have to be judged by the others; an explanation has to be given of the glossolalia; during the explanation there has to be complete silence; the whole has to serve the education, encouragement, and development of the community (vv. 26-33).

The Spirit was expressed not only in the various charismata but also at different times. Thus it is said that at the moment Peter was brought forward, he spoke boldly, "filled with the Holy Spirit" (Acts 4:8-13). When the community came together to thank God after Peter's release together with the others, "the place in which they were gathered together was shaken," according to the text, which continues by stating that "they were all filled with the Holy Spirit and spoke the word of God with boldness" (Acts 4:31). It was said that Stephen was "full of the Holy Spirit" as he "gazed into heaven and saw the glory of God" before he was stoned and died a martyr (Acts 7:55).

That the charismata are the work of the Spirit does not mean that human activity is unnecessary. Thus Paul ordered the following: "Pursue love and strive for the spiritual gifts, and especially that you may prophesy" (1 Cor. 14:1). One is expected to "strive for the greater gifts" (1 Cor. 12:31). He closes the part on the charismata with this warning: "So, my friends, be eager to prophesy, and do not forbid speaking in tongues; but all things should be done decently and in order" (1 Cor. 14:39). The right medium to receive the charismata is prayer (1 Cor. 14:13). Fasting provides the right preparation to the charismata: "While they were worshipping the Lord and fasting, the Holy Spirit said . . ." (Acts 13:2).

Spirit in the community

As we stated, there was the idea in these communities that everyone who believed and had been baptized had received the Spirit. The focus was not on an individual matter, as if the person in question had gone through a special pneumatic experience. Rather, the community one was joining was seen as the bearer of the Spirit. Those who participated in the community participated in the strength of the Spirit. The Spirit was felt to be present in the community and as active in the community. That is why the following passage was part of the letter addressed to the communities in Antioch, Syria, and Cilicia after the council of Jerusalem concerning circumcision: "For it has seemed good to the Holy Spirit and to us to impose on you no further burden than these essentials: that you abstain from what has been sacrificed to idols . . ." (Acts 15:28-29).

The presence of the Spirit in the community was especially experienced during the liturgical gatherings. Hence Paul set forth rules to put things in order because of the "pneumatic density" of these celebrations. Everything was in token of the Spirit: the citing of psalms, the teaching, the singing of songs, the prayer, the prophecy, the glossolalia, and the explanation. What applied as a criterion was the tuning of the gathering to the message of the gospel and the development of the community.

The Spirit was experienced as being present in each community separately. This is strikingly expressed in the passage of the first letter to the Corinthians, in which Paul defended himself against the handsome but deceptive teacher Apollos. Paul rants: "Do you not know that you are God's temple and that God's Spirit dwells in you?" (1 Cor. 3:16). This admonishing question implies that the community itself had to bestow care on the pneumatic foundation on which it was built. The Spirit did not work outside the activity of the community itself. The Spirit gave to the community the task to bring about its presence. This is nicely expressed in the first letter of Peter: "Come to him, a living stone, though rejected by mortals yet chosen and precious in God's sight; and like living stones, let yourselves be built into a spiritual house, to be a holy priesthood, to offer spiritual sacrifices acceptable to God through Jesus Christ" (1 Pet. 2:4-5). The community had to allow itself to be developed into a spiritual house. It was not as if it fulfilled the role of architect and builder, for the Spirit was the one to build the spiritual house from the community. What it had to do was dedicate spiritual sacrifices — not sacrifices of animals or food, but of prayer, faith, hope, and love.

However much the emphasis was placed on the presence of the Spirit in the community, it did not mean that the Spirit and the community were the same. By no means. The Spirit was not the church. The Spirit was not of the church, but of God and Jesus. There was a radical distance between the Spirit and the church, however great the connection was. This distance made the Spirit free from the church. There could be no other way, since the church was a *communio mixta:* a community of people that was just and sinful at the same time *(simul justus et peccator).* The church was not only a church of sinners, but it was also a sinner itself (chapter 11 sub 2). The symbolum says: "I believe in the Holy Spirit" *("credo in Spiritum sanctum").* After that it says: "I believe the holy church" *("credo sanctam ecclesiam").* We believe in the Spirit, not in the church; we believe the church (Küng 1967, 203). The Spirit is free with respect to the shortage and guilt of the sinful church. Haarsma puts it strikingly: "Holy is the last and definitive word about the church, sinful is the first that one has to say of the church. We may believe in [*sic!*] the holy church, but we experience it as the sinful church" (Haarsma 1967, 333).

That the Spirit is not identical to the community means that it is earlier, further, broader, and deeper than the community. What do earlier, further, broader, and deeper mean? The Spirit is *earlier* in the sense that it is the origin and source of the community. The community cannot exist without the working of the Spirit. He calls upon the church to *be* the church. This does not cancel out the coming together and joining of believers in the community, as we argued earlier. The Spirit gives believers the task of joining together. He calls upon them to call themselves together (chapter 2 sub 2).

The Spirit is *further* than the community, because it is ahead of it and inspires, summons, admonishes, and corrects the community from that position. He pulls the community into intercourse and connectedness, across denominational boundaries too, in the direction of the ecumenism of God *(oikoumene tou Theou).* Thus the Spirit is regarded as the principle creating unity between the churches in the texts of Vatican II (*Unitatis Redintegratio* 3). In the constitution on the church this is further explained as follows: "And so the Spirit stirs up desires and actions in all of Christ's disciples in order that all may be peaceably united, as Christ ordained, in one flock under one shepherd" (*Lumen Gentium* 15). The Spirit bears the church beyond the boundaries that separate the churches from each other: papalism, episcopalism, presbyterianism, synodalism, conciliarism, congregationalism, and independentism (Moltmann 1975, 318).

The Spirit is *broader* than the community, and broader than the Christian churches, since it flies where it wills, outside of the churches, in other religions and other philosophies of life. Those who deny this close their eyes to the "ecclesial fugitiveness" of God. God is always ahead of any religious institution; God's being ahead is his Spirit.

Finally, the Spirit is *deeper* than the community. It knows how to penetrate into layers of human existence that hardly or do not reach the surface of the church — the layers of spirituality and mysticism, of reflection and prayer, of contemplation and meditation. Here we are dealing with the deeper layers of awe and wondering at the secret of human existence in which people participate in a passive-active presence without words (Krueger 1989). Through this the Spirit opens up the community to God's presence in Islamic Sufi mysticism, Hinduistic Veda, and the Buddhist *Bhagavad Gita* (Walgrave 1961; Schoonenberg 1991).

Community of the Spirit

The fact that the Spirit is present in the community, but is also earlier, further, broader, and deeper than the community, leads us to the conclusion that it is the Spirit and not the community that deserves priority. It is in the community, but at the same time it surrounds and envelops the community. To put it differently, the relation of the Spirit to the community is of an immanent-transcendent nature. It is present in the community but does not dissolve into this presence; the Spirit does not exhaustively spend itself in this. It is both the foundation and destination of the community.

In order to develop an exact view of the pneumatological foundation of the community, we will turn to the first letter to the Corinthians. In this letter, Paul uses the metaphor of the field (orchard or garden). Besides the plant in the field, we are also concerned with the walls around the field. Paul uses the metaphor in his defense against Apollos, who manipulated his community in Corinth during his absence. He says: "For we are God's servants, working together; you are God's field, God's building. According to the grace of God given to me, like a skilled master builder I laid a foundation, and someone else is building on it. Each builder must choose with care how to build on it. For no one can lay any foundation other than the one that has been laid; that foundation is Jesus Christ. Now if anyone builds on the foundation with gold, silver, precious stones, wood, hay, straw — the work of each builder will become visible, for the Day will disclose it, because it will be revealed with fire, and the fire will test which sort of work each has done. If what has been built on the foundation survives, the builder will receive a reward. If the work is burned up, the builder will suffer loss; the builder will be saved, but only as through fire" (1 Cor. 3:9-15). It is clear what Paul suggests here. He himself raised the walls and planted the community of Corinth within them. Apollos came to water the plant, but God took care of the growth. It is not important who did the planting, nor who watered the plant. What is important is the one who looks after the plant's growth. Therefore Apollos and Paul are on a par with each other. For they are both only fellow workers, as is mentioned in the first line of the above quotation. The community itself is God's field, and — Paul now turns from the metaphor of the field to the metaphor of the wall — the community itself is God's building. But the foundation is the important thing. The foundation is Jesus Christ. Paul set it like a master builder. Apollos continued the building on the foundation. But it is not clear whether the material he used for this was satisfactory. The fire of judgment will tell. The precious metals will not be affected by it; wood, hay, or straw, of course, will be. Finally, Paul makes use of the scheme of retribution. The good builder will receive his reward, while the bad one will suffer loss. In short, the community has its foundation in God, but the further development and extension of the community have to take place with care and expertise (Cerfaux 1966).

In the letter to the Ephesians, there is a broad perspective on the destination of the community: peace. This is based on the gift of the Spirit. The author says: "So he came and proclaimed peace to you who were far off and peace to those who were near; for through him both of us have access in one Spirit to the Father. So then you are no longer strangers and aliens, but you are citizens with the saints and also members of the household of God, built upon the foundation of the apostles and prophets, Christ Jesus himself being the cornerstone. In him the whole structure is joined together and grows into a holy temple in the Lord; in whom you also are built together spiritually into a dwelling place for God" (Eph. 2:17-22). This verse has to be understood against the background of the turbulent times that Asia Minor was going through. It is a formula of pacification. The distinction between Jews and non-Jews that ran like a fracture through the peoples is overcome here; the fracture is healed. Jews and Gentiles became each other's housemates in the community of Christ. The Gentiles, who came from afar and were held at a distance, changed from strangers and aliens into co-citizens. They are the fellow citizens of the Jews who already belonged to the community. The community no longer had any partition walls. Christ brought the two groups in the church together and provided them access to God together. God, who is the all in all through the Spirit: "[is] making every effort to maintain the unity of the Spirit in the bond of peace. There is one body and one Spirit, just as you were called to the one hope of your calling, one Lord, one faith, one baptism, one God and Father of all, who is above all and through all and in all" (Eph. 4:3-6). Here the perspective is opened up to a universal ecumenism (Schillebeeckx 1977b, 175-95).

Functions

As we did with the previous religious codes, we will now discuss the three functions of the code *building of the Spirit:* the cognitive, emotive, and conative functions. As before, they can be distinguished from each other but not separated. The point is the emphases that they represent.

Cognitive

The religious information that lies in the church as building of the Spirit places an emphasis on the source and origin of the church: the Spirit. This Spirit is the Spirit of Jesus and of God. It is Jesus, the Messiah, who is felt to be the force *(dynamis)* in the anamnetic-pneumatic experience. It is God's in that it motivates the community through the proclamation of his kingdom as a healing force that makes things whole. This Spirit is present in the community insofar as the community is animated and it sees the animation itself as a sign of the Spirit's presence. The Spirit is present in the community insofar as it is truly inspired and sees this inspiring force itself as a reference to Jesus' inspirational power. In this it is signified and re-presented.

At the same time, however, the church as building of the Spirit draws attention away from the church and sets it above the church. In the perspective that then unfolds, we see the dream of universality looming: the unity of the church, the unity of churches, the unity of religions, the unity of all people — universal peace, as the letter to the Ephesians states. The Spirit flies where it wants to and when it wants to. It is earlier, further, broader, and deeper than the church.

The church as building of the Spirit combines the two poles of the presence of the Spirit in the church and its presence outside the church. This code symbolizes the identity of the church as a church and surpasses it at the same time. The church is the bearer of the Spirit because it is borne by the Spirit, and at the same time the church realizes it is a carrier beside other carriers. The Spirit is in it, but is greater than the church and at the same time comprises it and envelops it. In this combination we find the dialectics between the immanence and transcendence of the Spirit with respect to the church: the immanent transcendence.

The Spirit enables the church to realize itself. The Spirit gives the church as a task to itself. This implies that the presence of the Spirit has to be maintained in one's own church community, and that it has to be seen as being active in other communities at the same time. Church development is the development of one's own community and that of other communities from the perspective of the presence of the Spirit. Church development surpasses itself.

Emotive

The pneumatological prospect relativizes the church and motivates it do work for and in the church at the same time. The relativization and motivation are connected. If the relativization is absent, the church turns inward; it becomes oppressive and closed. This has a demotivational effect because all perspective is lacking. If the church is open to the Spirit in the communities outside it and walks the path of reconciliation and peace, spiritual room is made and an ideal arises, a prospect to live for.

The charismata of faith, hope, and love are then able to flourish, as well as the prayer and the thanks, the knowledge and the wisdom, the discernment of spirits, the ecstasy, the assistance and help, the leadership and prophecy. The gift of healing also belongs to this. People become strong of spirit: the psychosomatic unity that the human is becomes whole in a deepened sense. The gifts of tongues and of tears also belong to this, as the spiritual expression of feelings and moods in the comprehensible or incomprehensible layers in humans (chapter 16 sub 3). The Spirit does not work outside the powers of human beings, but it takes hold of these powers, intensifies them, and works through them (Schoonenberg 1985). The charismata raise the church above routinization (chapter 12).

Through these charismata the awareness of the fundamental equality of the members of the church can arise. As in the pneumatic communities of yore, every member has authority in the church on the basis of his or her own spiritual inspiration. Enthusiasm is catching. It permeates all ranks and classes. It is then that the charter of freedom of the first Christian communities can be rehabilitated, based as it is on Jesus, Messiah: "For in Christ Jesus you are all children of God through faith. As many of you as were baptized into Christ have clothed yourselves with Christ. There is no longer Jew or Greek, there is no longer slave or free, there is no longer male and female; for all of you are one in Christ Jesus" (Gal. 3:26-28).

It is important to note that Vatican II expressly teaches the equality of the members of the church: "It is not only through the sacraments and the ministrations of the Church that the Holy Spirit makes holy the people, leads them and enriches them with his virtues. Allotting his gifts according as he wills (cf. 1 Cor. 12:11), he also distributes special graces among the faithful of every rank. By these gifts he makes them fit and ready to undertake various tasks and offices for the renewal and building up of the Church, as it is written, 'the manifestation of the Spirit is given to everyone for profit' (1 Cor. 12:7). Whether these charisms be very remarkable or more simple and widely diffused, they are to be received with thanksgiving and consolation since they are fitting and useful for the needs of the Church" (*Lumen Gentium* 12).

There are some essential points in this text. The passage "the faithful of every rank" is naturally of great importance, especially for a church that for centuries has been marked by the gap between the ordained and the nonordained, the clergy and laypeople, subjects and objects. The faithful themselves are bearers of the charismata. Further, the charismata are not delegated to the believers by the ministers, nor even mediated. The Spirit grants them directly. He works in only one way: through the charismata. A more fundamental point of view in this context is not really imaginable (Haarsma 1991).

Conative

In the cognitive and emotive functions we find some regulative indications for the further development of the church as building of the Spirit. They form a support for the shaping of the church in the direction of an innovative strategy, which we argued for in this chapter.

We will work this out on two sides: the flow aspect and the self-organization aspect of the innovative organization.

What is called in religious terms "the working of the Spirit" finds its correlate in organizational terms in the innovative organization. The Spirit flies where and when it wills to. In the same way an organization streams where and when it will, depending on its flow character. In what way can the flying of the Spirit in the flow of the church as an innovative organization find its own channel? The characteristic thing about flow in an innovative organization is that from time to time it is somewhat anarchical. Such processes usually begin in the experience that there is a gap between what people want and what is being achieved. Following this a flood of suggestions pours down to bridge the gap that has been signaled. A great number of solutions are brought forward, which are found to be more or less attractive for the value they represent in themselves, even without the relation to the problem that has to be solved. There is a frequent coming and going of people who think along, put in a word, and join in. All of this continually flows through the whole of the organization. Such anarchical moments provide the organization with an unpredictable quality: a creative, coincidental quality (Daft 1989, 373-75). Such an organizational flow should be copied by the church to a certain extent. It creates conditions for the Spirit as the dynamic principle of the church. These dynamics do not eliminate the organization, but continually change and transform it. The Spirit continually rejuvenates the church, according to Vatican II (*Lumen Gentium* 4).

Such a flow could gain optimal realization in the church if it were to make use of a different principle that stems from the science of organization: flexible self-organization. This is the second aspect. What we mean by this is that people in the church are not organized; they organize themselves, taking the varying needs and interests of their own and of groups from the societal environment into account. This self-organization has its foundation in the direct gifts of grace from the Spirit to each individual, without delegation or mediation: the charismata. It finds its orientation in the charismata aiming at mutual support and community and the development of the church. This self-organization can be called a "today's command" *(Gebot der Stunde),* as it gives expression to the personal responsibility of the members of the church and to the legitimation of their participation (Schneider 1982).

The principle of self-organization could be given concrete shape in the setting up of a parish volunteer council with its own aims and tasks. It can focus itself on the coordination of pastoral work that is carried out by volunteers; the signalling of desirable developments and changes; the advising of other organs with regard to policy development. The volunteer council can be seen as the concrete shaping of the responsibility that the volunteers themselves bear with regard to the self-realization of the church. This is what Rahner already argued for in the *Schluss* of the *Handbuch der Pastoraltheologie,* as we mentioned before (chapter 19 sub 2). It is not only the matter of the self-organization that is at stake here, but also the problem of the juridical regulations. For one can ask whether it would not better serve the volunteer council to give it its own juridical statute, in order to emphasize the principle of self-organization. Naturally, this would have to be done in balance with the other organs of authority in the local church. Concretely this comes down to the right of association. In short, would it not better serve the volunteer council to set up a volunteer association? In the Codex the right of association has been treated like a stepchild. It has no balanced tuning of the powers and faculties of the association to those of the church hierarchy. It hardly has any real freedom with respect to the hierarchy (Huysmans 1986, 124-25).

One could carry this lack of any true right of association back to two more fundamental omissions in Vatican II. It is important to point this out since they both clarify why the positive working out of the right of association is lacking and what has to happen to make its further development possible.

The first omission relates to the lack of pneumatology in the texts of this council. In the first chapter of *Lumen Gentium,* the church is situated in the mystery of God, the Father, the Son, and the Spirit. However, this trinitarian approach did not lead to an elaborate pneumatology as the foundation of the church, even though this would have been possible in principle (*Lumen Gentium* 2-4). The text suffices with a re-sourcing of ecclesiology in the direction of the trinitarian approach of the church fathers of the first centuries, which in itself is important (Philipon 1966). No conclusions are drawn in the direction of a pneumatological ecclesiology, however. This would have been a sound base for the treatment of the charismata. In fact, a fundamental middle piece is missing between the treatment of the trinitarian basis of the church on the one hand, and that of the charismata on the other: a Spirit ecclesiology. If it had been worked out, then an easier answer could have been given to all sorts of thorny questions regarding the structure of the church and the ministry (Schoonenberg 1991).

The second omission relates to something that seems to be the complete opposite of a pneumatological elaboration of ecclesiology: a theology of ecclesial law. The texts of Vatican II almost entirely leave aside ecclesial law. They pay no attention to it. The cause of this is probably the deep gap that exists between theology and ecclesial law in general. Theologians like to keep a certain distance from ecclesial law because they fear that they will be forced to suit their ecclesiology to all kinds of rules and regulations. Canonists, on their part, are so occupied with juridical casuistry that reflection on all sorts of fundamental philosophical and theological ideas is left out (Walf 1984a).

A theology of ecclesial law based on a pneumatological ecclesiology would have to pay attention to the dynamics of the Spirit in the church: "Law may not and must not suffocate the Spirit. On the contrary, law is a part of the laws of life, it develops, it is not only protective, it bears dynamics in it too" (Walf 1984a, 22-23). Such a theology should also negotiate the charismata as being foundational for the community, and it should also involve the church as *communio* in its regulations. With this the law would not restrict or curtail, but it would serve and stimulate. It could, for instance, offer an open approach and a positive support to the rise of new customs in the church *(consuetudo)* instead of marking them down as deviations from what has been set down in the Codex. It could also lend juridical support to the positive meaning of the religious sense organ *(sensus fidei)* of the faithful in the church *(sensus fidelium)* and to the agreement among the faithful *(consensus fidelium).* It would also have to involve the meaning of the acceptance or nonacceptance of ecclesial law in its reflections *(acceptatio legis).* These are only a few examples of the importance of a close involvement of theology and ecclesial law with each other, especially with an eye to the development of ecclesiology (Walf 1984a, 23-24; 1985; Haarsma 1991, 185-88; Van der Ven 1992b).

Against this background we can understand why the two omissions mentioned (Spirit ecclesiology and theology of ecclesial law) are connected to each other. They summon each other. Without a Spirit ecclesiology, ecclesial law is caught in an inflexible, static attitude. Without a theology of ecclesial law, a trinitarian approach to the church floats in idle speculation (Legrand 1979).

PART VI

MANAGEMENT

In this part we will deal with the last core function of the church: management. The fact that we left this to last does not mean that it is the least important function. Its being discussed now is a consequence of the choice we made earlier for the liga model rather than the agil model. In the liga model one departs from the guiding force of latency (identity) via integration, via goal attainment (policy), to adaptation (management). In the agil model the emphasis is placed on the conditional working of adaptation (management) via goal attainment (policy), via integration, to latency (identity). Both models are complementary with respect to each other. They refer to the guiding impact from top to bottom and the conditional impact from bottom to top (chapter 4 sub 2). If we had departed from the agil model, then we would have started with management, which gives the conditions from all the things above it: policy, integration, and identity. To put it strongly, without management there is no building of the Spirit, no body of Christ, and no church as Jesus movement or as people of God. Without management, there is no community of believers.

However important and necessary management is, hardly any attention is paid to it in ecclesiology or none at all — at least not to the themes we classify under management: service quality, personnel development, and financial management. However, they may not be absent from an ecclesiology that is developed in the perspective of practical theology. So let us get down to earth.

We will start this part the same way we started the previous parts.

First, we will place the core function of management in the context of the societal process of modernization, and particularly that of calculation. By this we mean the increase in the endeavor to weigh off the costs and benefits in order to obtain a product or service (chapter 21). Then we will discuss the striving for service quality in the church (chapter 22). Next, we pay attention to the problems of personnel development proceeding from the viewpoint of both the pastoral professional — ordained and nonordained — and the pastoral volunteer (chapter 23). Finally, we will go into financial management. With this we will bring up not only the enlistment but also the allocation of financial means. In that context we will focus upon the religious code *church of the poor* (chapter 24).

Chapter 21

The Context of Calculation

Calculation can be called a societal process — and not just an economic one — because it radically interferes in the whole of societal and personal life. It can be pointed out in several institutions outside of the economic sector. Market thinking is snatching at more and more around it. It does not leave the church untouched. Not only do people meet the church proceeding from an attitude of calculation, but the church itself does not seem to be able to escape it. If this is the case, the religious identity of the church is in danger: its vision (people of God), its mission (Jesus movement), its community formation (body of Christ), and its universal aim (building of the Spirit).

In this chapter we will ask the following questions: (1) What does the process of calculation entail? (2) To what degree is the church itself determined by it? and (3) Is the church being absorbed into the market?

(1) Calculation and the market

First we shall dwell upon the term *calculation*. Then we will indicate which substantial elements comprise it, namely individualism, instrumentalism, hedonism, and consumerism. These gain their own aim through the influence of the market.

Calculation

By calculation we mean the process through which the societal and personal interaction between people is determined to an increasing extent by the calculative weighing of costs and benefits with an eye to the achievement of a commodity. This commodity can be a product or service. One can observe this process not only in the sphere of the economy or politics but also in that of social life and culture, and even in personal relations, friendship, marriage, and the family. It is not that all these areas are entirely determined by calculation; however, we can point out certain aspects in these processes that are characterized by calculation, like trade, giving and taking, fair play, and contract and compromise thinking. The calculating citizen is permeating all institutions and sectors of society. He is himself the product of the contract society (Fortuyn 1992). The appearance of the calculating citizen can be placed in the context of the colonization of society by the economy. The economy involves more and more areas in its sphere of influence (Habermas 1982). We will give two examples from the sector of culture: education and psychosocial service. We will restrict ourselves to the use of certain calculation codes. In doing this we do not do justice to either education or psychosocial service; however, the examples are only for purposes of illustration. We want to demonstrate that even these two institutions, which are of a particularly cultural nature, are colonized by the economy and therefore entangled in fundamental conflicts.

In the school and the university the focus of attention — proceeding from the perspective of calculation — is on the teaching and study contract. It is involved with human capital. To make this profitable, investments have to be made. This can be achieved through the improvement of the educational product: the pupils and the students who complete their educations. Besides that, it can be optimized through a contrived reward structure. This influences the returns: the enlargement of the output and the raising of efficiency. How are the returns measured? In the case of education, by the numbers of pupils and students who obtain a certificate or diploma at the fastest rate. In the case of research, by the numbers of publications, citations, and dissertations in the smallest amount of time. These codes shed a one-sided light on the whole of processes that take place at a school or university. There are other codes too, like the general, cultural, aesthetic, moral, religious, and personal formation of the students. However, there is a tense relationship, not to say conflict, between the calculation codes and those of formation *(Bildung)*. Educational economy and educational technology on the one hand, and *Bildungspaedagogik* on the other, are opposite each other (Gamm 1979; Mollenhauer 1972; Klafki 1976; Preul 1980; Nipkow 1990).

In the psychosocial services, intake is central and the sorting of complaints and disorders into the right treatment departments where service contracts are closed is crucial. The recovery of relationships that have run aground is measured by the costs and benefits of a renewed emotional investment. First the emotional balance has to be drawn up, to see whether the emotional household can be set in order by getting a profit from it. One has to be able to speak of a more or less equal trade between partners. The emotions themselves can also be conceived of in terms of investment and reward: when one is happy, both are in balance; while rage stems from a reward that is too low, and guilt stems from too small an investment made (Frijda 1983; 1984; 1986).

These codes also shed a one-sided light on the whole of processes that occur in the psychosocial services. Other codes apply as well, like connectedness, intimacy, commitment, and devotion. Besides contractual actions, there are acts that bear the character of gratuity — acts that take place from an existential connectedness in which the other is loved "for nothing." These are acts that one cannot count on and that cannot be commanded in a calculative sense. They rise above it. They are supererogatory acts (Rawls 1971). These, too, can be brought up for discussion in the psychosocial services. Human happiness does not merge into acts of trade but surpasses it in the direction of the mystery of human existence. The question is, however, whether or not the psychosocial services are characterized by a fundamental conflict between two anthropological orientations: trade and self-effacing love (Browning 1987b).

These two examples — in their one-sided exposure — make it clear that the market is not limited to the economy, but extends to all of societal and personal life. One can also define this process as commercialization. Commerce is the selfish trade of goods and services. Commerce permeates the personal life of humankind too, up to and including the emotions. One behaves like a sympathetic partner to another so that the latter will be sympathetic toward him. Sympathy is commercial sympathy. One can view commercial sympathy as the religion of secularized society (Van Leeuwen 1984).

Market

Where does the process of calculation come from? Its deepest tracks can be found in the so-called classic economy founded by Adam Smith, and in the neo-classic economy that followed. They contain the following elements: individualism, instrumentalism, hedonism, and consumerism. Each has its own orientation proceeding from the central position held by the market in societal and personal life (Etzioni 1988).

For a description of *individualism* we return to the process of individualization, which we discussed earlier, in the context of urbanization. Individualism is couched in the transition from the pre-industrial to the industrial or the post-industrial society respectively. It is the result of a process of centuries in which humankind is primarily seen as single, viewed as monad, as separate from the community, which is regarded as a collection of separate individuals (chapter 13 sub 2).

This individualism can be clarified in a number of aspects. The first is the autonomy of the individual and his needs. This autonomy is the highest good. It implies that it is the basic right of humankind to determine its own needs as well as the way to satisfy these needs. The emphasis on doing it oneself requires the assumption that one can arrange one's own life, that one can make a life for oneself. There is nothing else, no other, to which one has to give thanks for existence. With this we have arrived at the second aspect, which is defined by the term *poietic subjectivism* (derived from the Greek *poieo,* which means "doing" or "making"). The other, the others, the community, the society, form a threat and hindrance to autonomy and to one's ability to determine one's own life. This makes one man a wolf for another *(homo homini lupus)*. In order to secure the satisfaction of its needs in the future, humankind has to enlarge its power with regard to the other or others. The most effective way to do this is through the acquisition of property and the increase of property, to which the term *possessive individualism* refers — the third aspect. However, the struggle of all against all, the battle for power, threatens to escalate into an absolute jungle. Because of this, the whole societal system is in danger of collapsing. If this were to happen, then the free fall of society would also drag along the individual human with all his pretensions to autonomy and power. Now there is only one way to create order in the chaos: the contract. In the contract, humans not only plan their own lives (poietic subjectivism) but also make relationships with fellow humans by placing this in a balance of trade and setting it down juridically in an agreement — the fourth aspect (Willms 1969). Contract thinking places so much emphasis on the individualism of the calculation of one's own items of profit and loss that it makes all thought concerning the notion that several people could together form a corporate personality impossible (Rawls 1971, 28).

Instrumentalism serves individualism. It is characterized by the notion that humankind has to go about the processes with which it tries to satisfy its needs in as effective and efficient a manner as possible. *Effective* means that one has to run the thing for what it is worth. *Efficient* means that one has to work with the smallest amount of effort and with the least implementation of means, against the lowest possible costs. Everything that can contribute to this goal is used or instrumentalized, including lifeless nature, plants and animals, other people, oneself, one's body. These are judged not on their intrinsic value, but on what they can contribute to the aims that lie outside of them. This extrinsic valuation leads to exploitation. The body, too, is worked to the bone.

Time is also exploited. Whereas time was experienced as flowing in traditional society, it runs from point to point in modern society. Time is divided into spatial units so that it can be measured to achieve "the fastest time." In the society of the past, time was structured ritually according to the natural periods of the day, the night, the week, the month, the seasons, the year, and seven-year periods (sabbath year). Nowadays people speak of the technicalization and bureaucratization of time. Time is clocked in and out. The flow of time based on the rites of passage has made way for opening times, office hours, box-office hours, and consulting hours. Time is no longer experienced, but is calculated in advance and programmed. One's lifetime is being replaced by planned time. Time is recorded and compared to a ruler. Time has become space. Time is money (Zijderveld 1983, 129-35).

The needs that give direction to instrumentalism are predominantly determined proceeding from *hedonism,* which is focused on the sensational side of the satisfaction of needs. It is aimed at the acquisition of a feeling of pleasure *(hedone),* happiness, comfort, and satisfaction. This experience of delight can be both of a physical and a psychic nature (Schrey 1977; Heeger 1985). The tie between instrumentalism and hedonism provides us with the need to optimize the experience of delight, or even to maximize it. In its most extreme shape, everything is brought into action, or other things are set aside. A normative orientation underlies this: pleasure is good and pain is bad; more pleasure is better and more pain is worse. The accuracy of the action is measured by the degree to which it contributes to the satisfaction one wishes to achieve (Rawls 1971, 22-27).

Hedonism is closely related to *consumerism,* which relates to the endeavor to use as many products and services as possible, in order to satisfy one's own needs to the maximum. Money functions as a lubricant in this context. With money one can buy the satisfaction of one's own needs, particularly where it concerns our need for lust. If the lust is sufficiently satisfied, then the used product can be thrown away and the service relationship can be broken off until the need to satisfy one's lust announces itself again. Consumerism is not restricted to the market sector, however. It spreads out across other societal sectors too: people consume human relations (disposable relations), organization (disposable organizations), culture (disposable culture) and theories (disposable theories). Here satisfaction is central, and not truth, rightness, or reality. This extends to all of life. Thus, Zijderveld states: "Everyday speech reflects this consumerism. People no longer disagree with a certain statement; they say: 'I don't feel it that way.' Not only edible and drinkable goods are called nice, so are objects (a nice car), people (a nice girl), well-being (How are you doing? I'm doing nicely, thank you), work (a nice job), etc. All are marked with this adjective" (Zijderveld 1983, 149).

Through the influence of the market on individualism, instrumentalism, hedonism, and consumerism, the special attitude that characterizes the calculating citizen arises. The term *market* is thus not taken in an economic sense, but in a sociological sense. We are not dealing with the objective market that exists for raw materials, goods, products and services, capital, and labor. We are dealing with the subjective market, which refers to the experience and attitude of people from which they look at things, situations, other people, and themselves. The sociological term *market* refers to the degree to which people believe that goods, products, or services are available to them in exchange for money. It relates to the degree to which people are aimed at the price they have to pay for the above, and endeavor to reduce it as much as possible. It points to the extent to which people find they are in competition with each other. Proceeding from this description, it is clear that *market* not only refers to economic goods, products, or services but also to political, social, cultural, or even religious ones. They, too, are "for sale" (Weber 1965, 443).

We would like to tie in some other terms with the sociological term *market.* Thus, *marketability* relates to the regularity with which goods in the subjective sense function as market goods according to people's experience (Weber 1980, 43). It forms a kind of measure to trace this regularity. Some goods appear hardly ever or never to function as market goods. Thus people find that light, wind, and rain are free. They are not subject to the laws of the market. Other goods appear to be market goods only to a limited extent. Public toilets are a good example. In some situations one has to pay for them, although it is only a small amount, and in most cases one does not have to pay at all. Yet other goods, like foodstuffs, water, ventilation, and energy, which meet our most vital needs, have a strong marketability. Still others possess an extremely strong marketability. An indication of this is the price of goods that follows the fluctuations in the market, like for instance durable goods, particularly in the strongly urbanized areas.

By means of the term *marketability,* one can also ask the question to what extent the services function as market goods that are provided by cultural institutions like education, spiritual health care, welfare work, etc. This question can also be asked in connection with religion, as we shall see. Moreover, the developments in these areas can be described by means of the term *marketability.* Thus the marketability of education has greatly increased in the last few decades.

Other relevant terms are *market freedom* and *market regulation.* Market freedom involves the degree of autonomy of the participants in the market to set their own price and determine their own competition. Market regulation points to the degree of limitation that regulative organs impose (Weber 1980, 43-44).

Both terms can be applied to religion. The state church entails strong market regulation. It imposes all sorts of restrictions on other religious communities, because of which they come to be in disadvantageous competitive positions. The division of church and state and the neutral stance of the state with regard to religion imply a large degree of market freedom.

(2) The market and the church

This market freedom regarding religion compels us to go into more detail concerning the way in which the church is indeed subject to the laws of the market. Concretely, do the services that the church provides have a low or high marketability? Are they determined by a particular competitive position of the church? These questions can be divided into two dimensions. The first has to do with the relations of the church denominations among themselves (ecumenism). The second points to the relations between the church and nonchurch institutions for welfare and mental health care.

Ecumenism

Two of the most important authors who have approached the relations of the Christian churches among themselves proceeding from market thinking are the sociologists Berger and Luckmann (Berger 1963; Berger & Luckmann 1966). They view the churches as denominations (chapter 2 sub 1). From there they regard the churches as economic entities that are embroiled in a competitive battle. They substantiate this by pointing to the following three phenomena. First, all denominations are aimed at binding the middle class. Further, one can observe financial inflation because of which the financial position of the churches is becoming worrisome. Finally, the church bureaucracy, which is — as can be factually established — on the increase, has to be paid for, and for this there has to be more money.

Against this background the fluctuations in ecumenism can be understood, according to the authors. On the one hand, the denominations are occupied with the formation of a kind of cartel, and in connection with this, with the standardization of their product. This means that the differences between the denominations are less emphasized and that attention is more focused on connectedness and unity. This leads to doctrinal erosion, at least insofar as this concerns differences between the churches. Catholicism is not what it was, at least with regard to Calvinism, and the reverse also applies, according to the authors. On the other hand, this erosion of denominational identity implies a deterioration of the market position of the churches, which depends upon market specificity. The competition in the marketplace demands that one have one's own church profile with respect to the other churches (denominational image), which is founded in a particular church doctrine (denominational ideology).

The most striking example of the market sensitivity of ecumenism is the recent development in the relations between the Orthodox churches in Russia and the Ukraine and the Catholic Church. During the European synod of bishops on evangelization, which was held in Rome in the fall of 1991, the representatives of the Orthodox churches were deliberately absent, though they had been explicitly invited. The reason was the advantage the Catholic Church had taken of the confused situation after the collapse of the Soviet Union in 1991, in the eyes of the Orthodox churches. They accused the Catholic Church of unfair competition or, in ecclesial terms, proselytism — in plain English, the winning of souls.

Welfare and mental health care

Until a number of decades ago, the whole area of the meaning and value of life belonged to the natural competency of the churches. The question of meaning was answered proceeding from the faith, and that of value from ethics. The treatment of problems and disorders in this field was deemed to belong to the profession of the minister or the specialized minister.

Nowadays things are different. One finds, to an increasing extent, that workers in institutions for welfare and mental health care are occupied in their professional practice with the client's sense of the meaning and value of life. Sometimes it is even said that counselors who hesitate, or display resistance or discomfort, give expression to defective competency. They are guilty of counter-transference, thinking that the client wants nothing to do with an approach that proceeds from the question of meaning. Workers are thus shown a task that they have to fulfill objectively according to this viewpoint. There are also workers in these institutions who take up this task most actively, in contrast with the past.

What are the causes of this? It may be that the cultural climate, in which the belief in the psychologically supported regulation of behavior is fading, leads them to this. Perhaps the disappointing attempts to measure the effects of behaviorally focused psychotherapy have led to disillusionment in some regarding the techniques in question. It is also possible that, in a positive sense, people have reached the conclusion that in mental health care, you also have to deal with matters that cannot be expressed in terms of measurable effects. We are dealing with matters that surpass this (Kuilman & Uleyn 1986).

In some institutions for mental health care, besides ordinary psychotherapists, there are special professionals who look after spiritual care. It is made quite clear that they are not theologians or ministers. Their task is described as follows: "Spiritual care is aimed at the guidance of people with questions and problems concerning life, which are approached from and placed in the philosophical frameworks of the client and counselor, and which are discussed with an aim to support and stimulate the spiritual functioning of the client" (Mooren 1989, 65-66).

However one looks at this, it is certain that it places the churches in a competitive position with regard to these institutions. In a great many institutions where ministers have been appointed besides therapists and spiritual counselors, as in hospitals, or judicial and military institutions, one can observe traces of a kind of competition.

This becomes even more tangible, the more that secularization and de-ecclesialization increase (chapter 9 and 17). To put it in market terms, the weaker the demand, the more consumption drops. This may be caused by the insecurity people have about what one may expect from the church and whether that which the church provides meets the demands people have. The possible discrepancy between supply and demand can be clarified by means of an example. From research it appears that Protestant youths in Baden-Wuertenburg entertain four specific needs with regard to the Christian faith, but at the same time they are not sure whether this faith meets these needs. Thus they hope that the Christian faith will offer support in situations of suffering that occur in everyday life (theme of theodicy); that it offers an explanation as to the meaning of the existence of the world as a whole (theme of creation); that it provides access to an authentic life with God (theme of God); and that the church represents the faith in a credible fashion (ecclesiological theme). As we mentioned, these themes are connected to doubts at the same time. The theme of theodicy appears to be connected to experiences of disappointment; the theme of creation to feelings of insecurity because of the explanatory power of the "competitive" theory of evolution; the theme of God to doubts because of the danger of religious projection and illusion; the theme of ecclesiology to indifferentism, scepticism, and even cynicism (Nipkow 1988). This discrepancy between supply and demand makes the market position and competitive position of the church weaker.

(3) The church and the market

How can the marketability of the church be judged? There are theologians who believe that market thinking can contribute to the clarification of the functioning of the local church. In that context, people see it as a producer and supplier of religious services that are provided by paid people (priests, deacons, and pastoral workers). On the consumer side, we find members of the church, including marginal members, who make use of the services. Production and consumption are determined by the balance of supply and demand. However, according to this approach, there is a group among the members of the church that is not only part of the consumer side but also provides services even though it does its work without remuneration, literally "pro Deo"; namely, the church and pastoral volunteers. They strive after the growth of the market of the local church, which is expressed in a growing interest, a rising turnover of services, and an increase in financial means (Van Kessel 1985). From a sociological viewpoint, Berger added the notion that the central position that the volunteers hold in the local church can be understood proceeding from the principle of the market. The "volunteer church" is then assumed to be an ecclesial and theological ideologization of the need for binding regular and true customers (Berger 1967).

The fact that all this is not just idle speculation, but answers the concrete experiences of ministers in practice, becomes clear from the following quotation: "For however imperishable the value and truth of the Gospel may be, employers of ministers with a well-organized fixed appointment expect them to be sensitive to signals in the presentation of the Gospel, which stem from collections and financial contributions concerning the quality, or say market value of their pastoral work. In our market society such signals are of greater structural importance than all sorts of doctrinal magisterial or theological stipulations and criteria concerning ministerial work. In conferences with ministers, I have often felt this contradiction" (Van Kessel 1985, 215). In other words, ministers are concerned about the extent to which they may attune the presentation of their religious convictions (which they themselves hold to be true, valuable, and real) to the needs of the people. Concretely, this means attuned to what people want to hear with regard to matters like unemployment, foreign laborers, the third world, nuclear armament, marriage, sexuality, abortion, suicide, euthanasia, etc. If they do not do this, or do it too little, then this would be noticeable in the fluctuations in the financial streams in the local church, that is to say, fluctuations in the market. We deliberately formulated it thus: "would be noticeable." We are not sure since empirical research from theology has unfortunately not yet been carried out.

Objections can be raised to the market approach to the church. We refer here to two points of possible criticism that can lead to a certain relativization of the market approach. The first has to do with the presupposition that the term *market* covers the whole of the local church. Nothing is further from the truth. The insight that runs through this book as a guide is that the local church can be viewed under the aspect of not one but several social codes: association, people, movement, group, network, community, and organization. One would be quite right in adding "market." This term does indeed shed light on aspects of the church that would otherwise remain covered. However, we would be overshooting our mark by approaching the church from the standpoint of the market only. This would clash with the principle of complementarity (Introduction).

This can be clarified by proceeding from the functionalistic perspective that was developed by Luhmann. The church appears to function at three different levels: the macro, meso, and micro levels. At the macro level the church maintains relations with other societal institutions, for example, institutions for welfare and mental health care. In this field the church functions like a company aimed at the market, which guards and protects its competitive position. The meso level involves the church itself and the way in which it functions *ad intra*. In this area it works like an organization, with management, paid staff members, volunteers, ordinary members, buildings, and capital.

The micro level refers to face-to-face interaction in small social contexts in the various sectors: pastoral care, catechetics, liturgy, proclamation, and diacony. At this level the church functions as a group. Luhmann is of the opinion that the macro, meso, and micro levels have to be sharply divided, including the social codes that adhere to them (market, organization, and group). The reason is that the processes on the one level certainly do not always act upon those on the other level. The functioning of the church that is aimed at competition at the level of the market has no influence on the affective formation of relations at the micro level of the group, at least not immediately and not directly (Luhmann 1972; Scholten 1991).

The second point of criticism concerns the macro level of the market itself, in which the church finds itself among other societal institutions. Formulating it as sharply as possible: Is it true that the market always completely behaves like a market? Is it true that companies and factories (preeminent market-oriented organizations) allow themselves to be entirely determined by the laws of the market? The answer is no. It is an empirical fact that companies are not entirely controlled by competition: there is no perfect competition. Companies often appear to be satisfied with the second-best option. Competition is not the be-all and end-all in trade and industry. The only thing one can say is that there is more or less competition in companies, and therefore more or less market presence. *Market* is a complex term. One has to conceive of it in terms of a continuum. The two extremes are the absolute market and the nonmarket, with numerous intermediate types.

The statement that the absolute market and the nonmarket do not occur and the second best option does, lies in the market's being embedded in society. The market may exert a great influence on society, but it does not cover all of society. It is located within society. It is surrounded by political, social, and cultural contexts. That is why the market is a bound and encapsulated market, an embedded market, as Etzioni convincingly describes it (1988, 204). Absolute competition would lead to absolute conflict of all against all. It would work like a self-destruct mechanism, leading to a catch-as-catch-can war, which would ruin all of society. That is why the market is a restricted and delimited market (Etzioni 1988, 205).

Further, there are all sorts of social and affective ties between the actors on the market. What does this mean for the contract that they close? Earlier we stated that the contract is a way to secure one's own interests by creating an advantageous balance between costs and benefits. However, besides this, we must have an eye for what is called the precontractual base of the contract. This is formed of the mutual connections that are not an object of negotiation, but that simply exist and without which the contract would never come about. Naturally, these ties are dictated by personal interest in the long run. However, they appear to bind people, even if they entail "costs" for the person in question in the short or long run (Etzioni 1988, 210). Here one could also speak of the pre-market structure of the market.

All this means that we have to regard the relationship between the church and the market from a differentiated perspective. On the one hand, the church is influenced by the laws of the market. It possesses a certain marketability. The terms *market regulation* and *market freedom* (competition) are applicable to the church. It is influenced by the mechanisms of supply and demand. On the other hand, however, the church does not merge into its marketability. It also bears the features of a people, movement, group, and community with it. Besides, the market itself is not exclusively a market. It is also determined by social and affective relations of connectedness. That is why the market is both a danger and a challenge to the church.

Chapter 22

The Endeavor for Service Quality

In the last chapter we discussed the societal context of the core function of management: the process of calculation. We paid attention to the marketability of the church, seeing to what extent the market exerts an influence on it. In addition, we noted that the church guards its market position with respect to other denominations and religions and other institutions for welfare and mental health care. The mechanisms of supply and demand do not pass by the church. At the same time, however, we established that the church is not just a company. It is also a people, movement, group, network, and community. Besides, insofar as it belongs to the market as a company, it is not completely determined by the market. We discussed the pre-market structure of the market. Social and even affective connectedness precede action and negotiation on the market (chapter 21).

These dialectics in marketability (the church is and is not bound to the market) will be focused upon the endeavor for service quality in the church, especially in the following sectors: pastoral care, catechetics, liturgy, proclamation, and diacony. In the endeavor for service quality, what is important is what quality is, and from which angle it is approached. Insofar as it is determined by the endeavor to satisfy the needs of the users of the service, it is characterized by marketability. However, the question is, of course, how this relates to the aim of service in the church, which lies in the vision and mission of the church. More exactly, we wish to know whether the ecclesiological aim is superordinate or subordinate to the user orientation that is implied in marketability.

In this chapter we will discuss the following questions: (1) What does the quality of pastoral service entail, and (2) How can this quality be stimulated in an ecclesiologically justifiable manner?

(1) Service quality

In order to gain clarity concerning the term *service quality,* there is no better method than to discuss the terms *service* and *quality* themselves. Here we would like to recall the epistemological principle that we discussed earlier (Introduction). If we apply this principle to the present problem, this means that ecclesial and pastoral work is not service, but it can be *viewed* as service. Thus the minister is not a renderer of service, but he can be viewed as such. It is especially important to emphasize this in connection with the liturgy. The wish to reduce the liturgy to the rendering of service would do it no justice, especially if we consider its ritual, religious-communicative character, coupled with the ability to contribute to community formation and societal transformation. We can approach the liturgy as service, in this case the rendering of service, but with this only one aspect is brought to the surface.

Service

Earlier we discussed the transition from the preindustrial to the industrial and postindustrial society (chapter 13 sub 1). This was characterized by changes in the shares of the professional population in the agrarian sector, the industrial sector, and the service sector. Within the preindustrial society, the greater number of people worked in agriculture (primary sector); and within the industrial society, in the industrial sector (secondary sector). Within the postindustrial society, the greater number work in the service sector (tertiary sector). Already at the end of the last century, the number of workers active in the tertiary sector was larger than in the other two in the Netherlands. In 1986 it was even as much as 66%. The service sector encompasses both profit and nonprofit organizations, which are also distinguished as the tertiary and quartiary sectors. The church can be viewed as a nonprofit organization.

The difference between profit and nonprofit organizations is not easy to determine. Profit organizations are often seen as being aimed at profit, and nonprofit organizations as being not aimed at profit. However, on the one hand there are profit organizations that strive after profit, but not in order to make a profit but to ensure their continuance, their survival. This can be due to the societal appreciation they receive — for instance, the high-grade product they manufacture, the employment they stimulate, etc. On the other hand, there are nonprofit organizations that actually make a profit. Universities are an example of this. Therefore it is better not to depart from a direct contrast, but from a variety of accents in the aims of the organizations. This different emphasis in purpose can be expressed with the terms *for-profit* and not-for-profit. It makes a difference whether an organization is for-profit or not-for-profit (Kapteyn 1989, 249-51). The church and the services it renders can be regarded as not-for-profit.

What is a service? It is not simple to answer this question, especially if one involves the term *goods* (product). Often the terms *goods* and *services* are mentioned in one breath. In literature one can find the following description of service: "An action with which someone is of use to someone else — stimulates his interest — by enlarging his personal well-being or through the improvement of a property" (Neijzen & Trompetter 1991, 69). If one leaves out the things that are not applicable to the church (the improvement of property), there are still a number of problems. For what is the meaning of the remaining terms used in the definition: *use, interest, personal, well-being,* and *enlarging?* Why do we speak of "someone" as an individual? And what does it mean to stimulate someone's own interest by "enlarging his personal well-being"? Let us now go into these questions in more detail.

Earlier we placed the terms *use* and *interest* in the framework of the process of utilization. We mentioned the necessity of placing these terms in a normative frame of reference. This was because use and interest imply very different meanings of value depending on whether they stem from the desire of someone to have more income, or from the cry of the poor at the bottom of society for food and work. The same applies to the term *well-being.* Someone's endeavor at self-development is in stark contrast to the need for basic education in the deprived districts and slums. In other words, the terms *use, interest,* and *well-being* have been unjustly stripped of their normative implications in their descriptions; they are incorrectly used free of value (chapter 17 sub 3).

There is something else that strikes us in the description: the exclusive use of the word *personal.* Is it personal well-being only that falls under the heading "service," and is societal well-being left out? The interconnectedness of humankind in societal relations remains hidden from view because of this. The insight that well-being is determined through a combination of personal and societal factors is neglected. This formulation evokes the suspicion that it is determined by the kind of individualism that we described earlier (chapter 21 sub 1) in which the autonomy of the individual and his needs is central.

As far as the term *enlarging* is concerned, it contains a quantitative connotation, as if well-being could be extended in a quantitive sense. If the term *enlarging* could be conceived of in a qualitative sense too, then the objection would fall away. Besides that, the term requires supplementation, for there are enough situations one can think of, where one renders someone else a service by performing an action that is useful to him or stimulates his interest — still following the description — without being able to speak of the enlarging of well-being. Rather, it is the consolidation of well-being, or the reduction of the loss of well-being. In other words, an optimism about growth or belief in progress underlies the definition of the term *service.* It does not take the fundamental contingency of human existence — its limitedness, death, and guilt — into account (Van der Ven 1991d, 166-71). That is why a neutral term like *the stimulation of well-being* is more suitable. Stimulation is also applicable if the situation concerns the reduction of a loss.

In the description above, there is mention of an individual. This is an unnecessary restriction that has to do perhaps with the aforementioned individualism. For there are services performed for the benefit of dyads, triads, smaller or larger groups, communities, and collectives. That is why it is better to replace "someone" with "persons and groups."

Then we are left with the question of what it means to serve someone's interest by enlarging his well-being. In this formulation, what is implied is that well-being is a means for the realization of interests. This brings up the issue of instrumentalism, which we described above as an element of calculation (chapter 21 sub 1). In an anthropology inspired by the gospel, however, the perspective has to be turned around: the stimulation of well-being by serving people's interests. In such a perspective, one need not promote every (supposed or subjective) interest, but only the interest that contributes to the well-being of the person or persons in question.

In short, it is of great importance to take a critical look at the descriptions of "service" that occur in the literature. In the formulation quoted above, the terms *use, interest,* and *well-being* are used free of value. However, it is only an illusion that they are free of value. We have brought to light some indications for the normative frame of reference that is implicit in the description. The exclusive use of the word *personal* points to individualism, as well as being aimed at the individual. The exclusive use of the word *enlarging* refers to a belief in progress. The means/aims relationship between well-being and personal interest refers to instrumentalism. In other words, the terms *use, interest,* and *well-being,* which seem to be used free of value, can only be understood from the normative frame of reference of this individualism, instrumentalism, and belief in progress.

For these reasons, we have to supplement and correct this description, at least if we want to use the term *service* for the pastoral work of the church. This supplemental correction has to occur proceeding from the normative frame of reference of the gospel, from which the vision and mission of the church are given shape (chapters 11 and 12). Furthermore, it is important — as will appear — to give expression to the communicative character of the service. It is precisely this communicative character that distinguishes a service from a good (product). Finally, something can be dropped from the above description. It is not useful to make coordinative use of "use" and "interest." That is why one of the two can be scrapped.

Our description — which is focused on work in the church — is as follows: *service is a communicative action with which one serves the interests of persons and groups, with an eye to the stimulation of their personal and societal well-being in the perspective of the gospel.* Now the rendering of service can be viewed as the performing of this service.

As we have already said, services are often mentioned in one breath with goods or products. That is why it makes sense to dwell upon the relations between the two. Furthermore, there are authors who say that the church should sell its product better to the people. This product is believed to be made up of representations of God, images of Jesus, metaphors of the church community, consolation, help, happiness, and trust (Fauconnier 1987, 14). If one sees things like this, then how does the product distinguish itself from the service? Or are we just dealing with colloquial or untidy use of the language?

The differences between product and service can be brought back to two principles: the tangibility of the product, and the intangibility of the service; the divisibility of production and consumption with regard to the product, and their indivisibility with regard to the service. All this can be clarified further. Tangibility/intangibility is an important point of difference. A product can be felt, seen, heard, and touched. This is not the case for a service. That is why the quality of a service is more difficult to determine. Because services are intangible, they cannot be stored and are not subject to stock like products are. They cannot be demonstrated as products can be. With services there is no transfer of property, and they cannot be transferred secondhand. After the service has been rendered, nothing tangible is left; it cannot be used at a later date.

Divisibility/indivisibility is also an important point of difference. The production and consumption of a service occur at the same time; the production does not precede the consumption, as in the case of a product. Moreover, in a service, the consumer also produces; his share is necessary for the realization of the service, unlike for the product. That is why people speak of the *prosumer* in a service. In its turn, this participation in the realization of service means that one can speak of a communicative interaction process between the renderer and user of the service. This does not necessarily apply to the buyer and seller of a product: it can be ordered and delivered. In such a case, one can speak of (postal, telegraphic, and electronic) interaction, but not of communication. Through the communicative interaction process that characterizes the rendering of service, one can also speak of the feedback of the user to the renderer of service. Finally, a service is bound to its locality; it cannot be transported as a product can be (Kapteyn 1989, 254-56; Neijzen & Trompetter 1991, 70-75).

In application to the church, we can say that representations of God, images of Jesus, metaphors of the church community, happiness, and trust are not products. One should rather see them as convictions, views, stories, values, and attitudes that are stored in the culture and cultural tradition of Christianity. They only gain significance within religious communication (chapter 3). They do not function like products that are delivered, but as communicative vehicles for the disclosing of meaning, which the pastoral work is aimed at as a service.

Quality

We are concerned with the quality of service in the church, or the pastoral service respectively. The question of what this quality implies is important in this context. Certainly wishing to turn next to the endeavor for quality, having only a vague notion of what quality is, is not enough.

Several criteria are used to determine the meaning of the term *quality.* The five criteria most frequently mentioned in the literature are given here, albeit that their names are somewhat freely interpreted. The first is the *transcendent criterion,* in which quality is approached from the question of to what extent the product or service meets a certain ideal image, conviction, or value. Thus the Rolls Royce meets the ideal of the perfect car as the transcendent criterion. Naturally, "transcendent" has to be understood in a formal sense in accordance with the literature. It refers to that which surpasses the factual and that by which it is measured. The second is the *technical criterion,* in which the quality is measured by norms of soundness in technical production and realization. The third is the criterion of *content,* in which the quality is determined by means of features the product of service has to have in an objective sense. The fourth is the *user criterion,* in which the quality depends on the question to what extent the needs of the user are satisfied and how content the user is. The fifth is the *economic criterion,* in which the quality is involved with the question of whether the value and the price of the service correspond to each other in the experience of the user (Neijzen & Trompetter 1991, 28).

In principle all five criteria are relevant for the quality of the service in the church, with the exception of the last: the economic criterion. The reason is not that little money circulates in the church. On the contrary, further along we shall see that the church is characterized to a large extent by incoming and outgoing financial streams (chapter 24). However, in principle, one does not have to pay for the service that takes place in the church: it is free. This does not mean to say that a voluntary contribution does not have to be requested, but the services can be had for free. This applies to the sectors of pastoral care, catechetics, proclamation, and diacony. For liturgy there are stipends for special happenings. Participation, however, in the weekend or weekly liturgy of the Eucharist is free, just as that in the sacraments of baptism, confirmation, confession, anointing of the sick, and ordination to the priesthood. That is why we leave aside the economic criterion, which involves the relationship between the value and the price of the service.

The prioritization of the four remaining criteria with respect to each other (transcendent, technical, content, and user) is of decisive importance for what people understand by quality. At present there is a tendency to give the user criterion (the needs and experiences of the user) the highest rank. The other criteria become subordinate to it or are left unmentioned. When quality is identical to being aimed at the user, one can arrive at statements like: "In determining the norm for the quality of a service, the deliverer has to take care of a perfect attunement to that which the client requires." In other words "quality is fitness for use" (Kerklaan & Kingma 1991, 79). Aiming at the user is especially dominant in service-rendering profit organizations. In the nonprofit organizations, the emphasis can sooner be placed on the quality of service from normative viewpoints like convictions, ideals, values, and objective aims (Kapteyn 1989, 262-65).

If we use the term *quality* in the frame of pastoral service, we do not just follow the trend of being aimed at the user. This would conflict with the religious codes from which we described the identity of the church. It would also be in conflict with the plea to place the needs and interests from which people turn to the church in the normative frame of reference of the solidarity of the gospel (chapter 17 sub 3). This does not mean that the user criterion is not important, but it is not the only criterion, and it is not the first.

The highest priority has to be given to the transcendent criterion. In a formal sense, transcendent means, as we have said, that it surpasses all factuality and that all factuality is judged by it. If one tries this out on the church, one can reach no other conclusion than that pastoral service is eventually measured by the ideals, convictions, and values that lie in the vision and mission of the church: the church as the people of God, Jesus movement, body of Christ, building of the Spirit, and church of the poor. The highest priority is not being aimed at the user but at the gospel. It regulates the whole of the service.

The other criteria are of importance to the extent that they can be ordered from the highest criterion. To start with, let us take a look at the technical criterion, which involves the technical abilities in the sectors of pastoral care, catechetics, liturgy, proclamation, and diacony (chapter 23 sub 1). Next, the criterion of content involves the theological knowledge of content and insights that are implied in the service in these sectors (chapter 23 sub 1). The technical and content criteria fulfill conditional functions in the pastoral service. In other words, one can speak of pastoral service only if the technical and content criteria are met. They form the bottom line. Without the effective input of technical and content know-how there is no pastoral service. Finally, the user criterion fulfills an indicative function. It indicates what the pastor has to pay attention to in the communicative interaction: how does the service meet the requirements of the user insofar as that is possible and desirable?

In short, the transcendent criterion has the highest priority. It determines the course taken. It has a regulative character. The technical and content criteria are of a conditional nature. The user criterion fulfills an indicative function. It indicates the mode of communicative interaction in the pastoral service.

(2) The striving for quality of pastoral service

It is important to strive for the promotion of quality in the church, in this case, the pastoral service. The first question we asked ourselves is, Who is it meant for? Which target group or groups have we in mind? To whose benefit is the care for quality? After that, we will present a model in which the most prominent elements of which this this care is made up will be combined with each other: the pastoral service quality model. Finally, we will give some suggestions as to its execution.

Target groups

One could say that the church need not ask the question concerning target groups because its message is universal. The service, therefore, has to be of the highest quality for all persons and groups. In the religious codes (people of God, Jesus movement, body of Christ, building of the Spirit, church of the poor) one finds an all-encompassing perspective. Yet we cannot pass over the choice of target groups. In practice, the church nevertheless makes a choice. Therefore it is better to make this actual choice explicit and hold it to account.

The first thing that has to happen is to describe the entire population that belongs to the environment of the local church. Earlier, in our discussion of social stratification, we gave the most prominent factors by means of which this can be done. To these we can add: sex, age, kind of relation, resident children, length of residence, education, profession, work, country of origin, political orientation, localism, lifestyle, cultural attitude, religious orientation, church participation, and pastoral participation.

The next step is the division of this population into segments. This is done by combining the factors we just mentioned. Thus one can combine young age, low education, and extended unemployment to determine the segment of the marginal group of youths that can be of importance for youth pastoral care. One can combine age, terminated relations (divorce), and unemployment to determine the segment of divorced women without jobs. The division into segments has to be relevant from the viewpoint of the service of the church, of course.

Once one has set up a (greater or smaller) number of segments, one can turn to the allocation of certain segments to target groups. The term *target group* does not mean that one excludes other segments, but that one gives priority to one or more other segments. Here there are two possibilities: the concentrated or the differentiated choice of target groups. With the concentrated choice, one gives priority to one target group; and with the differentiated choice, to two or more groups.

The concentrated choice occurs proceeding from their being held accountable in an ecclesiological sense. One criterion could be the development of the community of the church. Another could be church of the poor. If one departs from the development of the community, one could, hypothetically, make a choice for the group that can support the church from a relatively strong attitude of localism (chapter 17 sub 2). If one departs from the church of the poor, one could focus one's choice on the group of people who belong to the lower class, who are young, poorly educated, and have been unemployed for a long time.

The differentiated choice is not focused on one but on two or more groups. This method is often applied in the church, albeit in a special manner. That is to say, in many parishes and communities the aim is at the whole of the population (first priority); however, within this, the church is specially aimed at a few subpopulations (second, third, and fourth priorities). The most important principles for division used (consciously or unconsciously) in determining these second, third, and fourth priorities are social-economic status, age, and type of relations (e.g., families with children). An example of social-economic status as a principle for division is the following. There are churches that organize a liturgical service in community centers for the inhabitants of a particular deprived district (old districts, industrial districts, railway districts, or red-light districts), besides the celebrations for everyone in the ordinary church building. An example of the age-bound principle is the development of special liturgical celebrations and catechetics programs for different age-groups, such as children, youth, young adults, the middle-aged, and the elderly (Kotler 1975, 109). An example of the type of relations as a principle of division is the system of children's services, extra children's services, youth services, and family celebrations. Often a local church applies the three principles mentioned in a combined form. Besides this or instead of this, other principles of division, such as sex, degree of church participation, etc. can be used.

We do not wish to and cannot give further indications as to the choice the local church has to make. The diversity is too great for this. The only thing we would like to emphasize is that the three steps mentioned (description of the population, division in segments, and choice of target groups) has to be done carefully enough to be able to account for it from an ecclesiological point of view. We would like to reiterate that we are not dealing with exclusion but with prioritization. The attention for the whole of the population is not done away with.

Pastoral service quality model

Once the choice for the target groups has taken place, quality care can be undertaken. Quality care is aimed at service to the target groups in question. In order to clarify this, we will make use of the *service quality model,* albeit in a more critical fashion, as will appear. In this model, the congruity or incongruity between the performance of the renderer of service and the needs of the user fulfills a central role. Its point of departure is that the quality is high if there are little or no gaps between the needs and the service. Quality is low if there are many gaps. The model is exclusively aimed at the user.

In order to be able to apply this model to pastoral service, we

FIGURE 22.1 Pastoral service quality model

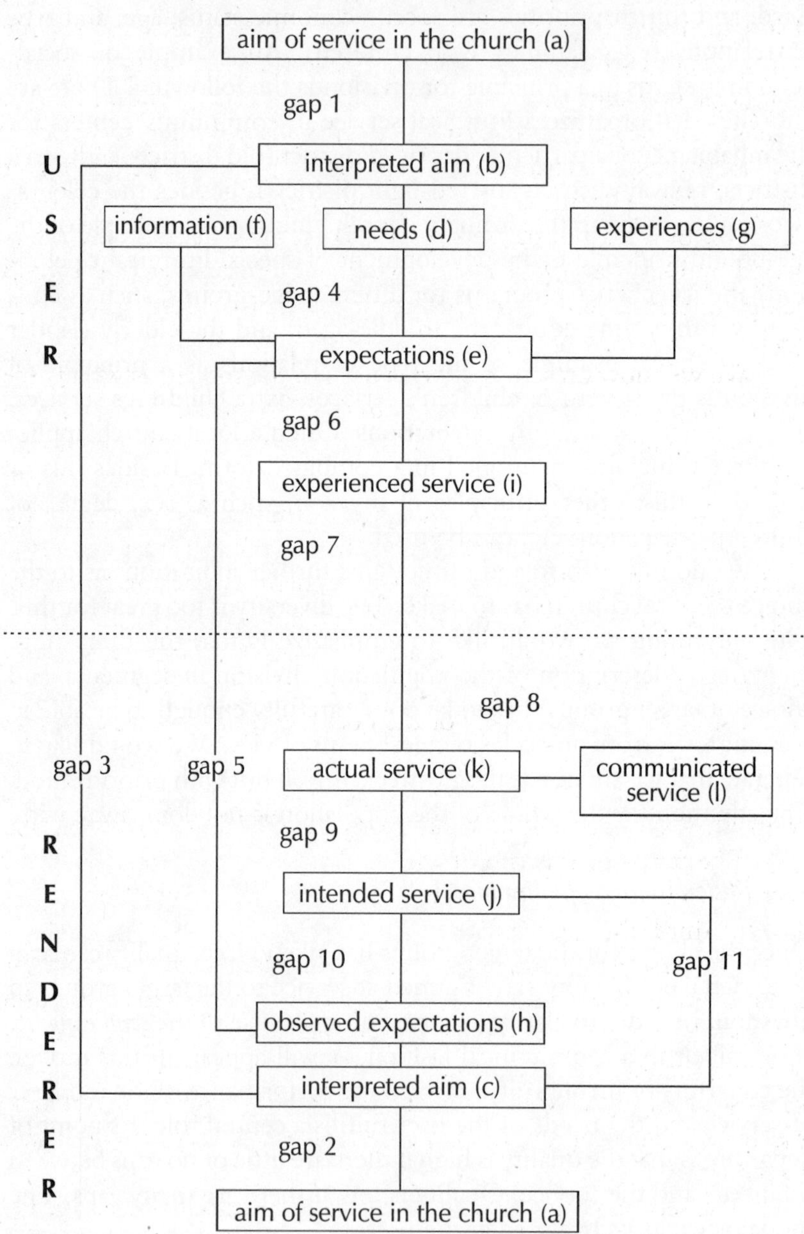

have to aim it at the transcendent criterion of the gospel that we mentioned above, and supplement it from there. We shall, therefore, distinguish two criteria in the use of the service quality model: the transcendent and the user criteria. That is why we define it as the *pastoral service quality model.* The two remaining criteria (technical and content) are set aside. They will be brought up when we discuss pastoral professionalization in the context of personnel development (chapter 23). The model is shown in figure 22.1, as it has been designed by Parasuraman et al. (1985), complemented and interpreted by Dijkstra (1989) and Neijzen and Trompetter (1991), and being supplemented proceeding from the transcendent criterion as well.

We will now present the terms used in the model, as well as the relationships between the terms. These relationships are shown in terms of possible gaps. The model is split in two by a dotted line: the upper half relates to the user; the lower half relates to the renderer of service. What envelops both, however, is the context in which the service takes place: the church. That is why the transcendent criterion is already involved. It lies in the transcendent aim of the service of the church. The model makes two assumptions: first, that this aim is formulated in terms of the vision and mission of the church (community of believers, people of God, Jesus movement, body of Christ, building of the Spirit, church of the poor); and second, that this aim is determined by the organs of authority (pastoral team, pastoral group of clergy and laity, finance council, pastoral council, and volunteer council). We conceive of it, therefore, as the officially determined aim.

The terms in this model can be divided into three groups: the first group involves the aim; the second, the needs and expectations; and the third, the service itself.

The first group encompasses the aim of the service (a) and the interpretation of the aim; in short: the aim as interpreted by the user (b) and the renderer of service (c). In the case of the user, one can speak of incongruity between aim and interpreted aim (gap 1). This can also apply to the renderer of service (gap 2). Further, there can be discrepancy between the user and the renderer of service with regard to the interpreted aim (gap 3).

The second group refers to needs and expectations (d, e, f, g, and h). Proceeding from the interpreted aim, the user turns to the church for certain needs (d). He cherishes certain expectations with regard to this (e). These are supported by information he has received from others (f) and by his own past experiences (g). In turn, the renderer of service believes he or she knows these expectations or has observed them — in short: the observed expectations (h). A possible gap exists in the relation between the needs (d) and expectations (e) of the user. It is possible that the user expects the church to satisfy only a part of his needs (gap 4). The relationship between the expectations of the user (e) and the observed expectations of the renderer of service (h) is important also. There, too, a discrepancy can occur (gap 5).

The third group involves the service itself: the service experienced by the user (i), the service intended by the renderer of service (j), the actual service rendered (k), and the communication about the service by the renderer or by others in his name — in short: the communicated service (l). All kinds of discrepancies can occur: between the expectations and the service experienced (gap 6), between the experienced and the actual service (gap 7), between the actual and the communicated service (gap 8), between the actual and the intended service (gap 9), between the intended service and the observed expectations (gap 10), and between the intended service and the interpreted aim (gap 11).

Proceeding from a service quality model aimed at the user only, quality care is made up of the reduction of the number and depth of the gaps or, better still, the filling in of the gaps. In this approach, there should be no gaps; they hinder the quality. However, we have made the user criterion subordinate to the transcendent criterion. That is why we introduced the aim of the service (a) and the interpreted aims (b) and (c) into the model. They are lacking from the service quality model. This means that not all gaps may be filled in, at least not if we proceed from the transcendent criterion. There may be some gaps that have to stay if the church is to do justice to its own vision and mission.

Which gaps cannot be filled in and why they cannot be, is a question of ecclesiological choice and responsibility. Let us give an example by means of figure 22.1. One day a resident of a certain district went to the consulting hour of the minister on call, proceeding from a certain interpretation (b) of the aim of pastoral service (a). He did this because he felt the need to join a group that looked for ways to gain access to the religious depths of the human existence (d). He had heard from friends of his that such groups are given guidance by the church (f). Because of this, his memory was activated and he recalled the positive experiences he had in a certain period, with a kind of pastoral group work in a university church (g). He now turned to the minister in the expectation that he would be offered a place in a religious encounter group (e). The minister responded positively to his request. He offered him the opportunity to participate in a group in which a certain book was being read under his guidance, *The Art of Loving* by Erich Fromm. The district resident agreed to this. It seemed to be just the thing for him (l). What the minister did, however, during the group meetings that followed, was to place what had been read in a deductive-theological frame of reference, from which Fromm could be critically evaluated (k). The district resident soon found that his expectation (e) and the experiences he gained in the group of this minister (i) did not fit. He decided to talk to the minister about this. He reached the conclusion that he had not been at fault in observing the direction in which the minister was guiding the group discussions (there was no gap 7). However, this was not in accordance with what he had expected. One could speak of a certain discrepancy (gap 6). The minister, however, did not allow himself to be moved. He explained that the way in which he gave guidance to the group about Fromm (k) stemmed from the specific aim he was trying to achieve with this group (j). This was the achievement of a religious-critical evaluation of Fromm's theory of love proceeding from the absolute-transcendent revelation of God. In the conversation they were able to establish that the expectations the district resident had (e) had been incorrectly observed by the minister (h). The district resident had expected to find an open attitude with religion as a quest in the group. The minister, however, thought that the district resident was in search of religious certainty, or religion as an end. Thus, it appeared there was another discrepancy (gap 5). Moreover, it appeared that the first conversation between the minister and the district resident had created an image of the group meetings that differed from the meetings themselves. There was therefore a third discrepancy (gap 8). All of this did not change the minister's mind. He stuck to his aim (j). Next, he based this on the general aim of ecclesial and pastoral work as he saw it (c). In questioning, however, it appeared that the interpreted aim of the minister (c) was not in accordance with the aim of pastoral work, as this had been determined by the organs of authority in his church (a). Therefore, one could speak of a fourth discrepancy (gap 2). However, a decision was made not to put further pressure on the relations between the minister and the organs of authority, which were already under a lot of stress because of other matters. As a consequence, the minister could stick to his point of view in his conversation with the district resident, which is what he did. The district resident took leave of him in disappointment and decided to turn elsewhere for having his needs satisfied.

We cannot tell from this example from which theology this minister operated. It could easily have been Catholic neoscholastic or Protestant dialectical theology. Proceeding from neoscholastic theology, one could have given ample space to a reflection on the nature of human love. But it would nevertheless have to be raised and elevated in a supernatural sense to divine love. Proceeding from this theology, Fromm would have to be supplemented in an absolute-transcendent sense. Proceeding from the dialectical theology, Fromm's theory would have to be placed under Jesus' cross and judgment and be opened up in the direction of the selfless, vicarious love. In addition, Fromm's vision would have to be corrected in an absolute-transcendent sense. Neoscholastic theology would lack the necessary supplement with Fromm alone, and dialectical theology would lack the necessary correction. These are two possible reasons why the minister did not give way and could not satisfy himself with the religion-as-quest approach in a religious encounter group, and made a choice for the religion-as-end approach (Batson & Ventis 1982). On the basis of these reasons, he made the decision not to adapt to the needs and expectations of the district resident. He did not fill in the gaps.

It becomes clear from this example that such a decision does not just involve a single part of the model (figure 22.1). It appeared that there were discrepancies between expectations (e) and the service experienced (i), between expectations (e) and observed expectations (h), between the actual service (k) and the communicated service (l), and between the interpreted aim of the minister (c) and the official aim of the church authorities (a) — four discrepancies in all (gaps 6, 5, 8, and 2). From this description, it appears that making a theological judgment not to fill in the gaps has far-reaching consequences.

Now we will consider this example further and reflect on it. This will be done from the distinction we made earlier in the three pastoral strategies: the deductive, inductive, and reductive strategies (chapter 9 sub 2). The neoscholastical and dialectical theologies both make use of the deductive strategy, in which they depart from the revelation of God, who is communicated from above *(senkrecht von oben)*. God reveals himself directly (dialectical theology) or indirectly through the *depositum fidei* that was entrusted to the doctrinal authority of the church (neoscholastic theology). Both are characterized by the image of God as absolute-transcendent and of humanity as heteronomous (Berger 1979). The reductive strategy is characterized by the elimination of any kind of transcendent perspective. The inductive strategy, however, is determined by the perspective of God as immanent-transcendent and of humanity as (relatively) autonomous. The text/context correlation is central in this approach (chapter 16 sub 2). In this one goes in search of the similarities and differences in the structure of texts from tradition and from the present situation, proceeding from both their contexts. The texts are mutually criticized. Thus, not only is the present criticized by the past, but the past is criticized by the present. The one-way traffic between tradition and situation that is characteristic of the deductive strategy is replaced by two-way traffic. A critical exchange between present and past takes place (Tracy 1981; 1989). The inductive-theological strategy is to be preferred to the deductive strategy because of the hermeneutical-correlational approach. In this religion sooner functions as a quest than as an end.

What does this mean for the pastoral service quality model? The transcendent criterion that is expressed in the aim of the service is of a regulative nature, we said. It is not exclusive but guiding; not eliminating but critical-orienting. It orders the pastoral service from an inductive-theological perspective rather than from a deductive one. It has to be handled in a pastorally prudent fashion. "Prudent" does not mean cautious here, but wise and intelligent, particularly where it concerns conflicts, as in our example. Ideal and reality have to be tuned to each other in a responsible manner, as we argued earlier in the context of the term *prudence* (chapter 15 sub 3).

Aspects of execution

We cannot give an entire survey of the way in which the model has to be executed. We will end with a particular function that is of importance: the monitoring of pastoral service. Monitoring is important because it offers a description of the actual ways in which things are run. If it appears from this description that the quality of service leaves something to be desired, then one can intervene and make course corrections. We will now go into two aspects: monitoring of the actual reaching of the target groups and the actual course of the service. Finally, we will discuss some facets of the collection of data that are of importance for monitoring (Rossi & Freeman 1989, 167-224).

The first thing one has to do is to check whether the target groups have been reached and to what degree this has occurred. In other words, is there coverage of the target groups by the service intended for them? In this there may be so-called bias: some subgroups are better reached by the service than others. This may be a consequence of the nature of the service, which is better tuned to these subgroups than to other ones. It also can be because these subgroups have positive self-selection: "this is really something for us." Further, there can be undercoverage and overcoverage. One speaks of undercoverage if the target groups one has in mind are being insufficiently reached. Overcoverage occurs if they are being more than sufficiently reached. What is sufficient has to be determined in advance. A measure for this is: the number of people from the target groups with which contact is maintained; the number of contacts that occur per person, divided into individual and group contacts; the sector in which the contact takes place; the kind of contact; and the scale of themes that are brought up for discussion.

Besides reaching the target groups, the description of the actual course of the service is important. A number of focused questions can be asked proceeding from figure 22.1. The point of departure is formed by the actual service rendered (k). From the perspective of the renderer of service, the following questions are relevant: Is there congruity between the actual and the communicated service (l)? Is the actual service similar to the intended service (j)? Is the intended service in accordance with the interpreted aim of the service in general (c)? And is this interpreted aim the same as the officially determined aim (a)? From the perspective of the user the following questions should be discussed: Is the actual service similar to the service experienced (i)? Does the service experienced meet the expectations (e)? Are the expectations (e) and the observed expectations similar (h)? Are the expectations in accordance with the needs (d)? In what sense are the needs related to the interpreted aim of the service (b)? Is there a similarity between the interpreted and the official aim (a)?

How do we get the data that are necessary to answer these questions? It is quite impossible to cover the whole field of pastoral service with these questions. But that is not necessary. However, if one wishes to raise the quality of the service in a certain sector, a particular choice can be made. Let us take a look at some methods and techniques for the collection of data, which can be used for answering these questions. What applies to all methods is that both qualitative and quantitative techniques can be considered; that is, narrative interviews, guided interviews, semi-structured interviews, checklists, shorter or longer questionnaires with open or closed questions, and group research. These techniques can be implemented depending on the aim one has in mind in the collection of data and the questions one wishes to answer (Hopewell 1987).

The first method is the observation of the actual service. Here one can make a distinction between systematic and nonsystematic, participative and nonparticipative, open and hidden, direct and indirect observation (Van der Ven 1990c, 140-43). The second method is the collection of service record data. These involve the number of contacts and the numbers of those involved, divided into individual and group contacts and divided into sectors. These can be gained through simple and small forms. The third method is the collection of data that are provided by the renderer of service regarding the process of service: the service provider data. In this the terms from the lower half of figure 22.1 can be an aid. The techniques we can use are all kinds of interviews, check lists, and shorter or longer questionnaires. Finally, the fourth method, which involves the user. In this the terms from the upper half of figure 22.1 can be useful. The techniques mentioned above can be used here too. Group research could be considered here as well.

We will close with an example from research among students of the University of Nijmegen (the Netherlands), regarding student pastoral care in this city. Among other things, students were given questions concerning their wishes and expectations regarding pastoral conversations with student chaplains. Here a distinction can be made between three kinds of conversations (Van Knippenberg 1987, 73-90): the kerygmatic conversation (in which the chaplain sets his aim on transferring the faith); the counseling conversation (in which the

TABLE 22.1 Wishes and expectations in % (N = 585)

	WISH			
EXPECTATION	keryg.	couns.	comm.	total
kerygmatic	0	12	12	24
counseling	1	19	18	38
communicative	1	15	22	38
total	2	46	52	100

chaplain listens to what the student himself has to say about his faith or worldview); the communicative conversation (in which the chaplain wants to achieve the deepening and improved understanding of the faith and/or worldview of both the chaplain and the student in a mutual exchange). The horizontal axis in table 22.1 relates to wishes with regard to the three kinds of pastoral conversations, and the vertical axis to expectations.

From this table it appears that only 2% want the pastoral conversations to be kerygmatic, while 46% want them to be aimed at counseling and 52% want them to be communicative. What the students expect is clearly different: 24% expect the pastoral care to be kerygmatic, 38% expect it to be aimed at counseling, and another 38% expect it to be aimed at communication.

Something else comes to the fore in this table. The percentage of students in which the wish and expectation agree amounts to (0% + 19% + 22% =) 41%. No less than 59% do not think this will be the case. The latter percentage is less unsettling than it seems. One can split the 59% in two: the communicative-counseling group and the rest. The communicative-counseling group wants to have a communicative conversation but expects a counseling one, or wants a counseling conversation but expects a communicative one. This group comes to (18% + 15% =) 33%. The rest is made up of students who want a kerygmatic conversation but expect either a counseling or communicative conversation (1% + 1% = 2%), or those who expect a kerygmatic conversation but want a counseling or communicative one (12% + 12% = 24%). Because the relation between pastoral care aimed at counseling and communication is closer than to kerygmatic pastoral care, one could say that there is a true discrepancy in over a quarter of the students (2% + 24% = 26%).

This example shows how important it is to do research into the elements we distinguished in the pastoral service quality model. Through this research, discrepancies can be brought to light. From there the pastoral work can be improved from the viewpoint of the rendering of service.

Chapter 23

Personnel Development

At the beginning of this part, we placed the core function of the management of the church in the context of the process of calculation. We focused upon the marketability of the church (chapter 21). Then we explored the meaning of the endeavor for quality in the service of the church. In this quality of service, the criterion of aiming at the user plays an important part. By this we mean the endeavor to satisfy as best we can the needs of those who wish to make use of the service. However, we made this criterion subordinate to the transcendent aim of pastoral service. On the basis of this, we developed the pastoral service quality model (chapter 22).

In the treatment of the quality of pastoral service, we came across two other important criteria: the technical and content criteria. We conceived of the technical criterion as the whole of the norms of soundness that apply in the process of realization of the service. The criterion of content has to do with the features that are typical of the service itself. We called these two "conditional criteria." We can speak of pastoral service only insofar as the technical and content criteria are met. They form the bottom line (chapter 22).

We will now bring both criteria up for discussion in the context of personnel development. Personnel development is an aspect of the provision of personnel. Other aspects in the provision of personnel are: recruitment, selection, formation, judgment, management, and care of personnel. Personnel development involves the stimulation of expertise in integrated training programs within the organization (Van Braam 1986, 541-50). We are concerned with two different groups of people: pastoral professionals and pastoral volunteers. The difference is that the professional expertise of ministers is aimed at the tasks of content and leadership, and the expertise of volunteers is aimed at the executive tasks. We therefore make a distinction between professional expertise and expertise in itself. What is professionally distinct is the capacity to trace and discover problem areas proceeding from the scientific knowledge acquired, and to reflect upon, analyze, and evaluate them in order to contribute to their adequate handling (Knoers 1987).

In this chapter we will discuss the following questions: (1) What does the development of the professional expertise of pastors entail? (2) And the expertise of pastoral volunteers?

(1) Development of professional expertise of pastors

Professional expertise is an aspect of professionalism. That is why we will first explore the term *professionalism* and then place the professional expertise of pastors within it. Next, we will focus upon the development of their professional expertise. So that there is no misunderstanding, we will again refer to the epistemological principle, which states that the pastor is not a professional but can be regarded as such (Introduction).

Pastoral professionalism

The question is in what sense the occupation of pastor can be called a profession and meets the characteristics of professionalism. In order to answer this question, it is necessary to define what profession and professionalism mean.

A prominent feature of professionalism is the expertise that is necessary for the performing of activities by the professional group in question. What is important in this is the degree to which the expertise rests on systematically ordered, transferable, theoretical knowledge. Another feature is the degree of autonomy from which one performs one's professional activities. Yet another feature involves the structure of the profession. Here we are concerned with the extent of specialized differentiation. The more specializations or even superspecializations there are, the more the professional group forms a profession. Still another feature lies in the conditions for entry into a professional group, the professional organization. These conditions involve the level of training (e.g., M.A. or Ph.D.). What we called the "context" is important too. By this we mean the size of the professional group. The smaller it is, the more exclusive it is. Furthermore, an important role is played by the fundamental orientation of the occupation toward the rendering of service. In a formal sense, this is expressed in a professional code or an ethical foundation in which the professional organization sees to its adherence. Finally, there is a cohesive professional culture and ideology, with strong values and norms that are supported and promoted by the professional organization.

The occupation of pastor answers to these features to a certain extent. We can point out the following restrictive facts: Pastoral expertise is based on one's own practical experience, besides the scientific knowledge one has. The autonomy of the pastor is bound to the juridical order of the church in which he or she works. Pastoral work is characterized by specialization to a modest degree. The conditions for the entry level do not exceed having completed a B.A. or M.A. program. There are professional organizations, but membership is not obligatory and provides one with no prerogatives. The size of the pastoral profession can hardly be called small. There is a strong orientation toward the rendering of service, but this is interpreted along diverse ecclesiological paths. There is also a professional code, but it does not apply to all pastoral professionals and has no binding force. A professional culture is being developed, but it is characterized by many variations.

The conclusion is that the pastor of today has a so-called restricted professionalism, rather than an extensive one. The difference between restricted and extensive professionalism has been further worked out for the profession of teacher in the literature. We will describe it only in formal terms, so that it can be applied to the pastoral profession directly. Among other things *restricted professionalism* is characterized by great faith in one's own practical experience; a strong orientation toward the micro level of one's own professional circle; little interest in and knowledge of the professional literature; and the conviction that one's own work is an intuitive art. Among other things *extensive professionalism* is determined by a high valuation of collective policy formation and professional collaboration; a positive aim toward the contribution of theory formation and research for one's own practice; keeping up with the professional literature; orientation from one's own micro situation to the meso and macro levels; and the conviction that one's own work is a rational science (Giesbers & Bergen 1991).

The factors that influence the restricted professionalism of the pastor are great in number and diverse by nature. They can be divided into two groups: societal and ecclesial factors. These enhance each other.

The societal factors have to do with the process of institutional differentiation and cultural generalization (chapter 1 sub 3). Through institutional differentiation, religion is losing its integrative function more and more and is being pushed into the margin as nonspecialistic by the increasing specialization in the societal institutions. Specialization and religion have historically always had a tense relation. Specialization forces religion into the role of a nonobligational cultural generalization. Religion covers only the societal institutions to the point that the foundation of the whole requires a last pillar of support that they cannot provide for themselves and that escapes them or transcends them: the transcendent. God is the last point of reference. With this observation, the complex character of the whole of the institutions is reduced to something more surveyable. Religion performs the function of reducing complexity because it is nonspecialist and has a culturally generalizing effect (Luhmann 1972; 1977). The pastor as the representative of this religion becomes the specialist of that which is nonspecialized (Kaufmann 1989, 167).

Besides this, ecclesial factors play a part. These have to do with the culture and structure of the church. Insofar as the ecclesial culture has a tense relationship with science and rationality, one cannot speak of an extensive professionalism. Thus the hypothesis was forwarded that the higher clergy is sooner selected on the basis of allegiance to the immutable tradition than on the basis of professionalism (Krijnen 1987). Insofar as the structure of the church clashes with the principles of the functional-rational development of organization and policy development, it hinders the formation of extensive pastoral professionalism. The pastor is not a free professional in the way that a general practitioner is a free entrepreneur. Neither is he a functionary in a professional organization like the independent medical specialist in a hospital, who can operate autonomously. However, he is not the nonindependent professional like the military surgeon in the army, who is also a professional officer. Does he perhaps seem more like the professional member of staff in a volunteer organization, albeit within a strongly developed hierarchical-bureaucratic structure?

However, one can establish the fact that pastoral professionalism is developing in the direction of an extensive professionalism step by step. This appears particularly from the program of the Federation of Associations of Pastoral Workers in the Netherlands (Basisprogram 1988). In the first two chapters, this document describes the context in which the development of pastoral professionalism has to be placed. In the first chapter, the present culture is outlined by means of two features: secularization and democratization. In the second chapter, the position of the church is determined with respect to this secularization and democratization. In the third chapter, professionalism is divided according to the professional statute, the professional code, and the professional organization. The whole is closed off in the last chapter with options for policy. From this document, it appears that the federation wants to promote the development of professionalism from the restricted to the extensive type. It makes the professionalization of pastoral work its explicit aim (chapter 16 sub 3).

Professional expertise

We have seen that professional expertise is only one aspect of professionalism, but that it is an important aspect. We will now take a further look at it. The question that keeps coming back in publications and discussions is what professional expertise entails, which components it comprises, and how it should be developed.

In a general sense, professional expertise can be divided into four aspects: (a) scientific knowledge, (b) scientific insight, (c) scientifically responsible skills, and (d) scientifically responsible attitudes.

The first two aspects (knowledge and insight) are provided with the adjective "scientific," while the latter two (skills and attitudes) have the adjective "scientifically responsible." Why this distinction? The professional pastor has or should have scientific knowledge and insight at his disposal because he needs it and uses it in doing his pastoral work. This does not apply to scientific skills and attitudes. The pastor does not fulfill the function of the researcher, who has the necessary scientific skills and attitudes at his disposal to generate new scientific knowledge and insights by means of complex methods and techniques. However, the professional pastor has pastoral skills and attitudes at his or her disposal, at least he or she should have them. The development and use of these pastoral skills and attitudes have to be founded in the insights and themes drawn from the theological disciplines. They have to be legitimized from there, hence be scientifically responsible. Let us now take a look at the four aspects separately.

(a) *Scientific knowledge* relates to having active access to concepts and theories from the main theological disciplines and their supplementary sciences, and to strategies for the independent acquisition of knowledge that is lacking.

(b) *Scientific insight* refers to the ability to apply concepts and theories in relatively new problematical situations. The aim of this is to localize these problematical situations and explore them, think about them in an argumentational manner, subdivide them into parts, and investigate their mutual connections in order to contribute to their adequate handling. Practical theology (or pastoral theology) holds a central position among the main theological disciplines in the context of pastoral professionalization. This applies to historical, fundamental, general, and methodological practical theology as well as to the subdisciplines of poimenics, catechetics, pastoral liturgics, homiletics, kerygmatics, and diaconology.

(c) The term *scientifically responsible skills* refers to a whole list of skills that are essential for the performance of pastoral work. They relate to religious developmental processes; religious learning processes; religious group dynamics; religious handling of conflict; ritual skills; homiletic skills; religious self-expression; religious handling of the media; pastoral policy development; pastoral activation; problem-centered theological reflection; problem-centered ecclesiological reflection; and, finally, psycho-religious introspection and self-reflection.

(d) The term *scientifically responsible attitudes* relates to attitudes regarding the gospel, the pastorees, the pastoral volunteers, the pastoral colleagues, and other professionals in the area of education, welfare, and mental health care. As far as the gospel is concerned, the central focus is on attitudes of personal openness to the gospel and openness to the formation of one's own pastoral spirituality. As far as the relation to pastorees, pastoral volunteers, and pastoral and other colleagues is concerned, the focus is on the attitudes of proximity, authenticity, balance, transparency, reliability, attention, involvement, and service-mindedness.

The mutual relations between he pastoral skills and attitudes can be divided on two sides. On the one hand, the attitudes form the background of the skills, which plays a continuous role in the implementation of the skills and colors their use. Without the attitudes, the skills easily become something purely instrumental and technical. Attitudes like proximity, authenticity, transparency, balance, and religious inspiration form the actual pastoral bed of the skills. On the other hand, these attitudes are given expression only in the skills. The claim that pastoral action is determined by the attitudes we just mentioned and others like attention and involvement easily finds itself floating in thin air. That is true unless this attention and involvement in the skills of paying attention and communicating involvement are given expression. The relationship between scientifically responsible skills and attitudes is therefore of a dialectical nature. They cannot be developed separately from each other.

Problematic situations

We have localized what is typical of the professional expertise of pastors over against nonprofessional expertise: being able to reflect scientifically upon problematical situations. This raises the question what problematical situations pastors of the present come across in pastoral practice.

In order to be able to answer this question, we will present some results gained from research among 255 pastors in the Catholic Church, the Netherlands Reformed Church, and the Reformed Churches in the Netherlands in 1989, which we referred to earlier. It concerns a list of 40 questions regarding the bottlenecks they encountered in their daily pastoral work. These 40 questions were reduced to 13 groups through multiple factor analyses, as appears from table 23.1. These 13 groups were placed under the four core functions of the church, which function in a theoretical sense as a guideline in this book: identity, integration, policy, and management.

The core function of identity covers questions that relate to the following themes: (1) the influence of secularization on individuals and small groups; (2) the influence of secularization on societal institutions; (3) the hermeneutical exchange between tradition and the

TABLE 23.1
Problematical pastoral situations (N = 255)

	Catholic		Protestant	
	aver. sc.	prior.	aver. sc.	prior.
Identity				
1 individual secularization	3.23	5	3.22	2
2 societal secularization	2.53	12	2.40	12
3 hermeneutical exchange	2.85	11	3.06	5
4 gap doctrine-faith	3.53	3	2.63	11
5 diaconal mission	3.46	4	3.05	6
Integration				
6 communication	2.99	9	2.87	9
7 unity and conflict	3.19	7	2.96	7
8 conventional members	3.00	8	3.07	4
9 nonconvent. members	2.46	13	2.91	8
Policy				
10 policy form. and org.	2.94	10	2.75	10
Management				
11 individual time pressure	3.60	1	3.66	1
12 colleague bound time pres.	3.58	2	1.97	13
13 volunteers	3.20	6	3.21	3

Source: Van der Ven & Biemans 1992b

present situation; (4) the gap between church doctrine and the actual faith; and (5) the diaconal mission of the church.

The core function of integration is expressed in questions involving (6) inter- and intrapersonal communication in the local church; (7) the tension between unity and conflict; (8) dealing with conventional members of the church; (9) dealing with nonconventional members.

The core function of policy was brought up for discussion in questions regarding (10) policy formation and policy organization.

Finally, the core function of management was made concrete in questions of (11) the individual experience of the pressure of time; (12) the colleague-bound experience of the pressure of time (availability of the number of pastors); and (13) the availability and training of volunteers. The pastors were asked to indicate to what extent they had been confronted with these problems.

In the first and third columns of table 23.1, the average scores of these problems are presented. The scale contains five points of measurement: (1) never a problem; (2) hardly a problem; (3) sometimes a problem; (4) often a problem; and (5) continuously a problem.

The first column relates to Catholic pastors, the third to Protestant ones (the Netherlands Reformed Church and the Reformed Churches in the Netherlands together). The second and fourth columns contain the figures that put the problems in order of priority. Problem 1 is experienced as the most important problem, followed by number 2, etc. The second column concerns the priority of problems among the Catholic pastors, while the fourth column concerns that among their Protestant colleagues.

In the discussion of this table, we focus upon the average scores that lie on or to the right of the middle of the scale (≥ 3.00). This means that we are dealing with themes that are sometimes, often, or continuously a problem. What strikes us is that there are eight such themes for Catholic pastors (1, 4, 5, 7, 8, 11, 12, and 13), and only six for the Protestant pastors (1, 3, 5, 8, 11, and 13). From the whole of this group, five are experienced as a common problem: (1) individual secularization, (5) diaconal mission, (8) dealing with conventional members, (11) individual pressure of time, and (12) volunteers.

Let us first examine these common themes. Both groups see (1) the secularization that is creeping into the lives of individuals, marriages, families, and primary types of relations as a phenomenon that they experience quite often. One could say that it gnaws away at the plausibility of the Christian faith, so that the identity of their pastoral work in the local church comes under pressure. This is not resolved by arguments that state that theologically secularization is not a problem because it stems from the Christian faith itself, or that secularization does not even exist because it is the ideology of sociologists. Pastors certainly do come across secularization in practice and experience it as a burden. Both groups place it in the top five of the pastoral problems (Catholics: priority 5; Protestants: priority 2).

There is a second problem that touches upon the identity of the church and that both groups experience as a problem: (5) the diaconal mission of the church. Here we are dealing with the contribution of the church to the solution of structural-societal problems and the counteracting of the crumbling of the welfare state. Both groups have quite a problem with this: the Catholic pastors more so than their Protestant colleagues. For Catholic pastors, the diaconal mission of the church belongs to the top five of the pastoral problems (priority 4); for the Protestant colleagues it just misses out (priority 6).

Both groups also have problems with (8) dealing with conventional members. This does not apply to (9) dealing with nonconventional members; these do not really present a problem to the pastors. The conventional members represent the established church, in which people participate in church activities from traditional self-evidence. Sometimes they make such high demands of the orthodoxy of those who think differently that they wish to shut them out of the church. Both groups of pastors have difficulties with this. For Protestant pastors, we are dealing with a problem that belongs to the top five (priority 4); their Catholic colleagues have less difficulty with this (priority 8).

The most sensitive problem that presents itself in both groups is (11) the individual pressure of time. For both groups it belongs to the top five, and forms the problem with the highest priority for both of them (priority 1). Here the focus is on finding enough time to take care of duties and list priorities in the work that one has to do. People also complain of the fact that they cannot set aside enough time for their own spiritual life. As both groups suffer a great deal from this, one can assume that we are dealing with a structural-pastoral problem rather than a denominational one. It cannot be done away with as a technical problem of guarding one's agenda — although this certainly plays a role. Rather, it is the lack of clear insight into the pastoral priorities in relation to the actual amount of time available. We shall return to this later.

Finally, the pastoral volunteers (13) are a problem for both the Catholic and Protestant pastors. There are several matters involved: the reduction of the number of available volunteers, the training of the volunteers, the adequate implementation of the right volunteer in the right place, and the motivation of the volunteers. Finally, the fact one continually has to take leave of them plays a role. For the Prot-

TABLE 23.2
Number of Catholics per pastor

year	1975	1980	1985	1990
number of Catholics	1850	2250	2700	3007

Source: Van Hemert 1992, 11

estant pastors this theme belongs to the top five (priority 3), for the Catholic pastors it falls just outside of it (priority 6).

Those were the common problems. The other problems that are found on or to the right of the scale (≥3.00) are experienced differently by the two groups of pastors. For the Protestant pastors only (3) the hermeneutical exchange between tradition and situation forms a special problem. For the Catholic pastors the following matters are special problems: (4) the gap between doctrine and faith, (7) the tension between unity and conflict, and (12) the colleague-bound pressure of time. Here we indeed are confronted by denominational problems.

The Protestant pastors have quite a few problems with (3) hermeneutically translating the Bible, so that it can be understood according to its current meaning. For them this belongs to the top five of the pastoral problems (priority 5).

The Catholic pastors are their opposites. For them it is not the Bible that is a problem, but (4) the gap between ecclesial doctrine and faith. This belongs to the top five for them (priority 3). Here we can still speak of a classic distribution of weight: for the Protestants it lies in Bible and faith, while for the Catholics it lies in ecclesial doctrine and faith.

Further, (7) the tension between unity and conflict is a special problem for Catholic pastors. Though it does not belong to the top five, it nevertheless is a worry for them (priority 7). It probably has to do with the problem that we just mentioned: the gap between doctrine and faith. This gap and the polarization that occurs as a consequence probably cause a large share of the tension between unity and conflict and vice versa.

Finally, there is a problem that is highly specific to Catholic pastors: (12) the colleague-bound pressure of time. The cause of this lies in the aging and reduction in the number of pastors. It belongs to the top five (priority 2). We are definitely dealing with a very serious problem here, as appears from practice (Zuidberg 1984). It also appears from the data in table 23.2, which relate to the rise in the number of Catholics per pastor between 1975 and 1990 in the Netherlands.

The figures in this table take into account the actual number of appointed priests, permanent deacons, and pastoral workers. From this it appears that the number of Catholics per pastor has increased by more than 60% in fifteen years' time. If one regards the figures for the last five years (2,700 in 1985 and 3,007 in 1990), we see that the increase comes to 11%. If one restricts oneself to the number of Catholics per priest (excluding deacons and pastoral workers), then the increase during the last five years (3,050 in 1985 and 3,750 in 1990) is almost 23% (Van Hemert 1992, 11). This deviates considerably from the figures on a global scale for the period 1984-1989. In 1984 the average number of Catholics per priest across the whole world was 2,069, and in 1989 it was 2,258 (excluding deacons and pastoral workers), which comes down to an increase of over 9% (*Annuarium 1991,* 75). Therefore, the percent increase in the number of Catholics per priest (23%) in the Netherlands was nearly 14% higher than the increase in percent on a global scale (9%).

The Dutch pastors — with the priests up front — are weighed down by an increasing workload. This appears from their own reactions too, seeing their experiences with individual pressure of time (priority 1) and colleague-bound pressure of time (priority 2). After a time, this can have only negative consequences for mental and bodily health, personal continuation in the function of pastor, and recruitment of new pastors.

We will now summarize the problems we described by placing them within the four core functions of the church: identity, integration, policy, and management. What do we find? The problems of management are the largest, followed by identity problems, and then by integration problems. The themes of policy are not really experienced as a problem. We will elaborate on this briefly.

The problems that belong to the management of the church have the highest priority, particularly the pressure of time and work with pastoral volunteers. The time pressure concerns setting priorities in relation to available time. The work with the volunteers involves the development of an effective and efficient organization, motivation, and development. For Catholic pastors there is the additional theme of the colleague-bound pressure of time.

The problems within the core function of identity are especially focused upon the church and secularization and on the diaconal mission of the church. For Catholics we can add the relation between doctrine and faith and for Protestants we can add that between the Bible and faith.

The problems that belong to integration are especially centered on dealing with conventional church members, and for Catholics we additionally have the tension between unity and conflict. As far as Catholics are concerned, the two problems are probably related. Probably this is of a dialectical nature: the pressure of the conventional members leads to the raising of tension between unity and conflict; the raising of tension leads to higher pressure on the part of the conventional members.

The themes that lie within the sphere of policy are not really felt to be a problem, as we mentioned. We can note, however, that the fact that no problem is experienced does not mean there is no problem.

All in all, Catholic pastors are confronted more often with the problems mentioned than their Protestant colleagues. The average score of the 13 themes together is above the middle of the scale (≥3.00) for Catholics. It comes to 3.12. For Protestants it is below it: 2.90. The average score of the top five problems that both groups experience is 3.48 for the Catholics and 3.24 for the Protestants. Therefore we can say that the Catholic pastors are weighed down more by their work than their Protestant colleagues.

Stimulation of professional expertise

From the data in table 23.1 we can point out the areas that should be considered for the stimulation of professional expertise, proceeding from the main theological disciplines and the supplementary sciences. We will hold on to the order of the core functions of the church in this: identity, integration, policy, and management.

With regard to *identity,* the priority has to be given to communicative ecclesiology in the context of secularization, theological hermeneutics, and diaconology.

Communicative ecclesiology in the context of secularization

forms a high priority. The emphasis should not be placed too much on the structural side of secularization, insofar as this is related to the societal institutions and depillarization. It is precisely the cultural side that forms a problem for the pastors, namely insofar as secularization penetrates the consciousness of the people and determines their perceptions, cognitions, affections, and actions (chapters 1 and 9). This brings the pastors to question how they can deal with it in an adequate way. It makes high demands of the field of religious communication to which they must give guidance proceeding from the church (chapter 3). For this skills are required in the area of pastoral-therapeutic and religious-educational counseling (Cantor 1953; 1961; Van der Ven 1982a, 430-32). Naturally, the cultural and structural sides have to be approached in connection with each other. But the cultural side deserves to have the most attention.

Theological hermeneutics likewise forms an important area for the stimulation of professional expertise. In this we are concerned with the hermeneutics of the Bible as well as that of church doctrine. Both would benefit from what we earlier called the development of the text/context correlation (chapter 16 sub 3). This would have to be worked out for five sectors: pastoral care, catechetics, liturgy, proclamation, and diacony (chapters 4 and 18).

Next, we have diaconology. In this field the pastors are at their wits' end. The insights from political and liberation theology would have to be translated to the context of Western society (not: applied) and then have to be made operational in the shape of projects. Therefore, there is a need for "project-bound diaconology" (Reinders 1989).

The stimulation of professional expertise with regard to the core function of *integration* would benefit from topics from communicative ecclesiology through which problems with conventional church members can be cleared up. These problems will increase in the future because the share of conventional church members in the whole of the church population is growing in percent and will continue to grow. The focus is on topics in which the group, network, and community formation, consensus, and confession are central, as well as the handling of conflicts (chapters 14 and 15). In this the problem of church leadership cannot be avoided (chapter 16).

With regard to the core function of *policy,* the pastors hardly experience any real problems. This does not mean, however, that there are no tasks waiting that demand a better approach. As soon as the term *policy* is made concrete in terms of a policy plan, program, and projects, one still winds up in a vacuum in many local churches. The more large-scale the local church becomes because of religious-demographic developments, the more the need for adequate policy development will grow proportionately. That is why topics from the pastoral science of policy must hold an important position in the stimulation of professional expertise (chapters 18, 19, and 20).

The core function of *management* deserves our special attention, since the pastors are confronted by the most problems in this field. Two themes that require adequate treatment proceeding from theology catch our eye: the pressure of time proceeding from "operational ecclesiology" and the volunteer problem proceeding from the pastoral science of activation.

From the viewpoint of what is called "operational ecclesiology" here, the pressure of time is not only a question of time management but also an ecclesiological problem. More accurately: in resolving the problem of time management, one automatically reaches the need to prioritize ecclesiologically. This centers on establishing and prioritizing the core and subfunctions of the church; establishing and prioritizing the aims and tasks within the pastoral sectors; establishing and prioritizing the time needed for these tasks by the pastors (professionals and volunteers) concerned. Each of these elements demands an ecclesiological account (chapter 4 sub 2).

In the pastoral science of activation, we are concerned with some seven problems that are raised: the recruitment, selection, development, implementation, and guidance of volunteers; and the evaluation and termination of their work. These problems require solid theoretical knowledge and the practical skills to handle them adequately. Further along we will discuss the aspect of development (training).

We would like to close this section with the remark that the stimulation of professional expertise has to focus itself on the four aspects we distinguished earlier: scientific knowledge, scientific insight, scientifically responsible skills, and scientifically responsible attitudes. From there the topics mentioned from hermeneutics, ecclesiology, diaconology, and the pastoral sciences of policy and activation can be approached.

(2) Development of expertise of pastoral volunteers

From research carried out in the diocese of Rotterdam (the Netherlands), it appears that pastors spend much time dealing with pastoral volunteers. The estimated average is 18% of the total number of hours worked. Now a distinction can be made between the time invested in organization, motivation, and development (training) of volunteers. The estimate is that over 5% of the time is invested in organization, over 5% in motivation, and almost 8% in development. It would seem that the pastors have taken this time from tasks they spent more time on twenty years ago: catechetics, personal study and reflection, and especially individual pastoral care (Scholten 1988). In the research among 255 pastors of the three larger denominations that we referred to earlier, questions were also asked with regard to time investment in the development (equipment) of volunteers. The pastors of the Catholic Church turned out to spend over 7% of their time on this; the pastors of the Netherlands Reformed Church spent 4.6% of their time; and the pastors of the Reformed Churches in the Netherlands spent 4.5% of their time (Van der Ven & Biemans 1992a).

We would now like to bring two aspects from this trichotomy (organization, motivation, and development) to the fore in particular: motivation and development. People sometimes raise the idea that the motivation of the volunteer finds its most important source in personal religiosity. The idea is that the more religious a volunteer is, the more motivated he or she is. On this ground, a plea is made for development (training) that aims to strengthen the religiosity of the volunteer. There are, however, voices that say that the motivation of the volunteer should be specially based on his or her feelings of expertise. What they seem to say is the more expert the volunteer is, the more motivated he or she will be. On this basis, people want to focus development (equipment) of the volunteer on the stimulation of expertise. Let us take a look at what motivational research has to say about the question whether personal religiosity or feelings of expertise are decisive.

Motivation

In the research on motivation, it is customary to make a distinction between two dimensions. The first relates to what one feels to be

TABLE 23.3
Motivation of pastoral volunteers

	religious	nonreligious
value	3.89	4.75
expectation	2.84	3.34

Source: Van Gerwen 1990, 106; Van der Ven & Van Gerwen 1990, 37

important. One is motivated to do a certain job as a volunteer because one feels it is meaningful. This is the value dimension. Besides this, we distinguish the expectation dimension. This relates to the extent to which one believes one will achieve this value by actually performing the task as a volunteer. We are dealing with the personal estimate of its achievability (Van der Ven 1985b, 19-24).

Now people distinguish themselves from others by scoring high or low on both dimensions. This also applies to volunteers. Four groups arise from this. The first group is formed by those who have a high score on both dimensions: they feel the job to be done is important and deem it achievable. They will be highly motivated to actually make an effort as a volunteer. But how are things for the other groups? The second group is characterized by a high score on the value dimension and a low score on the expectation dimension. They find the job to be done important, but they do not think it is achievable. These people will be less motivated. The third group displays a reverse image. They have a low score on the value dimension and a high score on the expectation dimension. They, too, will be less motivated. They find the job achievable but less important. Finally, the fourth group is made up of people who score low for both dimensions. They find the job of the volunteer neither important nor achievable. They will not be motivated at all.

Both dimensions can be further divided into a religious and nonreligious interpretation. Let us start with the religious interpretation. One may wonder whether the people in question understand the value dimension in a religious sense. Do they find the job important because they see it as a religious vocation? The same applies to the expectation dimension: do they believe that the job is achievable

TABLE 23.4

Influence of the motivation aspects

	% explained var.	β
non-religious expectation	42	.54
non-religious value	2	.13
religious expectation	1	.15

Source: Van Gerwen 1990,110; Van der Ven & Van Gerwen 1990, 38

because they will carry it off with their religious inspiration? Now for the nonreligious interpretation. Is it true that the people see their job as valuable but not because they experience it as a religious vocation? And as for the expectation dimension: is it true that they see their job as achievable but not because they feel actual religious support?

In table 23.3 the average scores of 279 pastoral volunteers who work in Catholic parishes in the Netherlands are shown on a scale. In 1986 they were asked about their motivation concerning the pastoral guidance of people in mourning. Proceeding from the terms we just mentioned, we can make a distinction, as the table shows, between the religious value of pastoral guidance; the nonreligious value; the religious expectation; and the nonreligious expectation.

Let us first consider the table from a vertical perspective: the columns religious and nonreligious. From the figures we discover that the pastoral volunteers researched are less motivated by the religious value (3.89) and more by the nonreligious value (4.75) of pastoral guidance. In other words, they feel it is more important to offer support to the people in question from a human perspective than from a religious point of view. Something similar can be observed for the expectation dimension: they believe that they are better able to give guidance on humane grounds (3.34) than on religious grounds (2.84).

If we view the table from a horizontal perspective along the value and expectation rows, another salient factor strikes us. The average scores for the value dimension are more positive than those for the expectation dimension. Those of the value dimension (3.89 and 4.75) indicate strong to very strong valuation. Those of the expectation dimension lie more in the area of doubt regarding personal abilities.

TABLE 23.5

Aims of training programs

	score	sd.
functional skills	4.21	.76
community-forming attitude	3.94	.76
personal religious attitude	3.90	.84
ability to critically participate	3.24	1.07

Source: Hermans & Van der Ven 1991, 312

Along with this, we can note that the religious expectation is on the negative side of doubt (2.84) and the nonreligious expectation is on its positive side (3.34).

Which of these four aspects is the most decisive in the motivation of the pastoral volunteers researched? In order to be able to answer this question a regression analysis was carried out.

From table 23.4 it appears that 45% of the total motivation can be explained by three of the four aspects together: the nonreligious expectation (42%), the nonreligious value (2%), and the religious expectation (1%). The religious value appears not to play a significant role and is therefore left out of the table. The nonreligious expectation takes up a dominant position (42%). The two other aspects of motivation exert a significant but almost negligible influence: the nonreligious value accounts for 2% and the religious expectation for 1%. From this one can deduce that the feeling that the task is achievable on humane grounds forms the most important source of motivation of the volunteers.

This is an important conclusion. The principal factor in motivation is not personal religiosity but the estimation that the volunteers themselves make concerning their humane skill to support people in need. Their personal religiosity plays a role only in the background. It is sooner a condition rather than an element of motivation (Van der Ven & Van Gerwen 1990).

Development

What does this mean for the training and guidance of pastoral volunteers? This question was looked into as well. In 1990 a survey was held among 350 participants in Catholic pastoral schools who were following a two-year training program with an eye to the function of pastoral volunteer. A number of questions were put before the members of the course concerning their preference for the aims of this program. In the research, four kinds of aims were distinguished. We mention them in the order listed in table 23.5: the learning of functional skills for the performing of specific pastoral tasks; the development of a community-forming attitude in the church; the development of a personal religious attitude; and the development of the ability to critically participate in church life in the parish.

In this table we find a reinforcement of the insight that came to the fore in the research into motivation. The pastoral volunteers have a primary preference for functional training in which they develop skills with an eye to performing specific pastoral tasks (4.21). What also lies in this is the principal factor in their motivation as a volunteer, as appeared from table 23.4. This does not detract from the relative importance of the other aims. This particularly holds for the aims of attitude: the community-forming attitude (3.94) and the personal religious attitude (3.90). The desire to develop the ability to participate critically in the local church contrasts somewhat with this: it lies in the area of doubt, albeit on the positive side of doubt (3.24). Here we must note that the standard deviation is remarkably high (1.07). This indicates a major lack of consensus among the members of the course on this point.

In summary, we can say that the motivation of pastoral volunteers especially rests on their feelings of being sufficiently able to fulfill the tasks they have. In addition, they would prefer to be trained in the skills that are part of this ability without disregarding the meaning of the development of the personal and community-forming attitudes. Just so we are not misunderstood: the emphasis on the development of functional skills does not imply a formal, empty, functional training without content. For we are dealing with pastoral, catechetical, liturgical, homiletical, and diaconal skills. The basic elements for these can be drawn from poimenics, catechetics, pastoral liturgics, homiletics, and diaconology.

Chapter 24

Financial Management

We started this part with a discussion of the societal process of calculation, bringing the marketability of the church up for discussion. Even though the church does not merge into the process of calculation, it certainly is determined by the laws of supply and demand to a degree (chapter 21). This influences service in the church, in this case pastoral service. So as to put things in the correct order, we made service aimed at the user subordinate to the transcendent aim of the church (chapter 22). Within the service itself, we attached great importance to the development of personnel in which the stimulation of pastoral expertise is central (chapter 23).

However, none of this could be kept going without financial means. For this we need adequate financial management that is aimed not only at obtaining financial means but also at their allocation (Van Braam 1986, 551-58). It is necessary to develop criteria for financial management. These are implied in the identity, vision, and mission of the church. They have to be worked out proceeding from the religious code *church of the poor.* This justifies and even compels us to give an explanation of the finances in the church. Even though this accountability may not be customary in ecclesiology, we cannot avoid it in an ecclesiology from a practical-theological perspective.

In this chapter we will discuss the following questions: (1) Which financial streams exist in the church and how do they work? and (2) What is the meaning of the religious code *church of the poor* in this context?

TABLE 24.1

Church income national averages in %

	church contr.	collect.	church serv.	inter./rent
1986	39	24	16	21
1990	39	22	15	24

Source: Kerkbalans 1990, 3; Kerkbalans 1991, 3

(1) Financial streams

We will begin with a description of the financial streams in the church. We will then try to give an analysis of the most prominent factors in these streams, particularly from the position of the pastor.

Description of the financial streams

Four financial streams are to be distinguished in the local church: the financial church contribution; the collections; the remuneration of church services; and finally the income from net interest benefits, rent, etc. The percentages of the national averages of these four streams in the Netherlands are shown in table 24.1. The two reference dates are 1986 and 1990.

Various items can be noticed in this table. The financial church contribution remained constant proportionally (39% for both years). In an absolute sense, it increased. The average contribution per Catholic was Dfl 39.10 in 1988, Dfl 39.30 in 1989, and Dfl 39.75 in 1990. This means that the church contribution is not subject to inflation.

The collections decreased; there is a drop from 24% to 22%. This is a consequence of the decrease in church attendance: the fewer participants there are in church celebrations, the less income there is from collections. We are here talking about the collections for the local church only. The special collections for churches elsewhere in the world and of the service of the church to society fall outside of this. We shall return to this later.

The remuneration for church services also shows a certain decline: from 16% to 15%. Here we are dealing only with the remuneration for special liturgical services. People do not pay for participation in the regular, weekday, and weekend services, nor do they pay for service in the sectors of pastoral care, catechetics, proclamation, and diacony. This remuneration is a relic of the rates system from the past, which can be characterized as problematic for more than one reason. First of all, this system was a class system. Depending on one's personal financial abilities, one could choose — and therefore pay — for a "service with a priest, a deacon and a subdeacon," or a "service with one priest only," with or without an organ, with or without a choir, with or without candles, with or without flowers, with or without a runner, and with or without carpets and curtains. Next, this system was dysfunctional: it led to a desacralization of the liturgy. Thus, the jurist Van der Ven made the following cynical remark in 1950: "What do we say of the pastor who, against church regulations, had differentiated his rates so precisely that he asked his parishioner, who had lost his wife and child in a bombing raid, to pay the stipend of Dfl 2.50 for a Holy Mass, but that he would charge Dfl 1.00 more if the same Holy Mass had to be read for the child too, whom this parishioner lost in the same bombing raid? Had he thus 'charged' an extra Dfl 1.00 or given Dfl 1.50 discount for the second victim?" (J. J. M. Van der Ven 1950, 124).

These kinds of practices led the bishops of Brabant, Bekkers (Den Bosch), and De Vet (Breda) in the Netherlands to a reorganization of church finances at the beginning of the sixties, so that the class system could be broken through: "We have searched for means in order to remove the differences between classes and milieus in the church," according to the bishop of Breda in "l'Enquete sur la Pauvreté dans l'Eglise" (De Vet 1965, 335). The bishops tried to reach a "reasonable balance between church and money," as the bishop of Den Bosch put it (Groothuis 1973, 112). According to this reorganization, reasonable, fixed, non-class-bound rates were determined for special services. The third column in table 24.1 focuses on this.

Finally, there is income from the net interest benefits, rents, etc. The things that fall under this category are, for instance: rent of the church, the presbytery, parish halls, houses, estates, and revenues from cemeteries. Here we are of course dealing with all sorts of local particulars and usages. Some churches have an annual jumble sale, others organize an annual church auction. One can even find "church sheep" mentioned in the financial parish documents (Geldwerving 1976).

Besides the national average income percentages, local income is worth a further look. In table 24.2 the average benefits are shown

Table 24.2

Average benefits per parish diocese of Rotterdam

	1986	1990
church financial contribut.	78,000	80,600
collections/pewage	36,400	34,700
collections third parties	11,400	12,100
stipends	17,800	19,800
other contributions parish.	12,700	12,800
total contrib. parishioners	156,300	160,000
investment benefits	51,000	62,100
total	207,300	222,100

Source: *Gekonsolideerde cijfers 1990*

per category per parish in the diocese of Rotterdam (the Netherlands) for 1986 and 1990.

It appears from table 24.2 that financial contributions to the church are increasing and collections/pewages are decreasing because of the decline in church attendance. The increase and decrease keep each other in balance. The collections for third parties and the stipends display a certain growth. This, therefore, applies to the total contributions of the parishioners. The investment benefits go from over 24% (1986) to nearly 28% (1990) of the total benefits.

Besides the financial inputs, there are also the outputs. In table 24.3 the average costs are given per category per parish in the diocese of Rotterdam (the Netherlands) for 1986 and 1990.

From this table it appears that the personnel and housing costs take the lion's share of the expenses made: over 61% in 1986 against nearly 60% in 1990. The liturgy and pastoral work account for only 10% of the expenses in 1986 and nearly 11% in 1990; the same amount as the payments to the vicariate and diocese. If one adds the management costs to this we find that almost 17% was spent on liturgy, pastoral work, and management in 1986, and almost 18% in 1990. The money from the collections for third parties, found under the benefits in table 24.2, were expended, as appears from table 24.3; they account for 5%.

Tables 24.2 and 24.3 are lacking the funds that are obtained

TABLE 24.3
Average costs per parish diocese of Rotterdam

	1986	1990
personnel costs and housing	127,800	128,000
liturgy and pastoral work	21,000	23,200
management costs	13,600	14,600
costs immovables	11,200	11,800
interest and costs for debts	1,900	1,900
contributions vicariate/dioc.	21,100	23,100
collections for third parties	11,400	12,100
Total	208,000	214,700

Source: *Gekonsolideerde cijfers 1990*

locally and nationally for the benefit of churches elsewhere in the world (interecclesial) and for the service of the church to society (diaconal). The figures that relate to the national campaigns and collections of 1984 are shown in table 24.4.

Under the heading interecclesial we find: Apostotale for the Eastern Churches, Missionary Works, Missionary Works for Children, Missionary Works for Native Priests, the National Bureau for Missionary Works, and Missionary Traffic Means Campaign. Besides this there are funds for the benefit of the Advisory Commission Missionary Activities, the Week for the Dutch Missionary, and Pension Fund for the Dutch Missionary. The diaconal collections comprise: Medical Missionary Campaign, Episcopal Lenten Fund-raising Appeal, and the Advent campaign Solidaridad. Besides this, there are funds for "People in Need." The total sum (over 81 million guilders) was nearly 10 million higher in 1984 than in the previous year.

In this table, the division between interecclesial and diaconal aid comes to the fore. The first places considerable weight in the scale, but it is outdone by the second. Interecclesial aid comes to over 40%, while diaconal aid is almost 60% of the national funds. What has to be added to these national fund-raising appeals is the amount that is collected at a local level for interecclesial and diaconal aims. For 1984 this was estimated at 59 million guilders (*Missie 1986*). Together this comes to over 140 million guilders.

TABLE 24.4

National funds 1984 × Dfl 1,000 and in %

	Absolute fig.	%
Interecclesial		
Eastern churches	228	0.2
Missionary works	4,793	5.9
Missionary works children	408	0.5
Missionary works priests	2,848	3.5
National bureau missionary work	2,204	2.7
Miss. traffic means campaign	7,500	9.2
Missionary activities	8,771	10.8
Dutch missionary week	4,321	5.3
Pension fund missionary	1,707	2.0
Diaconal		
Medical miss. campaign	11,356	13.9
Lenten fund-raising appeal	13,251	16.3
Solidaridad	4,149	5.1
People in Need	19,640	24.2
Total national campaigns	81,176	99.6

Source: *Missie 1986*, 33-34

Analysis of the financial streams

The question is whether we can gain more insight into the nature of the financial streams we have just described. In the Netherlands there is no fund-raising in the sense of that in the United States (Bassett 1978; McManus 1978), and there is no church tax as in Germany (Walf 1978). How can we conceive of the financial streams in the Dutch church? Where do they come from?

We base our discussion on four financial streams of input: financial contribution to the church, collections, remuneration for church services, and income from interest/rent (table 24.1). We shall divide these four streams of input into four types of organization, from which we can clarify church business.

This division departs from the question of which people or

groups the organization benefits: *cui bono* (Blau & Scott 1962). The reasoning is that the group that profits from it also contributes to the financial maintenance of the organization. The four types are: the service organization, the public service organization, the mutual assistance organization, and the social movement organization. The service organization, like the school and the hospital, benefits the users of the service: pupils or patients respectively. The public service organization, like the city manager's office, is for the benefit of the public. The mutual assistance organization, like the patient association, is useful for the members themselves (Blau & Scott 1962). The social movement organization, like the peace and environmental movements, wants to work for the benefit of the present and the future generations (Lammers 1984). In short, the beneficiary groups are: the users (service organization), the public (public service organization), the members (mutual assistance organization), and the present and future generations (social movement organization).

Now the church can be seen as a complex organization that is involved with four different beneficiary groups and that therefore incorporates aspects from all four types of organization. We did not mention the fifth type of organization, the business organization, which aim at profit and optimization thereof (Blau & Scott 1962). Since the church factory *(fabrica ecclesia)* is a thing of the past, this type of organization is no longer applicable to the church. The church does have a right to acquire, retain, administer, and get rid of temporal goods; but it has to use them in pursuit of its proper ends (Can. 1254 §1). These aims are: liturgy, support of pastors and others in the service of the church, evangelization, and charity, especially with regard to the needy (Can. 1254 §2).

As a *service organization,* the church renders services in the sectors of pastoral care, catechetics, liturgy, proclamation, and diacony (chapter 22). It does not receive financial compensation in these sectors, not even in that of the daily or weekend liturgical celebrations. There is one exception: the stipends for special liturgical services. According to table 24.1, they come down to 15 or 16% of the total income of the local churches.

As a *public service organization,* the church occasionally throws open its doors to the general public. This is true particularly when the public has need for a celebration in a serious atmosphere to ritualize the seriousness of life *("la vie sérieuse"),* according to the cyclical rhythm of the seasons (Christmas) and the linear rhythm of biographically determined life events (birth, marriage, and death), as Durkheim (1925) put it. The general public contributes to the maintenance of the church through the voluntary financial contribution to the church. This occurs even though such persons may not be seen regularly in the church. From research we know that 72% of the parishioners pay a fixed annual financial contribution (Van Hemert 1991, 68). In 1990 this came down to Dfl 39.75 per Catholic, as we mentioned earlier. Instead of the German church tax, we have a kind of voluntary tax in the Netherlands. People impose this upon themselves because they feel they are dealing with a "public good," for which the financial maintenance has to be guaranteed.

As a *mutual assistance organization,* the church takes care of the diacony among its members: the material and spiritual support of individuals and groups in need. It allocates part of the collections to the material side of this diacony. As we have seen, this comes to no more than 5% (table 24.3). Even though they live in a social welfare state, many among the poor (5%) in the Netherlands who belong to the church need material and spiritual support. They live on an income that is less than 95% of the social minimum (Sociaal en Cultureel rapport 1992, 158-61).

Finally, as a *social movement organization,* the church focuses on activities of which the aim is to give expression to the cultural and societal criticism that lies in the Jesus movement. For this purpose special funds are raised and passed on. From table 24.4 the size of the national interecclesial and diaconal programs, projects, and campaigns becomes clear. To this we have to add the funds that are raised at a local level for these aims. In 1984 the estimated total amount reached over 140 million guilders.

Analysis from the position of the pastor

Both in a formal and a material perspective, the pastor is separate from the financial streams of input and output. In a formal perspective, this is because the finance council is responsible for these matters. In a material perspective, this is because the pastor is not dependent on them. The ordained pastor is part of the diocesan or regular priests. The diocesan priest has a guarantee that his needs will be provided for by the bishop, who took on this obligation with his ordination.

The regular priest is assured of support because of his order or congregation. The nonordained pastor closed an employment contract with the finance council, and therefore has a right to a salary, social security, legal status, etc. Nevertheless, the pastor is stuck in the middle of a land with four financial streams, and he participates in the church as a service, public service, mutual assistance, and social movement organization.

Proceeding from the *ecclesial service organization,* the pastor functions as a provider of pastoral services. In this task, he finds himself in a spiritual or religious market where the law of supply and demand rules. His service has to be of high quality, competitive, user friendly, and of a reasonable price (chapter 22). Those who think this is a bit over the top would do well to remember the words of the theologian Van Kessel, who spoke of being "sensitive" to the collections and financial contributions and attuning the quality of the pastoral work to this (chapter 21). To this we would like to add the following quotation: "The iron law that holds in such a market, is that a fixed appointment in a well-regulated employment contract is only bearable for an employer with a guaranteed sale of the product in the long run. This demands continuous adjustment of the production with a maximum sensitivity to the continually fluctuating and fashion-conscious market demand" (Van Kessel 1985, 215). The customer is always right in the religious market too, according to Van Kessel (1986, 333). Those who feel this has been too strongly put, should remember the marketability of services in the church (chapter 21).

In this marketability there is a double danger. The first is that the interpretation of the gospel is modified to the varying taste of the market. The second danger is that the market dictates that fundamental questions have to be solved in a cheap way. But a cheap solution is only an apparent one.

This is so because the rhetoric of the tempting bargain, the low price, the extra quality, and the money-back guarantee do not fit these existential questions. Existential questions have no solution. They are about life, suffering, guilt, and death; they are about fate and fortune, finiteness and limitedness, disorder and chaos, contingency and tragedy. The only thing one can achieve is to learn an attitude with a positive outlook and hope, proceeding from the gospel (Van der Ven 1991d).

Proceeding from the church as a *public service organization,* the pastor finds himself in the comparatively anonymous relationship of the functionary of a public institution to the voluntary taxpayer. At a smaller or greater distance he supervises the group of people willing to go around collecting church contributions. They go from door to door to check annually — as it were — the financial church meter. They form the interface between the church and the general public. From this angle, the pastor represents a public machine, the church, which fulfills a public function, the civil religion: something that has to be paid for by the general public.

This puts the stress of a double bind on the performance of the pastor. On the one hand, he feels called to serve God and to serve the "least of my friends." On the other hand, he symbolizes civil religion, which founds the civil morals that in their turn underlie modern society. In this values like freedom, equality, and fraternity play a part (Ter Borg 1990). However, this happens in such an abstract fashion that the lack of freedom, the inequality, and the missing fraternity of the societal system are cloaked. For the sake of the gospel, the pastor may feel called upon to turn against this civil religion in order to be an atheist in that sense, just as the Christians in the first centuries were called atheists. But in doing this, he would be sawing through the very financial branch upon which he is sitting (Häring 1984).

Proceeding from the church as the *mutual assistance organization,* the pastor fulfills yet another role. Now he symbolizes neither the market nor the public machine, but the *communio.* One can see in this a distant derivation of the *convivium* that characterized the first Christian communities: "Now the whole group of those who believed were of one heart and soul, and no one claimed private ownership of any possessions, but everything they owned was held in common. With great power the apostles gave their testimony to the resurrection of the Lord Jesus, and great grace was upon them all. There was not a needy person among them, for as many as owned lands or houses sold them, and brought the proceeds of what was sold. They laid it at the apostles' feet; and it was distributed to each as any had need" (Acts 4:32-35). The pastor bears evidence to this *convivium* when he calls upon the community for mutual solidarity. Here he stands as a *pars pro toto* of another *pars pro toto:* he is the community personified through his founding of the community for the benefit of those who threaten to fall away from this community.

Proceeding from the church as a *social movement organization,* the political and liberation-theological option of the pastor is relevant. As a social movement, the church is driven by the Jesus movement, which interrupts justice based on exchange and turns it in the direction of social justice and love of the kingdom of God. Here one cannot speak of the calculation of the market, nor of the heavenly canopy of civil religion. Here the *convivium* of the solidary church community is aimed at the universal solidarity in which God will be all in all. This solidarity is only really given shape in the church of the poor.

(2) The church of the poor

The analysis of the complex organization that the church is and that the performance of the pastor determines, makes it clear that we are dealing with a fundamental ecclesiological problem here. Should priority be given to the supply and demand structure in the service organization, the civil religion in the public service apparatus, the *convivium* in the mutual assistance organization, or the universal solidarity in the Jesus movement?

The question is how the ecclesiology handled the problem of financial management during the course of history, what the significance is of the religious code *church of the poor* in this context, and which functions this code can fulfill.

Financial management in the church

At the beginning of his article on temporal goods in the church according to theological and canonical tradition, Congar remarks that the theme of financial management definitely has a place in ecclesiology. However, he adds to this that there have been only historical studies in this field, but hardly any systematic studies (Congar 1965b, 233). Thus the problems many pastors are faced with are in effect ignored, as we have seen. This pinches all the more because many people are bothered by the way the church handles money, and this injures its credibility (Bassett & Huizing 1978).

In the first centuries, the capital of the church did not constitute a problem. Thus, the story goes that the deacon Laurentius was burnt alive on the 10th of August, A.D. 258, because he refused to transfer the goods of the Christian community in Rome to the imperial powers. He had distributed them to the poor and referred the prefect to the poor. Whatever the historical import of this story is, it is clear that ecclesial goods should have been extensive in that time. However, it also is clear that the poor had plenty to do with them (Cereti 1978, 7).

There are authors who believe that the problem of ecclesial goods raised its head only in the third century. The moment the clergy entered the church, church property turned into a problem. According to these authors, the church of the poor changed into the church of the clergy. In order to resolve this problem, the goods were divided into four parts: one part for the bishop, one part for the priests, one part for the church building and the liturgy, and one part for the poor (Faivre 1976).

Meanwhile the legitimization of the ownership of the ecclesial goods formed a problem. How can the church justify owning goods? Patristics has brought several principles to the fore concerning this subject. Some authors said that the goods are not the property of the church but of God. Others claimed that they belonged to the church as a community, by which they meant that they were not the property of the clergy. Still others were of the opinion that they belonged to the poor. The latter is asserted most often by the Fathers: what transcends the theological and ecclesiological motive is the diaconal motive (Congar 1965b).

Just how strong the diaconal motive shone through in patristics, appears from the fact that he who embezzled the property of the poor was viewed as a murderer of the poor *(necator pauperum)*. Again and again we observe that it is the task of the bishops and the priests only to administer and distribute temporal goods. They were allowed to have their share, but no more than was necessary for their own maintenance. So as to underline the legitimacy and the limitations of this, constant appeal was made to the text of Paul: "Do you not know that those who are employed in the temple service get their food from the temple, and those who serve at the altar share in what is sacrificed on the altar?" (1 Cor. 9:13). The amount of money needed for the priests had to be measured by the local average cost of living, according to John Chrysostom (Congar 1965b).

In the time of the Fathers, one comes across the division into four parts more often. There are, for that matter, authors who point out a difference that gradually arose in a number of places during the course of the fourth century. Not only was there a further refinement of the division but also a shift in its balance. This was expressed by the fact that four parts were allocated to the bishop, two parts to the priests, two parts to the deacon, two parts to the lecturer, and one part to the widows. By the end of the fourth century, a further hierarchization of this division occurred: the two parts of the priest were raised to three parts (Faivre 1976).

Whatever we may say of this, the classic division into four parts held strong. The first official church signs can be found in the time of Pope Gelasius in A.D. 494. In the Carolingian period the division regularly appeared in the texts of the councils, like the council of Paris in A.D. 829. Those who did not keep to the stipulation that a quarter was intended for the poor ran the risk of being excommunicated. No arithmetical division was given with this, since both the bishop and the priests were bound to give to the poor that which they did not need for themselves (Brion 1975). This, of course, does not mean that they actually followed this rule in practice. The threat of excommunication was not for nothing.

In the early Middle Ages, the legitimization of the property of ecclesial goods took on ideological features. People started to ascribe this property, which belonged to ecclesial institutions like dioceses, parishes, and monasteries, to the patron saints of these institutions. The capital *(patrimonium)* of the diocese of Rome, which was dedicated to Peter as its patron saint, was renamed "patrimonium Sancti Petri." The charters of legacies and donations left to such institutions made mention of the patron saints as the beneficiaries. We have no choice but to see this as a kind of pious fraud *(pia fraus):* "As long as there is only one saint as patron or patroness of a church, chapel, monastery, etc., we do not have to worry. It becomes more complicated, however, if three, four or sometimes even five saints occupy the same altar at the same time, and one cannot even begin to imagine the patronage of the eleven thousand Holy Virgins. Should divine judgment intervene so as to divide the goods pro rato ascribed to these collectives?" (De Groot 1980, 6).

In A.D. 1142 Gratian tried to harmonize the mutually incompatible legal traditions and regulations in his "Concordia discordantium canonum" (or "Decreta"). In this he also systematized the instructions regarding ecclesial goods (Congar 1965b). He came across diverse rules concerning the private capital of the clergy. Some rules allowed this private capital, while others did not. Gratian solved the problem as follows: "But it should be remarked that eastern 'episcopoi' have wife and children, while some in our (western) regions achieve the higher ordinations, after they have become widowers, having once been laymen or minorists with wife and children, or have promised to live a life of abstinence in consultation with their wives. They are allowed to own property for the care of themselves and the ones they care for. All those who are destined for the holy ministry from when they were a child may not have any private property, as they have no excuse whatsoever, unless they are perhaps able to abandon the financial support by the church because of their own private property" (quote in De Groot 1980, 7). From this quote we can glean two interesting points. First of all, private property was not seen as being a good thing. There had to be an excuse for it. However, all clergymen — that is the second point — were allowed to have property, because it was advantageous to the church.

After this period of evangelical "weakness," as Mollat (1977, 49) puts it, the movements of the poor from the 11th to the 14th centuries stimulated the awareness of the inseparable bond between the church and the poor. They were strongly influenced by economic factors in their actions, particularly by the growing poverty among large groups of the population as a consequence of urbanization. However, their rise cannot be reduced to these factors. An authentic evangelical ideal lay hidden beneath it, which entailed that one had to seek out the poor, be in solidarity with them, and live among them: poor among the poor. Great examples of this are the canons of Prémontré: Bernard, Bruno, Dominic, and Franciscus.

Yet the movements of the poor and the religious orders that stemmed from them were, in the long run, unable to stop the Reformation from taking place. In part this came about as a protest against ecclesial abuses concerning indulgences, simonies, and benefices (only abolished in the Codex of 1983!). Thus Luther remarked in one of his table speeches that the initial letters of the Pauline verse *"Radix omnium malorum avaritia"* (greed is the root of all evil) together form the word ROMA (De Groot 1980, 11).

The capitalism that started to determine Western society at the beginning of the modern age did not stop at the church door. On the contrary, the spirit of capitalism also stemmed from the spirit of the Christian religion, at least from the Calvinism of the 17th century, as

Weber explained. This Calvinism was characterized by a calculating attitude, the keeping of an accurate accountancy, and the efficient and effective employment of money. In this the verse from the second letter to the Thessalonians played a part: "Anyone unwilling to work should not eat" (2 Thess. 3:10). It formed a religious legitimization of the will to do business and earn money with earnest and dedication (Weber 1969, 169). In this spirit, it was not fitting to wish to be poor: "God blesseth his trade" (Weber 1969, 172). Before the Reformation, this financially calculating attitude counted as a disgrace. Afterward it gradually became a kind of ethos in the church. Especially after the loss of ecclesial goods through economic secularization in modern times, we see the church entering into the capital market in order, from interest and dividend, to be able to lead an independent life (Cereti 1978).

In his historical studies, the canonist and sociologist Le Bras demonstrated the prestigious display of the clergy (clothing, titles, and cortege), as well as the misuse of its wealth. The purity of the church was increasingly compromised because of this, according to Le Bras (1959, 233-302, 571-84). The poor received no more than crumbs of the whole of church property: sometimes 3%, sometimes only 1% (Trouiller 1978, 82).

One of the few systematicians who has delved into the problem of temporal goods in his theology is Journet, who extensively refers to work by Thomassin from 1725. His solution comes down to the following: Whether we are dealing with buildings, other properties, or financial means, only one principle counts. It has two sides to it. On the one hand, there is the degree to which the temporal goods are aimed at the purpose of gospel, which contributes to the nature of the church becoming transparent. This applies if they are used for the maintenance of the clergy, the apostolate, and the poor. On the other hand, if they are used for making money, they darken the true nature of the church by becoming a danger for it. The church itself is not at stake here, for that matter, according to Journet, for it is holy and immaculate. We are concerned with "the mistakes, negligence, missings, boorishness and disloyalty of its children" (Journet 1951, 948). It is remarkable that the author knew of no sin of the church, nor even of sin in the church or sinful church ministers. He only knew of the faults of its children. Probably the image of the church as a mother (with its children) is incompatible with the *ecclesia mixta,* the *ecclesia sanctorum et peccatorum* (chapter 11 sub 2).

Between Vatican I and II the church was far too busy with the extension of the church as a perfect society *(societas perfecta)* to be occupied systematically with poverty, hunger, and misery. The draft text for the church constitution of Vatican II as it was to be bears witness to this. Due to pressure from the council hall, a brief passage on poverty was added in the final document, from which the dominance of the perfect society was removed — without the image itself being removed. It states that "Christ was sent by the Father 'to bring good news to the poor, . . . to heal the contrite of heart' (Luke 4:18), 'to seek and to save what was lost' (Luke 19:10). Similarly, the Church encompasses with her love all those who are afflicted by human misery and she recognizes in those who are poor and who suffer, the image of her poor and suffering founder. She does all in her power to relieve their need and in them she strives to serve Christ" (*Lumen Gentium* 8). Some authors are glad to be able to mention this addition (Chenu 1977). Others, however, deplore the fact that after the publication of the constitution on the church in the modern world (*Gaudium et Spes*), which is known as scheme 13 to insiders, no scheme 14 followed it up. This should have been dedicated entirely to the poor in the church, the church of the poor, and the poor church (Gutiérrez 1977).

The poor and the church

The church has a long history of misuse of money and power, of gain and accumulation of property. However, it has an equally long history of care for the poor. This already appears from the registers of the poor of parishes in the first millennium, the foundation and maintenance of hospitals, orphanages, poorhouses, guest rooms in the monasteries, and meals at the "gateway." However, there is much evidence that the poor did not really feel safe in the church and did not trust it because it made them just as marginal as society did. The poor were seen as a danger by both society and the church. They represented a threat (Chenu 1977). There are authors who believe that all church's care of the poor was aimed at channeling and curbing the disquieting power of the poor (De Swaan 1990).

Whatever the case may be, if we want to find an answer to the question how the church should handle money in order to carry out a responsible financial management, then we have no other choice than to be quite frank about the core problem. That is: How does the church relate to the poor? This relationship can take on three shapes: the church *for* the poor, the church *with* the poor, and the church *of* the poor (Boff 1985, 19; 1987b, 5). The church *for* the poor goes to the poor. It organizes the aid to combat the poverty of those who fall outside of it, as it were. The poor are the object of the church's care. The church *of* the poor is in contrast to this. It is formed by the poor themselves, who are the subject of their own project to liberate themselves from their poverty, in the perspective of the kingdom of God. In this project, the poor become a people to the extent that they are less of a mass and bid farewell to the accompanying mass spirit. In other words, they become a people to the extent that they take on the historic task of their own freedom and equality as a people (Boff 1985, 209), and to the extent that they express their own historic credo. The church stems from this people of the poor. The church of the poor is the church from within the poor. The people of the poor forms the people of God (Gutiérrez 1977). And what about the church *with* the poor? Those who come from the higher classes and who wish to belong to this people identify with the cause of the poor and are in solidarity with them. They are on the side of the poor and are occupied with them (Boff 1987a, 68).

The difference of the church *for* the poor on the one hand and the church *of* the poor on the other can also be worked out as follows. In its most optimal sense, the church *for* the poor refers to an ethical task of the church, a diaconal task that it has to fulfill proceeding from the gospel. The church of or from within the poor refers to the religious identity of the church itself. The poor do not form a category outside the church, nor do they form a segment of the people of God within it. The people of God that the church is, is born of the poor; it stems from them. The people of God have their origin and center in the poor. The church *for* the poor is an ethical task of the church; the church *of* the poor implies an ecclesiological approach to the church itself (Sobrino 1989, 92, 135).

However, the relationship between the church *with* the poor and the church *of* the poor is not without its problems. To put it sharply: in the church *with* the poor there is an appeal to the existing church to reform itself regarding the poor and to engage itself with them. In the church *of* the poor, we find the notion that the church is born from the poor. In this notion we can read an element of discontinuity with the existing church; some even see it as a rupture. In order to accomplish a certain balance between continuity and renewing discontinuity, some authors have proposed to interpret the birth of the church of the poor as the rebirth of the church of the poor. Gutiérrez himself sometimes conceives of the church of the poor in the sense of engagement of the church with the poor. With this he does away with the distinction between the church *with* the poor and the church *of* the poor, or at least its sharper edges (Van Nieuwenhove 1991, 176-77).

Whatever the case may be, this triangular field of tension between the church *for* the poor, the church *with* the poor, and the church *of* the poor characterizes the local church of today. It particularly applies to the local church in Western society, and more especially the local church of the white community in the north of Western Europe.

Church of the poor

In the gospel we do not find this field of tension. It took up a tradition that went back to the peasants' revolts in the Israel of old. At the time the rights of slaves were defended against exploitation by the monarchy, and people were waiting for the coming of a really benevolent king, the Messiah. In their desire for the kingdom of God, the poor held a favored position. All dividing lines and prerogatives are absent in that kingdom. Neither sex, nor class, nor origin counted there (Pixley 1984). The prophets of the Old Testament followed up this line, preaching about the God of justice: "Thus says the LORD: For three transgressions of Israel, and for four, I will not revoke the punishment; because they sell the righteous for silver, and the needy for a pair of sandals — they who trample the head of the poor into the dust of the earth, and push the afflicted out of the way; father and son go in to the same girl, so that my holy name is profaned; they lay themselves down beside every altar on garments taken in pledge; and in the house of their God they drink wine bought with fines they imposed" (Amos 2:6-8).

Jesus himself turned to the poor directly and promised them the kingdom of God. They were not called blessed because they were poor, but because Jesus came to them as the Messiah, and proclaimed the messianic kingdom in his person, words, and deeds. Happiness was their share: "Blessed are you who are poor, for yours is the kingdom of God. Blessed are you who are hungry now, for you will be filled" (Luke 6:20-21). In this kingdom the poor are favored, not the rich; the humble, and not the mighty. Luke added a fourfold woe to this: "But woe to you who are rich, for you have received your consolation. Woe to you who are full now, for you will be hungry. Woe to you who are laughing now, for you will mourn and weep. Woe to you when all speak well of you, for that is what their ancestors did to the false prophets" (Luke 6:24-26). A reversal of all values comes to the fore in the Magnificat: "He has brought down the powerful from their thrones, and lifted up the lowly; he has filled the hungry with good things, and sent the rich away empty" (Luke 1:52-53). Riches are a hindrance in entering the kingdom, as appears from the parables of the rich miser and poor Lazarus (Luke 16:19-31) and of the rich corn grower (Luke 12:16-21). Jesus warned the people: "Take care! Be on your guard against all kinds of greed; for one's life does not consist in the abundance of possessions" (Luke 12:15). He told the people: "Sell your possessions and give alms. Make purses for yourselves that do not wear out, an unfailing treasure in heaven, where no thief comes near and no moth destroys. For where your treasure is, there your heart will be also" (Luke 12:33-34). The whole point is to achieve detachment: "So therefore, none of you can become my disciple if you do not give up all your possessions" (Luke 14:33). Jesus took the side of the poor. He lived with them and among them.

The ancient community in Jerusalem was characterized by the realization of the promise of Deuteronomy: "There will, however, be no one in need among you, because the LORD is sure to bless you in the land that the LORD your God is giving you as a possession to occupy" (Deut. 15:4). Thus, Luke states in the verses mentioned earlier: "There was not a needy person among them, for as many as owned lands or houses sold them and brought the proceeds of what was sold. They laid it at the apostles' feet, and it was distributed to each as any had need" (Acts 4:34-35).

The letter of James, meant for the Jews converted to Christianity from the Dispersion, mentions the fact that not everything was going the way it should in an evangelical community: "For if a person with gold rings and in fine clothes comes into your assembly, and if a poor person in dirty clothes also comes in, and if you take notice of the one wearing the fine clothes and say 'Have a seat here, please,' while to the one who is poor you say, 'Stand there,' or 'Sit at my feet,' have you not made distinctions among yourselves and become judges with evil thoughts?" (Jas. 2:2-4). The same letter is opposed to the rich: "Come now, you rich people, weep and wail for the miseries that are coming to you. Your riches have rotted, and your clothes are moth-eaten. Your gold and silver have rusted. . . . Listen! The wages of the laborers who mowed your fields, which you kept back by fraud, cry out, and the cries of the harvesters have reached the ears of the Lord of hosts" (Jas. 5:1-4).

Next we have the community of Corinth. This was mainly made up of fools, the despised, people from the lower classes, though some wise and powerful people also belonged to it (1 Cor. 1:26-29). Paul turned against certain things that happened during their meetings. There were factions (1 Cor. 11:18-19), but there was also an unequal distribution of food and drink: "For when the time comes to eat, each of you goes ahead with your own supper, and one goes hungry and another becomes drunk" (1 Cor. 11:21). This was in stark contrast with Paul's directions concerning the meal of the Lord: "The cup of blessing that we bless, is it not a sharing in the blood of Christ? The bread that we break, is it not a sharing in the body of Christ?" (1 Cor. 10:16). The *koinonia* of the community was the *koinonia* of the bread and wine, in his view.

There was *koinonia* among the communities as well. This appears when there are calls for help and support from them. Thus, Paul did a lot of work on collections for distressed sister communities. He called upon the community of Corinth to set aside some money for the Christians in Jerusalem and Palestine each Sunday (1 Cor. 16:2; cf. 2 Cor. 8:1-9, 15; Rom. 15:26). It was not Paul's intention to make the community of Corinth poor, but to make it share its abundance: "it is a question of a fair balance between your present abundance and their need, so that their abundance may be for your need, in order that there may be a fair balance" (2 Cor. 8:13-14).

These aspects particularly played an important role in the thought of the community about the church as the body of Christ in the time of the Fathers. The church's being Christ's body was expressed in coming together for the meal of the Lord and in being there for each other in the interecclesial diacony. It took place in the eucharistic sacrament of community and solidarity (Congar 1965b).

Church of the poor today

The image of the church *for* the poor has a somewhat strained relationship, as we said, with that of the church *with* the poor, together with that of the church *of* the poor. Which aspects do we find in this field of tension? What difficulties present themselves, particularly for the white community of the local church in Western society?

Let us establish a number of matters, so as to avoid falling into ecclesiological phantasmagoria. First of all, the church of the poor does not only imply the poverty of the individual members but the church as a social formation, as a collective. The church of the poor is a community of poor. Secondly, this poverty is not only spiritual, or an attitude or lifestyle, but real material poverty. The church of the poor is a community of the poor in a material sense. Thirdly, the church of the poor is a church in a poor society. The church in rich Western society, whose members dispose of a legally guaranteed social minimum in principle, cannot call itself a church of the poor. This remains the case, even though the church's share in the total societal capital has been considerably decreased, and the church has become poorer in a relative sense (Rahner 1971). The church of the poor is a community of materially poor in a poor society. Fourthly, the gap between the church of the poor in the so-called Third World and the church of the West is so great that the latter may not call itself "church of the poor." It is not allowed to do this because it would ideologically disguise the fact that Western society, including the Western church, brought about this gap through centuries of colonization and still maintains it (Müller 1977).

The local white church in Western society may not and cannot call itself a church *of* the poor. What can it call itself then? The way open to it and that it is called upon by the gospel to follow is that of the church *with* the poor. With this, the image of the church of the poor is not pushed into the background, but remains present as a perspective. For the Western church has to create conditions, as the church with the poor, for the truly poor masses to become a people and within this the people of God. In this way the church is born or reborn from the poor.

This assumes that the Western church is learning to read its •wn history, which belongs to the history of Western society itself, in a new way: with the eyes of the poor. This demands a fundamental reinterpretation that touches upon the structure and culture of Western society and of the church itself. Only after such a rereading will it become clear that Jesus' kingdom of God is shaped in solidarity with "the least of these who are members of my family"; and finally, that it is shaped in "the least of these": the hungry, the thirsty, the imprisoned, the naked, the despised, and the sick (Matt. 25:32-46). For the rereading is not a purely intellectual deed: it assumes the praxis of evangelical *diakonia* and *koinonia* (Gutiérrez 1977). The interecclesial traffic between Corinth and Jerusalem lies within the memory of the church. It is this interecclesial, intercontinental *diakonia and koinonia* that forms the task of the church.

From there it can develop a better eye for all those groups that live on the margins of Western society, to which the verse cited by Paul from Exodus is applicable: "As it is written, 'The one who had much did not have too much, and the one who had little did not have too little'" (2 Cor. 8:15). Finally, the church has to focus its attention on all people and groups within its own walls who have wants and are distressed.

What does this mean for the actions of the pastor, whose position was described from the complex organization that the church is? The question was whether he should give priority to the exchange of supply and demand in the service organization, the civil religion in the public service apparatus, the convivium in the mutual assistance organization, or the universal solidarity in the Jesus movement. The complexity of this question cannot simply be undone by means of an argument, a declaration of adherence, or a declaration of principle. However, the following has become clear in the meantime: the local church and the pastor along with it have to give priority, within this field of tension, to the *koinonia* and the *diakonia* in the solidarity with the poor who are called by Jesus "the least of these who are members of my family."

Functions

As with other religious codes, we can discern three functions: cognitive, emotive, and conative. The description of these functions can help the local church to orient its financial management in reading its task with the eyes of the poor.

Cognitive function

It is part of the essence of the church that it is a church of the poor, and in connection with this a church *with* the poor. The orientation toward the poor is not just some addition. It is not merely evangelical advice, which is followed up by separate groups and persons. It is not *ad libitum.* This has to do with the fact that the church bears witness to the message of the kingdom of God, which was proclaimed to the poor, the sick, the outcasts, and those on the margins of society. It is the sacrament of the universality of God's liberation that is given expression in the particularity of its choice for the poor. In its praxis of solidarity, it refers to the partiality of this liberation: it signifies and re-presents it. Without the orientation toward the poor, the church stops being the church of Jesus, the Messiah. Without this aim, all that is left is a noncommittal religious society, an aesthetic company, an autocentric, self-experiential association.

At the same time, an interpretation of the deficiencies of the church in this area lies in this. It is not only a consequence of a kind of inertia and boorishness of the children of the church, as Journet believed. They are a sign of the sin not only *in* the church but *of* the church — a sign of the church as a sinner (chapter 11 sub 2). Here, repentance and conversion are fitting. On the part of the Western church, the historical *confessio* answers the historical *credo* of the poor, who take upon them the project of their liberation as a people. A confession of guilt corresponds to a confession of faith. This confession does not imply a difficult and depressing sense of guilt, but a liberating awareness of guilt that has been pushed aside and suppressed for too long. It implies a recognition of failure that frees one to change and reform (Uleyn 1969). By turning this recognition into transformatory action, the church realizes its holiness — that is to say, its practical, societal, and political holiness (Boff 1987a).

Emotive

By conceiving of the church as church of the poor, there is room for feelings of connectedness with the local, national, and especially the global community. This conception stimulates the psychic forces of pity and compassion. It opens us up to the awareness of the precipital depth of the vicarious suffering of the poor. Their example liberates us. It motivates us to accomplish the deeds they achieve: the deed of giving, the deed of receiving, and the deed of giving back. They are deeds that no one can claim for himself but which take place nevertheless: the supererogative actions. They are founded in mutual trust, bonding, and community. They do not occur in trade on the market; they do not fit the symmetry of costs and benefits, of debt and obligation. They surpass these in the direction of the giving of self and self-sacrifice.

The charisma of voluntary poverty fits in here too. It is a sign that the actual poverty people are forced to undergo does not have a final say. It is a vehicle of hope for the messianic kingdom, where suffering is past and tears are no longer shed. It is an expression of personal solidarity (Rahner 1971).

Conative

In the cognitive and emotive functions, we find a number of regulatory aspects. They can be divided into micro, meso, and macro levels.

At the *micro level,* the church must go in search of individuals and groups that are on the borders of society: the unemployed, the disabled, the divorced, widows, and orphans. With regard to the Netherlands, they belong to the group of 5% whose income amounts to less than 95% of the social minimum; they belong to the group of more than 10% who, according to their own feelings, live below the poverty level — the so-called subjective poverty line (Sociaal en Cultureel rapport 1992, 158-61).

To prevent this call from degenerating into a moral appeal, concrete work has to be done. Several steps have to be taken for this purpose: a description of the social stratification, so that the persons and groups in question can be localized and traced (chapter 17 sub 2); policy formation at project level, through which resolutions are turned into concrete policy actions (chapter 18 sub 1); formation of a special project group that goes about concrete work; placement of this group in a matrix organization, so that feedback can come from the project group for the established groups and councils within the church and vice versa (chapter 20 sub 1).

At the *meso level* the local church has to contribute to regional and national campaigns, projects, and organizations that coordinate aid for the larger groups, population groups, and collectives. Without the help of the churches at the base, these kinds of support and development would never get off the ground. In order to stimulate the awareness of connectedness and the efforts put forth, a responsible selection has to be made. For this purpose contact, adoption, visitation, and exchange projects are worth considering.

At the *macro level* the church must aim at the greatest possible contribution to intercontinental programs of relief aid, support, education, development, and upbuilding. It is important that these contributions should not only be focused on dealing with the negative consequences of the status quo. They should also be aimed at the transformatory processes in the church and society with an eye to restructuring the economic order. For the mischief that the present structures cause year in and year out is in flagrant opposition to the message of liberation that is implied in the messianic gospel of the poor. The reordering of the present world economy is therefore a matter of faith and confession: "Economics as a matter of faith" (De Lange 1989, 105).

The disadvantage one may spot here is that we are dealing with long lines: long-term matters, distant committees, established institutions, and abstract organizations. This, however, is only our experience, and not that of those who need a new economic order. How can we handle this contrast?

We can do no better than to refer to the image of the Last Judgment. It symbolizes our fundamental inability to point out clearly what the consequences are of our actions in daily life. It symbolizes the insight that we are not capable of an absolute judgment of our doings (Terpstra 1991, 113). The Gospel of Matthew paints the following picture: "When the Son of Man comes in his glory, and all the angels with him, then he will sit on the throne of his glory. All the nations will be gathered before him, and he will separate people one from another as a shepherd separates the sheep from the goats, and he will put the sheep at his right hand and the goats at his left" (Matt. 25:31-33). Which criterion will be used at the last judgment? What shall we be judged upon? The touchstone will be what we have done for individual people (Ricoeur 1968). What really matters is feeding the hungry, taking in a stranger, clothing the naked, and visiting the sick and the imprisoned. This is even without our being conscious of it. The awareness that we did this does not play a role, according to the Gospel. Thus, the text goes on to state: "Then the righteous will answer him, 'Lord, when was it that we saw you hungry and gave you food, or thirsty and gave you something to drink?'" (Matt. 25:37). That we reached individuals will be decisive. Probably this will sooner be in the extended relations of abstract institutions than in brief relations of face-to-face contact. The Last Judgment means that we will be judged on the basis of what has remained hidden to us because we do not know whether or when we have reached other individuals. We can be wrong about the significance of brief relations, and not see through to our own autocentric wants. We cannot survey the meaning of far-removed relationships. We often think we have not reached anyone in the abstract systems of economy, politics, and our own professions. Here, too, we can be wrong. All will be revealed to us. Whether or not we fed the hungry, quenched the thirst of the thirsty, clothed the naked, and visited the sick and imprisoned: in the end the judgment is not ours to make. We have neither the right nor the power. And the standard by which this is measured is outside our reach.

Summary of Parts III-VI

In the first two parts of this book, the functions and the religious codes of the church were discussed. The general function is religious communication. The core functions are identity, integration, policy, and management. The religious codes are community of the faithful, people of God, Jesus movement, body of Christ, building of the Spirit, and church of the poor. The first two parts concluded with the following question: In what sense can the core functions of the church, which signify and re-present the salvation from God that is implied in the religious codes, become bearers of the religious signs in the concrete practice of the church?

In the following four parts the four core functions were described one by one: identity, integration, policy, and management. Each time they were placed in the context of the societal process of modernization and described in several dimensions. Identity is localized in the context of secularization, integration in that of individualization, policy in that of utilization, and management in that of calculation. The context was always described as being both a restriction and an opportunity, a threat and a challenge to the church.

Further, each core function is related to one of the religious codes. The function of identity is related to two: the church as the people of God and as the Jesus movement. The function of integration is involved with the church as the body of Christ. The function of policy was clarified by means of the church as the building of the Spirit. Finally, the function of management was approached from the standpoint of the church of the poor.

We did not, however, base our discussion on the idea that there is a one-to-one relationship between core functions and religious codes. The breadth and depth of the codes cannot and may not be restricted by the separate functions. They do not merge with the various core functions. One can only emphasize certain accents. This was done proceeding from the assumption that there is a dialectical relationship between the functions and the codes. On the one hand, a particular code was discussed proceeding from the core function, through which certain facets of the code came to the fore more clearly than others. On the other, ample attention was paid to the effect the religious code had on the function in question. Each time this effect was discussed in terms of the cognitive, emotive, and conative aspects. The core function in question was clarified, supplemented, and corrected through this.

In Part III the core function of identity was central. As we mentioned, it was placed within the context of the societal process of secularization, which was clarified by means of its cultural and structural dimension. It was indicated that the church reacts to this secularization with three different strategies: deductive, inductive, and reductive (chapter 9). In these strategies the core of the identity of the church is at stake: its convictions. These can be divided into various levels (ultimate reality, ultimate order, spheres of life, and activities) and stem from different sources (religious socialization and praxis). It was demonstrated that they were influenced by both secularization and pluralization (chapter 10). The vision and mission of the church can serve as a guideline in dealing with secularization and pluralization. The vision of the church was clarified proceeding from the sociological term *people* and the religious code *people of God.* In this context the sin in the church and of the church was dealt with: the church as a sinner (chapter 11). The mission of the church was interpreted proceeding from the sociological term *movement* and the religious code *Jesus movement.* Here there was a critical discussion of the routinization of the charismata in today's church (chapter 12).

Part IV was dedicated to integration. It is localized in the context of individualization, which itself is the result of the fundamental process of industrialization and urbanization (chapter 13). Despite this individualization, many kinds of group, network, and community formations occur in all sorts of places in modern society. They provide the social infrastructure for the church as a community. The church as the body of Christ can lock onto this infrastructure. In this the freedom, equality, and mutual organic connectedness of the members of the church that are founded in Christ are central (chapter 14). Even though the communicative formation of consensus plays an important role in the church community as the body of Christ, it does not prevent the rise of conflicts. These need to be dealt with adequately. Here a complete solution in the spirit of the council of apostles in Jerusalem can work as a perspective, but a balanced compromise can often be seen as "today's command" *(Gebot der Stunde).* The term *prudence* is central in the balanced formation of compromise (chapter 15). Leadership in the church continually plays a role in the background in these matters. The practice of this leadership and its structure have to be oriented on two principles: ecclesiality and contextuality; for we are dealing with the development of the church in the context of today's society. Proceeding from the four types of authority that have been distinguished in accordance with the tradition of Max Weber (charismatic, traditional, legal-rational, and functional-rational), the church's authority has to be characterized by an evangelically inspired, apostolically oriented, democratic-participational, and pastoral-professional performance. This applies to both the ordained and the nonordained church leader (chapter 16).

In Part V the policy of the church was discussed. It was placed in the context of the societal process of utilization. By this we meant the endeavor to satisfy one's own needs and to realize one's own interests. In order to gain as clear a view as possible of the various needs and interests of the people in the church and its surroundings, their social stratification has to charted as accurately as possible. From there the church can explore the various needs and interests in a differentiated manner, albeit from the normative frame of reference that lies in the vision and mission of the church (chapter 17). So as to tackle this in an effective way, sufficient care has to be given to adequate policy development — both its formation and implementation. In the policy cycle the two are involved with each other (chapter 18). Adequate policy development demands an adjusted policy organization. The present formal organization structure, which can be typified as a bureaucratic and entrepreneurial organization, does not meet this demand (chapter 19). The development of church policy requires a shift in the direction of innovative organization. This can be given shape proceeding from the church as building of the Spirit. Here it is important to make a connection between a pneumatological approach of the church and a theology of ecclesial law that is to be developed (chapter 20).

Part VI dealt with the management of the church. This is localized in the context of the societal process of calculation and the law of supply and demand. The church as a service organization cannot escape a certain marketability, to the extent that it is dependent on being focused on the user (chapter 21). The endeavor for pastoral service quality places a special emphasis on aiming at the user; however, in the church it has to be made subordinate to the transcendent aim of pastoral service, which lies in the vision and mission of the church (chapter 22). This service depends on the expertise of those who render it: pastoral professionals and pastoral volunteers. Their development (education and training) deserves top priority (chapter 23). The church is incapable of realizing all its functions in the areas of identity, integration, policy, and management unless there is a solid financial infrastructure. The church cannot escape the problem of money. However, a problem presents itself that touches upon the very essence of the church: the relation of the church to the poor. In the perspective of the church of the poor, the church has to convert itself from a church of the rich to a church with the poor, and not to a church *for* the poor (chapter 24).

Bibliography

Achterhuis, H.

1980 *De Markt van welzijn en geluk.* Baarn.

Adam, I., and E. R. Schmidt

1977 *Gemeindeberatung.* Gelnhausen/Berlin.

Alberigo, G.

1984 "Het volk Gods in de gelovige ervaring." In *Conc.* 20 6:31-43.

Algemeen reglement voor het bestuur van een parochie van de Rooms Katholieke Kerk in Nederland.

1988 *Regelingen R. K. Kerkgenootschap in Nederland,* no. 3. Utrecht.

Ammer, H., ed.

1975-1978 *Handbuch der Praktischen Theologie,* I-III. Berlin.

Andree, T. G. I. M.

1983 *Gelovig word je niet vanzelf. Godsdienstige opvoeding van r.k. jongeren tussen 12 en 20 jaar.* Diss. RU Utrecht.

Andree, T., and P. Steegman

1987 Religieuze socialisatie. Utrecht/Franeker.

Annuarium statisticum ecclesiae 1989

1992 *Secretaria status, rationarium generale ecclesiae.* Vatican City.

Annuarium statisticum ecclesiae 1990

1992 Secretaria status, rationarium generale ecclesiae. Vatican City.

Aristotle *Ethica Nicomachea.*

Arnold, F. X.

1965 *Pastoraltheologische Durchblicke. Das Prinzip des Gott-Menschlichen und der geschichtliche Weg der Pastoraltheologie.* Freiburg/Basel/Wien.

———, K. Rahner, V. Schurr, and L. M. Weber, eds.

1964-1969 *Handbuch der Pastoraltheologie. Praktische Theologie der Kirche in ihrer Gegenwart I-V.* Freiburg.

Bibliography

Arroyo, G.

1980 "Afhankelijkheidstheorie. Een geldige bemiddeling voor de bevrijdingstheologie?" In *Bevrijding en christelijk geloof in Latijns-Amerika en Nederland,* 55-68. Baarn.

Aubert, R.

1974 "De kerk van de crisis van 1848 tot Vaticanum II." In L. J. Rogier, R. Aubert, and M. D. Knowles, *Geschiedenis van de kerk,* Dl. Xa. Bussum

Auer, J., and J. Ratzinger

1983 *Kleine Katholische Dogmatik, Band VIII: Die Kirche — Das allgemeine Heilssakrament.* Regensburg.

Aves, G. M.

1973 *The Voluntary Worker in the Social Services.* Ned vert. *De vrijwilliger in de sociale dienstverlening.* Amsterdam.

Avis, P.

1992 *Authority, Leadership and Conflict in the Church.* London.

Baart, A. J., J. G. M. Bakkers, and H. D. de Loor

1985 *Maatschappelijke activering en opbouw van de kerk.* Hilversum.

Barth, K.

1955 *Kirchliche Dogmatik* IV/1, IV/2. Zürich.

Basisprogram Federatie VPW

1988 *Uitgangspunten, professioneel statuut, beroepskode, organisatie, beleidsopties.* Utrecht.

Bassett, W.

1978 "Ondersteuning van de kerk door vrijwillige bijdragen." In *Conc.* 14 7:31-42.

———, and P. Huizing

1978 "Ten geleide. Het geld in de kerk." In *Conc.* 14 7:3-6.

Bastian, H.-D.

1972 *Kommunikation.* Berlin.

Batson, C. D., and W. L. Ventis

1982 *The Religious Experience. A Social-Psychological Perspective.* New York.

Bäumler, C., and N. Mette, eds.

1987 *Gemeindepraxis in Grundbegriffen. Ökumenische Orientierungen und Perspektiven.* München/Düsseldorf.

Bekke, H., and P. Kuypers

1990 *Afzien van macht. Adviseren aan een andere overheid.* Den Haag.

Bellah, R.

1973 "Religiöse Evolution." In *Seminar: Religion und gesellschaftliche Entwicklung.* Frankfurt.

Bellah, R. N., and Ph. E. Hammond

1980 *Varieties of Civil Religion.* San Francisco.

Bellah, R. N.

1985 *Habits of the Heart. Individualism and Commitment in American Life.* Berkeley.

Bellarminus, R.

1721 *Disputationes de controversiis Christianae fidei adversus hujus temporis haereticos.* Milan.

Berger, P. L.

1963 "A Market Model for the Analysis of Ecumenicity." In *Soc. Res.* 30:77-93.

1967 *The Sacred Canopy.* New York.

1969 *A Rumor of Angels.* New York.

1973 *Zur Dialektik von Religion und Gesellschaft.* Frankfurt.

1979 *The Heretical Imperative.* New York.

———, and Th. Luckmann

1966 "Secularization and Pluralism." In *Intern. Yearbook for the Sociology of Religion* II:73-86. Köln/Opladen.

1967 *The Social Construction of Reality. A Treatise in the Sociology of Knowledge.* New York.

Berger, W. J.

1984 *Logos en mythos.* Baarn.

Berkhof, H.

1985 *Christelijk geloof.* (5e dr.) Nijkerk.

Berkouwer, G. C.

1970 *De kerk I: Eenheid en katholiciteit.* Kampen.

1972 *De kerk, II: Apostoliciteit en heiligheid.* Kampen.

Berting, J.

1981 "Sociale stratificatie." In *Sociologische grondbegrippen,* 313-343. Utrecht/Antwerpen.

Bibby, R. W.

1987 *Fragmented Gods.* Toronto.

Bijzondere Synode van de Bisschoppen van Nederland. Rome

January 14-31 1980 *Documenten RK Kerkprovincie Nederland.* Utrecht.

Billiet, J.

1988 *Tussen bescherming en verovering. Sociologen en historici over zuilvorming.* Leuven.

Bilsen, B. van

1962 *Kerk in beweging.* Utrecht/Nijmegen.

Bitter, G., and R. Englert

1984 "'Hören, was der Geist den Gemeinden sagt.' Kairologische und pneumatologische Desiderate an die Theorie und Praxis der Praktischen Theologie." In O. Fuchs, ed. *Theologie und Handeln,* pp. 38-49. Düsseldorf.

Blake, R., and J. Mouton.

1984 *Solving Costly Organizational Conflicts.* San Francisco.

Blau, P. M., and W. R. Scott

1962 *Formal Organizations.* San Francisco.

Blommestein, H. J., J. Th. A. Bressers, and A. Hoogerwerf, eds.

1984 *Handboek beleidsevaluatie. Een multi-disciplinaire benadering.* Alphen a.d. Rijn/Brussel.

Bloth, P., ed.

1981 *Handbuch der Praktischen Theologie.* Gütersloh.

Bockmann, A.

1977 "Welke impulsen geeft het Nieuwe Testament aan de verhouding van de kerk tot de armen?" In *Conc.* 13 4:38-46.

Boekestijn, C.

1979 "De psychologie van relaties tussen groepen." In *Sociale psychologie in Nederland,* II:166-179. Deventer.

Boff, Cl.

1983 *Theologie und Praxis.* München.

Boff, L.

1972 *Die Kirche als Sakrament im Horizont der Welterfahrung. Versuch einer Legitimation und einer Strukturfunktionalistischen Grundlegung der Kirche im Anschluss an das II.* Vatikanische Konzil. Paderborn.

1984 "Wat betekenen theologisch volk Gods en kerk van het volk?" In *Conc.* 20 6:103-113.

1985 *Kirche: Charisma und Macht. Studien zu einer streitbaren Ekklesiologie.* Düsseldorf.

1987a *Und die Kirche ist Volk geworden.* Düsseldorf.

1987b "Leergezag en bevrijdingstheologen onder het oordeel van de armen." In *Conc.* 23 4:5-6.

1987c *Passion of Christ, Passion of the World.* New York.

Borg, M.B. ter

1990 "Publieke religie in Nederland." In *Religie in de Nederlandse samenleving,* 165-184. Baarn.

Bosch, D. J.

1991 *Transforming Mission. Paradigm Shifts in Theology of Mission.* New York.

Bosman, A., ed.

1981 *Planning en beleid bij profit en non profit organisaties.* Leiden/Antwerpen.

Bouwen rond de Hoeksteen

1989 *Een nota van het bisdom 's-Hertogenbosch.*

Braam, A. van

1986 *Leerboek bestuurskunde.* Muiderberg.

Brakel, J. van, and J. T. van der Brink

1988 *Filosofie van de wetenschappen.* Muiderberg.

Brief van de bisschoppen van Groningen, Utrecht, Haarlem, Rotterdam en Breda aan de pastoraal werk(st)ers in hun bisdom

1990 In *1-2-1.* Kerkelijke documentatie RK Kerkgenootschap. 18 4:13-18.

Brief van de bisschop van 's-Hertogenbosch aan de pastorale werk(st)ers in zijn bisdom

1990 In *1-2-1.* Kerkelijke documentatie RK Kerkgenootschap. 18 4:19-25.

Brief van de bisschop van Haarlem aan de pastoraal werk(st)ers en de pastoraal assistenten in zijn bisdom.

1990 In *1-2-1.* Kerkelijke documentatie RK Kerkgenootschap. 18 4:26-30.

Brion, M.

1975 "La paroisse dans l'organisation financière de l'Église." In *Lumière et Vie,* 37-51.

Brockhaus, U.

1972 *Charisma und Ambt.* Wuppertal.

Browning, D., ed.

1983 *Practical Theology. The Emerging Field in Theology, Church and World.* San Francisco.

Browning, D.

1987a "Practical Theology and Religious Education." In *Formation and Reflection,* 79-102. Philadelphia.

1987b *Religious Thought and the Modern Psychologies. A Critical Conversation in the Theology of Culture.* Philadelphia.

1991 *A Fundamental Practical Theology. Descriptive and Strategic Proposals.* Minneapolis.

Bruggen, K. van der

1986 *Verzekerde vrede of verzekerde vernietiging. Ontwikkeling van een theorie van gerechtvaardigde afschrikking.* Diss. V.U. Amsterdam. Kampen.

Brümmer, V.

1981 *Theology and Philosophical Inquiry.* The Macmillan Press.

Bulhof, I. N.

1990 "Het postmodernisme als uitdaging." In *Postmodernisme als uitdaging,* 11-50. Baarn.

Bultmann, R.

1965 *Theologie des Neuen Testaments.* Tübingen.

Buren, P. van.

1963 *The Secular Meaning of the Gospel.* London.

Byars, L. L.

1987 *Strategic Management. Planning and Implementation. Concepts and Cases.* New York.

Callahan, K. L.

1983 *Twelve Keys to an Effective Church.* New York.

1990 *Effective Church Leadership: Building on the Twelve Keys.* New York.

Cantor, N.

1953 *The Teaching-Learning Process.* New York.

1961 *Dynamics of Learning.* New York.

Carroll, J. W., C. S. Dudley, and W. Mckinney

1988 *Handbook for Congregational Studies.* Nashville.

Catechesi tradendae

1979 *Apostolische adhortatie van Paus Johannes Paulus II. Archief van de kerken,* no. 25.

Cereti, G.

1978 *De financiële bronnen en activiteiten van het Vaticaan.* In *Conc.* 14 7:7-23.

Cerfaux, L.

1966 "De symbolische beelden van de kerk in het Nieuwe Testament." In *De kerk van Vaticanum II,* deel I, 345-359, ed. G. Barauna. Bilthoven.

Challenge of Peace: God's Promise and Our Response

1983 Ned. vert. *De uitdaging van de vrede: Gods belofte en ons antwoord. Pax Christi Boekenreeks,* no. 7.

Chanlat, J. F.

1990 *L'individu dans l'organisation, les dimensions oubliées.* Quebec.

Chenu, M. D.

1964 *La Parole de Dieu. I. La foi dans l'intelligence.* Paris.

1977 "'De kerk van de armen' op Vaticanum II." In *Conc.* 13 4:57-63.

1979 *La "doctrine sociale" de l'Eglise comme Idéologie.* Paris.

Claassen, A.

1985 *Schipperen tussen school en kerk.* Nijmegen.

Clarke, H. D., and N. Dutt

1991 "Measuring Value Change in Western Industrialized Societies: The Impact of Unemployment." In *American Political Science Review* 85, 3:905-920.

Codex Iuris Canonici

1983 *Libreria Editrice Vaticana.* Vatican City. Ned. vert. *Wetboek van canoniek recht. Latijns-Nederlandse uitgave.* Brussels/Hilversum 1987.

Coleman, J. A., and G. Baum

1991 "Herdenking, evaluatie en verdere uitbouw van een traditie." In *Conc.* 27 5:9-13.

Commissaris, J.

1977 *Planning van kerkelijke vernieuwing.* Leiden.

Congar, Y.

1963 *Sainte Eglise. Etudes et approches ecclésiologiques.* Paris.

1964 *Jalons pour une théologie du laïcat.* Paris.

1965a "De kerk als volk van God." In *Conc.* 1 1:11-34.

1965b "Les Biens temporels de l'église d'après sa tradition théologique et canonique." In *Eglise et Pauvreté.* Paris, 233-258.

1967 "Apostolicité de ministère et apostolicité de doctrine." In *Volk Gottes,* ed. R. Bäumer and H. Dolch, 84-111. Freiburg.

1968 *Vraie et fausse réformé dans l'église.* Paris.

1970 *L'Eglise. De Saint Augustin à l'époque moderne.* Paris.

1972 "Vernieuwing van de Geest en hervorming van het instituut." In *Conc.* 8 3:36-47.

Conzemius, V.

1986 "Die Kritik der Kirche." In *Handbuch der Fundamentaltheologie* 3, Traktat Kirche. Freiburg, 30-48.

Corecco, E.

1983 "Theologie des Kirchenrechts." In *Handbuch des katholischen Kirchenrechts,* 12-23. Regensburg.

Coriden, J. A.

1979 "Mensenrechten in de kerk: een zaak van geloofwaardigheid en authenticiteit." In *Conc.* 15 4:70-79.

Cornelis, E.

1985 "De vloeiende grenzen van het begrip 'het uiteindelijke.'" In *Conc.* 21:10-20.

Daft, R. L.

1989 *Organization Theory and Design.* 3rd ed. New York.

Daiber, K.-F., and I. Lukatis

1984 *Die Praxisrelevanz von Theologie und Sozialwissenschaften.* Frankfurt.

Dalferth, I. U.

1981 *Religiöse Rede von Gott.* München.

Deaux, K., and L. S. Wrightsman

1984 *Social Psychology in the 80's.* California.

Dekker, G.

1987 *Godsdienst en samenleving.* Kampen.

Derksen, N. J. M.

1989 Eigenlijk wisten we het wel, maar we waren het vergeten. Een onderzoek naar parochie-ontwikkeling en geloofscommunicatie in de parochies van het aartsbisdom Utrecht. Diss. Heerlen, Kampen.

Dialogue and Proclamation

1991 "Reflections and Orientations on Interreligious Dialogue and the Proclamation of the Gospel of Jesus Christ." In *Origins,* July 4, 21, no. 8. *Ned vert. Dialoog en verkondiging. Kerkelijke documentatie 1-2-1,* 19:9. Utrecht.

Dietterich, I. T.

1991 *An Evaluation of Approaches to Church Transformation.* The Center for Parish Development. Chicago.

Dietterich, P.

1987 *Strategic Planning in the Church.* The Center for Parish Development. Chicago.

Dignitatis Humanae. Vaticanum II. Katholiek Archief. Amersfoort.

Dijkstra, J.

1989 *Opbouw in Spoorwijk.* Diss. K.U. Nijmegen.

Dingemans, G. D. J.

1986 *In de leerschool van het geloof. Mathetiek en vakdidactiek voor catechese en kerkelijk vormingswerk.* Kampen.

1987 *Een huis om in te wonen. Schetsen en bouwstenen voor een Kerk en een Kerkorde van de toekomst.* Den Haag.

1989 "Pleidooi voor een open kerk." In *De kerk verbouwen. Dingemans' ecclesiologie critisch bekeken,* ed. J. P Heering et al., 177-187. Nijkerk.

1991 *Als hoorder onder de hoorders. Een hermeneutische homiletiek.* Kampen.

Dobbelaere, K.

1988 "Vormen van godsdienstig isolement: Hutterienten en zevendedagadventisten." In *Tussen bescherming en verovering. Sociologen en historici over zuilvorming,* ed. J. Billiet, 279-308. Leuven.

Döbert, R.

1973 *Systemtheorie und die Entwicklung religiöser Deutungssysteme.* Frankfurt.

1984 "Religiöse Erfahrung und Religionsbegriff." In *Religionspädagogische Beiträge* 14:98-118.

1986 "Wider die Vernachlässigung des Inhalts in den Moraltheorien von Kohlberg und Habermas." In *Zur Bestimmung der Moral,* ed. W. Edelstein and G. Nunner-Winkler. Frankfurt.

Dolan, J. P., R. S. Appleby, P. Byrne, and D. Campbell

1990 *Transforming Parish Ministry. The Changing Roles of Catholic Clergy, Laity, and Women Religious.* New York.

Doorn, J. A. A. van, and C. J. Lammers

1959 *Moderne sociologie. Systematiek en analyse.* Utrecht/Antwerpen.

Doorn, J. A. A. van, and F. van Vught

1978 *Planning. Methoden en technieken voor beleidsondersteuning.* Assen/Amsterdam.

Dorenbos, J., L. Halman, and F. Heunks

1987 "Modernisering in West-Europa: een tweedeling?" In *Traditie, secularisatie en individualisering,* 234-254. Tilburg.

Drehsen, V.

1988 *Neuzeitliche Konstitutionsbedingungen der Praktischen Theologie,* Bd. I-II. Gütersloh.

Dudley, C. S.
1983 *Building Effective Ministry.* San Francisco.

Duffhues, T.
1991 *Generaties en patronen. De katholieke beweging te Arnhem in de 19e en 20e eeuw.* Baarn.

———, A. Felling, and J. Roes
1985 *Bewegende patronen. Een analyse van het landelijk netwerk van katholieke organisaties en bestuurders 1945-1980.* Baarn.

Dulles, A.
1974 *Models of the Church.* Dublin.

Dunn, W. N.
1981 *Public Policy Analysis: An Introduction.* Englewood Cliffs.

Durkheim, E.
1925 *Les formes élémentaires de la vie religieuse.* Paris.

Duroux, B.
1955 *Aspects psychologiques de l'analysis fidei chez Saint Thomas FZPHTH* 2, 148-172.
1963 *La psychologie de la foi chez Saint Thomas d'Aquin.* Tournai.

Dussel, E.
1984 "'Populus Dei' in het 'populus pauperum.' Van Vaticanum II naar Medellin en Puebla." In *Conc.* 20 6:44-54.

Dux, G.
1973 "Religion, Geschichte und sozialer Wandel in Max Webers Religionssoziologie." In *Seminar Religion und gesellschaftliche Entwicklung,* 313-337. Frankfurt.
1982 *Die Logik der Weltbilder.* Frankfurt.

Duyker, H.
1976 "De ideologie van de zelfontplooiing." In *Pedagogische Studiën* 10:358-374.

Ebach, J.
1986 "Die Welt 'in der Erlösung nicht vorweggenommen werden kann.'" In *Leiden, Religion und Philosophie.* Bd. 3, 20-27. Paderborn.

Eco, U.
1979a *A Theory of Semiotics.* Bloomington.
1979b *Lector in Fabula.* Ned vert. (1989). Lector in Fabula. Amsterdam.
1990 *The Limits of Interpretation.* Bloomington.

Edwards, J.
1976 "A Treatise Concerning Religious Affections in Three Parts." In *The Works of Jonathan Edwards,* Vol. I, 226-236. Edinburgh.

Edwards, R. B.
1982 *A Return to Moral and Religious Philosophy in Early America.* Washington.

Egan, G.
1989 *Organiseren in de non-profit sector.* Nijmegen.

Egmond, A. van
1986 *De lijdende God in de Britse theologie van de negentiende eeuw.* Diss. VU Amsterdam.

Eicher, P.
1977 *Offenbarung. Prinzip neuzeitlicher Theologie.* München.
1980 *Theologie. Eine Einführung in das Studium.* Kösel/München.

Eijsink, A. H.

1988 *Een staaltje van macht?* Utrecht.

Eisinga, R., and P. Scheepers

1989 *Etnocentrisme in Nederland.* Nijmegen.

Eisinga, R., A. Felling, and J. Peters

1990 "Church Involvement, Prejudice, and Nationalism." *Review of Religious Research* 4:417-433.

Elias, N.

1982a Über die Einsamkeit der Sterbenden. Frankfurt.

1982b *Über den Prozess der Zivilisation. Sociogenetische und psychogenetische Untersuchungen. Ned vert. Het civilisatieproces,* 2 dln. Utrecht/Antwerpen.

Ernst, H. et al.

1984 *Theologie en kerkvernieuwing.* Baarn.

Ernst, H.

1989 *Pastoraal beleid bij verscheidenheid in kerkbetrokkenheid.* Uitgave Bisdom Breda 5 April 1989.

1991 *De pastorale arbeid in de negentiger jaren.* Uitgave Bisdom Breda.

1992 "Visie en achtergronden bij de oprichting van de Diocesane commissie voor vrijwilligers in de kerk." In *Analecta Bisdom Breda* 6 6:184-187.

———, and J. A. van der Ven

1987 *Bisschoppen en theologen in dialoog. Verslag van gesprekken over de funktie van pastoraal werk(st)er in een werkgroep samengesteld vanuit kerkelijk beleid en theologie.* Kampen.

Etter, U. W.

1987 *Sinnvolle Verständigung,* Bd. I-II. Bern.

Etzioni, A.

1964 *Modern Organizations.* Englewood Cliffs.

1968 *The Active Society.* New York.

1975 *A Comparative Analysis of Complex Organizations.* New York.

1988 *The Moral Dimension. Toward a New Economics.* New York.

Evers, G.

1989 "Die Wetterecke gegenwärtiger Theologie. Stand und Probleme des interreligiösen Dialogs." In *Herder Korrespondenz,* 2:75-80.

Ezerman, G., and W. Mastenbroek

1991 *Kwaliteitsverbetering in de dienstverlening.* Deventer.

Faivre, A.

1976 *Clergé et propriété dans l'église ancienne."* In *Lumière et vie* 129/130, 51-64.

Fauconnier, G.

1987 "Kerk, media en marketing." *Katholiek Instituut voor Massamedia,* 2-26. Nijmegen.

Feige, A.

1990 *Kirchenmitgliedschaft in der Bundesrepublik Deutschland. Zentrale Perspektiven empirischer Forschungsarbeit im problemgeschichtlichen Kontext der deutschen Religions- und Kirchensoziologie nach 1945.* Gütersloh.

Feldman, K. E., and Th. M. Newcomb

1969 *The Impact of College on Students.* San Francisco.

Felling, A., and H. Hüttner
1981 "De analyse van sociale netwerken." In *Onderzoekstypen in de sociologie,* ed. M. Albinski, 244-261. Assen.

Felling, A., J. Peters, and O. Schreuder
1983 *Burgerlijk en onburgerlijk Nederland. Een nationaal onderzoek naar waardenoriëtaties op de drempel van de jaren tachtig.* Deventer.
1986 *Geloven en leven. Een nationaal onderzoek naar de invloed van religieuze overtuigingen.* Zeist.
1987a *Religion in Dutch Society.* Steinmetz Archive. Amsterdam.
1987b *Religion im Vergleich: Bundesrepublik Deutschland und Niederlande.* Frankfurt am Main/Bern/New York/Paris.

Fichter, J. H.
1961 *Religion as an Occupation.* Notre Dame.
1988 *A Sociologist Looks at Religion.* Wilmington.

Firet, J.
1968a *Het agogisch moment in het pastoraal optreden.* Kampen.
1968b *Praktische theologie als theologische futurologie.*
1986 "Het niveau van de intuïtie overstijgen." In *Prakt. Theol.* 13 5:595-605.
1987 *Spreken als een leerling.* Kampen.

Fortuyn, W. S. P.
1992 "De contractmaatschappij: een politiek-economische zedenschets." In *Overheid: Vernieuwer of vernieler,* 45-48. Leiden/Antwerpen.

Fowler, J. W.
1987 *Faith Development and Pastoral Care.* Philadelphia.
1990 "Practical Theology and the Social Science." Paper at the Conference on Practical Theology. Tübingen/Blaubeuren.

Frankemölle, H.
1981 *Kirche von unten.* München/Mainz.

Frankl, V. E.
1977 *Das Leiden am sinnlosen Leben.* Freiburg.

Freire, P.
1972 *Pedagogy of the Oppressed.* Ned. vert. *Pedagogie van de onderdrukten.* Baarn.
1974 *Extensao ou communicacao? Deutsche Übers. Pädagogik der Solidarität.* Wuppertal.

French, W. L., and C. H. Bell, Jr.
1984 *Organization Development: Behavioral Science Interventions for Organization Improvement.* Englewood Cliffs.

Freud, S.
1985 *Leonardo da Vinci and a Memory of His Childhood.* The Pelican Freud Library, vol. 14, 143-232. Penguin Books.

Friebe, J.
1973 *Pilgerndes Gottesvolk. Eine pastoraltheologische Untersuchung in der kritischen Gemeinde IJmond.* Diss. K.J. Nijmegen. Münster.

Fries, H.
1985 *Fundamentaltheologie.* Graz/Wien/Köln.

Frijda, N. H.
1983 "De structuur van emoties." In *Psychologie in Nederland.* Lisse.

1984 "Emoties." In *Intermediair* 8:17-21.

1986 *The Emotions.* Cambridge.

Fuchs, O.

1984 *Theologie und Handeln. Beiträge zur Fundierung der Praktischen Theologie als Handlungstheorie.* Düsseldorf.

1990 *Zwischen Wahrhaftigkeit und Macht. Pluralismus in der Kirche?* Frankfurt.

Gabriel, K.

1988a "Lebenswelten unter den Bedingungen entfalteter Modernität." In *Pastoraltheol. Informationen* 1:93-108.

1988b "De uitoefening van macht in de kerk van onze tijd in het licht van sociaalwetenschappelijke machtstheorieën: Max Weber, Michel Foucault en Hanna Arendt." In *Conc.* 24 3:33-40.

———, and F.-X. Kaufmann

1980 *Zur Soziologie des Katholizismus.* Mainz.

Gaede, St.

1981 "Review Symposium: Peter L. Berger's The Heretical Imperative." In *Journal for the Scientific Study of Religion,* 181-185.

Gagné, R.

1977 *The Conditions of Learning.* New York.

Gallup, G., and J. Castelli

1989 *The People's Religion. American Faith in the 90's.* New York.

Gamm, H.-J.

1979 *Allgemeine Pädagogik. Die Grundlagen von Erziehung und Bildung in der bürgerlichen Gesellschaft.* Reinbek (Hamburg).

Gamwell, F. I.

1984 *Beyond Preference. Liberal Theories of Independent Associations.* Chicago/London.

Gaudium et Spes. Vaticanum II. Katholiek Archief. Amersfoort.

Geerts, H.

1990 "An Inquiry into the Meanings of Ritual Symbolism: Turner and Pierce." In *Current Studies on Rituals,* 19-32. Amsterdam.

Geertz, C.

1969 "Religion as a Cultural System." In *The World Yearbook of Religion. The Religious Situation,* I:639-688. London.

Geffré, C., and J.-P. Jossua

1983 "Religieuze onverschilligheid. Ten geleide." In *Conc.* 19 5:5-7.

Gekonsolideerde cijfers van de parochies in het bisdom Rotterdam

1990 Nota Bisdom Rotterdam.

Geldwerving in de parochie

1976 Kaski, rapport no. 337. Den Haag.

Gerechtigkeit schaft Frieden

1983 *Wort der Deutschen Bischofskonferenz zum Frieden.* Bonn.

Gerwen, G. T. van

1983 "Privatisering als thema in de ecclesiologie." In *Tijds. v. Theol.* 23:125-146.

1985 *Catechetische begeleidinig.* Serie Theologie en Empirie, deel 3. Kampen.

1988a "De moeizame professionalisering van het pastorale beroep." In *Prakt. Theol.* 15 5:541-556.

1988b "Over organisatie en management in de kerk." In *Tijds. v. Theol.* 28 4:371-392.

1989 "Geestelijke verzorging in de knel. Pastoraaltheologische reflektie naar aanleiding van Hirsch Ballin." In *Prakt. Theol.* 16 4:453-470.

1990 *Pastorale begeleidinig door vrijwilligers. Empirisch-theologisch onderzoek naar de motivatie tot deelname aan pastorale zorg in levenscrises.* Serie Theologie en Empirie, Deel 7. Kampen.

Geurts, J., and J. Vennix, ed.

1989 *Verkenningen in beleidsanalyse.* Zeist.

Giesbers, J., and T. Bergen

1991 *Professionaliteit en professionalisering van leraren.* Focus 8. Culemborg.

Giesecke, H.

1979 *Didaktik der politischen Bildung.* München.

Glock, Ch.

1973 "The Role of Deprivation in the Origin of Evolution of Religious Groups." In *Religion and Social Conflict,* ed. R. Lee and M. Marty. New York.

Glock, Ch., B. Ringer, and E. Babbie

1967 *To Comfort and to Challenge. A Dilemma of the Contemporary Church.* Berkeley.

Glock, Ch., and R. Stark

1965 *Religion and Society in Tension.* Chicago.

Goddijn, H.

1981 "'Gemeinschaft' en 'Gesellschaft.'" In *Sociologische grondbegrippen,* 249-260. Utrecht/Antwerpen.

Goddijn, W.

1973 *De beheerste kerk. Uitgestelde revolutie in Rooms-Katholiek nederland.* Amsterdam/Brussel.

1981 *Hebben de kerken nog toekomst?* Baarn.

Goede, J. H. de

1983 "Urbanisatie en urbanisme." In *Schoorl J. W. Sociologie der modernisering,* 312-349. Deventer.

Goffman, E.

1975 *Totale instituties.* Rotterdam.

1977 "Der bestätigende Austausch." In *Seminar: Kommunikation, Interaktion, Identität,* 35-72. Frankfurt.

Gonzalez, O.

1966 "Het nieuwe kerkbewustzijn en zijn historisch-theologische vooronderstellingen." In *Der Kerk van Vaticanum II,* dl 1, ed. G. Barauna. Bilthoven.

Gordon, C. W., and N. Babchuk

1959 "A Typology of Voluntary Associations." In *American Sociological Review* 1:22-39.

Grabner-Haider, A.

1974 *Theorie der Theologie als Wissenschaft.* München.

1975 *Glaubenssprache.* Freiburg.

Graf, A.

1841 *Kritische Darstellung des gegenwärtigen Zustandes der praktischen Theologie.* Tübingen.

Granfield, P.

1982 "Het verschijnen en verdwijnen van de societas perfects." In *Conc.* 18 1:8-14.

Greeley, A. M., and P. H. Rossi

1966 *The Education of Catholic Americans.* Chicago.

Greinacher, N.

1968 "Soziologie der Pfarrei." In *Handbuch der Pastoraltheologie,* Band III, 111-139. Freiburg.

1971 "Gemeente zonder overheersing." In *Conc.* 7 3:70-86.

1974 "Das Theorie-Praxis-Problem in der Praktischen Theologie." In *Praktische Theologie heute,* 103-119. München.

1990 "Demokratisierung in der Kirche." In *Theologische Quartalschrift* 170:253-260.

1992 "Das Heil der Menschen. Oberstes Gesetz in der Kirche." *Theol. Quartalschrift* 172 1:2-15.

Gremillion, J., and J. Castelli

1987 *The Emerging Parish. The Notre Dame Study of Catholic Life Since Vatican II.* San Francisco.

Griesl, G.

1974 "Praktische Theologie als Lehre vom Selbstvolzug der Kirche." In *Praktische Theologie heute,* 141-149. München.

Grijs, F. de

1985 "Op zoek naar een signalement van de kerk." In *Toekomst voor de kerk? Studies voor Frans Haarsma,* ed. J. A. van der Ven, 78-88. Kampen.

Groethuysen, B.

1930 *Die Entstehung der bürgerlichen Welt- und Lebensanschauung in Frankreich,* I-II. Halle/Saale.

Groot, A. D. de

1968 *Methodologie. Grondslagen van onderzoek en denken in de gedragswetenschappen.* Den Haag.

———, and F. L. Medendorp

1986 *Term, begrip, theorie.* Meppel/Amsterdam.

Groot, A. J. de

1980 *Pecunia olet. Enige beschouwingen over kerk en tijdelijke goederen.* Rede KU Nijmegen.

Groothuis

1973 *De brabantse bisschoppen Bekkers en De Vet.* Tilburg.

Gross, E., and A. Etzioni

1985 *Organizations in Society.* Englewood Cliffs.

Grossouw, W. K.

1967 "Van het Reve en de religie of lezen en lezen is twee." In *Een overlevende uit de voortijd,* 232-239. Roermond/Hilversum.

Gustafson, J.

1961 *Treasure in Earthen Vessels. The Church as a Human Community.* New York.

Gutiérrez, G.

1974 *Theologie van de bevrijding.* Baarn.

1977 "De armen in de kerk." In *Conc.* 13 4:82-88.

1987 *On Job.* New York.

Haaften, A. W. van, et al.

1986 *Ontwikkelingsfilosofie. Een onderzoek naar grondslagen van ontwikkeling en opvoeding.* Muiderberg.

Haarsma, F.

1965 "Pastoraaltheologische beschouwingen over de priester." In *Tijds. v. Theol.* 5 3:272-295.

1967 *Geest en kerk.* Utrecht.

1970a "Pastoraaltheologie." In *Grote Winkler Prins,* Deel 15, 160-161.

1970b "Kerkelijk ambt als profetisme." In *Tijds. v. Theol.* 10 2:179-202.

1971 "Aufgaben der Pastoraaltheologie in den kommenden Jahren." In *Zukunft der Theologie, Theologie der Zukunft,* 179-190. Wien.

1971 "Alternatieve groepen in de kerk, I." In *Theol. & Past.* 4:308-316.

1972 "Alternatieve groepen in de Kerk, II." In *Theol. & Past.* 3:212-224.

1975 "Terugblik op de opleiding vanuit de staf. Pastorale opleiding, pastorale praktijk, kerkelijk beleid." In *Praktische Theologie* 2 1:23-27.

1981 *Morren tegen Mozes. Pastoraaltheologische beschouwingen over het kerkelijk leven.* Kampen.

1983 "Partiële identificatie met de kerk." In *Meedenken met Edward Schillebeeckx,* ed. H. Häring, T. Schoof, and A. Willems. Baarn.

1985 *Pastoraal in de stad van de mens.* Afscheidscollege. Baarn.

1990 "Tot zegen geroepen. Ecclesiologische reflektie bij de pastorale brief." In *Prak. Theol.* 17 1:14-25.

1991 *Kandelaar en korenmaat, pastoraaltheologische studies over kerk en pastoraat.* Kampen.

Haas, P. de

1972 *The Church as an Institution. Critical Studies in the Relation between Theology and Sociology.* Diss. Leiden.

Habermas, J.

1982 *Theorie des kommunikativen Handelns,* Bd. I-II. Frankfurt.

1983 *Moralbewußtsein und kommunikatives Handeln.* Frankfurt.

Hahn, F., et al.

1979 *Einheit der Kirche. Grundlegung im Neuen Testament.* Freiburg.

Hainz, J.

1982 *Koinonia.* Regensburg.

Hall, R. H., J. E. Haas, and N. J. Johnson

1967 "An Examination of the Blau-Scott and Etzioni Typologies." In *Administrative Science Quarterly* 12:118-129.

Hall, S., and T. Jefferson

1977 *Resistance through Rituals. Youth Cultures in Post-War Britain.* Birmingham.

Halman, L., et al.

1987 *Traditie, secularisatie en individualisering. Een studie naar de waarden van de Nederlanders in een Europese context.* Tilburg.

Halman, L.

1991 *Waarden in de westerse wereld.* Tilburg.

Häring, H.

1984 "Tussen 'civiele religie' en godsdienstkritiek." In *Tijds. v. Theol.* 24 4:333-354.

1985 "'Kerk, wat zeg je van jezelf?' De theologie van Johannes Paulus II." In *Tijds. v. Theol.* 25 3:229-249.

Harrison, P. M.

1960 "Weber's Categories of Authority and Voluntary Associations." In *American Sociological Review* 25:232-237.

Harskamp, A. van

1986 *Theologie: tekst in context.* Bd. I en II. Diss. KU Nijmegen.

1988 "Kerkelijk gezag: vluchtoord voor de moderniteit." In *Tijds. v. Theol.* 28 2:135-154.

1991 "Behoefte aan religie of verlangen naar God?" In *Tijds. v. Theol.* 31 3:223-245.

1991 *Verborgen God of lege kerk. Theologen en sociologen over secularisatie.* Kampen.

Hart, J. de

1990 *Levensbeschouwelijke en politieke praktijken van Nederlandse middelbare scholieren.* Kampen.

Hartshorne, C.

1948 *The Divine Relativity.* Yale University.

———, and W. L. Reese

1953 *Philosophers Speak of God.* Chicago.

Hasenhüttl, G.

1973 *Kirche als Institution.* Freiburg.

1974 "Kerk en instituut." In *Conc.* 10 1:16-25.

Heckhausen, H.

1972 "Some Approaches to Interdisciplinarity." In *Interdisciplinarity. Organization for Economic Cooperation and Development,* 83-89. Paris.

Heeger, R.

1985 "Utilisme en aanvaardbaarheid." In *Ethiek in meer voud,* 18-47. Assen.

Heering, G. J.

1981 *De zondeval van het christendom.* Utrecht.

Heidenreich, H.

1988 "'Evangelisierung in Europa.' Zur Thematik der Konferenz deutschsprachiger Pastoraltheologen in Wien 1987." In *PThI* 1:25-43.

Heiler, Fr.

1969 *Das Gebet.* München/Basel.

Heinz, G.

1974 *Das Problem der Kirchenentstehung.* Mainz.

Helm, A. van der

1992 "Functies en posities in het pastoraat: Naconciliaire ontwikkeling in Nederland vanuit het recht bezien." In *Tijds. v. Theol.* 32 1:57-82.

Hemert M. van

1991 *Achtergronden van kerkelijk gedrag. Een onderzoek in zeven roomskatholieke parochies.* Diss. KU Nijmegen. Den Haag.

1992 "Kerkelijke statistiek van het R.K. Kerkgenootschap in Nederland 1985-1900." In *1-2-1.* Kerkelijke documentatie. Secretariaat R.K. Kerk 20, 7.

———, and L. Spruit

1984 *Parochie, maatschappelijke kontekst en kerkelijke betrokkenheid. Een onderzoek in zeven parochies.* Kaski. Rapport 389 en 389A. Deel I en II (bijlagen). Den Haag.

Henau, E.

1988 "Pastoral theology: science or wisdom?" Paper at the International Colloquium on Pastoral Studies. St. Paul University, Ottawa. In A. Visscher, *Pastoral Studies in the University Setting,* 101-108. Ottawa.

1989a *De kerk: instrument en teken van heil.* Leuven/Amersfoort.

1989b "Pastoraaltheologie: wetenschap of wijsheid? Over de wetenschappelijke status van de pastoraaltheologie." In *Kerkelijk leven in Vlaanderen anno 2000,* ed. J. Bulckens and P. Cooreman. Leuven/Amersfoort.

Hendriks, J.

1990 *Een vitale en aantrekkelijke gemeente. Model en methode van gemeenteopbouw.* Kampen.

———, and S. Stoppels

1986 *Uitspraak, Tegenspraak, Samen spraak. Het profetisch spreken van de kerk als pastoraal handelen.* Kampen.

Hengel, J. Van de, P. O'Grady, and P. Rigby

1989 "Cognitive Linguistic Psychology and Hermeneutics." *Man and World,* 43-70.

Hermanns, M.

1979 *Kirche als soziale Organisation.* Düsseldorf.

Hermans, C. A. M.

1986 *Morele vorming. Empirisch-theologisch onderzoek naar de effecten van een katechese-curriculum in de morele vorming omtrent de milieucrisis.* Serie Theologie en Empire, Deel 4. Kampen.

1988 "Understanding Parables and Similes qua Metaphors." In *Journal of Empirical Theology* 1 2:21-51.

1990 *Wie werdet ihr die Gleichnisse verstehen? Empirisch-theologische Forschung zur Gleichnisdidaktik.* Kampen.

———, and J. A. van der Ven

1991 "Motivatie van pastorale vrijwilligers tot deelname aan toerustingscursussen." In *Prak. Theol.* 18 3:302-320.

Heron, A.

1978 "Het historisch geconditioneerde karakter van de Apostolische geloofsbelijdenis." In *Conc.* 14 8:22-29.

Heunks, F.

1987 "Patronen van sociale en politieke integratie." In *Traditie, secularisatie en individualisering,* 98-122. Tilburg.

Hijmans, E., and H. Hilhorst

1990 "Hedendaagse vormen van zingeving." In *Religie in de Neerlandse samenleving,* 137-164. Baarn.

Hill, M.

1987 "Sect." In *The Encyclopedia of Religion* 13:154-159.

Hiltner, S.

1958 *Preface to Pastoral Theology.* New York.

Hoeben, G., and N. Nooren

1984 *Onderweg naar pastoraatsgroepen in het Bisdom Breda.* Breda.

Hoedemaker, L. A.

1989 "De plaats van de gemeente." In *De kerk verbouwen. Dingemans' ecclesiologie critisch bekeken,* ed. J. P. Heering et al., 133-144. Nijkerk.

Hoekendijk, J. C.

1967 *The Church Inside Out.* London.

Hoesel, P. H. M. van

1985 *Programmering van beleidsonderzoek. Theorie en praktijk.* 's-Gravenhage.

Höfte, B.

1990 *Bekering en bevrijding.* Diss. KThU. Utrecht.

Höhn, H.-J.

1985 *Kirche und Kommunikatives Handeln. Studien zur Theologie und Praxis der Kirche in der Auseinandersetzung mit den Soziallehren Niklas Luhmanns und Jürgen Habermas.* Frankfurt a.M.

Hollweg, A.

1971 *Theologie und Empirie.* Stuttgart.

Homans, G. C.

1961 *The Human Group.* Ned. vert (1966): *Individu en gemeenschap.* Utrecht/Antwerpen.

Hoogen, T. van den, and P. van Gerven

1991 "Gemeenteopbouw in de spiegel van de diakonie." In *Prakt. Theol.* 18 4:414-435.

Hoogstraten, H.-D. van

1986 *Het gevangen denken. Een bevrijdings theologie voor het "vrije Westen."* Kampen.

Hopewell, J. F.

1987 *Congregation: Stories and Structures,* ed. Barbara Wheeler. Fortress Press.

Houtepen, A. W. J.

1973 *Onfeilbaarheid en hermeneutiek. De betekenis van het infallibilitasconcept op Vaticanum I.* Diss. KU Nijmegen. Brugge.

1983a "Kerkelijk gezag als garantie van christelijke identiteit." In *Meedenken met Edward Schillebeeckx,* 276-291. Baarn.

1983b *Mensen van God. Een pleidooi voor de kerk.* Hilversum.

1984 "Naar een gemeenschappelijk verstaan van doop, eucharistie en ambt?" In *Tijds. v. Theol.* 24 3:247-274.

1990 " 'Integrity of Creation': naar een ecologische scheppingstheologie." In *Tijds. v. Theol.* 30 1:51-75.

1992a "Gerechtigheid in honderd jaar sociale encyclieken." In *Tempora mutantur. Over maatschappelijke verandering en ontwikkeling in het sociale denken,* ed. W. A. Arts et al., 28-50. Baarn.

1992b "Een gebroken wereld? Fragmenten van een bevrijdende scheppingstheologie." In *Schepping, verlossing en het kwaad. Wijsgerige en theologische reflecties,* ed. P. van Tongeren, 44-72. Baarn.

Huels, J.

1986 "Het parochieleven in het nieuwe kerkelijke wetboek." In *Conc.* 22 3:61-67.

Huitema, H., P. Post, and R. Lantman

1986 *Catechese en parochie. Bouw stenen voor volwassencatechese.* Averbode-Apeldoorn.

Huizing, P., and W. Bassett

1976 "Geloven op bevel? Rechtsproblemen rond het leergezag." In *Conc.* 12 7:3-11.

Huysmans, R.

1986 *Het recht van de leek in de rooms-katholieke kerk in Nederland.* Hilversum.

1986 "De pastoraal werk(st)er en het nieuwe pause lijke wetboek." In *Van beroep: Pastor. De arbeidsverhoudingen van pastores in de rooms-katholieke kerk van Nederland,* ed. B. van Dijk and Th. Salemink. Hilversum.

———, and R. Scholten, ed.

1986 *De pastoraatsgroep.* Hilversum.

Iersel, A. van

1982 *Op zoek naar "gewetenloze" politiek. De tegen stelling tussen gezindheidsethiek en verantwoordelijkheids ethiek in het denken van Max Weber in het licht van de tegen stelling tussen conscientia en prudentia.* Doc. scriptie. Theologisch Instituut. KU. Nijmegen.

———, and M. Spanjersberg

1985 "Vredeseducatie in de kerk: een gevaar voor eenheid?" In *Pastoraal tussen ideaal en werkelijkheid,* ed. J. A. van der Ven, 141-156. Kampen.

1993 *De vrede leren in de kerk.* Serie Theologie en Empirie. Kampen.

Iersel, B. van

1970 "Structuren van de kerk van morgen." In *De toekomst van de kerk,* 116-126. Bussum.

1980 "De onderzoeksprocedure van de congregatie voor de geloofsleer." In *Tijds. v. Theol.* 20 1:3-25.

In Christus' naam. Herderlijk schrijven over woord, sacrament, ambt en wijding

1992 Bisschoppelijke Brieven. No. 29. Utrecht.

In Gezamenlijke Verantwoordelijkheid

1990 Beleidsplan Parochie Johannes en Jacobus, Dukenburg. Nijmegen.

Inglehart, R.

1990 *Cultural Shift in Advanced Industrial Society.* Princeton.

Izard, C. E., et al., ed.

1984 *Emotions, Cognitions and Behaviour.* Cambridge (USA).

Jäger, A.

1986 "Diakonie als christliches Unternehmen, Gütersloh. Jakobson R. (1985). Closing Statement: Linguistics and Poetics." In *Semiotics. An Introductory Anthology,* ed. R. E. Innis. Bloomington.

James, W.

1902 *The Varieties of Religious Experience.* Ned vert. (1963). *Varianten van religieuze beleving. Een onderzoek naar de menselijke aard.* Zeist/Antwerpen.

1975 *Pragmatism.* Cambridge.

Javierre, A.

1968 "Een oriëntatie in de klassieke leer over de apostolische opvolging." In *Conc.* 4 4:17-27.

Jenkins, D. T.

1974 "Congregationalists." In *Enc. Brit.,* 1127-1131.

Jeurissen, R.

1989 "Het sociale denken binnen de katholieke kerk: uitgangspunten en ontwikkelingen." In *Vernieuwing van het christelijk sociaal denken,* 26-45. Baarn.

1993 *Peace and Religion.* Diss. KU Nijmegen. Serie Theologie en Empirie. Kampen.

Jolles, H. M.

1972 *Sociologie van de participatie.* Alphen a/d Rijn.

1978 "Sociologie van de verenigingen." In *Sociologische Encyclopedie,* 776-780. Utrecht/Antwerpen.

Joncheray, J.

1992 *Le rapport sciences humines/théologie en théologie pratique. Conférence. Congrès international oecuménique et francophone de théologie pratique.* Lausanne.

Jong, A. de

1990 *Weerklank van Job.* Diss. KU Nijmegen. Serie Theologie en Empirie, Deel 8. Kampen.

Jossutis, M.

1976 "Dogmatische und empirische Ekklesiologie in der Praktischen Theologie." In *Theologie und Kirchenleitung,* ed. W. Erk and Y. Spiegel, 150-168. München.

Journet, Ch.

1951 *L'Eglise du Verbe Incarné, II, Sa structure interne et son unité catholique,* Paris.

Kagenaar, P. F.

1975 "Onderwijsplanning als instrument van onderwijsbeleid I en II." In *Ped. Stud.* 6:207-217; 7/8:239-257.

Kannengiesser, C.

1978 "Het Nicea van 325 in de geschiedenis van het christendom." In *Conc.* 14 8:29-37.

Kapteyn, B.

1989 *Organisatietheorie voor non-profit.* Deventer.

Kasper, W.

1970 *Glaube und Geschichte.* Mainz.

———, and G. Sauter

1976 *Kirche, Ort des Geistes.* Freiburg.

Katz, D., and R. Kahn

1978 *The Social Psychology of Organizations.* New York.

Kaufmann, F.-X.

1979 *Kirche begreifen. Analysen und Thesen zur gesellschaftlichen Verfassung des Christentums.* Freiburg.

1989 *Religion und Modernität. Sozialwissenschaftliche Perspektiven.* Tübingen.

1992 *Das Janusköpfige Publikum von Kirche und Theologie. Zur kulturellen und gesellschaftlichen Physiognomie Europas. Referat auf den Ersten Kongreß der Europäischen Gesellschaft für katholische Theologie.* Stuttgart/Hohemheim.

Kemenade, J. A.

1981 *Onderwijs: bestel en beleid.* Groningen.

Kerkbalans '91

1990 *Teken van geven. Informatie ten behoeve van Perskonferentie dd. 10 januari 1991. Interdiocesane Kommissie van Geldwerving.* Zeist.

Kerkbalans '92

1991 *Voor het nodige evenwicht. Informatie ten behoeve van Perskonferentie dd. 9 januari 1992. Interdiocesane Kommissie Geldwerving.* Zeist.

Kerklaan, L. A. F. M., and J. Kingma

1991 "Kwaliteitsdiagnose in de dienstverlening. De kwaliteitsbalans als auditinstrument; het observeren van klant/leverancierrelaties." In *Kwalitetisverbetering in de dienstverlening,* ed. G. C. Ezerman and W. F. G. Mastenbroek. Deventer.

Kertelge, K.

1986 "Die Wirklichkeit der Kirche im Neuen Testament." In *Hb. der Fundamentaltheologie,* 3; Traktat Kirche, 98-121. Freiburg/Basel/Wien.

Kessel, R. van

1985 "Arbeiders in de wijngaard." In *Toekomst voor de kerk?,* ed. J. A. van der Ven, 202-216. Kampen.

1986 "De krisis van de christelijke identiteit." In *Tijds. v. Theol.* 26 4:329-350.

Keuning, D., and D. Eppink

1986 *Management en organisatie. Theorie en toepassing.* Leiden/Antwerpen.

Kickert, W. J. M., ed.

1985 *Planning binnen perken. Nieuwe ziens wijzen op planning in het openbaar bestuur.* Assen/Maastricht.

1986 *Overheidsplanning. Theorieën, technieken en beperkingen.* Assen/Maastricht.

Klafki, W.

1976 *Aspekte Kritisch-konstruktiver Erziehungswissenschaft.* Weinheim/Basel.

Klein, Goldewijk B.

1991 *Praktijk of Principe. Basisgemeenschappen en de ecclesiologie van Leonardo Boff.* Diss. KU Nijmegen. Kampen.

1992 "Een gebroken perspectief op bevrijding en verlossing. Verlossingstheologie vanuit de praxis van bevrijding." In *Schepping, verlossing en het kwaad. Wijsgerige en theologische reflecties,* ed. P. van Tongeren, 73-100. Baarn.

Kloostermann, R. C.

1992 "Stedelijke vernieuwing in een post-industrieel tijdvak." In *Overheid: vernieuwer of vernieler,* ed. N. J. M. Nelissen et al., 107-118. Leiden/Antwerpen.

Klostermann, F.

1974 *Gemeinde, Kirche der Zukunft,* I-II. Freiburg.

———, and R. Zerfass, eds.

1974 *Praktische Theologie heute.* München/Mainz.

Knippenberg, H.

1992 *De religieuze kaart van Nederland. Omvang en geografische spreiding van de godsdienstige gezindten van de Reformatie tot heden.* Assen/Maastricht.

Knippenberg, M. van

1987 *Dood en religie. Een studie naar communicatief zelfonderzoek in het pastoraat.* Diss. KU Nijmegen. Serie Theologie en Empirie, Deel 6. Kampen.

Knitter, P.

1980 "Het christendom als religie: waar en absoluut? Een rooms-katholieke benadering." In *Conc.* 16 6:19-30.

1988 *No Other Name? A Critical Survey of Christian Attitudes Toward the World Religions.* New York.

1990 "Wohin der Dialog führt. Grundlagen zu einer Theologie der Religionen." In *Evang. Komm.* 10:606-610.

Knoers, A. M. P.

1987 *Leraarschap: Amb(ach)t of professie.* Assen/Maastricht.

Koffeman, L.

1986 *Kerk als sacramentum.* Kampen.

Komonchak, J.

1976 "Theologische overwegingen over het leergezag in de kerk." In *Conc.* 12 7:76-87.

1981 "De status van de gelovigen in de herziene Codex van het canoniek recht." In *Conc.* 17 7:46-54.

Koops, W.

1981 "Theoretische ontwikkelingsleer." In *Codex Psychologicus,* ed. H. C. J. Duijker and P. A. Vroon. Amsterdam/Brussel.

Korsten, H., H. Meertens, and A. Reijnen

1973 *Werken aan de basis. Opbouwwerk en pastoraat. Wegen tot pastoraat,* deel 12. Nijmegen.

Köster, R., and H. Oelke, ed. Lernende Kirche. Ein Leitfaden zur Neuorientierung kirchlicher Ausbildung. Kaiser.

Kotler, P. H.

1975 *Marketing for Nonprofit Organizations.* Englewood Cliffs.

Kreveld, D. van

1979 "Nederlands onderzoek over groepsactiviteiten en groepsstructuur." In *Sociale Psychologie in Nederland II,* 21-53. Deventer.

Krijnen, A.

1987 *Kennen binnen coördinaten. Een kennissociologische studie over de clericale elite in de r.k. kerk.* Diss. EUR. Helmond.

Krogt, T. van der

1981 *Professionalisering en collectieve macht.* Den Haag.

Krüger, J. S.

1989 *Metatheism. Early Buddhism and Traditional Christian Theism.* University of South Africa. Pretoria.

Kuilman, M., and A. Uleyn

1986 *Hulpverlener en zingevingsvragen.* Baarn.

Kuiper, F. H.

1977 *Op zoek naar beter bijbels onderwijs. Een exploratief onderzoek naar de eigenlijke problematiek van bijbels onderricht aan de hand van katechetisch materiaal.* Diss. RU Leiden.

Kuitert, H. M.

1985 *Alles is politiek maar politiek is niet alles. Een theologisch perspectief op geloof en politiek.* Baarn.

1992 *Het algemeen betwijfeld christelijk geloof.* Baarn.

Küng, H.

1962 *Strukturen der Kirche.* Ned. vert.: *Structuren van de kerk.* Hilversum/Antwerpen.

1967 *Die Kirche.* Ned. vert.: *De kerk.* Hilversum.

1973 "Partijen in de Kerk?" In *Conc.* 9 8:133-145.

Laan, H. C.

1967 *De rooms-katholieke kerkorganisatie in Nederland. Een sociologische structuur-analyse van het bisschoppelijk bestuur.* Utrecht.

Laeyendecker, L.

1984 *Sociale verandering.* Meppel/Amsterdam.

1992 "Het vervagend Godsbeeld. Enkele sociologische opmerkingen." In *Tempora mutantur,* ed. W. A. Arts, et al., 28-50. Baarn.

———, and W. J. Berger

1984 *Kiezen als noodzaak.* Baarn.

———, and M. Thung

1978 "Liturgie in een politiek geëngageerde kerk." In *Tidjs. v. Theol.* 18 1:49-71.

Lakeland, P.

1990 *Theology and Critical Theory. The Discourse of the Church.* Nashville.

Lammers, C. J.

1984 *Organisaties vergelijkenderwijs. Ontwikkeling en relevantie van het sociologisch denken over organisaties.* Utrecht/Antwerpen.

Lang, B.

1978 "Geloofsbelijdenissen in het Oude Testament en Nieuwe Testament." In *Conc.* 14 8:7-15.

Lange, H. M. de

1989 "Het christelijk sociale denken geconfronteerd met Sollicitudo Rei Socialis." In *Vernieuwing van het christelijk sociaal denken,* 99-106. Baarn.

Lans, J. M. van der

1981 *Volgelingen van de goeroe.* Baarn.

Lauwers, J.

1974 *Secularisatietheorieën. Een studie oer de toekomstkansen van de godsdienstsociologie.* Leuven.

Le Bras, G.

1959 *Les Institutions ecclésiastiques de la Chrétienté médiévalle. Histoire de l'Eglise depuis les origines jusqu'à nos jours, fondée par A. Fliche et V. Martin,* 12, I-II, Paris.

Ledegang, F.

1992 *Mysterium Ecclesiae. Beelden voor de kerk en haar leden bij Origenes,* 2 dln. Diss. KU Nijmegen.

Leeuwen, A. Th. van

1984 *De nacht van het kapitaal.* Nijmegen.

Leeuwen, H. van

1985 "Communicatie tussen kerk en maatschappij." In *Media en religieuze communicatie,* 60-68. Hilversum.

Leeuwen, P. A. van

1966 "De algemene deelname aan het profetisch ambt van Christus." In *De Kerk van Vaticanum II,* ed. G. Barauna, 479-506. Baarn.

Lefèbre, M.

1971 "L'interdisciplinarité dans l'action et la réflexion pastorale." In *Nouv. Rev. Théol.* 947-962, 1051-1071.

Legrand, H. M.

1979 "Grâce et institution dans l'Eglise; les fondaments théologiques du droit canonique." In *l'Eglise: Institution et Foi,* 139-172. Bruxelles.

Le Guillou, M.-J.

1968 "Ecclesiologie." In *Sacramentum Mundi.* Ned. vert., III:190-197. Hilversum.

Lehmann, K.

1971 "Bijdrage tot een dogmatische rechtvaardiging van een democratisering in de kerk." In *Conc.* 7 3:47-69.

Lemaire, A.

1972 "Van diensten naar ambten. De kerkelijk diensten in de eerste twee eeuwen." In *Conc.* 8 10:36-50.

Letterie, J. W.

1979 *Over machtsonderzoek.* KU. Nijmegen.

Likert, R.

1967 *The Human Organization.* New York.

Lima

1982 *Baptism, Eucharist and Ministry* (Faith and Order. Paper 111). Geneva.

Lin, J. van

1990 *Ontmoeting van hindoes en christenen.* Hilversum.

Linde, H. van der

1978 "Nieuwe geloofsbelijdenissen." In *Conc.* 14 8:80-87.

Lindsay, P. H., and D. A. Norman

1977 *Human Information Processing. An Introduction to Psychology.* New York/San Francisco/London.

Listl, J.

1983 "Die Rechtsnormen." In *Handbuch des katholischen Kirchenrechts,* 83-98. Regensburg.

Litt, Th.

1940 Führen oder wachsen lassen. Eine Erörterung des pädagogischen Grundproblems. Stuttgart.

Lohfink, G.

1986 "Jesus und die Kirche." In *Hb. der Fundamental-theologie,* 3; Traktat Kirche, 49-97. Freiburg/Basel/Wien.

Löhrer, M.

1964 "Die Feier des Mysteriums der Kirche: Kulttheologie und Liturgie der Kirche." In *Handbuch der Pastoraltheologie,* I:287-323. Freiburg.

Loor, H. D. de

1970 *Een analyse van het spreken der Nederlandse Hervormde kerk sedert 1945.* Baarn.

1986 *Nieuw Nederland loopt van stapel. De Oxford groep in Nederland. Een sociale beweging in het interbellum.* Kampen.

Luhmann, N.

1972 "Die Organisierbarkeit von Religionen und Kirchen." In *Religion im Umbruch,* 245-285. Stuttgart.

1977 *Funktion der Religion.* Frankfurt.

1978 "Erleben und Handeln." In *Handlungstheorien Interdisziplinär, II. Handlungserklärungen und philosophische Handlungsinterpretation,* ed. H. Lenk, 235-255. München.

Lukken, G.
1991 "De receptie van de Greimasiaanse semiotiek bij theologen: weerstanden en misverstanden." In *"Gelukkig de mens." Opstellen over psalmen, exegese en semiotiek aangeboden aan Nico Tromp,* 121-135. Kampen.

Lumen Gentium. Vaticanum II. Katholiek Archief. Amersfoort.

Luyckx, M.
1981 "Leken als kerkelijke ambtsdragers: het probleem van de wijding." In *Tijds. v. Theol.* 21 2:147-159.

Manenschijn, G.
1984 "Morele argumentatie." In *Onderwijs in de natuurwetenschappen en morele vorming,* 157-184. Baarn.
1991 "Terugkeer van de ethiek in de economie?" In *Tijds. v. Theol.* 31 2:140-162.

Mannheim, K.
1928 "Das Problem der Generationen." *Kölner Vierteljahresheft für Soziologie,* 157-185, 309-330.
1960 *Ideology and Utopia. An Introduction to the Sociology of Knowledge.* London.

Marsch, W. D., ed.
1973 *Plädoyers in Sachen Religion.* Gütersloh.

Martimort, A. G.
1961 *L'Eglise en prière. Introduction à la liturgie.* Paris.

Marx, K.
1971 *Die Frühschriften. Von 1837 bis zum Manifest der Kommunistischen Partei 1848; herausgegeben von S. Landshut,* Stuttgart.

Mauss, A. L., and D. W. Petersen
1973 "The Cross and the Commune. An Interpretation of Jesus People." In *Social Movements,* 150-170. Chicago.

McKenzie, J. L.
1976 "Het Nieuwe Testament." In *Conc.* 12 7:12-20.

McManus, F.
1978 "Geldinzamelingen en verantwoording." In *Conc.* 14 7:42-51.

McSweeney, B.
1980 *Roman Catholicism. The Search for Relevance.* Oxford.

Meijers, T.
1991 "Pastorale werkers en kerkelijk huwelijks-sluiting." In *Tijds. v. Theol.* 31 4:402-418.

Ménard, C.
1992 *L'approche herméneutique en théologie pratique. Conférence Congrès international oecuménique et francophone de théologie pratique.* Lausanne.

Merklein, H.
1983 *Jesu Botschaft von der Gottesherrschaft.* Stuttgart.

Merton, R. K.
1983 *Social Theory and Social Structure.* New York.

Mette, N.
1978 *Theorie der Praxis.* Düsseldorf.
1989 "Pfarrei versus Gemeinde?" In *Diakonia* 20.

1990 "Vom Säkularisierungs-zum Evangelisierungsparadigma." In *Diakonia* 21:420-429.

———, and M. Blasberg-Kuhnke

1986 *Kirche auf dem Weg ins Jahr 2000. Zur Situation und Zukunt der Pastoral.* Düsseldorf.

———, and H. Steinkamp

1983 *Sozialwissenschaften und Praktische Theologie.* Düsseldorf.

Metz, J. B.

1968 *Zur Theologie der Welt.* Ned. vert. (1970): *Theologie over de wereld.*

1971 "Kerkelijk gezag in konfrontatie met de vrijheidsgeschiedenis." In *Kerk tussen gisteren en morgen,* ed. J. B. Metz, 54-94. Baarn.

1973 "Kleine apologie van het verhaal." In *Conc.* 9 5:58-73.

1977 *Glaube in Geschichte und Gesellschaft.* Mainz.

1981 *Jenseits bürgerlicher Religion.* München/Mainz.

Milbank, J.

1990 *Theology and Social Change.* Cambridge.

Minear, P. S.

1960 *Images of the Church in the New Testament.* Philadelphia.

Mintzberg, H.

1979 *The Structuring of Organizations. A Synthesis of the Research.* Englewood Cliffs.

1989 *Mintzberg on Management.* Ned. vert. (1991): *Mintzberg over management. De wereld van onze organisaties.* Amsterdam/Antwerpen.

Missie In *Informatiebulletin R.K. Kerk 1-2-1,* 24 jan. 1986, 33-34.

Moberg, D. O.

1962 *The Church as a Social Institution.* Englewood Cliffs.

Mok, A. L.

1973 *Professie en professionalisering.* SISWO, Amsterdam.

Mollat, M.

1977 "Armoedebewegingen en armenzorg in de kerkgeschiedenis." In *Conc.* 13 4:47-56.

Mollenhauer, Kl.

1972 *Theorien zum Erziehungsprozess.* München.

Möller, Chr.

1987 *Lehre vom Gemeindeaufbau. Band I. Konzepte, Programme, Wege.* Göttingen.

Möller, J.

1990 "Het permanente diakonaat." In *1-2-1. Kerkelijke documentatie RK Kerkgenootschap,* 18, 4, 4-9.

Moltmann, J.

1966 *Theologie der Hoffnung.* München.

1975 *Kirche in der Kraft des Geistes. Ein Beitrag zur messianischen Ekklesiologie.* München.

1980 *Trinität und Reich Gottes. Zur Gotteslehre.* München.

Moor R. de

1987 "Religieuze en morele waarden." In *Traditie, secularisatie en individualisering,* 15-49. Tilburg.

Mooren, J. H. M.
1989 *Geestelijke verzorging en psychotherapie.* Baarn.
Morgan, G.
1986 *Images of Organization.* Beverly Hills.
Morris, C.
1985 "Signs and the Acts." In *Semiotics. An Introductory Anthology,* ed. R. E. Innis. Bloomington.
Mouroux, J.
1965 *Je croix en toi.* Paris.
Müller, A.
1977 "De armen en de kerk — poging tot een balans en synthese." In *Conc.* 13 4:112-118.
Munos, R.
1977 "De functie van de armen in de kerk." In *Conc.* 13 4:13-21.
Nauta, J.
1989 "Flexibele gemeentevormen in de eerste eeuw." In *De kerk verbouwen. Dingemans' ecclesiologie critisch bekeken,* ed. J. P. Heering et al., 11-28. Nijkerk.
Negenman, J.
1986 *De wording van het Woord. Over ontstaan en verstaan van de bijbel.* Turnhout/Kampen.
Negt, O.
1971 *Soziologische Phantasie und exemplarisches Lernen.*
Neijzen, J. A., and M. Trompetter
1991 *Kwaliteitszorg in dienstverlenende organisaties. De klant is koning, maar wie maakt er de dienst uit?* Deventer.
Neisser, U.
1976 *Cognition and Reality. Principles and Implications of Cognitive Psychology.* San Francisco.
Nelissen, N. J. M., T. Ikink, and A. W. van der Ven
1992 *Overheid; vernieuwer of vernieler?* Leiden/Antwerpen.
Nemeshegyi, P.
1977 "Godsbegrippen en Godservaringen in Azië." In *Conc.* 13 3:30-40.
Neunheuser, B.
1966 "Universele en plaatselijke kerk." In *De Kerk van Vaticanum* II, dl. I., ed. G. Barauna. Bilthoven.
Niebuhr, H. R.
1963 *The Social Sources of Denominationalism.* New York.
Niebuhr, R. R.
1964 *Schleiermacher on Christ and Religion.* New York.
Nieuwenhove, J. van
1991 *Bronnen van bevrijding. Varianten in de theologie van Gustavo Gutiérrez.* Kampen.
Nipkow, K. E.
1969 *Grundfragen des Religionsunterrichts in der Gegenwart.* Heidelberg.
1975 *Grundfragen der Religionspädagogik I-III.* Gütersloh.
1988 "The Issue of God in Adolescence." In *Journ. of Empirical Theology* 1:43-54.

1990 *Bildung als Lebensbegleitung und Erneuerung. Kirchliche Bildungsverantwortung in Gemeinde, Schule und Gesellschaft.* Gütersloh.

Nissen, P. J. A.

1991 "Het Tweede Vaticaans Concilie en het herstel van het permanente diakonaat." In *Kerk in Beraad,* ed. G. Ackermans, A. Davids, and P. J. A. Nissen, 301-319. Nijmegen.

Nitzsch, C. I.

1847 *Praktische Theologie.* Bonn.

O'Dea, Th.F.

1968 "Sects and Cults." In *Int. Enc. of the Social Sciences,* 14:130-136.

Ohlig, K. H.

1972 "Theologische doelstellingen van den kerkhervor ming." In *Conc.* 8 3:48-60.

Osendarp, P. J., and A. Ferron

1985 "Parochianen leren voorgaan." In *Pastoraal tussen ideaal en werkelijk heid,* ed. J. A. van der Ven, 175-190. Kampen.

Osmer, R. R.

1990 *A Teachable Spirit. Recovering the Teaching Office in the Church.* Westminster.

Ott, H.

1974 "Techne und Episteme. Funktionen praktischer Theologie." In *Theologica Practica,* 33-35.

Otto, G.

1974 "Praktische Theologie als kritische Theorie religiösvermittelter Praxis. Thesen zum Verständnis einer Formel." In *Praktische Theologie Heute,* ed. F. Klostermann and R. Zerfass, 195-205. München/Mainz.

1976 *Einführung in die Praktische Theologie. Ein Arbeitsbuch.* Stuttgart.

1986 *Grundlegung der Praktischen Theologie.* München.

Overheid, godsdienst en levensovertuiging

1988 *Eindrapport van de Commissie van advies inzake de criteria voor steunverlening aan kerkgenootschappen en andere genootschappen op geestelijke grondslag.* Den Haag.

Pannenberg, W.

1970 *Thesen zur Theologie der Kirche.* Gütersloh.

1973 *Wissenschaftstheorie und Theologie.* Frankfurt.

Parasuraman, A., V. Zeithaml, and L. Berry

1985 "A Conceptual Model of Service Quality and its Implications for Future Research." In *Journal of Marketing,* 49:41-50.

Parsons, T.

1937/1968 *The Structure of Social Action.* New York.

———, et al.

1953 *Working Papers in the Theory of Action.* Glencoe, Ill.

Parsons, T.

1959a *Structure and Process in Modern Societies.*

1959b "The Principal Structure of Community." In *Community. Nomos,* ed. C. J. Friedrich, II:152-179. Liberal Arts Press.

1965 "An Outline of the Social System." In *Theories of Society,* ed. T. Parsons et al., 30-79. New York.

1968 "Professions." In *Intern. Enc. of Social Sciences,* 12:536-546. New York.

Pastoraal plan binnenstad Amsterdam

1969 *Advies tot reorganisatie van de pastoraal en van de kerkvoorzieningen van de R.K. Kerk in de binnenstad van Amsterdam.* Nijmegen/Utrecht.

Pater, W. de

1978a "Theologische linguistiek: situering en bibliografie." In *Tijds. v. Theol.* 18 3:234-246.

1978b "Strukturele tekstanalyse: enkele achtergronden." In *Tijds. v. Theol.* 18 3:247-293.

Peeters, H.

1984 *Burgers en Modernisering. Historisch-sociologisch onderzoek naar burgerlijke groeperingen in het moderniseringsproces van de Duitse Bond 1810-1870.* Diss. KU Nijmegen. Deventer.

Peirce, C. S.

1985 "Logic as Semiotic. The Theory of Signs." In *Semiotics: An Introductory Anthology,* ed. R. E. Innis. Bloomington.

Pelchat, M., ed.

1992 *Les Approches empiriques en Théologie. Empirical Approaches in Theology.* Quebec.

Perrin, N.

1963 *The Kingdom of God in the Teaching of Jesus.* London.

1976 *Jesus and the Language of the Kingdom.* London.

Pesch, R.

1971 "Nieuwtestamentische grondslagen voor een kerkelijk-democratische levensvorm." In *Conc.* 7 3:47-69.

Peters, J.

1957 *Metaphysica. Een systematisch overzicht.* Utrecht/Antwerpen.

1977 *Kerkelijke betrokkenheid en levensbeschouwing. Een onderzoek naar de verbreiding en de sociale relevantie van kerkelijke betrokkenheid in een nieuwe stadswijk.* Diss. KU Nijmegen.

Peters, J., and O. Schreuder

1987 *Katholiek en Protestant. Een historisch en contemporain onderzoek naar confessionele culturen.* Nijmegen.

Petter, D. M. de

1964 *Begrip en werkelijkheid. Aan de overzijde van het conceptualisme.* Hilversum.

Peukert, H.

1978 *Wissenschaftstheorie, Handlungstheorie, Fundamentale Theologie.* Frankfurt.

Philipon, M.

1966 "De allerheiligste Drieënheid en de Kerk." In *De kerk van Vaticanum II,* ed. G. Barauna, I:302-323. Bilthoven.

Piaget, J.

1975 *Introduction à l'Epistémologie génétique. Tome III: La Pensée Biologique, La Pensée Psychologique et la Pensée Sociologique. Deutsche Übersetzung: Die Entwicklung der Erkennens III.* Stuttgart.

———, and B. Inhelder.

1978 *La psychologie de l'enfant.* Ned. vert.: *De psychologie van het kind.* Deventer.

Pieper, J. Z. Th.

1988 *God gezocht en gevonden? Een godsdienstpsychologisch onderzoek rond het kerkelijk huwelijk met pastoraaltheologische consequenties.* Nijmegen.

Pieterse, H. J. C.

1983 "Bureaucracy in the Reformed Tradition in South Africa." In *Journal of Theology or Southern Africa,* 43 June: 55-64.

1987 *Communicative Preaching.* Pretoria.

———, P. Scheepers, and J. A. van der Ven

1991 "Religious Beliefs and Ethnocentrism." In *Journal of Empirical Theology* 4:64-85.

Piret, J.-M.

1992 "Burgerreligie. De religieuze 'fundering' van de liberale rechtsstaat." *Nexus* 2:3-36.

Pixley, G.

1984 "Het volk Gods in de bijbelse traditie." In *Conc.* 17 6:23-30.

Plas, M. van der

1991 *Mijnheer Gezelle. Biografie van een priester-dichter (1830-1899).* Tielt & Baarn.

Pohier, J.

1978 "De gevolgen van twintig jaar omgang met de psycho-analyse voor mijn theologiebeoefening." In *Conc.* 14 5:54-63.

1985 *Dieu fractures.* Ned. vert. (1986): *God in fragmenten.* Hilversum.

Popper, K.

1978 *Unended Quest.* Ned. vert. *Autobiografie.* Utrecht.

Pottmeyer, H. J.

1983 "Die zwiespältige Ekklesiologie des Zweiten Vaticanums." In *TThZ* 92:272-283.

1986 "Die Frage nach der wahren Kirche." In *Handbuch der Fundamentaltheologie,* 3; Traktat Kirche, 212-241. Freiburg.

Praktische Theologie heute. Edited by F. Klostermann and R. Zerfass. München.

Prein, H. C. M.

1976 "Stijlen van conflicthantering." In Ned. *Tijds. v. Psych.* 31.

Preul, R.

1980 *Religion-Bildung-Sozialisation. Studien zur Grundlegung einer religionspädagogischen Bildungstheorie.* Gütersloh.

Pröpper, Th.

1988 *Erlösungsglaube und Freiheitsgeschichte. Eine Skizze zur Soteriologie.* München.

Rabbie, J. M.

1979 "Competitie en coöperatie tussen groepen." In *Sociale psychologie in Nederland* II:190-226. Deventer.

Rademaker, L.

1981 *Sociologische grondbegrippen 1: Theorie en analyse.* Utrecht/Antwerpen.

Raedts, P.

1990 "De christelijke middeleeuwen als mythe." In *Tijds. v. Theol.* 30 2:146-158.

Rahner, K.

1965a "Kleines Fragment 'Über die kollektive Findung der Wahrheit.'" In *Schr. z. Theol.* VI:104-110. Einsiedeln.

1965b "Marxistische Utopie und christliche Zukunft des Menschen." In *Schr. z. Theol.* VI:77-88. Einsiedeln.

1965c "Konziliäre Lehre der Kirche und künftige Wirklichkeit christlichen Lebens." In *Schr. z. Theol.* VI:479-498. Einsiedeln.

1966 "De zonde in de Kerk." In *De Kerk van Vaticanum II,* ed. G. Barauna, 431-447. Baarn.

1967 "De behoefte aan een 'beknopte formulering' van het christelijk geloof." In *Conc.* 3 3:69-80.

1969 "Die Zukunft der Kirche hat schon begonnen." In *Handbuch der Pastoraltheologie* IV:744-759. Freiburg.

1970 "Reflexionen zur Problematik einer Kurzformel des Glaubens." In *Schr. z. Theol.* IX:242-256. Einsiedeln.

1970 "Zur Struktur des Kirchenvolkes heute." In *Schr. z. Theol.* IX:558-568. Einsiedeln.

1971 "Theologie der Armut." In *Schr. z. Theol.* VII:435-480. Einsiedeln.

1972a "Der Glaube des Christen und die Lehre der Kirche." In *Schr. z. Theol.* X:262-285. Einsiedeln.

1972b *Strukturwandel der Kirche.* Freiburg.

1976 *Grundkurs des Glaubens. Einführung in den Begriff des Christentums.* Freiburg.

1978 *Schr. z. Theol.* XIII. Einsiedeln.

1980 "Warum lässt uns Gott leiden?" In *Schr. z. Theol.* XIV:450-466. Zürich.

Ravetz, J. R.

1980 "Science and Technology as Promise and Threat. The Scale and Complexity of the Problem." In *Faith and Science in an Unjust World* I:89-96. Geneva.

Rawls, J.

1971 *A Theory of Justice.* Cambridge.

Regeling persoonsregistraties parochies

1989 *Regelingen R.K. Kerkgenootschap,* no. 7. Utrecht.

Reinders, J. S.

1989 "Radicaliteit in het christelijke sociale denken." In *Vernieuwing van het christelijk sociaal denken,* ed. J. M. M. de Valk. Baarn.

Rendtorff

1973 *Christendom buiten de kerk.* Baarn.

Rhoads, D. M.

1976 *Israel in Revolution: 6-74 C.E. A Political History Based on the Writings of Josephus.* Philadelphia.

Ribeiro de Oliveira, P. A.

1984 "Wat betekent 'volk' vanuit analytisch oogpunt?" In *Conc.* 20 6:94-102.

Ricoeur, P.

1968 *Politiek en geloof.* Utrecht.

1970 *La Symbolique du Mal.* Paris 1960. Ned. vert.: *Symbolen van het kwaad,* dl. I-II. Rotterdam.

1971 *Le conflict des interprétations. Essais d'hermeneutique.* Ned. vert.: *Kwaad en bevrijding.* Rotterdam.

1987 *Hermeneutics and the Social Sciences.* Cambridge/Paris.

Rigaux, B.

1966 "Het mysterie van de kerk in het licht van de bijbel." In *De Kerk volgens Vaticanum II.* Bilthoven.

Righart, H.

1986 *De katholieke zuil in Europa.* Meppel.

Rikhof, H. W. M.

1981 *The Concept of Church. A Methodological Inquiry into the Use of Metaphors in Ecclesiology.* Diss. KU Nijmegen. London.

1983 "De kerk als 'communio': een zinnige uitspraak?" In *Tijds. v. Theol.* 23 1:39-59.

1987 "De ecclesiologieën van Lumen Gentium, Lex Ecclesiae Fundamentalis, Schema Codicis Iuris Canonici." In *Conc.* 23:66-75.

1990 "Vaticanum II en de bisschoppelijke collegialiteit. Een lezing van Lumen Gentium 22 en 23." In *Conc.* 26 4:12-22.

1992 "Brief congregatie over communio blijft steken in eenzijdigheden." In *1-2-1.* Uitgave R.-K. Kerk. 20, 12, 27-30.

Rip, A., and P. Groenewegen

1980 *Macht over kennis.* Alpen a/d Rijn.

Roes, J. H.

1991 "Diocesane synodes tussen hiërarchie en democratie. Een hernieuwde kennismaking met een kruispunt in de geschiedenis van de katholieke kerk in Duitsland tijdens de revolutiejaren 1848/49." In *Kerk in Beraad,* ed. G. Ackermans, A. Davids, and P. J. A. Nissen, 235-254. Nijmegen.

Rondeau, A.

1990 "La gestion des conflits dans les organisations." In *L'Individu dans l'organisation,* ed. J. F. Charlat, 507-527. Quebec.

Rosenthal, U.

1980 *Openbaar bestuur.* Alphen a/d Rijn.

Rössler, D.

1986 *Grundriss der Praktischen Theologie.* Berlin/New York.

Rossi, P. H., and H. E. Freeman

1989 *Evaluation. A Systematic Approach.* London: New Delhi.

Roumen, T., C. Hermans, and J. A. van der Ven

1991 "Lernen über Liebe." In *Sexualität im Wertpluralismus,* ed. H.-G. Ziebertz, 85-106. Mainz.

Rudge, P.

1968 *Ministry and Management.* London.

Ruggieri, G.

1981 "De hernieuwing van de kerk tot evangelische broederschap." In *Conc.* 17 6:29-38.

Ruiter, J. de

1985 "Het spreken van de kerk: een probleem van de kerken." In *Moet de kerk zich met politiek bemoeien?,* ed. A. W. Muschenga and W. Haan, 61-70. Amsterdam.

Sacrosanctum Concilium Vaticanum II. Katholiek Archief. Amersfoort.

Sandmel, S.

1969 *The First Christian Century in Judaism and Christianity.* New York.

Sauter, G., and T. Strohm

1976 *Theologie als Beruf in unserer Gesellschaft.* München.

Schaller, L.

1987 *It's a Different World: The Challenge for Today's Pastor.* New York.

1990 *Choices for Churches.* New York.

Schama, S.

1988 *The Embarrassment of Riches. An Interpretation of Dutch Culture in the Golden Age.* Fontana Press.

Scheer, A.

1985a "Als gemeente geroepen tot vrede." In *Toekomst voor de kerk? Studies voor Frans Haarsma,* ed. J. A. van der Ven, 240-256. Kampen.

1985b "De beleving van liturgische riten en symbolen." In *Pastoraal tussen ideaal en werkelijkheid,* ed. J. A. van der Ven, 105-120. Kampen.

1991 "Vivas in Deo. Aanzet tot een thematische analyse van de uitvaartliturgie." In *Tijds. v. Liturgie* 4:238-257.

Schelsky, H.

1957 "Ist die Dauerreflexion institutionalisierbar?" In *Zeitschrift für Evangelische Ethik,* 4.

Schepens, Th.

1992 "Nederlandse katholieken steeds verder werwijderd van de kerkelijke norm." In *1-2-1.* Uitgave R.K. Kerk 20, 12, 23-26.

Schillebeeckx, E.

1964 *Openbaring en theologie.* Bilthoven.

1965 *God en Mens.* Bilthoven.

1966 *Wereld en kerk.* Bilthoven.

1968a "De kerk als sacrament van dialoog." In *Tijds. v. Theol.* 8 2:155-169.

1968b *De zending van de kerk.* Bilthoven.

1973 "Stilte, gevuld met parabels." In *Politiek of mystiek,* 69-81. Brugge.

1974 *Jezus, het verhaal van een levende.* Bloemendaal.

1975 "Kritische bezinning op interdisciplinariteit in de theologie." In *Vox theologica* 2:111-125.

1977a *Gerechtigheid en liefde, genade en bevrijding.* Bloemendaal.

1977b "Godsdienst van en voor mensen." In *Tijds. v. Theol.* 17 4:353-371.

1980 *Kerkelijk ambt, voorgangers in de gemeente van Jezus Christus.* Bloemendaal.

1982 "De sociale context van de verschuivingen in het kerkelijk ambt." In *Tijds. v. Theol.* 22 1:24-59.

1983 *Theologisch geloofsverstaan anno 1983.* Baarn.

1985 *Pleidooi voor mensen in de kerk.* Baarn.

1989 *Mensen als verhaal van God.* Baarn.

1990 "Identiteit, eigenheid en universaliteit van Gods heil in Jezus." In *Tijds. v. Theol.* 30 3:259-275.

Schippers, K. A., et al.

1990 *Kerkelijke presentie in een oude stadswijk. Onderzoek naar buurtpastoraat vanuit behoeften en belangen van bewoners.* Kampen.

Schleiermacher, F.

1960 *Der christliche Glaube,* I-II. Berlin.

Schluchter, W.

1979 *Die Entwicklung des okzidentalen Rationalismus. Eine Analyse von Max Webers Gesellschaftsgeschichte.* Tübingen.

Schnackenburg, R.

1961 *Die Kirche im Neuen Testament.* Freiburg.

Schneider, G.

1982 *Grundbedürfnisse und Gemeindebildung. Soziale Aspekte für eine menschliche Kirche.* München.

Scholten, R. G.

1988 "De bemoeienis van de pastor met de vrijwilligers(arbeid)." In *De pastor als partner,* ed. H. J. van Hout, 94-104. Hilversum.

1991 "Bouwstenen voor een pastorale organisatieleer." In *Prakt. Theol.* 18 5:489-512.

Schoof, T. M.

1980 "Getuigen in de 'zaak Schillebeeckx': theologische lijnen in de publieke en persoonlijke reacties." In *Tijds. v. Theol.* 20 4:402-421.

Schoonenberg, P.

1955-1962 *Het geloof van ons doopsel,* I-IV. Den Bosch.

1968 "Historiciteit en interpretatie van het dogma." In *Tijds. v. Theol.* 8 3:278-311.

1969 *Hij is een God van mensen. Twee theologische studies.* Den Bosch.

1977 "Denken naar God toe." In *Tijds. v. Theol.* 17 2:117-130.

1985 "Charismata, talenten waar de Geest mee speelt." In *Toekomst voor de kerk? Studies voor Frans Haarsma,* ed. J. A. van der Ven, 47-58. Kampen.

1986 *Auf Gott hin denken.* Freiburg.

1991 *De Geest, het Woord en de Zoon. Theologische overdenkingen over Geest-christologie, Logos-christologie en drieëenheidsleer.* Kampen.

Schoorl, J. W.

1983 *Sociologie der modernisering. Een inleiding in de sociologie der nietwesterse volken.* Deventer.

Schreiter, R.

1984 *Constructuring Local Theologies.* New York. Ned. vert.: *Bouwen aan een eigen theologie.* Baarn.

Schreuder, O.

1962 *Kirche im Vorort.* Freiburg.

1964 *Het professioneel karakter van het geestelijk ambt.* Rede KU. Nijmegen.

1965 "Priesterbeelden." In *Tijds. v. Theol.* 5 3:258-271.

1967 *Gestaltwandel der Kirche.* Olten.

1969 *Gedaanteverandering van de kerk, aanbevelingen voor vernieuwing.* Nijmegen/Utrecht.

1980a "Bewegingen en veranderingen." In *Institutie en beweging,* ed. J. Thurlings, et al., 58-109. Deventer.

1980b "Overpeinzingen bij het gouden kalf." In *Prakt. Theol.* 7 3:140-148.

1981 *Sociale bewegingen. Een systematische inleiding.* Deventer.

1984 "Mediterende Nederlanders." In *Spiritualiteit,* 133-146. Baarn.

1985 "Religie en modernisering." In *Religie en politiek,* 197-213. Kampen.

1989 "Nederlandse katholieken tussen assimilatie en pluralisme." In *Tussen isole-*

ment en assimilatie. Katholieken en het hedendaagse culturele klimàat, ed. G. A. M. Beekelaar, 72-90. Baarn.

———, and L. van Snippenburg

1990 *Religie in de Nederlandse samenleving. De vergeten factor.* Baarn.

Schrey, H. H.

1977 *Einführung in die Ethik.* Darmstadt (2e dr.).

Schrojenstein, Lantman, R. van

1990 *Arbeid ter sprake brengen.* Hilversum.

Schüssler Fiorenza, E.

1983 *In Memory of Her.* New York. Ned. vert. (1987): *Ter herinnering aan haar.* Hilversum.

Schuurman, B.

1987 "Het draagvlak van de bevrijdingstheologie: de rol van het 'volk.'" In *Tijds. v. Theol.* 27 1:74-94.

Schwarz, F., and A. Schwarz

1987 *Theologie des Gemeinde-aufbaus. Ein Versuch.* Neukirchen-Vluyn.

Scott, J. C.

1957 "Membership and Participation in Voluntary Associations." In *American Sociological Review* 22:315-326.

Semmelroth, O.

1966 "De kerk, het nieuwe Godsvolk." In *De kerk van Vaticanum II,* ed. G. Barauna, 451-465. Bilthoven.

Siemerink, J. A. M.

1987 *Het gebed in de religieuze vorming. Empirisch-theologisch onderzoek naar de effecten van gebedseducatie bij volwassenen.* Diss. KU Nijmegen. Serie Theologie en Empirie, Deel 5. Kampen.

1989 "Prayer and Our Image of God." In *Journal of Empirical Theology* 2 1:27-44.

1992 *Voorgaan in de liturgie.* Kampen.

Sierksma, F.

1978 *Een nieuwe hemel en een nieuwe aarde. Messianistische en eschatologische bewegingen en voorstellingen bij primitieve volken.* Groningen.

Sills, D. L.

1968 "Voluntary Associations. Sociological Aspects." In *Int. Enc. of the Social Sciences* 16:362-379.

Silverman, D.

1970 *The Theory of Organisations.* London. Ned. vert. (1974): *Organisatietheorie.* Rotterdam.

Simons, E., and L. Winkeler

1987 *Het verraad der clercken. Intellectuelen en hun rol in de ontwikkelingen van het Nederlandse katholicisme na 1945.* Diss. K.U. Nijmegen. Baarn.

Simonton, D. K.

1990 *Psychology, Science and History. An Introduction to Historiometry.* New Haven/London.

Sleegers, P. J. C.

1991 *School en beleidsvoering.* Diss. K.U. Nijmegen.

Smeets, W.

1990 *Communicatief zelfonderzoek rond God en lijden. Empirisch-theologisch onderzoek van een pastoraatsmethode. Doctoraalscriptie vakgroep empirische theologie.* K.U. Nijmegen.

Smit, J.

1989 "De rangorde in de kerk; Retorische analyse van 1 Kor. 12." In *Tijds. v. Theol.* 29 4:325-343.

Smulders, P.

1966 "De kerk als sacrament van het heil." In *De kerk van Vaticanum II,* deel I, 372-395. Bilthoven.

Sobrino, J.

1989 *Resurrección de la verdadera Iglesia: Los pobres, lugar teológico de la eclesiología.* Engl. trans.: *The True Church and the Poor.* New York.

Sociaal en Cultureel Rapport 1992

1992 *Sociaal en Cultureel Planbureau.* Rijswijk.

Sonnberger, Kl., and J. A. van der Ven

1992 "Ekklesiologische Hypothesen zur kirchlichen Autorität." In *Bijdragen. Tijds. v. Fil. & Theol.* 53:4.

Spiegel, Y.

1969 *Kirche als bürokratische Organisation.* München.

Spilka, B., et al.

1985 "A General Attribution Theory for the Psychology of Religion." In *Journal for the Scientific Study of Religion* 24:1-20.

Spruit, L., and H. van Zoelen

1980 *Dopen . . . ja, waarom eigenlijk? Onderzoek naar motieven. Kaski.* Hilversum.

Steeg, L. ter

1985 "Religieuze beïnvloeding via massamedia als ethisch probleem." In *Media en religieuze communicatie,* 139-150. Hilversum.

Steggink, O.

1991 "Democratische organisatie, verkiezingen en besluitvorming bij de mendicanten in de dertiende eeuw, met name bij de Dominicanen." In *Kerk in Beraad,* ed. G. Ackermans, A. Davids, and P. J. A. Nissen, 79-86, Nijmegen.

———, and K. Waaijman

1985 *Spiritualiteit en mystiek,* I. Inleiding. Nijmegen.

Steinkamp, H.

1985 "Identität der Gemeinde?" In *Kommunikation und Identität,* 198-213. Freiburg.

1988 "Selbst 'wenn die Betreuten sich ändern.'" In *Diakonia,* 78-89.

Stillings, N. A., et al.

1987 *Cognitive Science. An Introduction.* Cambridge.

Stoetzel, J.

1983 *Les valeurs du temps présent: Une enquête européenne.* Paris.

Strauss, A. L.

1971 *Professions, Work and Careers.* San Francisco.

Suchocki, M. Hewitt

1989 *God, Christ, Church. A Practical Guide to Process Theology.* New York.

Sunden, H.

1966 *Die Religion und die Rollen.* Berlin.

Swaan, A. de
1982 *De mens is de mens een zorg.* Amsterdam.
1990 *Zorg en de staat.* Amsterdam.

Taylor, J. C., and D. G. Bowers
1972 *Survey of Organizations. A Machine-Scored Standardized Questionnaire Instrument.* Ann Arbor.

Terpstra, M.
1991 "Zo spreken de schuldigen. Over schuldbetrekkingen en schuldhuishoudingen." In *Schul en gemeenschap. Hoofdstukken uit een genealogie van de schuld,* 98-135. Baarn.

Tettero, J. M.
1972 *Medewerkers in het pastoraat. De inschakeling in de parochiële zielzorg van personen, die geen priester zijn.* Den Haag.

Theissen, G.
1977 *Soziologie der Jesusbewegung.* München.
1979 *Studien zur Soziologie des Urchristentums.* Tübingen.
1983 *Psychologische Aspekte paulinischer Theologie.* Göttingen.

Thomas Aquinas *Summa Theologica.*

Thung, M. A.
1976 *The Precarious Organisation.* The Hague/Paris.

———, et al.
1985 *Exploring the New Religious Consciousness.* Amsterdam.

Thurlings, J. M. G.
1977 *De wetenschap der samenleving, een drieluik van de sociologie.* Alphen a/d Rijn.
1978 *De wankele zuil.* Deventer.
1980 "Institutie in beweging. Bouwstenen voor de theorie der institutionalisering." In *Institutie en beweging,* ed. J. M. G. Thurlings, et al., 9-57. Deventer.

Tillard, J. M.
1986 "Final Report of the Last Synod." In *Conc.* 22:64-77.

Tillich, P.
1966 *Systematic Theology,* Vol. I-III. Chicago.

Tinbergen, J.
1977 *Reshaping the International Order.* New York. Ned. vert.: *Naar een rechtvaardiger internationale orde.* Amsterdam/Brussels.

Toepassingsbesluiten bij de Codex Iuris Canonici
1989 *Regelingen R.K. Kerkgenootschap,* no. 5. Utrecht.

Toffler, A.
1971 *Future Shock.* New York.

Tönnies, F.
1887 *Gemeinschaft und Gesellschaft.* Leipzig.

Tracy, D.
1981 *The Analogical Imagination.* New York.
1988 *Blessed Rage for Order. The New Pluralism in Theology.* San Francisco.
1989 "The Uneasy Alliance Reconceived." In *Theol. Stud.,* 548-570.

Troeltsch, E.
1912 *Die Soziallehren der christlichen Kirchen und Gruppen.* Tübingen.

Trouiller, L.
1978 "De kerk als rentmeester van de armen." In *Conc.* 14 7:79-86.
Turner, J. H.
1984 *Societal Stratification. A Theoretical Analysis.* New York.
1991 *The Structure of Sociological Theory.* Belmont.
Uden, M. van, J. Pieper, and E. Henau
1991 *Bij geloof. Over bedevaarten en andere uitingen van volksreligiositeit.* Hilversum.
Uleyn, A.
1969 *The Recognition of Guilt. A Study in Pastoral Psychology.* Dublin.
Unitatis Redintegratio. Vaticanum II. Katholiek Archief. Amersfoort.
Vall, M. van de
1980 *Sociaal beleidsonderzoek. Een professioneel paradigma.* Alphen a.d. Rijn.
Veen, P., and E. Wilke
1986 *De kern van de sociale psychologie.* Deventer.
Veen, R. van der
1982 *Aktivering in opbouw- en vormingswerk. Een vergelijking van vier benaderingen.* Baarn
Ven, J. A. van der
1968 "Horizontaal en verticaal in Schleiermachers dogmatiek." In *Vox Theologica,* 181-199.
1973 *Katechetische leerplanontwikkeling.* Den Bosch.
1981 "'En de oorlog leren zij niet meer' (Jes. 2:4): Pastoraaltheologische reflecties." In *Tijds. v. Theol.* 21 3:265-287.
1982a *Kritische godsdienstdidactiek.* Kampen.
1982b "Naar een leerproces van geloof en ervaring." In *Tijds. v. Theol.* 22 3:261-286.
1983a "Op weg naar een empirische theologie." In *Meedenken met Edward Schillebeeckx,* 93-114. Baarn.
1983b "Kerkelijk leiderschap in verband met oorlog en vrede." In *Kerk over kernbewapening. Reeks Pax Christi Boeken,* no. 10, 37-52. Pax Christi. Den Haag.
1984a "Unterwegs zu einer empirischen Theologie." In *Theologie und Handeln,* ed. O. Fuchs, 102-128. Düsseldorf.
1984b "De toekomst van de kerk als intergeneratief probleem." In *Conc.* 20 4:38-47.
1984c "Vragen voor een empirische ecclesiologie." In *Theologie en kerkvernieuwing,* ed. H. Ernst et al., 51-93. Baarn.
1985a *Toekomst voor de kerk? Studies voor Frans Haarsma.* Kampen.
1985b "Evaluatie van de pastoraal tussen ideaal en werkelijkheid." In *Pastoraal tussen ideaal en werkelijkheid,* ed. J. A. van der Ven, 9-34. Kampen.
1985c *Vorming in waarden en normen.* Kampen.
1986 "Konflikten rond vrede: Een gevaar voor de eenheid van de kerk?" In *Prakt. Theol.* 13 3:312-331.
1987a "Erfahrung und Empirie in der Theologie?" In *Religionspäd.* Beiträge, 132-151.
1987b "Empirische theologie: een repliek." In *Tijds. v. Theol.* 27 3:292-296.
1988a "Practical Theology: from Applied to Empirical Theology." In *Journal of Empirical Theology* 1 1:7-28.

1988b "Mogelijkheden van een Westeuropese bevrijdingstheologie," in *Bevrijdingstheologie in West-Europa,* ed. B. Klein Goldewijk, E. Borgman, and F. van Iersel, 90-116. Kampen.

1990a "Explorations on Church Development from a Theodicy Program." In *Pastoral Sciences* 9:75-108.

1990b "Practical Theology as Critical-Empirical Theology." In *Pastoral Studies in the University Setting,* ed. A. Visscher, 238-262. Ottawa.

1990c *Entwurf einer empirischen Theologie.* Kampen/Weinheim.

1991a "L'avenir de la théologie empirique, I. D'aujourd'hui à hier." In *Laval Théologique et Philosophique* 2:231-240.

1991b "Blijvende beweging in de Acht Mei-bewegin." In *Prakt. Theol.* 18 3:335-349.

1991c "Methodologische Pluriformität in der niederländischen Praktischen Theologie." In *PThI.* 11 2:111-124.

1991d "Religieuze variaties: Religie in een geseculariseerde en multiculturele samenleving." In *Tijds. v. Theol.* 31 2:163-182.

1991e "De identiteit van pastorale counseling." In *Prakt. Theol.* 18 2:230-256.

1992a "Congregational Studies from the Perspective of Empirical Theology." In *Les Approaches Empiriques en Théologie. Théologies Pratiques,* ed. M. Pelchat, 4:101-130. Laval University. Quebec.

1992b "God in Nijmegen. Een theologisch perspectief." In *Tijds. v. Theol.* 32 3:225-249.

1993 "Katholieke kerk en katholicisme in historisch en empirisch perspectief." In *Kerk op de helling.* Kampen.

———, and B. Biemans

1992a *Pastorale professionalisering. Intern rapport vakgroep praktische theologie.* KU Nijmegen.

1992b *Studentenpastoraat. Intern rapport vakgroep praktische theologie.* KU Nijmegen.

Ven, J. A. van der, and G. van Gerwen

1990 "Ecclesiological Explorations from Volunteer Ministry." In *Journal of Empirical Theology* 3 1:27-46.

Ven, J. A. van der, and L. van der Tuin

1990 "Communicatie omtrent lijden als aspekt van kerkopbouw." In *Lijden en pastoraat. Prakt. Theol.,* 103-118, Zwolle.

Ven, J. J. M. van der

1950 "Sociale banden en caritatieve werkzaamheid." In *Onrust in de zielzorg,* 114-141. Utrecht.

Vet, G. H. de

1965 "L'Enquête sur la pauvreté dans l'église." In *Église et pauvreté,* 335-336. Paris.

Vischer, L.

1978 "Een oecumenische geloofsbelijdenis?" In *Conc.* 14 8:95-109.

Visscher, A.

1990 *Pastoral Studies in the University Setting.* Ottawa.

Vogels, W.

1986 *God's Universal Covenant.* Ottawa.

Voorlopig statuut voor de pastoraatsgroep in het bisdom Breda

1992 *Analecta Bisdom Breda,* 6 2:27-31.

Vossen, H. J. M.

1985 *Vrijwilligerseducatie en pastoraat aan rouwenden.* Diss. KU Nijmegen. Serie Theologie en Empirie, Deel 2. Kampen.

1990 "Empirische theologie: reductie of verrijking van de theologie?" In *Verslag Stegon-symposium "Uitdagingen aan de theologie,"* 24-32. Kampen.

Vrede en Gerechtigheid

1983 *Een brief van de Nederlandse bisschoppenconferentie over de kernbewapening.* Utrecht.

Vught, F. van

1979 *Sociale planning. Oorsprong en ontwikkeling van het amerikaanse planningsdenken.* Assen.

1982 *Experimentele beleidsplanning. Bestuurskundige expedities in de jungle van het planningsdenken.* 's-Gravenhage.

Waldenfels, H.

1976 "Woord en woordeloosheid in het boeddhisme." In *Conc.* 12 2:26-43.

Walf, K.

1978 "Kerkbelasting als bestaansmiddel." In *Conc.* 14 7:24-31.

1984a *Kirchenrecht.* Düsseldorf.

1984b *Einführung in das neue katholische Kirchenrecht.* Köln.

1985 "Jurisdictie: alleen voor gewijden?" In *Pastoraal tussen ideaal en werkelijkheid,* ed. J. A. van der Ven, 133-140. Kampen.

Walgrave, J. H.

1961 "Standpunten en stromingen in de huidige moraaltheologie." In *Tijds. v. Theol.* 1 1:48-70.

Wallace, R. A., and A. Wolf

1991 *Contemporary Sociological Theory, Continuing the Classical Tradition.* Englewood Cliffs.

Ward, K.

1990 "Truth and the Diversity of Religions." In *Relig. Stud.* 1:1-18.

Watzlawick, P., J. H. Beavin, and D. D. Jackson

1967 *Pragmatics of Human Communication.* Ned. vert. *De pragmatische aspecten van de menselijke communicatie.* Deventer 1986.

Weber, M.

1920/1978 *Gesammelte Aufsätze zur Religionssoziologie.*

1965 "The Market." In *Theories of Society,* ed. T. Parsons et al., 443-446. New York.

1968 *Gesämmelte Aufsätze zur Wissenschaftslehre.* Tübingen.

1969 "Die protestantische Ethik und der Geist des Kapitalismus." In *Die protestantische Ethik I.,* ed. M. Weber. München/Hamburg.

1980 *Wirtschaft und Gesellschaft. Grundriss der Verstehenden Soziologie,* 1. Halbband. Tübingen.

1982 *Politik als Beruf.* Berlin.

Welte, B.

1965 "Zum Strukturwandel der katholischen Theologie in 19. Jahrhundert." In *Auf den Spur des Ewigen,* 380-409. Freiburg.

Welten, V. J.

1991 "De surfer op de golven: psychologie van cultuur en gedrag." In *Cultuur en sociale wetenschappen,* ed. A. Felling and J. Peters, 31-50. Nijmegen.

1992 *Greep op cultuur. Een cultuurpsychologische bijdrage aan het minderhedendebat (afscheidscollege).* KU Nijmegen.

Weren, W.

1984 "Israel en de kerk." In *Tijds. v. Theol.* 24 4:355-373.

Wess, P.

1983 *Ihr alle seid Geschwister, Gemeinde und Priester.* Mainz.

1989 *Gemeindekirche — Ort des Glaubens. Die Praxis als Fundament und als Konsequenz der Theologie.* Graz/Wien/Köln.

Weth, R.

1986 *Diskussion zur "Theologie des Gemeindeaufbaus."* Neukirchen-Vluyn.

Wheeler, B.

1990 "Uncharted Territory: Congregational Identity and Mainline Protestantism." In *The Presbyterian Predicament,* ed. Milton S. Coatter et al., 67-89. Westminster.

Wilhelm, Th.

1969 *Theorie der Schule.* Stuttgart.

Wilke, H.

1979 "Sociale invloed." In *Sociale Psychologie in Nederland II,* 88-127. Deventer.

Willems, B. A.

1967 *De verlossing in kerk en wereld.* Roermond-Maaseik.

1980 "Komt er een derde kerk?" In *Tijds. v. Theol.* 20 4:361-380.

Willems, A.

1983 "Naar het ambt van een minderheid." In *Meedenken met Edward Schillebeeckx,* ed. H. Häring, T. Schoof, and A. Willems. Baarn.

1985 "De wezenlijk relativiteit van de kerk." In *Toekomst voor de kerk?,* ed. J. A. van der Ven, 105-117. Kampen.

1986 "Het mysterie als ideologie: de bisschoppensynode over het kerkbegrip." In *Tijds. v. Theol.* 26 2:157-171.

Willis, J. R.

1967 "Congregationalists." In *New Catholic Enc.,* 173-176.

Willms, B.

1969 *Revolution und Protest oder Glanz und Elend des bürgerlichen Subjekts.* Stuttgart.

Winquist, C. E.

1980 *Practical Hermeneutics.* Chicago.

1987 "Re-visioning Ministry: Postmodern Reflections." In *Formation and Reflection. The Promise of Practical Theology,* ed. L. S. Mudge and J. N. Poling, 27-35. Philadelphia.

Witte, H.

1983 "Verschil in geloven binnen één kerk." In *Tijds. v. Theol.* 23:359-380.

1986a *Al naargelang hun band met het christelijk geloof verschillend is.* Tilburg.

1986b "Er zullen altijd accenten vallen. Het perspectief van de 'hierarchie' van waarheden." In *Prakt. Theol.* 13 4:445-462.

1991 "De kerk over zichzelf." In *Op grond van vertrouwen. De RK kerk in Nederland op de drempel van de 21e eeuw,* 117-148. Baarn.

Witteman-Devillee, A., J. Helderman, and M. van Hemert

1989 *Kerk metterdaad.* Hilversum.

Wolde, E. J. van

1984 "Semiotiek en haar betekenis voor de theologie." In *Tijds. v. Theol.* 24 2:138-167.

1989 *A Semiotic Analysis of Genesis 2-3. A Semiotic Theory and Method of Analysis Applied to the Story of the Garden of Eden.* Assen.

1990a "Van tekst via tekst naar betekenis: Intertekstualiteit en haar implicaties." In *Tijds. v. Theol.* 30 4:333-361.

1990b "Uitdagingen aan de theologie: exegese en de semiotische methode." In *Verslag Stegon-symposium "Uitdagingen aan de theologie,"* 8-18. Kampen.

Yinger, J. M.

1970 *The Scientific Study of Religion.* New York.

Zerfab, R.

1974 "Praktische Theologie als Handlungswissenschaft." In *Praktische Theologie heute,* ed. F. Klostermann and R. Zerfab. München.

Ziebertz, H.-G.

1990 *Moralerziehung im Wertpluralismus.* Serie Theologie en Empirie. Kampen/Weinheim.

1991 *Sexualität im Wertpluralismus.* Mainz.

Zijderveld, A. C.

1983 *De culturele factor.* Den Haag.

Zirker, H.

1984 *Ekklesiologie.* Düsseldorf.

Zoest, A. van

1978 *Semiotiek. Over tekens, hoe ze werken en wat we ermee doen.* Baarn.

Zuidberg, G.

1984 *Zeven is voldoende. Krachtlijnen in de spiritualiteit van pastores in Nederland.* Hilversum.

Zulehner, P. M.

1976 *Heirat, Gęburt, Tod. Eine Pastoral zu den Lebenswenden.* Wien/Freiburg/Basel.

1988 "Ecclesiastical Atheism." In *Journal of Empirical Theology* 1 2:5-20.

1989-1900 *Pastoraltheologie.* Bd. 1-4. Düsseldorf.

Zwart, C. J.

1983 *Gericht veranderen van organisaties. Theorie en praktijk van het begeleiden.* Rotterdam.